TEXTBOOK ON
CRIMINOLOGY

TEXTBOOK ON
CRIMINOLOGY

Third Edition

Katherine S. Williams

Lecturer in Law, University of Wales, Aberystwyth

BLACKSTONE
PRESS LIMITED

First published in Great Britain 1991 by Blackstone Press Limited, Aldine Place, London W12 8AA. Telephone 0181 740 2277

© Katherine S. Williams, 1991

First edition, 1991
Reprinted 1993
Second edition, 1994
Reprinted 1996
Third edition, 1997

ISBN: 1 85431 692 3

British Library Cataloguing in Publication Data
A CIP catalogue record for this book is available from the British Library

Typeset by Style Photosetting Ltd, Mayfield, East Sussex
Printed by Bell & Bain Limited, Glasgow

Contents

Acknowledgments

Thanks to UW Aberystwyth whose financial support financed trips to acquire materials necessary to the new edition.

Special thanks to my father, John Williams, who lent continuous support and made helpful suggestions for improvement, and also to my mother, Mair Williams, who typed the corrections for me.

My loving gratitude to Alex whose continuous support and understanding makes my work not only possible but more enjoyable.

CHAPTER ONE
Introduction

This book is intended to introduce students to the broad study of criminology. Stated thus the project sounds very simple, but the breadth of the disciplines and theories involved in the study of the subject renders it rather more elusive. It seems logical to begin with an explanation of what criminology is. Criminology includes the study of: the characteristics of the criminal law; the extent of crime; the effects of crime on victims and on society; methods of crime prevention; the attributes of criminals; and the characteristics and workings of the criminal justice system.

In earlier times there was a greater belief in the supernatural and in the effects of God on good behaviour and the Devil on bad behaviour. This gave rise to methods of resolving disputes like trial by battle and such methods of deciding guilt or innocence as trials by ordeal. These were perfectly understandable and logical if there was a reasonably wide acceptance of the premise that God would watch over the good and see that they got their reward – God would protect the innocent and see to it that the guilty were punished. It is a perfect example of how comprehension of certain social phenomena, such as crime, depends upon the important concepts of the day. In a more sceptical society, and as the importance of science and empirical enquiry increased, these views of criminality and criminal justice became less accepted. People became more and more interested in 'why' certain things occurred. It is not possible to prove or disprove the existence or effects of metaphysical or divine factors. Especially with the rise of rationalism through the eighteenth century, belief in heavenly or ethereal explanations declined and criminal justice moved on to set its bases on 'fact'.

Much of the modern work purports to be factual and claims to be scientific. It records information, often in statistics; uses the results of studies or tests; and embodies the conclusions drawn from such results. Even in this scientific era there is a place for speculation. Most scientific study begins with an idea of why something happens or works, and criminology is no different. The main difference between the old metaphysical ideas and those of today is that the modern theories lend themselves more readily to ideas of 'proof', or as Popper would put it, are capable of disproof. In criminological study the change is sometimes more apparent than real because the range of influences to be considered is wide and includes such intangibles as the effect of the environment on an individual's behaviour. Thus although modern criminology claims to be more scientific, that claim needs to be treated with care: some theories remain incapable of proof.

Part of the problem is that inherent in the nature of the subject are many concepts which are difficult to define and hard to measure. Even the central idea of what is a crime and who is a criminal has no single definitive answer. In fact, a number of the more recent theories are concerned with a consideration of why some behaviours are defined as criminal whilst others which may also be damaging are not, and why certain individuals are convicted of crimes whilst others who have also committed offences are allowed to escape conviction. Such approaches centre on the workings of the official systems of control rather than on trying to explain why people commit crimes. Their central reference is the definitions of the behaviour rather than the reasons for that behaviour. But, as we shall see, definitions which appear to be objective may turn out to have subjective elements: in this area of study the elusive nature of objectivity is a recurrent obstacle. Definitions always need careful scrutiny, but they are also indispensable. They are, for example, important to efforts to establish or explain why crime is committed or what should be done about it. For example, many researchers do not work within the legal definitions of crime, tied in with technicalities of defences, but rather consider what causes are behind a particular type of behaviour or what might help to prevent that behaviour. What the researcher accepts as criminal may be presented as objective but might in fact have subjective elements drawn, perhaps unconsciously, from the researcher's view of the world and how to improve it. Subjectivity is likely to be present throughout the study of criminology, including the present book, and its effects should always be considered.

Criminologists must take care to remember that their experimental material is human and that any testing will have effects on people. For this reason most of the scientific 'testing' is actually based on observation and use of available or collected data rather than experiments in any laboratory sense. However, in the area of punishment and treatment any effect given to theories has a very direct, and in some cases, unpleasant effect on those convicted of offences (some theorists would also treat those who might commit crimes) and their rights to be dealt with humanely must never be forgotten.

The present text contains a collection of theoretical and factual material. When dealing with what claims to be factual or objective proof of an idea it is important to be very wary. Some of the difficulties with such information have been mentioned above: a few need further consideration. Firstly, just because one idea has more studies which uphold it does not mean it is correct: each of those studies may be based on a false premise or be flawed through being subjective or through an unscientific work base. Similarly, although one theory may appear 'true' this might be misleading, as it may be limited by the knowledge available at the time – once we thought the world flat; our knowledge has since been extended and we now think we know it is a globe; knowledge may one day move us on again. Such shifts are more common in the case of criminology, partly because we are dealing with less solid proof than is available to other sciences and much of a proof may depend on attitudes. Indeed, in this area shifts in interpretation are necessary and desirable since they are affected by a constantly changing social and institutional environment. Most of the ideas put forward to explain criminality are based on some reasonably plausible premise. They can usually call upon some 'facts' to 'prove' that they explain criminality. Since no-one can encompass all possible data, which is literally limitless, the 'facts' are necessarily selective. At the same time, since in dealing with complex human issues there is never likely to be just one single cause, the process necessarily involves giving more weight to some factor or factors than to others. And since some, if not most, of these factors are likely to be impervious to measurement, an exercise of judgement is entailed. In assessing their significance, readers will be influenced by their own view of the world, which may also be shaped by the disciplines from which they approach the subject and by their preconceptions of the subject matter. Although it is necessary to warn about the perils of subjectivity and to indicate the limits to the scientific basis of the subject, it needs also to be remembered that what this book is reporting represents the fruits of a great deal of study by many fine minds over a long period of time. In the nature of the subject, certainty is rarely on offer, but it is hoped to extend understanding.

Criminology is a subject with a fairly long and varied history. Our study will begin at the end of the last century and will consider theories which have gained credence over the past century or so. There have been many approaches to the subject drawn from many different disciplines. The student of the subject is likely therefore to be confronted with a range of ideas drawn from numerous disciplines. The object of the book is to attempt to bring together the main currents and to act as a basic introduction to each and to provide a survey of the existing state of our knowledge in each area. Such a survey is particularly useful because there is no single accepted approach or answer to the problem of who commits crimes. Although the subject matter is largely set out in the various disciplines, it is hoped that students might be encouraged to consider the subject as a whole and from each discipline apply those parts which might be most useful.

Inevitably, a book of this kind which is trying to survey as large a part as possible of the literature and its origins and at the same time to put it into both its historical and contemporary contexts, will entail a great deal of enforced categorisation. No doubt other writers might organise all this somewhat differently. It is therefore necessary to say something briefly about how the present work has been ordered.

It is necessary to begin the study by indicating the basic constituents of the central subject, crime. One essential prerequisite is to place definitions on some of the major terms, and so Chapter Two looks at the definition of crime and how it is differently interpreted.

Crime is a subject about which nearly everyone has views. This is not a trivial consideration because criminology is not the property of the experts. Indeed, generally held views are important because notions of crime and how it and criminals should be dealt with are matters of public policy. Chapter Three considers some of the influences which shape public perceptions and in so doing places special importance on the media. Chapter Three goes on to consider some of the most problematic misconceptions about crime.

Perception of the problems caused by crime and the fear of it are largely shaped by popular impressions of how common it is, of – so to speak – the amount of crime that is about. This interacts with the influence of the media, e.g., every year when crime statistics are published all the papers carry features and stories about the amount and kinds of crime. The journalists' treatment is, however, necessarily selective and occasionally misleading. It is thus of crucial importance to the study of criminology both to know the sources of statistics, official and other, and to have some clear understanding of the use and limitations of this information. This area is considered in Chapter Four.

Beside needing to know about the amount of crime and the numbers of criminals, it is also important to have some information about victims of crime. Chapter Five considers the victim, the effects on victims and whether victims can be 'blamed' for their own victimisation. It also considers whether criminology and criminal law processes are sufficiently concerned with the victim.

The book then moves on to the various explanations and theories that have been developed over the years to account for the characteristics of criminals or of criminality. It is based around three main types of theory. Firstly, those which argue that criminality is caused by forces beyond the control of the individual. This characterises many of the chapters in this section, particularly the earlier ones, and is based on a positivist idea that behaviour is pre-determined. It appears in biological and psychological as well as sociological disciplines and tries to explain what causes criminality. Although often illuminating, it is essentially limited as it ignores the human factor of choice. One might say that entering a pool of water causes someone to become wet but that explanation does not explain why the person fell into or chose to enter the pool. The second group of theories allow for free choice in taking part in crime and therefore recognises a basic human trait: the ability of people to think and choose what is perceived as their own best interests. This is the basis of so-called classical theory. It has more recently been given extra weight by adding the possibility that people can by social process be influenced to believe that law-abiding behaviour is best for them and for society. This characterises a number of the learning and control theories. The third body of theories are less interested in crime and criminals than in the way society decides what and who to control and how it goes about these functions. These ideas grew up in the 1960s and are called the 'New Criminologies'.

There is a rough chronology about this in the sense that the type of general explanations which were initially developed are first treated before proceeding, in each area, to the more modern developments. The actual sequence is outlined below.

Chapters Six and Seven consider the effects of physical and biological factors on criminality and are largely deterministic. Chapters Eight, Nine and Ten then deal with the connection between psychological and mental factors and criminality. Most of these are deterministic in character. Parts of these, especially of Chapter Ten, also consider the effects of learning and socialisation on criminality. They involve a willingness to take part in criminal behaviour which introduces an element of choice or at least opens up the subject to such possibilities. Chapter Eleven goes on to discuss the effects of the environment on criminality. It considers factors such as ecology, poverty, unemployment and lower-class culture. Many of these are built upon in Chapter Twelve, where the effects of some social structures are considered and special attention is paid to juvenile criminality. Both of these chapters are largely positivist in approach. Chapter Thirteen leaves more to free will and is concerned with the way society might persuade individuals to be law-abiding. It looks at the social structures which may help law-abiding behaviour: by implication if they are absent criminality might well arise. Chapters Fourteen and Fifteen take a very different approach, either attributing criminality to the official control mechanisms or questioning the efficacy of the present definitions of criminality and the way in which we choose to control those who live in society. The ideas set out in Chapter Sixteen use elements drawn from all three approaches and relate these to what these writers regard as the real problems of crime and the practicalities of solving them. Chapters Seventeen and Eighteen deal with female offending. Although the author is unconvinced that different explanations are relevant to explain male and female criminality and believes that much of the earlier chapters apply equally to males and females, many criminologists have considered it necessary to look for differing explanations, often because they perceive that the two groups act differently. It would not be correct to ignore these other explanations but it is hoped that the reader will not thereby dismiss the earlier ideas from any relevance in considering female criminality.

The student may feel disappointed that relatively little emerges in the form of settled conclusions. Instead the intention has been to indicate the present state of a continuing debate and to point, where appropriate, to those interpretations and proposals which currently command the most general acceptance. Given what has been said about the complexities of criminology, the difficulties of suppressing subjectivity and even prejudice, the disputes over definitions and the resistance of many of the key concepts to precision and measurement, definite conclusions and certainties are probably inappropriate. The book is intended to give a broad overview to the scope of criminology, to the ideas which have influenced the area of the subject, and to the practical uses to which these have been, or might be, put. In the course of the work a wide range of authorities has been drawn on; they have necessarily been treated rather briefly. If this encourages students to turn to the original texts a major object of the book will have been achieved.

CHAPTER TWO

Definitions, Terminology and the Criminal Process

2.1 INTRODUCTION

Criminology is concerned with crime: to understand the materials every criminologist should thus have a good grounding in the criminal law. This chapter can only act as a very brief introduction to that field and students should have recourse to one of the more detailed texts on this subject (see for example Smith and Hogan (1996); Ryan and Scanlan (1991); *Blackstone's Criminal Practice* (published annually); Allen (1997); or Cross, Jones and Card (1995)). In this chapter some of the technical terms will be briefly explained and some of the theories about the sources and limits of criminal laws will be considered.

2.2 THE JUDICIAL PROCESS

In England and Wales the legal system consists of two separate sets of hierarchies of courts. One set (together with the police, the Crown Prosecution Service, the court officers and the penal institutions) enforces the criminal law on behalf of the State. The other set enforces the civil law between and on behalf of aggrieved individuals in society. Civil law is largely concerned with making one individual pay compensation to another for some wrong done to him under the law of tort (civil wrongs which include such things as liability for negligence, defamation, damage to premises and injury to animals) or compensating the injury arising from a breach of contract or a breach of trust. Otherwise it is concerned with settling disputes as to entitlement or relationships as in dealing with matters of land law, succession or family law. In contrast, criminal law, irrespective of what its aim or purpose should be, is punitive. It punishes any act or omission forbidden by the criminal law.

There are differences in the aims and procedures of criminal as opposed to civil courts, but it is difficult to define what is criminal, especially since most acts or omissions which are crimes, or at least serious crimes, will also (simultaneously) be civil wrongs (i.e., torts). Thus in a recent high-profile case in the United States, O.J. Simpson was charged under the criminal law with the murder of his wife. He was acquitted and that verdict cannot be reversed: none the less, the family of the murdered woman brought a civil case against him and a large sum of money was awarded in damages. However, many activities may be torts which are not also crimes. Generally, any act or omission may give rise to two consequences, one criminal and the other tortious (i.e., civil). One act or omission may result in an individual being prosecuted and punished by the State and also in the person injured bringing an action (i.e., suing) in the civil courts for compensation called damages. Only in the former will the police and prosecuting authorities be involved and the liberty of the individual be in jeopardy. In the latter, only that person's, or his insurers', wallet will be in any danger.

2.3 FORMAL SOURCES OF CRIMINAL LAW

Textbooks on the English legal system (this applies to England and Wales and will be used in this sense throughout this book) will tell you that there are various sources of law: custom, the judiciary (common law), the prerogative (of the Crown), legislation and directives from the institutions of the European Community. As far as the principles of criminal law dealt with in this book are concerned, an appreciation of only two of these creative sources of legal rules is required: common law and legislation. Common law consists of the rules established by the decisions of judges. These decisions in our system become precedents which are binding on, and therefore must be applied by, courts lower in the hierarchy than the one which made the decision. Legislation consists of statutes or Acts of Parliament and delegated legislation (rules made by persons or bodies other than Parliament but authorised to do so by Parliament). English criminal law is made up of rules contained in statutes and precedents, in court precedents (the common law) and in the judicial interpretations of those statutes, which interpretations become the law unless and until Parliament or a higher court alters any such judicial interpretation.

In most instances Parliament lays down the conduct which is to be criminalised and also sets out the maximum penalties and sometimes whether there are any special powers, for example of search or arrest, which should attach to the detection of this type of conduct. The courts through the judges (legal matters) and the jury (matters of fact) set the limits in any particular case. In this phase the judges are very important, because in most cases various elements such as what are the limits of mental intention or of particular defences arise, which are questions of common law for the judge to rule upon. It is then for the jury to decide what factually occurred. The judges can thus play a very powerful role in the outcome of any trial, and do this without appearing to be making any decisions and claiming that they are merely applying the will of Parliament. For offences which are considered to be less serious (mainly non-indictable cases) the process may be carried out by magistrates.

This lays out the formal sources of the law but does not consider where these laws arise or why they are chosen. There are numerous theories on the sources of the laws themselves. Some believe that they are derived from torts or wrongs done to the individual and that those which were most serious or which were perceived as having consequences for the State also became crimes. Moral standards have also been given as a source of our criminal laws. Others believe that they are the product of customs or mores which the society found or finds particularly important. In all cases they are supposed to alter and be repealed as society decides that they are no longer of import. Unfortunately, they often are left sitting on the statute books or in the common law long after their usefulness has been outlived, only because no-one bothers to repeal them. Such oversight can give rise to problems and to anomalies. This is what happened to the blasphemy laws, which many people consider to be inappropriate in a modern multi-cultural, multi-racial, multi-religion society and which had lain dormant for over 50 years. Many believed that they no longer represented the laws of Britain, then in 1979 they were revived by Mary Whitehouse (see *Whitehouse* v *Lemon* [1979] 2 WLR 281). This revival, together with subsequent events, seemed to aggravate racial and religious tensions in Britain in the late 1980s and early 1990s.

Most of these ideas are based on a consensus idea of society, that is, that society functions as an integrated structure whose members agree on the norms, rules and values which are to be uniformly respected: the criminal law is then merely the embodiment of what the members in a society disapprove of and find most unacceptable. As can be seen from the case of blasphemy, this idea breaks down from time to time. More recently, two other ideas have emerged about the sources of the criminal law. The first contends that rather than acting as a consensus, society is made up of a series of conflicting and competing groups – the conflict theory. Under this idea the criminal law is said to be built on what is important to the wealthy and powerful in the society, and particularly protects them against those who might try to usurp their position. At the same time, some of the proponents of conflict theory assert that the criminal law often fails to criminalise activities from which these groups may gain even if others in society suffer (these ideas will be further considered in Chapter Fifteen). The last idea is also a more recent interpretation and is again based on the hypothesis that the criminal law is built up by those in political and legal power. In this case, however, it is not claimed that the law arises only to protect their interests; rather that it represents the preferred definition of these privileged groups as to where the line should be drawn, and they may make their decision depending upon their values, norms or morals as well as on their position in society (see Chapter Fourteen).

Criminology has totally different origins. Its aim is to ascertain the causes of crime, to pre-empt or prevent crime by 'treating' its perceived causes, to study the effects of crime on society, and to analyse societal reactions to crime. Consequently its source is a combination of theory and empirical research. Its aim is to be more scientific than forensic.

2.4 UNDERLYING INFLUENCES

The English or common law system is adversarial not inquisitorial, and generally it does not permit the judiciary to consider and rule on points (or give interpretations of the meanings of statutes) which are not in issue on the facts of the case brought before the court (in civil law by a party, and in criminal law generally by or on behalf of the State) or arising on an appeal. The courts cannot take the initiative and clarify criminal law principles *ad hoc*. They must wait until the obscure or difficult points come before them. Even then the court's ruling will be authoritative only on the particular point in issue. As a consequence, the courts frequently consider an issue relating to criminal liability in one case without reference to the effect such a decision may have on other parts of the criminal law because that effect is not in issue. Because the judiciary cannot consider and rule on points which are not in issue on the facts of the case before the court, such areas of potential conflict between the rules and principles of criminal law may only be resolved where an individual case raises such issues simultaneously or where the point in conflict is raised specifically in a subsequent case or on appeal. Considerable time may pass before any of these events occur. Meanwhile academics may be critical and pressure may grow amongst the public for Parliament to change or clarify the law by legislation.

The courts, however, sometimes voluntarily undertake the creation of principles of criminal law. For example, at one time the rule was that where an accused intended his conduct to produce certain consequences (such as the death or serious injury of another) or he foresaw as a matter of high probability the occurrence of those consequences he could, if his conduct caused the death of another, be convicted of murder. It has now been determined that foresight of consequences is in law neither an alternative nor an equivalent of intention. Nevertheless, the judiciary tell us that foresight of such consequences may still lead to an irresistible inference that those very consequences were in fact intended by an accused. A jury may, therefore, come to the conclusion as a matter of evidence or fact that if an accused foresaw certain consequences resulting from his actions, he intended to bring them about, but a jury is no longer compelled because of a rule of law to come to that conclusion.

Sometimes the judiciary create or change law which remains part of the realm of common law (i.e., those areas of our law not legislated but traditionally derived from court decisions) by an express pronouncement or reformulation of a rule of substantive law. A good example is in the cases concerning conspiracy to corrupt public morals and conspiracy to outrage public decency. Although academics may debate the point, it would appear that the judiciary in those instances clearly created new criminal offences. Sometimes, however, the judiciary alter the law by more arcane methods. In the example noted above relating to murder, the courts had classified an element of the offence as a rule of substantive law which permitted but one conclusion, and later reclassified that element as a matter of adjectival law, in other words as a matter of evidence or fact for a jury to determine from its own conclusions. Whether or not this particular change will have any practical effect upon the law, or on the number of persons convicted of murder, is at present uncertain. Nevertheless, such a development illustrates the subtle ways in which the judiciary may work a reformulation of the criminal law; it should thus be of great interest to, but rarely appears to have been taken into consideration by, criminologists. It should be clear that the judiciary are contracting or expanding the net within which persons may be made liable for particular offences whenever they expand or contract the definition of intention (by saying that foresight is or is not included) or the definition of recklessness (by saying that failure to consider a risk either is or is not included), or if they impose an objective test as opposed to a subjective test for *mens rea* (the mental state of the accused in respect of the elements of the offence). Likewise, if the judiciary declare an offence to be one of strict liability as opposed to one requiring proof of *mens rea*, they are widening the net and increasing the possibility of persons being found guilty of that particular offence. This is seldom, if ever, referred to by criminologists despite the fact that it must have some bearing at least on the way criminal statistics are perceived.

The reasons why the judges seek to change our criminal law in such a covert way are partly social and partly political. Today the constitutional position of the judiciary is such that they must avoid being seen overtly to create new offences or to widen the ambit of existing criminal liability. This function is now, in theory at least, the responsibility of Parliament, but in reality the judges always have played a part, either directly in developing the common law, or by the process of interpreting the will of Parliament in pronouncing on the meaning of statutes. What affects the judges' views, amongst other things, may well be what they perceive, rightly or wrongly, to be socially desirable or what they consider a danger to society, its culture, its ethos, its Judaeo-Christian morals and its liberal-democratic tradition. Their views may in turn be affected by whether or not they perceive crime generally, or particular crimes, to be on the increase in their community. There is no doubt that the judges play a very significant role in our society. Two things should be evident, first that at various stages in the criminal process (prosecution, adjudication and sentence) there are few guide-lines or rules and much discretion is left in the first instance to the prosecutors and in the latter instances to the judiciary. The beliefs and attitudes of judges about criminals and crime, and about public policy (which is a guise for public opinion or more often public acceptability) become very important. If their views are too idiosyncratic or flexible they may not attain proportionality by way of punishment and equality of treatment or justice between offenders, and may create uncertainty in society because there would be no predictability. On the other hand, if their views are too stereotyped or ultra-conservative or radical, they may detract from the second constitutional function of the judge, which is to protect our traditional freedom and liberties. If they show evidence of prejudice for or against the ways of life or traditions of particular groups of people, again they may attack the constitutional rights of citizens and residents of Britain. Some discussion of the importance and effects of this judicial power is made in Chapters Fourteen and Fifteen, where it is shown that it is only relatively recently that criminologists have acknowledged the importance of the judiciary and their opinions.

A criminologist should be aware of the factors and policies which mould the criminal law causing the creation, and constant reshaping, of criminal offences. Also needed is an appreciation of the nature of, and reasons for, the criminal law and of the judicially controlled mechanisms for its reformulation. A realisation of the influences and policies behind the judicial or parliamentary mind, which in a constantly changing society are themselves necessarily unstable, gives an understanding of the impetus for change in the criminal law and an explanation of its fluidity. An understanding is also required of the motivation of individuals and pressure groups (including the prosecutors, the magistracy and the judiciary), since these are seeking to change or to prevent change in the law. Such motives can range from direct vested interest to a deep belief that it is in the best interests of society as a whole, essential for the protection of individuals or a class, or an unwarranted detriment to freedom. These are some of the basic skills and qualities which it would be desirable to find in a criminologist: simply to specify them is enough to indicate that they represent a sort of ideal.

2.5 DEFINING A CRIME

2.5.1 Formal legalistic definition

It is difficult to define what is criminal or to distinguish a crime from a tort. One cannot even declare that crimes are always more serious in their effects either on the individual or on society. For example, the negligent manufacture and marketing of a product which turns out to be dangerous may be far more injurious to both individuals and society than the theft of a pencil, yet the former would normally only constitute a tort whereas the latter is criminal. There are similarities: each is a wrong, each is a breach of a legal obligation or rule. What, then, is the difference? Although it is circular, the best definition and the best distinguishing feature is that only if the breach of a legal rule (the wrong) has criminal consequences attached to it, will it be a criminal offence. An offence or a crime, then, is a wrong to society involving the breach of a legal rule which has criminal consequences attached to it (i.e., prosecution by the State in the criminal courts and the possibility of punishment being imposed). This gives a legalistic view of a crime but fails to impart the types of activity which may fall under that head. Above all, it must be re-emphasized that it is a circular definition – a crime is something the law calls a crime and uses criminal prosecutions and sanctions to deal with. Despite these shortcomings with the definition, it is essential that one never forgets that no matter how immoral, reprehensible, damaging or dangerous an act is, it is not a crime unless it is made such by the authorities of the State – the legislature and, at least through interpretation, the judges.

2.5.2 Basic elements of most crimes

Most criminal laws forbid certain types of behaviour, and therefore before a person can be convicted, it must be proved that he or she acted in a fashion proscribed by law: this is generally known as the *actus reus* of an offence. Some defences go to the very core of the action and claim that part of the *actus reus* was missing. For example, the offence of assault requires that an individual unlawfully injures another: a claim that an injury was caused as the result of self defence is thus claiming that the action has not been completed, i.e., it renders the injury lawful. Another example arises in the offence of rape, which involves sexual intercourse with a woman without her consent; if the man claims that she consented he is claiming that part of the *actus reus* is absent. In both cases the defence goes to the heart of the action. Other defences may admit the action but ask that it be excused because of, for example, duress or certain types of mistake. In stealing, someone intentionally deprives another person of property and thus clearly commits an offence: but if that offence is committed because a third party forced it at gunpoint, the offender could plead lack of choice.

Generally, omitting to do something will not amount to the *actus reus* of an offence. For example, if I decide to watch a young child drowning in inches of water and do nothing to save its life, I am not guilty of any criminal offence though clearly my inaction is morally indefensible. Basically, the law usually only punishes individuals for positive conduct and not for inaction. There are, however, some notable exceptions. In a few instances the law requires certain types of behaviour, and therefore the individual may be convicted for failure to act in that prescribed fashion, for example, failure to submit the accounts of a public limited company. In others, there may be a duty to act. This duty may arise through statute, for example, the duty to report road accidents to the police. The duty may arise out of a person's job or out of holding public office, for example, a police officer may have a duty to prevent an assault. The duty may also arise out of the obligation to care for a dependent.

The second important element which is required in most cases is a mental state. There must be a state of mind with respect to the *actus reus*: this is called the *mens rea*, that is an intention to act in the proscribed fashion or to bring about the unacceptable ends, or in some cases reckless indifference to causing a particular harm. It is important to distinguish *mens rea* from motive. If I decide to kill a close relative, such as my grandmother, because she is helpless and begs me to put her out of her misery, some might argue that my motive is honourable and understandable. But if I premeditate my action and intend its consequences, my conduct is murder just as if I had shot an enemy with hatred in my heart. The conviction must in both cases be murder; the motive does not alter the fact that the crime has been committed. Motive, however, may be taken into account in sentencing or in carrying out the sentence. In the above example, the court has to pass a life sentence on all murderers, but the time actually spent in prison may vary depending on the conduct of the prisoners and possibly also on the motive for the crime, as this may touch on the possibility of the offence being repeated. In cases where the court has a discretion, they may decide to punish the person who acted in a criminal way but with a good motive less severely than if the individual acted out of greed, hatred or other unacceptable motives. Foucault (1988) has claimed that all too often the law gets caught up with motive rather than with intent. He also questions the idea that motive should be used at the sentencing stage, although most would have more sympathy for a merciful killing than for a cold-blooded killing, and most would prefer to see the former sentenced less severely than the latter.

There are some defences which question the *mens rea* of an offence, such as a plea of insanity, diminished responsibility and automatism, all of which are discussed in Chapter Nine.

In some cases the *mens rea* of an offence may be established if the individual intended to do wrong, though a greater harm than intended occurs as a result of the actions. For example, if I intentionally hit someone it is an assault, and I could be convicted of that crime, but if the person is particularly weak and dies as a result of the injury, then I may be convicted of manslaughter or, if it can be proven that I intended to cause grievous bodily harm, murder. Although I did not intend to kill, the death is the direct result of a crime which I did intend.

Some offences do not require any *mens rea*, as to all or some of the *actus reus*, on behalf of the offender. These offences are known as strict liability offences. Many strict liability offences are set by Parliament and are sometimes referred to as 'state of affairs' offences or as absolute liability offences. They often fall into the area of public welfare offences or regulatory offences, and regulate potentially dangerous activities, like motoring, or they protect people against other dangers of modern life. In these cases, all that needs to be proven is that the state of affairs existed and the crime is complete; it is no defence to say that one did not intend this state of affairs or even that one was unaware of it. Examples of this arise in many road traffic violations (e.g., driving with defective brakes, or more generally the use of defective and dangerous motor vehicles); possession of dangerous objects or substances such as firearms or controlled drugs (where all that is necessary is knowledge of possession, not that the thing possessed is a controlled drug); public health legislation such as the sale of food containing extraneous matter; or control of pollution. These types of activities fall into the category of strict liability to force people to exercise higher standards of care to ensure that offences are not committed, especially when their activities could present a danger to the public. Furthermore, because they often involve an omission, for example failure to renew the tyres on a vehicle, it would be difficult to prove the *mens rea* as to all or some of the *actus reus*.

Lastly, for all crimes there is a legally prescribed punishment. The punishment is usually set out in terms of a maximum and the actual punishment in any particular case is left to the discretion of the judge, although in addition to the established minimum life sentence for murder, the Crime (Sentences) Act 1997 has further curtailed their discretion by requiring minimum sentences for repeat offenders of certain serious crime. In addition, both the defence and the prosecution can now appeal the sentence, and the Court of Appeal can lay down guide-lines for sentencing. In a few cases there is a minimum punishment. For example, murder carries with it a life sentence, drunk driving carries with it the loss of a driving licence.

2.5.3   What actions are criminalised?

Why certain acts or omissions are declared criminal and others are not is a difficult question. So are the questions: what aggravating factors warrant being made the subject of a separate offence? and which mitigating factors should be recognised as defences? As with the terminology (see 2.8), there is an element of fashion involved in attempts to answer these fundamental issues, but the underlying rationale is largely governed by the traditional ethos and ethics of the society. In our case this relates mainly to the largely white, male-oriented, Judaeo-Christian tradition and the conservatism that accompanies the desire for stability, order and predictability. Morality and notions of blameworthiness based on harm may explain the formulation of the early fundamental crimes (murder, theft, etc.) but do not necessarily fully explain the modern social welfare, moral improvement and traffic offences created by statute. No one philosophy or cause can adequately explain why differing forms of activity are deemed criminal. Morality, economics, politics, public administration, public order and public safety all play a part. Also, there is an interrelationship with the equally complex question: why do people commit crimes? As in defining a crime, there are numerous conflicting views and theories. As we shall see, attempts to provide explanations have to confront such fundamental issues as: does crime occur because man is inherently evil; or because of socio-economic conditions; or because of physical or mental illness; or because of genetic, inherited defects; or are there other factors or combinations of factors which are responsible? Such questions form the core of this book and are considered in Chapters Six to Seventeen. They represent an attempt to get away from studying the principles of criminal law and the theories of criminology in a vacuum, and to enquire about their aim and purpose; whether these ends are achieved; and whether claims made by criminologists and others are substantiated by sound research. It is not claimed that such an approach gives, or can give, clear-cut conclusions, but it is strongly contended that it is essential for anyone seeking understanding of a hugely complex field.

2.5.3.1   Consensus approach

This assumes that the activities which are criminalised are firmly based on the generally agreed mores for conduct. The criminal law thus seeks to identify and control the types of behaviour which the community finds unacceptable. Perhaps the most universally assumed aim of the criminal law, and that which is said to be the strongest unifying element in the consensus theory is that of averting harm. Mill accepted that the State could always intervene in the liberty of personal conduct to prevent one individual harming another. This basic liberal ideal has guided the consensus theory in its main aim, the prohibition of crimes which are *mala in se*, harmful in themselves. This includes activities which attack the person such as assault, murder and rape as well as acts which attack property or the possession or ownership of property such as theft, arson or intentional damage. Many of these offences are criminalised in most societies and there is often claimed to be a general consensus about their prohibition. Consensus theorists see that another of the main aims or functions of the criminal law is the maintenance of order in society. Even that is not free from ambiguity, but it is clearly not its only function. But the defining of function obviously affects the ambit of what is and is not criminal, and consequently again must be of interest to criminologists. For example, Lord Simonds in *Shaw* v *DPP* [1962] AC 220 dwelt on another function (in his view) when he said its aim is 'to conserve not only the safety and order but also the moral welfare of the State'. That raises two basic points: firstly, it is not a viewpoint that would command universal agreement (see, e.g., 2.5.3.2, below), and secondly, it illustrates that criminal laws are perceived as having numerous aims. These laws do maintain public order and the safety and integrity of individuals, but also they raise revenue (e.g., the laws punishing those who evade income tax); they regulate business (e.g., they punish the charging of excessive prices and they punish unhygienic and unsafe practices); they protect employees; they conserve the environment; they preserve heritage; and they enforce morality. The basic effect is thus to maintain society in its present form and to ensure its smooth functioning.

Today in this country there are literally thousands of offences created by statute which are designed to enforce certain standards in the practice of lawful activities where such activities may result in harm to the public. The rules relating to road traffic, to public hygiene, rules about health and safety at work and rules governing the entry into and conduct of certain businesses or professions are examples. These rules are generally enforceable by way of criminal sanction. Unlike the traditional common law notions of crime, these newer statutory offences generally punish omissions as well as positive acts.

Furthermore, they are more often than not created as offences of strict liability for which an accused may be held liable without any proof of a blameworthy state of mind with regard to one or more element of the *actus reus*. This last innovation has produced practical advantages but it means that if a minor prohibited act, omission or event occurs for which a person is responsible, that person may be guilty. Guilt does not necessarily depend, as it must in the old common law offences, on state of mind. People may be deemed guilty irrespective of what they intended, thought or believed. Consensus theories accept this as necessary to the smooth running of society and also as a way of permitting activities which may cause harm, whilst minimising the danger. Generally, the ordinary man or woman in society does not consider persons convicted of these sorts of offences, including traffic violations, 'criminals', that term being popularly reserved to express moral condemnation for the acts of murderers, rapists, thieves and the like; yet these regulatory or social welfare type offences can cause individuals and society no less suffering and harm. Should society and the law treat such offenders as being as blameworthy and reprehensible as the traditional 'criminals'? Why is there a consensus that they should not?

Finally, where there are offences the sole purpose of which is the enforcement of morality, the question needs to be asked: are the types of conduct declared criminal matters of private morality with which the criminal law should not be concerned at all? If the prohibited conduct does no harm to society or to the participants, should that conduct be criminal? In a sense, by declaring certain immoral conduct to be criminal, society is creating or causing crime. The abrogation or repeal of such laws would delete a mass of criminal statistics and prevent large numbers of people being labelled criminals. It would not mean that these acts and their perpetrators would be acceptable, because they may still be considered antisocial by the majority of the community. Clearly, repeal would be to those persons' advantage, but it could also be to the advantage of the community generally. Law enforcement agencies may, for example, then be able to concentrate their resources in the prevention or pursuit of serious criminal offenders: the muggers, rapists, robbers, those who cause grievous bodily harm, and the like. Are the criminal offences relating to alcohol, gambling, pornography, bigamy, blasphemy, bestiality, criminal libel, conspiracy to corrupt public morals, conspiracy to outrage public decency and possibly also controls on drugs outmoded and unreasonable restrictions on our liberty? Would individuals and society be at risk if current laws on these matters were abolished? If these laws are essential to our society, why are adultery, fornication and seduction not criminal? Occasionally, popular demands lead to legislation to withdraw certain conduct from the ambit of the criminal law. One of the best examples is the public debate following the Wolfenden Committee Report (1957) which led to Parliament passing the Sexual Offences Act 1967, which declared that homosexual acts between consenting adult males (then over age 21, altered to 18 by the Criminal Justice and Public Order Act 1994) in private were no longer a crime.

The limit of the criminal law is a topic which has taxed lawyers, criminologists, sociologists, philosophers and others for many years. The theorists touching on this point can generally be split into three camps. The first suggests that the criminal law should not intervene unless there is a harm to some discernible individual. This gives rise to problems when considering activities, such as tax evasion, which may harm society more generally. There is also the problem of defining how direct the harm needs to be. Does it include harm to one's family if a parent gambles all his or her income, does it include harm to an individual by being offended, e.g., if a woman is faced with a flasher, or is it only concerned with very direct physical harm? One of the most famous answers to these questions was provided by Mill (1974, first published 1859) who argued that:

> the only purpose for which power can be rightfully exercised over any member of a civilized community, against his will, is to prevent harm to others. His own good, either physical or moral, is not a sufficient warrant. (*On Liberty*, Chapter One).

This individual freedom he extended to the 'freedom to unite for any purpose not involving harm to others.' (*On Liberty*, Chapter One.) More recently this idea has gained support from the Wolfenden Committee Report (1957), although its support for the harm principle is not so unquestioning as was Mill's.

A second viewpoint is that, as well as protecting individuals from harm caused by others, the criminal law should be used to protect individuals from themselves, to protect them from dangerous substances such as drugs, or to regulate the way in which they participate in dangerous activities such as driving or working machinery, possibly by requiring the wearing of protective gear such as helmets, seat-belts, goggles or ear protectors. Hart (1963), although largely agreeing with Mill, shows some sympathy for these arguments: '. . . paternalism – the protection of people against themselves – is a perfectly coherent policy.' (*Law, Liberty and Morality*, Part II.)

The third approach would use the criminal laws in order to uphold morality. Clearly most crimes are morally wrong, but some observers would criminalise activities purely because they were immoral, irrespective of whether they harmed another individual (Devlin (1965)). The moral basis for law is very old. In medieval times, under the name of natural law, it was adopted by famous Christian philosophers such as St Thomas Aquinas to claim that law was God-given for the protection of people. Some of the moral laws date back to this time although now they are often supported on non-Christian grounds – grounds of the mores of a society which it is necessary to respect in order to prevent society disintegrating for lack of control. These various viewpoints, besides indicating the enduring mysteries of the human condition, also reflect the variety and subjectivity of the aims and functions of the criminal law. A further set of nuances is explored in the next subsection.

2.5.3.2 Modern sociological approaches

The above approaches generally assumed that there was something about the nature of an act itself or its consequences which made it unacceptable. The present approach will consider whether the crime consists not in the act itself, but simply in it being defined by society as criminal. The implication is that crime is constructed by the society or group. This idea has given rise to a number of explanations of criminality (discussed in Chapters Fourteen and Fifteen) but here we are concerned with how this might have affected the definitions of crimes. Virtually all societies are too large for everyone to define the rules which are thus constructed by some group or groups. Acceptance of this as a sociological fact has led to various interpretations of the ways in which such crimes are defined.

The first of these is the conflict school which views the constructs of modern society as fluid or dynamic and claims that new issues are resolved, or old ones redefined, by the resolution of conflict (Dahrendorf (1959)). In this analysis society is not built on harmony and consensus but rather is constructed of competing groups who struggle for power. Conflicts between workers and employers; between the sexes or the races; between religions; between political groupings. Each of these conflicts is resolved by the more powerful group enforcing its views and using the law as its weapon. In criminal terms this is done through controlling their opponents' behaviour, by calling it illegal. On this view the criminal law is constructed to protect the interests of powerful groups. Neither individuals nor their behaviour is inherently criminal: the social order has constructed the proscribed areas of behaviour (see Quinney (1970) and Turk (1969)). It is further argued that the law is applied more vigorously to the less powerful than to others, making criminality almost by definition the normal response of the powerless or disadvantaged to their position in life. Conflict theorists also claim that public opinion is manipulated by the same powerful groups so that the proscribed behaviour becomes widely accepted as necessary for the protection of many in the society. This might explain why certain actions are either not criminal or are treated very leniently (for a fuller discussion of conflict see Chapter Fifteen and for some illustrations see Chapter Three).

In the 1970s critical criminologists took this position one step further (see Taylor et al. (1973)). They criticised the conflict theorists for still viewing criminality as pathological and proposed a view, based on Marx, which studied crime as a wider subject, including the relationships between crime, criminal, victim and State. The areas of behaviour which are defined as criminal are those necessary to a capitalist society. Under these the upper classes can exploit the weak, put them in physical danger, and transgress their human rights either with total impunity or with only very light punishment (for a full discussion see Chapter Fifteen). This very politicised attack helped many to question the *status quo* and to confront the possibility that the criminal law was designed to control certain types of behaviour for reasons other than the general well-being of those in the society. The anti-capitalist slant naturally alienated many.

More recently theorists have moved on again. The critical school of thought splintered into Marxist and more conservative sections. Most of the latter group still provide socialist perspectives but do not accept the Marxist alternative to the *status quo*. They retain the attack on early theories but do not accept that the criminal system emerges solely out of the capitalist domination of society. They see power as just one element – others include culture, personality, prejudice and even chance – in determining the social order. They agree that the criminal law tends to define the activities of those who are dominant as legitimate and those of the weak as less acceptable, but the reasons are not always capitalistic. Many activities are deconstructed to discover interactions and to understand and analyse behaviour. Law may be constructed by the powerful and in their interest, but this may often be with the blessing of the weaker in society. These writers have a wider view of the concept of crime. They look not only at the criminals and their behaviour, and the State and its need for a definition of criminal, but also at society's constructs of social control, and at the views, actions and input of the victims.

Each of these theories sees crime as an artificially constructed social reality: it is made by particular people to protect the interests of some over those of others. To illustrate the point, even violent behaviour is not always viewed and treated the same way. Criminal violence is created by those who make and enforce the law rather than by the nature of the behaviour. In the media and general discussions on the level of violence in our society it is usually only this officially constructed area of behaviour that is considered. Thus most of the controls on violence only protect against violence on the street. Until recently domestic violence was not taken seriously. Even as recently as the last century the law permitted husbands physically to chastise their wives; it still permits parents (and other carers) to treat children in ways which if committed against an adult, would be a crime. Only in the last 20 years has excessive violence against partners or children been accepted as an activity needing strong enforcement measures to punish and control it. Assaults committed by law enforcers themselves are rarely prosecuted whereas similar acts by others might well culminate in imprisonment. Corporations and governments may take decisions they know or suspect will result in death or injury and yet will not necessarily face criminal prosecution: asbestos, thalidomide; use of soldiers to test mustard gas or the effects of atomic bomb radiation. The criminal law does not protect against all the dangers we face, nor even against all the worst dangers (e.g., food, air, environment). It tends rather to concentrate attention on the activities of a few who endanger others, and then to claim that the criminal law is objective and protects all in our society.

2.5.4 Particular cases

In the above discussion a number of theories were briefly mentioned which might help students of criminology to understand the complexity of the idea of the subject and to see that the factors on which it is based are not necessarily objectively defined and universally accepted. It is important to keep this problem in mind through some of the discussions which arise later. Before we leave the subject of the definition of crimes we will look at some areas which give substance to these difficulties.

2.5.4.1 *Victimless crime*

What is the utility of controlling behaviours which do not have any direct harm on others? It picks up on one of the central elements to the consensus theory of crime.

Bedau (1974) set out in four principles what is generally meant by victimless crimes. First, there must be a consensual participation of all the people involved in the activity. Second, no participant complains to the police. The fact that a non-participant may make a complaint, he argues, is irrelevant. Third, the participants generally believe that they are not harmed by the activity, although others may disagree with their assessment of the situation. Finally, most of these offences involve the willing exchange, among adults, of desired goods or services. He recognises that some offences which may be classed as victimless may not fit in with all these elements, for example, public drunkenness and the mere use of drugs involving no transaction.

Each author who writes in this area has a slightly different view of what activities fall within this concept, but the following are frequently included: drunkenness and related offences; sale and use of prohibited substances; vagrancy and begging; gambling; prostitution (or rather the offence of soliciting); homosexuality (still an offence for males below the legal age of consent); various adult consensual sexual offences such as bestiality and buggery. Some also include abortion, bigamy, private fighting, bribery, flashing between adults and obscenity and pornography between adults. There are some clear inconsistencies in this area; for example, why is bigamy illegal whereas both adultery and living with a person of the opposite sex as if married are legal?; why are the use and sale of some substances which may be considered harmful to the user, such as heroin, made unlawful whilst sale and use of others, such as tobacco, is legal?; why are soliciting in public, setting up a brothel, kerb-crawling and living off immoral earnings illegal whilst prostitution itself, although unlawful, is not criminal?

Whether and how these activities are regulated varies very widely from State to State. They vary on habitual and cultural grounds, but most frequently they vary on moral grounds, and most of these have a basis in authority. It appears that the legality or illegality of these activities depends mostly upon the morality and the economic interests of the groups with the most political power in the State.

Many elements in society now call for these offences to be decriminalised. Some have been *de facto* decriminalised in that they are either not policed and/or when discovered their perpetrators are not prosecuted. In many police areas this has happened to the possession and use of small amounts of soft drugs. Others have been *de jure* decriminalised, such as homosexuality between legally consenting adults in private. Many people who argue for their decriminalisation do so on the basis that criminalising them has failed to control the problem and in some cases it may have exacerbated the difficulties. Many of those, including some in the police and other enforcement agencies, who question the use of this criminal law to control drug-taking, do so on this basis. Non-criminal methods, such as programmes to help drug addicts, may be more appropriate (see Schur (1974)).

There is an additional case for decriminalisation on wider cost/benefit arguments, which have been laid out by Packer (1968); Morris and Hawkins (1970); and Schur (1974). First, they argue that the police and court time spent in dealing with these offences is not efficient use of these precious and expensive resources. Secondly, that the type of police investigations required to control this behaviour is often unsavoury and degrading to the police officers, and that they should not be required to participate in this activity. Thirdly, that criminalising the behaviour causes a black market to open up and operate in this field and allows those who are willing to take the chance to make large profits out of such deals. Fourthly, that law enforcement officers are exposed to bribes, some of which could be very tempting. Fifthly, that in order to obtain these substances or services the individual has to turn to criminals, and may become cut off from law-abiding citizens and learn further criminal behaviours. Sixthly, if the substance is illegal and there is a market, then the providers of that service or item are taking a risk providing it, and will require a high price which may force the customers to perform crimes in order to obtain the necessary money. Each of these suggests that the cost of criminalising and policing these types of offences is too high, and that society should therefore find some other way of controlling them, if control is warranted.

There is now a realisation that crimes do not fall neatly into victimless and predatory offences. If the term 'victimless' means consensual participants there are some offences where all those who participate are consenting. In the case of drugs there are producers, importers, dealers and sellers and each of these generally consents to his or her crime, although people may unwittingly carry the drugs, hidden in their luggage or in a vehicle (a particular problem for international lorry drivers). There are other clusters of offences of a primarily predatory nature, such as assault, where there is a victim who does not consent. Lastly there are clusters of offences which have both consensual and predatory elements. Property offences are often of this sort. The initial theft or burglary is predatory with a definite victim, but it is followed by much consensual activity in receiving and dealing in stolen property. Many of the predatory offences would be unlikely to occur without the consensual offence which occurs later. Conceptualising offences as victimless can thus sometimes be counter-productive when they may be organically connected with a predatory crime. In assessing victimless offences and considering them for decriminalisation it is therefore necessary to be aware of the wider context and their possible connections with predatory offences.

2.5.4.2 Sexism
Criminal laws can originate in a conflict between two groups where the interests of one group are subordinated to those of the other. Critical theorists initially raised this in the context of the laws, consciously or unconsciously, favouring the interests of the rich over those of the poor. More recently attention has been given to the ways in which the criminal law discriminates against women. Two areas – provocation and rape – are discussed as examples of what some view as deliberate discrimination against women not only by the criminal justice system (see Chapters Seventeen and Eighteen) but also by the criminal law itself.

Violent crimes committed by women are rare, killings by women are even less common. Where they occur they mostly victimise a male partner (Edwards (1989)). When a woman kills her partner the two most frequently used defences are provocation and diminished responsibility. Both are only partial defences to an accusation of murder. If someone is convicted of murder there is a mandatory life sentence. Successful pleading of one of these defences will reduce the conviction to manslaughter and allow the judge a discretion over what sentence to pass. The defence many would prefer to use is self-defence which is a full defence, successful pleading of which will result in an acquittal. None of these defences appears to be gendered. Here we will consider provocation.

Provocation is set out in s. 3 of the Homicide Act 1957 as having two parts: first, a subjective element, that there were words or conduct or a combination of these which caused the accused to lose self-control; and secondly, that the jury determines that a reasonable person would have lost his or her temper, the objective element. The final element which has consistently been considered necessary to the defence of provocation is that there must be 'a sudden and temporary loss of self-control, rendering the accused so subject to passion as to make him for the moment not master of his mind' (per Devlin J in *R* v *Duffy* [1949] 1 All ER 932). Originally this clearly meant immediate and temporary loss of self-control. The reason behind this rule was that without immediate response there was time to calm down, making any ensuing violence premeditated and nullifying the use of provocation as a defence. Feminists and their supporters have always claimed that the immediacy principle is less applicable to women who may not be physically capable of responding immediately and might, whilst still very angry or frightened, respond somewhat later. One illustration of this is the case of Sara Thornton whose appeal against her conviction for murder was turned down in 1991. Everyone accepted that she had suffered violence and threats of violence from her alcoholic husband over a period of years and that he had threatened her that evening, but her claim of provocation failed because she waited for him to fall asleep before she killed him and because there was some question as to whether she had lost self-control (*R* v *Thornton* (1992) 96 Cr App R 112; see also the retrial which was ordered by the Court of Appeal in response to a reference by the Home Secretary: *R* v *Thornton (No. 2)* [1996] 1 WLR 1174). This contrasts with cases where husbands have successfully pleaded provocation due to nagging wives because they have suddenly lost control (see the *Daily Telegraph*, 1 January 1992, in which it is reported that Rajinder Bisla was convicted only of manslaughter when he strangled his wife in front of their three children; she was nagging him but he was in no physical danger). Other information is available in the evidence from numerous organisations offered to the Home Affairs Committee of the House of Lords in 1993 which claimed to prove the biased nature of the defence. The old common law rule and the interpretation of s. 3 is carried out by judges who are almost exclusively male and it is claimed that they have defined the defence in keeping with their own perceptions of provocation, a male-oriented definition. This may have been intended to be objective but in application it proved to be discriminatory. Recently, the case of *R* v *Pearson* [1992] Crim LR 193 suggested that this position may have changed. The provocation in this case was not immediate and yet the defence was put to the jury. However, in *R* v *Ahluwalia* [1992] 4 All ER 889 the Court of Appeal approved *Duffy*, because, in their opinion, 'important considerations of public policy would be involved should provocation be redefined so as possibly to blur the distinction between sudden loss of self-control and deliberate retribution' (per Lord Taylor of Gosforth CJ at p. 896). The loss of self-control must be sudden and temporary but the Court of Appeal recognised that it need not be immediate. The important element is that at the time of the killing the perpetrator is temporarily not in control of his or her mind. An interval of time between the provocative act and the violence could indicate either that there had been time to gain self-control and plan revenge, or that the accused lost control more slowly or was still out of control when the act occurred. The appellant in *Ahluwalia* claimed that expert evidence shows that women who are subjected to frequent bouts of violence over a period of time may react to provocative words or acts with a 'slow burn', a slower loss of self-control than 'sudden and immediate' might imply. Although the Court of Appeal did not fully endorse this as being applicable to the defence of provocation it did accept that such arguments could be put before the jury for them to decide whether the necessary lapse of self-control existed at the time of the violence, that it was temporary and that it arose and departed fairly quickly. But if the situation is a little better than ten years ago, many still question whether men are in fact more likely to suffer sudden and temporary losses of control than are women.

Even if the jury accept that the woman suffered a sudden and temporary loss of self-control they still need to decide whether a 'reasonable man' in the defendant's situation might similarly lose self-control and go on to act as the defendant did. In deciding this issue they can take account of the defendant's sex, age and other physical attributes, as well as other characteristics which are relevant to the provocation. A person's racial background may be relevant where a defendant has been taunted about his or her race, but not where taunted about wearing glasses. They can take account of the fact that the last provocative acts or words were only the last in a series, but it is less clear whether they are permitted to consider the state of mind of the accused as a characteristic. Can they take into consideration the fact that the woman was suffering from battered women's syndrome? In the New Zealand case of *R v McGregor* [1962] NZLR 1069, which is of persuasive authority in Britain, it was decided that for a characteristic to be part of personality it must be something definite and reasonably permanent. Difficulties thus arise when considering mental peculiarities. In *R v Newell* (1980) 71 Cr App R 331 the Court of Appeal refused to take account of the male accused's drunken condition (because it was temporary) and the fact that he was grieving the death of his girlfriend despite the fact that the provocation concerned his girlfriend. Many argue that the importance of a person's frame of mind, even if this may not be permanent, is an issue which should be taken into account, especially where factors – relevant to the provocation – can affect a person over a period of time. This is not merely a feminist argument but it does have particular relevance to most cases of killing carried out by women.

Part of this argument has now been accepted by the House of Lords in *R v Morhall* [1996] AC 90, where Morhall's addiction to glue sniffing was accepted as a characteristic because the provocation related to the addiction. But, as the Privy Council stated in the persuasive case of *Luc Thiet Thuan v R* [1996] 3 WLR 45, the mental state must not be something which merely affects the powers of self-control rather than the provocation. Where this leaves a plea based on the characteristic of battered wife syndrome is not entirely clear, but it should be aided by the decision in *Morhall*. Whether this is seen as being advantageous to women is questionable as it forces women to rely on asserting that they were, for some reason, mentally less in control or less strong than others or than the 'norm', whatever that may be. It could also disadvantage women who react after one or only a few beatings and who are not diagnosed as having the syndrome. It may be that the law needs more radically to assess its approaches to ensure that no one group is disadvantaged by rules which, although having the appearance of neutrality, in fact render it easier for one group (in this case males) to rely on the defence than for another (in this case women).

The second example is that of rape as defined by ss. 1 and 44 of the Sexual Offences Act 1956 and s. 1 of the Sexual Offences (Amendment) Act 1976, both of which have been amended by s. 142 of the Criminal Justice and Public Order Act 1994. This is a male-defined act – that of non-consensual entry of a penis into the vagina or anus. Penetration must occur – the use of any other object or the penetration of any other orifice are defined as indecent assault, although these may be equally abhorrent and invasive to the female victims. To some women the definition has more to do with male ownership of women and their offspring than with protection of women, especially as rape has had a lower conviction rate than any other offence (Grace et al. (1993)). Although s. 2 of the Sexual Offences (Amendment) Act 1976 was intended to protect women from objectionable cross-examination, especially that concerning their sexual history, Tempkin (1993) shows that judges have been interpreting it more and more narrowly so that its protection of women is very limited.

Lastly in this area it may be useful to consider the case of rape within marriage. Until recently this was considered to be a legal impossibility as intercourse within marriage is lawful and at the time of the marriage the woman was said to consent such activities, to have 'given herself up in this and unto her husband, which she cannot retract' (Hale (1736), p. 629). In *R v Clarke* [1949] 2 All ER 448 a husband was convicted of raping his wife because her consent was revoked by the order of a court that she no longer needed to cohabit with her husband. The extent of this exception was expanded over the years, but the rule was still that a wife could not be raped by her husband because she had submitted to him in the marriage vows, no matter whether she was ill or whether she desired intercourse at the time. This position was reinforced by the Sexual Offences (Amendment) Act 1976 which used the word 'unlawful' in defining rape, indicating that for intercourse within marriage there still did not need to be consent. In *R v R* [1992] 1 AC 599 the House of Lords altered this, deciding that the position of women had altered so radically that the ideas considered so clear to Hale as being a necessary result of marriage should no longer pertain. They decided that the use of the word 'unlawful' merely meant without consent, making rape within marriage possible. Husbands as well as all other men now have to be sure that their wives are consenting to intercourse, not merely submitting to it out of fear or some other compelling reason. Although this decision is to be applauded it is legally less than ideal since it alters a piece of legislation so as to widen the criminal law. This is interesting as the usual rule is that, when ambiguous, a criminal statute should be construed so as to favour the accused. It is an indication that the predominantly male judiciary do not always disadvantage women, and also illustrates the complexity of the conflicts evident in the forming of the criminal law.

Sexism is not only evident against women, sometimes it is prejudiced against men. In law only men can commit rape: attacks on men by women are only sexual assaults. Thus although s. 142 of the Criminal Justice and Public Order Act 1994 makes it an offence for a man to rape another man, rape by women remains legally unrecognised. Homosexuality between men under the age of consent is a crime; this contrasts with heterosexual intercourse which can lawfully commence at 16, whilst lesbians have no age limit other than that set by indecent assault.

2.5.4.3 *Control of the powerful*

Lack of control over the powerful has often been a complaint of conflict and critical criminologists. As will be seen in Chapter Three, it is the powerful who are often involved in white-collar crimes (which this author considers are crimes they commit for their own gain) and in corporate crimes (which are committed by employees in a corporation for the good of the corporation). Many argue that the criminal sanctions in these areas are too narrow and inadequate to control the dangerous activities of these people and bodies. In this section we will briefly consider how the criminal law controls corporations in the way it is defined and enforced, and whether there are better methods of control.

In order for the State to control the dangerous or harmful activities of corporations they need to be both defined as criminal and properly enforced. This may seem straightforward since the dangers are often known and their causes are clear; yet the activity may not be defined as criminal, nor the corporation made liable. In part this is defended on the grounds that corporations provide wealth for society and have a social utility in a way which is not recognised in, for instance, burglars. More tendentious is the argument that enforced State control will push up production costs, and corporations will threaten to locate new production lines in States where regulation is not so strict. The implication is that the State must choose between these possible costs of over-regulation, and the possible harmful effects for the community of under-regulation. Conflict and critical theorists argue that the corporations use their political and economic powers to ensure that neither the definition of criminal activities nor their enforcement are sufficiently controlling of harmful behaviour. They also see that the situation has, to an extent, worsened with the reduction in union powers, now no longer able to protect the workers. They often call for tougher criminal laws, more effective controls and harsher sanctions. Against this, it is argued that corporations are now too complex and their creators and controllers too ingenious to be controlled effectively by criminal law structures and by punishments designed to deal with individual transgressions. Other approaches have been suggested.

A number of authors (Braithwaite (1993); DiMento (1993); and van de Bunt (1994)) have suggested a middle ground of reasonably strict criminal laws, but then aiming to influence corporate behaviour by a discriminating use of prosecutions. The call for restraint by enforcement agencies is partly based on the understanding that most of the employees in an organisation both have a conscience and are members of the general society as well as of the organisation. There are three parts to the equation leading to corporate

social responsiveness: first employees at all levels and therefore the organisation must be aware of the possible harm a particular action will cause;
secondly the employees and therefore the corporation must realise the social
unacceptability of the conduct; and finally they need to be aware of the
possible criminal sanctions, the negative consequences for them, which might
ensue if they proceed. These conditions are necessary for responsible decision-making in the organisation, but they may not be sufficient if the bonds
of employees to the corporation, or their identity within it, become more
important than their commitment to the outside world. Braithwaite is
sanguine that the consciences and professional ethics of employees will
constitute an essential enforcement factor in preventing corporate criminality,
increasing the likelihood that serious breaches of regulation will be uncovered. These writers would thus leave some regulation to the corporations
themselves, or to the social conscience of employees within them.

One implication, as van de Bunt argues, is that the job of the regulatory
body is to inform corporations of their duties, make them aware of the norms
with which they must comply, talk with them about the most effective means
of compliance and give reasonable weight to real problems and constraints on
compliance whilst not accepting excuses for non-compliance. Therefore
regulatory agencies are consultants first, advising on how to comply, and
police officers second, only prosecuting where all else fails. Such a system can
work only if there is a strong criminal law and fierce sentencing on its
transgression. Without this enforcers have no leverage to persuade corporations to act.

Critics of such a strategy attack it as being permissive of breach, too
accepting of the problems claimed to be faced by businesses and too prone
to a cosy solution between business and regulator. It is predicated on a view
that corporations are basically conforming organisations which can be trusted
to act responsibly. There could be contradiction between this and the basic
ethos of business to make a profit. Businesses certainly wish and aim to
control as much of their working environment as possible, a consideration
which grows in significance as corporations grow in size enabling them to
exercise such control more effectively, through pressure on government and
workers. Some would therefore argue that what is necessary is to make it
more expensive to breach than to comply, and urge an approach which
involves both civil and criminal law: that is, realistic and effective criminal
sanctions which are harmful to the corporation; and civil payments in
compensation to workers and their families.

Pearce and Tombs (1992) combine these ideas. They see a need to require
a change to corporate structure such that criminal actions become simpler –
marking out those responsible for worker safety, pollution control and
product safety – and thus making any necessary prosecutions simpler,
cheaper and more likely to succeed. It would also make the corporation
perform some of the work for the enforcers, as has been done in relation to
financial responsibility by s. 89 of the Insolvency Act 1986. But beyond more,
and more certain, prosecutions they also call for closer policing (to detect
breaches), more pressure on firms (to alter practices), and willingness to

challenge financial reasons given for non-compliance. Even if there are some increases in production costs these could be minimised by social pressure on shareholders to accept lower or steadier returns on their investment, and to take responsibility for the long-term viability of the company rather than merely being interested in a quick return. Here again strict regulation may help: without it those who transgress can increase profits by harming others, but with strong regulation there will be a profit in conformity. Under a regime of strict and effective State regulation of corporate criminality, at both national and international levels, large corporations would have a strong incentive to conform and push others to do so. For most of this to operate there might need to be statutory criminal laws which place clear responsibility on corporations and an interpretation of these which permits criminal responsibility to be imputed to corporations and/or their senior officers. Some movement in this direction was made by Lord Chief Justice Taylor in his interpretation of 'gross negligence' in manslaughter cases (see *R* v *Prentice* [1993] 3 WLR 927).

It may be difficult or impossible effectively to punish certain targets at all. No State has the powers fully to control corporations either by reforming them or their main actors, or by incapacitating their unacceptable behaviours; nor would such activities be either economically viable or desirable as they would bankrupt firms and leave many innocent people unemployed. If it is thus necessary to note that not all can or should be controlled, it is also necessary to recognise that deterrence can be strengthened by the targeting of some corporations and individuals. In addition to these criminal justice approaches it may be possible to affect behaviours by public questioning of the activities of powerful operators within a corporation, who may not themselves have taken part in the criminal activity but who could have prevented it: these individuals might be shamed into preventing future activities by threatening to expose their moral responsibility for the activity. The criminal justice system can expose them through careful questioning of witnesses but would need support. In particular, as suggested in the next chapter, the media may be better placed to perform such functions and professional and other regulatory bodies may also be used. Full investigation by professional bodies such as that relating to accountants, or by a judicial inquiry rather than by criminal justice agencies, may be more effective. Fisse and Braithwaite (1993) suggest that what may be needed is a much wider accountability model, an holistic problem-solving approach, whereby all systems are utilised to try to achieve the desired outcome of more responsible corporate activity. This may mean using civil actions either as well as or instead of criminal means where these may be more effective at reaching the desired ends – a more responsible trading system. Lastly, what may work best is to force the law-abiding sections of the corporation to investigate and deal internally with the criminal elements. This may not punish the wrongdoing, but it can effectively prevent its continuation.

The discussion of victimless crime, sexism and corporate crime illustrates the large and complex issues involved in defining the criminal law and in its enforcement. It illustrates the problem of trying to consider the criminal law in a vacuum without studying its relationship with other aspects of society, and without discovering or considering the reasons for the criminal nature of the activity. The discussion also shows how an apparently neutral law can in fact be strongly prejudicial to one or more sections of society, even perhaps (as in rape) prejudicial to the very section it purports to protect. The examples can also indicate that the law does alter and respond over time, but such adjustment is normally slow, extending the anguish and suffering of those who feel discriminated against.

2.5.5 Definitions and usage

Having briefly considered the concept of crime and illustrated the problems arising from the acceptance of the legal limits, the debate becomes still more complicated when sociological considerations of crime or rule-breaking are included. One of the first aspects to grasp is that without law – the criminal law – there would be no crime and no criminals, so that criminalising an act usually takes place only because some people want to do that act and others wish to prevent them. On this reading an act is not controlled by use of the criminal law because the nature of the act is essentially criminal, but because those whose job it is to formulate such matters within a society define it or name it as criminal. The acts which are criminalised are acts which some people wish to do; it is thus unlikely that any criminal law will totally prevent a particular activity. The more realistic object is to control its frequency and to punish when it occurs; in this way the State (society) has exhibited its disapproval of the act.

If the act itself is not considered to be inherently wrong, everyone will have his or her own conception of acceptable limits of behaviour, based partly on his or her present circumstances and upbringing. Even if individuals recognise an activity as criminal, they may still be willing to accept its occurrence or even to participate in it. For example, some may be willing to accept theft of limited amounts from large institutions though not from individuals; employees often steal from employers and view their activities as 'perks' of the job or as minor fiddles. Others may have more permissive attitudes to sexual matters than those which are permitted in the criminal law; if they are caught and dealt with by the criminal justice system, the wider society will define them as criminals, even if many sympathise with their activities. A few break the most accepted laws, they murder or steal large amounts. Even some of these cases may be widely accepted – killing to release someone from appalling pain, especially when it is at that person's request, or failing to disclose full earnings to the Inland Revenue, or insider dealing. In other cases where generally serious crimes are committed the participant may claim the moral high ground by stating that the killing or other crime was necessary in pursuit of a political ideal: although these people often consider themselves as basically law-abiding they claim to be freedom fighters, forced to perform these activities out of political necessity, in order to correct intolerable situations. At the same time most people in that society view them as terrorists, dangerous criminals who will stop at nothing and will hit any target which might further their cause, seeing them as totally amoral (even evil) and very dangerous. Outside their immediate society, the way in which their acts will be judged often depends on the acceptance or otherwise of their political aims.

More generally, others, indignant at behaviour of which they disapprove, argue that the law should be altered to make it criminal (as Chapter Three shows, the press often feeds on and fuels these attitudes): others call for decriminalisation, particularly in areas of life they consider private (see the discussion above concerning victimless crime).

The perception of people is often coloured by their position in relation to the particular activity. For example, the drug user (his or her family and friends), drug addict (his or her family and friends), police officer, psychologist, doctor, magistrate, judge, academic lawyer and sociologist may view the use of various drugs in very different ways. Some argue for legalisation and control merely through medical/therapeutic channels; others accept criminalisation of drug dealing though not of use, preferring the treatment approach for the latter; others want full criminalisation. Personal assessments also condition reasons for varying positions: economic; moral; political; or paternalistic.

These differences between individuals and groups are significant and act as important indicators of the societal tolerance of behaviour over time and the need to change criminal laws. However, the democratic need to accommodate differences should not obscure another central feature of the relationship between democracy and law: in a democracy the law would lose its legitimacy if it was not perceived as reflecting most people's ideas of morality or which activities are in need of control. If this disjuncture became widespread the trust in the criminal justice system and ultimately, possibly, in the state would dissolve.

The contrived nature of criminal law should be borne in mind when considering theories on why people participate in these activities. The theories often suggest that such people are 'different' or even 'abnormal', or that they have been less 'moral' in the way in which they have allowed their free will and choice to rule their activities. If the activities are not manifestly unacceptable then ideas of 'normal' and 'moral' become less firmly and clearly acceptable. Explanations therefore need to keep in mind the activities of the State in criminalising and enforcing certain activities.

2.6 ENFORCEMENT OF CRIMINAL LAWS

Before progressing to define a criminal, it might be useful to consider the effects of the workings of the enforcement agencies. This work is carried out by a plethora of organisations which together make up the criminal justice system. The main agencies involved are: the police; the Crown Prosecution Service; the courts; prisons; the probation service; and social services. This list is not exhaustive – the Inland Revenue, Customs and Excise, Factories Inspectorate, fraud squads, etc. all have investigation powers and sometimes also prosecution powers. Fines and similar sorts of punishments may be administered by court officials. Although not part of the official system, lawyers (both solicitors and barristers) are an essential part of its workings and are generally considered as part of the criminal justice system. Outside the official system are many private agencies, particularly private security firms. This is now a very big business, and over 150,000 people are employed in the private sector covering tasks such as credit investigation, information services, private investigations, transport for prisoners, private security patrols, and as bailiffs; more recently Group Four, one of the larger firms, began to operate the first private prison, Wolds Remand Prison (the contract was signed in 1991, since then others such as Blakenhurst and Doncaster have followed suit). Increasingly the State is using these private agencies to fulfil its obligations to its citizens in the criminal justice system. This may be seen as sensible economic management, but does it address the needs of society and does it help to solve the crime problem? Many argue it does not and see this move as the State refusing to face its responsibilities and relying on private firms which have their own economic and other objectives to place above the good of society (for further discussion see Chapters Sixteen and Nineteen).

As the above makes clear, the criminal justice system is large and complex. It has many goals or aims, though its ultimate goal is generally said to be to make society safer for its citizens. More specific and generally accepted aims include:

- enforcing the criminal law and so exhibiting society's disapproval of criminal activity through catching, convicting and punishing criminals on a principled basis;
- protecting the public by preventing and deterring crime; by advising citizens on how to avoid victimisation; by making crime commission both more difficult and more likely to be detected through control, surveillance and design of public space; by attempting to rehabilitate offenders; and by incapacitating those who might otherwise prove to be a danger to the public;
- protecting society through maintaining law and order;
- helping victims;
- efficient and fair application of the law, ensuring the proper treatment of suspects, defendants, those held in custody and witnesses, and ensuring that the innocent are acquitted and the guilty punished in a fair and equitable manner, all of which should help to promote respect both for the law and for the criminal justice system;
- ensuring that each aspect of the system is accountable to society.

Each of the agencies mentioned above plays its part in trying to achieve these aims. Thus the police investigate and help to prevent crime and maintain order. They are usually the link between the public and the system, playing a key role in advising victims and the public on such issues as crime prevention. The Crown Prosecution Service prepares cases for trial and decides which cases are too weak to justify proceeding. The courts are intended to ensure the efficient and fair application of law by protecting the rights of all parties and making decisions as to bail or remand, guilty or not guilty and on what types of sentence to pass. The probation service provides information on many defendants so that correct decisions concerning bail and sentencing can be made, but its largest single role is intended to be rehabilitative, working with offenders on community orders and with those released from custody. While hoping to rehabilitate and deter some people, the main role of prisons and other custodial institutions now appears to be the humane detention of individuals refused bail and offenders sentenced to custodial orders. The private security firms and others acting outside the system may have the above aims in mind but their position may be complicated by their overriding loyalty to their shareholders which can cause problems for the criminal justice system (see below).

The above suggests that the aims and activities of the system are not in dispute, but this is too simplistic a picture since the aims may conflict with each other. There is a plethora of approaches to this problem: King (1981) refers to six, of which the main two (due process and crime control) will be discussed here, while the others (rehabilitative, bureaucratic, denunciation and degradation, and power) will be outlined only. Due process and crime control are given prominence because, as suggested by Herbert Packer in 1968, the whole criminal justice system turns around balancing these two conflicting value systems, one of which prioritises justice and protecting the innocent (due process) while the other centres on swift prosecution and early punishment (crime control).

Due process maintains that the purpose of the criminal justice system is to require the State to prove the guilt of a defendant beyond reasonable doubt in a public trial as the condition for the imposition of a sentence. It is based upon an idealised form of the rule of law. This recognises the State's duty to protect the community from crime and criminals by requiring agencies of the State to seek out and to punish the guilty, but to ensure that only the guilty are punished by requiring the State to prove the guilt of those it wishes to accuse. If an innocent person is convicted it is viewed as a double failure, being both a breach of his or her rights as well as a failure to protect society because the guilty person has escaped conviction and punishment. Central to this idea is the presumption of innocence – that is that every suspect and accused is presumed innocent until proven guilty and no-one should have to incriminate him or herself – the defendant's right to a fair trial, equality before the law and justice being seen to be done. A due process model requires and enforces rules governing the powers of the police and the admissibility and utility of evidence. Due process notes the power of the State in the application of criminal laws and, to prevent misuse of this position of power by agents of the State, requires checks and balances to protect the interests of suspects and defendants, which helps to reduce the inequality between the parties: informal or discretionary powers are seen as less acceptable.

The due process model recognises the possibility of error in any State system of adversarial justice. Due process theorists understand that the authorities may be convinced that they have arrested and charged the right person but recognise that there may have been an error: a witness may mis-remember, may twist his or her recollection or may just wish to appear helpful and caring and so feign memory or over-exaggerate its accuracy; suspects may be willing to confess because they feel under pressure, whether or not pressure is intended; officials may 'twist' evidence because they are sure they have the guilty person, etc. Recognising the fallibility of humans and the possibility of error, due process theorists stress the need for formal procedures to reduce the possibility of that error affecting any particular situation – all processes should be controlled by formal rules governing the powers of the police and the admissibility and utility of evidence. These rules should be applied even where it may lead to an offender escaping justice because the approach requires that the criminal justice system does not profit by illegalities. If one of the enforcement agencies breaks the process rules and in so doing obtains evidence which proves beyond reasonable doubt that that individual committed the offence in question, be it shop lifting or murder, strict application of the due process system would exclude that evidence from the court as being unfairly obtained. The rationale for this is neatly encapsulated by Zander in his dissenting opinion in the Runciman Report (1993) when he says that allowing such evidence:

> . . . would I believe encourage serious wrongdoing from some police officers who might be tempted to exert force or fabricate or suppress evidence in the hope of establishing the guilt of the suspect, especially in a serious case where they believe him to be guilty. . . . The integrity of the criminal justice system is a higher objective than the conviction of any individual. (pp. 234–5)

Even so, errors can still occur: the possibility of a re-trial in light of new evidence must therefore be kept open.

If, within these constraints, the State is believed and proves a person guilty, it can then punish the individual or other guilty party to the extent which reflects that party's responsibility and the severity of the offence. Note that the finding of guilt does not necessarily mean that the individual is guilty – it does not even mean that a crime has been committed – it merely denotes that 12 people believed one set of facts over another.

A strict due process approach recognises that some guilty people will go free and unpunished; this is considered necessary to prevent wrongful conviction and punishment. The value judgement which is being asserted here is that the arbitrary or excessive use of State power is a worse evil.

Even if one accepts the ideals of due process it is not a panacea: it can be misused and can disintegrate into a type of legal formalism where the technical details of the rules are applied but the underlying intentions ignored, so perverting any idea of justice. It also needs to be made explicit that due process, or any approach which prioritises suspects and defendants, tends to ignore or give less priority to the interests of victims or of society at large unless such interests can be accommodated with no alterations to the legal rights of the suspects or defendants.

A quite different approach results if the stress is placed instead on the need to control the level of crime – if, within the constraints imposed by the need for evidence of guilt, the central function of the criminal justice system is seen to be the repression and punishment of criminal conduct. In this way society can express its disgust for criminal activities, and this communal expression then tends to strengthen the moral standards and cohesion within society. From this standpoint it is desirable that there should be as few fetters as possible on the authorities in pursuing criminals. Here the criminal justice system must be seen to be strong, providing a high rate of conviction and low acquittal rate, and harsh and certain punishment. A high acquittal rate makes it look as if the criminal justice agencies are not performing their functions correctly or are inefficient, either in not catching the right people or in not providing sufficient evidence so that too many criminals are getting away with it. The effect would be a failure to deter others from indulging in criminal activity.

To prevent this the crime control model prioritises efficiency and getting results: to catch, convict and punish the offender is paramount. Inherent in crime control models is the idea that once the police and prosecutor believe in the guilt there is almost a 'presumption of guilt' (King (1981)), which means that the practitioners within the system all predict that the individual should and will be found guilty – 'guilty' is the expected plea or verdict. This model places great faith in the police and Crown Prosecution Service as professionals, who would accuse and bring to court only those who they are confident are guilty. The model is less respectful of legal controls which exist to protect the individual defendant; these are seen as practical obstacles which need to be overcome in order to get on with the crime control and the punishment. The trial becomes more ritualistic, with an expected outcome of conviction based on the presumed reliability of the police (or other enforcement agency) in identifying the true offender. There is, at best, a much-reduced presumption of innocence at trial since the presumption of innocence only really rules the way in which the court process is conducted – guilt is the expected outcome. In this approach the balance between due process and crime control has been shifted towards the latter: the central element is seen to be the control of crime which requires a high rate of apprehension and conviction of criminals and quick results. If occasionally some innocent individuals are sacrificed to the ultimate aim of crime control this may be a necessary evil. However, it needs to be emphasised that such errors are intended to be kept to a minimum through the careful application of justice by the agents of the law, whose professionalism ensures that they apprehend the guilty and allow the innocent to go free.

Once guilt is pronounced punishment begins and should be sure, unpleasant, and sufficient to recognise the seriousness of the offence. It should also reflect the extent of blame attaching to the offender, since there is a presumption that all people are responsible for their behaviour. Even if the final criminal act is one resulting from a loss of self-control there is some blame because the individual allowed himself or herself to get into a situation where he or she might lose control. Any failure to punish severely might be seen as weakness and a failure to uphold standards of behaviour, so allowing people to believe that criminal acts may be acceptable.

In the crime control model the interests of victims and society are thus given priority over those of suspects and defendants. The justification is that swifter processing makes the system appear more efficient and that this will deter greater criminality – if you offend you are likely to be caught and punished, therefore it is not worth it. In seeking to achieve this aim the model is willing to convict the innocent (though not in large numbers). Formal procedures are kept to an absolute minimum and their breach should not lead to the exclusion of evidence which is otherwise thought reliable – the guilty should never be acquitted on a technicality. The primary aim of crime control is to punish the guilty and deter crime as a means of reducing crime and creating a safer society.

A very different approach is taken by those with a rehabilitative aim, which is more individualised and asks, at each stage of the process, how best to deal with this person. Criminal activity is the catalyst for official intervention usually designed to help, or even 'treat', the offender whose free will and responsibility are seen as limited. This is based upon ideas that offenders may not be wholly responsible for their acts, which arise, at least in part, due to individual or social factors (see Chapters Six to Twelve). Information concerning every area of offenders' lives may be collated and wide discretionary powers are permitted to professionals to decide what to do. Formal rules and legal protections may be kept to a minimum.

King's fourth model, the bureaucratic, derives from classical Weberian sociology and its intention is the management of both crime and criminals by such means as the standardisation of procedures, political neutrality, precision and efficiency. Lengthy periods before trial, extended trials and claims of miscarriages of justice all serve to undermine trust in the administration of justice and so lead to less confidence being placed in the system and less respect for the law. All agencies in the criminal justice system should keep clear records and be able to substantiate allegations with clear documentation; this minimises conflict and so reduces expense. In the bureaucratic model the success of the system is tested by how well it achieves internally set targets such as response times for incidents, percentage of cases in which there is a guilty plea or a finding of guilt, or the time it takes to get a case through court, regardless of the effects this has on such wider problems as levels of criminal activity, public safety, and levels of rehabilitation of offenders. In its extreme form managerial efficiency is seen as an end in itself, rather than as a means to create a better society. The agencies of criminal justice can be said to succeed even if levels of crime are rising: if they have properly performed their bureaucratic function they cannot be blamed for the rise in the levels of criminal activity or for the fact that society is less safe. The approach provides a powerful political tool for avoiding responsibility and is utilised, to a greater or lesser degree, by most governments in the western world.

The fifth approach centres on the denunciation and degradation of criminals and derives from the sociology of Emile Durkheim. Stigmatisation and the reinforcement of social cohesion are the central features. To stigmatise offenders (and even defendants) is to set them out as separate from the other, law-abiding, members of the community, who are thus made to feel like a more cohesive group. The public shaming of individuals is meant to persuade them of the stupidity of their actions and to reassure others of their own virtue. Furthermore, the use of media coverage to disseminate information is valuable since it leads to wider denunciation and knowledge of the processes and consequences of unacceptable behaviour. Braithwaite in 1988 suggested that a reasonable level of shaming was necessary to permit proper rehabilitation – an understanding of the consequences and a feeling of shame for having made others suffer is necessary for one to decide not to act in that way again – what he terms re-integrative shaming.

Questioning of the interests served by crime and crime control is central to King's last model – the power model – which derives largely from Marxism, post-Marxist critical theory and post-modern theory. Each of these tends to attack criminal laws and the criminal justice system for maintaining the position of the powerful in society, a power which might be based on class, wealth, race or sex. The system is seen as one the central intention of which is to maintain order and the *status quo* rather than to enforce the criminal law to protect the whole of society. The attack is that most official crime control is just about order, controlling the weak to the advantage of the strong. This may be done in a number of ways: for example, by having very clear and set rules which are then implemented in ways that ensure a discriminatory outcome; or by having loose rules within which there is a wide area of discretion which may then be exercised in a discriminating manner. In simplistic terms, theorists in this area point to the way in which criminal law and its enforcement often tend to exclude some, painting them as welfare-dependent, undeserving, generally irresponsible and different from the other good citizens who are self-reliant and law-abiding. The majority are thus enticed into supporting a system the main object of which is to preserve the position of the ruling group or groups.

King's six models are not exhaustive; other approaches could put the stress on rights or notions of just deserts. But the six which have been mentioned are sufficient to illustrate how the system can be pulled in different, and possibly inconsistent, directions. The criminal justice system of England and Wales does not conform to any one approach, and there is much debate as to which approach is paramount.

An early commentator on this was Herbert Packer (1968). Initially he studied the system in the USA and concluded that although the legal rules and the apparent values of the criminal justice system appeared to conform with the due process approach, in practice the crime control approach was most often used. He suggested that similar findings would be made in most common law jurisdictions. Certainly the system in England and Wales, like any adversarial system, starts with the due process presumption that a person is innocent until proven guilty; but what an adversarial system actually does is to say that a person will be treated as innocent unless the evidence is sufficient, beyond reasonable doubt, to prove guilt. In effect, then, a trial never establishes innocence; it either purports to establish guilt, or finds that there was insufficient evidence to prove guilt or that the jury (or magistrates) were unwilling to convict. In this legal environment it might be said that the crime control approach is prevalent in that a trial can never establish innocence. Doreen McBarnett (1978) on looking at the British system claimed that law, values and practice all take on a crime control approach, while McConville and Baldwin (1981) found that the practice in Britain is geared towards conviction and crime control. Bottoms and McClean (1976) and Robert Reiner (1992) came to a similar conclusion, but suggested that the reason was not ideological but rather that the participants in the criminal justice system were simply led by the application of rules.

It can thus be seen that, although the professed intentions give weight to due process, some commentators see the outcomes of the system in England and Wales as being closer to the crime control approach. Which approach wins out is indicative both of the way in which society controls behaviour and of the insight it gives to the weighting of the aims set out above, and of the way in which criminal behaviour is viewed within our society. How many innocent people are we willing to see convicted, or how many guilty people are we willing to see go free? In an ideal world the answer to each would be none, but neither that nor a perfect balance between due process and crime control is likely to be achieved. An official tendency to lean one way or the other will have an impact on the way in which justice is experienced by a society. The issue is obviously of high importance, and a recurring theme in the discussions of the numerous studies outlined in this work centres on the question: where should the balance be between the demands for crime control and those for justice and humanity?

At this point it is important to note that despite the fact that most of the above models centre around the narrow aspects of controlling and punishing crime, it is still essential to retain the wider view of the criminal justice system as being necessary to provide a public service, aimed at promoting public safety, protecting the weak and vulnerable, justice for all promoting and encouraging civilised behaviour, and making society a safer, more pleasant place for the whole of society. A criminal justice system must treat victims, defendants and criminals with respect; a system which excludes individuals and makes them the subject of fear and suspicion even after their punishment is served is one where continued criminal behaviour is almost guaranteed. The simplistic idea that crime will be solved and society made safer if more criminals are harshly punished may not be the most successful or efficient approach. It may not even be the best way of responding to the needs of victims and redressing the wrongs done to them. Impacting on the real problem of crime means addressing the wider aspects mentioned above, which can sometimes involve new criminal justice solutions such as mediation, but in other cases the need may be for earlier, very different solutions such as town planning, helping the disadvantaged overcome difficulties, providing opportunities for all. Some of these possibilities will be explored in later chapters, but for the moment it needs only to be recognised that crime reduction and a safe society cannot simply be provided by criminal justice agencies. Criminal justice is basically about the society in which one lives: a healthy society treats all its citizens with respect and punishes only when necessary to redress a balance; its criminal laws are to restrain activities which reduce the freedom of others, not to interfere with individual freedom; its end is to increase the freedom of all citizens. Such a high ideal can only be the product of a responsible, holistic and reasoned approach to crime which treats all individuals as citizens and as deserving of respect.

2.7 THE CRIMINAL

Who is a criminal? Most people would probably argue that a criminal is a person who commits a crime. By this idea, everyone in almost any modern State is a criminal, as most of us have breached a law at one time or another. In a technical legal sense a person is not a criminal until he or she has been convicted by a court of law of having committed a criminal offence.

For criminology it is sometimes important and useful to be able to use the idea of a criminal more widely than the very technical legal concept would permit. If the purpose is to understand why individuals are willing to participate in certain forms of behaviour, the looser idea of someone having performed an act which appears to be a crime may be more useful, regardless of whether or not that person has been caught and convicted. Most of the theorists referred to in this book take this wider, less precise, less technical and in some ways less correct meaning of the word criminal. Some also use the word delinquent, which is even more imprecise. First, it may be used to designate a young criminal and can therefore take on either the technical legal meaning or the wider criminological meaning. It is also frequently used to denote a young person who performs acts which some members of society find unacceptable, but which have not been criminalised. It has to be said that theorists are not always clear how they are using the term, and this causes even greater problems. The reader should be aware of these facts in reading this and other texts.

The wider use of the word criminal or delinquent raises the question: how long should the term 'criminal' be used to describe a person who has committed a crime? In a technical legal case this is often decided by statute, for example, after a certain period of time most convictions become spent for most purposes. Where the term is used in the wider criminological sense there are no such rules. As the term is being used in a social sense as a stigma, the exact meaning and the time it will last are impossible to predict; they will depend on the interaction of the individuals concerned.

Use of the official term 'criminal' is very limiting and excludes most of those who commit offences: from Home Office figures only 2 per cent of offences result in a conviction. In fact many who commit offences are excluded by most definitions: of every 100 offences committed, the Home Office estimates that only 47 are reported; the police record only 27 (see Chapter Four for an explanation of this); five are cleared up; three result in a caution; and only two result in a conviction. This not only shows the limit in using official labels of criminality, but also indicates the narrow effects that the criminal justice system is likely to have, particularly one based on harsh punishments.

2.8 TERMINOLOGY AND CLASSIFICATION

What is currently in vogue in terminology, as in fashion, changes from time to time. The words 'crime' and 'offence' are synonymous, but generally 'crime' is used only in relation to serious offences such as rape or murder, which are technically called indictable offences (see below). Throughout the book an individual who has been charged with and prosecuted, but not yet convicted, for a criminal offence is referred to as the 'accused' or the 'defendant'.

An accused may be tried and found not guilty or acquitted, or that person may be found guilty (i.e., convicted) and sentenced. In some instances (see below) a person who has been convicted may appeal either against the severity of the sentence imposed, or against the conviction seeking to have it quashed. In these instances the individual concerned may be referred to as the appellant or accused.

2.8.1 Felonies and misdemeanours

The terminology for the classification of offences has changed with time. It is necessary to be aware of some of the old terms in order to understand the older, reported English cases and some of the texts, old and new. American texts also generally use the old terminology. Criminal offences used to be categorised at common law either as felonies or as misdemeanours. Felonies were those crimes which had as their penalty on conviction the forfeiture of land and goods, and if Parliament had declared a crime to be a felony without benefit of clergy (originally exemption of clergymen from criminal process before a secular judge, but later extended to cover the first offence of all those who could read), then the penalty was death as well as forfeiture of property to the State. The Forfeiture Act 1870 abolished forfeiture for felony. A misdemeanour was any offence not amounting to a felony; these were regarded as less serious offences and never incurred the death penalty or forfeiture of property. They were punished by fines or imprisonment at the court's discretion. The distinction between the gravity of these two categories of offences and their differing consequences had all but disappeared in Britain by the time they were formally abolished by s. 1 of the Criminal Law Act 1967. That Act, by s. 2, put in place of those old categories a new classification – arrestable and non-arrestable offences.

2.8.2 Arrestable and non-arrestable offences

The definition of an arrestable offence was first contained in s. 2 of the Criminal Law Act 1967, which concentrated upon the procedural consequences of a crime. It has been incorporated into and expanded by the Police and Criminal Evidence Act 1984, which came into force on 1 January 1986. Where an individual has committed an arrestable offence, a police officer or a member of the public may arrest him without a warrant. This classification encompasses all offences for which the penalty upon conviction is fixed by law (e.g., the mandatory life sentence in case of murder) or for which a person of 21 years of age or over (not previously convicted) may be sentenced to imprisonment for a term of five years or more. For example, theft contrary to s. 1 of the Theft Act 1968 has a maximum penalty of ten years' imprisonment and thus is an arrestable offence. In addition, s. 24(2) and (3) of the Police and Criminal Evidence Act 1984 declare numerous specific offences to be arrestable offences even though the prescribed penalty on conviction is less than five years' imprisonment. An arrestable offence which is a 'serious arrestable offence' as defined in s. 116 of that Act has enhanced powers of arrest for the police attached to it. The majority of arrestable offences will be indictable offences (see 2.8.3). In addition, s. 25 of the Act gives the police a general power to arrest for any non-arrestable offence, no matter how petty, provided one of the general arrest conditions specified in s. 25(3) is satisfied. For example, the name of the relevant person is unknown to, and cannot be readily ascertained by, the constable, making the service of a summons impracticable or inappropriate. This new general power of arrest permits arrest without warrant for summary and otherwise non-arrestable offences if one of the general arrest conditions is satisfied. But, broadly speaking, arrestable offences are in the main indictable, i.e., serious, offences.

2.8.3 Indictable and summary offences

Another classification of criminal offences is by reference to the modes by which offences may be tried. Criminal offences are either tried summarily before a magistrates' court (less serious types) or are tried on indictment in the Crown Court (the more serious types).

Summary trial, i.e., before magistrates, takes place with regard to offences which are so minor that they must be so tried, or offences for which an accused can normally elect either to be tried before magistrates or before the Crown Court and has chosen to be tried before the former. (These offences are known as offences triable either way.) A list of such offences is contained in the Magistrates' Court Act 1980; statutes may also specifically provide that the offences contained therein must or may be tried summarily. A magistrates' court is comprised of two or more lay magistrates, i.e., individuals who are neither salaried nor in most cases legally qualified. In some cases a magistrates' court may comprise a single stipendiary magistrate (a professional salaried judge who is legally qualified).

Trials on indictment in the Crown Court take place in relation to offences where an accused may elect such a trial (and has so chosen) or where the offence can only be tried in the Crown Court because of its seriousness. Trials on indictment are so named because the trial is commenced by a document known as a bill of indictment which sets out the offence and its particulars with which the accused is charged. A Crown Court trial is before a judge and jury. The trial of an accused is preceded by an initial investigation of the accused's potential criminal liability by magistrates who, if convinced that an accused has a case to answer, commit him to the Crown Court for trial. This process is known as committal proceedings.

2.9 APPEALS

An accused convicted by a magistrates' court of an offence may appeal by way of a full rehearing of the case to the Crown Court. In this instance the Crown

Court consists of lay magistrates and a judge as chairman (usually a circuit judge but with no jury). Any further appeal can only be on a point of law and can be from either the Crown Court following a rehearing as noted above, or from the magistrates' court direct. The appellate court in such instances is the Divisional Court of the Queen's Bench Division, which comprises two or more High Court judges. There is a final appeal from the Divisional Court to the House of Lords. Such appeals are restricted to instances where a point of law of general public importance is raised and where either court has given leave to appeal.

Where an accused has been convicted of an offence following a trial before the Crown Court (i.e., before judge and jury) he may appeal to the Court of Appeal, Criminal Division on a point of law, and ultimately to the House of Lords upon the restricted ground that the point of law concerned is of general public importance and leave has been given by either court because it is an issue that should be settled by the House of Lords.

The prosecution may appeal against an accused's acquittal in all cases except where the accused has been acquitted by a jury's verdict – that decision is always final.

2.10 LIMITS OF PROSECUTION

Each of the limitations listed below acts as a bar or barrier to prosecution, but that is not to say that no crime has been committed. Criminal conduct will have occurred and a victim often will have been harmed, but for various policy reasons the State chooses not to prosecute.

Unlike civil wrongs, there is generally no limitation period for criminal offences. Prosecutions can be brought against an accused at any time, even years after the act or omission has been committed. Parliament, however, may by statute provide exceptions in specific instances to that general rule (e.g., s. 127 of the Magistrates' Courts Act 1980 provides that all summary prosecutions must be brought within six months of the commission of the offence, again unless a specific statute provides to the contrary).

Certain persons are in effect absolutely immune from prosecution (e.g., the monarch, foreign sovereigns and their emissaries, members of diplomatic staff and persons working for international organisations). Others receive a limited immunity (e.g., the administrative and technical staff of an embassy are only immune for acts or omissions done in the course of their duties; visiting armed forces are given a very technical and limited immunity).

Certain children in effect receive immunity from criminal prosecution in the form of a presumption of incapacity to commit crimes. Age can furnish a defence in that the law maintains that no child under ten years of age can be guilty of an offence (see the Children and Young Persons Act 1933, s. 50 as amended. In Scotland the relevant age is eight). For a child between the ages of ten and fourteen years there is a rebuttable presumption of incapacity to commit a crime, known as *doli incapax*. The prosecution may rebut that presumption by proving not only that the accused child committed the offence but also that he or she knew that it was seriously wrong, not just naughty.

Almost all prosecutions are brought on behalf of the Crown, which is a synonym for the State, and generally they are instituted in the name of the monarch or an officer of the Crown such as the Attorney-General or the Director of Public Prosecutions. For less serious offences the prosecution may be brought by the Crown Prosecution Service in the name of the police, or the actual police officer, or by a representative of a local authority, or by a representative of a government department, such as the Inland Revenue, the Factories Inspectorate or Customs and Excise. A few prosecutions can be brought by a private citizen. In some of these cases a limitation of sorts arises in that the permission or leave of the Attorney-General, or the Director of Public Prosecutions, or the Home Secretary or some other Minister is sometimes required. Without the necessary approval specified in the particular statute from whichever of those representatives of the Crown, the trial cannot proceed, and if commenced the proceedings are deemed void. Examples of prosecutions requiring such approval are incest, homosexual offences, theft of or unlawful damage to a spouse's property and offences under the Official Secrets Act 1911. In most instances private prosecutions are permitted under s. 6 of the Prosecution of Offenders Act 1985, but such actions are in fact rare and in practice most prosecutions are brought by the Crown Prosecution Service on behalf of the police.

Appeals aside (see above) there is a principle of criminal law that if a competent court finds in favour of an accused and acquits him, the prosecution cannot re-open that issue in another trial involving either the same accusation or another necessarily dependent on the issue already adjudged in the accused's favour. This principle against double jeopardy applies equally where a person has been convicted of an offence. This prevents anyone being tried more than once for any one particular act or omission.

Jurisdiction can be a further limitation to prosecution. In the main, English criminal law is concerned with where an offence is committed. If it occurs within the territorial boundaries of England or Wales, or on or over the territorial sea of those countries, then the offence is triable in either England or Wales irrespective of the nationality of the accused. There are exceptions to this general rule in that certain offences (like piracy) are tried here no matter where in the world the offence occurred. British ships and aircraft are considered by the law to be British territory; consequently offences committed on board such vessels, no matter where in the world they are, may be tried in England or Wales, again irrespective of the accused's nationality. Certain statutes, the best example of which is the Offences against the Person Act 1861, ss. 9 and 57, provide that British citizens who commit certain offences abroad may be tried in England and Wales. Lastly, an individual liable to be tried in England and Wales who flees or escapes to another country may be retrieved by the formal procedure of extradition, provided there is an extradition treaty in existence between Britain and the country in which the fugitive has sought refuge or, by virtue of a special extradition arrangement where there is no general extradition treaty, under s. 2 of the Extradition Act 1989.

2.11   EVIDENCE

In criminal prosecutions the law applies the maxims: 'The party that alleges must prove' and 'The accused is presumed innocent until proved guilty'. To obtain a conviction, the prosecution must prove all the constituent elements of the substantive offence in question beyond reasonable doubt. Although in theory this concept has never been attacked or altered, it has been diluted by ss. 34–37 of the Criminal Justice and Public Order Act 1994, which allow inferences to be drawn from the failure of a suspect or an accused to answer questions or to mention facts when questioned by those (police or others) properly charged with the duty of investigating offences: this does not include private persons or bodies, such as store detectives. Likewise, if a defence is raised the prosecution must disprove it beyond reasonable doubt. In the very few rare instances where the burden of proof relating to a defence is imposed on the accused, then the law specifies that the accused need only prove on a balance of probabilities (the usual civil standard) rather than beyond reasonable doubt.

2.12   PUNISHMENT

There are various theories concerning the purpose of punishment ranging from retribution, through prevention, deterrence and education to rehabilitation. In this country the criminal courts have available to them a number of punishments which they may impose following conviction, ranging from deprivation of liberty to absolute and conditional discharges. The death penalty was abolished for murder by the Murder (Abolition of Death Penalty) Act 1965, although it is possible today that a sentence of death could be imposed in limited and exceptional circumstances (e.g., for treason or piracy). Except in the case of murder, for which a mandatory sentence of life imprisonment is automatically imposed, there are as a general rule no minimum sentences prescribed. However, the Crime (Sentences) Act 1997 imposes normal minimum sentences for repeat offenders: life for certain serious sexual and violent offenders; seven years for certain drug offences; and three years for domestic burglary. This Act also abolishes automatic remission. The effect will be a rise in the prison population of at least 10,000 in the next few years, when the prison population at mid-1997 was already at an all-time high of over 60,000.

Generally, the maximum sentence imposable is specified and it is left to the judges' discretion, having considered all the circumstances, what term of imprisonment to impose short of the maximum. The length of the prison sentence is usually commensurate with the seriousness of the offence (Criminal Justice Act 1991, ss. 1(2) and 2(2)). Section 2(2) empowers a court to imprison a person convicted of a violent or sexual offence for longer than the seriousness of the case requires (but not exceeding the maximum) if it is necessary for the protection of the public. In view of the fact that the Crime (Sentences) Act 1997 removes remission, there is an expectation that judges will reduce prison sentences by 20 per cent to take account of this. However, as the press and public are used to the longer sentences this may be difficult to implement. Indeed, in the case of offences for which there is now a minimum for a second offence, judges may indicate seriousness by increasing sentences for first-time offenders. One safeguard against such a use of judicial discretion would be to move towards the universal use of a computerised sentencing system which is (1997) being tested in the Scottish High Court. Computers would be used to assess the variables in a particular case and suggest a 'norm' which, presumably, judges could still vary. Such an approach has its own dangers, and certainly does not necessarily deliver greater justice.

Apart from prisons there are remand homes, attendance and detention centres and approved schools. Those accused who are either mentally unfit to plead or found not guilty on grounds of insanity will be detained in a mental institution at Her Majesty's pleasure (until certified safe for release). Where the circumstances warrant it, the judge may impose a suspended sentence or give a conditional or an absolute discharge. Where the convicted person may be punished by the imposition of a fine (whether or not in conjunction with a term of imprisonment), generally the maximum fine imposable is prescribed, leaving it to judges' discretion to fix the actual amount. The Powers of Criminal Courts Act 1973, ss. 35 and 38 as amended by the Criminal Justice Act 1982, s. 67 and Part VII of the Criminal Justice Act 1988, permit all criminal courts to award compensation to individuals who have suffered loss as a result of the convicted person's criminal activity.

REFERENCES

Allen, Michael J. (1997), *Textbook on Criminal Law*, 4th edn, London: Blackstone Press.

Bedau, Hugo (1974), 'Are There Really "Crimes Without Victims?"' in Edwin Schur and Hugo Bedau (eds), *Victimless Crimes: Two Sides to a Controversy*, Englewood Cliffs, New Jersey: Prentice-Hall.

Blackstone's Criminal Practise, published annually, ed. Peter Murphy, London: Blackstone Press.

Bottoms, A.E. and McClean, J.D. (1976), *Defendants in the Criminal Process*, London: Routledge & Kegan Paul.

Braithwaite, John (1988), *Crime Shame and Reintegration*, Cambridge: Cambridge University Press.

Braithwaite, John (1993), 'Transnational Regulation of the Pharmaceutical Industry', in Gilbert Geis and Paul Jesilow (eds), *Annals of the American Academy of Political and Social Science*, Newbury Park: Sage Periodicals Press.

Cross, Sir Rupert, Jones, Phillip Asterley and Card, Richard (1995), *Introduction to Criminal Law*, 13th edn, London: Butterworths.

Dahrendorf, Ralf (1959), *Class and Conflict in Industrial Society*, London: Routledge.

Devlin, Patrick (1965), *The Enforcement of Morals*, Oxford: Oxford University Press.

DiMento, Joseph F. (1993), 'Criminal Enforcement of Environmental Law', in Gilbert Geis and Paul Jesilow (eds), *Annals of the American Academy of Political and Social Science*, Newbury Park: Sage Periodicals Press.

Edwards, Susan (1989), *Policing Domestic Violence: Women the Law and the State*, London: Sage.

Fisse, Brent and Braithwaite, John (1993), *Corporations, Crime and Accountability*, Cambridge: Cambridge University Press.

Foucault, Michel (1988), 'The Dangerous Individual', in Lawrence D. Kritzman (ed.), *Foucault: Politics, Philosophy and Culture*, trans. by Alan Sheridan and others, New York: Routledge.

Grace, Grace, Lloyd, Charles and Smith, Lorna (1993), *Rape: from Recording to Conviction*, Home Office Research and Planning Unit Paper 71, London: HMSO.

Hale, Sir Matthew (1736), *History of the Pleas of the Crown*, vol. 1.

Hart, H.L.A. (1963), *Law, Liberty and Morality*, Oxford: Oxford University Press.

Home Affairs Committee of the House of Lords (1993), *Third Report, Domestic Violence*, vol. 1, London: HMSO.

King, Michael (1981), *The Framework of Criminal Justice*, London: Croom Helm.

McBarnett, Doreen (1978), 'False Dichotomies in Criminal Justice Research', in John Baldwin and A. Keith Bottomley (eds), *Criminal Justice: Selected Readings*, London: Martin Robertson.

McConville, Michael and Baldwin, John (1981), *Courts, Prosecution and Conviction*, Oxford: Clarendon Press.

Mill, J.S. (1974) (first published 1859), *On Liberty*, Middlesex: Penguin Books.

Morris, Norval and Hawkins, Gordon (1970), *The Honest Politician's Guide to Crime Control*, Chicago: University of Chicago Press.

Packer, Herbert (1968), *The Limits of the Criminal Sanction*, Stanford, California: Stanford University Press.

Pearce, Frank and Tombs, Steve (1992), 'Realism and Corporate Crime', in Roger Matthews and Jock Young (eds), *Issues in Realist Criminology*, London: Sage.

Quinney, Richard (1970), *The Social Reality of Crime*, Boston: Little Brown.

Reiner, Robert (1992), *The Politics of the Police*, 2nd edn, London: Harvester Wheatsheaf.

Runciman Report (1993), *The Royal Commission on Criminal Justice*, Cm 2263.

Ryan, Christopher and Scanlan, Gary (1991), *Swot: Criminal Law*, 3rd edn, London: Blackstone Press.

Schur, Edwin (1974), 'The Case for Abolition', in Edwin Schur and Hugo Bedau (eds), *Victimless Crimes: Two Sides to a Controversy*, Englewood Cliffs, New Jersey: Prentice-Hall.

Smith, J.C. and Hogan, Brian (1996), *Criminal Law*, 8th edn, London: Butterworths.

Taylor, Ian, Walton, Paul and Young, Jock (1973), *The New Criminology*, London: Routledge & Kegan Paul.

Tempkin, Jennifer (1993), 'Sexual History Evidence – The Ravishment of Section 2', *Criminal Law Review*, p. 3.
Turk, Austin T. (1969), *Criminality and Legal Order*, Chicago: Rand McNally.
van de Bunt, H.G. (1994), 'Corporate Crime', *Asset Protection and Financial Crime*, vol. 2(1), p. 11.
Wolfenden Committee Report (1957), *Report of the Committee on Homosexual Offences and Prostitution*, Cmd 247, London: HMSO.

CHAPTER THREE

Public Conceptions and Misconceptions of Crime

3.1 INTRODUCTION

This chapter will review popular ideas of criminality and how these are affected by the media. It will then illustrate the limitations of public conceptions with two brief case studies which outline specific areas of criminal activity which are not normally perceived as criminal, namely, 'white-collar crime' and 'corporate crime'. Later chapters will discuss related issues such as the effect of the media on the amount of crime that is committed (e.g., whether it causes crime) and on perceptions of criminal types which are not usually in the public mind (such as female criminals).

The way people perceive crime and criminals is important to criminologists for a number of reasons. First, it is vital for new students to this area to be aware of any prejudices, preconceptions or opinions which they may hold. The mere awareness of these can often prevent those views interfering with an objective approach. It will allow students to evaluate the usefulness of such views in the light both of extra information and of other, possibly conflicting, views. Secondly, the public's attitude to crime and criminals may be used by certain theorists to explain why people might commit crimes, see for example, labelling in Chapter Fourteen. Thirdly, the perception of crime as being 'wrong' or 'abhorrent' may be questioned when one looks at crime in its wider sense rather than looking just at the acts most commonly associated with the idea of crime (see also Chapter Two where the relationship between crime and morality was discussed). Lastly, perceptions of crime are all important when it comes to looking at punishment. If perceptions, although inaccurate, determine or even influence punishment the result may be unfairness and inefficiency.

3.2   POPULAR AND MEDIA PERCEPTIONS OF CRIME

The word 'crime' generally evokes images of murder, rape, drug abuse, drug trafficking, terrorism, aggravated assault, aggravated burglary, armed robbery, arson, theft or similar dramatic acts. The 'criminal' is often perceived as thoroughly 'bad' or an out and out villain: not the sort of person one knows and is friendly with – an unknown and feared creature. Often, if one does know a person who has been convicted, that person is perceived differently; not a true criminal but rather someone basically good who has perhaps been led astray by others. Or their crime is an activity which is not considered as truly criminal: driving offences or petty dishonesty offences for example. Actions, indeed, which one might even have committed oneself without being apprehended.

Images of criminals are particularly interesting as most of us will know someone who has offended, even if they have not been caught and officially labelled a criminal. Offending is common, especially for men: one third of males have a conviction for a relatively serious offence (standard list offence) by the time they are 30 (Home Office (1995)); and, as Graham and Bowling (1996) suggest, many more young people commit offences and are never caught. Moreover, many offenders commit more than one offence; a quarter of males and a tenth of females admit committing five or six offences. This might suggest a habit of offending, but for most this is a brief phase which will pass and which the young person will grow out of. The ideal is to try to prevent their offending in the first place or, where this is not possible, to limit the damage they cause. All this should make us confront the possibility that those who commit offences are not others but rather ourselves and those we know, even if we, or they, have no overt contact with the criminal justice system.

With this in mind it is particularly difficult to assess how these perceptions are constructed, still less how they are maintained, but some understanding of these issues is useful. Our awareness of any social phenomenon is clearly affected by all our personal experiences. Contact with crime may come directly as criminal or victim, or in contact with the police, or indirectly through police information, family, friends, work, education, the community or the media. It is difficult to assess the effect each of these may have on public opinion.

It is, however, safe to assert that one of these sources, the media, plays some role in forming people's perceptions of crime. One eloquent confirmation of this is implicit in the much greater attention paid to the media in recent times by all the main interested bodies. Not just the Home Office and the police, but the professional associations and trade unions as well as the many pressure groups all work hard to influence media coverage which they see as influencing public attitudes (see, e.g., Schlesinger and Tumber (1994), Part 1). How great its effect is more debatable. Media take various forms (newspapers, television, etc.) and are made up of a number of aspects – news, editorials and documentaries, each of which is assumed to be largely non-fiction. There are also stories, drama and films which are largely fictitious.

Here most attention will be paid to the non-fiction areas, particularly news reporting. Without news reports we would remain ignorant of occurrences outside our direct social groups. News therefore provides us with an important point of contact with the rest of society. In evaluating its effect on popular perceptions of crime it becomes important to consider where most of the information comes from and how representative it is of actual criminality.

To illustrate our points attention will be concentrated on newspapers although, allowing for differences of style and technique, many of the points would broadly apply to radio and television. Journalists largely have the same access to criminal data as most other individuals, but they have a professional motive to make use of these sources. Most crime stories come to them from official sources such as the police, the courts and the Home Office. Some may originate from unofficial sources such as victims, witnesses or informants. Generally, information from these latter sources must be checked against official sources before printing or presenting. The more official the source, the more credible the account, and the more likely it is to be reported as fact rather than allegation. The seeming objective nature of facts lends further weight to the report. Rarely does the criminal's own view or interpretation appear in the media, and when it does the reference will tend to be more anecdotal than factual.

The newspapers themselves sift this information, choosing only those areas which are 'newsworthy'. The distortion of information arises from the commercial and highly competitive nature of newspapers and their fight to obtain a wider readership which is generally achieved by titillating their patrons and/or by stimulating their lives with sensational information. Crime reports, particularly of violent and/or sexual crimes, sell newspapers, which gives the media a powerful incentive to give most prominence to the more graphic cases of criminal behaviour (Schlesinger and Tumber (1994)). Lord Shawcross in his introduction to the Press Council Report (1977) referred to:

> an avid appetite in the readership, leading for the most part humdrum and uneventful lives, to know about what goes on in the more exciting world. In reporting crime or violence in a sensational way the media may well be giving that section of the public the sort of food they want. But the appetite grows with the eating.

Why are certain items reported while others remain in the dark? Clearly it would be impossible to report every item, so some selection is necessary, but how do the press decide which crimes are newsworthy? Jock Young (1974) claims that newspapers 'select events which are atypical, present them in a stereotypical fashion and contrast them against a backcloth of normality which is overtypical'.

Reporters are not generally interested in the most common crimes involving those people who are most usually the victims of crime, but concentrate rather on more serious crimes or on ones whose victims are particularly vulnerable or 'newsworthy'. Moreover, they present these crimes in a deliberately shocking, blunt, or brutal manner, and emphasise the contrast with what is implied to be a quiet and law-abiding community. To achieve this the papers simplify events, sensationalise them with shock headlines, and present the story as good threatened by evil, or law and order threatened by crime and chaos. Reports will be presented in a dramatic and unusual way so as to capture the readers' imagination; for example, reporting of rape focuses on dramatic attacks by strangers in public places, whereas women are more likely to be raped in private by someone they know (see Soothill and Walby (1991)). Furthermore, once an individual is convicted, the papers often print as factual sensational information concerning that individual or the crime, irrespective of the accuracy of that information; often the criminal has no reputation to be protected and so the papers have no fear of a prosecution. In this way the 'story' is supposedly rendered more interesting to the public. For example, Schlesinger and Tumber (1994, pp. 234–40) studying press coverage of a conviction in a sex murder case, show how the popular press used such headlines as 'He should never have existed' and 'Weirdo's sick lust' as well as titillating reports which, they say, 'invite the reader to watch the voyeur at work'.

Steven Chibnall (1977) noted five items which enhance the likelihood of being reported. They are:

(a) visible and spectacular acts;
(b) sexual or political connotations;
(c) graphic presentation;
(d) individual pathology;
(e) deterrence and repression.

The clear implication is that the violence most likely to receive coverage in the press is that which involves sudden physical injury to seemingly innocent strangers, preferably committed in public. So, the escapades of football hooligans outside football grounds are particularly newsworthy, as are those of muggers, vandals, rioters and terrorists. If there is also a controversial political content, its interest is enhanced. For example, racial attacks are particularly newsworthy where the majority race is threatened. Such broad and permanent characteristics should not be taken to imply that the list of what is newsworthy is static – until fairly recently, the newspaper coverage of child- and baby-battering was rare; now it is reported fairly frequently. This may reflect an increase in such offences, or it may simply portray a change in what is judged to be newsworthy. There are still some areas of violence which are rarely reported, such as wife-battering, injuries or deaths at work resulting from unsafe working conditions, and illness caused by pollution. On the other hand, some sexual and/or violent crimes seem always to have a high value in news reporting.

Another factor involved in deciding whether an item is newsworthy or not is the vulnerability of the victim. If the victim is very old or very young, or female (especially if photogenic), there is particular interest. Violent acts committed by individuals, for example women, who are generally thought of as passive are also newsworthy. The conflict is often given more dramatic impact by being simplified into clashes between opposing factions: young versus old; hooligans or rioters versus police; black versus white. The criminal is often labelled as a psychopath, a beast, a madman or just a bored yobbo. In these ways the crime and the criminals are simplified, and the intricacies necessary to provide a full picture are almost never provided. The crimes mentioned above may be far from typical, but are presented as if they were the usual activity of most criminals. The criminals themselves are perceived as violent, immoral and a threat to society, being depicted as people who attack the normal harmony of our existence.

Activities may be condemned not because they have any direct effect on the interests of those who read or hear of them, but simply because they represent the breaking of unwritten rules. If a person lives by a code which forbids certain pleasures, or which involves strict abstention until the right to some benefit or indulgence has been earned, then that person is likely to react in a powerful but negative way against those who do not live by that code. Examples can readily be found in sexual acts or relationships. Such reaction may be unsurprising in the case of sexual acts which may be illegal – rape, child molesting, buggery, bestiality, soliciting. But similar reactions may be provoked by sexual acts which some people simply perceive as unacceptable – intercourse before marriage, extra-marital sex, prostitution – or by acts which some people regard as purely immoral but which, in certain circumstances, may become illegal – homosexuality, abortion. The press can be seen both to form and to play on these values in its reporting of such events, which may blur the question of whether an activity is criminal or not. In this way, sensational reporting of 'immoral' or socially unacceptable acts serves to represent them as either akin to criminality or as possibly leading into it.

Normality would be boring to read about, so the papers naturally pick out the unusual. This leads to seeing things in extremes, so that young people are either drugtaking, sexually permissive and partaking in wanton violence, or they are saving lives, taking part in Outward Bound courses, or performing great charitable works. To gain newsworthy status it is therefore necessary to fall outside many people's experiences. But being unusual does not necessarily guarantee a place in the newspapers. The story must normally also contain an element of human interest, which often arises by violating what most people see as being acceptable. The reporting then takes on what Young (1974) calls a stereotypical style, using basic ideas of what it sees as moral and portraying the criminal acts as wholly alien to that morality.

What has been said above has assumed a bias in media news reporting, albeit a bias which in part arises more or less unavoidably out of what is generally seen as constituting 'news'. Dr Johnson said: 'dog bites man is not news; man bites dog is'. Thus what we have described as 'bias' in newspapers is inherent in their own functions (informative, entertaining, making money etc.) and is not necessarily a criticism. But for our purposes it does raise the question: are the types of crime most commonly reported the ones which are actually most commonly committed? Is crime reporting representative of the amount and type of crime committed?

Over an extended period researchers have discovered a clear bias in news reporting. In 1981 Box claimed that:

90 per cent of media space devoted to the reporting of crimes concentrates on serious crimes such as wilful homicide, forcible rape, aggravated assault, robbery, burglary and theft and crimes currently fanning social hysteria such as drug trafficking and abuse.

Similar findings arise out of other studies carried out, for example, Rochier (1973) and Cumberbatch and Beardsworth (1976) have discovered an over-emphasis on crimes of violence, and Sherizen (1978) and Ditton and Duffy (1982 and 1983) discovered a similar over-emphasis on crimes involving indecency, while they found that those involving dishonesty, malicious conduct and petty assaults were reported roughly proportional to their incidence in the official statistics, and some crimes, particularly motoring offences, were consistently under-reported. More recently, Tumber (1995) shows that most coverage was given to violence against the person and to sexual offences. Soothill and Walby (1991) note the frequency with which sexual crimes are reported, while Schlesinger and Tumber (1994) and Schlesinger et al. (1995) in a study of the whole range of the national press demonstrate both the proportion of coverage given to different types of crime and the variations between different sections of the press.

As Tables 3.1 and 3.2 demonstrate, most coverage in all types of newspapers was given to violence, although there are interesting differences in the coverage by different newspapers. Non-sexual violence occurred in a quarter of the cases mentioned in the 'quality press' as against 45.9 per cent of those in the tabloid press; the corresponding figures for sexual offences were 7 per cent and 11 per cent (Table 3.1). These percentages, and the differences between types of newspaper, remained much the same for non-sexual violence when attention was limited to front-page coverage (Table 3.2). But for sexual offences there was now a dramatic difference: in the 'quality' papers these accounted for 2.8 per cent of all front-page treatment of crime; in the tabloids it was 22.7 per cent.

Table 3.1: Percentage of crime-related items in national daily newspapers mentioning various types of offence

Type of offence	Type of newspaper		
	Quality	Mid-market	Tabloid
Non-sexual violence against the person	24.7%	38.8%	45.9%
Sexual offences	7.2%	9.3%	11.3%
Non-violent offences against the person	3.7%	5.1%	4.4%
Drug offences	3.1%	5.4%	6.4%
Offences against animals	0.4%	0.2%	0.3%
Property offences	25.7%	23.2%	18.8%
Corporate offences	5.6%	2.9%	2.1%
Public order offences	5.3%	5.9%	4.1%
Offences against the justice system	1.9%	2.4%	2.3%
Offences against the state	5.0%	4.6%	2.8%
Number of items	835	410	388

Table 3.2: Percentage of crime-related items on the front pages of national daily newspapers mentioning various types of offence

Type of offence	Type of newspaper		
	Quality	Mid-market	Tabloid
Non-sexual violence	22.0%	45.0%	45.5%
Sexual offences	2.8%	20.0%	22.7%
Non-violent offences against the person	5.5%	10.0%	22.7%
Drug offences	–	5.0%	4.5%
Property offences	35.8%	40.0%	27.3%
Corporate offences	6.4%	–	–
Public order offences	6.4%	5.0%	–
Offences against the justice system	0.9%	–	13.6%
Offences against the state	8.3%	10.0%	–
Number of items	109	20	22

Source: Schlesinger et al. (1995)

As with newspapers, Schlesinger et al. (1995) note that television coverage is varied both in substance and style. Of the national channels ITV comes closest to the tabloid coverage, but local bulletins are even more clearly of this type, being most likely to focus on violent crime.

Also of interest is the focus of programmes such as *Crimewatch UK*. Again their intention is to entertain viewers, which means that they both use powerful visual images such as reconstructions and:

Select their crime stories from the popular end of the market, with murder, armed robbery with violence, and sexual crime as their staple items of coverage. Corporate crime, which is seen as difficult to visualise, and political crime, which is seen as sensitive (especially in the case of Northern Ireland), do not figure in *Crimewatch's* menu. (Schlesinger et al. (1995), at p. 106)

Ditton and Duffy (1983) studied the Scottish press. The aims of their research were to assess whether the newspaper coverage of crime in Scotland was selective; whether it was representative of the actual crimes committed; and whether it tended to suggest that more or less of one particular type of crime was committed than was actually the case. They studied the official crime statistics for the Strathclyde region and compared them with the crime reporting in six papers produced in that area. First, as an indication of the 'weight' given to crime as compared to other news, they discovered that the six papers devoted an average of 6.5 per cent of their news space to crime news.

When the newspapers were examined in detail and compared with the official figures, it became obvious that they were necessarily highly selective about their crime reporting. Of 47,970 offences either made known to the police or recorded as court proceedings for the month taken, only 120 were reported (0.25 per cent). Only 62 of the 34,763 'made knowns' were reported, and 58 of the 13,207 court cases were reported. It was therefore clear that court cases were twice as likely to be reported. The reports of the court cases were also allotted 1.3 times as much space as the 'made knowns'. The fact of selection is of course inescapable: on its own it is neither surprising nor worrying as long as the result is a balanced cross-section of the recorded crimes. However, as Table 3.3 shows, the reporting emphasis was on crimes of violence. The same result has generally been found to exist in studies of this sort. Beyond this, however, there was also a clear over-emphasis on sexual crimes. Since previous researchers, despite looking for such a bias, have only rarely found it, the finding of Ditton and Duffy may have portrayed a recent cultural change, a possibility reinforced by the findings of Schlesinger and Tumber, and Soothill and Walby, reported above.

Susan Smith (1984), in a survey of local Birmingham newspapers, found similar media bias. She discovered that personal offences, including robbery and assault with intent to rob, occupied 52.7 per cent of the space allocated to crime stories in newspapers, but represented less than 6 per cent of recorded crimes, whereas burglary and theft not involving direct contact only occupied 3.8 per cent of the allotted space, but represented 83.9 per cent of recorded offences. She concluded that the most emotive crimes were played up whilst the less exciting crimes were played down, even though the public had a far greater risk of experiencing them. She discovered a further distortion in that the part of Birmingham which the press portrayed as the worst area for crime (quoting it in 34 per cent of all reports) turned out to be third in terms of overall crime rate.

All these studies indicate that in selecting reports of individual crimes there is a bias towards the more serious, but it is interesting to note that, particularly in the 'quality' papers, crime reporting has begun to move away from reporting of individual incidents towards an analysis of what is being done about the problem of crime. The quality papers seem to believe that their readers are more interested in the wider issues of solving the crime problem because such information touches more clearly on their own lives and well-being; the public wants to know what is being done to tackle burglaries or violence on the streets. These papers may therefore utilise more column inches in considering the performance of the professional crime control agencies of the criminal justice system than in discussing individual criminal activity (see Schlesinger and Tumber (1994)).

Fictional accounts, particularly television, cinema and video presentations, are also relevant. Most of us are subjected to such representations from an early age and are probably more interested in them and watch them for longer periods than our exposure to news or other non-fiction criminal information. If the news presentations have an effect on our perceptions, attitudes are arguably equally likely to be formed by the impact of fiction. In Chapter Ten the effect of media on criminality will be considered; here we are concerned only with its effect on perceptions of crime.

Fiction is full of representations of crime, criminals, victims and enforce-ment agencies. Such images are so common that we take them for granted.

Table 3.3: Distortion: a comparison of coverage with incidence

	1 ACTUAL INCIDENCE No. of MKs and CCs (% of total MKs & CCs)	2 NUMERICAL COVERAGE No. of MKs and CCs (% of total MKs & CCs)	3 AREA COVERAGE Area given to MKs+CCs (% of total MKs & CCs)	4 NUMERICAL BIAS INDEX % covered divided by % actual i.e. % in Col. 2 divided by % in Col. 1	5 AREA BIAS INDEX % covered divided by % actual i.e. % in Col. 3 divided by % in Col. 1
I Violence	830 (1.7%)	45 (37.5%)	845,085 (44.0%)	22.1	25.9
II Indecency	309 (0.6%)	10 (8.3%)	195,143 (10.2%)	13.8	17.0
III Dishonesty	17,028 (35.5%)	29 (24.2%)	349,877 (18.2%)	0.7	0.5
IV Malicious	3,311 (6.9%)	8 (6.7%)	128,563 (6.7%)	1.0	1.0
V Other Crimes	666 (1.4%)	9 (7.5%)	113,371 (5.9%)	5.4	4.2
VI Misc. Offences	11,143 (23.2%)	13 (10.8%)	196,997 (10.3%)	0.4	0.4
VII Motoring Off.	14,683 (30.6%)	6 (5.0%)	92,796 (4.8%)	0.2	0.2
CRIMES AND OFFENCES	47,970 (100.0%)	120 (100.0%)	1,921,832 (100.0%)	1.0	1.0

Source: Ditton and Duffy (1983), at p. 163

MK – the official record of those offences made known to the police in the Strathclyde Region.

CC – the official record of all those proceeded against in the Strathclyde Region's Courts.

What is more difficult is to understand the images and the effects they have on our understanding of the world. Like the news media they tend to over-represent sensational crimes which makes for good drama, but they do not represent what are most people's real experience of crime. However, they are even more complex than the news reports: they are imbued with other meanings, a moral representation. Thus they can sometimes evoke favourable sentiments for a particular individual despite that individual's unacceptable behaviour. One of the best examples of the moral ambiguities are the *Dirty Harry* films starring Clint Eastwood. He is a police officer fighting against people depicted as dangerous criminals, but the methods he uses in his enforcement techniques are often as morally bad as those of his adversaries. Yet the story line and images are constructed to persuade the viewer to back him, not only against the criminals, but also against his superiors who would prefer a more civil libertarian and less aggressive form of law enforcement. This simplistic representation of the complex interactions in such films is sufficient to give rise to the question of what such films teach about the operation and perception of crime and enforcement. Furthermore, fiction has an even greater bias towards criminality than non-fiction: it is one of the commonest themes of dramas, films and serials. And like non-fiction accounts, sex and sensationalism are heavily over-represented. But what are the effects? Do, as is often asserted (e.g., Pearson (1994)), popular entertainments like 'video nasties' cause the perceived rise in the crime rates of young offenders?

Allegations of a bias in both crime reporting and fictional representations would therefore seem to be towards the more sensational crimes of violence and possibly also of sex. Given that such bias exists, what is its effect, if any, on the public's perceptions of crime?

3.3 EFFECTS OF MEDIA ON PUBLIC PERCEPTIONS OF CRIME

Sparks (1992) warns against assuming that television necessarily influences people's perception of crime, particularly that it might do so in specific ways. He notes that we view fictional crime programmes for entertainment not enlightenment. It is a common argument and obviously has some substance; but more as a caution against exaggeration than as a total dismissal of the effects of the media. At the least, it seems plausible that many fictional accounts encourage fears and insecurity. And it is interesting that it is often difficult to tell the difference between fiction and the crime reconstruction that takes place in a programme such as *Crimewatch UK*. Here the non-fiction programme employs the techniques of fiction programmes so as to grab the imagination and appear more entertaining, thereby using our preoccupation with fictional depiction of fear as a weapon in crime detection.

Jock Young (1974) suggests that the media affect public opinion in one of three ways, namely:

(a) by mass manipulation,

(b) by a commercial *'laissez-faire'*, or
(c) by the 'consensual paradigm'.

Those who argue that the media seek mass manipulation envisage the public as a gullible mass into which the media can pour chosen information in order to mould that society's opinions. The theorists who support this thesis generally see the press as dangerous because of the possibility of political manipulation. Often, however, the form taken by this fear depends on the political views of the writer – a left-wing theorist tends to see the media as a source of manipulation towards property, commercialism and the dominant classes of our society: a right-wing writer may see the media as the propagators of permissiveness.

Those who argue for commercial *'laissez-faire'* say that the media offer a variety of differing views allowing the public a choice of opinions. They would argue that a person is not just a void into which ideas can be poured and accepted without question, but rather that an individual's attitudes already exist and so he or she will choose the paper or programme which best reinforces that view. Of course they see it is possible to alter some of these views, but the ease with which this may be done is inversely proportional to the importance of a particular view to the person.

Those who support the 'consensual paradigm' theory would argue that there are not many views portrayed in newspapers, largely because they are all owned and run by a few people. They also dispute the idea that most people have set ideas about the world around them, saying instead that an individual is often torn between differing arguments. People's ideas are vague or contradicting: the press plays upon this uncertainty and fickleness of thought. Furthermore, many attitudes may be the products of the media rather than of direct experience, for example, occurrences many miles away may not be understood except so far as and in the way they are portrayed in the media.

It would clearly be helpful if we could discern how the press affects public opinion. Equally clearly this is an elusive goal, but some guidance can be obtained from the attempts that have been made. For example, as already indicated, Susan Smith (1984) studied the effects of media reportage of crime on the inhabitants of a small area in Birmingham. Her survey suggested that 52 per cent derived their main source of information about crime from the media, 35.8 per cent from hearsay or the supposed experience of friends and neighbours, 3.2 per cent from their own experience and only 1.3 per cent from the police. The study suggested that those who had gleaned most of their information from the media were more likely to believe that local crime consisted mainly of personal violence or vice, and more likely when considering crime generally to think of it in terms of personal or violent incidents. The subjects of the survey lived in the area which the newspapers had most often portrayed as having criminal connections, and those who gleaned their information from newspapers were more likely to believe that portrayal than were others. A similar view of that area was found when she questioned 117 representatives from voluntary organisations about their views on crime rates in various districts of Birmingham.

The study therefore lent some support to the view that there was a clear link between the public's opinion of crime and the media reporting of crime. It also suggested another possible relationship – that between hearsay and public opinion. It may be that information gained from hearsay provides more balanced information than the press and so allows the public to fill in the gaps left by press reporting. Schlesinger et al. (1995), in what they admit to be a very limited study, found a relationship between the types of media to which individuals were exposed, those reading tabloid papers and watching a large amount of television (especially ITV), and their level of fear of victimisation. The link was particularly marked so far as fear of violent attacks was concerned. The researchers suggest that the media may be reinforcing personal fears and insecurities and may build on life experiences. All this is highly conjectural, but at least the studies establish reasonably firmly that press reporting of crime creates a broad public awareness of crime which is substantially different from any contained in the official statistics and, as will become apparent in Chapter Four, is different again from actual criminal activity. Other factors which affect public awareness and beliefs about crime are specific social and environmental stress and various forms of gossip, rumour and prejudice.

Further support for this connection is discovered in the Grade report (Home Office (1989)) which implicates the mass media in sustaining and distributing information about crime, leading to a fear of crime. In particular it pinpoints programme reconstructions about crimes such as *Crimewatch UK*, *Crime Stoppers* and *Crimebusters* as having irresponsible features: portraying crimes out of context; being very selective about those they cover; using language which tends to increase fear and insecurity; and stereotyping criminals, crimes, enforcement agencies, enforcement agents and victims. The report is, however, less worried about motivation than are critics such as Young (1974). The report does not see the programme distortions as a purposive and deliberate slant used to sell more papers or attract more viewers, but as a naïve action which will alter once journalistic awareness is heightened. Whatever its views on intentions, however, the Grade report clearly sees the media playing a strong role in building people's perceptions of crime and victimisation.

A related problem (Sparks (1992)) is that the fictional representation of crime depicts ordinary citizens as victims or helpless onlookers, unable to enforce the criminal law or counter crime. Stopping criminality and corruption is left to heroes (and very occasionally heroines). The images are steeped in strong feelings, which hugely simplify the complex social reality. Of course this simplicity is probably partly what renders them enjoyable but, if they do affect our perceptions of crime (and there is no firm proof that they do) then this simplicity may render their effects actually, or potentially, dangerous.

While much in this area is conjectural, there is some positive support for the initial hypothesis. The media, or at least the press, do distort crime reporting and the public do, to a large extent, rely upon that information to form their picture of crime and criminals, and of the possibility of either affecting themselves.

This perception of crime has a number of undesirable side effects such as increasing moral indignation, causing public panic, or individual fear of crime. All of which may cause people to modify their lives so as to take account of these, e.g., by staying in at night, which may be sensible if the perceptions are true but may be totally unnecessary if they are exaggerating the problem. Glass (1989) argues that increasing a person's internal fear of the outside world can lead to a feeling of loss of freedom and cause withdrawal and isolation from society. Even those who are only moderately influenced in this way can have their lives and social interactions affected. By playing on anxieties for commercial purposes both fictional and non-fictional portrayals of crime may be increasing fear and decreasing feelings of citizenship, safety and social community. Possibly most serious is the effect such perceptions may have on the criminal justice system by causing the public to support, or appear to support, severe sentences, so making certain reforms of the penal system more difficult to carry out, even if these may in fact improve the situation. Newspapers often carry stories in which they purport to be outraged by what they consider to be lenient sentences for particular offences. They rarely complain of sentences which may be too punitive. In this way they portray our criminal justice system as over-sympathetic to the criminal, and render the introduction of less punitive sentences or alternative sentences very difficult, if not impossible.

An historical and particularly blatant example of press vilification of proposed changes to make sentences more lenient came in 1978 following the publication of the report by the Home Secretary's Advisory Council on the Penal System (ACPS). After three years' work, the Council had come up with a long and complicated document suggesting a two-tier system in which the maxima laid down by Parliament would indicate the highest penalty appropriate in most cases, with special provision for extended sentencing powers in very serious cases. The new maxima were to be based on the actual levels of prison sentence passed in 90 per cent of cases over the previous ten years. This would lead to some maxima being reduced, for example, the maximum for theft would be reduced from ten years to three years. Furthermore, they suggested that life sentences might be inappropriate outside homicide, and suggested a test period of using determinant sentences for these crimes with, for example, a seven-year maximum in most rape cases. Newspapers greeted these suggestions with headlines such as: '7 YEAR MAXIMUM URGED FOR RAPE', 'A CHARTER FOR RAPISTS' and 'CRIMINALS' CHARTER'. The content of the reports and editorials was similarly damning of the report, without really considering the reasons for the suggestions. The report was therefore strangled before it could be given full consideration.

The perception the public seems to have of the sentencing structure, and certainly that portrayed by most popular newspapers, is that sentencing is too lenient. This is particularly galling when studies such as the *British Crime Surveys* (1982 and 1984) and Hough and Moxon (1985) all point out that when individuals are asked what sentences they would pass on certain offenders for particular offences, their decisions are very closely in line with actual sentencing practice, and that the public believed that the courts were more lenient than they actually are. Interestingly, Hough and Moxon point out that older individuals are more punitive than young ones; that manual workers are more punitive than non-manual workers; and that those who are most fearful of crime (whether that fear is based on actual likelihood of victimisation or not) are more punitive than others.

Despite these findings the media continue to affect penal sanctions. In the Criminal Justice Act 1991 a new form of fining was introduced (it came into operation in the autumn of 1992), the unit fine system, in which the number of units to be paid would represent the seriousness of the offence while the amount of each unit was dictated by the wealth of the offender. This was intended to allow fines to be used more frequently in cases involving the less well off in society whilst ensuring that those with funds were sufficiently affected to be deterred by the punishment. The adverse media reporting on this strategy was so forceful that it led to the total repeal, rather than just reform, of the provision (by the Criminal Justice Act 1993) within the first year of its operation. There was no time even to assess its effectiveness. In this particular case media power was magnified by government vulnerability in the form of an embarrassing by-election defeat at Newbury. On 30 April 1992 the Home Secretary stated that he supported the principle of fines being linked to disposable income, but by 14 May (after the election) he was announcing the abolition of the system to the House of Commons so that the only practical way of ensuring such a link was lost.

Altogether there is much evidence that in recent years the media have sometimes had a powerful effect on public perceptions of the dangers posed by particular actions or behaviours. To take but one example: arising from a few incidents a media-led campaign appeared in all newspapers, radio and television news items attacking certain types of dogs which were thought to pose a particular threat to people, especially children. Breeds such as Rottweilers were particularly picked on for attention. This led to the passing of the Dangerous Dogs Act 1991 which was intended to control these more problematic animals rather than provide what many thought would be a more considered approach, a licensing system to keep track of, and control, all dogs. Since the law was altered there have been almost no reports of attacks by such animals. Either the law has been almost 100 per cent effective or, more likely, the media have lost interest in the subject and moved on to other issues – the subject is no longer newsworthy. The emotive power of the media can sometimes lead to illogical and ill-conceived alterations in the law. None the less, there is a temptation and a tendency to lay too much at the door of the media. For example, in the run-up to the 1997 general election it was often asserted that the competitive bidding over tougher criminal laws was media-driven, but it is probably more accurate to see it as attempts by the politicians to manipulate the media.

It seems reasonable to conclude that the media seem, on occasions at least, to affect perceptions of crime: but equally it needs to be noted that the way this occurs is complex. Motivation is also difficult. Many theorists believe that crime depiction in the media is deliberately skewed towards a particular bias which distorts reality, and that this holds for both fiction and non-fiction.

Fictional representations are likely to be especially misleading; and some would argue that their effects are more powerful because they are deliberately imbued with morals and sentiments intended to engage the reader's feelings, reactions and understanding. And perceptions, wherever they originate, are significant because they have fairly strong effects on the lives of individuals and on their reactions to crime and harmful behaviours. An indication of the significance of this can be obtained by looking at a couple of areas where activity which is undoubtedly criminal has traditionally been given little coverage or condemnation.

3.4 TWO UNPERCEIVED AREAS OF CRIME

3.4.1 Introduction
Two areas of crime which, to date, have had little media coverage and which are not topics that most people think of when they consider what is crime, are white-collar and corporate crime. Today both have a well established place in criminology text books (see, e.g., Croall (1992), Nelken (1994), and Bologna (1993), but until the late 1980s the former was not something generally recognised or readily perceived by the general public to be criminal in the United Kingdom. That changed when the full ramifications of the Guinness affair and the prosecution of Geoffrey Collier for the relatively new offence of insider dealing were given prominent media coverage, and was reinforced in the early 1990s by the high-profile media coverage of the scale of fraud involved in both the collapse of the Bank of Credit and Commercial International (BCCI) and the Robert Maxwell pensions scandal. Corporate crime remains relatively unrecognised as crime even today, despite many national and international events that should have altered the general public perceptions. In brief, both types of crime are given relatively little media coverage, and corporate crime (because of its magnitude, possibly because of powerful lobbying factions and for other legal reasons) is still rarely, if ever, dealt with in the media as crime.

Both categories of crime, therefore, fit very appropriately into a discussion of the relation between the public perception of crime and the ways in which crime is reported in the media. Clearly, strong grounds exist to support the view that there is a connection, but equally it is clear that proving this in an unequivocal manner is difficult. The media treatment of white-collar and corporate crime lends further evidence, albeit circumstantial, to the case for a connection.

3.4.2 White-collar crime
What is white-collar crime? Edwin H. Sutherland was the first to bring this topic to the forefront of criminological study. He did this in works such as *White-Collar Criminality* (1940) and *White-Collar Crime* (1949). His work in this area is still the best known and continues to be both highly regarded and controversial. Most introductions to this subject begin with Sutherland's study (see, e.g., Coleman and Moynihan (1996), pp. 8–10).

Carson (1970) broadly summed up Sutherland's thesis as follows:

. . . the behaviour of persons of respectability and upper socio-economic class frequently exhibits all the essential attributes of crime but it is only very rarely dealt with as such. This situation emerges, (Sutherland claims), from a tendency for systems of criminal justice in societies such as our own to favour certain economically and politically powerful groups and to disfavour others, notably the poor and the unskilled who comprise the bulk of the visible criminal population. (p. 384)

Sutherland's definition of white-collar crime consists of four criteria, namely:

(a) a crime;
(b) committed by a person of respectability; and
(c) of high social status;
(d) in the course of his/her occupation.

Many writers have included a fifth element, namely:

(e) a violation of trust.

Sutherland, however, was at pains to add that his definition was merely approximate. Nevertheless, that definitional aspect of his thesis has caused the most sustained and heated disagreement. Despite that, his definition is important and repays study, together with the additional notion that such crimes involve a violation of trust.

3.4.2.1 What is a crime?
The first element, that the conduct in issue must be a crime, may seem rather obvious but it is also too often forgotten. The nature or seriousness of the conduct is irrelevant so long as it is a crime. Non-criminal activities, however unacceptable, should not be included, but they often are. Indeed, Sutherland himself occasionally fell victim to this practice, and tried to support his claims by including activities which in reality were only administrative or civil wrongs and not crimes. Carson (1970) maintains that Sutherland's:

motives in doing so were to show that under such a definition the white-collar criminal would figure much more prominently and that legis-latures, themselves, are not precluded from the possibility of bias in their determination of the limits of criminal justice.

This idiosyncratic and subjective definition of 'crime' laid Sutherland's thesis open to immediate criticism by such people as Tappen (1947), who pointed out the lack of certain (i.e., definite) criteria for determining white-collar criminality and suggested that, as described by Sutherland, 'it is the conduct of one who wears a white collar and who indulged in . . . behaviour to which some particular criminologist takes exception . . .'.

Sutherland's argument that the activities of certain persons are not criminal simply:

. . . because of their social status (white-collar criminals) have a loud voice
in determining what goes into statutes and how the criminal law as it affects
themselves is implemented and administered,

will not be dealt with here. It may well be that some of these activities should
become criminal, but that is not the immediate concern of a review of
white-collar crime (see Chapter Two and Chapters Fourteen and Fifteen).
Our direct interest is with instances where a crime is committed but no
criminal sanction is incurred because of its white-collar nature, and what can
be referred to as the 'substantial immunity (it enjoys) at the operational level'
(see Carson (1970) and Aubert (1952)). That 'immunity' comes about
arguably because the public do not perceive it to be, and the media do not
treat it as, criminal: indeed, many of those administering the criminal justice
system act as if these were 'not really criminal offences' (see, e.g., Croall
(1992), ch. 5).

3.4.2.2 Who are 'persons of respectability' and 'status'?

The second and third elements in Sutherland's definition – that the crime was
committed by a person of respectability and of high social status – are equally
fraught with difficulty. For example, what is meant by 'respectability'? It
seems likely that Sutherland meant absence from convictions for crimes other
than white-collar crimes. If this is taken as the meaning, it would at least
usefully eliminate from the study those with criminal records for non-white-
collar crimes, and concentrate attention on why people commit white-collar
crime as opposed to any other.

The element of 'high social status' indicates how Sutherland used the term
'white-collar'. Clearly, his is a far narrower meaning than is given to that term
in everyday usage. In Britain there are a number of large white-collar trade
unions with thousands of members, but Sutherland did not intend to draw
his candidates from such a wide pool, so he limited the area to those of high
social status. The reason Sutherland included the requirement of high social
status was to call attention to a vast area of criminal behaviour which is
generally overlooked, and to prove his theory of 'Differential Association' (see
later, 10.2.3). To do that, it was necessary to separate criminals by social
status. Despite these reasons for its inclusion, Sutherland did not stick to
examples drawn from high social status, but included frauds and thefts at
work committed by middle- or even lower-middle-class workers. Although it
was accepted that these examples could be validly included as white-collar
crime, this also led to great criticism, on the ground that these examples did
not prove his particular claims and indicated that he was unable to find
examples from the high social status groups. Sutherland's third element is
therefore not considered to be essential to the definition by many theorists
who choose to ignore it so as to include, if not every social strata, then at least
those included in the wider and more generally accepted use of the term
'white-collar', i.e., using the term 'white-collar' crime more literally. Others
argue that the study should go wider and include all crime committed at
work. Where this is done, the study should perhaps be more accurately called

'occupational crime', of which 'white-collar crime', in Sutherland's sense of the term, is but an instance. Overall, it is essential to be clear exactly which definition is being used, and why.

3.4.2.3 When is someone acting in 'the course of an occupation'?

The fourth part of the definition ('in the course of his/her occupation') is not contentious. If upper-class people commit robbery, rape, murder or other ordinary crimes, this is not automatically classifiable as white-collar criminality. White-collar crimes are crimes committed in the course of one's employment or occupation. The important element is not the socioeconomic status of the individual, but rather the type of crime and the circumstances of its commission. Typical of the types of crime usual to this category are: over-charging, charging for unnecessary work, pilfering, misuse of the employer's telephone, photocopier and other equipment or facilities, false accounting, time fiddling, false allowance claims, bribery, the use of fictitious or over-valued collateral, embezzlement and insider dealing. Certain crimes, however, are commonly included in this category, for example tax evasion, which are not authentic white-collar crime, at least not in terms of Sutherland's definition. These activities, although associated with work, are not committed in the course of an occupation, but are included by many commentators.

3.4.2.4 What is a 'violation of trust'?

The final criterion generally added to the definition, namely that 'the crime should be a violation of trust', is closely related to its being committed by a person of high or middling social status, as it is largely in these positions that this type of trust arises. Sutherland mentioned seven methods of trust violation, which included the obtaining of positions of power which could then be exploited to advantage; the payment of vast salaries to directors even when the company is in financial difficulty; the use of power to obtain smaller corporations at a low price only to ruin them and so dispense with competition. Basically, it includes abuse of power, evasions of regulations, and violations of law carried out in order to secure greater profit without concern for the injury inflicted on the public.

In general, Sutherland considered all crimes committed at 'office-type' work by people of high social status as white-collar crime. Others have studied white-collar crime in a wider context, i.e., so as to include crimes committed by all white-collar workers, not just those of high social status. Still others have chosen to work at the even wider field of occupational crime, which includes all crimes committed in the course of an occupation, no matter what status the employee holds. Each of these is important in its own way, and each has importance for our purposes, as they all cover crimes which rarely appear in newspaper reports and are rarely an important part of public perceptions of crime. Until recently, occupational crime or white-collar crime has been treated as one type of crime, with little or no distinction between crimes committed for the corporation and those committed against the corporation. This can been seen in the preceding paragraph, where some of the examples which Sutherland used to illustrate white-collar crime are committed for the corporation and some against it. More recently, criminologists have preferred to distinguish between these two in order to facilitate the search for reasons why people commit crimes.

A useful distinction can be made between job-related crimes committed for the corporation, and those committed against it. The easiest way to do this is to remove the former category (i.e., where employees commit crimes for the benefit of the company or corporation) and label it 'corporate crime'. Then white-collar or occupational crime may be used to describe the remainder, that is, all crimes committed by persons of respectability in the course of their occupation involving a breach of trust and where the victim is the employer, or at least where the employer does not gain. This would include crimes such as embezzlement and theft from the employer (company, firm or individual) and from other employees.

3.4.2.5 White-collar crime and its enforcement
In legal terms the social class of the offender is irrelevant, it is the nature of the offence and the mental intention which are of importance. Almost all white-collar offences are financial offences and involve frauds. Some frauds are wider than the white-collar crimes discussed above, they involve cheque or credit card frauds committed by people outside the workplace. These are dealt with under the same legal and enforcement provisions as other frauds and are the frauds about which most people are aware because they involve direct and obvious victimisation of the general public. Other frauds involve actions such as embezzlements from companies (very often those for whom the offender works), insider dealing (which can be committed by the directors or the secretarial and other staff) and deceptions to obtain money by false pretences which could be committed by a person in work or by others (collecting money from senior citizens whilst claiming to be from the gas board). Most frauds are for fairly small amounts and committed by offenders who are not rich and famous. These frauds are dealt with by local police and Crown Prosecution Service, but their complexity makes them expensive to investigate and prosecute both in terms of finance and labour. A police force which focused on fraud would be seen to have poor overall performance in terms of cost and efficiency. Furthermore the general invisibility of fraud means that there is less political, and popular or media pressure on chief constables to deal with it. For these reasons fraud tends to have a low priority and low profile in most forces outside London.

Beyond these common frauds there is a smaller number of very different white-collar offences where the sums involved are very high, where the victims may not know of their victimisation, and where clever and calculated investments or deals are used to line the pockets of a few, already very rich individuals. Recent examples of these are the Blue Arrow rights issue fraud of 1987, the Guinness insider dealing affair of 1986, the Bank of Credit and Commerce International, which collapsed in 1991, and Robert Maxwell's use of his workers' pension funds in an attempt to shore up his failing business ventures which all collapsed in 1992. Each of these involved large sums of money and would now be dealt with by the Serious Fraud Office (set up under the Criminal Justice Act 1987). It deals with cases where there is at least £5 million at risk, but in effect it rarely accepts frauds which involve less than £6 million. Under s. 2 of the Criminal Justice Act 1987, the Director of the Serious Fraud Office was given powers to require a person under investigation, or any other person whom he or she has reason to believe has relevant information, to produce documents and to provide an explanation of them even where the information may be incriminating to that person or to another person. These powers were necessary partly to protect employees who might be willing but frightened to give evidence, but were also intended, and have been used, to force information to be provided to help with investigations. This clearly marked an intention to deal with these kinds of offences and possibly suggested that they were at last being treated seriously by the authorities. The power has been successfully challenged in the European Court of Human Rights where, in the case of *Saunders v UK* (1996) 23 EHRR 313, the Court decided that the powers used by the prosecution did contravene Article 6 of the Convention on Human Rights (right to a fair hearing) but that in the particular case it did not affect the outcome. This decision suggests that in order to remain within the basic standards of rights set out in the Convention, s. 2 will need to be altered. No such change has yet occurred, and the Court of Appeal in *Re Arrows Ltd (No. 4)* [1995] 2 AC 75, specifically left it to Parliament to complete the alteration, though it seems unlikely that judges will be minded to allow evidence discovered under s. 2, at least where it is self-incriminating, to be used in evidence, although of course such information may have been used to build the case and to locate other evidence. To alter the law so as to respect the right against self-incrimination may not undermine the prosecution case to any great extent because the provision has anyway not proved very successful in obtaining guilty verdicts.

Bringing these cases to trial is very expensive and the complexity of the cases means that trials tend to be very lengthy (three to 18 months) and the information is very complex for jurors to understand. There have been a number of acquittals, and even on conviction there seems to be little possibility of imprisonment; where imprisonment does ensue it has in practice been for a short period. So in the famous Guinness affair where there were a few convictions the sentences were very low compared with other property offences committed in non-white-collar environments and involving relatively tiny amounts: the chairman, Ernest Saunders, originally faced a five-year sentence, reduced to two and a half years because he was suffering from Alzheimer's disease (fortunately he made a miraculous recovery following the change in his sentence) (Saunders has since successfully challenged in the European Court of Human Rights the powers used in his prosecution (see *Saunders v UK*, above)); the stockbroker, Anthony Parnes was given a 21-month sentence; the multi-millionaire, Gerald Ronson got one year and a £5 million pound fine; and Sir Jack Lyons got a £3 million fine and was later stripped of his knighthood. In a very interesting article by Michael Levi (1991) the aspects of the sentencing of the Guinness four are laid open and compared with other sentencing. The discrepancies are especially unfortunate because they can plausibly be interpreted as a reluctance by judges to send their own kind to prison even when they have let the side down. If this is so, it is uncertain whether, as some suggest, the recent sentence of 14 years (plus a £2.9m confiscation order) on the shipping magnate, Abbar Gokal, for his part in the BCCI case, can be seen as signalling a new sentencing policy. All the enforcement problems make it very difficult for there to be any bargaining for guilty pleas when: the accused has nothing to lose from a full case; is unlikely to be convicted; if convicted unlikely to be severely sentenced; and when so many offenders escape with impunity. Change seems dubious because, apart from any social discrimination, these crimes do not induce fear in the community and the media condemnation – though growing – is still muted. Indeed, some argue that the issue of high-level fraud should not be pressed very hard because a strong economy needs to encourage enterprise: but whether a strong society can be built by tolerating injustice is a wider issue (for a more detailed discussion see Croall (1992) and Levi (1993)).

3.4.3 Corporate crime or organisational crime
Corporate crime is more difficult to define. Partly this is because it covers such a wide range of offences (a useful categorisation is given in Bologna (1993), ch. 2) and is complicated by a problem of terminology. It is variously called corporate, business or organisational crime. Most writers are referring largely to the same area of activity (see Conklin (1977), Schrager and Short (1977) and Shover (1978)). Here it will be defined as: an illegal act of omission or commission, punishable by a criminal sanction, which is committed by an individual or group of individuals in the course of their work as employees of a legitimate organisation, and which is intended to contribute to the achievement, goals or other objectives thought to be important to the organisation as a whole or some sub-unit within it, and which has a serious physical or economic impact on employees, the general public, consumers, corporations, organisations and governments.

The first part of this definition makes it clear that the concern is with criminal acts rather than just unlawful acts. An activity may be unlawful in civil or administrative law without being criminal or illegal. Generally, for lawyers the word 'illegal' is synonymous with the word 'criminal', but sometimes criminologists are not so precise. As with white-collar crime, it is important to appreciate that in this discussion 'illegal' is to be confined to actual, recognised criminal conduct, namely acts or omissions declared by the law to be criminal in that society, as opposed to civil wrongs.

The definition covers omissions as well as commissions, and may include both intentional and unintentional harms. The need for *mens rea* (a guilty, blameworthy or criminal state or mind) was discussed in Chapter Two. In certain types of crime it is unnecessary. The mere fact that machinery in a factory is dangerous may be sufficient to prove a crime even if those in charge of the factory did not intend to injure anyone, or even did not know it was dangerous. They ought to know, and have a duty to ensure it is safe. Similarly, if a drug company distributes a product before adequately testing it, if that product is harmful they may be liable to criminal prosecution even if they neither intended harm nor knew of the danger: they are liable as long as in distributing it they break a criminal regulation. In each case a prosecution could occur even though no-one is actually hurt but merely because the criminal law is breached. Some theorists have argued that such crimes are actually worse than intentional crimes, as they show a general disregard for humanity and could lead to the injury of numerous victims, whereas an intentional crime is usually directed towards one victim (for a further discussion of this idea see Box (1983)).

The definition does not concentrate on economic goals but rather allows a wider understanding of organisational goals. It also recognises that the impact of such crime upon victims may well be, and often is, physical rather than economic (e.g. environment dumping), and that the victims may be corporations, organisations and even governments. Such victims may result from tax evasion, bribing governmental officials, industrial espionage, illegal mergers and takeovers, trademark or patent violations, insider dealing, fraudulent advertising, and so on. Their inclusion is therefore necessary.

Is corporate crime important? Is it surprising that many people do not consider corporate crime as crime? Arguably it is surprising, because of the extensive harm corporate crime causes to the community generally. But the relative lack of public concern is more understandable when consideration is given to the information made available to the public in a readily accessible and digestible form. Corporate crime receives very little exposure in the media or, if it is covered, it is often confined to the 'city' pages or portrayed as a disaster or accident rather than a crime.

Corporate crime can be a cause of injury, or even death. Death does occur in the course of, and as a result of, legitimate corporate activities such as exploration, mining and machine failure. Sometimes, however, the corporate activities which resulted in deaths or serious injuries are illegitimate in that the corporation has shown wanton disregard for, or been reckless or negligent of, the health and safety of its employees or its customers. Dowie (1977) claims that in the United States a motor-car manufacturer (Ford) continued to sell a particular model with the knowledge that it was unsafe. The company had rushed it onto the market despite knowing of a hazardous defect. It is alleged that the company had calculated that the amount it would pay out in compensation would be less than the loss in profits by delaying production until the problem was solved. Ford was prosecuted for manslaughter caused when one of its Pinto cars burst into flames after a rear impact in 1978. The company was acquitted on formal grounds but many civil claims for damages were successful and, despite the failure to convict, it is probably the most famous corporate case (see Cullen et al. (1984)).

Deaths resulting from corporate activity have occurred from time to time: some are purely accidental or involve death by misadventure; others may be the result of some criminal breach on the corporation's part. Carson (1981) refers to 106 fatalities between 1969 and 1979 on or around installations in the British sector of the North Sea, and he suggests that many of these deaths were avoidable and occurred because of lower safety standards applied offshore (for further examples, see the annual reports of the Health and Safety Executive and Health and Safety Commission). Similar problems arise in the case of major disasters. For example, in Bradford in 1986 many people died and there were numerous injuries when the football stadium caught fire. In the enquiry which followed, it transpired that the club was aware that it was in breach of safety regulations, but no prosecution ensued. In 1987 a Townsend Thoresen ferry, *The Herald of Free Enterprise*, sank off Zeebrugge with the loss of hundreds of lives and many injuries; the cause of this was identified as being the omission to close the bow doors before sailing. An unsuccessful prosecution for corporate manslaughter was brought against the firm. Braithwaite (1984; 1993) refers to many examples in the pharmaceutical industry. Corporations often disregard the interests of society as a whole in pursuit of their corporate goals, so they may dump toxic waste, emit dangerous fumes into the atmosphere, fit faulty equipment to products such as cars, and expose employees or others to dangers. In 1994 the West Midlands Health and Safety Advice Centre (a non-governmental organisation) investigated 28 deaths at work and the official response to them (see Bergman (1994)). They both attempted to judge the level of criminal responsibility of the companies and the senior officers involved and to evaluate the work of the enforcement agencies involved in investigating the incidents (the Health and Safety Executive and the Environmental Health Department). They concluded that in 13 cases the criminal responsibility of the companies and/or the senior officers was greater than suggested by the official action (in 11 cases there should either have been a prosecution for manslaughter or a referral for consideration to prosecute for manslaughter) and 11 others deserved further investigation. This suggests the level of corporate criminality is considerably higher than official statistics suggest and that the enforcement agencies are not performing their function correctly, in particular they fail to take account of the previous history of the company and of the action of the officers involved and they fail to consider cases for a charge of manslaughter (and referral to the police). Part of this failure arises out of a starvation of resources supplied to the regulatory bodies but part is also attitudinal and may also arise because they had either not picked up on problems at earlier visits or failed to ensure compliance with their findings. Reporting of situations where the lives of either workers or members of the public are tragically lost, or put in danger, is generally factual and suggests the accidental nature of the disaster. Sometimes these could reasonably be reported, not as unavoidable or regrettable accidents, but rather as culpable infractions of the criminal law which warrant punishment in addition to any civil sanctions.

The fact that the press often do not report these incidents in such a way is unsurprising for a number of reasons. First, the areas of law involved are often regulated by some autonomous body such as the Factories Inspectorate. These bodies often do not see themselves as there to punish breaches of the law, but·rather to make those in authority aware of the rules involved and allow them a chance to bring their organisation within those regulations. Therefore, where a breach of the factories' legislation is discovered, it is often dealt with by a polite letter pointing out the infraction and requesting that it be attended to. This may be followed by a letter threatening prosecution. Carson (1970) studied the workings of the Factories Inspectorate more closely, and claimed that prosecution usually occurred only where an injury took place, but not all injuries led to prosecutions. Normally guilt is admitted and the fine is small, often below £500 (at the time Carson wrote, it was often as low as £50). As journalists glean most of the official crime news from the police and the courts, they are unlikely to come across many instances of this type of corporate crime. Secondly, if a newspaper carelessly accuses a company of some criminal activity it could risk large libel payments, so great care is needed to verify any facts. Thirdly, corporate crime may not fit within the parameters of what is 'newsworthy'. In particular, such cases do not generally lend themselves to simple, catchy headlines, but involve complex factual situations needing full, lengthy and often technical analysis. The exceptions are where, as in the Guinness and Maxwell cases, the offences overlap with the media's abiding obsession with the lives of the rich and the famous (see, e.g., Tumber (1995) and Levi and Pithouse (1994). Fourthly, the general public may be the only victim, and they may often be unaware of the criminal activity and be unable to obtain the information necessary to discover whether a crime has occurred or not. Fifthly, the lack of media attention may be due to the powerful lobbying which large companies can use (e.g., by withdrawing advertisements).

The incidents of death and injury caused by corporations, their services or their products are not unimportant, nor are they uncommon. The general public may suffer if pollutants are illegally released by a company into the environment, or if products are unsafe, or if services in the form of lifts or aircraft or ships or other vehicles are defective in law, or their method or manner of deployment legally negligent. Employees may suffer from 'accidents' at work which spring directly from conditions at work which are in violation of statutory safety standards. Employees may also suffer from work-induced diseases such as lung cancer, asbestosis and mesothelioma. In 1987 the Health and Safety Executive estimated that 750 people die every year as a result of such work-induced diseases, whilst others, such as the Work Hazards Group, would describe this figure as a gross underestimate.

The extent of the problem is difficult to quantify but it has been estimated that in 1972 in the USA 114,000 died from occupational diseases or accidents, compared to the 20,600 who died from being shot, stabbed, beaten or poisoned and were recorded as homicide cases. In Britain there is a similar discrepancy. Table 3.4 shows the figures for 1973-79, and the number of work-related deaths far outweighs other homicides.

During the same time span there was an annual average of 330,000 non-fatal accidents at work (see Box (1983)). Clearly, not all the work-related deaths and injuries are a result of criminal conduct (acts or omissions) on the part of companies and their directors, but it does give some idea of the extent of the problem.

When one considers that these accidents only relate to the working population which is less than 50 per cent of the whole, the danger of

occupational injury to those at work appears to be more striking. (Box
(1983))

**Table 3.4: Homicides finally recorded by the police compared with
fatal occupational accidents and deaths from occupational diseases,
England and Wales, 1973–79**

	1 Fatal occupational accidents[1]	2 Deaths from occupational diseases[2]	3 Col. 1 + Col. 2	4 Deaths finally recorded as homicides by the police[3]
1973	873	910	1,783	391
1974	786	911	1,697	526
1975	729	957	1,686	444
1976	628	976	1,658	489
1977	614	916	1,530	418
1978	751	866	1,617	472
1979	711	752	1,463	551
total	5,146	6,290	11,436	3,291
adjusted for population at risk (approx)			22,872 7 : 1	

[1] Health and Safety Executive (1980) *Health and Safety Statistics,* 1977,
London: HMSO, p. 4 and (1981) *Health and Safety Statistics,* 1978–9,
London: HMSO, p. 12.

[2] Health and Safety Executive (1980) p. 58 and Health and Safety Executive (1981) p. 63.

[3] *Criminal Statistics England and Wales,* 1980, London: HMSO, p. 61
(Murder, Manslaughter, etc.).

(Table taken from Box (1983), at p. 28)

For the 1970s it is possible to give an idea of the extent of the violations
and how many may have been caused by the employers' managerial decisions.
Health and safety records show that in each of the years from 1973 to 1979
more than 600 people died and a further 18,000 were injured as a result of
work-related incidents (Health and Safety Executive 1987), and also estimated that in three out of five deaths at work the management had violated
ss. 2 and 3 of the Health and Safety at Work etc. Act 1974 (general duties to

employees). There are other indications that these infractions are widespread: the Occupational Safety and Health report for 1987 refers to a mass inspection of building sites in which one in five of those visited was so unsafe that work had to be stopped immediately, and many others were violating in less blatant ways. What is involved is clearly a problem which is both large and widespread in business and industry.

Most of these deaths do not result in prosecutions. In investigating 28 workplace deaths the West Midlands Health and Safety Advice Centre discovered that even when company directors and senior officers within companies committed acts which might amount to manslaughter they could easily avoid prosecution because the investigations into the deaths were inadequate and because there seemed to be a reluctance to criminalise the activities of employers (see Bergman (1991) and (1994)). So even with the most serious offences corporate crime goes largely uncontrolled, and part of this seems to be due to an unwillingness to prosecute. Nationally, over 1,500 workplace deaths occurred between 1988 and 1991, but there were only 249 prosecutions. Even where prosecutions took place, the average fine following deaths in 1990–91 was just £2,488 (Labour Research (1994) 11, pp. 9–12; (1996), 12, p. 7).

There are economic losses as well. Fraud on the grand scale can go as far as raising the possibility of destabilising the economic framework by using corporate structures, as in the BCCI case where national laws and regulations were largely evaded through a complex transnational corporate structure. At a less grandiose level some of the economic losses are suffered by other companies, for example through industrial espionage, price-fixing and patent violation. Others are suffered by the public, for example through corporate tax evasion. In the end it is generally the public who are the final losers, and most authors would agree that the losses suffered as a result of corporate crime far outweigh those suffered as a result of economic street crimes such as robbery, theft, larceny and motor vehicle theft.

As Box (1983) put it (at p. 25):

All the . . . examples of deaths, injuries, and economic losses caused by corporate acts are not the antics of one or two evil, or mentally disturbed, or relatively deprived senior employees. Rather they represent the rational choices of high-ranking employees, acting in the corporation's interests, who intend directly to violate the criminal law or governmental regulations, or to be indifferent to the outcome of their action or inaction, even though it might result in human lives obliterated, bodies mangled, or life-savings lost.

Lastly, there is the possibility of almost unquantifiable environmental damage even when, as it should be for this purpose, consideration is limited to corporate acts which are criminal, i.e., the illegal cleaning of oil tanks at sea or the dumping of toxic pollutants in rivers.

Corporate crime is therefore a real social problem. Some go so far as to argue it is more dangerous than conventional crime. Whether or not that is over-stating the case is unimportant. What is important is the realisation that each of these criminal acts represents a very real danger to society and yet corporate crime, like white-collar crime, is not usually among the first to spring to mind when crime is being considered. Why not? They are no less morally reprehensible, and in terms of suffering inflicted or damage caused they are as bad, and often because of their magnitude, worse than conventional, run-of-the-mill crimes committed by individuals.

The media are at least partially responsible for this situation. When a murder is committed and reported in the papers, it is clearly reported as a life criminally taken by another. But when life is lost as the result of a corporate crime, it is often reported as a disaster or an 'act of God' rather than as the result of human culpability. In this way, these activities are not perceived to be the result of criminal acts or omissions but as unfortunate accidents. This is one illustration of the way in which the media do have power to shape the general public's view of crime, and indirectly the consequences for the class of person and the corporations that perpetrate these crimes.

Publicity, by providing information, can discourage corporate crime. Certainly, in some of these infractions publicising the breaches of particular companies would have a powerful enforcing effect. The corporations rely on consumers for their well-being; consumers can take legal action in civil courts for damage done to themselves; or can boycott, or threaten to boycott, goods which offend regulations; or can write letters, individually or collectively, drawing the problems to the attention of the corporation. The corporations involved are usually basically legal and responsible, wish to retain a positive corporate image and profile, and will wish to avoid a bad press or possible boycott if they ignores the original letter or letters. To be effective the consumer pressure needs to be well organised. Braithwaite (1993) gives examples of the power of such action in altering the behaviour of major pharmaceutical companies. Corporations are interested in their public image and the media could, by drawing attention to problems, do much to persuade companies to work within the regulations and, possibly, to even more acceptable standards.

Interestingly, where perceptions of crime could do most for enforcement they have a low media profile; where their most effective result is to increase fear of victimisation by reporting of street crime, often in a distorted and startling way, they proliferate.

REFERENCES

Advisory Council On the Penal System, Report (1978), *Sentences of Imprisonment: A Review of Maximum Penalties*, London: HMSO.

Aubert, V. (1952), 'White-Collar Crime and Social Structure', *American Journal of Sociology*, vol. 58, pp. 263–271.

Bergman, David (1991), *Deaths at Work: Accidents or Corporate Crime*, London: Workers Educational Association.

Bergman, David (1994), *The Perfect Crime? — How Companies can get away with Manslaughter in the Workplace*, West Midlands: West Midlands Health and Safety Advice Centre.

Bologna, J. (1993), *Handbook of Corporate Crime*, London: Butterworth-Heinemann.

Box, Steven (1981), *Deviance, Reality and Society*, 2nd edn., London: Holt.

Box, Steven (1983), *Power, Crime and Mystification*, London: Tavistock.

Braithwaite, John (1984), *Corporate Crime in the Pharmaceutical Industry* London: Routledge & Kegan Paul.

Braithwaite, John (1993), 'Transnational Regulation of the Pharmaceutical Industry', in Gilbert Geis and Paul Jesilow (eds), *Annals of the American Academy of Political and Social Science*, Newbury Park: Sage Periodicals Press.

British Crime Survey (1982), see Mike Hough and Pat Mayhew (1983), *British Crime Survey*.

British Crime Survey (1984), see Mike Hough and Pat Mayhew (1985), *Taking Account of Crime*.

Carson, W.G. (1970), 'White-Collar Crime and the Enforcement of Factory Legislation', *British Journal of Criminology*, vol. 10, p. 383.

Carson, W.G. (1981), *The Other Price of British Oil*, London: Martin Robertson.

Chibnall, Steven (1977), *Law and Order News. An Analysis of Crime Reporting in the British Press*, London: Tavistock.

Coleman, C. and Moynihan, J. (1996), *Understanding Crime Data*, Buckingham: Open University Press.

Conklin, J.E. (1977), *Illegal but not Criminal*, New Jersey: Spectrum.

Croall, Hazel (1992), *White Collar Crime*, Buckingham: Open University Press.

Cullen, F.T., Maakestad, W.J. and Cavender, G. (1984), 'The Ford Pinto Case and beyond: Corporate Crime, Moral Boundaries, and the Criminal Sanction', in E. Hochstedler (ed.), *Corporations as Criminals*, Newbury Park: Sage.

Cumberbatch, C. and Beardsworth, A. (1976), 'Criminals, Victims and Mass Communications', in E. Viano (ed.), *Crimes, Victims, and Society*, Lexington: D.C. Heath.

Ditton, Jason and Duffy, James (1982). 'Bias in Newspaper Crime Reports: Selective and Distorted Reporting of Crime News in Six Scottish Newspapers during March 1981', *Background Paper Three*, Department of Sociology: University of Glasgow.

Ditton, Jason and Duffy, James (1983), 'Bias in the Newspaper Reporting of Crime News', *British Journal of Criminology*, vol. 23, p. 159.

Dowie, M. (1977), 'Pinto Madness', *Mother Jones*, vol. 2, p. 18.

Ericson, R.V. (ed.) (1995), *Crime and the Media*, Aldershot: Dartmouth.

Glass, J. (1989), *Private Terror: Public Life*, Ithaca, NY: Cornell University Press.

Graham, J. and Bowling, B. (1996), *Young People and Crime*, Home Office Research Study No. 145, London: HMSO.

Health and Safety Commission (1980), *Health and Safety Commission Report 1978-79*, London: HMSO.

Health and Safety Executive (1980), *Health and Safety: Manufacturing and Service Industries, 1978*, London: HMSO.

Health and Safety Executive (1987), *Statistics 1984–85*, London: HMSO.

Home Office (1989), *Report of the Working Group on the Fear of Crime*, London: HMSO.

Home Office (1995), *Criminal Careers of those Born Between 1953 and 1973*, Home Office Statistical Bulletin, London: HMSO.

Hough, M. and Moxon D. (1985). 'Dealing with Offenders: Popular Justice and the Views of Victims', *Howard Journal of Criminal Justice*, vol 24, p. 160.

Hough, M. and Mayhew P. (1983), *The British Crime Survey: First Report*, Home Office Research Study No. 76, London: HMSO.

Hough, M. and Mayhew P. (1985), *Taking Account of Crime: Findings From the Second British Crime Survey*, Home Office Research Study No. 85, London: HMSO.

Labour Research (1994 and 1996), London: LRD Publications.

Levi, Michael (1991), 'Sentencing White-Collar Crime in the Dark? Reflections on the Guinness Four', *Howard Journal of Criminal Justice*, vol. 30, p. 257.

Levi, Michael (1993), 'White-collar Crime: the British Scene', in Gilbert Geis and Paul Jesilow (eds), *Annals of the American Academy of Political and Social Science*, Newbury Park: Sage Periodicals Press.

Levi, M. and Pithouse, A. (1992), 'The Victims of Fraud', in D. Downes (ed.), *Unravelling Criminal Justice*, London: Macmillan.

Nelken, D. (ed.) (1994), *White-collar Crime*, Aldershot: Dartmouth.

Occupational Safety and Health Report (1987), *Annual Statistical Report*, London: HMSO.

Pearson, G. (1994), 'Youth Crime and Society' in Mike Maguire, Rod Morgan and Robert Reiner (eds), *The Oxford Handbook of Criminology*, Oxford: Oxford University Press.

Press Council Report (1977), London: Press Council.

Rochier, R. (1973), 'The selection of Crime News by the Press', in S. Cohen and J. Young (eds), *The Manufacture of News*, London: Constable.

Schlesinger, P. and Tumber, H. (1994), *Reporting Crime: The Media Politics of Criminal Justice*, Oxford: Clarendon Press.

Schlesinger, P., Tumber, H. and Murdock, G. (1995), 'The Politics of Crime and Criminal Justice', in R. Ericson (ed.), *Crime and the Media*, Aldershot: Dartmouth.

Schrager, L.S. and Short J.F. (1977), 'Towards a Sociology of Organisational Crime', *Social Problems*, vol. 25, p. 407

Sherizen, S. (1978), 'Social Creation of Crime News: All The News Fit to Print', in C. Winnick (ed.), *Deviance and Mass Media*, Beverley Hills: Sage.

Shover, N. (1978), 'Defining Organisational Crime', in M.D. Ermann and R.J. Lundman (eds), *Corporate and Governmental Deviance: Problems of Organisational Behaviour in Contemporary Society*, Oxford: Oxford University Press.

Smith, Susan (1984), 'Crime in the News', *British Journal of Criminology*, vol. 24, p. 289.

Soothill, K. and Walby, S. (1991), *Sex Crime in the News*, London: Routledge & Kegan Paul.

Sparks, Richard (1992), *Television and the Drama of Crime: Moral Tales and the Place of Crime in Public Life*, Buckingham: Open University Press

Sutherland, Edwin H. (1940), 'White-Collar Criminality', *American Sociological Review*, vol. V, pp. 1–12.

Sutherland, Edwin H. (1949), *White Collar Crime*, New York: Dryden Press.

Tappen, Paul W. (1947), 'Who is the Criminal?' *American Sociological Review* vol. 12, pp. 96–102.

Tumber, H. (1995) '"Selling Scandal": Business and Media', in R. Ericson (ed.), *Crime and the Media*, Aldershot: Dartmouth.

West Midlands Health and Safety Advice Centre (1994), see Bergman.

Work Hazards Group (1987), *Death at Work*, London: WEA.

Young, Jock (1974), 'Mass Media, Drugs and Deviance', in Paul Rock and Mary McIntosh (eds), *Deviance and Social Control*, London: Tavistock.

CHAPTER FOUR

The Extent of Crime: A Comparison of Official and Unofficial Calculations

4.1 OFFICIAL STATISTICS

4.1.1 Introduction

Almost all discussions of the level of crimes in any area start with a consideration of the official criminal statistics. These are the statistics gathered by the police, the courts and the punishment establishments. Court records have been kept since medieval times and until very recently it was to these that people turned for information concerning the crime rate. In 1778 Jeremy Bentham suggested that these should be centrally collected and used to measure the moral health of the country. Gradually, information concerning the imprisonment of individuals, and later the crimes reported to the police, began to be kept. The methods of recording were generally localised, making comparison difficult. It was not until 1856 that tables showing crimes known to the police were first included in the official statistics for England and Wales (then called the *Judicial Statistics*), and only since 1876 have such offences been systematically collected and collated. It was much later that these figures became used as the main indicators of the crime levels in the country. Now the police statistics are almost universally taken as the best official indicators of the level of crime. The court and other statistics will naturally record a substantially lower level of crime, since many crimes are either not solved or not taken to court. The police and court statistics for England and Wales are collected and published annually as the *Criminal Statistics*. Quarterly bulletins present supplementary information.

This chapter is mainly concerned with the statistics collected by the police as these relate to the measure of crime of which the authorities are aware. In England and Wales the police record serious offences about which they are aware, but this does not represent all crimes committed in the country. In fact, the statistics collected by the police are a poor indication of the full extent of criminal activity in the country. There are a number of reasons for this, which can be studied in some detail in recent accounts of the nature and limitations of criminal statistics (see, e.g., Coleman and Moynihan (1996); and Walker (1995)): the immediate purpose, however, is simply to make a few broad points about the deficiencies of police statistics as indicators of the overall level of criminal activity. First, although the police detect some crimes for themselves, for example drugs-related offences, driving offences, public order offences or street brawls, football hooliganism and offences against unoccupied property, the majority of offences come to light because they are reported by the victim or victims. In both instances some crimes may never come to light. There will be cases where the police do not discover crimes which fall into the category of those most likely to be detected by them, and there will be many offences which victims fail to report to the police. Secondly, the police may not record all the activities which are reported to them, or may not record them as crimes, e.g., they may be recorded as lost goods instead of stolen. Thirdly, there are many crimes which are not controlled by the police but which fall under the auspices of some other authority such as the Customs and Excise. The official statistics are a better reflection of society's attitudes towards crime and criminals than an objective measure of criminal behaviour.

4.1.2   Reasons for reporting and non-reporting of offences
As mentioned above, there are many crimes which are never reported to the police, and these often remain wholly undetected by officials. There are various reasons why some are not so reported:

1.   The victim may be unaware that a crime has been perpetrated. This is especially likely if the crime is one against a large corporation, such as shop-lifting and pilfering by the staff, or if there are a number of victims, none of whom realises they have been victimised. Similarly, the victim may be unaware that what has occurred is a crime. This is especially a problem with offences committed against children.

2.   The victim may participate willingly, or there may be no victim, so that no-one is likely to report the activity, e.g., many sexual offences, illegal abortions, prostitution, drugs offences, obscene publications.

3.   The victim may be unable to report the offence. This occurs, for example, in most offences against children or other offences against relatively weak victims where the victims may be threatened (e.g., with loss of a job) to prevent revelation. Problems of this type occur also with illegal immigrants, who are afraid of reporting offences committed against them as it may result in their being deported.

4.   The victim may consider that the offence is too trivial to bother reporting it to the police.

5.   The victim may not wish to participate in the time-consuming procedures to which reporting may give rise.

6.   The victim may be worried about other consequences of reporting, such as not being believed or having to face very personal and attacking questions in court.

7. The victim may not want to see the offender punished because he is a child or a relative, friend, employee or employer.

8. The victim may not have any confidence in the criminal justice system.

9. The victim may consider that, in the circumstances, the official system is inappropriate, possibly because the property is returned or some form of compensation is forthcoming, or because the victim is not altogether blameless or wishes certain activities to remain secret.

In the last five *British Crime Surveys* (BCS) (1984, 1988, 1992, 1994, and 1996), the reason most often given for non-reporting of crimes was that the crime was too trivial to report (between 40 and 55 per cent; in contrast, the Islington Survey found that 75 per cent were not trivial); next was that victims felt that the police would not have been able to do anything (between 23 per cent and 32 per cent); and around 10 per cent (19 per cent in 1996) said they did not feel that it was a matter for the police or that they had dealt with it themselves. In 1992, 13 per cent did not report because they thought the police would not be interested: this had risen to 20 per cent by 1996. Victims rarely cited inconvenience (2–4 per cent); fear or dislike of the police (0.4 per cent to 1 per cent); or fear of reprisals (1–4 per cent). Police-related reasons for non-reporting have increased from 24 to 49 per cent in the period between 1984 and 1996.

The 1992 and 1996 BCS found that offences which had the most serious consequences for the victim were most likely to be reported (two thirds were reported as against a quarter of the least serious cases). This still meant that in 1992 approximately 1.9 million of the most serious offences went unreported, a large number when one considers that only 3 million offences involving similar seriousness get reported to the police. In the non-reporting of serious offences the belief that the police could do nothing or would not be interested were more often cited than when the offence was less serious. In the case of assault the most frequent reason for non-reporting of both serious and other offences was that the victim had dealt with it personally or thought it inappropriate for the police (37 per cent of serious offences and 29 per cent of least serious offences in 1992). This was particularly important where the victim knew the offender. Fear of reprisals was stronger in the case of serious offences, particularly assault (20 per cent). Over the 14 years that the BCS have been conducted, the proportion of all contact crime (crimes of violence) which has been reported increased from 30 to 38 per cent, the greatest increase being in the reporting of domestic and acquaintance violence.

The degree to which crimes are or are not reported to the police varies with the type of offence. Murders tend to have high rates of reporting. People often report their loved ones as missing; the police normally search for them; it is difficult to dispose of bodies; and discovered bodies are nearly always reported to the police. But even in the case of murder there is not 100 per cent reporting. The actual victim is clearly unable to report the offence, and sometimes discovery may depend on chance, as the case of Nielson showed. Nielson was finally convicted of murdering 15 men, but his offences lay hidden for many years as the bodies were not found. Crimes to property are increasingly likely to be reported, probably largely due to increased insurance. This is borne out by the General Household Surveys (for 1972, 1973, 1979, 1980, 1985, and 1986) and the 1982, 1984 and 1988 BSCs, which indicate that the proportion of residential burglaries involving loss which were reported to the police increased greatly over the period 1972–1987. In 1972 approximately 78 per cent of burglaries involving loss were reported; this rose to 90 per cent in 1987, but fell back to 84 per cent in 1995 (BSC, 1988 and 1996). Actual burglaries involving loss increased only 17 per cent, whilst recorded offences increased 127 per cent (nearly 8 times more). Insurance policies make it a normal condition of payment that the offence should have been reported. The reporting seems also to have affected recoveries. In 1972 only 19 per cent of property stolen as a result of burglaries was recovered through insurance, whereas in 1987, 58 per cent was so recovered (figures drawn from the BCS (1988)). Other offences are, for various reasons, rarely reported. For example, child sexual or other child abuse, wife-battering, rape (although recently the rate of reporting has increased due to better police response to and treatment of the victims, but it still remains a little-reported crime) and other sexual offences, driving offences, drugs related offences, fraud, blackmail and corporate crime. The 1996 survey shows that a low reporting rate is normal when the victim knows the offender, and this, along with a fear of reprisals, helps to explain the lowish reporting rates in wounding (39 per cent) and assault (34 per cent).

The 1984 and 1996 BCS asked victims why they had reported offences, and the answers are quite illuminating. Just over half of victims in 1996 (but only 36 per cent in 1984) stressed motives which were to their own advantage – recovery of property, reducing their risk of further victimisation, getting help from the police, and notifying the police to satisfy the requirements of insurance companies, etc. In 1996, nearly two thirds (as against 33 per cent in 1984) of victims mentioned that they felt obligated to report the crime, because offences such as these should be reported, because it was a serious crime, or because it might reduce the risk to others. Retribution explained another third in 1996 but only 16 per cent in 1984, who reported the offences in order to see the offender punished. The 1996 report makes it clear that serious offences are more likely to be reported to the police: 67 per cent of serious offences were reported to the police, against 41 per cent of offences generally.

4.1.3 Police recording of crimes

The police have a statutory obligation to record crimes. There are a number of rules for the collecting of criminal statistics by the police, but the basic criteria for recording an incident as a crime are:

(a)   there must be *prima facie* evidence, in the eyes of the police, that a notifiable offence has been committed (notifiable offences are basically the more serious offences such as violence against the person and serious property offences, and include all those which are indictable, see Chapter Two);

(b)   the case must be sufficiently serious to merit police attention – i.e., any identified offender should in the normal course be prosecuted, cautioned or dealt with in some other formal way.

Clearly, these criteria allow different interpretation by different forces, different divisions within the same force and even different police officers. The police could not operate if they had to record and deal with every minor infraction of which they became aware: operational requirements demand selectivity. Each force has some discretion about how to operate in their area, and therefore to deploy their resources. Similarly, each police officer has to use discretion in performing his or her duties, resulting in further imprecision. None of this is surprising, nor does it indicate that police officers are not performing their jobs; it is necessary for the smooth running of the force.

From the above it should become apparent that there are two ways in which the police recording of crimes may affect the figures. Firstly, the rules for classifying and counting these incidents might change, and secondly, these rules and the incidents have to be interpreted by police officers when faced with a recording decision. Therefore, variations in the recorded statistics over time or place may reflect the way in which they are compiled more than the phenomenon they are intended to record.

The most important source of discrepancy comes in the rules for the recording of crimes by the police. The rules are set by internal force regulations, which can lead to differences between forces, and by Home Office directives concerning how criminal statistics are recorded. A famous example of the effects these can have over time comes from London. In 1932 the Commissioner of Police for the Metropolis ruled that the 'suspected stolen book' should be closed, and that they should only operate a 'lost property book' and a Crime Book. All property which went missing under suspicious circumstances was thereafter entered in the Crime Book, with the result that recorded thefts rose from 26,000 in 1931 to 83,000 in 1932 (over 300 per cent increase). Nottinghamshire provides an example of how internal force regulations can give rise to differences between the forces. The Nottinghamshire Constabulary consistently reported a very high offence rate per 100,000 population, more consistent with cities such as London and Liverpool. However, in 1985 Farrington and Dowds proved that this high official rate resulted from differential public reporting of crimes and/or differential police recording of crimes. The methods of recording offences had made it appear as if Nottinghamshire had a considerably higher crime rate than other Midland counties when in fact that was not the case.

The recording rules which most affect the level of crime reporting are those known as the 'counting rules'. These rules are set centrally and apply to all forces. There are a number of different heads to the rules. For example, in the case of property offences, if a number of different offences are committed at the same time, then one of each group of more or less homogeneous offences is recorded (usually, but not always, the most serious one); if they are crimes of violence or sexual assaults then one offence per victim is generally counted. Furthermore, in a situation involving several distinct offences, generally only the most serious offence is recorded. Therefore, although many offences may have been committed, only a few will be recorded. Sometimes, if an offence, such as fraud or blackmail, is repeated over a period of time, it may be recorded as a single continuous offence rather than as many offences.

Another statistical problem with police recording is that after an offence is classified in one way, this classification will generally not be altered, even if it later transpires that the offender is only convicted of a lesser offence. For example, the offender may agree to plead guilty to a lesser offence, and so the more serious charges are dropped, but the more serious offences will still appear in the recorded statistics. The same thing happens when the jury acquit of the more serious charge but convict of a lesser offence. The only exception to this is the murder statistics, where if the offender is only convicted of manslaughter the figures can be altered at a later date. Similarly, incidents which may once have appeared as accidental deaths may later, on forensic or other evidence, be defined as murders and then again the statistics may be altered. These considerations necessarily affect the accuracy of the figures for any particular year.

Individual police officers can also affect the crime statistics by the way they make their decisions to record an incident as an offence or not. If an activity is reported to the police as a crime they may decide not to record it as such; a reported theft may be treated as lost property if the circumstances suggest that theft is unlikely. Or the police may decide that it is not a case which warrants reporting. For example, if it is not sufficiently serious, the police may still investigate but it will only be officially recorded if it comes to court. Again, the police may decide that the offence was committed too long ago to warrant investigation and therefore not record it (for further details see Coleman and Bottomley (1986)).

4.1.4 Other official effects on crime statistics

The final way in which the official *Criminal Statistics* may be inaccurate arises because many types of crime are controlled by bodies other than the police. The records of these bodies are not usually recorded in the *Criminal Statistics* unless they are brought to court, in which case they appear in the court records. Examples of such criminal activity are tax evasion, which is controlled and recorded by the Inland Revenue; VAT evasion and smuggling or related offences, controlled and recorded by the Customs and Excise; and breaches of factories legislation controlled and recorded by the Factories Inspectorate. The number of offences in this category may be very high, although the number of prosecutions and of convictions is often very low (see Carson (1970)).

4.2 COMPARATIVE PROBLEMS WITH OFFICIAL STATISTICS

In the following sections other methods of assessing the extent of criminal behaviour will be considered, the most useful of which are crime surveys. In 1983 the first *British Crime Survey* (here referred to as the 1982 report) was published covering information for England and Wales, and in 1984 the *British Crime Survey: Scotland* was published (Chambers and Tombs (1984)). These two publications can usefully serve to make two preliminary points: that the information on crime surveys is also dependent on the methods used and the accuracy of the recording, and that comparisons between surveys in different countries need extreme caution. The English and Scottish surveys highlight this point because they covered the same time period in the two areas and used the same approach to tackling the problem (see Table 4.1). Mayhew and Smith (1985) studied these two reports and concluded that the differences in the official statistics between England and Wales and Scotland was mostly one of reporting rather than a real difference in crime rates.

Table 4.1: Rates per 10,000 population of recorded crimes in Scotland and notifiable offences in England and Wales, 1981

	England and Wales	Scotland
Violence against the person	20	15
Sexual offences	4	4
Burglary[1]	147	185
Robbery	4	8
Theft and handling stolen goods	325	389
Fraud and forgery	22	42
Criminal damage[2]	78	120

Notes
[1] Residential and non-residential burglary.
[2] Including damage to the value of £20 or less.

Table drawn from Mayhew and Smith (1985).

In fact, comparisons between England and Wales and Scotland should be relatively precise, because they have broadly similar criminal laws. There are greater difficulties in using statistics from other countries whose criminal laws may differ. These difficulties must be borne in mind when such comparisons are made.

Despite these problems, comparisons can be interesting and constructive, especially when they are gleaned from research such as the highly respected International Crime Victimisation Survey (ICVS), which is alive to the problems of comparison and tries to reduce or eliminate their effects. The ICVS is a victim survey carried out in eleven Western industrialised countries (Austria; Canada; England and Wales; France; Finland; The Netherlands; Northern Ireland; Scotland; Sweden; Switzerland; and the United States of America). In the 1996 survey (published in 1997) The Netherlands (31 per cent of respondents had been victimised once or more and there were 63 crimes per 100 correspondents) and England and Wales (31 per cent of respondents had been victimised once or more and there were 61 crimes per 100 correspondents) came out with the worst crime rates (over a third of those questioned had been victimised); and when the seriousness of offences was taken into account England and Wales came out worst. Interestingly, contact crimes (including robbery, assaults and sex attacks on women) were worst in England and Wales (3.6 per cent suffering this type of attack) with the USA not far behind (3.5 per cent), though the use of knives and guns in these offences was less common in England and Wales. England and Wales has by far the highest rate of burglary (over 6.1 per cent). Unsurprisingly, the public in England and Wales have the greatest levels of fear of crime (measured by issues such as their propensity to protect their property, feelings of security when out at night and their feeling that burglary is very likely in the next year). More surprising is that despite the high crime rate in England and Wales the public have a strong measure of confidence in the police. Interestingly, Scotland is a lot less prone to crime, being lower on overall rates (26 per cent of respondents had been victimised once or more and there were 46 crimes for every 100 correspondents) and on contact crime (2.7 per cent), though the use of knives in such attacks is more common, as is burglary (3.6 per cent). However, the public in Scotland are still worried about going out alone at night and tend to take measures to secure their homes, but fewer of them consider burglary is very likely in the next year. Satisfaction with the police is 69 per cent, about the same as in England and Wales (68 per cent). (All figures drawn from Mayhew and van Dijk (1997)). Although this is only a brief analysis it puts the crime levels in England and Wales in context: crime is a serious social problem in need of policies which are able to address the issue. This level on international tables is only a recent phenomenon: crime in England and Wales approximately doubled between 1979 and 1991; it fell slightly in the following few years, but the overall trend has been upwards and it is this which must be addressed.

4.3 THE DARK FIGURE OF CRIME

From the above it should be evident that the criminal statistics do not represent all criminality which occurs in England and Wales. The criminal activity which falls outside this area is often referred to as the 'Dark Figure of Crime'. Many criminologists have tried to assess the size of the dark figure. There are three methods used. First, estimates (or guesses). Many people have tried to estimate the real level of criminality in Britain, either for a particular offence or for crime in general. The estimates differ enormously, but all agree that a great deal of criminal activity (many estimate well over 50 per cent) goes undetected. Nothing further need be said about this approach, but the two other methods – self-report studies and victim surveys – need additional comment.

4.3.1 Self-report studies

In these, subjects are asked whether they have ever committed any particular type of offence. The survey can take the form of a questionnaire, in which respondents are asked to tick which offences they have committed and to record the frequency with which they have committed them; or of an interview, in which they may be asked about these activities in greater detail.

Most of these studies require respondents to provide details of their social characteristics, such as class, race, religion, sex, age and certain other factors which sociologists may have used to explain criminality. This is because this research method is mostly used to test hypotheses about the reason for crime rather than to assess how much crime is actually committed. Nonetheless, self-report studies do also record levels of criminal statistics above the official figures and so may be useful in assessing the dark figure, at least in respect of particular offences. For a fuller consideration of these see Box (1981), pp. 65–89.

However, their use raises a number of problems. First, and most important, is the problem of validity. Are the subjects telling the truth? Theoretically, cross-checking is possible with family and friends, peer group members, and/or with official statistics, the police, teachers, employers and others in authority over the subject. Or lie detectors could be used. Such checks can never be exact or definite, and are often impractical.

Validity is also suspect because subjects may forget crimes they have committed, or have rationalised them so that they do not consider them as crimes. Subjects may also wrongly characterise something as criminal when in fact it is not, or when they would in law have a legitimate defence; or, of course, they may do the opposite. These last problems can in part be tackled by using full interviews conducted by legally trained personnel in order to ensure that the activities reported would fit within the legal parameters of what is a crime.

The third difficulty with these studies is that the sample is often not representative of the population as a whole. For example, nearly all actual self-report studies have been carried out on adolescents. These studies can be used for a discussion of the extra amount of juvenile crime, or for testing the correctness of explanations of juvenile crime, but not more generally. Moreover, many of the studies have been carried out on young people in school. In thus missing truants and drop-outs, some say that they have excluded the two groups most likely to be criminal.

If one wishes to compare the results of self-report studies, a problem arises because each researcher chooses different crimes to include in their samples. Clearly, no research could include all crimes committed by juveniles, but the lack of uniformity complicates the comparison of results. This is especially true if the object is to test theories about why offences are committed when the types of crimes chosen may make it likely that certain groups will admit to more (or less) crime, which will slant the results.

Although they cast some light on the extent of the dark figure of crime, the main use of self-report studies is as a means of testing theories of criminality. In some cases these two uses are joined. For example, self-report studies have consistently shown that trivial offences are far more common amongst all social classes than official statistics suggest. Therefore they indicate a much higher actual rate of criminality than is indicated in the official statistics and than many of the theories would have us believe. Such qualifications are especially damaging for theories which predict that crime is related to some special physical (for example, increased testosterone, see Chapter Seven), mental (for example, a psycho-analytical problem, see Chapter Eight) or social (for example, class differences or strain, see Chapters Eleven and Twelve) characteristic, rather than related to the likelihood of being caught and punished, as is suggested for example in control theories (see Chapter Thirteen). Furthermore, self-report studies indicate that the serious crime rates for different social classes are not as great as the official statistics would have us believe: the dark figure seems to indicate less of a class split in criminality. For a full discussion of the findings in self-report studies see Box (1981) Chapter Three and Rutter and Giller (1983) Chapter Four. Self-report surveys could be given a new, wider and interesting lease of life because, in the 1992 BCS, those between the ages of 16 and 19 were asked about their own offending, and those between 16 and 59 were asked about misuse of drugs. The questions concerning drug taking were repeated in 1994 and 1996 (not yet analysed). The 1994 report (Ramsey and Percy (1994)) notes that almost half 16–29 year olds have taken prohibited drugs at some time, but only 20 per cent reported doing so in the month preceding the questionnaire. It also discovered that drug use tends to peak at 19 and fall thereafter. This suggests that although young people often become involved with drugs, it is not something that most of them do regularly or become permanently attached to. The most common drug tried by 16–29 year olds was cannabis (one third had tried it); only 14 per cent had ever tried a stimulant (and only 6 per cent had tried Ecstasy); and only 4 per cent reported having tried opiates. These figures tend to question the myth that drug use is either common or normal, and question the claims often made for drugs such as Ecstasy and some of the opiates that they are prevalent in the youth culture. Interestingly, it seemed that drug misuse in the 16–19 age group was often associated with alcohol consumption, with frequenting pubs and with being out in the evenings. This link can be explained partly by the extra opportunity (such young people would be more likely to come into contact with drugs), as well as the reduced control of parents and others in authority. In the 20–29 age group, lifestyle played a reduced role in drug-taking which now became more associated with socio-economic factors, which seemed particularly important in the case of opiate use. Entering the labour market and setting up home with a partner both made drug use less likely in this age group.

These studies have reinforced much of the work which had been carried out on drug use and the information is likely to be used to advise government policy in the area. The 1995 Government White Paper *Tackling Drugs Together: A Strategy for England 1995–1998* cited surveys as a major way of obtaining information, and because the BCS is now repeated every two years it should give a good indication of any changes over time which will allow trends to be assessed, which is a new use for this type of survey.

4.3.2   Victim or crime surveys

4.3.2.1   Introduction
These are the most frequently used and claim to be the most reliable indicators of the true level of criminality in a society. Victim surveys, or crime

surveys as they are often called, measure rates of victimisation by questioning a randomly selected sample of the population about their experiences as victims of selected crimes. The results can be used to make fairly reliable estimates of the extent of those particular crimes in the society studied, and if similar surveys are carried out over intervals of time, then crime trends (for these offences) can be discerned. It is important to note that these surveys do not record the true level of crime in the State; they only help to estimate the level of particular crimes. Victim studies can never give a true picture of crimes such as those which do not have clearly identifiable victims, for example, pollution, violation of safety codes, dangerous products (but see Second Islington Crime Study). Most crime surveys only study crimes against the person and/or property of private individuals. Even within this remit they are not well placed to measure consensual offences such as those involving drugs and consensual sexual offences. Corporate victims, such as companies, businesses, shops, clubs, schools and public services, are less often studied because victimisation is more likely to go unnoticed and no one person is likely to be aware of all offences committed. For example, fare evasion and shop-lifting may occur but go undetected; employees may commit crimes, particularly fraud or theft, and be well placed to hide their criminality; and companies may violate laws which have other companies as their unknowing victims.

Within these limitations crime surveys are a fairly good measure for individual victims and for the crimes they actually cover. They can also be useful in assessing whether any increases or decreases reflected in official crime statistics are genuine or whether they arise because people are reporting the incidents in an increasing or decreasing number of cases. The authors of the three BCSs admitted that for certain crimes which are exceptionally well reported to the police (for example, thefts of vehicles and high-value burglaries) police statistics may be more accurate than the surveys. In the case of crimes such as robbery and rape, which are thought to be relatively rare, both official statistics and BCS are bad indicators of the real levels in society, although the BCS is probably slightly more accurate.

A virtue of crime surveys is that most of them do not only count crimes. Most, including the BCSs (see below), collect additional information about crime, the victim, and the police. Official statistics provide very little information about victims, offences and offenders. Although many police forces have been trying to increase their information, crime surveys still collect, for the crimes which they cover, more of this extra information than do the police and other officials. Such surveys give a better idea of the groups of the population which are most at risk and why this extra risk arises, and can assess whether the high risk groups are also those who fear crime (these questions will be addressed in Chapter Five). Crime surveys can record both reported crimes and unreported crimes, and discern the differences between them and suggest why some offences are not reported (see above, section 4.1.2). They can look at public attitudes to the police and to preventing and dealing with crimes. They can study special areas such as crime committed against workers, or such special groups as ethnic minorities or the young. In these and other ways, therefore, crime surveys are a very valuable tool.

Crime surveys are not new. Sparks (1982) has discovered a reference to this idea in eighteenth-century Denmark. However, the modern use of them grew up in the 1960s in the United States, and the first modern national survey was carried out in 1972, again in the United States. The surveys reflected a growing and widespread scepticism with the official statistics. National Crime Surveys have now been conducted in many countries such as Australia, Canada, Israel, The Netherlands, Republic of Ireland, Scotland, Sweden, and Switzerland. In Britain since 1972 the General Household Survey has intermittently recorded levels of victimisation of residential burglary. The first BCS covered crimes in England and Wales; a separate report covered Scotland, and was carried out in 1982 (the report for England and Wales was published in 1983, Hough and Mayhew; the report for Scotland was published in 1984, Chambers and Tombs). Since then there have been five more BCSs, 1984 (published in 1985, Hough and Mayhew), 1988 (published in 1989, Mayhew, Elliot and Dowds), 1992 (published in 1993, Mayhew, Aye Maung and Mirrlees-Black), 1994 (published in 1994, Mayhew, Mirrlees-Black and Aye Maung) and 1996 (published in 1996, Mirrlees-Black, Mayhew and Percy), but no follow-up reports have been prepared for Scotland. There have also been a number of local surveys such as Kinsey's 1985 Merseyside study, the Nottingham study in 1985 by Farrington and Dowds, the Sheffield study carried out by Bottoms, Mawby and Walker and reported in 1987, the two Islington crime studies (Jones et al. (1986); Crawford et al. (1990)), the 1989 Hammersmith and Fulham study (Painter, Lea, Woodhouse and Young) and the Aberystwyth crime survey (Koffman (1996) which is one of the first to look at the levels of crime in more rural areas. The national surveys give an overall idea of the extent of crime, whereas the more localised surveys can pin-point problems of a particular area and can also be used to discover whether small environmental, particularly housing, differences affect criminality.

As well as national and local surveys there are now, as indicated above, international crime surveys. Particular care must be taken in interpreting these as the figures will hide strong cultural differences between the victims in each State, between the law enforcement agencies, and in definitions of criminality in the various jurisdictions. International studies will not form part of the discussion in the rest of this work.

4.3.2.2   How are surveys conducted?

As an example of how these are conducted, the basic methodology of the BCS will be described. In an ideal world, every member of the population would be questioned about their victimisation, but cost does not permit such a survey to be conducted. Therefore, all surveys are based on a sample of the population. The larger and the more representative the sample the greater the accuracy of the results, but such surveys are more expensive to conduct; there is always a trade-off between expense and accuracy. In any survey a sample of the population under study is selected for questioning. In the 1996 BCS one person over 16 was selected for interview in each of about 16,300 households in England and Wales. Households were chosen from the Postal Address File by a system of random sampling. More inner city areas were chosen than would strictly have been included in such a sample. Already several problems arise. By choosing the sample according to households, the homeless, those living in temporary accommodation, and those living in institutions are completely excluded. This may bias the sample away from the least well off in society, who may also be most likely to be victimised. In addition, the inclusion of high levels of inner city constituencies is likely to give rise to high crime rates being discovered.

All surveys from 1988 onwards included a booster sample of ethnic minorities. West Indians, Africans, Indians, Pakistanis and Bangladeshis were separately studied to discover their victimisation and their attitudes to, and experiences of, the police. In the 1992 survey a sample of children between the ages of 12 and 15 who lived in the selected households were also included, as was a booster sample of teenagers.

Each participant in the survey filled out a main questionnaire which included some questions on attitudes, but the main aim of which was to discover whether the individual (in the case of assaults, robberies, thefts from the person, other personal thefts and sexual offences) or any member of the household (in the case of car thefts, other theft, vandalism of household property and domestic burglary) had been the victim of a crime in the last 12 months. The questionnaire was couched in everyday language such as, 'in the last 12 months has anyone done X to you?', where X is a layman's way of describing a crime, such as, 'has anyone got into your house without your permission, in order to steal?'. All respondents also completed a questionnaire about their personal details, and in more recent studies gave information on their attitudes towards local crime or fear of crime. Those respondents who had been victimised were asked to fill out detailed information on the incidents (up to a limit of six in 1996) indicating where the incident took place; what happened; the offenders; whether the incident was reported to the police; satisfaction with the police and information concerning victim support. All studies then asked further questions of some or all of their respondents which were designed to record extra elements. In the 1982 report these included: fear of crime; contact with and attitudes to the police; self-reported offending; and routine activities and lifestyle. In the 1984 report they included: fear of crime; self-reported offending; attitudes to punishment; crime seriousness; and crime prevention. In the 1988 and 1992 surveys all respondents filled out one of two follow-up forms; one covered attitudes to security, sentencing and prevention, and the other covered the public's contact with and attitudes to the police. In the 1992 survey, personal details were collected from all respondents, including – for those aged 16 to 19 – drug misuse and self-reported offending, and – for those aged 20 to 59 – just drug misuse. The 1996 survey again asked all 16–59 year olds about drug taking, but also quizzed half the sample about their contacts with and attitudes to the police; membership of Neighbourhood Watch; household and vehicle security measures; and attitudes to and knowledge of the criminal justice system.

The results obtained from all the various questionnaires are then 'multiplied up' to give a crime rate which represents the whole population with which the survey is concerned.

The defects of any type of survey carried out in this way include:

(a)   Respondents may forget about crimes, particularly the less serious ones, which gives an undue weight to serious crime and reduces the usefulness of the survey as an indicator of the real level of criminality in our society. As crime rates rise, this problem may – as the 1992 survey acknowledged – increase: victims will remember only the most important incidents, creating the illusion that the gap between reported and unreported offending is narrowing.

(b)   Respondents may be mistaken about when the incident occurred. They may therefore include incidents which occurred before or after the relevant dates, or may exclude items which occurred within them.

(c)   Respondents may remember an incident but not wish to reveal it to the interviewer. For example, if it was a sexual offence which the respondent finds embarrassing or difficult to talk about, or if an offence was committed by a member of the family or a close friend.

(d)   The respondent may not understand the question and therefore fail to report incidents.

(e)   The respondent may not consider that a particular incident falls within the terms of a question.

(f)   The respondent may invent an offence, possibly to appear interesting, to obtain the sympathy of the interviewer or to 'help' the interviewer.

(g)   The respondent may purposely omit offences so as to speed up the process and get rid of the interviewer. This is particularly likely if they know that they will be asked for further particulars of offences.

(h)   The surveys record that better-educated respondents are more able to recall relevant events, and this may give the survey a bias.

(i)   The surveys record that middle-class respondents are more ready to define certain types of incidents as assaults, again giving the appearance of a relatively higher rate for this class than is actually the case.

(j)   The British Crime Surveys always exclude those in institutions whose experience of crime may be very different from the rest of the population. They also exclude victimless crimes, and crimes against organisations and children. Nor do they specifically ask about crimes committed by organisations. Some of the local surveys are better in these respects.

From the above it is obvious that certain inaccuracies are inevitable in these surveys (for a fuller account of the problems see Block and Block (1984) and Skogan (1986)). On balance, the inaccuracies are thought to undercount offences rather than overcount them (see Skogan, (1981)).

4.3.2.3   *What crimes do crime surveys count?*

In 4.1.3 it was stated that police did not record all crimes. What do these surveys usually do? As was stated in 4.3.2.1 (above), crime surveys only research into and record a small number of crimes, those against clearly identifiable victims and their property. Within these categories, however, they may include offences which would be too trivial to be recorded by the police.

Unlike the police (see 4.1.3), the surveys record all crimes which are reported to them. This suggests that the survey counts are more accurate than the police count. Such a conclusion assumes that crime is a concrete and definite term, but the concept of a crime can vary from individual to individual. For this reason it is important that any survey or official figures should stick to a legalistic idea of crime. In Chapter Two above, crime was defined as a wrong to society involving the breach of a legal rule which has criminal consequences attached to it (i.e., prosecution by the State in the criminal courts and the possibility of punishment being imposed). Both police and survey counts depart from this strict rule but in different ways.

As was seen above, the police tend not to record crimes which they consider too trivial to require a prosecution, a police caution or other formal response, or those with insufficient evidence that a crime has occurred: they tend towards recording only those crimes which *would* be punished. They generally do not record: if they do not believe the victim; if it is unclear whether it is a crime or an accident (e.g., stolen property or lost property); if moral consensus is weak (for example, some forces do not prosecute or record possession of small quantities of certain drugs which are only for personal use).

Crime surveys tend to approach the problem in different ways depending upon the reason for the survey. The BCS believe all reports of crime, and count all incidents which fall within the letter of the criminal law: they record all offences which *could* be punished. Therefore the BCS contain crimes which are very trivial, and record as assaults and threats some incidents which, although falling within that idea, are not 'notifiable offences'.

Some incidents such as burglaries or thefts of, or from, cars will be considered as crimes by the general public, police and surveys alike. Other incidents such as some domestic troubles or family fights; scuffles in pubs, clubs or football grounds; fights outside such establishments; fights at school; incidents on sports fields; and minor criminal damage are technically criminal but may not be reported to the police, and even if reported they may not be recorded. However, if reported to the BCS, they will always be recorded. Therefore some of the extra crimes recorded by the BCS may be fairly minor, but many are very serious indeed.

4.3.2.4 Size of the 'Dark Figure' as indicated by the BCS

The BCS indicate a much higher level of crime than is recorded by the police. In those offence categories covered on the 1996 BCS and which can be directly compared with police figures, the BCS estimated 12 million offences whereas the police recorded only 2.8 million. (In total the BCS estimated 19.1 million offences – and this still did not cover all categories of criminal offence.) The implication is that, if the BCS are relied upon, the police figures record less than one quarter of all offences. If the police statistics and BCS information are combined it is possible for 1991 to obtain an estimate of the 'dark figure' for certain specific offences. Figure 4.1 shows the number of recorded incidents for certain crimes (gained from the criminal statistics for 1991, adjusted to be more compatible with the survey data); the number of reported but unrecorded crimes (estimated from information given to the crime survey); and the number of unreported crimes (estimated from BCS results grossed up to the population of England and Wales, and rounded). It also indicates the percentage of these crimes which were officially recorded in the criminal statistics. In all cases except the theft of motor vehicles, less than 50 per cent of these crimes were recorded by the police, and in most instances it was under 30 per cent. The BCS figures suggest that in 1991, 50 per cent of offences were reported to the police, which was a higher percentage than in 1987 when it was 41 per cent, or in 1983 when it was 36 per cent, indicating a general rise in reporting.

The reasons for the increase in reporting are difficult to discern. The 1992 survey suggested that this may be due to the fact that more people take out insurance (those who are insured are more likely to report victimisation); that older people are more likely to report and Britain has a growing elderly population; and that as more telephones are fitted into homes it becomes easier to report victimisation. The extra offences reported in 1992 also tended to be less serious suggesting that certain offences victims previously considered too trivial are now reported. It is uncertain whether this indicates increased sensitivity to crime or less tolerance of antisocial activities. The apparent increase in the proportion of offences reported may also simply reflect a facet of the survey rather than represent a real change: frequent victims may forget the less serious incidents and victims may not bother mentioning all incidents. These tendencies would reduce the total number of crimes noted by the BCS, increase the level of seriousness of offences noted, and (as more serious crimes are those most likely to be reported) make it appear that a greater portion are now reported. The interpretation of the figures is therefore unclear and awaits further investigation.

Both Figure 4.1 and Table 4.2 indicate that a large number of crimes which are reported to the police are never recorded by them. For example, it seems that the police recorded only about two-thirds of the property offences which were reported to them. The reasons for this shortfall have been discussed above. In addition, some of the difference arises because the BCS use slightly different categorisations from those used by the police, and there may also be some sampling error. However, all BCS reports have shown a similar shortfall in the police figures which reinforces the view that these under-record crime.

If it seems worrying that the recorded figures are a significant underestimate of actual criminality, some perspective is gained from the 1982 BCS estimate that the average person over 16 could expect:

a robbery once every five centuries (not attempts)
an assault resulting in injury (even if slight) once every century
the family car to be stolen or taken by joyriders once every 60 years
a burglary in the home once every 40 years.

In this context it is important to note that aggregates produced by the BCSs, which portray victimisation as a fairly rare occurrence, only portray national trends and gloss over the different expectations in, for example, inner-city

Figure 4.1: Unreported, Reported but not recorded, and Recorded incidents for 1991: from the British Crime Survey (1992, p. 14).

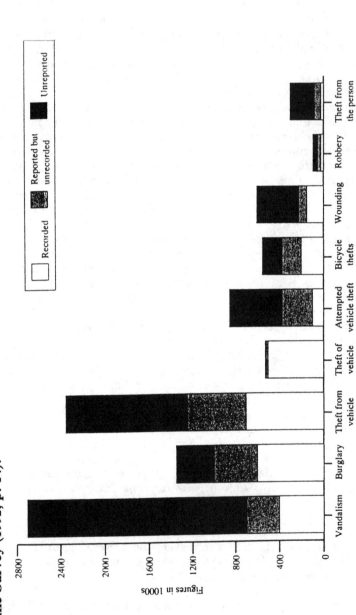

Note: The figures for the total number of crimes are best estimates from BCS results grossed up to the population of England and Wales, and rounded. Recorded crime in each category is derived from *Criminal Statistics, 1991* of notifiable offences recorded by the police, adjusted to maximise comparability with survey data. Comparable comparisons for later years were not available.

Table 4.2: Figures obtained from the 1992 British Crime Survey concerning rates of offending and reporting and recording of offences

	Vandalism	Burglary	Theft from vehicle	Theft of vehicle	Attempted vehicle theft	Bicycle theft	Wounding	Robbery	Theft from the person
Total number of crimes	2,731,900	1,365,000	2,300,600	517,400	889,800	564,000	626,000	183,000	439,000
Percentage reported to the police	27	73	53	99	41	69	48	47	35
Percentage recorded in criminal statistics	15	46	32	93	14	40	25	22	9
Percentage of all crimes found by the BCS	38	9	44	9	16	10	4	1	3

areas and rural areas. Those living in the inner city have a higher expectancy of being victimised. In the Hammersmith and Fulham study, 40 per cent of women who lived in the area were frightened to go out after dark due to fear of crime, and one household in two had experienced serious crime within the previous twelve months. Fear of crime was high; dissatisfaction with the police was similarly high; and after unemployment, crime was the most important public issue facing the residents.

It is clear that each of the BCSs usefully sheds some light on the dark figure of crime – how large it is, what sort of crimes are included. Beyond this these surveys add to our understanding of crime because they are carried out regularly, allowing trends in crime and victimisation to be assessed. One of the most prominent claims made in recent years is that crime has risen by record amounts, making it a major political issue, with politicians vying for position in solving the 'crime problem'. All records of crime, including both official statistics and the BCS, show some increase. However, careful analysis of the trends indicated by the BCSs suggests that the increase may be less dramatic than has been claimed. One reason for this view is to be found in the trends in the proportion of crime which is reported. The 1982 report shows that only 31 per cent of all incidents were reported; by 1996 this had risen to 41 per cent (and in 1992 had been 43 per cent); and for recorded offences the rate of reporting has risen from 36 per cent to close to 50 per cent. A similar trend can be seen in the fact that the BCS also shows a 130 per cent increase in the number of crimes which were reported to them where the victim said that the offence had been reported to the police, which would seem to be partially confirmed by the fact that the number of crimes recorded by the police rose by 91 per cent between 1989 and 1995, a faster rate than the overall increase in crime (83 per cent) revealed by the successive BCS. The strong indication is that a higher percentage of offences are now reported to the police, implying that some of the apparent increase in crime is in fact due to an increase in its reporting. There is a variety of factors which lend further plausibility to such a conclusion: more coverage by insurance necessitating reporting; greater confidence in police action; increased ease in reporting due to larger numbers of private telephones and better access to working public telephones; higher owner-occupation; increased sensitivity to crime; and, importantly, the suggestion of the BCS that victims may now be less tolerant towards anti-social behaviour and criminal activity.

The BCS can also be used to assess the validity of claims about trends in crime based on single years of the official statistics. Usually these take the form of a government claiming to have achieved a reduction in some categories of crime. For example, in March 1989 the Home Secretary stated that the 1988 burglary rate was 'one of the patches of blue' in the otherwise stormy sky of crime and violence. Later that year the Minister responsible for crime prevention credited Neighbourhood Watch with what was claimed to be a 9.5 per cent drop in burglaries. However, the 1988 BCS indicated that between 1981 and 1987 burglary rose by 59 per cent, and that although most of this increase took place in the first part of the period, there was no evidence of a decline. The claims and perceived drops based on the official statistics were probably not real. One suggestion was that the supposed drop was produced as a result of a specific increase in the price of insurance at that time, the argument being that this led to a (temporary) decrease in the numbers taking out property insurance. Since many people report burglary only to facilitate an insurance claim, they may not bother reporting if they are not insured (Jones and Young (1989)). A more contemporary example is that official figures for 1993 to 1995, claiming that crime fell by 8 per cent, can be questioned because for comparable offences the BCS notes a rise of 2 per cent for the same period. The continued rise seems to throw doubt on the claims of a fall in crime being made by the authorities; on the other hand, the rise in the BCS is the smallest recorded.

Lastly the BCS may be used to indicate changes in policy on the part of the authorities. For example, the rate of vandalism registered in successive BCS has remained almost level (with perhaps a slight decrease in household, as against vehicle, vandalism) although the overall crime statistics have doubled: more vandalism crimes must be being recorded. Interestingly, as will be seen in Chapter Sixteen, the increased perception of the seriousness of offences, particularly those of vandalism, is in line with the authorities having accepted some of the policies of right realists which suggests that policing is being seen as a public, rather than just a law enforcement, issue.

Although victim surveys suffer from inaccuracies of their own, they are none the less useful for testing actual levels of offending and are even more important for measuring trends in both rates of victimisation and rates of the reporting of crime.

4.4   CONCLUSION

Official statistics give a distorted picture of criminality in Britain. The more involved the incident becomes with the criminal justice system, the less representative it is of the offence type. The least reliable statistics to use for an idea of the size of the crime problem, or the types of crimes committed, or the types of people who commit crimes, are the prison statistics. These are probably a better indication of the types of incidents which, and persons who, are institutionalised, rather than having any bearing upon crime more generally. Awareness of the various deficiencies which have been discussed is particularly important because criminologists necessarily use official statistics in support of their theories. An additional problem is that the statistics are probably a better measure of why people are caught and prosecuted than of why they commit crimes which is the central interest of criminolgists. The most obvious example of this is the use of official statistics to prove a class bias in criminality – usually that crime is more prevalent amongst the poor than the rich. As already shown, self-report studies suggest that the bias is not as strong as is indicated by official statistics, and if certain white-collar offences (see Chapter Three) were included then possibly there would be even less of a discrepancy. These problems with criminal statistics and with any estimate of the full crime problem should be borne in mind when studying the arguments of theorists about the reason for criminality (see Chapters Six to Eighteen).

REFERENCES

Block, C.B. and Block, R.L. (1984), 'Crime Definition, Crime Measurement and Victim Surveys', *Journal of Social Issues*, vol. 40, p. 137.

Bottoms, A.E., Mawby, R.I. and Walker, Monica A. (1987), 'A Localised Crime Survey in Contrasting Areas of a City', *British Journal of Criminology*, vol. 27, p. 125.

Box, Steven (1981), *Deviance, Reality and Society*, 2nd edn, London: Holt, Rinehart and Winston.

British Crime Survey (1982), see Hough, Mike and Mayhew, Pat (1983), *British Crime Survey*.

British Crime Survey (1984), see Hough, Mike and Mayhew, Pat (1985), *Taking Account of Crime*.

British Crime Survey (1988), see Mayhew, Pat; Elliot, David and Dowds, Lizanne (1989), *British Crime Survey*.

British Crime Survey (1992), see Mayhew et al. (1993).

Carson, W.G. (1970), 'White-Collar Crime and the Enforcement of Factory Legislation', *British Journal of Criminology*, vol. 10, p. 383.

Chambers, G. and Tombs, J. (1984), *The British Crime Survey: Scotland*, A Scottish Office Social Research Study, Edinburgh: HMSO.

Coleman, Clive A. and Bottomley, A. Keith (1986), 'Police Conceptions of Crime and "No Crime"', *Criminal Law Review*, p. 344.

Coleman, C. and Moynihan, J. (1996), *Understanding Crime Data*, Buckingham: Open University.

Crawford, A., Jones, T., Woodhouse, T. and Young, J. (1990), *Second Islington Crime Survey*, London: Middlesex Polytechnic, Centre for Criminology.

Farrington, D.P. and Dowds, E.A. (1985), 'Disentangling Criminal Behaviour and Police Reaction', in D.P. Farrington and J.C. Gunn (eds), *Reactions to Crime*, Chichester: John Wiley.

Hough, M. and Mayhew, P. (1983), *The British Crime Survey: First Report*, Home Office Research Study No. 76, London: HMSO.

Hough, M. and Mayhew, P. (1985), *Taking Account of Crime: Findings From the Second British Crime Survey*, Home Office Research Study No. 85, London: HMSO.

The Islington Crime Survey (1986), see Jones, T., Maclean, B. and Young, J. (1986).

Jones, T., Maclean, B. and Young, J. (1986), *The Islington Crime Survey: Crime Victimisation and Policing in Inner City London*, Aldershot: Gower.

Jones, Trevor and Young, Jock (1989), 'Why Aren't the Police Out Catching Burglars?' *The Guardian*, 28 August.

Kaufmann, L. (1996), *Crime Surveys and Victims of Crime*, Cardiff: University of Wales Press.

Kinsey, R. (1985), *Merseyside Crime and Police Surveys: Final Report*, Edinburgh: Centre for Criminology, University of Edinburgh.

Mayhew, P., Aye Maung, N. and Mirrlees-Black, C. (1993), *The 1992 British Crime Survey*, Home Office Research Study No. 132, London: HMSO.

Mayhew, Pat, Elliot, David and Dowds, Lizanne (1989), *The British Crime Survey: Third Report*, Home Office Research Study No. 111, London: HMSO.

Mayhew, Pat, Mirrlees-Black, Catriona and Aye Maung, Natalie (1994), *Trends in Crime: Findings from the 1994 British Crime Survey*, Research Findings No. 14, Home Office Research and Statistics Department, London: HMSO.

Mayhew, Pat and Smith, L.J.F. (1985), 'Crime in England and Wales and Scotland: a British Crime Survey Comparison', *British Journal of Criminology*, vol. 25, p. 148.

Mayhew, Pat and Van Dijk, Jan J.M. (1997), *Criminal Victimisation in Eleven Industrialised Countries: Key Findings from the 1996 International Crime Victims Survey*, London: Home Office.

Mirrlees-Black, Catriona, Mayhew, Pat and Percy, Andrew (1996), *The 1996 British Crime Survey for England and Wales*, Home Office Statistical Bulletin, Issue 19/96.

Painter, K., Lea, J., Woodhouse, T. and Young, J. (1989), *Hammersmith and Fulham Crime and Policy Survey*, Middlesex: Centre for Criminology, Middlesex Polytechnic.

Ramsey, Malcolm and Percy, Andrew (1994), *Drug Misuse Declared: Results of the 1994 British Crime Survey*, Home Office Research Study No. 151, London: HMSO.

Rutter, M. and Giller, H. (1983), *Juvenile Delinquency: Trends and Perspectives*, Harmondsworth: Penguin.

Skogan, W.G. (1981), *Issues in the Measurement of Victimisation*, Bureau of Justice Statistics, US Department of Justice, Washington, DC: Government Printing Office.

Skogan, W.G. (1986), 'Methodological Issues in the Study of Victimisation' in E.A. Fattah (ed.), *From Crime Policy to Victim Policy*, Bassingstock: Macmillan.

Sparks, R.F. (1982), *Research on Victims of Crime: Accomplishments, Issues and New Directions*, Rockville, Maryland: National Institute of Mental Health, Centre for Studies of Crime and Delinquency, US Department of Health and Human Services.

Van Dijk, J.M., Mayhew, Pat and Killias, Martin (1991), *Experience of Crime across the World: Key Findings of the 1989 International Crime Survey*, 2nd edn, Deventer: Kluwer Law and Taxation Publishers.

Walker, M. (ed.) (1995), *Interpreting Crime Statistics*, Oxford: Clarendon Press.

CHAPTER FIVE

Victims, Victimisations and Victimology

5.1 INTRODUCTION

The study of victims is said to be a new field. Twenty years ago it would have been difficult to have found any criminological agency (official, professional, voluntary or other) or research group working in the field of victims of crime, or which considered crime victims as having any central relevance to the subject apart from being a sad product of the activity under study – criminality. To officials the victim was merely a witness in the court case, to researchers either the victim was totally ignored or was used as a source of information about crime and criminals. Until very recently there was a striking lack of information about victims, and even now the knowledge is still fairly sketchy, limited to certain crimes and often to certain types of victim. This ignorance is astonishing when one considers that the criminal justice system would collapse if victims were to refuse to cooperate. Some victims have found that their treatment by the officials in the criminal justice system – the police, lawyers, court officials, judges and compensation boards – to be too stressful, demeaning, unfair, disregarding of their feelings, rights, needs and interests. Sometimes they see the system as a second victimisation which can be more unpleasant than the original crime. In such cases they may become disenchanted with the system and choose not to report or to cooperate in the future; their experiences may also affect their friends and family, and even the general public, spreading a general reluctance to cooperate. This syndrome is best known in rape cases where few women are willing to cooperate, but it also exists in other areas.

Various reasons might be suggested for this neglect of victims. Phipps (1986) points to a number of these. In the earlier part of this century many criminologists followed a positivist idea of crime, which involved the idea that an individual's criminal behaviour was determined by certain social or biological forces which they could neither control nor understand. In this model the criminal is seen largely as a victim. The notion of offender as victim implies his or her relative lack of responsibility for their criminality, and tends to focus attention on their need for help rather than on the needs of the actual victim. Marxist or left wing criminology often sees the criminal as the victim, but in these writings the victimisation is through the use of power in labelling the offender, and in the bias of the way the law operates. The effect is again to make the literal victim invisible. Marxist theories may also serve to distance the victim from study by arguing that crime is an expression of political opposition to capitalism. In all these approaches the criminal and not the crime or its consequences is studied (for further discussions in each of these areas see Chapters Six to Eighteen). Part of the reason for this is that in Britain most of the funding for criminological research comes from central government, which was interested only in the problem of crime and not with the problems of vulnerability. In consequence, the attention of such research centred on the criminals rather than the victims. It is thus not surprising that much of the early interest in victims in Britain came from non-government funded research, and often from victim support schemes and from feminist writers on rape, sexual assaults and violence against women and children. Much current critical analysis still comes from these sources. More recently, central government has become interested in victims and more money has been made available.

Over the last twenty years interest in victims has increased and today it is central to the subject, to professionals, to officials and to the public. The media have given increased attention to the victim, and politicians have responded by appearing to improve the lot of the victim: there are now improved compensation awards which courts can both offer and make more important than such sentences as the fine; there are new funds available to agencies who offer help and support to victims, especially to Victim Support Schemes (VSS); and in some cases children can give evidence by video-link or video recording (see the Criminal Justice Act 1988, s. 32 as amended by the Criminal Justice Act 1991, s. 54). The police have also reacted positively, especially in areas where they had obtained a reputation for insensitivity. For example, they now occasionally provide rape suites and arrange screening for witnesses in identification parades. Unfortunately such provision is still rare. Some have argued the victim's place in the criminal justice system has been over-strengthened, upsetting the balance between the State and the offender where a crime is seen as an attack against the State or the society as a whole, and not just an attack on the victim.

Although extensive research began only about twenty years ago, there were isolated pockets of research long before that, mostly in the United States, and mostly hypothetical with little empirical or practical basis. The most notable early contributors to what they called 'victimology' were Mendelsohn (1947) and Von Hentig (1948). Their work centred on the extent and way in which crime may be said to be 'precipitated' by the behaviour or lifestyle of the victim. This early work has had a partial revival in recent years when, in certain controversial cases, particularly rape cases, it has been suggested that victimisation is precipitated or even caused by the victim. As one judge put it in 1989: 'As gentlemen of the jury will understand, when a woman says no, she doesn't always mean it.' In these accounts the criminal is portrayed as almost as much a victim as the victim herself. There has also been study of what victims can do to prevent crimes, suggesting again that the victim may in some way cause or precipitate criminal acts.

At the beginning of the 1970s there emerged in the US a number of groups interested in various areas of victimisation or victims. These included groups concerned with: restitution or compensation for victims; the welfare of victims; groups of victims of particular crimes such as survivors of concentration camps, prisoners of war (especially Vietnam); the relatives of the victims of drunk drivers; the often hidden victimisation of women and children; and the victimisation of mental health practitioners. Although these groups were drawn from different backgrounds and have differing interests, they generally agreed on two issues: that punishments should be harsher; and that criminals should be made to pay. If the two could be merged through restitution, compensation or reparation, all the better. It was possibly more than coincidental that these groups were growing at a time when the belief that a criminal could be rehabilitated within, or by, the criminal justice system was dying: their stance was largely one of revenge. But they also argued that victims had certain rights which they could expect to be met, and needs which should somehow be addressed. These have been taken up internationally by the United Nations in its 1985 charter for victims' rights entitled *Declaration on the Basic Principles of Justice for Victims of Crime and Abuse of Power*. This charter firstly specifies ways in which victims should have access to judicial and administrative procedures, be treated fairly and have their views considered; secondly, encourages restitution (or compensation) by offender to victim; thirdly, encourages government funded compensation where the victim is poor; and finally suggests ways in which the victim may need assistance to recover from the ordeal. The Council of Europe has similarly addressed the problems of victims' rights and has produced one Convention, the European Convention on the Compensation of Victims of Violent Crime (1983, this entered into force in Britain on 1 June 1990) and guide-lines, *Recommendation on the Position of the Victim in the Framework of Criminal Law and Procedure*, 1985 (Council of Europe Recommendation No. R(85)11 of the Committee of Ministers to member States). The Convention deals with compensation for the victims and the guide-lines deal with the treatment of victims by State agents such as the police and courts, and the assistance which victims need. In Britain this was taken on board in the spring of 1990 by the production of a booklet entitled *Victims' Rights*, but this is vague and largely unknown, so it has had little impact.

In Britain, as in much of the rest of Europe, most of the focus has been on providing practical services to victims rather than on addressing their rights in a criminal justice or legalistic way. Much of the work has been done by VSS, which started in 1974 in Bristol to fill a gap in provision for those involved with crime. It was started by the National Association for the Care and Resettlement of Offenders, on the assumption that victims too had needs which were not being met. These needs soon became very apparent and the VSS grew very quickly. Almost all of its work is done by volunteers, but as the numbers of serious cases needing long-term support grows it is being forced towards professionalism in order to cope. VSS has largely avoided any political arguments on the position of victims in the British system. Other important victim agencies in Britain are the Rape Crisis Centres (RCC) and shelter homes or refuges. These deal with survivors of sexual abuse and violence perpetrated against women. They provide them with three types of support; advice and information; help in resolving such practical difficulties as lack of shelter; and emotional support in helping to deal with the offence. Each of these, although taking a fairly strong political view on the reason for the problem, has so far played a small and secondary role in altering the position of victims in our system. There has been little collaboration between the various organisations. The victim services in Britain have not really formed themselves into a general lobby to argue for an increase in victims' rights. Rather, each works separately and concentrates on dealing with immediate practical and emotional needs as they arise. Despite this, in 1990 the Home Office issued a booklet entitled 'Victim's Charter' which sets out how victims should be treated. Although a step in the right direction, it is only a statement of what should be good practice on the part of the criminal justice organisations; it does not give the victim any legal rights.

Before victims can be properly helped, and particularly before they can be carefully studied, more information is needed about them and their needs. Similarly, before work on the precipitation of crime by victims can be seriously considered more needs to be known about victims, both those who report their victimisation to the police and those who do not. In recent years more information has been obtained both on victims and on the fear of victimisation.

This chapter will act as an introduction to an interesting, still developing and dynamic area of study. Before embarking upon that study it should be noted that the rather narrow conception of victimisation which is being accepted in this chapter, should not obscure the possibility of criminals also being victims. As the United Nations *Declaration on the Basic Principles of Justice for Victims of Crime and Abuse of Power* makes clear, far more victimisation occurs as a result of the actions of governments and of business institutions than ever arises from what are defined as crimes under national laws, and furthermore that much traditional criminal victimisation is caused by social victimisation often resulting from the actions of governments and businesses. Therefore to see, as will become apparent later, the authorities using the plight of victims to sustain or back up particular criminal justice and sentencing policies should lead us to enquire behind their motives and question who will be the real winners if such policies are accepted and become law. In addition, before embarking on a consideration of the plight of victims of crime, it must be remembered that this will include a consideration only of those who suffer from what the State has defined as criminal behaviour and, as the last two chapters should have made clear, this is sometimes a fairly arbitrary group of activities – other, excluded individuals may suffer as much. Lastly, the press, as is clear from the last chapter, have their own idea of 'victim', particularly 'deserving victim', and use their immense influence to convince others of that idea. Interestingly, the press conception of victim often coincides with that of the State, except that it is even narrower because there are some victims of crime which the press do not consider worthy of consideration. All of which reinforces the initial caveat that the definition used here is necessarily restricted.

5.2 THE EXTENT OF THE PROBLEM

One of the first ways in which the extent of the problem became known was as a side product of the crime surveys described in the last chapter. In these surveys people are asked whether they have fallen victim to certain crimes over a fixed period. These crime surveys, often referred to as victim surveys, started in the US in the 1960s and soon began to reveal fascinating information about the extent of financial loss and physical injury due to crime. Winslow as early as 1968 summed up that:

> Every American is, in a sense, a victim of crime. Violence and theft have not only injured, often irreparably, hundreds of thousands of citizens, but have directly affected everyone. (p. 1)

As already indicated, they also showed that crime and victimisation were more widespread than had hitherto been believed, while demonstrating that not everyone was equally in danger of victimisation:

> . . . risks of victimisation from forcible rape, robbery and burglary, are clearly concentrated in the lowest income group and decrease steadily at higher income levels. (p. 9)

As their value as indicators of information about victims became more obvious, so more questions were included to discern the position of victims, their satisfaction or otherwise with the criminal justice system, and the feelings and fears of the general public about crime. Different surveys, by including different questions, consider discrete areas of these puzzles. This chapter will be mainly concerned with the British Crime Surveys (BCS) of 1982, 1984, 1988, 1992, 1994 and 1996 (Hough and Mayhew (1983 and 1985); Mayhew, Elliot and Dowds (1989); Mayhew, Aye Maung and Mirrlees-Black (1993 and 1994); Mirrlees-Black, Mayhew and Percy (1996)), each of which contained important questions about victims and victimisation. Other surveys will also be considered where these provide more detailed information on a particular area (see Chapter Four): a more general assessment of victim surveys is provided by Zedner (1994), pp. 1207–17.

Before further consideration is given to such surveys, one of their main limiting factors must be recalled. Victim surveys study only personal vic- timisation and largely street crimes. Therefore, 'victimless' crimes·are ex- cluded from study, as are many crimes committed at work where the employer or company is the victim or where another company, the general public, a government body or other body is victimised by a company. One survey which redresses this balance is the second Islington crime survey (Pearce (1990)) which included questions concerning victimisation of individuals by corporations and businesses and found high levels of such victimisation. Victimisation of individuals as consumers, tenants and workers was perceived to be more extensive than their victimisation in street crimes, although this heightened awareness perhaps reflected the impact of such disasters as the King's Cross fire and Bhopal which immediately preceded the survey. The design and approach of most of the surveys tend to exclude victimisation which takes place in private, or between friends or relations, especially domestic violence, and to miss sensitive crime areas such as rape and sexual assault even where these are between strangers (Mirrlees-Black (1995). Finally, in almost all such surveys it is adults who are questioned: the extent and type of criminality against children is not understood or documented, and the effects of crime on children are also largely ignored. This is now changing. Recently Morgan and Zedner (1991) carried out a detailed study of child victims, whilst the 1992 and later BCS included those between the ages of 12 and 16.

With these limitations in mind, some interesting and useful figures are forthcoming. As outlined in Chapter Four, the 1982 BCS assessed the frequency with which an average person or household could expect to be a victim of various offences.

A typical person over 16 can expect:
(a)   a robbery once every five centuries (excluding attempts);
(b)   an assault resulting in injury (even if slight) once every century;
(c)   the family car to be stolen or taken by joyriders once every 60 years;
(d)   a burglary in the home once every 40 years.

To put the figures another way:
(a)   serious woundings, cases where severe injury was intentionally inflicted, occurred in only 5 cases in the 11,000 individuals surveyed;
(b)   other wounding, any other assault involving more than minimal injury, had a rate of 98 per 10,000 adults per year;
(c)   common assault, those resulting in very little or no personal injury, had a rate of 400 per 10,000 adults per year.

Later surveys did not break their figures down in this way, but would be unlikely significantly to have altered the above estimates.

The 1984 BCS estimated that victims who had vehicles stolen lost about £160 million in 1983; the victims of burglary lost £110 million; thefts from vehicles and vandalism gave rise to a loss of around £100 million; and losses from robbery and snatch thefts were in the region of £13 million. Except in the case of thefts of vehicles, the loss to individual victims was usually under £500 and often under £100, and therefore many people were affected. Even if the individual risk is low, the offences clearly present a great social problem and many people suffer as a result of them. In any event these averages for England and Wales mask the fact that certain groups (e.g., those living in the inner cities, the young, ethnic minorities) will suffer far higher victimisation. Apart from the uneven distribution, those who suffer most are those who can least afford the loss and to whom even a small loss may be devastating. According to the second Islington crime survey these groups are more likely to become victims of both commercial and conventional crime (see Pearce (1990); Crawford et al. (1990)).

What the figures cannot record are the practical and emotional consequences which often accompany victimisation. Among the practical difficulties might be having to cope without a car, or without some other object, time spent in giving evidence or completing insurance claims. For those suffering a physical crime, practical problems might include loss of earnings, pain, inability to perform certain tasks either in the short term or at all. Emotional problems might include anger, frustration, annoyance, depression, fear, loss of confidence, stress, difficulties in sleeping or other health problems. These emotional consequences were more common and strongest among those who suffered a personal attack or a burglary.

The figures cannot record the severity of the crime to the victim. A burglary or robbery may involve a few pennies or thousands of pounds. Crimes range from being a minor inconvenience to great personal suffering, even totally ruining a person's life. But the figures do show that victimisation is widespread.

5.3   WHO IS AT RISK AND WHY?

The general risks of victimisation disguise the greater real risks for some groups. Individuals within certain groups may fall victim to many offences in a year whereas others in different subgroups may never, or only very rarely, experience a crime. Furthermore, Gottfredson (1984) points out that a person's lifestyle may affect the likelihood of victimisation (p. 31). He found that going out at night, heavy drinking, working out of the home and using public transport all adversely affected victimisation. Successive BCS found that those most at risk of robbery were young males who live in inner cities or other densely populated areas and who go out a lot in the evening. Therefore, the figures given earlier overestimate the likelihood of criminality occurring to many in society, but underestimate the probability for those who are prone to victimisation.

For example the 1982 BCS found that, unlike most other offences, the chances of being assaulted were no greater if one lived in the inner city than if one lived in the country. The 1992 BCS partially reversed this, finding that, for violence as a whole, living in the inner city had a higher risk attached to it; but it also confirmed that, more generally, being young, single etc. carried a higher risk. Besides replicating this, the 1996 BCS added the further observations that living in rented, especially privately rented, accommodation further increased the likelihood of falling victim to violence, while being a repeat victim is more likely for crimes of violence than for most property offences.

Analysing the information into stranger violence and acquaintance violence produces interesting differences especially on a sex basis. In every group the most important connector is still youth, the 16–29 age group carried with it the highest risk. But in acquaintance violence other high–risk factors, for both men and women, were: being unmarried; having children under 12; and living in an area where the rate of incivilities was high. Against this the rates for stranger violence differed for men and women. For men, age and lifestyle variables (drinking, going out frequently etc.) were important; for women only area of residence and marital status were important, but when cases of mugging were removed from the victimisation of women, lifestyle and age again became strong risk factors (most muggings involving women are of older married women).

It is admitted that the surveys do not adequately assess crimes of violence against women, particularly rape or crimes committed against them in their own homes by friends or relatives. Some women may not see offences committed in the home as criminal or may not be able to reveal them, perhaps because their assailant is in the same room when the interview is being conducted, or because they are embarrassed. From other evidence it is known that women suffer a large amount of violence, much of which is committed in their own homes by people known to them. Such violence is often perceived as less 'criminal' than offences committed on the street and by strangers (see Stanko (1988)). Police and society often treat the latter more seriously than the former even if the physical effects are the same. The survey evidence, suggesting that violence against women appears to be very low, is thus obviously misleading.

In the case of rape, about 5,700 cases were reported in 1996. A higher percentage is now being reported than previously, but it still represents only about 15 per cent of all offences. In crimes of violence repeat victimisation is common: for contact crime 21 per cent of victims were victimised three or more times; whereas for burglary only 7 per cent and for car theft only 8 per cent were so victimised. The scale of the problem can be ascertained from the following:

For all contact crimes, a third of victims were involved in incidents more than once, often cutting across different types of violence. The fifth of victims subject to three or more incidents generated half of the total number of incidents measured by the survey. (Mirrlees-Black, Mayhew and Percy (1996), *The 1996 British Crime Survey, England and Wales*, p. 30)

Burglaries tended to be a phenomenon of lack of security devices and of the inner city, where there are twice as many burglaries as in other built-up areas and five times as many as elsewhere. Flats and end terraces were more likely to be targets, council houses were at a higher risk than owner-occupied dwellings and, unsurprisingly, homes left empty for several hours a day were more at risk than those constantly occupied. In the 1992 BCS the highest risk areas were:

(a) high status non-family areas, with considerable numbers of big old houses separated into flats, or furnished flats mostly let to single people;
(b) multi-racial areas, or metropolitan areas with a mix of poor, private renting housing with owner occupation;

(c)   poorest council estates, often those with high unemployment, overcrowding and/or with the worst poverty, located either in inner cities or in the
outer rings of conurbations.

Vehicles were more at risk if they were parked on the street at night; if their
owners lived in metropolitan areas, particularly inner cities; if their owners
lived in council houses; and if they had a high mileage.

The 1988 BCS studied two new groups – those at work and ethnic
minorities.

5.3.1   Those at work

It suggested that those in paid employment are about three times more likely
to be victimised than non-workers (housewives, the sick and the retired) but
are less likely to be victimised than the unemployed and those in full time
education (who are five times more likely to be victimised than the non-
workers). Part-time workers' risks were slightly lower than full-timers, and
female workers were only slightly less frequently victimised. The differential
rates were partly a result of the age differences – the non-workers contained
many older people, the workers represented a cross section of the adult
population below 65, but the unemployed and those in further education
were heavily weighted towards the younger end of the population.

The victimisation of workers was most likely to take place at work where
71 per cent of their cases of stolen property took place, and where 56 per cent
of all this type of offence occurred. The work place presumably provided a
favourable environment for crime, possibly because it was less secure and had
more public or semi-public space. Workers also blamed their jobs for crime
in nearly a quarter of violent offences they experienced, for more than a third
of the threats and for more than a quarter of the personal thefts. Unlike theft,
in the case of violent offences and threats it was the public rather than fellow
employees who were the perpetrators. Some occupations had a higher risk of
victimisation than others. For example, those in health, education, and
welfare (teachers, welfare workers, health care workers) had higher than
normal incidence of victimisation, as did entertainment managers and security men. Different types of victimisation were prevalent in different professions.

Care needs to be exercised in interpreting these findings. Some of the job
categories are wider than they seem: housekeeper, for example, includes
travel stewards, ward orderlies, hospital and hotel porters; in other cases jobs
which are high risk, such as ambulance men, may be left out completely as
they do not fit the categories. There may also be reporting bias. The
categories which report most crime at work seem to be the white-collar
workers who are perhaps more prone than other workers to categorise an
incident as criminal, especially where violence may be concerned. Other
research has shown some workers to be particularly open to victimisation. For
example, post office workers (Ekblom (1988)), building society staff (Austin
(1988)) and health service workers (Health Services Advisory Committee

(1987); and Smith (1987)). More recently, teachers and those administering social security rules have been high profile victims. If workers are more victimised than other sectors, this may also help to explain the lower victimisation of women, since a somewhat lower proportion of women work and many of them have only part-time jobs.

5.3.2 Ethnic minorities

When the 1988 BCS studied ethnic minorities they discovered that both Afro-Caribbeans and Asians suffered more victimisation than did Whites. This finding was true over many of the crime areas studied (one exception was that Afro-Caribbeans seemed to suffer lower rates of household vandalism than did Whites, whilst thefts of personal property when there was no offender-victim contact were about even for all three groups). Part of the discrepancy is explicable by locational and demographic differences between Whites, Afro-Caribbeans and Asians. Both Afro-Caribbeans (70 per cent) and Asians (40 per cent) are more likely than Whites (17 per cent) to live in the highest crime risk inner city areas, and to be more transient and less residentially stable. They tend to have lower household incomes. They have a larger proportion of young people and higher rates of unemployment. Asians tended to fall in between Whites and Afro-Caribbeans on all these lifestyle differences, and they also tended to have more stable family backgrounds than either Whites or Afro-Caribbeans. Asians were more socially tied to the family, rarely going out at night. However, even having taken this into consideration, the risk to these ethnic minority groups still tends to be higher than for Whites. Later crime surveys have found similar associations (Aye Maung and Mirrlees-Black (1994)).

Interestingly, Afro-Caribbeans were more likely than Asians and significantly more likely than Whites to be victimised by other Afro-Caribbeans. This appears to back up the assertion often made that crime is more often intra-racial than it is inter-racial, and that black criminality is a problem mostly because it victimises other Blacks rather than because of the small victimisation of Whites which may occur (see Stevens and Willis (1979) and Roshier (1989)). As a general statement it is, however, misleading to present crime as largely intra-racial. There is no doubt that both ethnic minority groups, but particularly the Asians, see much of the victimisation as being racially motivated. An analysis of the BCS of 1988 and 1992 suggested that the offences most often seen as racially motivated were assaults, threats and incidents of vandalism (Aye Maung and Mirrlees-Black (1994)). Asians were more often victimised by groups of strangers than were the others, and they tended to suffer more serious victimisation. The racial nature of much of the criminality against racial minorities is borne out in many other studies and has been well documented both here and in the States. In Britain, much of this victimisation is perpetrated by Whites against Asians, and much of it may fall short of what the police consider worthy of recording or even what the BCS records. Incidents of racial harassment can constitute very serious criminal offences like arson or serious physical attacks, such as the infamous case of *R v Hunt* [1958] *Criminal Law Review* 709 in which nine youths armed with iron bars and other weapons sought out five minority-race citizens and cruelly and viciously attacked them. Or they can simply be minor incidents of racial abuse or spitting.

There is much evidence that many members of the ethnic minorities suffer name calling, rubbish or excreta dumped on their premises, urine through the letter box, racist graffiti on their premises, damage to property, being spat at, having missiles such as milk bottles or rotten fruit thrown at them, and being punched or kicked. For some, everyday life is frightening, never knowing when the next attack may descend. Families, particularly the women and children, end up almost as prisoners in their own homes, but even here they do not feel safe. Normal activities such as shopping or visiting friends can be hazardous. If the more minor incidents are reported to the police the victim may well be advised that the police will not act, and if protection is wanted then a private prosecution is the only way of obtaining it. There are now welcome signs that such racial victimisation is being taken more seriously by the police.

5.3.3   Other groups at risk

Some crimes and victims are rarely assessed by the BCS and yet have been calculated to be large problems for certain sectors of the population. Sexual and domestic violence against both women and children falls into this category. The group least studied, at least until very recently, is that of child victims. Before 1992 child victims had never been the subject of a BCS, which only questioned those over 16. The plight of children was brought to the fore mainly through the work of feminist writers who often included them in studies of women as victims or survivors. More recently children have been the centre of a few studies. The areas which have received most emphasis have been child physical abuse and child sexual abuse. As yet there has not been much study of the effects of more ordinary crime on children and the effects of indirect victimisation.

Child physical and sexual abuse became the subject of much media coverage in the late 1980s and early 1990s. It was claimed that these crimes were increasing in our society but it may be that, although they have always occurred, only now are they being recognised. The levels of these offences are difficult to assess. Like rape and other sexual and physical abuse of women, they rarely come to light and are rarely studied. These offences also raise problems of definition. They are often not legally defined separately from offences committed on adults or, at least, are not all legally defined together. Therefore something other than legal definitions are needed to study this area. Gil (1978) provides one of the best definitions of physical abuse of children:

Physical abuse of children is intentional, non-accidental use of physical force, or intentional, non-accidental acts of omission on the part of a parent or other caretaker in the interaction with a child in his care, aimed at hurting, injuring, or destroying that child (p. 48).

This deals with cases of active and of passive abuse. It does not deal with psychological abuses which may be much more difficult to pin-point and to fit into any form of criminal behaviour. Such psychological abuses are probably best left out of the present discussion whilst still noting that they may occur and have great effects upon the children involved. In an American study of parents, Gil discovered that 15.9 per cent of respondents had come near to abusing their own children and 0.4 per cent admitted actual abuse. Given the clear social stigma involved with such admissions, the actual number of abusers and abuses, the dark figure is likely to be considerably larger than this suggests, but there have been very few studies to assess it. Certainly it can be said that child physical abuse is a prevalent occurrence, and that both sexes suffer it and both perpetrate it. Note that the abusers in this definition could actually fall outside the family, or at least outside the immediate family. It only requires a relationship of care, which may be one in which the abuser is a baby-sitter, child minder, nanny, teacher or a friend of the family into whose care the child has been entrusted. When these relationships are also included, the instances are even more widespread.

Child sexual abuse is also difficult to define. Russell (1984) helpfully splits it into two distinct types of behaviour, namely, extra-familial child sexual abuse and incestuous child abuse. Both include any form of sexual contact or attempted sexual contact, but in extra-familial abuse the victim must be under 14 (or 18 if the offence is rape), whereas incestuous abuse goes up to 18. In San Francisco, Russell conducted one of the clearest and most detailed assessments of the extent of such offences and discovered that 31 per cent (two thirds of whom were under 14) experienced extra-familial sexual abuse, and 16 per cent (three-quarters of whom were under 14) suffered incestuous sexual abuse. Paediatricians support the existence of these sorts of levels, and the Cleveland affair suggested that the levels of child sexual abuse within families might be significant and that the victims were often very young. In that particular case many of the children were under five and one was allegedly only nine months old (see Butler-Sloss (1988)). Furthermore, although there were 121 children involved in the Cleveland case, there were only 40 or 50 families, thus suggesting that one abuser perpetrates sexual acts against more than one victim and that all children, or at least all children of the same sex (usually female), within the family are likely to be victimised.

Child sexual abuse has normally been portrayed either as a violent street offence or as taking place in the child's own home and with members of its family, but recent police work has uncovered large numbers of child abusers or paedophiles. The first official estimate of the scale of the paedophile problem in England and Wales was conducted by the Home Office in 1997. It found that there were 110,000 men who had been convicted of offences against children (*Guardian*, 19 June 1997). Such criminals, all of whom have so far been found to be male, work in rings or networks passing on videos of their experiences and even sharing the victims, often young boys, between them. More recently concerns have been expressed at the use of the Internet for these purposes and at technical obstacles confronted by attempts to prevent or control such usage. Very often the criminal activity begins because the first abuser is a friend of the child's family, but some children are bribed with offers of sweets or other inducements into trusting these men. These are the least studied and least suspected types of criminal sexual behaviour. In the late 1980s special police work was started in this area, and a number of rings have been discovered and their members prosecuted and gaoled. It may even be that some of the Cleveland children, if sexually abused, were the victims of such groups, and not of their fathers or other relatives, the only suspects at the time. Clearly abuse is common and if the claim by 'Public Eye' (BBC2, 19 October 1990) that as many as 40 per cent of abusers have themselves been abused is true, then this criminal victimisation of children might be effectively reduced by the careful counselling of both abused and the abusers. The government expects that the paedophile register, which came into operation in August 1997, will help to address the problem, but by mid-September only about 800 of the expected 2,200 such offenders had so far registered (*Guardian*, 15 September 1997).

In both child physical and sexual abuse, figures now show that a large and grave problem exists which is still little recognised. Little is done for the children who suffer this violence, which very often comes from those closest to them – parents or step-parents. In child sexual abuse, Wilson (1983) estimates that 90 per cent of the victims are female and 95 per cent of the offenders male (but this was mainly sexual abuse within the family: outside this environment, although men continue to be the main perpetrators, more of the victims appear to be male). In child physical abuse there would not be nearly so great a gender division, although men would still tend to be the main perpetrators.

Children may also be very badly affected by other offences committed against them. Unfortunately, the spotlight which has been placed on child victims of sexual and violent crimes has not carried over into the less dramatic victimisation of children: the routine, but not trivial, acts of violence committed against children both by adults and by other children (especially bullying); acts of theft committed against them, and such acts as harassment. In these cases their victimisation, though often ignored, can cause great emotional distress. They need to be addressed.

Lastly, there are the indirect victimisations which may occur. Children may be aware of, or actually witness, crimes, especially those committed by one member of the family against another or by one peer against another. They may witness other crimes committed by strangers against members of their family, or committed by strangers against strangers. Even if they do not witness crimes against members of the family, they may be badly affected by them. They may be affected by household crimes such as burglary which affect the whole family. None of these may in themselves constitute specific crimes against the children, but they can be distressing to the child and could have lasting detrimental effects. The children are often the ones who take longest to recover from the violation. In a study of burglary, robbery, assault and theft, Maguire and Corbett (1987) found that '. . . seventy per cent [of those with children] stated that the children had been badly frightened or upset'.

From this it is clear that victimisation is a more common and everyday experience for some groups than for others; that some suffer more from certain crimes; and some are more adversely affected than others. The estimations given earlier (5.2) of the likelihood of victimisation can be understood only in this context.

5.4 WHO FEARS CRIME?

Fear of crime has been perceived as an increasing phenomenon. As was seen in Chapter Three, many people are influenced by the media portrayal of crime which bears little relation to the actual situation. Some radical and left-wing criminologists such as Harman (1982) questioned the very existence of a crime problem, suggesting it had been manufactured by right-wing papers and politicians to control the working class and Blacks by portraying them as the perpetrators. More recent left-wing writers, such as Kinsey, Lea and Young (1986), have recognised that there is a crime problem but attack the way in which this is used as an excuse to control society and maintain social order (see Chapters Thirteen and Sixteen).

Whatever the reason for the media portrayal, or the use to which the fear it manufactures is put, it undoubtedly makes people fear that they may be victimised. Many alter their lifestyles to reduce this possibility. The reality is that serious crime is less common than is portrayed by the media. In this regard, what criminologists, police officers and others in the criminal justice field regard as irrational fear is then often seen as more of a problem for many than is crime itself.

All the BCS have studied this aspect and discovered that two groups – women and the elderly – were particularly vulnerable to the fear of crime, although the victimisation rates for these groups were actually found to be relatively low (see Table 5.1).

Table 5.1: Fears of personal safety after dark and risks of 'mugging'

	% feeling very unsafe[1]	% victims of mugging on one or more occasions
Men		
16–29	2	3
30–59	2	0.4
60 +	8	0.2
Women		
16–29	12	1.3
30–59	13	0.5
60 +	31	0.5

([1] Question: 'How safe do you feel (or would you feel) walking alone in this area after dark?')
(Table drawn from information in the 1996 British Crime Survey)

In the 1996 survey, just under a third of women (29 per cent) but only 17 per cent of men admitted having altered their routines or behaviour in the last couple of years as to where they went and what they did outside their own home. The number who, simply as a precaution against crime when out after dark, avoided people (54 per cent of women but only 27 per cent of men) or who got someone to go with them (44 per cent of women but only 5 per cent of men) is even more striking. As Hough (1995) discovered from the 1994 BCS: the elderly were less anxious than others about burglary and car crime but more anxious about being out at night (particularly elderly women); those on a lower income were more worried; while high levels of disorder in the area (as indicated by aspects such as noisy neighbours, teenagers hanging around and bad street lighting) and lower levels of social support were related to almost all measures of fear. Interestingly, Hough also discovered two clear links with careful and intelligent assessment of risk – he found that fear arose where people judged their risk to be highest and that those who were vulnerable in terms of size, confidence etc. or in their ability to defend themselves were most fearful. This might help to explain the fear felt by women and the elderly.

The group consistently exhibiting least fear is young men, and yet the group which is most likely to be victimised consists of young, working-class males who inhabit inner cities and who spend a lot of their time in public places, particularly pubs and clubs.

The 1996 survey inquired about people's worries of becoming victims of certain crimes (such as burglary, being mugged and, for women, rape). In no category were even 20 per cent of men 'very worried' about such victimisation, whereas for every crime over 25 per cent of women were 'very worried' and 44 per cent of women between 16 and 30 were 'very worried' about being raped. The early BCS studies claimed that the fear of crime often reflected the interviewee's perception of their likelihood of falling victim but that their perception of risk was unrealistic, and conclude that fear of crime was, to this extent, irrational. The fear itself was thus thought to be a problem over and above that which would be justified by actual crime levels. This was a convenient official interpretation since it suggests that it is an irrational fear which exaggerates the significance of crime. Such a cosy view would have to confront much inconvenient evidence.

The question needs to be asked: is the level of fear to which these and other surveys give witness actually as illogical, irrational and ill-founded as some reports and criminologists suggest? (See Pearson (1983)). It could be that those who fear crime conduct their lifestyles to reduce their likelihood of falling victim to a criminal act. Their fear would thereby contribute to their low victimisation, which would suggest that it is not as irrational as the figures might suggest.

There are other possible grounds for doubting whether the fear is 'illogical or irrational'. The Islington Crime Survey (1986) discovered higher rates of female crime than had usually been recorded. They found that 20 per cent of women knew someone who had been sexually assaulted or molested in the previous 12 months, and that women were 40 per cent more likely to be victims of non-sexual assault than are men. This survey and its follow-up (Crawford et al. (1990)) demonstrated that the women had a firm grasp about their likelihood of becoming victims. These figures on female victimis-ation tie in closely with work carried out by other criminologists such as Dobash and Dobash (1980 and 1992), Stanko (1987, 1988 and 1990) and Russell (1982). If these figures are accurate then possibly women's fear is not so irrational. Both Stanko and the Dobashs further suggest that most sexual and violent attacks experienced by women occur in the home, often on a regular basis, and the perpetrators are generally male friends or relatives. They claim the women concerned often see this as private punishment rather than criminal behaviour, in which case any survey data are likely to be a serious underestimate of the problem. Many of the chapters reproduced in Rock (1994) indicate a more rational basis for fear of crime.

Furthermore, both the Islington and the BCS discovered that when women and the elderly are attacked they often suffer severer injury than do the young or men. This too may contribute to making their fear of crime more rational.

Lastly, many women are subjected to sexual and other harassments. Although these may fall short of actual crimes, they add to their fear and feeling of vulnerability. This is very similar to the experiences of ethnic minorities who also tend to fear crime. In addition, women, the elderly and people who are from one of the ethnic minority groups tend to be relatively powerless physically, financially and socially, and this adds to their vulnerability.

Much of the research noted above ignores the effects of secondary vic-timisation which Morgan and Zedner (1991) found to be particularly strong in the case of children. It also ignores structural aspects of fear, produced by the social environment and/or feelings of marginalisation. The general patri-archal nature of our society tends to be made invisible even though many women's lives are controlled by male violence (see Painter (1992)). Women's victimisation is often trivialised or treated as less important (see the way police treat domestic violence as opposed to other violence), and this is sealed by the patriarchal way in which women are treated within and outside the criminal justice system. Sliding over these aspects can make victimisation appear to be illogical: their recognition makes the fear more rational.

There are other aspects to this equation which have been pointed out most carefully by the left realists (see Chapter Sixteen), who recognise that fear includes emotional responses, as well as social and cultural expectations. These can be rendered illogical by definition, but that does not render them less real. Left realists also argue that the rational calculation of risk is simply not possible for the average person. Fear may indeed have as much to do with the unknown as with actual risk, making myths as important as are the facts, and general feelings of insecurity as important as real dangers. Essentially, what the left realists are arguing is that the rationality or irrationality of fear cannot be objectively assessed: what is important is the reality of the fear and the effect this has on a person's life, limiting enjoyment and their spheres of activity (this is a major aspect of left realist theory, see Chapter Sixteen).

When all these factors are collected together, the fear felt by these groups is possibly less irrational than is sometimes expounded (for a more complete discussion of these arguments see Young (1988); Mawby (1988); Box et al. (1988) Mawby and Walklate (1994) and Hale et al. (1994). For these reasons and after more careful analysis of the evidence, as indicated above, the recent assessments of BCS data have been careful not to claim any irrational assessment of crime (BCS (1996), Hough (1995) and Mirrlees-Black and Aye Maung (1994)). Moreover, these and other texts (such as Crawford et al. (1990)) now recognise the social and structural causes of fear – related to vandalism, boarded-up buildings, noisy neighbours, teenagers hanging around, poor street lighting and a feeling of powerlessness to alter these negative factors. There is now a realisation that fear is a real experience which needs to be addressed, and that both crime and fear of crime reduce the quality of life in a State. Such awareness can produce policy conflicts: thus many of the crime prevention schemes raise the public's awareness of the risks and so tend to increase rather than decrease fear of crime, even where the programme may lead to some decrease in actual crime. The awareness also calls in question some of the more prurient elements of press reporting which tend to feed on the interest/fear of criminality to sell news and to entertain.

Perhaps the irrationality which really needs addressing is: why are young men not more fearful of victimisation when they are seemingly the highest risk group? Are they really fearless, or just frightened of admitting their fear to the researcher, or even of articulating it to themselves? Is any lack of fear part of the image of their male virility and street credibility? Should someone try to raise their fear, or at least their appreciation of their own vulnerability, to help them protect themselves? At present these are neglected issues.

5.5 SUPPORT AND SERVICES FOR VICTIMS

Victims have to compete with all other disadvantaged or unfortunate groups for the aid that they may require. Therefore groups working for the victims must both state their case and point out why their particular demands should be met. The plight of victims received recognition from both the Council of Europe (in its 1983 Convention and its 1985 guide-lines) and the United Nations (in their 1985 Declaration). Both international bodies included similar lists of victims' needs: the need to be treated with respect and dignity; to be allowed access to the mechanisms of justice and to legal processes which will provide them with redress for the harm done; offenders should make restitution for the harm done to victims, their families or dependants, and such restitution should be possible as a sentencing option in criminal cases; information for victims concerning the progress of the case; allowing the views of victims to be considered where their personal interests are affected (as long as the accused is not prejudiced); assisting victims through the legal process; use of informal dispute resolution such as mediation where appropriate; and material, medical, psychological and social assistance for victims through governmental and community-based means (these are taken from the UN document). In 1990 in the United Kingdom the *Victim's Charter* was published which largely set out, in general terms, the existing arrangements for victims. It includes items under most of the heads covered by the international documents, but interestingly it omits any mention of informal dispute resolution. The Charter's main limiting factor is that there is no means of enforcement so that it does not give victims any rights, but it does represent an official recognition of the interests of victims and provides victims organisations with a powerful tool to lobby Parliament. Its strength lies in the provision of welfare-based support rather than rights in the criminal justice system. This perpetuates the way in which the needs of victims were anyway being addressed in Britain, by two very different approaches: first, officially through the criminal justice system; and, secondly, unofficially through a largely voluntary network of support schemes, most notably the VSS. In both approaches the victim is generally provided with opportunities rather than rights.

5.5.1 Victims in the criminal justice process

Until the establishment of a true police force in the middle of the last century, often the victim was the most important element in the bringing to justice of any criminal. The police slowly took over the prosecuting function of the victim. Today, private prosecutions are possible but rare and only arise where the State refuses to prosecute. It is usually the State, originally through the police and now through the Crown Prosecution Service, which carries out most of these functions. The victim's role has been reduced largely to one of reporting offences and giving evidence if so requested. Although these are essential to the system, they do not furnish the victim with any decision-making power. Some would argue that this reduces the feeling that the victimisation has been atoned: the prosecution seems to have little to do with them or what occurred and far more to do with State or even police policy. Until the 1960s this feeling was enhanced by the lack of compensation or restitution for the victim. Although there was some, fairly minimal, legislative provision for compensation it was rarely used, and the victim had no right to compensation and no expectation that it would be paid.

Apart from feeling ignored by the criminal justice system, victims often feel they are being used by the courts. They are expected to report to the police but are not always made to feel comfortable in doing this; for most victims the police station remains a fairly uninviting environment. This reduces the effectiveness of crime control, as it increases the offender's chances of getting away undetected. If victims are asked to identify offenders they are rarely screened and may, through fear of facing the offender, fail to identify him or her. When called to give evidence, they are rarely permitted to relate their experiences in their own words but are forced to answer questions which may actually misrepresent their account of what occurred. Furthermore if they refuse to cooperate they may be prosecuted because they would thereby be obstructing the course of justice. The proceedings are indeed mostly adapted to the needs of the State, which has also been victimised in that its peace and its rules have been broken. The State has an interest in social control of offenders and therefore has a right to require anyone to give evidence. To alleviate some of the stress caused by these difficulties, Crown Court Witness

Services are now available to offer support, but these on their own cannot redress the difficulties which are inherent in an adversarial system. The feeling that the system is not particularly friendly to victims has persisted: in an evaluation of the court system in 1991, the overwhelming finding was that victims and witnesses were dissatisfied (Raine and Smith (1991)), while Wright (1995) reports findings of a similar nature.

There have been some improvements. The first compensation scheme was set up in 1963 when New Zealand introduced a State compensation scheme, supposedly removing the need for the victim to rely upon the offender being wealthy. Britain followed a year later with a State compensatory scheme for victims of violent crime. This scheme was non-statutory and was only formalised in legislation in the Criminal Justice Act 1988. Under it, victims have no rights to compensation and payment is at the discretion of the Criminal Injuries Compensation Board (CICB). Indeed, the system was set up without any consultation of victims, and there was no real evidence that victims of violence wanted to be compensated by the State. It originated more from a wish to forestall possible complaints of lenient punishments at a time when criminal justice was pursuing a rehabilitative ideal, whilst it was also seen as an extension of the welfare principle of State support of those in need which was strong at the time. It was never considered as part of a wider idea for victims' rights.

One of the most important qualities necessary to qualify for compensation is that the victim be adjudged 'innocent', in other words, that the claim is not fraudulent and that in suffering the injury the victim was not at fault. This condition generally excludes cases where the victim may have participated in the violence. Any payment is reduced by an assessment of the amount for which the victim can be said to be responsible or to have contributed to the injury. It is important to note that compensation is not means tested, nor is it set to meet a particular need. It is set by the amount of injury the CICB assesses the victim to have suffered and not by the help which that person may need. The system compensates only those who suffer due to criminal violence, and therefore excludes those who suffer physical injury following other crimes, e.g., after breaches of the factories legislation or as a result of driving offences. The criminal is not permitted to gain from any payment; therefore claims in cases of domestic violence will be countenanced only if the parties are now living apart and look unlikely to co-habit in the future. More recently, the Criminal Injuries Compensation Act 1995 set out a statutory tariff for injuries which ran from £1,000 to £250,000 plus an additional payment against expenses and for loss of earnings or earnings capacity. For victims, a more supportive change might have been to reduce the minimum (perhaps to £100) and then to allow the CICB to compensate all crime victims and not just victims of crimes of violence (Mawby and Walklate (1994)).

The scheme is therefore limited in the help it offers, the people who qualify, and the way in which they qualify. None the less, it is a recognition of the suffering of the victim. One of the largest problems arises not out of the scheme itself, but rather out of public ignorance of its existence. Shapland,

Willmore and Duff (1985) found that most people who miss out on possible claims do so because they do not know that they can apply. There is no automatic mechanism in the criminal justice system to inform them of the possibility of compensation even if they would have a good case. This could be held as a further indication of the low status of victims and their problems in the criminal justice system. In the recent pamphlet entitled *Victim's Charter*, the Home Office has tried to correct this position by suggesting that the police should give every victim a pamphlet entitled *Victims of Crime* which sets out the compensation system. Unfortunately the police are not required to help victims; the pamphlet only sets out good practice.

Many argue that rather than the State helping the victim, the offender should be ordered to do so. In this context reparation as well as compensation has been considered, each being a means of repaying the victim for the wrong suffered. This 'payment' may be in the form of restitution of the objects stolen; monetary payment for harm done (as in compensation orders, see below); work done for the victim (direct reparation); or work for the victims of other offenders (indirect reparation). A very indirect form of reparation exists in the form of Community Service Orders (brought into operation by ss. 14–17 of the Powers of the Criminal Courts Act 1973 as amended) where the offender performs a useful task for the public at large, not for victims in particular. Reparation might be particularly useful for impecunious offenders.

Another possibility is mediation, which may be used as a way of removing or reducing the hostility between victim and offender, and is brought about by them meeting to discuss their differences. It often involves some form of agreed reparation, and when used is usually arrived at with the help of an intermediary such as a social worker. It may then be given the force of law by a court order or may be left less formally. Reparation and mediation are not generally used in this country. The 1982 and 1984 BCS attempted to assess the support that such projects might attract from victims and from the general public. In both cases they seemed to attract more than 50 per cent support, but as is clear from these reports, the question asked did not clearly separate financial repayment or compensation from services to be rendered. Therefore it is not clear whether reparation *per se* would be popular or acceptable. Its true popularity can possibly be assessed only by an evaluation of actual schemes which offer reparation. In the early 1980s the Home Office established four pilot reparation projects. These are described by Marshall (1984) and Marshall and Walpole (1985). Marshall (1984) remarks that many of the schemes offering the offenders' services suffer from low up-take on the part of victims. This could have a number of causes: the victim may not feel ready to meet his/her offender or even other offenders; they may not trust the offender to perform the agreed tasks; and they may be wary of having the offender close to them to perform services, especially if that requires access to their home. Some schemes require the victim to agree to relinquish further legal action. Victims are understandably reluctant to sign away any further legal rights, even if they are unlikely ever to be able to afford to act on them, or their offender is unlikely ever to pay. There are other complicating factors, such as the effects of reparation on any insurance claim, which may make them less attractive.

In view of these potential problems for victims and the fact that the possible benefits are small – performance of a job; satisfaction that the offender has paid a little back – it is unsurprising that these schemes are of little interest to victims. The benefits to the offender may be greater, in that agreeing to reparation may reduce the sentence. The benefits to the State of possibly reducing its prison population while still making the offender pay are greater still. The 1990 White Paper asks whether reparation benefits the offender more than the victim, and dismisses official use of reparation by the courts through court orders, arguing that the choice of the appropriate sentence should not be influenced by a victim's decision to accept reparation. It did recognise that reparation and mediation could continue on an informal basis if both victim and offender were freely willing. The machinery for this exists in the organisation called Forum for Initiatives in Reparation and Mediation (FIRM) which co-ordinates and monitors many of the voluntary schemes.

The early schemes were largely separate from the criminal justice system itself, often arising through the probation service. More recent projects have been more closely associated with the criminal justice process. Thus the Northamptonshire project works alongside it and was reasonably well received by the victims whose cases were referred to it: 71 per cent of the corporate victims and 62 per cent of the individual victims expressed satisfaction (Dignan (1991); see also (1992), (1992a) and (1994)). One of the advantages of a completely separate mediation scheme is that the victim does not feel pressurised into agreeing to take part, although in reality the outcome of mediation is sensibly taken into account in decisions as to whether to prosecute/divert an offender and what sentence to impose. As Wright (1995) suggests, the way forward might be to separate reparation and mediation, the offender being given the opportunity to make reparation to the victim or to the community (depending on the wishes of the victim), which would be taken into account in sentencing; but any mediation and apology would occur after sentencing thus removing any pressure on the victim to take part. More recently Mackay and Moody (1994 and 1996) have found considerable support for the use of community mediation to resolve neighbourhood disputes which are traditionally rather difficult for the official criminal justice authorities and in which the court system is not very effective. With these facts in mind, it arguably is time to take another look at reparation and mediation, especially in the light of Zedner's analysis that these systems serve the interests of all parties and of the wider community at least as well as, and in some ways better than, the traditional criminal justice system.

More recently there has been interest in a rather different initiative, here referred to as diversionary conferencing. It is very similar to reintegrative shaming (used to some extent in reparation and mediation), a theoretical idea proposed by Braithwaite which suggests that constructive use can be made of respect and relationships between the offender and those who care for him or her and for whom he or she cares. Diversionary conferencing uses community ties to help to deal with offenders. It has been introduced in both New Zealand (adapted from a traditional Maori practice) and Australia. It is based on the idea of requiring offenders to confront their criminal activity and the consequences of their crime – offenders are made to realise that their acts have real and often far-reaching consequences for individual victims, to do this in front of individuals for whom the offender feels some respect and to begin the process by which the offender may form attachments which will reinforce law-abiding behaviour. In trials still under way, conferencing is carried out by police officers as an extra part of the caution for offenders whose cases might otherwise have been passed on to the Crown Prosecution Service. A successful conference should cause the offenders and their family or friends to feel shame, prompt an apology and open up the possibility of acceptance back into the community by means of an agreed plan of action which may involve the offenders in certain responsibilities (reparation or community work) and the community in certain responsibilities to them (finding employment, help in dealing with problems such as drink or drug habits). Conferencing is very different from mediation and reparation schemes because it is an integral part of the criminal justice system, including the element of a clear show of displeasure/punishment; it is carried out by police officers as part of their enforcement role and requires the involvement of both victim and offender. The initiative is intended both to make offenders more accountable and to allow victims to feel a part of the official system of criminal justice, reducing their feelings of powerlessness. The initiative, when used in appropriate cases, has been fairly successful in both New Zealand (Morris et al. (1993)) and Australia (Strang (1993) and Forsythe (1994)) and is presently being tested by Dyfed Powys Police Authority, where the rural location and fairly close community ties should suit its strengths.

In contrast to these possibilities, compensation from the offenders has recently become an important element in the criminal justice system. The change began with the Criminal Justice Act 1972. This Act provided that in addition to dealing with the offender in any other way, the court may require the payment of compensation for any 'personal injury, loss or damage' resulting from the offence (the provisions are now set out in the Powers of Criminal Courts Act 1973, amended by the Criminal Justice Acts 1982 and 1988). The orders were only permitted in addition to other sentences, partly to indicate that they were not intended as a substitute for punishment, nor as a way of allowing rich offenders to buy their way out of the normal consequences of their conviction. As Scarman LJ (as he then was) explained, the purpose of the compensation order was to provide the victim with:

. . . a convenient and rapid means of avoiding the expense of resorting to civil litigation when the criminal clearly has means which would enable the compensation to be paid. (*R* v *Inwood* (1975) 60 Cr App R 70)

This clear separation of the purpose of the compensation order remained until the Criminal Justice Act 1982 enacted that a compensation order could be made instead of (or in addition to) any other sentence of the court. This was the first time compensation was seen as an alternative to punishment. Whatever the intention, the offender often perceives compensation as if it were punishment and is as resentful of it as of any fine. To the offender the result is the same, and is especially resented if the compensation is paid to a person who is far better off than the offender.

The 1982 Act indicated the growing importance of compensating the victim. It amended the compensation provisions so that in the case where the court considers that both a fine and a compensation order would be appropriate, but that the offender has insufficient funds for both, then the court should give preference to the compensation order. The Criminal Justice Act 1988 further obliges courts to give reasons for not ordering compensation for injury, loss or damage. Unfortunately many victims still fail to receive compensation largely because courts are not provided with sufficient information to assess the level of damage, and victims have no right of audience on this matter (see Newburn and Merry (1990)). Despite general approval of the system of making offenders pay, many victims get frustrated with having to wait for their compensation to be paid in instalments.

The main problem with obtaining compensation orders is that many victims remain unaware that compensation orders are available, or are unable to take the time off work to attend court in order to apply for one. An application for a compensation order is particularly unlikely if certain offences are to be 'taken into consideration' (TIC) by the court when sentencing the offender for another offence. The victims of those offences to be TIC are rarely informed of the possibility of compensation, or even that their case is to be TIC. In some areas the police do routinely inform the victim of the right to put in for compensation. Prosecutors can, and sometimes do, put forward the suggestion that compensation should be paid, and the court has the power to order compensation even when it is not requested. It is relatively uncommon for any of these possibilities to be exercised. Shapland, Willmore and Duff (1985) discovered that the most important factor in deciding whether a compensation order would be made was whether the prosecution mentioned its possibility, and/or whether the prosecution gave any details of the level of injury suffered. Possibly the Scottish system could be used to correct this problem. In Scotland the procurator fiscal scans every case to discover whether there is an identifiable victim. Any such victim is sent a form to complete with the information of the extent of the loss suffered along with information about compensation orders and about the CICB. This form is handed by the procurator fiscal to the sentencer at the time of the sentence. In this way, the sentencer is aware both of the possibility of making a compensation order and furnished with the information necessary to make one.

In England and Wales, obtaining information concerning the level of loss is still a problem which mitigates against the compensation order, so that it is still rare for the order to be the only sentence of the court. Following the 1988 changes there has been a slight increase in the number of orders made, but this is unlikely to continue unless the practical problems are addressed – getting information to the sentencer concerning the level of loss; offenders being permitted to pay orders over extended periods; and offenders failing to complete the order. Adoption of the Scottish system might address the first, while State payment of the compensation order and later recovery of the funds from the offender would help to alleviate the last two.

Particularly prominent amongst the victims of the criminal justice system are children. If they are the victims of child physical or sexual abuse they are removed from the family; or occasionally the perpetrator, usually the father or step-father, leaves the family. Either of these actions may have dramatic effects on the child, possibly causing feelings of guilt about the whole victimisation. Occasionally the other parent, generally the mother, or other siblings, also accuse the child of being at fault, which increases this guilt.

The major problem all children face in the criminal justice system is the giving of evidence. Until 1988 all children were required to give evidence in the alien and oppressive environment of the courtroom where they would be confronted with the accused, who might have perpetrated appalling acts upon them, or acts which they witnessed. In some cases the child would break down, and if he or she was an essential witness the case might fold. The consequent immense emotional distress might be as bad or worse for the child as the offence itself. For these reasons s. 32 of the Criminal Justice Act 1988 as amended by the Criminal Justice Act 1991 allows video-taped evidence in cases of violence, up to the age of 14, or sexual misconduct, up to the age of 17, where the tape is of an interview between an adult, other than the accused, and the child. This allows videos constructed after the event to be used and for interviews to be carried out by any adult, whether legally trained or not. There are safeguards incorporated and provision is made for extra questioning where this is necessary, although the scope for such extra questioning has been reduced by s. 62 of the Criminal Proceedings and Investigations Act 1996, which states that a pre-trial ruling that a tape is sufficient will normally prevent the child being asked to give evidence unless this is strictly necessary to prevent an injustice. The basic object is to protect the child from the trauma of giving evidence in court and of facing the accused. Little else is done for child victims, and in cases which do not involve violence or sexual misconduct the child is still required to give evidence in open court.

This section shows that although more is now done for victims, the State has still not taken victims seriously. For example, many victims need information about the criminal justice process in general, about where they may obtain help, about their rights, about ways they may improve their lot (through CICB or otherwise), and about the progression of their own case. Such information could be provided by insisting that the police give every victim an information sheet and by requiring them to keep victims informed of progress in their case. Although certain recent guide-lines for dealing with cases of domestic violence have called for the victim to be given information about aid agencies and the progress of the case, particularly the release of the alleged offender, and in a further pamphlet the police are called on to give more information to all victims, these are not requirements: the victim has no right to be told (Home Office Circular No. 60/1990; circular from the Home Office to Chief Constables; and Home Office pamphlet entitled *Victim's Charter*). The real initiatives which have increased the welfare of victims have occurred in the voluntary sectors, briefly described in the next section.

5.5.2 Victims and the voluntary sector

If help is to be offered it is important to assess the needs of victims. This task is not easy, as individuals differ. But Maguire (1985) identified a number of needs which can be summarised into three broad areas. First, victims need information, which, in the absence of positive action, means that the voluntary agencies are often the main and sometimes the only source. Unfortunately, they cannot help with information concerning particular cases. Secondly, there may be a need for practical help in completing insurance claims, repairing property, transport to hospital or court, etc. Most of these needs arise immediately after the crime and generally abate shortly thereafter. Thirdly, victims may need emotional support. The extent of this is impossible accurately to assess, but one estimate (Maguire (1985)) claims that on a conservative basis several hundred thousand people suffer from traumatic distress every year in England and Wales. For many the problem will be short lived, but for some, post-traumatic stress disorders may persist for extended periods of two years or more. These are usually associated with rape, kidnapping and other serious offences (even some victims of serious property offences). This may overstate the case, but clearly distress suffered by victims is a serious problem and one which in Britain is virtually ignored by the State. The voluntary sector has addressed these problems through two main types of agency. One type deals only with the problems of violence towards women and the other with victims more generally.

The feminist movement has been very active in helping female victims. They refer to them as survivors, as this gives the women a more positive and less depressing and passive view of their position. Feminist organisations have been especially useful in helping the survivors of domestic violence and rape or other sexual offences. They have also been supportive of child survivors (victims), either along with the women who suffer domestic violence, or more broadly in support groups such as the incest support group.

The help given to survivors of domestic violence is usually in the form of a place in a refuge, many of which are attached to the National Federation of Women's Aid. Shelter homes or refuges were set up as safe havens for women who were being criminally battered or whose children were being assaulted by people living with them, generally their husbands and/or lovers. These provide very practical help by giving the victim a roof over her head and a place to care for her children, outside the violence of the home and with the help and support of other women in the same predicament.

The refuge is a feminist response to a problem which had largely been ignored by the official criminal justice agencies of police and courts. Although some of these attitudes are beginning to alter (see Home Office Circular No. 60/1990), the police still do not see domestic violence as their business and they do not see prosecution as the most appropriate way of dealing with the problem. In domestic violence the woman is not generally seen as a separate entity: she is seen as part of the relationship, and the criminal justice agencies often feel it more appropriate to maintain that unity than to protect her individual person. In some cases it is this unity or, more realistically, the financial dependence of the woman which forces her to stay and be physically abused: it is this power element and the resultant helplessness which the refuges help women to cope with and to overcome.

Female survivors of rape or other sexual assaults can attend rape crisis centres (clearly, if these attacks have occurred at home, they may also turn to a refuge). Many survivors of rape feel that the criminal justice system does not meet their needs; the woman often feels as victimised by the police and court processes as she does by the initial act of violence. Sometimes women are even blamed for their own attacks (see Chambers and Millar (1983) and Smart (1989)). In response to the plight of these women the first Rape Crisis Centre (RCC) was opened in 1976 in London, and there are now many such centres in Britain. RCC operate by means of telephone 'hotlines' or drop-in centres. They allow women to make their own decisions about, e.g., reporting to the police or visiting a psychiatrist or other health professional. Each local unit is largely autonomous; there is no national association. They are generally intended as places where women survivors can talk with supportive women. The centres offer emotional support as well as legal and medical information.

Both refuges and RCC also play a political and educational role. They try to inform the public about the reality of rape and domestic violence. They try to change the law, social attitudes and social policy towards these problems. This politicisation has probably led to their being under-funded as far as government financing is concerned (see Mawby and Gill (1987)) and has limited their influence on government. The improvements which have come about arise more from public reaction to incidents covered in the press; to such TV documentaries as that on the treatment which Thames Valley Police gave women who complained of rape (BBC1, 18 January 1982); and to the pronouncements of judges about the contributory negligence of women victims and the need to protect otherwise respectable men (Adler (1987)). Part of this public pressure and press coverage may of course have been influenced by feminist organisations, but their lack of direct influence can lead to changes which are well-intentioned but inappropriate. For example, Home Office Circular No. 60/1990 set out a code of conduct for the police in cases of domestic violence which stressed the criminal nature of domestic violence, but proposed to keep a register of 'women at risk' rather than of violent men, which most women would find unacceptable. Some have argued that if the organisations were less political, or rather if their political stance were more acceptable, they might be able to obtain more finance and be consulted more often when changes to the law are being contemplated. The organisations argue that this would not be as supportive to the women survivors, as it would ignore part of their victimisation (see Dobash and Dobash (1980) and (1992) and Clarke et al. (1987)) and would reduce their usefulness in law reform, as they would not then address the real needs of women. A better method of dealing with this problem is considered by Roberts and Roberts (1990) who suggest careful crisis management of the situation; while Lloyd et al. (1993) report favourably on an initiative to prevent repeat victimisation and to ensure a swift response by the authorities by the use of a personal alarm for victims of domestic violence and other such offences.

Solving the problems of rape victims is more complex and probably involves a far-reaching policy of intervention. The criminal justice system is almost completely failing to protect women who report rape: fewer than one third of reported rapes get to court (less than 1,900 out of 5,700 which are reported); and fewer than 1 in 10 results in a conviction (only about 500). This figure is significantly worse than in the early 1980s when fewer rapes were reported but 1 in 3 resulted in a conviction. It seems very unlikely that 9 out of 10 women are lying or, if one just looks at cases which get to court, that three quarters of women are lying. There have to be structural explanations. One reason why so few cases come to court is because the efficiency of the Crown Prosecution Service (CPS) is partly judged by its conviction rate. Thus it does not want to prosecute hard cases (prostitutes, rapes in marriage, or cases where it is the word of the man against that of the woman). A clear indication that even strong cases are dropped is that in 1996 two prostitutes mounted a private prosecution after their case was dropped by the CPS for 'lack of evidence', and in 1995 £50,000 was awarded in a civil case after the CPS had dropped the case. Once cases are brought, the law and judges often fail to give women reasonable protection: in 1996 the judge allowed one woman (Julia Mason) to be cross-examined for six hours by the man she had accused, while another judge allowed a victim of a multiple rape to be cross-examined for 12 days by six separate defence counsel. Judges also continue to make unacceptable statements in rape cases – Judge Ian Stanforth Hill questioned the purity of an eight-year-old rape victim (1993), while Mr Justice Alliot sentenced below the recommended minimum because 'the victim was a whore' (1991) and Judge Raymond Dean said that 'when a woman says no she does not really mean no'. Jack Straw, the Home Secretary, is considering a new regime which will involve more appropriately trained prosecutors and aims to bring more of the hard cases to trial to demonstrate that rapists will not get away with it. The approach is based on one which was instigated in New York by Alice Vachss and, if introduced, could be a turning point for women and their protection against male violence. (See Mills (1997) and Vachss (1993)). Minor changes have occurred: women are afforded more dignity in medical checks and in questioning; women's identities are not revealed in rape cases; and, more recently, the Sexual Offenders (Protected Materials) Act 1997 ensures that certain sensitive information is not made freely available to the defendant or to any third parties.

Still less has been done to help the much wider range of general victims, most of whom have suffered property offences. For this large group, practical support has come from Victim Support Schemes (VSS). VSS are the only part of the voluntary sector which has really received any central support. The VSS organisation was less political, especially at the outset. It did not try to alter the criminal justice system, nor did it attack that system. Originally it offered short-term help to victims on a good neighbour principle: it now sometimes offers more long-term help on the same basis. In fact in 1979 its low political profile was reinforced when it became a charity, limiting its scope for campaigning or political agitation. The approach has gained the support of the police, from whom the VSS obtain information concerning victims who may need help. This less political approach also made the organisation's schemes more palatable to central government, who in 1987/88 awarded the VSS a £1.5 million budget increasing to £4 million by 1989/90 in order to help pay for the co-ordinators and to buy in some more professional help. This was welcome and a substantial achievement for the organisation. It also reflected a change in the public perception of the plight of victims which perhaps made it expedient for the government to be seen to be doing something for victims. It was also cheaper and easier to plug into an already existing voluntary system than to set up its own initiative (see Rock (1990)).

It is important to note that, as with the CICB, the government are not here admitting that victims have a right to aid, they are only conceding that the State has a moral obligation to help victims, or at least the deserving ones. The provision of aid has had a profound effect on an organisation which had hitherto survived on locally raised funds. There is some danger that the funding of VSS may lead to no funding for any other victim groups, and also to the police refusing to cooperate with other victim groups (see Corbett and Maguire (1988)). This is pertinent since the VSS model, good as it is, does not necessarily best meet the needs of all cases. They have always relied on the cooperation of the police in informing them of victims, and many schemes now operate a direct referral system. This involves the police informing them of the victims of all appropriate crimes whether or not the victim wants help, and generally without the consent of the victim even being sought. What are appropriate crimes or even appropriate victims depends on the policy of the local police force and, in the last analysis, on the discretion of individual police officers (see Maguire and Corbett (1987)). Certain types of offence seem therefore to have been largely excluded from the schemes. Corbett and Maguire (1988) remark that:

. . . victims of domestic violence, threats, racial or sexual harassment, repeated minor vandalism, and even quite serious cases of "multiple victimisation" . . . are relatively unlikely to be referred to or assisted by schemes.

They observe that schemes tend to deal only with one-off stranger to stranger offences, and contrast this with the system operating in Georgia, where the co-ordinators choose the cases they will deal with for themselves and end up dealing with the types of victim which are almost excluded from the British system. More recently, some VSS schemes have tackled some of these problems (especially racial attacks, harassment and cases of rape): they still mostly exclude domestic violence, arguing that the VSS method of sending a volunteer to a victim's house could endanger both the victim and the volunteer (Zedner (1994)).

In any event, the 1984 BCS estimated that only 1 per cent of victims are actually referred to VSS: by 1987 this had risen to 3 per cent, and by 1991 to 6 per cent. In 1992, when the BCS asked victims whether they would have liked to be contacted, only 4 per cent of all victims were interested, but this rose to 10 per cent of those who had reported their offences. Thus the system, though useful, fails to reach many who might benefit from its help. Some suggest that part of the problem lies in the way they contact victims, arguing for 'cold calling', but although two thirds of the BCS study said they would not have minded this, many preferred an initial letter; the least popular method was by telephone (see Mayhew (1993); Reynolds et al. (1993)). Furthermore, a greater injection of finance could alter this position by paying for more professionals to be appointed, and for more effective training of volunteers to deal with more complex victim problems. But it is clear that the non-campaigning, non-lobbying stance of VSS is very different from the position in America where the victim organisations join together to argue for the rights of the victim. It is arguable that VSS should do a lot more in this field, and as they gain a higher public profile their ability to bring about real changes will increase. But they would have to ensure that they did not jeopardise their charitable status nor alienate their volunteers and donors: to do so would impair their ability to help victims in more practical ways.

One conclusion is that the voluntary service provides invaluable and much needed help and support for victims or survivors of crime. But it is a conclusion needing qualification. Partly this is because the voluntary or-ganisations do not cover all victims – child victims are, for example, only patchily and incidentally included. Partly it is because they have not yet been effective in fighting for the rights of victims, either singly or as a coalition. It is in this latter area that the position of victims in Britain is now most in need of attention.

5.6 VICTIM PRECIPITATION AND LIFESTYLE

There seems to be a 'common-sense' or commonly accepted idea or concep-tion of a victim. One is that a victim is vulnerable, so that the victim of a street robbery (or mugging) is often thought of as being elderly, usually female. A victim of rape is necessarily female (men cannot legally be raped), usually young, and must have fought vigorously to defend herself. Her male attacker must be a stranger to her. She must also be 'respectable', otherwise she is deemed to have no honour to protect. Insurance companies often refuse to insure homes unless certain security measures are taken and may refuse to pay out if the victim of a theft has not been diligent in protecting their property. A victim is therefore seen as someone who has not contributed to the criminality in any way; they are helpless and wholly innocent. As has been seen above (5.5.1), this idea of an innocent victim is important in deciding whether compensation should be paid; whether and to what extent the criminal should compensate or perform reparation to the victim; whether victims should be believed; and lastly, it might also affect the criminal's sentence by the court after conviction. Therefore these perceptions are central to the criminal justice system.

5.6.1 Victim precipitation
Ideas of what constitutes a victim have long been a part of the discussion of whether victims precipitate the offence against themselves. This question is

one of the earliest issues in the study of victims. Von Hentig (1948) suggested that the relations between criminal and victim were complex and central to the criminal act. He argued that the law tended to separate criminal from victim almost totally, but that such a division was unrealistic. At times, he claimed, it may be unclear who is acting and who is being acted upon, and at others, the eventual victim may actually precipitate the activity which results in the victimisation, for example, by being the first to resort to violence. Therefore he is postulating that in certain instances it is the victim who determines whether there will be any criminal activity. Von Hentig's work was not based on any empirical study and was intended only as a starting point to further discussion.

Mendelsohn (1947) looked more closely at the idea of victim-precipitated incidents and classified victims by reference to the degree of their culpability for the crime. In this way, to a greater or lesser extent, he blamed the victim. He had six categories of victim ranging from the totally innocent, to the largely guilty victim, often one who had been the first aggressor but who had come off worst. This idea of victim precipitation was expanded and more carefully considered by Wolfgang (1958) when he considered homicide cases. He concluded that in certain cases the victim, by his actions, actually determined whether the crime was committed, for example, by being the first to turn to physical violence.

The idea of the precipitation of the offence is particularly strong where cases of violence and rape are concerned. In the case of rape, the notion of precipitation has been central to the way in which the criminal justice system has treated women who complain of having been raped. It is generally thought that if a woman has 'led on' the man who raped her then she may have provoked the attack, and this should lead to a reduced sentence. Similarly, it can be argued that if the victim places the criminal in a tempting situation this can be seen as precipitating the criminal activity, as when someone walks down the street alone at night with a bag bulging with money. Again this idea has been used in rape cases, where even asking for a lift with no suggestion of sexual invitations has been found to be provocative. In one case, for example, the judge stated, 'It is the height of imprudence for any girl to hitchhike at night. That is plain, it isn't really worth stating. She is in a true sense asking for it', and in sentencing the man to a fine of only £2,000 rather than the usual prison sentence he stated that the woman had 'been guilty of a great deal of contributory negligence' (Richards J in *R* v *Allen* (1982), unreported).

This case was attacked from all sides, both in and outside the legal arena, and led to official statements about the need for a custodial sentence in all rape cases and a closer look at the idea that women provoke rapes. It is an example of the danger involved in taking the concept of victim precipitation too literally. Can it illuminate the phenomenon of criminality without moving responsibility from criminal to victim? Probably not. Even stating that the crime happened here and now against this victim because the victim did or said something suggests that if the criminal had not been so stimulated, the crime would not have occurred. Victim precipitation is therefore a fairly dangerous concept, which leads to victim blaming. According to Miers (1992), victim blaming, or at least placing more responsibility on all citizens to avoid victimsation, is one of the dangers inherent in the enhanced position given to victims under modern responses to the victim movement.

5.6.2   Victim lifestyles and criminality
The claim is made that different lifestyles, particularly how much time is allocated to leisure activities, affect the probability of being in places where crime is likely, at times when crime is likely, and with people who are likely to commit those crimes. It might also lead to leaving property accessible for others to take advantage.

Above (5.3) it was noted that the BCS had discovered that individuals who tended to have an increased risk of victimisation were: male; under 30 years old; single, widowed or divorced; spent several evenings a week out; drank heavily; and assaulted others. The last three of these are obviously lifestyle variables. They relate to activities which increase the likelihood of such people being victims. The basis for viewing these behavioural factors in this way is obvious enough. For personal victimisation to occur, there needs to be a meeting between criminal and victim. Thus for street crime the element of going out more frequently will clearly increase the likelihood of such meetings, placing the individual at higher risk. Similarly it has been noted that many such offences take place in the evening, particularly in or around drinking establishments or between those who have been drinking, which suggests that going out in the evening and frequenting drinking establishments will increase the likelihood of victimisation. And property offences are more likely to occur if the property is left empty, open, or not protected by locks or alarms.

The first three of the variables in the above example are demographic variables, but they too are related to lifestyle. In most cultures, certain lifestyles are thought normal for given groups, and are therefore more or less socially encouraged or discouraged within such groups. Western cultures usually encourage young single men to socialise widely, and therefore the normal and encouraged lifestyle for this group within society is also the one which exposes them to most risk from street crimes. It is also the same group who commit most of this type of criminality.

An important reservation is that the lifestyle victimisation criteria so far discussed hold only for street crime or for crime committed on personal property. They totally ignore the private victimisation, referred to above in the areas of domestic violence and of sexual violence committed within relationships of family ties or of trust. Victims of these offences may find that they are safer outside the home rather than in it. They also ignore the fact that certain groups are sought out to be victimised. These are thus likely to suffer relatively high rates of victimisation, whether they remain in the home or venture out onto the street. Racial minorities are especially prone to such treatment.

One theory which goes some way to answering some of these problems about identifying victims was postulated by Sparks (1982). He highlighted six factors which he considers important in this area – vulnerability; opportunity; attractiveness; facilitation; precipitation; and impunity.

Vulnerability is used by Sparks to cover a number of possibilities. The first resembles the victim types discussed by Von Hentig (1948). These are at special risk, not because of something they do, but just as a result of their personal attributes such as being weak (mentally physically or both), old, or young. Other areas of vulnerability beyond the control of the individual may arise from variations of status, economic position or environment. Status vulnerability may arise because that individual belongs to a weak grouping such as minority races, women or children. Similarly, people living in a particular area or environment may increase their vulnerability. This may be connected to economic vulnerability.

Opportunity has two levels. First, it refers to availability. It is not possible to steal something which is securely locked away or which the victim does not possess. At this level, the concept is trite. Sparks uses it rather to consider the occasions on which the victim has made victimisation more likely, perhaps by a particular behaviour pattern. This is lifestyle by another name. More general lifestyle changes, such as increased leisure, may also have increased the opportunity for criminality (Smith (1982)). The danger of giving too much weight to such considerations is that it may lead to a reduction in the culpability and denunciation of criminals.

Attractiveness refers to how tempting something may be to a particular criminal. It is a relative idea, where the criminal is supposed to weigh up the ease of attaining the item against the possible gain from its possession. Where risk is low and the possible gain high, then the object is attractive, especially if it is spatially accessible. Attractive targets, both from the point of view of ease of access and possible gains, tend to be heavily concentrated in inner city areas: it is thus unsurprising that these areas experience high crime rates.

Facilitation refers to whether a position of special risk has been deliberately, negligently or unconsciously created by the victim. An example might be failure to fit locks or alarms in an area with high rates of burglary. It is a dangerous extension of moving blame away from the criminal and onto the victim.

Precipitation was seen by Sparks as particularly relevant to cases of inter-personal violence and rape, and most of these ideas were discussed above. He expands on these by seeing them as of most relevance when the offender and victim are known to one another, often very close. For example, he writes of the wife who kills her husband in his sleep because he has repeatedly beaten her.

Impunity is the final category defined by Sparks and related to situations where the victim is unlikely to complain, or to be believed if they do complain. The crime can thus be perpetrated without fear of being detected. This is often the case when sexual offences are committed against women and children where the victim is both unlikely to complain and unlikely to be believed. It also applies to cases against criminals, especially prisoners; down-and-outs; racial minorities; illegal immigrants; prostitutes (male and female), etc.

Most of Sparks's categories carry with them the notion that the victim carries some responsibility for crime. His message seems to be that potential victims should be encouraged to avoid dangerous situations for themselves or their property by staying indoors or keeping their property out of sight. If these cannot be avoided, they should protect themselves by only going out in groups, or in well lit streets, or by securing their property. Similar ideas were used by the Conservative Government in 1990 when explaining high crime rates, and they suggested that individuals alter their lifestyle so as to reduce criminality. These suggestions not only push the responsibility for crime towards its victims, but would also be very restrictive on the liberty of the potential victim. That is not to say that certain reasonable measures such as locks on doors and good neighbourly activities which might reduce crime should not be encouraged, but it does warn against using these ideas ostensibly to protect the individual whilst actually vastly decreasing their personal freedoms (see Morgan et al. (1994)).

5.7 CONCLUSION

Recently the interests of victims have gained a prominence in both media and political rhetoric. This shift has usually been associated with a call for greater 'law and order'. Some argue that in media and political discussions and in policy changes, the interests of victims have been hijacked to serve the needs of media entertainment and political power (for some discussion of this see Mawby and Walklate (1994), (especially pp. 13–21) and Elias (1993)). It is thus necessary to ask how many of the changes which are claimed to be in the interests of victims actually serve those interests? To respond to such a question some assumptions about the needs, interests and desires of victims have to be made. Here it is assumed that victims wish to be afforded dignity and have assurances that their lives will not be blighted by victimisation in the future. They may also wish to see the perpetrator dealt with. With this in mind, a number of new initiatives and suggested changes will be considered.

One prominent recent change is in increased powers of the police and other criminal justice agencies. The policy began under the Police and Criminal Evidence Act 1984 and culminated in the Criminal Justice and Public Order Act 1994, which vastly increased the powers of criminal justice agencies and criminalised certain types of protest and ways of life without providing much in the way of protection for individuals. It has had detrimental effects on the rights of suspects and defendants (Field and Thomas (1994)). At the same time it is dubious whether these enhanced powers and new criminal laws have increased the rights or interests of victims. Powers which do not respect the rights of suspects and defendants may well lead to miscarriages of justice – wrongful convictions, which not only breach the rights of the person convicted but are also clearly contrary to the interests of victims and of justice (see also the discussion concerning the crime control model in Chapter Two). This type of initiative, although usually presented as being in the interests of victims, in fact rarely improves their lot and may ultimately be damaging to them.

There is a plethora crime prevention and control initiatives: neighbourhood watch (using individuals to keep an eye on each other, see above); closed circuit television (using cameras to watch the public, see Fyfe and Bannister (1996)); the carrying of identity cards (mooted but not yet introduced); bans on guns and tighter controls on the sale of knives (see the Firearms (Amendment) Act 1997 and the Knives Act 1997); designing cities and towns in ways which might reduce crime (see Chapter Eleven); increasing awareness of the individual's responsibility to protect his or her own goods and person; more recent initiatives to persuade communities to take responsibility and be active in criminal justice initiatives (this type of strategy is supported by Wilson and Kelling (1982); the use of community to counter crime is questioned by Crawford (1995) and the idea is discussed at more length in Chapter Sixteen); and various other prevention initiatives which seem to draw citizens more and more into the control of crime. Such initiatives could be said to benefit victims if they actually reduce criminal activity, but the crime figures suggest that this has not yet occurred on any great scale. Each initiative needs to be considered in it own right, taking into account not only possible advantages to potential victims and society but also such negative effects for individuals and society as intrusions into privacy and the increased responsibilities placed on victims or potential victims (victim blaming, see Miers (1992)). It needs to be asked: do the possible advantages outweigh the reduction in freedom?

There are also calls for increased information for, and participation by, victims in the process, often in decisions as to bail, diversion, and levels of sentence. Britain has, as indicated above, substantially increased information and ensured that the victim's experience of the criminal justice system is made smoother. However, such provision still largely depends on where the victim is located since agencies in some localities are better equipped to serve victims, while much depends on the personalities of the officials in a particular case (see Mawby and Walklate (1994), pp. 195–6).

If the provision of information has improved, little has yet been done to increase the participation of victims in the criminal justice process. Schemes such as reparation, mediation and conferencing, which might most effectively move in that direction, have not gained much official backing. Occasionally victims may have been allowed some say in sentencing. Thus in *R v Kavanagh* (*Attorney-General's Reference No. 18 of 1993*) [1994] Crim LR 467, the family of the dead victim wrote to the courts expressing the view that the offender had already suffered enough and he was made subject to a probation order; in sharp contrast is the case of Jamie Bulger, where the petition from Jamie's parents demanding a lengthy sentence for his child killers led to the Home Secretary making a statement that they would be held for at least 15 years (this has now been successfully challenged in the Court of Appeal and is before the European Court of Human Rights). A more formal way of providing for victim's views to be taken into account is through a Victim Impact Statement (VIS), which allows victims to make known their views on what sentence should be imposed on their offender, and might even allow the victim a say in parole decisions regarding offenders. Such provisions have been introduced in America, though not always with positive effects (see Kelly (1990)): initial attractions have given way to severe criticism (see JUSTICE (1989) and Ashworth (1993)). Sentences should not depend on the accident of the forgiveness or anger of the victim; the victim could be subjected to cross-examination over allegations made in the VIS; if the offender felt that a severe sentence resulted from a VIS, he or she might seek revenge on the victim in the future; if the sentencer appeared to ignore the VIS this might make the victim feel even more frustrated and angry. Ashworth (1993) suggests that a better way forward might be to spend time educating those in criminal justice agencies (police, court officials, prosecutors, defending lawyers, judges, probation officers, magistrates and parole boards) about the physical and psychological effects of crime on victims.

Rejection of the idea of a full-blown VIS should not necessarily be seen as a reason to undermine the very different process whereby the victim is encouraged to provide information to the court so that a compensation order can be made. However, even these orders are not without difficulties; some victims may exaggerate compensation claims, and if these become increasingly used by courts, victims may be called to answer questions as to the level of damage suffered. Some, such as Ashworth (1986), would question the compensation of victims: compensation of individual victims might confuse whether the intent of the criminal justice system is to serve society or individual victims.

Most prominent in political and media initiatives has been the concept of tougher sentencing. The core of the crime control or law and order lobby is that one must force offenders to take responsibility for their actions and, as part of this, to face heavier sentences in the hope that these will incapacitate some offenders for a limited period of time and will deter others. In the 1990s this has been the main focus of initiatives culminating in the Crime (Sentences) Act 1997, the most important provisions of which introduce mandatory minimum sentences for repeat burglars, drug dealers, violent and sexual offenders, and abolish automatic remission. Whether this type of crime initiative 'works' is at best debatable; since the 1970s it has led crime policy in the United States, where crime rates have risen sharply despite the fact that the prison population has more than quintupled in the last 25 years (Currie (1996)). As Elias (1993) puts it:

> Conventional crime policy promotes harsh criminal punishments, which are ineffective, repressive, and even counterproductive. . . . Most prisoners initially are not a threat to society, but they become increasingly dangerous the longer they are imprisoned. Building more prisons does not stop crime, it only warehouses increasing numbers of outcasts from American culture. (p. 130)

There seems no sound reason why such initiatives should be more successful in Britain than in the USA. Harsh punishments are powerful political rhetoric and make good media hype, but they may well make bad criminal justice policy and may not serve the interests either of victims or of the rest of society.

Another victim-led initiative which is seen by many as a further punitive element, is embodied in the Sex Offenders Act 1997. This introduces a system whereby there will be a register of certain categories of sex offenders, registration to continue for periods of five, seven, ten years or life, depending on the length of the sentence imposed for their offence. Had the register been in force at the time of the Act's passage it would have held some 125,000 names, about 100,000 of whom would be paedophiles even though not all convicted paedophiles will be included. The intention is that the register should permit the authorities to keep sex offenders under surveillance so, it is hoped, rendering it less likely that they will re-offend. The police are entrusted with keeping the register, but access is a contentious issue which has yet (mid-1997) to be settled. Victim bodies are arguing that communities should be informed, or be able to find out, if a sex offender (particularly a paedophile) moves into their neighbourhood (this is the case in most states in the USA). Such information might make communities feel safer, but previous offenders must have some right of settlement; and the emotive nature of the issue can lead to a mob law, as was evidenced recently when neighbours set fire to the home of an alleged paedophile and burnt to death a child who was inside (*Guardian*, 19 February 1997). A register, particularly if the information is widely disseminated, may in fact be counterproductive as it might lead to what Braithwaite (1988) terms 'disintegrative shaming', where the criminal is not only punished but is also considered to be a criminal for life, beyond forgiveness and not worthy of being welcomed back into society – an outcast. The register may then become a self-fulfilling prophesy whereby such individuals become more and more dangerous and necessarily re-offend.

As was noted in Chapter Two, those who define crime and control the criminal justice agencies narrow the concepts of offenders and crime. These are then still further narrowed by what the media choose to depict as crime. The same process is true for victims: we have a narrow and controlled view of those who suffer harm and who are entitled to the concerns that go with the title of 'victim'. Victims of corporate or government offences or atrocities are rarely recognised as such. They are generally marginalised: they are not usually represented by victim groups, nor do they obtain the support offered by organisations such as VSS. Nor, indeed, do they get much notice in this book. However, it should at least be registered that they must be included in any consideration of how to respond to victimisation, especially as the sections of society who are most likely to fall victims of 'conventional' crime, and whose victimisation is therefore most accepted, are often the same sections as fall victim to 'commercial and governmental' crime whose victimisation is least likely to be recognised (see Pearce (1990) and Crawford et al. (1990)). Furthermore, feminist writers point out that the conceptions of victimisation which are most frequently given recognition fail fully to understand the concept of 'victim' for women and other groups who suffer discrimination (see Cain (1990) and Elias (1993)). Much feminist work in this area has opened up areas for recognition as crimes and has given the 'victims' some status – especially in the areas of child abuse (particularly child sexual abuse), rape and domestic violence. Such concerns have also started to break down the reluctance felt by the crime control agencies for entering the private domain, while demonstrating the resilience of many victims to survive their position. This too should be respected, forcing recognition that victims are a diverse group with different needs.

Paradoxically, one approach which might meet these requirements is to consider providing guaranteed and universal rights for victims. Great care would be needed to ensure that such rights do not interfere with the rights necessary to the suspect or defendant. The aim would be for a rights strategy which would go much further than the provision of legal powers towards ensuring that rights, legal and social, are enjoyed by all in a society. Many believe this wide rights base might reduce criminality more effectively (Elias (1993), ch. 8 and see also Chapter Eleven of this volume). In such a rights-based society, discrimination would be reduced and equality as citizens would be actively promoted. The contention is that this might bring with it reduced criminality, or at least fewer crimes of hatred which are very dangerous for both victims and societies (see Elias (1993)).

Victims are now an integral part of criminological study. Their importance in the criminal justice system is increasing, but they still lack basic powers and rights or interests which will be legally protected within that system. It is important that the study of the victim does not take over from the study of the criminal, and so allow the criminal to escape culpability and social condemnation. If the needs of victims must be kept in perspective, they must also be taken more seriously by those in authority, not least because without their cooperation the system quite literally could not operate.

REFERENCES

Adler, Z. (1987), *Rape on Trial*, London: Routledge & Kegan Paul.

Ashworth, Andrew (1986) 'Punishment and Compensation: Victims, Offenders and the State', *Oxford Journal of Legal Studies*, vol. 6, p. 86.

Ashworth, Andrew (1993), 'Victim Impact Statements and Sentencing' *Criminal Law Review* 498.

Austin, C. (1988), *The Prevention of Robbery at Building Society Branches*, Crime Prevention Unit Paper No. 14, London: Home Office.

Aye Maung, N. and Mirlees-Black, C. (1994), *Racially Motivated Crime*, Home Office Research and Planning Unit, Paper 82, London: HMSO.

Box, S., Hale, C. and Andrews, G. (1988), 'Explaining Fear of Crime', *British Journal of Criminology*, vol. 28, p. 340.

Braithwaite, John (1988), *Crime, Shame and Reintegration*, Cambridge: Cambridge University Press.

British Crime Survey 1982, see Hough, Mike and Mayhew, Pat (1983), *The British Crime Survey*, HMSO.

British Crime Survey 1984, see Hough, Mike and Mayhew, Pat (1985), *Taking Account of Crime*, HMSO.

British Crime Survey 1988, see Mayhew, Pat, Elliot, David and Dowds, Lizanne (1989), *British Crime Survey*, HMSO.

Butler-Sloss, E. (1988), *Report of the Inquiry into Child Abuse in Cleveland 1987, Short Version*, London: HMSO.

Cain, M. (1990), 'Realist Philosophies and Standpoint Epistimologies or Feminist Criminology as Successor Science', in L. Gelsthorpe and A. Morris (eds), *Feminist Perspectives in Criminology*, Buckingham: Open University Press.

Chambers, G. and Millar, A. (1983), *Investigating Sexual Assault*, Edinburgh: Scottish Office.

Clarke, J., Cochrane, A. and Smart, C. (1987), *Ideologies of Welfare*, London: Hutchinson.

Corbett, Claire and Maguire, Mike (1988), 'The Value and Limitations of Victim Support Schemes', in Mike Maguire and John Pointing (eds), *Victims of Crime: A New Deal*, Milton Keynes: Open University Press.

Council of Europe (1983), *European Convention on the Compensation of Victims of Violent Crime*, European Treaties Series No. 116.

Crawford, Adam (1995), 'Appeals to Community and Crime Prevention', *Crime, Law and Social Change*, vol. 22, p. 97.

Crawford, A., Jones, T., Woodhouse, T. and Young, J. (1990), *Second Islington Crime Survey*, London: Middlesex Polytechnic, Centre for Criminology.

Currie, Elliott (1996), *Is America Really Winning the War on Crime and Should Britain Follow its Example?* Conference Paper given to the 30th Annual Conference of the National Association for the Care and Resettlement of Offenders, London: NACRO.

Dignan, Jim (1991), *Repairing the Damage: An Evaluation of an Experimental Adult Reparation Scheme in Kettering, Northamptonshire 1987–89*, Sheffield: Centre for Criminological and Legal Research, Faculty of Law, University of Sheffield.

Dignan, Jim (1992), 'Repairing the Damage: Can Reparation be Made to Work in the Service of Diversion?', *British Journal of Criminology*, vol. 32, p. 453

Dignan, Jim (1992a), 'Just Deserts or Just Outcomes? Reparation Comes of Age' *The Magistrate*, vol. 48(3), 49.

Dignan, Jim (1994), 'Reintegration Through Reparation: a Way Forward for Restorative Justice?' in A. Duff, S. Marshall, R.E. Dobash and R.P. Dobash (eds), *Penal Theory and Practice: Tradition and Innovation in Criminal Justice*, Manchester: Manchester University Press.

Dobash, R.E. and Dobash, R.P. (1980), *Violence against Wives: A Case Against Patriarchy*, Somerset: Open Books.

Dobash, R.E. and Dobash, R.P. (1992), *Women, Violence and Social Change*, London: Routledge.

Ekblom, C. (1988), *Preventing Robberies at Sub-Post Offices*, Crime Prevention Unit Paper No. 9, London: Home Office.

Elias, Robert (1993), *Victims Still: The Political Manipulation of Crime Victims* Newbury Park, Calif: Sage Publications.

Field, Stewart and Thomas, Philip (eds) (1994), *Justice and Efficiency: The Royal Commission on Criminal Justice*, Oxford: Basil Blackwell.

Forsythe, Lubica (1994), 'Evaluation of Family Group Conference Cautioning Program in Wagga, NSW', Conference Paper Presented to the Australian and New Zealand Society of Criminology 10th Annual Conference.
Fyfe, Nicholas R. and Bannister, Jon (1996), 'City Watching: Closed Circuit Television Surveillance in Public Spaces', vol. 28, *Area* p. 37.
Gil, D.G. (1978), 'Violence Against Children', in C.M. Lee (ed.), *Child Abuse: A Reader and Sourcebook*, Milton Keynes: Open University Press.
Gottfredson, M. (1984), *Victims of Crime: The Dimensions of Risk*, Home Office Research Study No. 81, London: HMSO.
Hale, C., Peck, P. and Salked, J. (1994), 'The Structural Determinants of Fear of Crime: an Analysis Using Census Data and Crime Survey Data from England and Wales', *International Review of Victimology*, vol.6, p. 3.
Harman, C. (1982), 'The Law and Order Show', *Socialist Review*, vol. 1.
Health Services Advisory Committee (1987), *Violence to Staff in the Health Services*, Health and Safety Commission, London: HMSO.
Home Office Circular No. 60/1990, *Domestic Violence*, issued by the then Home Office Minister John Patten.
Hough, M. (1995), *Anxiety about Crime: Findings from the 1994 British Crime Survey*, Home Office Research Study No. 147, London: Home Office Research and Statistics Directorate.
Hough, M. and Mayhew, P. (1983), *The British Crime Survey: First Report*, Home Office Research Study No. 76, London; HMSO.
Hough, M. and Mayhew, P. (1985), *Taking Account of Crime: Findings From the Second British Crime Survey*, Home Office Research Study No. 85, London: HMSO.
Islington Crime Survey 1986, see Jones, T., Maclean, B. and Young, J. (1986).
Jones, T.; Maclean, B. and Young, J. (1986), *The Islington Crime Survey: Crime Victimisation and Policing in Inner City London*, Aldershot: Gower.
JUSTICE (1989), *JUSTICE, Sentencing: A Way Ahead* (chaired by Lady Ralphs), London: *JUSTICE*.
Kelly, Deborah (1990), 'Victim Participation in the Criminal Justice System', in A.J. Lurigio, W.G. Skogan and R.C. Davis (eds), *Victims of Crime: Problems, Policies and Programs*, Newbury Park, Calif: Sago.
Kinsey, R., Lea, J. and Young, J. (1986), *Losing the Fight Against Crime*, Oxford: Basil Blackwell.
Lloyd, S., Farrell, G. and Pease, K., *Preventing Repeated Domestic Violence; the Results of a Demonstration Project in Merseyside Police 'C' Division*, Home Office Crime Prevention Paper, London: HMSO.
Mackay, R.E. and Moody, S.R. (1994), *Neighbourhood Disputes in the Criminal Justice System*, Edinburgh: Scottish Office Central Unit, HMSO.
Mackay, R.E. and Moody, S.R. (1996), 'Diversion of Neighbourhood Disputes to Community Mediation' The Harvard Journal, vol. 35(4), p. 299.
Maguire, Mike (1985), 'Victims Needs and Victims Services', *Victimology*, vol. 10, p. 539
Maguire, Mike and Corbett, Claire (1987), *The Effects of Crime and the Work of Victim Support Schemes*, Aldershot: Gower.

Marshall, T. (1984), *Reparation, Conciliation and Mediation: Current Projects in England and Wales*, Home Office Research and Planning Unit Paper 27, London: HMSO.

Marshall, T. and Walpole, M. (1985), *Bringing People Together: Mediation and Reparation Projects in Great Britain*, Home Office Research and Planning Unit Paper 33, London: HMSO.

Mawby, R.I. (1988), 'Age, Vulnerability and the Impact of Crime', in Mike Maguire and John Pointing (eds), *Victims of Crime: A New Deal*, Milton Keynes: Open University Press.

Mawby, R.I. and Gill, M. (1987), *Crime Victims: Needs, Services and the Voluntary Sector*, London: Tavistock.

Mawby, R.I. and Walklate, S. (1994), *Critical Victimology*, London: Sage.

Mayhew, Pat, Elliot, David and Dowds, Lizanne (1989), *The British Crime Survey: Third Report*, Home Office Research Study No. 111, London: HMSO.

Mayhew, Pat, Aye, Maung, Natalie and Mirrlees-Black, Catriona (1993), *The 1992 British Crime Survey*, Home Office Research Study No. 132, London: HMSO.

Mendelsohn, B. (1947), 'New Bio-psychosocial Horizons: Victimology', *American Law Review*, vol. 13, p. 649.

Miers, David (1992) 'The Responsibilities and the Rights of Victims of Crime', *Modern Law Review*, vol. 55, p. 482.

Mills, Heather (1997), 'Legal Hit Teams to Target Rapists', *Observer*, 1 June 1997.

Mirrlees-Black, C. (1995), *Estimating the extent of domestic violence*, Home Office Research Bulletin No. 37, London: HMSO.

Mirrlees-Black, C. and Aye Maung, N. (1994), *Fear of Crime: Findings from the 1992 British Crime Survey*, Research Findings No. 9, London: Home Office Research and Statistics Directorate.

Mirrlees-Black, C., Mayhew, P. and Percy, A. (1996), *The 1996 British Crime Survey: England and Wales*, London: Home Office Research and Statistics Division.

Morgan, Jane and Zedner, Lucia (1991), *Child Victims: Crime, Impact and Criminal Justice*, Oxford: Clarendon Press.

Morgan, Jane, Winkel, Frans and Williams, Katherine (1994), 'Protection and Compensation for Victims of Crime', in Phil Fennell, Chris Harding, Nico Jörg and Bert Schwarts (eds), *The Europeanisation of Criminal Justice*, Oxford: Oxford University Press.

Morris, Allison, Maxwell, Gabrielle M. and Robertson, Jeremy P. (1993), 'Giving Victims a Voice: A New Zealand Experiment', *The Howard Journal*, vol. 32(4), p. 304.

Newburn, T. and Merry, S. (1990), *Keeping in Touch: Police–Victim Communication in Two Areas*, Home Office Research Study No. 116, London: HMSO.

Painter, Kate (1992), 'Different Worlds: the Spatial, Temporal and Social Dimensions of Female Victimisation', in David J. Evans, Nicholas R. Fyfe and David T. Herbert (eds), *Crime, Policing and Place: Essays in Environmental Criminology*, London: Routledge.

Pearce, Frank (1990), *Second Islington Crime Survey: Commercial and Conventional Crime in Islington*, London: Middlesex Polytechnic Centre for Criminology.

Pearson, G. (1983), *Hooligan: A History of Respectable Fears*, London: Macmillan.

Phipps, A. (1986), 'Radical Criminology and Criminal Victimization: Proposals for the Development of Theory and Intervention', in R. Matthews and J. Young (eds), *Confronting Crime*, London: Sage.

Raine, J. and Smith, R. (1994), *The Victim/Witness in Court Project: a Report on the Recent Programme*, London: Victim Support.

Reynolds, T., Viney, A., Aye Maung, N. and Phillips, M. (1993), *A Survey of Victim Support Volunteers*, London: Victim Support.

Roberts, A.R. and Roberts, B.S. (1990), 'A Mode for Crisis Intervention with Battered Women and their Children' in A.R. Roberts (ed.), *Helping Crime Victims* London: Sage.

Rock, Paul (1988), 'Governments, Victims and Policies in Two Countries', *British Journal of Criminology*, vol 28, p. 44.

Rock, P. (1990), *Helping Victims of Crime*, Oxford: Clarendon Press.

Rock, P. (1994), *Victimology*, Aldershot: Dartmouth.

Roshier, Bob (1989), *Controlling Crime*, Milton Keynes: Open University Press.

Russell, Dianna (1982), *Rape in Marriage*, New York: Macmillan.

Russell, Dianna (1984), *Sexual Exploitation*, Beverly Hills, California: Sage.

Shapland, J; Willmore, J. and Duff, P. (1985), *Victims in the Criminal Justice System*, Aldershot: Gower.

Smart, Carol (1989), *Feminism and the Power of Law*, London: Routledge.

Smith, L.J.F. (1987), *Crime in Hospitals*, Crime Prevention Unit Paper No. 7, London: Home Office.

Smith, Susan J. (1982), 'Victimisation in the Inner City', *British Journal of Criminology*, vol. 22, p. 386.

Sparks, R.F. (1982), *Research on Victims of Crime: Accomplishments, Issues, and New Directions*, Rockville, Md: National Institute of Mental Health, Centre for Studies of Crime and Delinquency, US Department of Health and Human Services.

Stanko, Elizabeth A. (1987), 'Typical Violence, Normal Precaution: Men, Women and Interpersonal Violence in England, Wales, Scotland and the USA,' in J. Hanmer and M. Maynard (eds), *Women, Violence and Social Control*, London: Macmillan.

Stanko, Elizabeth A. (1988), 'Hidden Violence Against Women', in Mike Maguire and John Pointing (eds), *Victims of Crime: A New Deal*, Milton Keynes: Open University Press.

Stanko, Elizabeth A. (1990), 'When Precaution is Normal: a Feminist Critique of Crime Prevention', in L. Goldthorpe and A. Morris (eds), *Feminist Perspectives on Criminology*, Buckingham: Open University Press.

Stevens, P. and Willis, C. (1979), *Race, Crime and Arrest*, Home Office Research Study No. 58, London: HMSO.

Strang, Heather (1993), 'Conferencing: A New Paradigm in Community Policing', Paper delivered to the Annual Conference of the Association of Chief Police Officers.

United Nations (1985), *Declaration on the Basic Principles of Justice for Victims of Crimes and Abuse of Power*, A/RES/40/34.

Vachss, Alice (1993), *Sex Crimes*, New York: Random House.

Von Hentig, H. (1948), *The Criminal and his Victim*, New Haven, Connecticut: Yale University Press.

White Paper (1990), *Crime, Justice and Protecting the Public*, London: HMSO.

Wilson, E. (1983), *What is to be Done About Violence Against Women?*, Harmondsworth: Penguin.

Wilson, J.Q. and Kelling, G. (1982), 'Broken Windows: The Police and Neighbourhood Safety' *The Atlantic Monthly*, March 1982, 29–38.

Winslow, R. (1968), *Crime in a Free Society*, (selections from the President's Commission on Law Enforcement and Administration of Justice), California: Dickenson.

Wolfgang, M.E. (1958), *Patterns of Criminal Homicide*, Philadelphia, Pennsylvania: University of Pennsylvania Press.

Wright, M. (1992), 'Victims, Mediation and Criminal Justice', *Cambridge Law Review*, 187.

Wright, M. (1995), 'Victims, Mediation and Criminal Justice', *Criminal Law Review*, 187.

Young, Jock (1988), 'Risk of Crime and Fear of Crime: a Realist Critique of Survey-Based Assumptions', in Mike Maguire and John Pointing (eds), *Victims of Crime: A New Deal*, Milton Keynes: Open University Press.

Zedner, L. (1994), 'Reparation and Retribution: Are they Reconcilable?', *Modern Law Review*, vol. 57, p. 228.

Zedner, L. (1994), 'Victims', in M. Maguire, R. Morgan, and R. Reiner (eds), *The Oxford Handbook of Criminology*, Oxford: Clarendon Press.

CHAPTER SIX

Influences of Physical Factors and Genetics on Criminality

6.1 INTRODUCTION

The aim of this chapter is to consider, from both an historical and a contemporary viewpoint, the assertion that there are biological explanations for crime. In the past, theories which advanced this type of explanation tended to adopt the stance that crime was a sickness or illness which afflicted individual criminals, and was the result of some biological disfunction or disorder. Many contemporary criminologists have doubted these biological, particularly genetic, explanations of crime. They perceive such ideas as an admission of hopelessness and untreatability which carry with them the inference that the public will demand the removal of these individuals from society for good, an approach of 'lock them up and throw away the keys'. These fears are, to an extent, understandable as some of the past research favoured this conclusion (see, for example, 6.4.1).

Modern biological theorists do consider that genes are influential because they have a strong influence on brain function and therefore, it is believed, on behaviour and criminality. Since all human beings (except identical twins) are genetically unique this can help explain differences in behaviour by individuals who have been subjected to similar environmental and social influences. However, most modern researchers do not view the part played by biology in any explanation of criminality as indicating an illness or a dysfunction; rather it suggests the possibility of a slightly different configuration of normal genes giving rise to a temperament which is more receptive to antisocial types of behaviour. Furthermore, many do not view such differences as immutable, recognising instead that biological and genetic differences can be altered. Some of the results, they accept, may be unpleasant but assert that this should not prevent the scientific investigation of the phenomenon of crime. The claim is that science should be allowed to seek for truth and leave it to the politicians and moral philosophers to decide how to deal with the results. In any event, there is an awareness that biology and genetics cannot be an answer in themselves. Modern biologists generally acknowledge the importance of environmental and social influences on criminal behaviour and suggest that they should be studied in parallel with genetics – they call this a biosocial perspective (Ellis and Hoffman (1990)).

Any interaction of the 'ologies' (particularly criminology, sociology, biology and psychology) poses problems. One of the main difficulties lies in the nature of the different types of research involved. Despite being one of the less exact 'sciences', biological research tends to be more precise than its sociological and psychological counterparts in that the variables studied are generally more exact. For example, an individual only has so much adrenalin in the body at any one time, and this level can be precisely measured. On the other hand, a sociologist may be attempting to measure or assess parental discipline, which will involve the researcher in more subjective and necessarily less exact conclusions. This may lead to problems when comparing the relative importance of each type of research.

For example, exact calculations based on precisely measurable data, such as the amount of a certain chemical in the body, may appear to show a stronger correlation between one variable and criminality than that which exists between a more imprecise variable, such as parental discipline, and criminal behaviour. It does not necessarily follow from this that the former is really more important than the latter, or is a better guide to predicting criminality. It may simply be that the element of say, parental discipline, has not been, and cannot be, measured and presented so clearly and in isolation from other social factors. Similarly, even if criminality is shown to be linked to, say, genetics, this, as already indicated, does not mean that genes are the sole cause of criminality. It may be that an individual has inherited the potential to act in a criminal manner, but whether or not that potential is realised may depend upon the interaction of the physical and social environment with those individual traits.

If it is appreciated that neither biological nor social explanations offer anything like a complete solution, but that their interaction may provide a more balanced perspective, then it may be possible to arrive at a better understanding of crime and its prevention. In any event, the interaction between biological and social factors is clearly very complex. It is an area where research, especially interdisciplinary research, might well prove fruitful. What is said about biological theories in this chapter should therefore be read with an awareness that they may also need to be considered in a social context.

6.2   EARLY CONSTITUTIONAL OR BIOLOGICAL THEORIES

Work on biological explanations for crime began with the phrenologists in the eighteenth and early nineteenth centuries (for a full history, see Fink (1985)). These theorists maintained that there was a relationship between the skull, the brain and social behaviour. The general claim was that a close relationship existed between the exterior shape of the skull, unusual cranial protuberances or other cranial abnormalities, and the structure of the brain. The

ideas of these phrenologists have virtually no significance for modern criminology. None the less, their ideas represented a useful and fruitful departure:
their contribution was to focus attention on the individual criminal rather
than on very vague and generalised theories of criminality. The logic of both
the criminal law and the penal system is to blame the individual for the action,
and theories which point towards the crime being caused by the individual
rather than by society fit in well with this. More recent theorists have made
similar links, but the most famous proponent of them was Lombroso.

6.3 LOMBROSO

6.3.1 Introduction
Cesare Lombroso has been called the father of modern criminology. An
Italian who lived between 1835–1909, he was educated in medicine and
became a specialist in psychiatry. He spent some time working for the military
and with the mentally afflicted, but his principal career was that of an
academic at the University of Turin. His main publication was *L'Uomo
Delinquente* (The Criminal Man), first published in 1876 and comprising
some 252 pages. By the fifth and final edition in 1897 it held 1,903 pages.

Lombroso's working methods were very different from most of his predecessors; he claimed to be scientific rather than philosophical or juridical.
Whereas earlier workers studied crime in the abstract, Lombroso turned
towards a study of the criminal himself. He decided there was a need for
direct empirical and analytical study of the criminal, as compared with
normal individuals and the insane. He believed strongly in the need for first
hand clinical observation and measurement in individual cases. Unfortunately, he was also willing to draw on the untested clinical observations of
others as well as on historical methods and data which were often merely
anecdotal (or at least were not readily verifiable), and on already questionable
anthropometric and statistical techniques in an attempt to build up proof for
his theories. Finally, he drew on the unscientific tools of both analogy and
allegorical illustration. One of the main drawbacks with his work was his
assumption that congenital and physical characteristics were static, and so
always available for observation. He paid little heed to transient characteristics or physical processes. On reading both his work and that of some of his
followers, it becomes clear that this aspect of his work was unsatisfactory. For
example, he, like others before him, carefully measured skulls in order to
determine the cranial capacity of criminals. He did this without knowing
either the stature or the age of the criminal, factors which affect the capacity
or size of the brain within the skull. Another major drawback with his work
arose in his sampling. First, many of the criminals he studied were mentally
ill and were therefore unrepresentative of the general criminal population.
Secondly, he often worked with no, or an inadequate, control group. For
example, some of his work was based upon samples from prison populations
where, compared to the population as a whole, there was an over-representation of those of Sicilian origin. The characteristics which Lombroso indicated as being atavistic (see 6.3.2) may have been more prevalent in that

part of Italy, but he has been criticised for assuming that these physical attributes led to criminality. The relative poverty and low social conditions experienced by Sicilians may have been a more plausible explanation. In effect, the prison sample he used had not been matched with a representative control group from the same racial and social background.

These criticisms are not intended to cast doubt on the importance of his work in the historical development of modern criminological theory, but rather to point out some of its methodological shortcomings. Leaving aside those imperfections, considerable though they are, the weight of his scientific observation and the amount of his statistical analysis was, at the time, remarkable. This alone was a formidable contribution to criminology and moved it away from a purely religious and philosophical debate towards an empirical scientific methodology.

6.3.2 Atavisms

Lombroso's theory assumes the existence of a distinct anthropological type – the born criminal – who is likely or even bound to commit crime. The type he isolated was, he claimed, the result of an 'atavism', a term borrowed from Darwin, from whom Lombroso gained much of his inspiration. According to this idea, a criminal is supposed to be a throwback in the evolutionary chain, a reversion to an earlier and more primitive being who was both mentally and physically inferior. In other words, the criminal reflected our lower and more ape-like ancestors; their physical characteristics, he claimed, resembled those of apes. His theory used physical characteristics as indicators of this degeneracy or inadequacy and therefore as indicators of criminality. The physical characteristics measured by him included the following:

(a) peculiar size or shape of head;
(b) peculiarities of the eyes;
(c) asymmetry of the face;
(d) enlarged jaw and cheekbones;
(e) ears which are too large, too small or too handle-shaped;
(f) nose twisted, upturned or flattened (indicative of thieves) or aquiline or beak-like (indicative of murderers);
(g) lips fleshy and protruding;
(h) peculiarities of the palate;
(i) abnormal teeth;
(j) chin too long, too short or too flat;
(k) abundance of wrinkles;
(l) abundance of hair which is often black and frizzled;
(m) sparse beard in men but abundance of facial hair in women;
(n) excessive length of arms;
(o) retreating forehead;
(p) dark skin.

From time to time the list was changed, but it was always made up of similar types of physical anomaly. If a person portrayed five or more of these atavisms or anomalies, then by Lombroso's reckoning that individual was a born criminal. In his earlier works he always claimed that all criminals fell into the category of born criminals, a claim which he was later to revise.

In addition to the purely physical characteristics he claimed that the born criminal portrayed certain other factors, such as:

(a)   Sensory peculiarities, including greater sensibility to pain and touch, more acute sight, less acute hearing, taste and smell.

(b)   Functional peculiarities, including greater agility, more ambidexterity and greater strength in left limbs.

(c)   A lack of moral sense, including an absence of repentance and remorse, the presence of vindictiveness, cynicism, treachery, vanity, impulsiveness, cruelty, idleness, participation in and love of orgies, a passion for gambling and an irresistible craving for evil for its own sake.

(d)   Use of a special criminal argot or slang.

(e)   A tendency to express ideas pictorially.

(f)   An excessive use of tattooing.

(g)   Excessive idleness.

He also connected epilepsy (see 7.3.2) to criminality. Initially, he claimed that all criminals were also epileptics, but stopped short of the allegation that all epileptics were criminals (see Wolfgang (1960)). Subsequently, in later works, he amended this claim and maintained that only about 30 per cent of criminals were epileptics (Lombroso (1906), p. 365).

In his early works (such as the early editions of *L'Uomo Delinquente*), Lombroso wrote almost exclusively about the physical characteristics of criminals, but later writings (Lombroso (1906)) include such things as climate, rainfall, the price of grain, sex and marriage customs, banking practices, the structure of government, church, religion, criminal laws and poor education as factors which have an effect on criminality. This huge extension of the number of variables obviously threatened to swamp his original thesis, but added to his reputation as the father of modern criminology because it encompassed the three major strands of most contemporary works – biology, psychology and environment. However, the emphasis throughout his work is always on human physical traits.

6.3.3   Three categories

Lombroso's early view, that almost all criminals were 'born criminals', was later revised to represent only a third of all criminals (Lombroso (1906), p. 365). The other two thirds fell into two other criminal groups. There were 'insane criminals' in which he included idiots, imbeciles, paranoiacs, sufferers from melancholia, and those afflicted with paralysis, dementia, alcoholism, epilepsy or hysteria. Finally, he conceded that there were what he termed 'occasional criminals'.

This last group he then divided into three distinct sub-groups, namely: 'pseudo-criminals', 'criminaloids' and 'habitual criminals'. The first of these, 'pseudo-criminals', comprise those who commit crime involuntarily, either due to perverse laws or in defence of the person or the family. The second group, 'criminaloids', was more difficult to characterise because its members possessed neither very obvious physical anomalies nor recognisable mental disorders, but their mental and emotional facilities were such that in certain circumstances they would indulge in vicious and criminal behaviour. In their case, the most important element of their criminality was the environment or the opportunity to commit crimes. Further, although these criminals could not always be pin-pointed by particular traits, they did have some innate peculiarities which were similar to, but far less obvious than, those evident in the born criminals. They therefore differed from each other in degree rather than in kind. Lombroso eventually consigned more than half the criminals to this category. The third and final sub-group, 'habitual criminals', portray no inbred anomalies or tendencies such as might predispose them to crime, but turn to it rather for reasons of poor education and training at an early age, or are drawn into crime by close association with criminals.

6.4   AFTER LOMBROSO

6.4.1   Critical analyses of Lombroso

Lombroso's theories equating propensity to commit crime with physical make-up have long been discredited as naive. Even before his death, anthropology had advanced to the point of accepting that the idea of uniform and linear evolution was too simplistic (see Vold and Bernard (1986), p. 38). This realisation rendered meaningless any claims that atavisms directly caused criminality. Similarly, psychiatry and psychology were demonstrating that the relationship between crime and either epilepsy or insanity was vastly more complex and involved than Lombroso had suggested. Subsequently, modern criminology has also moved away from the notion of a single criminal gene which clearly separates criminals from non-criminals, but the possibility of some genetic role in the explanation of crime is still debated.

These defects, however, must not blind today's readers to the importance of Lombroso's work. He is often said to be the father of the positivist school of criminological study. Positivism is the view that all true knowledge is 'scientific', and thus entails careful research and methodology by painstakingly collecting measurable and verifiable data, subjecting any assumption to empirical verification, and taking nothing for granted. Positivist theories play down the element of free will. The argument is that either the individual has some predisposition to criminality, and so does not choose it in any truly free sense, or that the environment forces him towards criminality, and therefore again no clear 'choice' exists for that individual.

Today, Lombroso's claim to fame lies in his scientific methodology and his rejection of choice, intent or free will. It should be remembered that Lombroso was not the first to utilise either these methods or this approach to criminology. Others before him (for a discussion of these see Ellis (1900)) had done both, but Lombroso's range and attention to detail has given him a new and lasting prominence, as well as the perpetuation of the myth that he was the first to take such an approach. It is a view which can be attributed to a number of factors.

First, his use of Darwinian-type theories was very popular at the time. It was daring to suggest that criminality was tied to the still questionable doctrine of evolution, and it was also a very intriguing concept. More importantly, he let society 'off the hook'. He provided a scapegoat. By widely expounding the concept of the born criminal, Lombroso let 'society' believe that criminality was not its fault; that it had nothing to do with poverty, environment or acquaintances, and everything to do with the individual self. For years, social reformers had claimed that criminality was a product of lifestyle. Lombroso gave governmental administrators the opportunity to disclaim any responsibility for the problem and, as is only natural, the opportunity was taken.

Having become accepted by some of those in authority, his theories were used to support certain methods of dealing with criminals (see Garland (1985)). In earlier classical writings, the punishment was supposed to fit the crime; the criminals paid for their past actions (see Beccaria (1964), first published 1776). In positivist writings the purpose of punishment may be seen differently. One function of punishment is the protection of society. Usually this is dependent on the harm done, but some positivists argue that punishment could also be increased or decreased by reference to the potential harm to society. Therefore, if the individual is of a type who is likely to commit further crimes (e.g., a born criminal), a long sentence may be necessary in order to prevent future criminality and thereby protect society. In the early twentieth century some saw eugenics as an added benefit of long term incarceration: imprisoned criminals would not reproduce, and so criminal traits might become less common, thus improving the race (see Garland (1985)). For many this strengthened the arguments for long sentences. These ideas are not generally explicitly accepted in our criminal justice system.

A second penal aim that many positivists saw was reform. Lombroso's belief in the born criminal did not mean that all such people would become criminal: they might be reformed. For reform to overcome natural tendencies the individual needs to be treated over a long period, and therefore long sentences are needed. In fact, it is partly from the early positivists' ideals that we get the notion of trying to reform criminals whilst they are in prisons (but see Foucault (1977), Part Two). In Britain, the prison system has often claimed to be attempting to reform prisoners, and this may be one, but only one, of the reasons we have relatively long prison sentences and a large number of inmates compared with the rest of Europe. This type of sentencing also fulfils the aims of the previous positivists' ideals without necessarily accepting them.

Logically, acceptance of the idea of a born or natural criminal would lead to the conclusion that punishing such individuals is not acceptable because the criminality is not their fault. In this situation, the individual should be helped by treatment or careful tuition, and this should be done not as part of punishment but instead of punishment. This would involve a court discovering the guilt or innocence of offenders and then handing them over to treatment agencies for indefinite periods of time, to be released only when they are 'cured' and presumed safe to resume their places in society. The length of the treatment may bear no relation to the crime committed. The next logical but extremely dangerous step (given the lack of scientific certainty), is to maintain that where the 'born criminal' has certain external characteristics which are capable of being recognised early on in life, it should be permissible to insist on 'treatment' before any crime is committed. Society would be protected from dangerous criminal acts before they occur, but only at the cost of individual freedom. Even more intrusive and dangerous is the idea that certain physical types could be operated on or subjected to drug 'therapy' in order to alter them and so pre-empt their criminal propensities (see 7.1.2), or to prevent them passing on these traits to their progeny by sterilisation or by genetic engineering (see 10.7). This argument takes the theory to the extreme; but illustrates just how easily it could be misused.

However, positivism is not solely concerned with anthropological theories. In its biological approach it also embraces arguments concerning, for example, genetics and biochemistry. One point which is paramount in the positivist approach is that, besides the biological, there are also very important psychological and sociological perspectives (see Chapters Eight to Thirteen and Sixteen). The positivist school shares both the methodology of the biological school as well as its exclusion of free will.

6.4.2 Biological research since Lombroso

There were several early attempts to test Lombroso's theories. Charles Buchman Goring tried to disprove Lombroso's claims, and E. A. Hooton tried to prove them. Goring (1913) attacked Lombroso's ideas and set out a theory of his own. In so far as his refutation of Lombroso is concerned, he made comparisons between 3,000 criminals and a large number of non-criminals, and found no more physical anomalies in the criminal group than in the non-criminal. He then compared groups of different kinds of criminals, but found no significant differences between them, for example, burglars and murderers or forgers and thieves. When matched for occupational groups, the criminals were one or two inches shorter than the non-criminals and about seven or eight pounds lighter. Goring attacked the idea that people were more or less criminalogenic, depending upon their physical characteristics. He was particularly insistent that the term 'born criminal' was dangerous and inexact because, until the first act of criminality, the individual was not a criminal. He did, however, consider that a tendency towards criminality could be inherited (see 6.6.4). He also argued (Goring (1913), p. 175) that even if there were physical differences between criminals and non-criminals, that did not indicate an abnormality amongst criminals; such a conclusion would be a circular argument. His thesis may be illustrated by using an example drawn from basket ball. If we apply a Lombrosian type theory to basket ball players, the argument might be that they are abnormal because they are tall, whereas Goring's argument would be that they may have been selected for the sport because of their stature. Similarly, Goring would claim that any physical differences between criminals and non-criminals would indicate a selection of the qualities most often useful to the commission of crime rather than any abnormality.

Goring has been criticised (see Driver (1972)) because in his eagerness to disprove Lombroso he put more weight on the statistics than they could objectively be made to bear. Driver (1972) showed that Goring's figures did not refute Lombroso's findings as categorically as Goring had claimed: but equally he did not find that the statistics supported Lombroso (see p. v).

Hooton (1939) studied about 14,000 criminals and 3,000 non-criminals drawn from ten US states and found real physical differences between criminals and non-criminals. Despite having no independent proof that the characteristics which appeared most often in criminals were examples of inferiority, he attributed the differences to an hereditary inferiority on the part of the criminals. To do this assumes that factors found most commonly in criminals are examples of inferiority merely because they occur most often in criminals. The argument suffers from the weakness that it is too circular. Despite this, Hooton argued strongly for the segregation of criminals so as to eliminate these types from the race.

6.5 SOMATOTYPES AND CRIMINALITY

Lombroso's work has often been referred to as the beginning of somatotyping, that is, the diagnosing of the individual's constitution and behaviour by the shape of their body. As we have seen, the early ideas of a link between body type and behaviour were relatively crude, but Lombroso's painstaking measurement of body characteristics provides a link with later work. Another early researcher in this area was Erenst Kretschmere (1921), but the first modern systematic linking of body traits with delinquency came from William Sheldon (1949), who drew many ideas from earlier works. The somatotype theory is that:

(a)   the shape of the body reflects the individual's constitutional make-up;

(b)   both shape and constitution are strongly influenced by factors existing at birth; and

(c)   the basic body shape at birth and therefore the constitutional make-up or temperament remain constant and are relatively little affected by nutrition.

Sheldon maintained that elements of three basic body types could be found in all people:

(a)   endomorphic – generally soft, rounded and fat, and characterised by extroversion and love of comfort. They tend to be friendly and sociable.

(b)   mesomorphic – hard, muscular and athletic, with a strongly developed skeleton. Their personality is strong and assertive, with a tendency to be aggressive and occasionally to be explosive.

(c)   ectomorphic – thin, weak and generally frail, with small skeleton and weak muscles. They tend to be introverted, hypersensitive, shy, cold and unsociable.

Sheldon tested his theory by studying 200 males held in a rehabilitation home in Boston and comparing these with a control group of 4,000 students. He concluded that most delinquents tended towards mesomorphy. The Gluecks (1950), a husband and wife team, attempted to test this conclusion, but although their initial findings were supportive, closer analysis led them to conclude that delinquency was related to a combination of biological, environmental and psychological factors. This, too, was the broad finding of the more sophisticated study carried out in Cortes and Gatti (1972).

The exact relationship between body type and crime remains controversial and uncertain. More detailed research has undermined the direct linear connection between body type and criminality and added other possible contributors to the criminality debate, such as adverse social conditions and psychological factors. Most studies do seem to suggest that there is a predominance of mesomorphs amongst delinquents, but in the absence of a feasible biological explanation it is dangerous to place much weight on this. Apart from coincidence, there would be other reasons for the apparent connection. For example, certain body-builds may simply be better adapted for certain types of crime; or perhaps the link simply illustrates closer policing of the types of crimes most often committed by mesomorphs; or body-build may be one attribute in attracting police attention and influencing juries. There is some evidence (see Bull (1982)) to suggest that there is a perceived stereotype of a criminal, and the criminal justice agents may therefore just be selecting or picking on that type more frequently than other types.

6.6 GENETIC FACTORS

6.6.1 Introduction
In recent years the study of genetics has become one of the fastest moving and most significant areas of modern science. The exercise of such techniques as genetic engineering, already commercially used for cereals and vegetables, raises possibilities which are at once exciting and frightening. It certainly raises major moral issues. Most of the work relating genetics to human characteristics has so far been more concerned with linking genetics with particular diseases, rather than with criminal behaviour, but the recent genetic advances clearly have possible implications for criminology and some of them will be indicated later (see 6.6.8). It is first necessary to survey the various attempts which have previously been made to explore the possible biological bases of crime and criminal behaviour.

6.6.2 Uninherited genetic abnormalities
Uninherited genetic abnormalities are usually the result of chromosomal mutations at the time of conception. In criminology, the interest is in XXY and XYY chromosomes. Each plant and animal cell has in its nucleus all the genetic characteristics of that particular organism. In normal human beings this genetic information, held on 23 pairs of chromosomes, controls the colour of the hair, the length of the legs, etc. One pair of these are the sex chromosomes which determine the sexual characteristics of the individual. In the normal female these sex chromosomes are represented by XX, and in normal males, by XY chromosomes.

At the time of conception the sperm and ovum (each of which normally holds 23 single chromosomes) unite to form a single cell (containing the normal 23 pairs of chromosomes, i.e., 46 in all). A normal male has the X chromosome from his mother via the ovum and his Y chromosome from his father via the sperm. Unfortunately some sperm and ova contain more than one sex chromosome. This can lead to abnormalities in the sex characteristics of the individual, so that abnormal males can be either XXY, if there is an extra X or female chromosome, or XYY, if there is an extra Y or male chromosome.

The first of these, the XXY, is known as Klinefelter's syndrome and is generally related to degeneration of the testes, sterility, a tendency towards homosexual fantasies or a general disinterest in sexual activity. Most of these problems are treatable with male hormone replacement (adding testosterone). It is possibly over-represented in institutions for the subnormal, but it probably has no connection with criminality.

The second chromosome abnormality is XYY. As maleness has always popularly been linked with criminality, an extra male, or Y, chromosome was popularly thought to give rise to an individual who was a 'supermale'. This person would, it was argued, be more aggressive and more criminal. In research, as represented by Jacobs, Brunton and Melville (1965), the syndrome was found to appear far more frequently in mental institutions than in the general population. Men possessing this characteristic were also found to be on average 6 ins taller than the average man (6 ft 1 in as opposed to 5 ft 7 ins). The tendency towards institutionalisation found amongst these men was first taken as proof of their enhanced criminality because it was believed to be linked to increased violence. Jacobs defines them as having 'dangerous, violent or criminal propensities.' Later studies such as that of Sarbin and Miller (1970) question this claim, and in fact assert that an individual with XYY syndrome would be less aggressive than a normal male. The argument is upheld by the research of Watkin and associates (1977). They discovered that although a high proportion of XYY men had committed crimes, they were mostly petty property offences, and such individuals were no more likely to commit dangerous crimes than normal XY males. They explained the over-representation of XYY men in institutions as a result of their slight mental retardation.

There is now some agreement that chromosome abnormality and criminality are not closely related, and, more significantly if general explanations are wanted, the incidence of XXY and XYY males is so rare as to be of little practical significance.

6.6.3 Inherited genetic factors: study of family trees
The early attempts to prove a genetic link with criminality were unsophisticated. They usually involved studying the family trees of known criminals. The most famous of these was undertaken by Richard Dugdale (1877). The Jukes were a New York family who were infamous for criminality, prostitution and (apparent) poverty. Dugdale postulated that all three factors were related and were fixed, so that criminality would always run in the family. It was true

that in the Jukes family there was a very high proportion of criminals, but that does not prove any link between criminality and genetic or inherited factors. Such a close family similarity might be explained by similar environmental factors acting on all members of that family, or by arguing that all had learnt the ideas and methods of criminality from one another, making it difficult for any member to remain non-criminal. Some more recent studies, such as those of Sheldon and Eleanor Glueck (1950), have claimed to show that a father's criminal conduct was one of the best predictors of his son's future criminal behaviour. But, genetically speaking, these too prove nothing because hereditary and environmental influences are intertwined. The natural parents are also usually the persons who rear or bring up the child. It could be their influence rather than their genes that cause their off-spring to go astray.

6.6.4 Goring and heredity

Goring (1913), referred to earlier (see 6.4.2), rejected explanations based upon physical characteristics. More positively, he argued that criminalistic tendencies are basically inherited. He attributed little relevance to environmental factors. He only studied persons who had been imprisoned, and so spoke of the convict rather than the criminal. He had a particular interest in the more serious offenders, which he characterised as those who had faced both frequent and lengthy prison sentences. In his study he found high correlations between the criminality of spouses, parents and children and between siblings. The correlation between father and son – and between brothers – for criminality was very similar to that for physical traits such as eye colour and stature. Goring's argument is that the shape, size, etc. of a criminal's nose (or any other physical trait) does not determine likely criminality: the important factor is the contents of the genetic material passed on from the parents. If the parents were criminal, they would pass the tendency on to their children exactly as they might pass on any other trait (Goring (1913), pp. 365–67).

He argued that these findings had to indicate an hereditary link to criminality. The similarity of behaviour of spouses was not environmental, as both were usually involved in criminality prior to marriage, and their criminality was therefore, he argued, inherited from their respective parents. The similarity in behaviour between parents and children could not, he said, be environmental because the correlation was too closely related to other clearly hereditary factors, such as physical appearance. Further, the coefficient was found to be no higher in crimes such as stealing, where one might expect fathers to act as examples for their sons and so teach them, than for sex crimes where one would expect the father to try to hide his involvement so the example would not be present. He also discovered that where parents were removed from the home when the child was still very young (usually the removal was the result of imprisonment), the child was as likely if not more likely to turn to criminality than if the parents were removed at a later stage. He accordingly claimed that a longer period of contact did not increase the criminality, which must have derived from some other source. Thus for Goring criminality was the result of hereditary factors, and from this he drew the conclusion that people with those inherited characteristics should have their reproduction regulated: 'Moderate opportunity for crime by segregating the unfit . . .' (see Driver (1960), pp. 345–6). This is a frightening conclusion, particularly when it is drawn from research that is so weakly based.

There are said to be three principal defects in Goring's argument (Sutherland and Cressey (1978) p. 120):

1. He did not measure the influence of 'environment'. He considered only eight environmental conditions, which represent a relatively small part of the total environment.

2. His comparison of stealing and sex offences is based on an assumption that parental contagion is restricted entirely to techniques of crimes, and he did not consider the possibility that transmission of values is more important.

3. He restricted his study to male criminals, although he mentions the fact that the ratio of brothers to sisters in respect to imprisonment is 102 to 6. If criminality is inherited to the same extent that colour of eyes is inherited, it must affect females to the same extent as males unless it is sex-linked. However, according to Goring, since the biological predisposition to crime is made up entirely of physical and mental inferiority, sex linkage is not plausible. (p. 120).

Goring's claims have since been rejected. This, as will be clear from 6.6.8 below, does not necessarily mean that there is no link between crime and heredity, but rather that the link is not of the nature described by Goring. His research, conclusions and suggested action to reduce criminality highlight the grave ethical dilemmas that exist in biological theories about criminality, and indicate how easily these can lead to suggested 'reforms' which might be incompatible with a free and humane society.

More careful and realistic study of the relationship between criminality and heredity can be seen in the areas of twin studies and adoption studies.

6.6.5   Twin studies

Does heredity or environment cause criminality? Theorists realised that if you could hold one of these variables constant, then similarities in criminality would suggest that crime was related to the constant, whereas differences would suggest a connection with the variables. The only way they saw of doing this was to study twins. There are two sorts of twins — monozygotic (MZ) or identical twins, who are from a single egg and single sperm and therefore genetically identical, and dizygotic (DZ) or non-identical twins, who are born from two eggs simultaneously fertilised by two sperm (i.e., they share only 50 per cent of their genes) and so are no more similar than ordinary brothers and sisters. The claim was that, if identical twins act in identical ways, their behaviours could be the result of identical inheritance, but any difference in behaviour would have to be the result of the environment. If criminality was caused by genetics, then if one MZ twin was criminal then the other would also be criminal, i.e., they would depict concordant behaviour patterns, whereas there need be no such relationship between DZ twins whose behaviour would be different or discordant. If criminality was related to the environment, then both MZ and DZ twins would show similar concordance rates.

Certain individual studies suggest, but do not necessarily prove, such a correlation. For example, Jenaway and Swinton's 1993 study of one set of triplets discovered that the genetically identical pair were behaviourally and temperamentally very similar, whereas the third triplet, who was genetically distinct, had a very different temperament and behaviour pattern. Although the researchers did not conclude that genetics had caused the difference they did suggest that it may have played a part. Small studies such as this are only, however, of limited value; more useful are the larger and wider twin studies.

Early studies of this sort suggested that criminality was closely related to genetics (see Lange (1929)). The MZ twins did show greater rates of concordance than did the DZ twins. Even so, it is important to note that the MZ twins also showed some discordance and that the DZ twins showed some concordance: clearly, criminality could not be wholly explained by genetics. Some part had to be played by other factors, such as the environment. In any event, most of these early studies suffered from very basic research problems. Firstly, in most of the studies at least one of the twins was drawn either from prison or from a psychiatric clinic, giving an unrepresentative cross-section of the twin population. This could have one of two effects. If there is a borderline decision about whether the other twin is also criminal, the researcher may only attribute that criminality where it is convenient to do so. If the first twin is discovered in a mental institution, this might test whether mental instability is inherited but not necessarily whether crime is passed on as part of the genetic material. Secondly, the zygosity tests were very crude and imprecise, often done just by looking at the twins and if they appeared identical calling them MZ twins, if not, then DZ twins. This might have the effect of making the MZ category larger than it should be. If wrongly classified DZ sets of twins were removed, the relationship between criminality and genetics might be strengthened if these DZ twins made up a large proportion of the discordant group found in the MZ category.

Two well-known recent twin studies by Christiansen (1968 and 1974) and Dalgaard and Kringlen (1976) try to take account of the above inaccuracies.

Christiansen drew his twins from the official twin register of Denmark, and collected information on some 6,000 pairs of twins born between 1881 and 1910 and who lived up to the age of 15. He then separated them into MZ and DZ twins, and finally used the Penal Register to discover whether either or both twins had been convicted. In the MZ or identical group he found that for males there was a 35.8 per cent concordance rate, whereas in the DZ or fraternal group this was only about 12.3 per cent, i.e. if one male MZ twin was convicted of a criminal offence the likelihood that the other twin would also be convicted was 35.8 per cent; for male DZ twins the corresponding figure was only 12.3 per cent. For females the differences were even more marked: 21.4 per cent for MZ twins but only 4.3 per cent for DZ twins. It has been claimed that these figures show a significant role is played by inherited factors. It does portray a possible connection, but care must be taken. The sample of female twins is too small for any pattern to be relied upon, while that for the men could possibly be explained by the closer upbringing of identical twins. Possibly of greater importance is that when Christiansen separated out serious crime, i.e., illegal acts that have been punished with imprisonment of those over 15 (the age of adult responsibility in Denmark) he found these to be more closely correlated with genetics than were the lesser offences. None the less, in all cases Christiansen himself recognised that no study had yet provided conclusive evidence of the complete dominance of either genetics or environment. He recognised that none of his results could be interpreted as indicating that heredity played a predominant part in the causation of crime, but stated that it is an *a priori* hypothesis that heredity and environment always interact in a dynamic fashion to bring about and shape criminal behaviour.

Dalgaard and Kringlen studied 139 pairs of Norwegian male twins and discovered a 25.8 per cent concordance rate in MZ twins as compared with only 14.9 per cent in DZ twins. Again this portrayed a slightly higher rate of similar behaviour in the identical twins but, as with Christiansen, Dalgaard and Kringlen suggested that this might be explained by the close similarities in upbringing in the case of identical twins. To test this idea, they grouped all the twins according to their mutual psychological closeness. They discovered that more of the MZ twins were close than were the DZ twins, and that among those who were psychologically close there was no difference in their concordance rates by zygosity. They therefore concluded that this wiped out the apparent involvement of genetics in criminality, leaving the environment as the only appreciable influence. On the evidence they present, this conclusion seems at least as doubtful as would be a simple acceptance of heredity.

When Cloninger and Gottesman (1987) studied the same figures, they came up with a rather different interpretation of the results. They argued that if Dalgaard and Kringlen were correct, then the environmental effects would cause psychologically close identical twins to act the same, and psychologically distant identical twins to act differently, but that did not occur. Taking Dalgaard and Kringlen's own figures, Cloninger and Gottesman 'proved' exactly the opposite conclusion. Cloninger and Gottesman use this to suggest that Dalgaard and Kringlen chose the wrong experimental data to prove an environmental rather than genetic bias. They should have gone for the closeness in the early home environment, rather than for psychological closeness. Cloninger and Gottesman argue that if it is the environment which causes criminality, then MZ twins brought up in very close environmental conditions should be concordant, whereas those brought up in rather different environments should be discordant. This, they said, was not proven by the study. This type of research can, as we shall see, better be carried out in adoption studies.

More recently a slightly different twin study gave rather different results which can be used to uphold both social and genetic reasons for criminality. Rowe (1990) refers to the Ohio twin study which he and Rodgers conducted (Rowe and Rodgers 1989). They collected information from self-report questionnaires on personal delinquency, temperament, perceptions of family environment, and association with delinquent peers from 308 sets of twins. They drew all their twins and control groups from schools in the Ohio State area and included 265 sets of same-sex twins and 43 opposite-sex twins, as well as a small non-twin-sibling control group. By drawing the children from the school system and taking self-reported information they avoided bureaucratic bias. They also calculated the effects of sibling interaction on antisocial behaviour. They concluded that genetic influences partly determine the similarity of behaviour of same-sex and monozygotic twins. They recognised that interaction between siblings could cause initially discordant siblings to become concordant in their levels of delinquency. Therefore genetics can explain some of the concordance but sibling and twin interaction also play a large part in shaping behavioural patterns. Rowe claims that some of the disparities found in other twin studies can be explained by a failure to recognise fully the importance of interaction between siblings. He goes on to explain three ways in which genetics and environment might interact to cause certain types of behaviour:

> One type of genotype-environment correlation is passive: the tendency of family environments to reflect genes shared by parent and child. For instance, antisocial parents may model aggression for children who may inherit temperamental traits predisposing them towards aggression. A second type of correlation is reactive, whereby inherited traits provoke reactions from the social environment – for example, physically unattractive individuals may receive negative social attention, which may in turn lead to delinquency. Finally, a third type – the active correlation – occurs when people with particular genetic dispositions select environmental conditions that serve to reinforce them. (Rowe (1990), p. 129)

He claims that the Ohio twin project provided evidence of active selection of environments by twins. The argument is that an individual chooses the peer group and environment which will reflect and reinforce his or her genetically based personality inclinations, suggesting that these groupings – and so the environmental influences on an individual – are partly dictated by the genetics. Thus in looking at family environmental effects, peer-group effects etc. it is necessary to take into account the genetic correlation with antisocial behaviour and vice versa. Behavioural and social scientists should be aware of possible neurophysiological reasons for personality traits or behaviour and biologists should not ignore either the psychological or the social causes of certain behaviours.

None of the above studies is decisive as to the significance of heredity for criminality, mainly because twins are brought up together as a general rule, and as Rowe (1990) notes, this makes it virtually impossible to reach any firm conclusion as to the role of genetics alone. It is still possible that a predisposition to crime could be genetically transmitted. Attempts to test this hypothesis have been based on studies of adoption, which permit a better delineation between genetics and environment.

6.6.6   Adoption studies

The intention is to discover whether there is a correlation between biological parental, particularly paternal, criminality and the adoptee's criminality. The tests are based on the adoptee having been removed from the criminal influence of its natural parent at an early age. If such a relationship is found, the argument is that it indicates a correlation between criminality and genetics. Whereas if family environmental elements are most important there will be no such correlation, and, instead, a link to the behavioural patterns of the adoptive parents will be discovered. Adoption studies are considered particularly important because they isolate one factor, genetics, from the other, environmental influences.

Hutchings and Mednick (1977) studied all Copenhagen male adoptions where the adopting parents were not related to the child and where the adoptee was born between 1927 and 1941. They discovered that boys with criminal biological fathers were more likely to be criminal than those with law-abiding fathers. Further, they found that those with criminal adoptive fathers were also more likely to be criminal than those with law-abiding adoptive fathers, but that the effects of a criminal biological father were more noticeable than a criminal adoptive father (22 per cent and 12 per cent respectively). This finding suggested that genetics were in this respect more important than environment. Lastly, they found the most significant effects when both the biological fathers and the adoptive fathers were criminal. In these cases, the effect upon the rate of criminality of the adoptee was quite marked, at 36 per cent. This suggests a possible gene-environment interaction, i.e., the genetic link may predispose an individual to criminality but that individual is only likely to act in a criminal fashion if the environmental influences are favourable to such behaviour. If environmental conditions favour criminality, it is more likely to occur for a person who possesses a genetic predisposition to crime than for someone who does not. In 1984 they replicated their research in a wider study which encompassed all non-familial adoptions in Denmark between 1924 and 1947 (Mednick et al. (1984)). In this wider study they found a similar though slightly less strong correlation between biological parents (note this study compared parents rather than just fathers) and their adoptee children (20 per cent). The relationship between adoptive parents and their adopted children was 15 per cent. Again they found the most significant results when both biological and adoptive parents were criminal (25 per cent). After checking for other possible explanations for the results they concluded that there was a genetic element which was transmitted from the criminal parents to their children which increased the likelihood of the children taking part in criminal behaviour.

From these results, Hutchings, Mednick and Gabrielli have claimed that criminality is related to genetics. It is important to note, however, that adoption agencies try to place children in homes situated in similar environments to those from which they came. If environmental forces are significant, this would tend to exaggerate the apparent genetic effects because their environment will remain relatively unchanged: but it may still be the upbringing and not the genetic material which causes criminality. In addition the claims have been questioned by Gottfredson and Hirschi (1990), who begin by observing that in the wider study, against expectations, the genetic correlation was reduced rather than increased. It is, indeed, difficult to categorise the second study as a true replication study because there were differences between the way in which the material was collected and collated. Gottfredson and Hirschi claim that this strengthens their criticism since the comparison was no longer with fathers and children but by including mothers had become a comparison between adoptive parents and children: if the important factor was genetic, Gottfredson and Hirschi claim this alteration should have strengthened the link. But in fact the link was weakened. Furthermore, they noted that although the number of adoptions studied rose by 3,403 cases, the actual number of cases in the category of criminal biological parents only rose from 58 to 85. From this Gottfredson and Hirschi concluded that:

> the true genetic effect on the likelihood of criminal behaviour is *somewhere between zero and the results finally reported by Mednick, Gabrielli and Hutchings*. That is, we suspect that the magnitude of this effect is minimal.

They went on to conduct their own calculations and concluded that the strongest possible case for a link between heredity and crime was a correlation of 0.031 between the crimes of fathers and sons, a figure which is statistically insignificant.

The link between criminality, genetics and the environment has been stressed by at least three other studies. Bohman (1978) suggests that there is a genetic predisposition to alcoholism, and that because there is also a link between alcoholism and criminality there is therefore a more distant relationship between crime and genetics. Cadoret, Cain and Crowe (1983) suggest that both genetic make-up and the environment, affect an individual's tendency to be active in criminality (and in unacceptable behaviour which is not criminalised). They argue that the environmental factors are probably stronger, but the most significant results are obtained if the individual is subjected to both environmental and genetic factors favourable to criminality. This follows from their suggestion that the correlation between crime and genetics is measurable, if limited, and is partly confirmed by the work of Walters (1992) who analysed 38 of the significant family, twin and adoption studies. He concluded that there was a small, though not insignificant, correlation between genetics and crime (11 to 17 per cent); that the common environmental element (that suffered or enjoyed by others in the same conditions) seemed to be 24 to 32 per cent; and the remaining 51 to 65 per cent is attributable to specific environmental influences (experiences unique to a particular individual), and to error. He notes that the better designed and more recent gene–crime studies were less supportive of a link between genetics and crime than were the earlier and less well designed studies. Despite this he concludes that one should not ignore a genetic link when studying reasons for criminality and suggests that the genetic and environmental and sociological elements combine in contributing to delinquent and criminal activity. This approach would be supported by many of the biosocial theorists (see Ellis and Hoffman (1990)).

6.6.7   Race, crime and genetics

As was seen in Chapter Four, there is broad agreement that there is a large and relatively stable correlation between race and crime: Afro-Caribbeans consistently have the highest conviction rates for crime; Whites are the next most likely criminal group; followed at some distance by Asians. Many theorists have suggested sociological reasons for the differences although, as was also mentioned in Chapter Four, some of the variation may be explained by prejudiced crime enforcement rather than by difference in crime commital. In contrast to the considerable body of sociological work linking race to crime, there have been few recent attempts to connect the racial differences in crime to genetic difference. One recent writer, Whitney (1990) argues that such research is long overdue because of what she regards as strong suggestive evidence for a link. She quotes the now widely accepted difference between the crime rates in various racial groups and compares this with studies which consider the genetic differences between the racial groups. A number of these (Latter 1980; Rushton 1985; Rushton 1988; Rushton and Bogaert 1987) suggest that there is an Afro-Caribbean – white – Asian ordering of differentiation between races with regard to certain testable genetic traits. As there is a similar breakdown of crime rates, she argues that there is enough evidence to support the need for research to assess whether genetics can provide a partial explanation for the criminality. Clearly her hypothesis will be supported if it is accepted that there is a genetic basis for some of the individual differences in criminality (still a contentious issue, see 6.6.6 above).

Whitney recognises the sensitivity of her suggestions but considers that science should not shrink from discovering the truth merely because it may be misused by society. She admits that once racial difference becomes an issue in the political and legal spheres, major moral problems will be raised, but insists that these should not dissuade scientists. Of course, although this is surprisingly never considered by Whitney, such scientific research may categorically disprove any genetic links between crime and race. Even so, the apparent rationality of Whitney's argument should not obscure two facts: firstly that such studies are scientifically questionable as we do not yet possess the information necessary to perform them: and secondly that information linking racial genetic differences to crime could prove to be very dangerous and might lead to increased discrimination with potentially very serious consequences. This should never be forgotten. With little of obvious positive value to be gained from any conclusions, the justification for pursuing this line of research must be questionable. Until the way in which the possible genetic difference operates is more fully understood the very powerful negative effects which might arise should be very clearly considered by scientists, politicians and lawyers.

6.6.8   Can genetics explain crime?

In recent years the advances in genetic science have given rise to widespread claims that not only human physical characteristics, but also aspects of human behaviour derive from genetic sources. In this context it is thus unsurprising to find claims, not necessarily by the scientists themselves, that aspects of criminality can be accounted for by genetic factors. Here two strands of this tendency will be examined: the first drawn from speculation based on analogies with theories of animal behaviour; the second deduced from the expansion of scientific knowledge about genes.

6.6.8.1 Theories of animal behaviour

The first approach is exemplified in the work of Ellis (1990a), who looked to processes of natural selection operating on genetic evolution to explain both some aspects of criminal behaviour and some of the major characteristics of the criminal justice system. In terms of behaviour, the argument is that some criminal activities – especially rape, assault, child abuse and property offenses – are related to powerful genetic forces. Thus it is contended that forcible rape could have evolved from the part of the male makeup which aims to mate with many females in order to guarantee the gene line, and from the natural resistance of females to this as it interferes with their control over choosing sex partners with suitable genetic characteristics. To support this speculation Ellis points to numerous studies revealing forcible copulation in many non-human species; to the fact that most rapes are on females in the fertile age group; and to the further observation that the risk of pregnancy from rape is quite high. Similarly he argues that assault often occurs as part of the ritual of finding and retaining a sex partner, involving fighting off rivals and controlling partners.

The link between natural selection and child abuse drew its speculative basis from findings of animal studies that such behaviour occurred where the parents were unable to rear all their young, where one of the parents abandoned its parental duties, where the offspring had a low probability of being reproductively viable, and where there was a lack of close genetic connection between the offspring and the abusing parent (adoption or replacing defeated or deceased parent). Ellis then proposed a connection between the large category of property-based crime with a characteristic feature of gene-based evolutionary theory. The evolutionary claim is that every species aims to ensure the survival of its offspring, and one way of doing so is by (females) mating with (male) partners who are best able to provide the resources necessary for survival. The speculative claim is that many property crimes, as well as much violent crime, result from a genetic drive to attract and retain a mate. A supporting argument is that such a theory would explain why such crimes are apparently most commonly committed by those males with a low ability to provide, especially those in the lower social and economic groups.

It is clear that none of this offers any proof of genetic connections with crime and criminality: it is rather providing suggestive hypotheses drawn on the analogy of presumed explanations of animal behaviour. Much the same stricture applies to the attempt by Ellis (1990b) to explain aspects of the criminal justice system in similarly evolutionary terms. This draws mostly upon studies of primate groups where the dominant males patrol the groups to protect females and offspring, to control the rest of the group, and to protect their own mating interests. The hypothesis is that human control systems, and particularly that of criminal justice, reflect similar evolutionary imperatives. The exercise of control by the dominant group obviously favours the perpetuation of the *status quo* and hence safeguards the existing social structure and those individuals and groups already in positions of power. Even if the genetic and evolutionary impulses which are presumed to be behind these control systems have plausibility (but not proof) for primate groups, their explanatory power for accounting for complex human systems of criminal justice seems much more tenuous.

6.6.8.2 Genetic influences
The second strand relating genetics to criminality also contains elements of speculation. However, in sharp contrast to those considered above, these aspects arise more from the current limitations of scientific knowledge rather than from the inherent problems involved in basing imaginative leaps on dubious analogies. This second strand reflects the giant strides recently taken in the science of genetics. As little as a generation ago textbooks on genetics had little to say on humans, although, as already indicated in the first part of this chapter, this had not prevented strong assertions about the significance of human inheritance in determining the tendency of individuals towards criminal behaviour. As one prominent practitioner recently put it: 'Within ten years we will have the complete sequence of the three thousand million letters in the DNA alphabet which go to make up a human being. Enough of the genetic message has already been read to make it obvious that the instructions are far more complicated than was ever thought' (Jones (1993), p. x).

Apart from the sheer intellectual excitement of such advances, the developments in genetics are having major practical implications. It is clear, for example, that the propensity to contract many diseases is strongly affected by inheritance; and the particular genes related to particular diseases are being identified. Such features can have large social implications; already there are suggestions that insurance companies (and credit institutions) might wish to examine the genetic characteristics of potential clients. Not surprisingly, attention – and research – has tended to concentrate on such links with health, particularly since the genetic origins of some diseases prompt the possibility of genetic cures. Prudent geneticists are, however, much more cautious in claiming or expecting that human behaviour is primarily an inherited characteristic – that our genes determine how we act.

None the less, given the enormous potential implications of work in this field, it is not surprising that projections about its results have reflected on the possibility of using genetic engineering to manipulate human behavioural, as well as physical, characteristics. There has been a deluge of articles and features on these lines, some of which, even in the quality press, can be wildly speculative: one such piece was recently headed 'Divorce is in our genes'. Such coverage, if not such particular treatment, does reflect intelligent public concern, as was indicated by the number and passion of the letters published in response to a newspaper article on genetic determinism (*Guardian*, 11 and

13 June 1997). The relevance of such trends for theories of criminal behaviour is obvious, although little work directly relating genetic make-up to criminal behaviour has yet been carried out. If criminals can plausibly claim that they have no control over their actions which are the result of their genetic inheritance, both the practical and ethical bases of criminal justice systems would be substantially undermined.

The implication is that advances in genetics could foster a new determinism, more soundly based not only than the biological determinism sponsored by Lombroso's earlier experiments, but also than the economic determinism derived from Marx. Some prominent scientists are already far down this road: influential writers like Dawkins (1976, 1981) certainly seem to be saying that they see Darwinian natural selection as possibly providing a direct explanation of the complexities of culture and behaviour. It is much more complicated than that, and Dawkins himself has given (1981, pp. 9–16) a spirited refutation of the charge of genetic determinism. The significant point is that recent developments in this scientific field have given new life and liveliness to the ancient philosophical debate of Nature (inheritance) *versus* Nurture (environment): many would also claim that the result has been to shift the balance towards Nature.

More pertinently, many geneticists would say that it is imprudent to claim too much knowledge for this area: rapid as the advances have been, there is still only limited understanding about the ways in which inheritance of characteristics takes place even in relatively simple organisms. One major finding that is now generally established and accepted is that acquired characteristics are not inherited. This is not to deny that the offspring of musicians may not be above-average musically, or that the offspring of criminals may not be somewhat more likely to commit criminal offences; but the reason for this is not found in genetic inheritance. The loving pursuit by some sociologists (see Chapter Thirteen) of 'criminal families' cannot, as often claimed, demonstrate simple inheritance but can illuminate environmental influences: families share the same environment as well as the same genes. Even characters which are inherited 'involve', as one authority expresses it:

> gene and environment acting together. It is impossible to sort them into convenient compartments. An attribute such as intelligence is often seen as a cake which can be sliced into so much 'gene' and so much 'environment'. In fact, the two are so closely blended that trying to separate them is more like trying to unbake the cake. (Jones (1993), p. 171)

Where there is so much uncertainty, even over characters which can be measured, extra caution is needed in looking to genetics for explanations of such ambiguous concepts as criminal behaviour. None the less, the discovery that some traits of personality, such as aggressiveness, have a genetic component (Jones (1993), p.178) greatly strengthens the possibility that some criminal behaviour can be explained by a genetic susceptibility being then triggered by environmental factors.

6.6.9 An assessment of genetic factors

None of these studies conclusively proves that either 'Nature' or 'Nurture' are the only factors involved in criminality. It seems that each plays some part, but that it is impossible to ascertain their relative importance at this stage. The problem has been further exacerbated by the now fairly widely accepted claims (see Shah and Roth (1974)) that a foetus is affected by its environment before birth, so that even claims that a new-born child portrays a distinct personality is not proof that that personality was simply genetically inherited. What can be said with some certainty is that the evidence of these studies is insufficient to found a claim that genetics provides a complete explanation for criminality. The most that can be claimed is that some members of society, because of their physical or psychological make-up, which to some extent may be a genetic endowment, are more prone to criminality if other environmental factors are also present.

Furthermore, there is as yet no adequate biological explanation as to what exactly is being inherited. There is much research into this area but the topic is new and, although developing quickly, the precision of the information is insufficient to provide an explanation. To give some idea of the complexity, McKusick (1982) estimates that there are between 50,000 and 200,000 genetic loci making up the human genome, and then reports that by 1982 only 2,911 discrete genetically variable traits had been located, each of which represents a single genetic locus. When one considers that each locus has allelic variations which will alter the genetic make-up and that up to half of the gene loci may be connected to the functioning of the nervous system, the full complexity can be partially grasped. Although work is progressing very rapidly, sufficiently detailed knowledge does not yet exist to explain how the genetic information might be affecting the propensity towards criminality. As with the research into somatotypes, until such an explanation is forthcoming any discussion in this area is of limited value. Unless geneticists can explain how inheritance affects criminality, there is no acceptable way to help limit criminality except through controlling the environment so that fewer individuals are tempted to, or have the opportunity for, criminality. Even that carries the assumption that we know which aspects of the environment give rise to criminal behaviour.

What the biological theorists claim now (see 6.6.5 to 6.6.8) is not that criminality is inherited but rather that we inherit certain biological predispositions. In claiming this the researchers are not saying that there is a link between a specific gene and criminality or antisocial behaviour. Indeed, it is unlikely that a single gene pair could ever produce the complex traits which are generally associated with criminality. Instead genetic links may arise from the interrelationship of many genes each producing a relatively small effect. Therefore criminal behaviour, if it is related to genetics, may arise from particular combinations of normal genes rather than from defective genetic structures. Many physical traits are the result of polygenetic groupings and it is therefore likely that behaviour results from such complex interrelationships. Geneticists point out that: the formation of the central nervous system is dictated by genetics; that the central nervous system is the organ which dictates human behaviour including criminal behaviour; therefore, there must be a link between genetics and criminality. It is not claimed that any polygenetic groupings force an individual into criminal behaviour but rather that some may predispose them to certain types of behaviour. It is not clear how far this would justify claims increasingly being made that genetic and therefore biological factors are significant factors influencing certain types of criminal behaviour. What is not explained is how this predisposition is expanded and developed into antisocial or criminal activity in some individuals, but is subdued or channelled into non-criminal activities in others. The development of the predisposition could thus be wholly decided by the environment. The genetic explanations are not as yet sufficiently precise to be of any real use: they do not explain how this predisposition is passed on or what it is. The above studies do suggest a connection between crime and genetics, but thus far this information is of limited practical use as we do not understand how it operates.

6.7 CONCLUSION

Biological theories have been out of vogue for some time. On reading the earlier theorists and some of their suggestions for change, it is easy to understand how this distaste for biological theories arose. In the older writings, the argument is often that the biological reason is the only reason for criminality. These biological and genetic explanations have been seen as proving that a criminal is untreatable, lending plausibility to the idea that society might turn towards sterilisation of the carriers of these genetic or biological disorders to breed a less antisocial society. Other suggested remedies, such as locking them away for good or utilising the death penalty, raised similar ethical questions (for a further discussion, see 10.1.7).

Today it is unusual for such Draconian measures to be countenanced, but new ideas may bring with them implications which are equally unpalatable. Recent genetic work could certainly produce highly intrusive possibilities for the future. Scientists are trying to understand and link specific genetic structures with types of behaviour (see *Guardian*, 14 September 1989). Some of the behaviour may be antisocial or criminal. As yet this research is not far enough advanced to draw any conclusions, but the possible implications are disturbing. If firm links are drawn between types of behaviour and genes, this could lead to calls for selective breeding or genetic engineering to eradicate unwanted genes and unwanted behaviour. Such selection could be carried out in a number of different ways – sterilisation of those with unwanted genes; mass execution of these same groups of people; or by laws specifying legal and illegal breeding groups. Lastly, it may be possible to perform surgery on a very young foetus (under 14 days) and remove the unwanted genetic material before returning the foetus to its mother. Some of the issues in this area will be regulated by the Human Fertilisation and Embryology Act 1990. Most of these possibilities should be unacceptable in a democratic society, and yet if the evidence was sufficiently strong the arguments for such measures could be extremely persuasive. The work is still in its early stages, but we need to be aware that modern and seemingly objective scientific research could give results which could be used in wholly unacceptable ways. Biological research is not, of course, mostly being conducted to solve the problems caused by criminal behaviour. Its applications to this area can thus be ambiguous. For example, up to the present some of this research has had a far more positive part to play in crime control in the guise of genetic or DNA fingerprinting. The structure of each individual's DNA is very distinctive, and the possibility of two being the same is very low. For this reason it has been used in a number of cases of rape and murder in Britain and other western countries, although its reliability has been questioned (see Alldridge et al. (1994)). The analyses can be obtained from samples of hair, nails or from body fluids. If such materials are found at the scene of a crime, they can be matched up with possible suspects in order to solve a crime. Even here, however, there are potential dangers. For example, a future discovery could be that certain patterns of DNA are more prevalent among criminals than non-criminals. Such information could be used to control the lives of people, possibly even before they commit any crimes, or to control their right to have children. The dangers of this become even greater when one considers that a databank of DNA fingerprints is being constructed by the police to help in future cases, and Part IV of the Criminal Justice and Public Order Act 1994 invests the police with greater powers to obtain and retain intimate body samples. The danger is already growing and only awaits interpretation. Furthermore, if certain types of profile are discovered to be more prevalent amongst criminals or individuals who commit certain types of offences, this could lead to very severe punishments or other intrusive actions (see Alldridge et al. (1994)). Therefore even where a genetic process has possible positive outcomes, it may also generate problems or negative elements.

The lesson would seem to be that while criminologists cannot and must not obstruct biological research, they should be watchful to ensure that any discoveries made are used in humane, acceptable and positive ways. Even more importantly, they should be vigilant in ensuring that such knowledge is never used for negative or unacceptable intrusions. The need is the greater since the power of science on political and social decision-making can no longer be ignored.

REFERENCES

Alldridge, Peter, Berkhout-van Poelgeest, Sanneke and Williams, Katherine (1994), to be published in Chris Harding, Phil Fennell, Nico Jorg and Bert Schwarts (eds), *The Europeanisation of the Criminal Justice System*, Oxford: Oxford University Press.

Beccaria, Cesare (1964), *Of Crimes and Punishments* (first published 1776 as *Dei delitti e delle pene*) (6th edn), trans. by Fr. Kenelm Foster and Jane Grigson with an introduction by A.P. D'Entreves, London: Oxford University Press.

Bohman, M. (1978), 'Some Genetic Aspects of Alcoholism and Criminality', *Archives of General Psychiatry*, vol. 35, p. 176.

Bull, R.H.C. (1982), 'Physical Appearance and Criminality', *Current Psychological Reviews*, vol. 2, p. 269.

Cadoret, R.J., Cain, C.A. and Crowe, R.R. (1983), 'Evidence for Gene-Environment Interaction in the Development of Adolescent Antisocial Behaviour', *Behaviour Genetics*, vol. 13, p. 301.

Christiansen, K.O. (1968), 'Threshold of Tolerance in Various Population Groups Illustrated by Results from the Danish Criminological Twin Study', in A.V.S. de Reuck and R. Porter (eds), *The Mentally Abnormal Offender*, Boston: Little Brown.

Christiansen, K.O. (1974), 'Seriousness of Criminality and Concordance among Danish Twins', in Roger Hood (ed.), *Crime, Criminology and Public Policy*, London: Heinemann.

Cloninger, C.R. and Gottesman, I.I. (1987), 'Genetic and Environmental Factors in Antisocial Behaviour Disorders', in Sarnoff A. Mednick, Terrie E. Moffitt and Susan A. Stack, *The Causes of Crime: New Biological Approaches*, Cambridge: Cambridge University Press.

Cortes, Juan B. and Gatti, Florence M. (1972), *Delinquency and Crime: A Biopsychological Approach*, New York: Seminar Press.

Dalgaard, Steffen Odd and Kringlen, Einar (1976), 'A Norwegian Twin Study of Criminality', *British Journal of Criminology*, vol. 16, p. 213.

Dawkins, R. (1976), *The Selfish Gene*, Oxford: Oxford University Press.

Dawkins, R. (1982), *The Extended Phenotype*, Oxford: Oxford University Press.

Driver, Edwin D. (1960), 'Charles Buckman Goring', in Hermann Mannheim (ed.), *Pioneers in Criminology*, London: Stevens and Sons.

Driver, Edwin D. (1972), The introductory essay of C. Goring, *The English Convict: A Statistical Study*, Montclair, New Jersey: Patterson Smith.

Dugdale, Richard (1877), *The Jukes: A Study in Crime, Pauperism, Disease and Heredity*, Putnam: New York: reprinted (1977), New York: Arno.

Ellis, Havelock (1900), *The Criminal*, 2nd edn, New York: Scribner.

Ellis, Lee (1990a), 'The Evolution of Violent Criminal Behaviour and its Nonlegal Equivalent', in Lee Ellis and Harry Hoffman (eds), *Crime in Biological, Social, and Moral Contexts*, New York: Praeger.

Ellis, Lee (1990b), 'The Evolution of Collective Counterstrategies to Crime: from the Primate Control Role to the Criminal Justice System', in Lee Ellis and Harry Hoffman (eds), *Crime in Biological, Social, and Moral Contexts*, New York: Praeger.

Ellis, Lee and Hoffman, Harry (eds) (1990), *Crime in Biological, Social, and Moral Contexts*, New York: Praeger.

Fink, Arthur E. (1985) (first published in 1938), *Causes of Crime*, London: Greenwood.

Foucault, Michel (1977), *Discipline and Punish: The Birth of the Prison*, trans. by Alan Sheridan, Harmondsworth: Penguin.

Guardian, 14 September 1989.

Garland, David (1985), *Punishment and Welfare: A History of Penal Strategies*, Aldershot: Gower.

Glueck, Sheldon and Glueck, Eleanor (1950), *Unravelling Juvenile Delinquency*, New York: Commonwealth Fund.

Goring, Charles Buchman (1913), *The English Convict: A Statistical Study*, London: HMSO.

Gottfredson, Michael R. and Hirschi, Travis (1990), *A General Theory of Crime*, Stanford, Calif: Stanford University Press.

Hooton, E.A. (1939), *The American Criminal: An Anthropological Study*, Cambridge, Mass.: Harvard University Press.

Hutchings, Barry and Mednick, Sarnoff A. (1977), 'Criminality in Adoptees and Their Adoptive and Biological Parents: A Pilot Study', published in Sarnoff A. Mednick and Karl O. Christensen (eds), *Biosocial Bases of Criminal Behaviour*, New York: Gardner Press.

Jacobs, P.A., Brunton, M. and Melville, M.M. (1965), 'Aggressive Behaviour, Mental Subnormality and the XYY male', *Nature*, vol. 208, p. 1351.

Jenaway, A. and Swinton, M. (1993), 'Triplets where Monozygotic Siblings are Concordant for Arson', *Medicine, Science and the Law*, vol. 33, p. 350.

Jones, S. (1993) *The Language of the Genes*, London: Harper Collins.

Kretschmere, Erenst (1921), *Physique and Character*, 2nd edn, translated by W.J.H. Sprott, and reprinted (1936), New York: Cooper Square Publishers.

Lange, Johannes (1929), *Verbrechen als Shicksal: Studien an Kriminellen Zwillingen*, trans. by Charlotte Haldane, (1930), *Crime as Destiny*, New York: Charles Boni.

Latter, B.D.H. (1980), 'Genetic Differences within and between Populations of the Major Human Subgroups', *American Naturalist*, vol. 116, p. 220.

Lombroso, Cesare, *L'Uomo Delinquente*, first published (1876), 5th and final edn, (1897), Torino: Bocca.

Lombroso, Cesare (1906), *Crime: Causes et Remèdes*, 2nd edn, Paris: Alcan.

McKusick, V.A. (1982), 'Genetic Disorders of the Human Nervous System: a Commentary', in O. Schmitt, S.J. Bird and F.E. Bloom (eds), *Molecular Genetic Neuroscience*, New York: Raven Press.

Mednick, Sarnoff A., Gabrielli, T., William F. and Hutchings, Barry (1984), 'Genetic Influences on Criminal Convictions: Evidence from an Adoption Cohort', *Science*, vol. 224, p. 891.

Rowe, David C. (1990), 'Inherited Dispositions toward Learning Delinquent and Criminal Behaviour: New Evidence', in Lee Ellis and Harry Hoffman (eds), *Crime in Biological, Social, and Moral Contexts*, New York: Praeger.

Rowe, David C. and Rodgers, J.L. (1989), 'Behaviour Genetics, Adolescent Deviance, and "d": Contributions and Issues', in G.R. Adams, R. Montemayor and T.P. Gullotta (eds), *Advances in Adolescent Development*, Newbury Park, Calif: Sage, pp. 38–67.

Rushton, J.P. (1985), 'Differential K theory: the Sociobiology of Individual and Group Differences', *Personality and Individual Differences*, vol. 6, p. 441.

Rushton, J.P. (1988), 'Race Differences in Behaviour: a Review and Evolutionary Analysis', *Personality and Individual Differences*, vol. 9, p.1009.

Rushton, J.P. and Bogaert, A.F. (1987), 'Race Differences in Sexual Behaviour: Testing and Evolutionary Hypothesis', *Journal of Research in Personality*, vol. 21, p. 529.

Sarbin, T.R. and Miller, J.E. (1970), 'Demonism Revisited: The XYY Chromosome Anomaly' *Issues in Criminology*, vol. 5, p. 199.

Shah, Saleem A. and Roth, Loren H. (1974), 'Biological and Psycho-physiological Factors in Criminality', in Daniel Glaser (ed.), *Handbook of Criminology*, Chicago: Rand McNally.
Sheldon, William H. (1949), *Varieties of Delinquent Youth*, New York and London: Harper.
Sutherland, Edwin H. and Cressey, Donald R. (1978), *Criminology*, 10th edn, Philadelphia: J. B. Lippincott Company.
Vold, George B. and Bernard, Thomas J. (1986), *Theoretical Criminology*, New York: Oxford University Press.
Walters, Glenn D. (1992), 'A Meta-analysis of the Gene–Crime Relation-ship', *Criminology*, vol. 30, p. 595.
Watkin, Herman A. et al. (1977), 'XYY and XXY Men: Criminality and Aggression' published in Sarnoff A. Mednick and Karl O. Christiansen (eds), *Biosocial Bases of Criminal Behaviour*, New York: Gardner Press.
Whitney, Glayde (1990), 'On Possible Genetic Bases of Race Differences in Criminality', in Lee Ellis and Harry Hoffman (eds), *Crime in Biological, Social, and Moral Contexts*, New York: Praeger.
Wolfgang, Marvin E. (1960), 'Cesare Lombroso', in Herman Mannheim (ed.), *Pioneers in Criminology*, London: Stevens & Sons.

CHAPTER SEVEN

Influences of Biochemical Factors and of the Central and Autonomic Nervous Systems on Criminality

7.1 BIOCHEMICAL FACTORS

7.1.1 Introduction

It was in the last century that hormones, the secretions of the endocrine gland, were first discovered and artificially copied in laboratories. The interest in the effects of these substances grew and their significance to the personality began to be studied (see Berman (1921)). Eventually, interest turned towards the effects of hormonal imbalance on criminal activity. Berman (1938) conducted one of the early studies on 250 inmates of Sing Sing prison in New York compared with a non-criminal control group. His results suggested that the incidence of hormonal imbalance in the prisoners was two or three times greater than in the control, which led him to the conclusion that hormonal imbalances had an adverse effect on crime commission. That is to say that the imbalances affected the brain's thinking powers and motor control, which might lead to criminality. More recently, researchers (see Shah and Roth (1974), p. 122) have not found the same results, and the general consensus seems to be that most hormone imbalances do not significantly affect criminality. It is unsurprising that researchers have found it difficult to discover any causal link between hormonal activity and criminality or other behaviour because hormones have only an indirect effect on behaviour. Therefore, although hormones may act as a catalyst for behaviour or may provide a biological environment favourable to other causal factors, they have rarely been found to be connected to criminality.

There are a few exceptions to this, most of which involve an imbalance in the sex hormones. A factor which affects women is the unusually large hormonal changes which occur just before and during menstruation, often referred to as premenstrual tension (PMT) and menstrual tension (MT).

These have been accepted as factors which can mitigate the sentence in some cases (see 17.2.4). The other main exception seems to be in the relationship between the level of the male sex hormone, testosterone, and criminality, particularly violent criminality (see below, 7.1.2).

The preponderant opinion amongst criminologists that hormone imbalances do not effect criminality has occasionally been disregarded in the criminal law. These discrepancies have not led to any public dissension. For example, criminal law and society generally accept that the recognised defence of infanticide (Infanticide Act 1938, s. 1) is an acceptable and, prior to the abolition of the death penalty, a very necessary defence against one category of murder charge. It is a recognition that a mother who kills her child within twelve months of giving birth to it should be given some allowance, either because her mind was disturbed by reason of having given birth or because of lactation consequent on the birth. The assumption is that the reason the mother kills must be the effect on her mind of one of these events. The acceptance of infanticide as a defence to a murder charge is a recognition that hormone imbalance, though not other biochemical imbalances, might in such cases be a cause of crime.

If hormone imbalance is not responsible for criminality, then it would seem to follow that the defence of infanticide should be abolished or justified on psychiatric, psychological or mental grounds. What is not in doubt, however, is that society is ready, irrespective of the origin or underlying cause, to accept that a mother should not be convicted of murder in those circumstances (for a further discussion of infanticide see especially 9.2.5). On the other hand, the view that hormonal imbalance does not produce criminal conduct (see Shah and Roth (1974), p. 122) has been instrumental in preventing premenstrual or menstrual tension from being generally recognised by the criminal courts or Parliament as a full defence. If used at all, it tends to be as a reason for reducing the sentence of the court (see 17.2.4).

There are a number of body fluids or chemicals which have been said to affect criminality, and more particularly aggression. Fishbein (1990) has noted that individuals who have psychopathic tendencies, antisocial personalities, or who exhibit violent behaviour or conduct disorders often have biochemical imbalances in hormones, neurotransmitters, toxins and metabolic products; he has also linked levels of psychopathy to different electroencephalogram (EEG) traces and cardiovascular rates and variations in electrodermal changes. Although it is a relatively new area, the initial research suggests some connection between biochemical factors and criminality. This chapter will consider its use as a tool to explain crime and possibly to prevent or control criminal activity. Work in this area is once again gaining political interest, and financial backing. How much this has to do with biological causes of criminality and how much is to do with a desire to locate the reasons for social problems, such as crime in the individual rather than in society, is something which will be considered in the conclusion.

7.1.2 Testosterone

Testosterone has been popularly related to the most aggressive and antisocial crimes such as rape and murder. The claim is that the male sex hormone, plasma testosterone, adversely affects the central nervous system causing aggressive behaviour. The exact meaning of aggressive or violent behaviour is rarely defined in these studies, but most of the writers are interested in interpersonal violence such as rape, murder and assault. Here, only a general introduction to some of the central research in this area will be undertaken and some of the more interesting results presented.

In tests on monkeys, Rose, Bernstein, Gorden and Catlin (1974) discovered that testosterone, the male hormone, was related to the aggressive behaviour of the monkeys. They proved that once a monkey finds his position in the social structure the level of testosterone does not affect that position, nor does it affect his aggression, but that a change in social setting will affect the testosterone level. This means that the testosterone level would increase if the monkey was put into a weaker colony, so encouraging him to use his superiority against other monkeys, and would decrease if he was introduced into a stronger colony, so dissuading him from challenging stronger males. The implication is that remembered environmental experience will trigger biological hormonal changes. Keverne, Meller and Eberhart (1982) discovered that males held in separate cages had very similar testosterone levels, and that when each was individually introduced to a single female the increases in testosterone were of a similar size, but that when they were introduced into a mixed social grouping the high ranking, dominant monkeys produced large quantities of testosterone but the low ranking monkeys produced only very small quantities. Interestingly, the high ranking monkeys showed greater sexual interest in the females than the low ranking ones, but they were not more aggressive than the others. The low ranking monkeys were more frequently the objects of other monkeys' aggression. When they were returned to separate cages there was again no difference in the testosterone levels of high and low ranking monkeys.

From the above there seems to be a close relationship between the environment and the hormonal balance in some monkeys, but as yet this is not fully understood. It is not clear whether the obvious association between aggression and testosterone in monkeys is proof of biological causation or not. In monkeys a further indication of the connection between aggression and testosterone can be found by implanting that hormone into females. This produces male-like behaviours such as enhanced aggressive behaviour and an increased interest in sex. The effects are most marked if the implant takes place prior to birth or immediately thereafter, i.e., while the central nervous system is still forming.

In humans the same male hormone exists and is thought to have similar effects. In studies on humans, men's testosterone levels are measured and then a psychological rating scale is used to measure aggression and social dominance. In some studies, aggressive male criminals are tested and their past records of aggressive behaviour are considered along with the other factors. In most men the testosterone levels probably do not significantly affect levels of aggression (for example, see Persky, Smith and Basu (1971), and Scarmella and Brown (1978)). In studies of proven violent male prisoners the results suggest that testosterone levels had an effect on aggressive and sexual behaviour, but even these results were not as strong as might be expected from the animal studies (see for example Kreuz and Rose (1972), and Ehrenkranz, Bliss and Sheard (1974)).

One factor which some have argued limits the usefulness of these studies on humans is that they do not separate out differing forms of aggression. They usually consider only actual bodily violence, whereas human aggression is frequently verbal. Furthermore, within both verbal and physical aggression or violence there is a distinct difference between persons who wantonly seek out or cause violent situations and those who defend themselves if violence is forced upon them. This distinction also needs to be studied. Lastly, the complexity of human personality requires attention to be paid to elements such as social dominance, sensation seeking, assertiveness, extroversion, sociability and other social factors as well as aggression. Dan Olwens (1987) and Daisy Schalling (1987) have each conducted studies which address some of these problems. Dan Olwens' study was conducted on young men with no marked criminal career. Daisy Schalling's study was conducted on a group of young male inmates with a control group of males of a similar age.

Dan Olwens first found a clear connection between testosterone and both verbal and physical aggression. He then noticed a distinction between provoked and unprovoked aggressive behaviour. Provoked aggressive behaviour, which tended to be verbal more often than physical, was a response to unfair or threatening behaviour by another; any other aggression would be unprovoked. The most interesting form of unprovoked violence was destructive, and included activities such as gratuitously starting fights and making unpleasant comments. Olwens carried out some preliminary research of his own and also considered a large amount of research carried out by others. These all suggested a connection between testosterone and aggression, so he set out to discover, for a group of boys, first whether there was a connection, and, secondly, whether or not the testosterone caused the activities. He used path analysis to discover the causal relationship. Path analysis takes account of the statistical relationship between various factors (including such things as upbringing and parental use of power as well as testosterone) and the behaviour studied, e.g., unprovoked violence or antisocial behaviour. The results suggested that provoked violence was directly associated with levels of testosterone. In these boys, the provocation resulted in heightened testosterone production and so more aggressive behaviour. The testosterone production was directly related to the aggression, but was only produced in response to environmental circumstances.

The relationship between testosterone and unprovoked violence and antisocial behaviour was indirect and would depend on, among other things, how irritable the individual was. The relationship is here rather more complex and needs explaining. In young boys, Olwens explains, unprovoked aggression tends to result from certain types of upbringing – parental use of power and aggression, parental and particularly maternal permissiveness of aggression. Low frustration tolerance will often result if the mother is permissive of aggression. Until puberty, unprovoked aggression and low frustration tolerance appear to be unrelated. In puberty, high levels of testosterone have marked effects upon the low frustration levels. Boys who already have a low frustration level become more impatient and irritable and are increasingly willing to participate in unprovoked and often destructive aggression. The testosterone thus seems to have an indirect effect on aggression by acting on the tolerance level. Olwens also found a weak but indirect relationship between testosterone and general antisocial behaviour. He concluded that there was an interesting and important connection between testosterone and aggression which merited further study. Testosterone was, however, only one of many factors affecting aggression, and possibly only a minor one.

Daisy Schalling discovered that high testosterone levels in young males were associated with verbal aggression but not with actual physical aggression or fighting. This, she said, portrayed a desire, on behalf of the high testosterone boys, to protect their status by threats. The low testosterone level boys would tend not to protect their position, preferring to avoid conflict and remain silent. High testosterone boys tended to shun monotony; to enjoy physical and competitive sports; to be more extrovert and sociable; and cared less about conventional rules and attitudes. Schalling thus portrays high testosterone boys as assertive, self-assured, sociable, and liable to become angry when aroused.

These findings are largely consistent with Olwens' finding that high testosterone levels in males cause low levels of tolerance, making them easily provoked and more likely to respond aggressively. Neither study suggests that there is a direct link between aggression and testosterone, but simply that if the correct social circumstances arise, especially a provocative situation, then those with an ability to secrete high levels of testosterone are most likely to resort to violence or aggression. The ability to secrete a high quantity of testosterone is a biological characteristic. Whether large amounts of testosterone are secreted depends upon the situations in which the individual finds himself. If that situation is provocative, it may lead to aggression and criminality may arise; if it is merely the setting for physical activity, e.g., sport, the high testosterone might be secreted but have its effects in more positive and acceptable ways. It is still unclear how the testosterone level interacts with social factors.

High levels of testosterone have also been related to crime generally and to sexual aggression. Ellis and Coontz (1990) note that testosterone peaks during puberty and early 20s, which correlates with the highest crime rates, and they claim that socio-environmental researchers have failed to explain why this distribution exists across almost all societies and cultures. They claim that this is persuasive support for a biological explanation and draw on testosterone to explain both property and aggressive criminality. The evidence for such a connection is very tenuous and does not arise from direct experimental data: a similar criticism can be made of the claim that testosterone is linked with sexual crime. Sexual assaults by males, particularly rape, tend to be committed by men at an age when their sex hormones are very strong. This is not sufficient to prove a causal relationship, and generally rapists and non-rapists have not been found to have very different levels of testosterone but the most violent rapists have been found to have very high levels of the hormone (see Rada et al. (1983)). Despite these findings there is no evidence that there is any causal relationship between the behaviour and the level of testosterone. The link may be more facilitative – providing the biological environment necessary for sexual aggression – rather than strictly causative. Despite this some causal link has been suggested as a result of therapies which have been used to try to reduce sexual violence. Earlier this century some countries, such as Denmark (1920), Germany (1933), Norway (1934), Estonia (1937) and Sweden (1944) (amongst others) legalised castration for sex offenders. Thousands of such operations were conducted, but it was never proved that such methods would reduce levels of sexual aggression. More recently a system of chemical castration has become available so that the physical operation is rarely conducted. The chemicals operate by latching on to the cellular binding sites in the brain, and elsewhere in the body, which testosterone would use to have its effect. The drugs therefore prevent or limit the effects of the hormone. Therefore today antiandrogen drugs such as cyproterone acetate and medroxyprogesterone acetate are offered to aggressive sex offenders as an alternative to castration. These drugs have been found to reduce some of the effects of testosterone and have proved to be fairly effective in certain cases (see Walker et al. (1984), p. 440 and Rubin (1987), p. 248). In this way, the causative link is, to an extent, implied although Walker considered that the drugs were of real use only in high doses and when other positive environmental conditions exist: the individual volunteers for treatment; lack of substance abuse; there is a sexually consenting partner. Certainly none of the studies or the treatments explains the link, and in the absence of any convincing explanation its practical significance is limited, particularly as it may be that social and environmental factors trigger the testosterone levels which are being claimed as the cause of the criminality. If this is the case it might be better to address these rather than the levels of testosterone. To decide this it is necessary to assess which would be less intrusive of individual liberty and which provides the clearest reduction in criminality. The choice is then a social and political decision.

Ellis and Coontz (1990) try to provide a partial explanation for the effects of testosterone. As mentioned above they note that the age and sex rates for criminality have about the same variation as levels of testosterone, and claim that this shows a possible causative link with both property crimes and aggressive behaviour against victims. They explain that the androgen testosterone has a strong presence in the male foetus before birth and is central to the formation of the sex of the child. At this stage it passes into the brain where they claim it affects development. The effects are strongest in male foetuses as the levels of testosterone are much higher. Female androgens might have similar effects, but as they do not pass into the brain this does not occur. Ellis and Coontz claim that testosterone in the brain at this early stage and again later produces three main effects, each of which they see as related to criminality.

First, the rate at which stimuli reach the brain is controlled by reticular arousability – the level of development of a bundle of fibres located at the base of the brain controls the way in which external stimuli will be passed on to the brain. The development is dictated by genetics, some of which are located on the Y-chromosome. As evidence of this they show that certain medical problems such as cot death, hyperactivity and sex differences to the toleration of pain are all gender dependent, the first two occurring more frequently in males than females and the latter being sex dependent. They then link this low reticular arousal with criminality (see 7.1.3 and 7.3.1, below), that is, a person who needs very high levels of stimulation will perform such behaviours (including criminal behaviour) to produce this result. He will then be less affected by negative stimulation, which in others would deter behaviours with very high stimulation levels.

Secondly, the limbic system which controls emotions such as rage, love-hate, jealousy, envy and religious fervour can be affected by testosterone levels in the brain. Problems with the limbic area may cause sudden and unpredictable emotions to arise, even in response to normal occurrences. These have been linked with epilepsy and epileptic seizures, and the proof for their relation to testosterone is that they are far more common in men. Ellis and Coontz then draw on research which links criminality to epilepsy and epileptic tendencies to suggest, therefore, a link between testosterone and criminality (see 7.3.2, below).

Thirdly, they point to a link between domination of a particular brain hemisphere and criminality, suggesting that heavy reliance on the hemisphere that is least open to reason, logic and linguistic statements and most closely related to the limbic system is related to criminality (see 7.3.3.2, below). Reliance on this hemisphere is more common in males than females: proof of this arises from the fact that there are more left-handed or ambidextrous men than women.

These three factors they put forward as an indication that criminal behaviour which involves a victim, but particularly aggressive behaviour, is more likely amongst those whose brains have been or are being affected by high levels of androgens, particularly testosterone. If correct, this moves us a step closer to explaining a causal link, if one exists, between criminality and testosterone, but it does no more than that. Probably the most that can be said is that the relationship between testosterone and crime, particularly aggressive crime, is sufficiently strong to merit further study.

Even with further study one needs to consider what can be done with the results. Are all male criminals to be placed on antiandrogen drugs, or even all aggressive male criminals? Despite the fact that the effects of these drugs are generally reversible and that they have relatively few side-effects, some people do react with increased weight, higher blood pressure, abnormal glucose tolerance and gall-bladder malfunctions, all of which could be serious. In addition, there would be a marked reduction in offspring among those subjected to these drugs and they are therefore a form of control on birth levels to these individuals: such interference should never be lightly treated. Therefore even if there is a proven link to testosterone, the way in which this might be treated carries with it many problems and so the usefulness of the information is reduced.

7.1.3 Adrenalin

The relationship between adrenalin and aggressive behaviour is a similar area of study to that involving testosterone. Each involves the relationship between a hormonal level and aggressive antisocial behaviour. In the case of adrenalin, Olwens (1987) found a negative relationship between adrenalin and aggression. Adrenalin levels are outwardly shown by the level of cortical arousal. Cortical arousal is a psychological state which usually involves all the outward portrayals of fear or excitement – high blood flow leading to more moisture on the skin, general alertness, etc. It is this which is measured by a lie detector, as most people have a 'fear' of being discovered lying. When a subject is being studied in non-stressful situations a low level of adrenalin and a low cortical arousal are often found in those with an habitually aggressive tendency. Hare (1982) also found that, when threatened with pain, criminals exhibited both fewer signs of stress and heightened cortical arousal than did other people. Furthermore, Mednick et al. (1982) discovered that not only do certain criminals, particularly violent criminals, take stronger stimuli to arouse them, but also that once they are in a stressed state (heightened cortical arousal) they recover more slowly to their normal levels than do non-criminals. Mednick et al. linked rapid recovery to an ability to learn from unpleasant stimuli, including punishment, suggesting that criminals, particularly violent criminals, are less able to learn acceptable behaviour from either negative or positive stimuli. Each of these studies links cortical arousal to adrenalin. Such a link is unsurprising and permits explanation and findings to be borrowed from those who research into cortical arousal. Eysenck (1959) reasons the relationship in this way: an individual with a low cortical arousal is easily bored, becomes quickly disinterested in things, and craves exciting experiences which will suspend this state of disinterest. For such subjects, normally stressful situations are not disturbing; rather they are exciting and enjoyable, something to be savoured and sought after. This alone would not necessarily be sufficient to enhance the use of aggression. It is important to note that those who enjoy high stimulation may turn to sport, exciting jobs or other outlets. The choice will depend on social and environmental influences rather than on biology, but when a desire for high stimulation is coupled with social and environmental conditions (such as parental aggression or parental permissiveness of violence) an individual may find excitement and arousal in that aggressive behaviour. Subjects with a similarly low cortical arousal who have not been exposed to habitually aggressive behaviour need not portray such antisocial aggressive behaviour. They are unlikely to seek out violence but may well resort to violence when provoked. At the other end of the spectrum, subjects with high cortical arousal generally avoid stressful aggressive or arousing situations.

Mednick et al. (1977) have suggested that the link between arousal and violent criminality is stronger in individuals from higher socio-economic groups. It would follow that because aggression is more normal behaviour in the lower socio-economic groups, it may be learned as being acceptable and will not therefore be so dependent on a person being neurologically incapable of responding to socialisation, whereas, in higher socio-economic groups, aggression is less acceptable conduct and will not be learned as normal behaviour, so will be more dependent on low arousal rates. These are generalisations of behaviour patterns which might well be affected by other stimuli. The results do suggest an inverse relationship between adrenalin and aggression, which stimulate interesting hypotheses for testing. The results could contribute to an understanding of how upbringing affects criminality.

Baldwin (1990) suggests that the link between age and crime rates can be partially explained by considering arousal rates and certain other biological aspects. He notes that all individuals enjoy stimulation at some level and that children quickly become used to stimuli which formerly frightened them and seek other, more exciting input. Of course if a stimulus gives unpleasant results the individual will usually learn to avoid the behaviour but the more pleasant the experience the more quickly the child will become used to it and, certainly if he or she enjoys high arousal, will wish to move on to more stimulating behaviours. Therefore the enjoyment of high stimulation will be fed if there are rewards and no painful experiences from the activities. The second factor which runs along with stimulation is skill: as a child develops, he or she learns new skills. Each child has a capacity for learning which Baldwin suggests is in part biological, but he recognises that much more important are the social and environmental inputs which dictate the types of skill or behaviour learned. He concludes that criminal activity in young people depends in part on the arousal levels which may be led by adrenalin, but also on strong socialisation for certain behaviours and on the types of behaviours that are available – sport and rewarding, exciting, legal activities or only crime and delinquency. Biology may predispose to enjoyment of exciting behaviour, but socialisation and environment will dictate the type of activity learned. Finally Baldwin turns to an explanation of the reduction of crime with age. First he notes that certain crimes appear only later in life or decline much more slowly than others (white-collar crimes) but that, for the most part, crime declines quickly during the early 20s. He explains this partly by the fact that the stiumulus received from (criminal) types of behaviour tends to decline over time, and partly by the fact that many crimes depend on physical fitness, strength or agility and as this declines so the ability to perform certain criminal acts declines. Interestingly, both in explaining the decline in criminality and its learning it seems that environmental factors may lead to a change in the effects of the stimulation and so in the desire to seek stimulation. This then raises the question whether the production of adrenalin is biologically or environmentally dictated. If the levels of adrenalin may be linked with criminality, are these causally linked or are the levels of adrenalin and criminality both caused by other factors?

7.1.4 Neurotransmitters
Substances such as serotonin, dopamine and norepinephrine all transmit signals between neurons in the brain. In animal studies, each of these substances has been linked to violent or aggressive behaviour, and low levels of serotonin have been linked to violence and suicide in humans. These

substances, rather like adrenaline, may be produced by aggression rather than cause it, so here again there is a serious problem associated with the nature of the link. In the case of serotonin it is an unusually low level which causes the problem, whereas excesses of dopamine and norepinephrine are considered to be undesirable. In each case it seems that mechanisms in the brain which affect moods or control behaviour may be impaired.

7.1.5 An assessment of biochemical factors

Many of the writers in this area admit that these biochemical effects cannot be studied in a void, and they note that attention needs to be given to the interaction of behavioural changes, the environment and the psychological characteristics of the individual. But often such links are not clearly defined. The connections between biochemical factors and school problems, or biochemical factors and personality problems, clearly suggest themselves as fruitful areas for future investigation.

What does emerge from this research is that behaviour, including criminal behaviour, is probably linked in some way to biochemical factors. The first problem facing criminologists is to explain that link and to determine whether criminal or antisocial behaviour is caused by biochemical changes or imbalances or *vice versa*; or, indeed, whether both are related to other causes. If, in the future, it should be demonstrated that crime is caused by biochemical imbalances, it would be necessary to consider what response would be appropriate – to try to change the biochemical balance of high-risk individuals through drug therapy; to alter their environment so that the behaviour is not triggered; or to incarcerate offenders for extended periods so as to incapacitate them.

7.2 NUTRITIONALLY INDUCED BIOCHEMICAL IMBALANCES

7.2.1 Introduction

Another theory is that criminality is the result of some biochemical imbalances which are due to external factors such as nutrition. There have been claims recently that foods such as 'chips' or 'sweets' cause criminality. These are ill-founded; scientists have never suggested such a simplistic causal relationship. There have, however, been some claims that food can cause biochemical imbalances in the brain that lead to behaviour changes, some of which may induce criminal actions. These ideas have been used particularly in the case of juveniles, and have sometimes been referred to as 'orthomolecular medicine'. The imbalances caused by the diet can, it is argued, lead directly or indirectly to delinquent behaviour by lowering the child's ability to learn and obey social rules (see Hippochen (1978) and 10.2). Of course, similar brain imbalances may be caused by other factors such as brain damage after an accident or a traumatic experience, or by an illness which affects the brain.

Study into diet as a cause of criminality is not new. At the end of the last century a number of individuals, particularly some of those in charge of institutions, were claiming that diet could affect behaviour as well as health (see Egleston (1893)). Claims of this sort have continued to be made this century (see Price (1945)). Some of these were based on scientific observations, others on mere conjecture, but there was little truly scientific study undertaken. Two animal studies suggest that nutrition may affect behaviour. Pottenger (1983) discovered that cats fed on cooked foods were likely to suffer certain illnesses and exhibited poor learning ability and poor social interaction. Nor were these ill effects corrected simply by altering the diet; they lingered through as many as three generations. McCarrison (1981) found that rats fed with a refined diet resorted to high levels of aggression. The suggestion was that humans would be similarly affected by their diet.

Research on a fully objective basis is complicated in this area because each individual is different. Nutritional needs vary, and so do reactions to different nutrients or combinations of nutrients. Thus, exact scientific measurement of the effects of different foods or diets is difficult. For this reason it is hard to assess the effects of food generally on behaviour: in this section an attempt is made to assess the effects of particular food-stuffs.

7.2.2 Blood sugar

It has frequently been suggested that blood sugar levels are connected with antisocial and criminal behaviour. Shoenthaler (1982) describes experiments in which he discovered that by lowering the daily sucrose intake of juveniles who were held in detention it was possible to reduce the level of their antisocial behaviour. It seemed to have a particular effect upon the levels of violence, where reductions of up to 50 per cent were claimed. He later found similar changes in behaviour by altering diet in rather different ways, and therefore concluded that both the level of sugar products added to nutritional foods and the ratio of carbohydrates to protein were associated with violent behaviour. Basically, he seems to be concluding that no one particular food type is causing the misbehaviour, but rather that it will occur if the whole diet of the individual is unbalanced and not providing proper nourishment. A discussion of the effects of under-nutrition on the central nervous system and thus on aggression can be found in Smart (1981) where the causal connections are discussed in more detail.

The most common claim in this area is that there is a connection between hypoglycaemia (a deficiency of glucose in the bloodstream) and criminality. The main symptoms of hypoglycaemia are emotional instability, nervousness, mental confusion, general physical weakness, delirium and violence. In severe cases, the individual may also be prone to automatic behaviour and to retrograde amnesia (see Clapham (1989)). Although not all these symptoms are evident in any one case or at any one time, they encourage claims that hypoglycaemia affects criminality (see Shah and Roth (1974), pp. 125–6).

Within hypoglycaemia, some claim that there is a particularly strong relationship between violence and reactive hypoglycaemia, that is, a tendency towards very low blood sugar levels as a reaction to being given a large dose of glucose. Reactive hypoglycaemia has been noted in adults who have both violent and antisocial personality problems. In a study carried out by

Virkkunen (1987), violent, antisocial males were compared both to violent males who did not suffer from similar antisocial personality problems and to normal law-abiding males. Each individual fasted overnight and was then given a set dose of glucose. The blood sugar levels were tested immediately prior to the glucose and then at hourly intervals thereafter for the next five hours. The blood glucose level in the violent and antisocial personality group fell to a very low level and remained at that low level for markedly longer than the smaller drops suffered by either the violent controls or the normal controls. In other studies the same author has linked hypoglycaemia with other activities often defined as antisocial, such as truancy, low verbal IQ, tattooing, stealing from one's own home in childhood, more than two criminal convictions, and violence of the individual's father under the influence of alcohol. The most interesting of these is possibly the connection with alcohol. Hypoglycaemia is often linked with alcohol, and if alcohol is imbibed regularly and in large quantities, the ethanol can induce hypoglycaemia and increase aggression. In many studies, habitual violence and alcohol are linked (see 9.5).

An interesting example of the very excessive effects which may be brought about by hypoglycaemia was referred to by Clapham (1989). He cites a case in which a man who had stabbed his wife and caused her death and also slit his own wrists (not fatally) was found not guilty of murder because at the time he was acting as an automaton. The husband had been on a very severe diet for the two months preceding his wife's killing, losing three stones in weight. The diet was basically one of Ryvita, cheese and apple, and he was allowed no sugar, bread, potatoes or fried food. On the morning of the killing he had drunk two whiskeys. Immediately after the killing he was found to be suffering from amnesia. He was subjected to some blood sugar tests while in prison. These were administered a few weeks after he had been returned to a normal diet, but they showed that he was still suffering from reactive hypoglycaemia. Medical experts testified that the hypoglycaemia was sufficient to impair normal brain functioning and substantially impair his mental responsibility, perhaps even to render him an automaton. The jury cleared him of all blame. This shows that the effects of reactive hypoglycaemia have been accepted in a court as a defence to murder and therefore as the sole cause of the actions of the individual.

In the above case the reason for the hyperglycaemic condition was fairly obvious – lack of a stable diet. In some cases the explanation is not necessarily directly related to food, and it has been related to the intake of alcohol and even to an allergy to tobacco.

It is possible for some foods and other substances to cause adverse effects on behaviour if the individual is in some way allergic to them. Such behavioural changes and their exact effects will vary from individual to individual, but it may be that some foods, and in particular certain additives, have effects which may lead to criminality or hyperactivity (see Prinz, Robert and Hantman (1980)). An American case provides a notable use of a defence on these grounds: a San Francisco murder in which the defendant had shot the Mayor. The shooting had clearly been premeditated, but the defendant pleaded diminished responsibility because he claimed there was a chemical imbalance in his brain which affected his behaviour and was caused by his eating too much 'junk food' including chocolates. In particular, he claimed he had consumed too many Twinkies (a particular sort of 'junk food'). The jury accepted this defence, and so he was convicted only of manslaughter. This type of defence became known as the 'Twinkie Defence'. It was one of the main factors in the abolition of diminished responsibility as a defence in California. In at least one case in Britain a similar defence has been used (see Martin (1987); Curran and Renzetti (1994)).

7.2.3 Cholesterol

A more recent line of research involves the effects of cholesterol levels on criminality. In 1966 Hatch, Reisell, Poon-King, Canellos, Lees and Hagopain discovered that criminals had very low and consistent cholesterol levels. Low cholesterol levels have been related to those who have difficulty in internalising norms and have a tendency toward irresponsibility and self-criticism. Low cholesterol levels have also been linked with people who take less than usual notice of the usual conventions of society. A low level of cholesterol has often been linked with hypoglycaemia, particularly when connected with alcohol – see Virkkunen (1987).

Hypoglycaemia, low cholesterol and high intake of alcohol have all also been related to enhanced insulin secretion. It is not at present possible to ascertain which of these is the cause of any consequent problems, or whether all are related and caused by some other factor. Clearly some further research in this area might lead to reasonable and acceptable suggestions for crime control such as alterations in diet.

7.2.4 Vitamins and minerals

Another suggested connection is between crime and the levels of vitamins or minerals in the human body. Generally, the claim is that either deficiencies of certain vitamins or the toxic effects of an excess of certain minerals is the cause of criminality.

Lead – In this category, the toxic effects of lead and its adverse affects on learning are widely accepted. As will become evident later (7.3.3.1), it is often claimed that delinquents are slow learners, but interestingly the connection between lead levels and criminality has only recently been suggested (see for example Bradley (1988)). Modern modes of life have raised the lead levels in the air and other parts of the environment, increasing the levels of lead absorbed by most individuals. There is now a disturbing link made between lead levels and learning abilities, and between levels of lead, intelligence levels and hyperactivity. High levels of lead have also been linked to low levels of independence, persistence and concentration, and high levels of impulsiveness, daydreaming and frustration (see Bryce-Smith (1983)). The problems caused by high levels of lead absorption may be compounded by a deficiency of vitamin C which reduces the ease with which lead is excreted.

Cobalt (which occurs in vitamin B_{12}) – Other minerals have been similarly linked to negative behaviour patterns. Most notably, two studies, Pihl (1982) and Raloff (1983), suggest a link between cobalt and violent behaviour. Each of them found that the lower the level of cobalt, the more violent was the behaviour pattern. Although these studies each claim a close relationship between cobalt and violence, neither explains the role of cobalt in a human body or how its level could be related to violent behaviour.

Vitamin B – A deficiency of the vitamin B complex is common amongst both criminals and hyperactive children. A shortage of vitamin B_1 can give rise to aggression, hostility, sensitivity to criticism and irrational behaviour, all of which are common in many delinquents. Those deficient in B_3 may, it is claimed, become fearful and act immorally because they are less able to discern right from wrong (see Lesser (1980)). Presumably, due to the link with cobalt, B_{12} must also be connected with criminality.

7.2.5 Assessment of nutritional factors

If this is a promising line of research, it is still too early for any proper assessment to be made. A lot of the claims in this area are anecdotal (see, for example, Bradley (1988)), but even the better work (for example, Hippochen (1978)) does not contain systematic proof of the effects of these matters on behaviour or criminality, nor does it explain exactly how these factors work to increase criminality. The literature certainly seems sufficiently weighty to indicate that some connection exists, but the extent and precise operation of the mechanisms require further investigation. This has not deterred Hippochen from making the surprising claim that rates of recidivism could be reduced by between 25 per cent and 50 per cent by controlling diet or prescribing drugs to control the biochemical balance in the body. Such assertions are, as yet, insufficiently supported by research to command widespread support.

Many of the writers in this area admit that the biochemical effects caused by food cannot be studied in a void, and note the need to consider interaction of behavioural changes, the environment and the psychological characteristics of the individual. Such links are not easily defined or identified. Further study of the connection between biochemical factors and school problems, or biochemical factors and personality problems, would be useful. Much of the work so far has been based on small numbers of individual case histories: larger samples might clarify more general links between nutrition and criminal behaviour and indicate whether nutritional programmes gain positive results. A particular requirement in this area is for all the research to be double-blind, so that neither the researcher nor the participants know which individuals are receiving treatment, and that information is held by a third party who plays no part in the research.

Even if a link is found between diet and criminal behaviour, what should then be the response? Can a change of diet be dictated, particularly prior to offending or after a sentence has already been served?

By using diet to explain criminal behaviour we may be providing criminals with at least a partial excuse for their behaviour, and we may therefore be relieving them of responsibility. If a person is not to be held responsible for his or her actions, it is difficult to insist upon self-restraint or to use the full weight of any punishment system if that person steps out of line. If such considerations are thought to be important, great care should be taken before accepting that diet can relieve a criminal of even partial responsibility. Such claims require clear proof of the effects of diet and an understanding of how the diet and the behaviour are related. In other words, it is necessary to be sure that there is a causal relationship and of the precise nature of that causal relationship. (For other suggestions for this area of work, see Bradley and Bennett (1987).)

7.3 CRIMINALITY AND THE CENTRAL NERVOUS SYSTEM

The central nervous system (CNS) is found in the brain and spinal column and is responsible for conscious thought and voluntary movements. As such it seems reasonable to assume that it controls behaviour of all sorts: learned, unlearned, and behaviour which is partly learned and partly unlearned. Assuming that the brain does control behaviour and that each individual's brain is slightly different both in its structure and the way it operates then it is unsurprising that for many years criminologists have been interested in the CNS and have connected it with criminal behaviour in a number of distinct theories. Some, usually rare, diseases may affect behaviour by affecting brain functioning. Wilson's disease, which can have both physical and psychological effects (see Kaul and McMahon (1993)), is one such problem. These will generally not be discussed here although they may be alluded to in later chapters, especially Chapter Nine.

7.3.1 Electroencephalography
Electroencephalograph (EEG) processes measure brain wave patterns by monitoring the electronchemical processes in the brain. Between 5 per cent and 20 per cent of non-criminals are said to have abnormal wave patterns, but in criminals the abnormality rate rises to between 25 per cent and 50 per cent (see Mednick and Volavka (1980) for a review of the materials). The difference is even more marked if violent recidivist criminals are studied. Williams (1969) studied habitual aggressives and used those who had committed only one aggressive act as controls. He excluded all those with histories of mental retardation, epilepsy and head injuries and discovered that the rate of EEG abnormality was 57 per cent in the persistently violent group but only 12 per cent for the control group.

From Mednick and Volavka's review it is clear that most of the studies have related criminality to an excessive amount of slow brain wave activity, although some have recorded an excessive amount of fast brain wave activity. Slow brain wave activity is often found in young children, and slow learning ability has often been related to criminality, which has led researchers to claim that criminality is linked to slow brain development (i.e., because their brains have not matured and grown as quickly as their bodies, their socialisation is retarded). The other commonly supported explanations are that in a laboratory setting criminals experience a low level of cortical arousal, or that they have suffered head or brain injuries.

possibly more important, it does not address the question of what causes the disability, and so its usefulness as a means either of explaining criminality or of bringing about any change in criminal behaviour is minimal.

7.3.3.2 Brain dysfunction

How do differences in the constitution of the brain affect behaviour? Buikhuisen (1987) reviewed all the available literature and research which attempted to answer this question. He noted that almost without exception the researchers discovered that delinquents do not perform as well as control groups. This can be used to uphold the claims that delinquents have a lower IQ than non-delinquents (for a fuller discussion of IQ see Chapter Nine). Buikhuisen's research showed that the delinquents had problems in comprehending, manipulating and using conceptual material (this includes problems with sequencing and with perceptual organisation). They also had problems of recall and with organising visual information, and they consistently performed badly when a task involved sustained concentration.

Many of the learning problems were found to arise in the brain's (pre)frontal lobes. The frontal lobe is important to the regulation of behaviour. It allows people to plan their actions, assess their outcomes and change the actions if necessary. Any damage to this area could therefore seriously affect ability to understand the consequences of actions; seriously impair ability to learn by experience; reduce ability to concentrate; cause a lack of self control and an increase in impulsive actions; induce a lack of understanding of others' feelings; and an inability to feel shame, guilt or remorse. It will also reduce the normal inhibitions which would prevent most people becoming aggressive and/or sexually antisocial. Lastly, it will increase sensitivity to alcohol.

From this it can be deduced that those suffering from this type of brain dysfunction are most likely to commit poorly planned crimes and will often act on impulse. The crimes could be of a relatively serious nature, although they will not involve ingenuity or planning. The fact that they are unlikely to learn from past punishment, are unable to understand the consequences of their actions, and tend to act on impulse, means that they are likely to become recidivists. Another possible association is with what is termed 'mild brain dysfunction', more recently referred to as 'attention deficit disorder', which may appear alone or with hyperactivity. The cause of the problem is not understood but it is diagnosed by the external results which include behavioural, psychological and cognitive responses. In 1988, Loeber assessed a number of studies which measured these difficulties and found that there was a suggestion that the problems were associated with offending behaviour in young males. A more interesting study was completed in 1990 by Farrington, et al. who analysed a longitudinal study of males who were tested at fixed intervals between the ages of 8 and 21. The data included information not only on their attention deficit and hyperactivity but also on conduct problems at home and school, information on home background and official and self-reported delinquency. Farrington et al. discovered that both attention deficit (with and without hyperactivity) and conduct problems were related to higher rates of delinquency. The attention deficit problems tended to be cognitive or low IQ and were in turn related to criminal parents, large family size and to official criminal convictions at a young age and to early chronic offending. The conduct problems were associated with inadequate parenting and led to self-reports of minor youthful delinquency and to offending at a later age. Farrington et al. concluded that although attention deficit problems and conduct problems are linked to criminality their causal relationships with that behaviour are different and not necessarily wholly biological. It thus appears that in young males (most studies have excluded females and this reduces the worth of their claims) there may be a link, but its causal relationship is not understood and it is very heavily affected by social and environmental conditions.

The central nervous system is split into two hemispheres, each of which is responsible for different functions of the brain. Yeudall, Fromm-Auch and Davies (1982) suggested that juvenile recidivists suffered a higher incidence of dysfunction in the nondominant hemisphere. The nondominant hemisphere is usually on the right, and it plays an important role in the understanding of and reaction to negative emotional stimuli such as fear and punishment. Normally, pain or other unpleasant experiences are remembered and connected to the action for which the punishment is used, so that if the individual considers similar action, fear of further punishment will stimulate the pituitary gland to release hormones which will force reconsideration of the action and thus possibly avoid its repetition. If the hemisphere regulating this behaviour is damaged, the fear will not be experienced, so sanctions become meaningless and continual criminal behaviour is likely to occur. Interestingly, in these people the dominant hemisphere is usually undamaged. This regulates responses to pleasant stimuli such as joy or praise, and if the right hemisphere is damaged they might be dissuaded from criminality by the rewards for good behaviour rather than punishment for bad or criminal behaviour. Our criminal justice system is unable to cope with this type of approach.

The theorists recognise that these brain dysfunctions alone cannot explain criminality; their effects can only be understood in the social context. The expectations of each culture may vary, but whatever its norms, society expects each individual to learn to live within them. To do this, each child needs all the normal powers of receptive and communication skills as well as the ability to understand and remember external stimuli. A large part of this learning requires the skills which have been shown above to be lacking as a result of certain brain dysfunctions. If the child fails to learn the social or parental norms, the parents may find that they are unable to cope, become frustrated, and begin to reject the child. At school similar problems may arise between the child and teachers, and a similar result of rejection may follow. The child will probably have a negative self-image and may try to look elsewhere for stimulation, acceptance and an enhanced self-image. This they may well find in subcultures, particularly delinquent subcultures, but the place they find this acceptance and enhanced self-image is often a question of chance. If it is in a criminal subculture, then the types of crime they may commit are also a question of chance. Often the chance may be weighted one way or the other, depending on the type of neighbourhood in which they live, their social class, or other matters of that type (for a discussion of such subcultures see Chapter Twelve).

Although this research suffers from problems such as small, unrepresentative samples and unmatched controls, the results are sufficiently convincing to offer fairly strong evidence that brain dysfunction could explain a perceptible amount of criminality. Equally, certain positive methods of coping with criminality could well emerge from this work in the future. Rather than a particular type of medical treatment, this might well lead to proposals which advocate changes in upbringing, both in the home and at school, as well as suggesting alterations which might be made to the criminal justice system in order to encourage law-abiding behaviour.

7.4 CRIMINALITY AND THE AUTONOMIC NERVOUS SYSTEM

The autonomic nervous system (ANS) controls many of the involuntary functions of the body. It will set the bodily functions so as to obtain maximum efficiency. It speeds up and slows down the heart, dilates the pupils of the eyes, controls the rate of breathing and regulates the temperature of the body by means of dilating and contracting blood vessels and by regulating the sweat glands. The most commonly used method of measuring or recording ANS is that used in lie-detectors, i.e., the measurement of the electric activity of the skin (this is generally referred to as GSR or galvanic skin resistance) usually taken from the activity of the sweat glands in the palms of the hands, recorded on a polygraph. In a calm, unemotional state the skin will be dry and disinclined to conduct a current, but if the person to whom the electrical current is applied is emotionally aroused or frightened, then that person's ANS causes the sweat glands in the palms to operate, creating less resistance to the current. Recording the variations in resistance will be indicative of the extent of ANS arousal.

Criminologists are interested in the aspect of this system which depicts emotional moods or feelings. The ANS is one of the best tests of a person's involuntary and therefore natural reaction to external stimuli. If the individual is frightened, then the body takes certain precautions in case it needs to react quickly. This is commonly called the 'fight or flight' situation, and involves increasing the heart rate, re-routing the blood from the stomach to the muscles, increasing the rate of breathing and stimulating the sweat glands. To do this, the ANS stimulates the production of certain enzymes which tell the body to make ready for action.

The enzyme production can be measured, as can all the above mentioned changes in bodily functioning. A lie detector works by measuring these changes, and similar measurements are taken to discern the efficiency of the ANS. These measurements are supposed to decide how well the individual has learnt to live in society, in that they measure conditionability. The theory is that most children are punished when they act in an antisocial manner, and so they will anticipate punishment when they misbehave. This anticipation brings on the involuntary bodily changes associated with 'fight or flight'. As these body changes are associated with unpleasantness, most children learn to avoid situations where they might arise, and so they become conditioned. The body changes and their associated feelings are often popularly referred to as conscience or guilt. Where the body changes are only affected very slowly or only at a very low level by the use of punishment, or when the return to the normal state is very slow, then the child will be difficult to control and its behaviour is more likely to become criminal.

One of the main proponents of this theory was Hans Eysenck (1977). He argued that personality is central to criminality, but that personality is largely determined by physiological characteristics such as those mentioned above. He pinpoints two key personality traits which are essential to criminality – extroversion or outward looking personality, and introversion or inward looking personality. The introvert tends to be quiet, serious, pessimistic, cautious and controlled. The extrovert will tend to be sociable, carefree, optimistic, impulsive and aggressive. The extrovert thus possesses lower inhibitory controls, and so can act without constraint and will possess an enhanced desire for stimulation, all of which renders him more likely to turn to criminality. These traits are seen as being a result of the poor conditionability of the extrovert which arises due to the different functioning of his ANS.

The research studies into this area are not unanimous about the acceptance of these ideas. In a study in 1970, Hoghughi and Forrest compared a number of persistent property offenders with a control group, and discovered that there was either no difference in the levels of extroversion or that the delinquents were more introverted. In a review of biological tests for comparisons of the operations of the ANS of delinquents/criminals and controls, both Siddle (1977) and Venables (1987) conclude that those with antisocial behaviour portray problems in their ANS such as low levels of electrodermal response and an irregular heart rate acceleration pattern. The tests seem to show a particularly strong connection between antisocial behaviour and slow recovery rates (see S.A. Mednick (1977)). The reason they offer is that when a person can recover from a state of fear quickly, they experience a high degree of relief which greatly strengthens the conditioning. If recovery is low the level of relief is low, and so conditioning is less likely to occur. Slow ANS recovery rates are, in these studies, seen as the answer to the question Mednick's work was designed to explain: why are nearly 50 per cent of all offences committed by just 1 per cent of the population?

From this it might appear possible to conclude that the relationship between crime and ANS is strong. No such definite conclusion, however, is possible, as many of the researchers often work with small samples which may not be representative of the whole group. They do not tend to match the criminals and controls for similar backgrounds. Furthermore, most of the researchers took official information of criminality as being correct without question. There is some doubt as to whether the characteristics of the ANS which have been linked with criminality are actually the result of that activity rather than the reason for it. This criticism was attacked by Mednick (see above) when he carried out a longitudinal study (that is, he studied the same people over a considerable period of time) where he still found a connection between the ANS and criminality. The research certainly suggests a link between criminality and ANS, but it is still early days. In addition, it would be very useful to see research into the part played by the environment in that relationship, and particularly the effects of different types of upbringing.

Few people recognise the possible connection between the CNS and the ANS, which might ultimately show the problem of the ANS to be merely the result of wider problems in the CNS. A scientific study of the relationship between the two will be interesting and instructive, and eventually might indicate whether either of them could ethically and effectively be treated so as to socialise the presently antisocial criminals.

7.5 CONCLUSION

In the last chapter some of the worst consequences of biological theories were discussed, e.g., sterilization. In this chapter the possibility of using other very problematic methods of control are implied, e.g., drug therapy and psychosurgery. The fear of these gross but possible consequences, together with the unlikelihood that purely biological factors are solely responsible for crime, has led intellectuals, researchers and reformers to shy away from supporting biological explanations of criminality in favour of wholly social or environmental factors. These have generally been seen to lend themselves to more acceptable methods of dealing with or treating the problem. Unfortunately, to date attempts to explain criminality and to recondition criminals on this basis have been pitifully unsuccessful.

If the real aim of every criminologist is to seek a clearer understanding of antisocial behaviour in general and crime in particular, then nobody can afford to have a closed mind to any area or any avenue of explanation. Totally to disregard biological explanations because of repugnance of what they might lead to is rendered even more dubious in light of the fact that those who presently research in this area do not usually claim that the individual's biological make-up alone explains criminality. Generally the claim is that biology can possibly explain why some people may be more susceptible to criminality if certain environmental conditions are also met. People may have a propensity for antisocial behaviour, but that does not mean that they automatically become criminal.

If biological explanations are accepted as a partial explanation, there is still a fear that although they may not lead to sterilisation or permanent imprisonment, they may involve other unethical and unacceptable treatments such as psychosurgery or the forcible administration of psychotropic drugs. This is not necessarily the case. The information could perhaps be used to discern which types of environmental intervention might be most effective to deter or prevent criminal behaviour, such as pin-pointing the effective types of social learning. For example, providing high-risk adolescents with stable home environments in which to grow up might prove to be an effective way of controlling those young people who are biologically predisposed to criminality. It recognises their enhanced likelihood of becoming criminals, but places them in an environment where criminality is least likely to occur. This has been tried on a small scale in some areas by arranging for those who have a stable relationship to foster young delinquents, but as yet it is too early to form any firm conclusion as to its success. Furthermore, although it appears relatively humane, care must be taken to ensure that it does not conceal any prejudice, e.g., it does not lead to the removal of black children from their homes into white homes or areas simply because these white families may be seen as more stable. This type of racial stereotyping, or even of social stereotyping – rich better than poor – needs to be avoided, but otherwise the provision of adults with whom relatively stable relationships could be fostered certainly has potential. It might be possible to provide such environments by paying people in relatively stable relationships to care for children and adolescents from unstable settings and with a propensity for antisocial behaviour (see Baker and Mednick (1984)).

Other more acceptable suggestions may come from the effects of diet upon behaviour. If any close relationship is proven to exist between eating habits and criminality or aggression, then it may be possible to devise dietary advice for families, schools and institutions such as prisons which could be used in order to reduce the incidence of antisocial behaviour. As long as such diets were also healthy in other respects, and could be afforded, then their use should remain relatively uncontroversial.

From the above, it can be seen that biological theories do not necessarily involve overly intrusive methods of control, and this is commendable, but the student of criminology must always be aware that there is work being carried out both on the possible use of drugs and on psychosurgery and other surgery to control crime. These may not be so commendable if they interfere too radically with the personality, physique or ability of individuals to lead normal lives. They may have a role to play if they do not involve the use of force, if they have no side-effects and where their effects are sufficiently localised: but altering nature is rarely so clean and acceptable. From the point of view of civil liberties and humane treatment, the dangers in these methods are self-evident. The use of psychosurgery is slowly losing ground, as it has been found to be difficult to control the exact changes which occur and to prevent side-effects. In both Britain and America such methods are reputedly used only after the consent of the individual has been obtained. Choice or consent in such cases is often debatable; when an inmate is presented with a choice between psychosurgery or surgery (for example, castration in sex cases) or very long terms of imprisonment, it is not truly a free choice. Similarly, the agreement to take drugs in these circumstances may not be freely made. Before drugs and surgery become acceptable in this field, there needs to be a clearer understanding of the causative role played by human biology and the effects of the suggested remedy. Even if such incontrovertible proof were to exist, no remedy should be used unless it is clearly beneficial not only to society but also to the individual. No such remedies should ever be used merely because they are cheap.

Furthermore, constant vigilance is needed as scientific boundaries are extended. New biological 'causes' of criminality may arise all the time. In the 1960s and 1970s such research was widely ignored, but it has recently come to the fore again and seems to have been more readily accepted by scientists, politicians and the public. Interestingly, most of the present biological theories are not new, rather they are a reworking and advance of older ideas. They begin from the premise that there is something wrong with the individual criminal – one must look inside criminals to ascertain the reasons for criminal behaviour. Since the late 1970s we have been in a period of political conservatism – even the traditional socialist parties have moved to the right. The strain of conservatism which has been prevalent has stressed individuals' responsibility for their lives and actions, stressed respect for tradition and traditional values, stressed the need for law and order, and has tended to play down or ignore social circumstances or feelings of exclusion from society as being significantly linked to behavioural problems. The fashionable theories, both in explaining crime and in suggesting remedies, have stressed the individual not society – individuals are responsible and therefore must be punished, or there is a biological or mental problem with them which explains their negative behaviour patterns and requires acting on them, not on society. Such individualistic theories also seem more plausible because social theories do not explain why most individuals in unpleasant environments are law-abiding. The political climate thus seems favourable for the acceptance of criminological causes based on biology and for solutions which address or control those biological 'problems'. These theories also lend themselves to simple headlines and make the public receptive to explanations of criminality from which most people are obviously excluded. So, when a study carried out by New York University Medical School on 15 convicted murderers discovered that they had all suffered head injuries, this was reported in the *New York Times* for 3 June 1986 as if it was a trait in all murderers. On 17 September 1985, the same paper carried a story that brain defects had been found in 90 per cent of excessively violent people, and that brain defects are also found in those who report violent acts. *The Sunday Times* (15 January 1989) reported that aggression amongst boys in the classroom was linked to the production of the male hormone, testosterone, and that although environmental factors might dampen or exaggerate its effects, they could not reverse these natural instincts. Such reports, by presenting matters in an over-simplified way, may create misleading impressions on the public.

It is important that criminologists do not ignore or try to prevent biological research from taking place and being publicised, as positive and acceptable uses may be found for the work. None the less, it is essential to be aware that it is always possible for such research to be used to justify unacceptable intrusions into civil liberties. Most of the more modern biological theorists recognise that any connection between their research and crime is only a part of the causal relationship which may have led to the perpetration of the crime. They generally recognise the need to work closely with sociologists, social scientists, psychologists and others in order to gain greater insight into the causes of crime.

7.6 POSTSCRIPT ON BIOLOGY AND CRIME

There are some positive factors which may arise out of the medicalisation of criminality: a sick individual may be blameless. This has very clear knock-on effects for sentencing, because if there is a medical reason for the behaviour it removes the justification for punishment in favour of treatment. If the condition is treatable both the individual and society can benefit from improved behaviour, making recidivism less likely. Of course these positive effects are often elusive because, as has been seen above, the link between crime and biology, if it exists, is rarely clean and almost never clearly causative. The negative aspects are many. For example, shifting the explanation of criminality away from the social order on to the individual suggests that certain individuals need to be altered, with all the appalling consequences to which this may give rise. Or, if the individual's biology is deemed to be the cause of the criminality and the condition is untreatable then that individual may be assessed too dangerous to release and may be held to protect the public from possible future criminal (usually violent) activity. This suggests confinement for the good of society and not to punish the individual, but the effect, permanent incarceration, feels the same if not worse (see ss. 1(2)(b) and 2(2)(b) of the Criminal Justice Act 1991, as amended and Part I of the Crime (Sentences) Act 1997). For a fuller discussion see 8.4 below. Another negative aspect arises if there is an acceptance that science does not lie and is morally neutral. This is very debatable because the questions asked will often colour the answers: certainly without full explanations of causative paths the utility and moral neutrality of scientific discovery are debatable. Science also seems to be politically neutral which makes it more difficult to contest: once more the questions asked are crucial and the findings can be politically interpreted. Again without full causative understanding their validity and utility is questionable. The essential point is that science in the modern world is endowed with great authority, partly because of its apparent neutrality and reliance on apparently disinterested experts. The apparent neutrality allows the experts to gain power over the control systems (see Foucault (1980)).

As has been seen above, although some of the biological remedies such as drug therapy and surgery may appear to lead to a lowering of criminal behaviour, we do not fully understand the full effects of what is happening. Should we therefore be 'experimenting' with criminals? As the possibility of genetic manipulation of humans becomes more reality than science fiction, we also need to consider how to deal with these advances. Do we want all humans to be the same? Is some difference, even if rather destructive, not enriching of society in many ways? Even if very strong causative explanations are ever found, which looks dubious, do we really wish to alter human beings irreversibly just to reach certain moral behavioural standards? Are the moral values of today always to exist, or do they portray protection of certain values or particular groups? Even violence is not universally condemned in any society – most societies have warriors to protect them and these warriors may need some biologically violent elements to their characters, if any such thing exists, in order to carry out their function. For these reasons any biological explanation should not lead to irreversible or even permanent (meaning a need for drug therapy for life) intervention. At most, if any biological explanation is found to be causative it may be acceptable to allow transient medical intervention whilst certain socialising elements can be learned or an acceptable environment found for the individual. Permanent intervention, either surgical or genetic, would seem never to be acceptable as its knock-on effects for humanity as well as the individual can never be understood or controlled.

REFERENCES

Baker, R.L. and Mednick, B. (1984), *Influences on Human Development: A Longitudinal Perspective*, Boston: Kluwer Nijhof Press.

Baldwin, John D. (1990), 'The Role of Sensory Stimulation in Criminal Behaviour, with Special Attention to the Age Peak in Crime', in Lee Ellis and Harry Hoffman (eds), *Crime in Biological, Social, and Moral Contexts*, New York: Praeger.

Berman, Louis (1921), *The Glands Regulating Personality*, New York: Macmillan.

Berman, Louis (1938), *New Creations in Human Beings*, New York: Doran.

Bradley, G. and Bennett, P. (1987), 'The Relationship Between Nutrition and Deviant Behaviour', *The Criminologist*, vol. 11, p. 133.

Bradley, Gail (1988), 'If Food be the Cause of Crime', *The Law Magazine*, 22 January 1988.

Bryce-Smith, D. (1983), *Nutrition and Health*, vol. 1, p. 179.

Buikhuisen, W. (1987), 'Cerebral Dysfunctions and Persistent Juvenile Delinquency' in Sarnoff A. Mednick, Terrie E. Moffitt and Susan A. Stack (eds), *The Causes of Crime: New Biological Approaches*, Cambridge: Cambridge University Press.

Clapham, His Honour Brian (1989), 'A Case of Hypoglycaemia', *The Criminologist*, vol. 13, p. 2.

Curran, D. and Ranzetti, C. (1994), *Theories of Crime*, Boston: Allyn and Bacon.

Egleston, G.W. (1893), Letter to Sterling Morton, 26 May, General Correspondence, US Dept. of Agriculture, Office of Experiment Stations, National Archives, Washington, DC.

Ehrenkranz, J., Bliss, E. and Sheard, M. H. (1974), 'Plasma Testosterone: Correlation with Aggressive Behaviour and Social Dominance in Man', *Psychosomatic Medicine*, vol. 36, p. 469.

Ellis, Lee and Coontz, Phyllis D. (1990), 'Androgens, Brain Functioning, and Criminality: the Neurohormonal Foundations of Antisociality', in Lee Ellis and Harry Hoffman (eds), *Crime in Biological, Social, and Moral Contexts*, New York: Praeger.

Eysenck, H.J. (1959), *Manual of the Maudsley Personality Inventory*, London: University of London Press.

Eysenck, H.J. (1977), *Crime and Personality*, 3rd edn, London: Routledge & Kegan Paul.

Farrington, D.P., Loeber, R. and Van Kammen, W.B. (1990), 'Long-term Criminal Outcomes of Hyperactivity-Impulsivity-Attention Deficit and Conduct Problems in Childhood', in L. Robins and M. Rutter (eds), *Straight and Devious Pathways from Childhood to Adulthood*, Cambridge: Cambridge University Press.

Fishbein, D.H. (1990), 'Biological Perspectives in Criminology', *Criminology*, vol. 28, p. 27.

Foucault, Michel (1980), *Power/Knowledge*, ed. and trans. C. Gordon, Brighton: Harvester.

Hare, R.D. (1982), 'Psychopathy and Physiological Activity during Anticipation of an Aversive Stimulus in a Distraction Paradigm', *Psychophysiology*, vol. 19, p. 266.

Hatch, F.T., Reisell, P.H., Poon-King, T.M.W., Canellos, G.P., Lees, R.S. and Hagopain, L.M. (1966), 'A Study of Coronary Heart Disease in Young Men: Characteristics and Metabolic Studies of Patients and Comparison with Age-Matched Healthy Men', *Circulation*, vol. 33, p. 679.

Hippochen, Leonard J. (ed.) (1978), *Ecologic-Biochemical Approaches to Treatment of Delinquents and Criminals*, New York: Van Nostrand Reinhold.

Hoghughi, M.S. and Forrest, A.R. (1970), 'Eysenck's Theory of Criminality: An Examination with Approved School Boys', *British Journal of Criminology*, vol. 10, p. 240.

Kaul, A. and McMahon, D. (1993), 'Wilson's Disease and Offending Behaviour – a Case Report', *Medicine Science and the Law*, vol. 33, p. 352.

Keverne, E.B., Meller, R.E. and Eberhart, J.A. (1982), 'Social Influences on Behaviour and Neuroendocrine Responsiveness in Talapoin Monkeys' in *Scandinavian Journal of Psychology*, vol. 1, p. 37.

Kreuz, L.E. and Rose, R.M. (1972), 'Assessment of Aggressive Behaviour and Plasma Testosterone in a Young Criminal Population', *Psychosomatic Medicine*, vol. 34, p. 321.

Lesser, M. (1980), *Nutrition and Vitamin Therapy*, New York: Bantam.

Loeber, R. (1988), 'Behavioural Precursors and Accelerators of Delinquency', in W. Buikhuisen and S.A. Mednick (eds), *Explaining Criminal Behaviour: Interdisciplinary Approaches*, Leiden: E.J. Brill.

McCarrison, Sir Robert (1981), *Nutrition and Health*, The McCarrison Society, first published in 1953, London: Faber and Faber.

Mark, Vernon H, and Ervin, Frank R. (1970), *Violence and the Brain*, New York: Harper and Row.

Martin, D. (1987) 'Justice, Mercy and an Allergy Test', *The Criminologist*, vol. 11, p. 29.

Mednick, Sarnoff A. (1977), 'A Bio-Social Theory of the Learning of Law Abiding Behaviour', in Sarnoff A. Mednick and Karl O. Christiansen (eds), *Biosocial Basis of Criminal Behavior*, New York: Gardner Press.

Mednick, S.A., Kirkegaard-Sorensen, L., Hutchings, B., Knop, J., Rosenberg, R. and Schulsinger, F. (1977), 'An Example of Biosocial Interaction Research: the Interplay of Socioenvironmental and Individual Factors in the Etiology of Criminal Behavior', in S.A. Mednick and K.O. Christiansen (eds), *Biosocial Bases of Criminal Behavior*, New York: Gardner Press.

Mednick, S.A., Pollock, V., Volavka, J. and Gabrielli, W.F. (1982), 'Biology and Violence', in M.E. Wolfgang and N.A. Weiner (eds), *Criminal Violence*, Beverly Hills, Calif: Sage.

Mednick, S.A. and Volavka, J. (1980), 'Biology and crime' in N. Morris and M. Tonry (eds), *Crime and Justice: An Annual Review of Research*, vol. 2, Chicago: University of Chicago Press.

Morrison, H.L. (1978), 'The Asocial Child: A Destiny of Sociopath?', in W.H. Reid (ed.), *The Psychopath: A Comprehensive Study of Antisocial Disorders and Behaviours*, New York: Brunner/Mazel.

Murray, Charles A. (1976), *The Link Between Learning Disabilities and Juvenile Delinquency*, Washington, DC: US Government Printing Office.

New York Times, 17 September 1985.

New York Times, 3 June 1986.

Olwens, Dan (1987), 'Testosterone and Adrenalin: Aggressive and Antisocial Behaviour in Normal Adolescent Males', in S.A. Mednick, T.E. Moffitt and S. Stack (eds), *The Causes of Crime: New Biological Approaches*, Cambridge: Cambridge University Press.

Persky, H., Smith, K.D. and Basu, G.K. (1971), 'Relation of Psychological Measures of Aggression and Hostility to Testosterone Production in Man', *Psychosomatic Medicine*, vol. 33, p. 265.

Pihl, R.O. (1982), 'Hair Element Levels of Violent Criminals', *Canadian Journal of Psychiatry*, vol. 27, p. 533.

Pottenger, F. (1983), *Pottenger's Cats*, Price-Pottenger Nutrition Foundation.

Price, Weston (1945), *Nutrition and Physical Degeneration*, Price-Pottenger Nutrition Foundation.

Prinz, R.J., Roberts, W.A. and Hantman, E. (1980), 'Dietary correlates of Hyperactive Behaviour in Children', *Journal of Consulting and Clinical Psychology*, vol. 48, p. 760.

Rada, R.T., Laws, D.R., Kellner, R., Stivastave, L. and Peak, G. (1983), 'Plasma Androgens in Violent and Non-Violent Sex Offenders', *American Academy of Psychiatry and the Law*, vol. 11(2), p. 149.

Raloff, J. (1983), 'Locks – a Key to Violence', *Science News*, vol. 124, p. 122.

Rodin, E.A. (1973), 'Psychomotor Epilepsy and Aggressive Behaviour', *Archives of General Psychiatry*, vol. 28, p. 210.

Rose, R.M., Bernstein, I.S., Gorden, T.P. and Catlin, S.F. (1974), 'Androgens and Aggression; A Review and Recent Findings in Primates', in R.L. Hollway (ed), *Primate Aggression: Territoriality and Xenophobia*, New York: Academia Press.

Rubin, Robert T. (1987), 'The neuroendocrinology and neurochemistry of antisocial behaviour', in Sarnoff A. Mednick, Terrie E. Moffitt and Susan A. Stack (eds), *The Causes of Crime: New Biological Approaches*, Cambridge: Cambridge University Press.

Scarmella, T.J. and Brown, W.A. (1978), 'Serum Testosterone and Aggressiveness in Hockey Players', *Psychosomatic Medicine*, vol. 40, p. 262.

Schalling, Daisy (1987), 'Personality Correlates of Plasma Testosterone Levels in Young Delinquents: an example of Person-Situation Interaction', in Sarnoff A. Mednick, Terrie E. Moffitt and Susan A. Stack (eds), *The*

Causes of Crime: New Biological Approaches, Cambridge: Cambridge University Press.

Schoenthaler, S.J. (1982), 'The effects of blood sugar on the treatment and control of antisocial behaviour: A double-blind study of an incarcerated juvenile population', *International Journal for Biosocial Research*, vol. 3, p. 1.

Shah, Saleem A. and Roth, Loren H. (1974), 'Biological and Psychophysiological Factors in Criminality', in Daniel Glaser (ed.), *Handbook of Criminology*, Chicago: Rand McNally.

Siddle, David A.T. (1977), 'Electrodermal Activity and Psycholopathy', in Sarnoff A. Mednick and Karl O. Christiansen (eds), *Biosocial Basis of Criminal Behavior*, New York: Gardner Press.

Smart, J.L. (1981), 'Undernutrition and Aggression', in P.F. Brain and D. Benton (eds), *Multidisciplinary Approaches to Aggression Research*, Amsterdam: Elsevier/North Holland.

Sunday Times, 15 January 1989.

Venables, Peter H. (1987), 'Autonomic Nervous System Factors in Criminal Behaviour', in Sarnoff A. Mednick, Terrie E. Moffitt and Susan A. Stack (eds), *The Causes of Crime: New Biological Approaches*, Cambridge: Cambridge University Press.

Virkkunen, Matti (1987), 'Metabolic Dysfunctions Among Habitually Violent Offenders: Reactive Hypoglycaemia and Cholesterol Levels', in Sarnoff A. Mednick, Terrie E. Moffitt and Susan A. Stack (eds), *The Causes of Crime: New Biological Approaches*, Cambridge: Cambridge University Press.

Volavka, Jan (1987), 'Electronencephalogram among Criminals' in Sarnoff A. Mednick, Terrie E. Moffitt and Susan A. Stack (eds), *The Causes of Crime: New Biological Approaches*, Cambridge: Cambridge University Press.

Walker, P.A., Meyer, W.J., Emory, L.E. and Rubin, A.L. (1984), 'Antiandrogenic Treatment in the Paraphilias', in H.C. Stancer et al. (eds), *Guidance for the Use of Psychotropic Drugs*, New York: Spectrum Publications.

Williams, D. (1969), 'Neural Factors Related to Habitual Aggression: Consideration of Differences between those Habitual Aggressives and Others who have Committed Crimes of Violence', *Brain*, vol. 92, p. 503.

Yeudall, L.T., Fromm-Auch, D. and Davies, P. (1982), 'Neuropsychological Impairment of Persistent Delinquency', *Journal of Nervous and Mental Disease*, vol. 170, p. 257.

CHAPTER EIGHT

Psychological Theories of Criminality

8.1 INTRODUCTION

Psychology is usually used to mean the study of people's mind or spirit (although animals are sometimes studied under this head). Chambers Twentieth Century Dictionary defines psych(o) as – 'In composition, soul, spirit: mind, mental: psychological.—n.' – and defines psychology as – 'science of mind: study of mind and behaviour: attitudes, etc., characteristic of individual, type, etc., or animating specific conduct'.

More specifically, psychology is the study of individual characteristics or qualities such as personality, reasoning, thought, intelligence, learning, perception, imagination, memory and creativity. Psychology is often separated into two groups of theories or schools of thought: cognitive and behavioural. Cognitive theories place the study of psychology in the mind; they see human action as the result of driving or compelling mental forces or to be the result of mental reasoning and beliefs. These theories take account of internal feelings such as anger, frustration, desire and despair. In fact, all activity is seen as the result of internal mental processes. In contrast, the behavioural theorists, whilst taking account of internal factors, place them in a social context. They see that internal mental processes can be affected and even altered by certain factors in the environment which either reinforce or discourage the behaviour. Clearly there is no strong dividing line between these two. A degree of overlap is likely, whilst some psychological theories may not fit neatly into either school.

There are psychologists who place weight on a biological link in the workings of the mind and link certain types of behaviour and certain thought processes with, for example, genetic or neurological factors (some of this research is sometimes referred to as psychophysiology). Others place so much weight on the environmental factors that they become closer to sociological theories. Either way it is clear that psychological theories should not be studied in a void, but be assessed and balanced in the criminological arena as a whole.

This chapter is concerned with psychological explanations for the behaviour of those who are generally seen as 'normal', in that they are not suffering from a mental defect. Mental abnormality will be considered in Chapter Nine. In both Chapters Eight and Nine there will be some mention of clinical psychology, which is often thought of as the study of those suffering from mental abnormality, but is also concerned with the study of lesser psychological disturbances and, possibly more importantly, with the treatment of all these mental difficulties. For a fuller and more precise account of general psychology, see an introductory text such as those by Gleitman (1986), Carlson (1986) and Gross (1989).

As with the biological theories, most of the ideas in this chapter fall into the positivist school of thought. They therefore explain crime as a result of some factor – in this case mental or behavioural constructs – rather than as a result of choice or free will.

8.2 PSYCHOANALYSIS AND CRIMINALITY

A number of different ideas are drawn together under psychoanalysis, but the general stand-point is that inner, dynamic forces are used to explain human behaviour. Psychoanalytical theorists perceive criminal behaviour to be the result of some mental conflict of which the criminal may be virtually unaware (i.e., the conflict arises in his sub-conscious or unconscious mind). Furthermore, they claim that this conflict is always present as an internal conflict between the demands of reason and conscience, and those of instinct. A 'victory' for instinct can lead to thoughts and deeds which will often be socially unacceptable. Everyone experiences this conflict, but some manage to control the instinct better than others. If the conflict is not resolved in a socially acceptable way, it may be expressed in ways which are criminal. The behaviour will tend to get worse unless the resolution of the conflict is helped or treated. Criminality is then seen as one of the outward signs of the disease, or of the problematic resolution of the mental conflict, just as physical deformity may be the manifestation of a physical disease.

Modern psychoanalysis began with the work of Sigmund Freud (1856-1939). He lived most of his life in Vienna and published most of his famous works between 1900 and 1939 (see especially Freud (1935)). His theories have had a profound effect on many aspects of modern life, on philosophy and literature for example, and have been widely used to explain human behaviour. Freud did not write a great deal specifically about criminality, but it is possible to see how some of his behavioural theories can be used as explanations of criminality, and later theorists have expanded on these to offer slightly different explanations. Psychoanalysis is a complex field, and only a brief introduction to those areas of Freud's writing which are of direct interest to criminology will be offered here. Areas such as those relating to dreams or to the mechanism of transference will be largely excluded, as will suggestions for treatments. There are many detailed texts dealing with Freud's work, for example Kline (1984).

8.2.1 The constituents of the personality

Freud split the personality into three parts – the id, the ego, and the super-ego. The id is an unconscious area of the mind; it is the most primitive portion of the personality from which the other two are derived. It is made up of all the basic biological urges – to eat, drink, excrete, to be warm and comfortable and to obtain sexual pleasure. It is driven by desire; it is illogical and amoral, and seeks only absolute pleasure at whatever cost. It characterises the unsocialised and unrestrained individual, and its drives need immediate gratification and have no conception of reality. It is the part of the personality with which one is born. It holds all the desires, even those society considers wrong or bad, and to that extent Freud says it needs to be repressed. The repression or control of the id is carried out by the ego and the super-ego.

The ego does not exist at birth, but is something the individual learns. It is largely conscious, although some of it is unconscious. It tempers the desirous longings of the id with the reality of what might happen if it is not controlled, and it also learns the reality of how best to serve the id. A baby learns that it is fed only after crying, and a child learns to say 'please' in order to obtain things. It learns that in some circumstances, giving in to the id leads to punishment or unpleasantness, and so it may not follow its desires in order to avoid these consequences. For example, the child's id may desire a biscuit, but when it takes one, some form of punishment or unpleasantness ensues. The pleasure of having the biscuit is marred by this unpleasantness, and so the child may decide that taking a biscuit is not worth it. The ego has developed and learned to reason with the id about the worth of the action. Slowly, the ego develops and controls or tempers the id.

The super-ego is largely part of the unconscious personality. It may contain conscious elements, for example, moral or ethical codes, but it is basically unconscious in its operation. It is the conscience which exists in the unconscious areas of the mind. The super-ego characterises the fully socialised and conforming member of society.

8.2.2 Formation of the super-ego

Possibly the most important influences on the individual are the precepts and moral attitudes of the parents or those *in loco parentis*. These are the people most loved, most respected and most feared. They are also the people with whom a child has his or her earliest contacts and relationships. These are essential to the child. The super-ego is often seen as the internalised rules and admonitions of the parents and, through them, of society. The super-ego acts on the ego; thus when a child desires a biscuit it may not take one even if it could not be punished because the child starts to reprove itself. The super-ego may therefore praise and punish the child in the same way as the parents do and so the child slowly learns an inner set of rules or values. If the behaviour or thoughts of the child live up to the super-ego, it experiences the pleasant feeling of pride but if they do not the child's own super-ego punishes it by self-reproach and feelings of guilt.

The ego therefore has two masters, each to be obeyed and each pushing in different directions. The id demands pleasure; the super-ego demands control and repression. The result is inner conflict which can never be fully resolved. Freud argued that for the super-ego to develop, the parents scold the child or otherwise show their displeasure, and this leads the child to become anxious that their love will be removed. The next time the child considers a 'bad' deed, he or she will feel anxiety that the parents may leave. The anxiety is unpleasant and leads to repression of the deed. As the child does not understand the difference between thought and action, the mental desire is also repressed in case the parents discover it: thoughts as well as deeds become repressed.

The basis of control or repression is therefore seen as built upon relationships with parents or those *in loco parentis*. This analysis to an extent has been upheld by the work of Aichhorn (1963), who found that environmental factors alone could not account for the delinquency of the children at the institution he supervised. The super-egos of many of the children were underdeveloped, which he maintained rendered them latent delinquents, psychologically prepared for a life of crime. If environmental conditions or some other element stimulated delinquency or criminality, then that, along with the unregulated or poorly regulated id, meant that criminal or delinquent behaviour was likely to result. He postulated that the failure to develop a super-ego was the result of the parents being unloving or absent for much of the child's upbringing. Each of these conditions would prevent the child from forming the dependant, trusting and intimate relationships necessary to the development of the super-ego. From this account, the socialising processes had failed to work on these children whose latent delinquency had become dominant; the children were therefore 'dissocial'.

Aichorn treated these youths by attempting to provide a happy and pleasant environment which might foster the type of relationships with adults which would facilitate the formation of the super-ego. He argued that the severe environments offered by most homes for juvenile delinquents merely exacerbate the problem begun by the parents, or by their absence, pushing the youths towards more criminal acts and confirming their 'dissocial' state. Parental neglect was not seen as the only reason for the super-ego to be underdeveloped: over-indulgent parents, allowing the child to do anything, would have a similar effect. It was also possible for children to learn all the lessons of their parents but still end with less than fully developed super-egos because the parents' ability to teach had been impaired by diluted moral standards, often because they were criminals themselves or were not themselves fully socialised. It has to be stated, however, that Aichorn realised that not all delinquents had poorly developed super-egos and that he never claimed that the failure to develop a super-ego explained all criminality.

These ideas have been further supported by other psychoanalysts such as Healy and Bronner (1936), who studied 105 families with two sons where one brother was a persistent criminal and the other was non-criminal. They concluded that the criminal brother had failed to develop strong emotional ties with his parents, and turned to pleasure to gratify the id. As a result they did not progress either to the reality of what will ultimately happen if desires are gratified immediately, or to the formation of a super-ego. John Bowlby

(1946 and 1953), found similar results when he focused on early maternal deprivation as being the cause of criminality. His argument rested on two basic premises: firstly, that a close, unbroken and loving relationship with the mother (or permanent mother substitute) is essential to the mental health of the child, and secondly, that rejection by the mother or separation from her (or her substitute) accounts for most of the more permanent cases of delinquency. This last sweeping claim has been attacked by both psychologists and sociologists, some of whom reject his methodology while others question his findings and claims. Many do, however, recognise that strong, though not necessarily lasting, damage can be done to a child's mental development if it is rejected by or separated from its mother during the first five years of its development.

A further factor which some argue has a profound effect upon the development of the super-ego, and one of the ideas most commonly associated with Freud, is the Oedipus complex (in boys) and the Electra complex (in girls). These develop during the process of sexual growth. Each is depicted by the child, normally when about three years old, being attracted to the parent of the opposite sex whilst feeling general hostility toward the parent of the same sex. In the Oedipus complex (male) the rivalry would be between the father and son. The latter, realising the supremacy of the father, fears castration and this fear forces him to control his desire for his mother. Freud believes that it is from the resolution of this conflict that the male's super-ego, social restraint or conscience, develops, and that all this occurs before the age of about five or six years. If the conflict is not resolved in this way, then serious personality or behavioural problems may arise. If there is no formation or incomplete formation of the super-ego, then the individual may have little or no conscience and so have no reason to restrain his desires. If the super-ego is overdeveloped then it may lead to guilt feelings or to his developing a neurosis (see below).

The resolution of the equivalent Electra complex in women is more complex and, Freud believes, less complete (see Chapter Sixteen).

Psychologists recognise that other factors such as relationships with individuals outside the family and the general social environment can also affect the formation of the super-ego. Hewitt and Jenkins (1947) categorised a group of 500 juveniles into three types:

(a) inhibited, shy and seclusive (an over-developed super-ego);
(b) unsociable and aggressive (under-developed super-ego); and
(c) members of a socialised, delinquent gang (having a dual super-ego).

The gang members possess a normal super-ego with respect to the rules of the gang, which therefore they obeyed, but they have inadequate or under-developed super-egos with respect to the rules of society. The behaviour of each individual gang member depends on whether or not he is with the gang. If he is, he obeys gang rules. If he is in the outside world, he feels no compulsion to obey the ordinary, everyday rules of society. Such a pattern indicates the strong influence which the environment can exert.

8.2.3 Balancing the id, ego and super-ego

The balance between desire and repression is kept by the ego, and in most people the desires of the id are shaped so that they are acceptable to the super-ego whilst still satisfying the id. This is often done by sublimation or displacement. For example, the desire for aggression may be channelled into sport where it can be usefully dissipated, or destructive instincts might be channelled in childhood away from harming people or animals and towards pulling toys apart and learning how to rebuild them. In this way the potentially aggressive or destructive person would become well balanced and would be unlikely to turn to criminality. The balance does not come from total repression of the id, but rather from channelling those desires into more useful activities which are acceptable to the super-ego. In this way both the id and super-ego are satisfied.

Psychoanalysts therefore argue that criminals are those who have not channelled their desires into useful, or at least harmless, pastimes. The id remains uncontrolled, and so the desires are allowed to take over and may give rise to socially unacceptable acts, some of which may be criminal. Occasionally, a criminal may be a person who has over-controlled or repressed these desires. Criminals may have a weak ego and hence be unable to balance the demands of the id and the super-ego; a weak super-ego where the conscience is insufficiently developed, making their moral standards lower than those of the rest of society; or an overly repressive ego and super-ego.

For example, guilt may be felt at the very existence of the desires (especially sexual desires), or at the performing of an act which, though not criminal, is wrong by super-ego standards. The guilt gives rise to a need to be punished as a form of relief or a purging of the guilt. The individual therefore commits a crime, often a very minor crime, and is caught and punished. The hope is that the punishment will be enough to atone for both the original guilt and the criminal act. Even if it does, the original desires are still there, in the unconscious, and so the guilt reasserts itself. On this interpretation it is understandable that further crimes are committed: crime brings punishment; punishment brings relief, but only for a time. A vicious circle develops and an habitual criminal comes into existence.

Psychoanalytical explanations are therefore based upon the idea that it is the inner processes and conflicts which determine behaviour. Unresolved inner conflict and lack of emotional stability are seen as the main causes of unacceptable behaviour; environment plays a subsidiary role. Because some of this inner conflict is unconscious the theory is very difficult to test.

8.2.4 'Normal' criminals

So far, most of the criminal tendencies referred to in this section on psychoanalysis have been those of 'abnormal' criminals whose behavioural problems arise from inner conflict (for example, individuals who suffer from a personality problem, such as neurotics). Psychoanalysis may also be used to explain some 'normal' criminality. The main trait of a 'normal' offender is that the whole personality, including the super-ego, is criminal. As there is no conflict between super-ego and the rest of the personality, there is no personality problem and so they are 'normal' offenders. This means that, presumably because of their environment and upbringing, these people regard crime as normal and acceptable (i.e., as natural) and they suffer no qualms about their criminal conduct. This does not mean that the 'normal' offender is willing to commit any crime, but that upbringing allows certain acts which are condemned by the rest of society, whilst condemning, along with the rest of society, many other activities considered to be criminal. This possibly suggests that society is not homogeneous but is made up of many subcultures (see Chapters Eleven and Twelve).

8.2.5 Extroversion and neuroticism

The idea that extroversion and introversion may play a part in criminality was popularised by Jung (1875–1960), originally a follower, but later a critic, of Freud. In 1947 Jung said that there was a continuance from introversion to extroversion, and that everybody could be placed somewhere along the spectrum. An hysteric condition, fitful or violent emotions, are more likely to be evidence of an extrovert, whereas an anxious condition, apprehensive or obsessive, indicates introversion. These concepts are often used in criminology as an explanation for recidivism – it is said that the introvert, being more careful, is better able to learn societal norms and so easier to condition and less likely to become a recidivist. Arguably, this is not necessarily the case. The flaw in presenting this as a general proposition is that whilst introverts may quickly learn the law-abiding behaviour taught in penal institutions, they will similarly have the capacity to re-learn antisocial behaviour after being released. There are both extrovert recidivists and introvert recidivists.

The main work in this area is that of Eysenck (1959), but see also (1977) and (1987), and Eysenck and Gudjonsson (1989), whose work covers a number of disciplines and draws upon psychoanalysis and personality theories as well as learning and control theories. Eysenck's starting-point is that individuals are genetically endowed with certain learning abilities, particularly the ability to be conditioned by environmental stimuli. He also assumes that crime can be a natural and rational choice where people maximise pleasure and minimise pain. An individual learns societal rules through the development of a conscience, which is acquired through learning what happens when one takes part in certain activities: punishment for being naughty and reward for being good. Personality is then based upon a combination of these biological and social factors. Eysenck saw two main dimensions to each personality which affected the individual's learning ability: extroversion, which runs from extroversion to introversion and is often referred to as the E scale; and neuroticism, which runs from neurotic or unstable to stable and is often referred to as the N scale. These dimensions are continuous and most people fall in the middle range, but with some at the extremes of each. The traits of each are depicted in Figure 8.1 (from p. 631 of Gleitman).

As with Jung's idea, the extroverts are seen as more difficult to condition, but so are the highly unstable or neurotic personalities. Eysenck argues that there is a hierarchy of conditionability:

(a) stable introverts (low N low E) are the easiest to condition;

(b)   stable extroverts (low N high E) and neurotic introverts (high N low E) are less malleable but do not encounter great difficulty in social learning;
(c)   neurotic extroverts (high N high E) experience most difficulty in social learning.

Figure 8.1

UNSTABLE

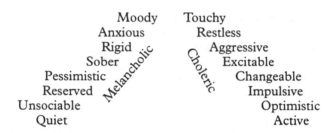

INTROVERTED   EXTROVERTED

STABLE

Later Eysenck introduced a third personality dimension which he called psychoticism, which could well be referred to a pschopathetic dimension since it is generally evidenced by aggressive, cold and impersonal behaviour. The individual will tend to be solitary, uncaring, cruel, will not fit in with others and will be sensation seeking. It is slightly less well understood than the first two and is associated with the frontal lobe of the cortex. Eysenck associates extremes of this dimension with criminality – the higher the P score, the higher the level of offending. In some studies Eysenck's claims have gained support; see particularly McGurk and McDougall (1981), where they found that neurotic extroverts and neurotic psychotic extroverts were only present in the delinquent group and stable introverts were only found in the non-delinquent group, whereas both neurotic introverts and stable extroverts were found in both groups.

There have, however, been many critics of Eysenck's work. Some attack the very basis of his claims: he has argued for a genetic basis for these traits and drawn his evidence from studies based on twins; thus his theory suffers from the difficulties encountered by such approaches (see 6.6.5). More fundamentally, some scholars such as Little (1963) and Hoghughi and Forrest (1970) assert that his findings are totally discredited. Little questioned whether there was any relationship between recidivism and either extroversion or introversion. For this, he drew upon research at three Borstal training institutions which purported to prove that neither release from these institutions nor recidivism rates connected to them were in any way linked to either extroversion or introversion. His research therefore questioned not only Eysenck's work but all work in this area.

The overall position is at present unclear and uncertain, especially as Eysenck himself accepted that the theory cannot explain all crime, since not all criminals will be at the extremes of these scales. However, Farrington (1994) reports that this approach seems to identify a link between offending and impulsiveness (see Chapter Seven and 8.3.6 below).

8.2.6 Criticism of psychoanalytical theories

Psychoanalysts profess, with good reason, that they are scientists. Their central concepts, however, are incapable of being directly observed, making their existence impossible to prove. The id, ego and super-ego are assumed to exist because of particular external manifestations which also exhibit the extent to which each part of the personality has developed. Often these external manifestations alone are not sufficient to diagnose the difficulties. They are supplemented by techniques such as dream analysis, verbal association and hypnosis, but these techniques are subjective since psychoanalysts differ over their interpretation. At the very least, this makes it a very inexact science.

One of the more dubious aspects of psychoanalysis, as applied to this area, is its assumption that because a person commits a crime he has some unconscious or subconscious personality conflict. The argument is circular, in that the problem to which a solution is sought is itself used as the proof that the explanation is correct. Moreover, the link between the crime and the alleged psychoanalytical reason for it is often obscure and dependent upon tortuous reasoning. The criminal will not normally recognise the analysis of himself, but the psychoanalyst does not see this as an objection, as the problem usually exists in the subconscious or unconscious mind. An unknown obsession with a particular type of sexual problem, or with one parent, or with a type of emotion, may give rise to acts involving symbols which represent that problem, e.g., using a gun as a power symbol and therefore as a sexual symbol. In some cases, it is asserted, a certain class of person is injured who represents the real target. For example, a particular criminal might habitually commit a crime against an older, female victim who represents his mother. The implication is that it is really his mother which the offender wishes to harm, perhaps stemming from a feeling that the mother wronged him earlier in his life. Whatever reason may be given, the real reason for the crime would not be admitted and may not even be known by the offender, whose motives may be hidden deep in the subconscious or the unconscious.

In such interpretations, the criminality is the outward manifestation of a disease or problem of the mind and personality, which exists in the subconscious or the unconscious. By using subjective methods on information gathered either from anecdote or methods such as dream therapy or hypnosis, the analyst follows the problem into these normally inaccessible areas of the mind and diagnoses the mental or personality problem. When asked to prove the existence of the problem, they point to the criminality. In this way the criminal act becomes both proof of the existence of the problem and the result of the problem. Proof of the worth of these theories is therefore difficult to obtain, but they can be useful, since in some cases the treatment has been successful. Nonetheless, it seems unlikely that all or even most criminality is associated with psychoanalytical problems. Nor does psychoanalysis add up to a clear understanding of crime or lead to widespread methods of preventing it - any successes have mainly been at an individual level. This does not mean that crime is not associated with the personality of the offender. In any event, psychoanalysis is not the only source of personality theories.

8.3   THE NORMAL CRIMINAL PERSONALITY

8.3.1   Introduction
Most theories using a concept of normal criminal personality assume that individuals possess definable and dominant sets of rules which determine how they will behave in virtually any situation. This is often called the central or core personality. Psychologists and psychiatrists believe that criminals tend towards certain well-defined personalities, and that their criminal tendencies can be overcome by controlling or altering those core personalities.

8.3.2   What is normality?
The line between normality and abnormality is impossible to draw exactly. Normality itself is elusive and difficult to define in any positive sense. It is usually negatively described as the state of mind or personality that cannot be classified as having a mental abnormality, (i.e., which cannot be classed as mentally defective, psychopathic, neurotic, psychotic or compulsive).

The mere fact that something is numerically common does not make it normal or healthy, and similarly the bare fact that something is uncommon does not make it abnormal or unhealthy. An event is not made normal or healthy because it frequently occurs and will certainly re-occur. For example, there will always be murder but this does not make it a normal, healthy or socially acceptable activity. Neither does the fact that an activity is socially unacceptable and unhealthy mean that those who take part in it are necessarily psychologically abnormal or unhealthy. If it did, it would follow that all criminals are mentally abnormal, and this is patently not the case.

Although all this is true, the plain fact is that in most of the studies normality is assessed in relation to the average person or the mental standard which is portrayed by most of the population (i.e., a numerical analysis). Furthermore, most of the studies of personality are heavily based on value judgements, such as assuming that because individuals have committed crimes they should portray a different personality from the law-abiding citizen (namely, a criminal personality). The assumption here is that those who participate in socially unacceptable activities must have something wrong with them, or at least must have something which is different from what the researcher, or society generally, considers normal.

This attitude can most clearly be seen in relation to murder, especially when there appears, on the face of it, to be no logical explanation for the killing. In such cases the press and public often refer to the events as motiveless crimes and term the murderer a 'monster' or a 'madman'. The activity is portrayed as something which any 'normal' person would find abhorrent and would not commit (or would like to think that they would not commit). Since most studies are tested against what society considers acceptable and normal, this is in effect the reality of the situation, and it is clear that as values in society change, so too will ideas of normality. For example, at one time homosexuality was a crime and generally considered to be a wholly unacceptable practice. It was considered to be an abnormal activity, and those taking part were deemed to be in need of medical or psychiatric treatment as well as punishment (see the Wolfenden Committee on Homosexual Offences and Prostitution (1957)). Homosexuality (between consenting adults over 18 in private) is now legal (according to the Sexual Offences Amendment Act 1967, s. 1 as amended by the Criminal Justice and Public Order Act 1994) and, although such activity is sometimes still considered biologically different or abnormal, it is less generally considered that its participants are in need of medical or psychiatric attention. From this it can be seen that the ordinary man in the street – or even the ordinary reasonable doctor, psychiatrist, psychologist, sociologist or criminologist – does not possess an absolute or constant definition of normality, personality or mental illness.

Any move away from the concept of normality may involve either together or separately at least three aspects: psychological suffering (the affective aspect), judgmental errors (intellectual aspect), and behavioural problems (moral or social aspect). None of these is necessarily a value-free norm and so variations from the 'norm' are laden with subjective assessments. These are particularly strong in the moral or social aspect where society or the expert defines what is to be categorised as 'problem behaviour'; and as seen above, that concept may not be static.

In Britain, in relation to criminology the issue of diagnosing normality and any deviation from normality (or illness) is further complicated by the proximity of the clinical work and the criminal justice system. This renders the diagnosis particularly difficult. In Britain, the psychiatrist, psychologist or probation officer is expected to report at the pre-sentencing stage. To make an assessment of the individual at this stage blurs the role of the diagnosis. Is it meant to determine the level of punishment by assessing the responsibility of the individual for the criminal act of which he or she has been found guilty? Is it to assess whether there is a likelihood of repeat offending of a sort likely to cause much damage to victims (particularly violent or sexual attacks)? Or is it rather to be used to diagnose the individual, mentally and medically, so as to propose methods of treatment or alter the personality and enable the offender to live within the requirements or boundaries set by society? This schism causes problems: it is confusing for the professional concerned; it may provide sentencers with ambiguous information; and it may relieve the offender of any feeling of responsibility. (For a fuller discussion of these aspects see Debuyst (1995).)

Despite these problems in the British tradition, it has been the psychiatric and psychological fields of criminal explanation which have generally carried more weight than the biological; they adapted more readily to the due process system of criminal trial and sentencing which is a feature of the British system (Gilling (1997)). It was generally believed that any necessary treatment could be carried out while the offender was being punished in a prison or elsewhere; and the approach also fits well with a system which is rooted in controlling or altering behaviour so that it conforms to an accepted type. It is also a useful tool because the 'diagnosis' or assessment by the expert is difficult to refute.

It is important to keep these ideas in mind when studying the remainder of this chapter, as well as Chapters Nine and Ten.

8.3.3 Personality tests

Psychologists are still searching for a general explanation of human personality. Over the years almost every aspect of human personality has been studied – emotions, temperament, morals and ethics as well as specific traits such as aggression, conformity, self-esteem and timidity. The types of tests and the ways of conducting them have been numerous and include self-administered questionnaires (such as the MMPI, see later), performance tests, free association tests and the Rorschach test (a test designed to show intelligence, personality and mental state, in which the subject interprets ink-blots of standard type). Despite extensive study, the human personality is still an enigma.

Many researchers have tested the difference between criminal and non-criminal personalities. Schuessler and Cressey (1950) carried out a comparison of 113 studies which used 30 different types of personality tests, all of which sought to detect a personality difference between criminals and non-criminals. They found that 42 per cent of the 113 studied showed differences in favour of the non-criminal, while the remainder were indeterminate. These links were too tenuous to conclude that personality traits were consistently and systematically linked to criminality.

Seventeen years later, Waldo and Dinitz carried out a similar comparison of some 94 studies which had been undertaken during the intervening years. They claimed that the comparisons they made were more accurate because they were methodologically more sound, involved larger sample groups, made better use of control groups and had taken account of other variables which might affect criminality, especially the environmental variables. In 76 of the studies (81 per cent) they found a difference between criminals and non-criminals. Although these tests seemed to provide evidence of a personality difference between criminals and non-criminals, Waldo and Dinitz felt that the findings were far from conclusive. Thus they too concluded that no personality traits were consistently and systematically linked to criminality. In order to comprehend this conclusion it is necessary to understand the main personality test: the MMPI.

8.3.4 MMPI test

Between the 1950 and 1967 comparative studies a new, and allegedly more reliable, test became more widely operative for assessing the criminal personality. This test was called the Minnesota Multiphasic Personality Inventory, or the MMPI for short. It consists of 550 items which were developed to assist the diagnosis of adults who sought psychiatric help. The subjects decide whether the 550 statements are true or false when applied to themselves. There are a number of checks included in the questionnaire in order to catch untruthful answers. The test is split into ten scales and the subject is given a score on each scale; there is no overall score. The individual's full personality is then constructed from a score profile obtained by entering the scores from each scale onto a graph. The ten scales indicate an assessment of: hypochondria; depression; conversion hysteria or disorder (where unexplained physical symptoms are assumed to be linked to psychological factors); psychopathic personality; masculinity-femininity; paranoia; neurosis; schizophrenia; hypomania (a condition marked by over-excitability); and introversion. As the MMPI is now used for the assessment of the personalities of normal individuals, the scales do not usually bear any names but are usually identified only numerically, e.g., scale 1, scale 2, scale 3, etc. (see Table 8.1).

Table 8.1: MMPI clinical scales

Scale Number	Scale Name	What the Scale Discloses
1	Hs–Hypochondriasis	Tired; inactive; lethargic; feels physically ill.
2	D–Depression	Serious; low in morale; unhappy; self-dissatisfied.
3	Hy–Hysteria	Idealistic; naïve; articulate; ill under stress; social.
4	Pd–Psychopathic deviation	Rebellious; cynical; disregards rules; socially aggressive; selfish.
5	Mf–Interest pattern of opposite sex	High score: sensitive. Low score: exaggerated own sex interest pattern. High score in males: gentlemanly; scholarly; feminine. High score in females: rough; ambitious.
6	Pa–Paranoia	Perfectionist; stubborn; hard to know; or, with moderate scores, socially acceptable.
7	Pt–Psychasthenia	Dependent; desires to please; feelings of inferiority; indecisive; anxious.
8	Sc–Schizophrenia	Negative; difficult; odd; pathetic; lacks social grace.
9	Ma–Hypomania	Expansive; optimistic; decisive; not bound by custom.
0	Si–social introversion	Unassertive; self-conscious; shy; or, with low score, socially active.

Source: From Lundman (1993), p. 30.

The items which the study by Waldo and Dinitz had found most often distinguished the criminal from the non-criminal lay in the Psychopathic personality (Pd) scale, or scale 4 of the test. However, rather than simply accepting the findings, they looked behind them and discovered that this part of the test could produce a systematic bias because it included a number of items which were most likely to be answered differently by a criminal. The most obvious was: 'I have never been in trouble with the law'. Other questions which appeared in this scale and to which the delinquent is more likely to answer differently from the non-delinquent were: 'I liked school'; 'My relatives are nearly all in sympathy with me'; 'I often was in trouble in school, although I do not understand for what reasons'. In the studies where personality differences were said to be found, this was based on the different answers given to only four questions out of 50. The small differentiation resulted in a significant difference between criminals and non-criminals in the final statistical analysis. In any event, an explanation could be found in the different environments or situations of the two groups, rather than personality differences.

It is unsurprising that the delinquent scores higher on this Pd scale, as it was designed specifically to differentiate delinquents from other groups, a factor which Waldo and Dinitz seem to have ignored. The more surprising fact is rather that the score differences on this scale were not greater. But its utility for identifying delinquents is weakened because it has been found to predict characteristics besides delinquency. For example, those who drop out of school have been found to have a higher Pd score than others, as have those who are less shy, particularly if they are more aggressive. The archetypal 'yuppie' or the hard-nosed businessman is also likely to score high on this scale. Professional actors also have high Pd scores and so do those who have 'carelessly' shot someone in a hunting accident (see Gleitman (1986) at p. 616). Used as a predictor, one would expect those who scored high on this scale to drop out of school, be outgoing, possibly more aggressive, become professional actors and be involved in hunting accidents. It would seem that what is being measured is not a predictor of action but rather something which indicates a disposition towards a certain type of personality. And the personality tendencies involved (the significance attached to what other people think of them) are too slight to point to any direct link to criminality. The practical application of such tests in criminology is thus severely limited.

One of the main reasons why these personality tests attracted so much interest was that it was hoped that they would provide predictive information on those most likely to offend in the future, raising the possibility of being able to offer special help before such persons' personalities began to cause criminally defined behavioural problems. Lundman (1993) reports on the utility of the MMPI test as a predictor of criminality. He found that three of the scales were associated with offending: scale 4–Pd Psychopathic deviation; scale 8–Sc Schizophrenia; and scale 9–Ma Hypomania. Of these, scale 8 was the best predictor, with 23.8 per cent of those who obtained a high score on this scale becoming officially delinquent within four years. This still means that there is a very high over-prediction – 76.2 per cent of those with a high rating on scale 8 did not offend within four years. A slightly better rate of prediction is obtained when high scores on at least two out of three of the above scales are combined: 34.5 per cent of those in this category offended within four years, but this still leaves 65.5 per cent who fall within this category but who did not offend. Crucially, the test was not able effectively to separate out the offenders from the others: it thus gives too many false positives to be a good predictive tool (Farrington (1994)).

8.3.5 Interpersonal maturity tests

A further level of tests which came out with very similar results was based on the social maturity levels of individuals. These are often called 'interpersonal maturity' tests or 'I-Level' tests. In these studies, individuals are tested for their social and interpersonal skills and they are then placed on one of several levels of maturity. These levels are simply given numerical values, but each of the numerical levels is also linked with descriptions of the person's 'core personality'. Both Warren (1970) and Palmer (1974) discovered that most convicted delinquents appeared in Levels 2, 3 and 4 and all were socially immature. Level 2 personalities are asocial, aggressive and power orientated, which is very similar to the descriptions found in the MMPI tests. Individuals on Level 3 are characterised by their conformity to the delinquent group, which bears marked similarities to claims by Hewitt and Jenkins ((1947), see 8.2.2), and those on Level 4 are often called neurotic. They claimed that 90 per cent of delinquents fell into one or other of these three levels.

8.3.6 Assessment of personality tests

The MMPI tests and the I-Level studies all suggest that there is a link between criminality and assertiveness, hostility, resentment of authority, dynamic personalities and psychopathy. However, while in the first two of these research studies the findings were statistically significant, their actual sizes were small. This has given rise to doubts about their reliability, and they have been questioned by later researchers. Each study compares delinquents or criminals (those who have been officially convicted) with non-delinquents or non-criminals (a group of those who have not been officially convicted but a number of whom may have committed acts which are as unacceptable or criminal). Some of the personality traits found in the criminal group could derive from their treatment by the justice system, rather than from something inherent in their characters. Such a reaction might be natural and normal, especially if they know of other people, possibly friends, who have committed similar crimes but not been caught. A hostile reaction would in those circumstances be understandable, as would a feeling of injustice and resentment of authority. The small personality differences found in these studies may not have been there prior to their contact with police or courts, and they might be the result of those encounters rather than the reason for them.

Conceptually, it would be better to begin testing at a very young age and follow the children through to adulthood. Ideally, the tests should cover not only personality and official criminality, but also self-reported criminality. The researcher would then be better able to assess whether their personalities were inherent, learnt from normal socialisation, or were the result of a brush with the criminal justice system. The proposed method of assessment might also show whether these personality types actually commit more crime or whether they are just more likely to be caught. There would still be problems: the perceived personality traits may be the result of earlier conflict with figures of authority such as teachers.

In any event, it seems that the personality trait will not determine the criminal behaviour, but will only predict a certain type of behaviour, of which criminality is but one example. Some even doubt whether there is any real personality trait, claiming instead that the way each individual acts depends rather upon the situation they are in. They point out that a person who is said to have a more aggressive personality will not be generally aggressive; the trait will show only in certain situations. Thus they may be aggressive on the sports field, or whilst driving and at work, but be very gentle in their personal relationships. The argument is that it is the situation, not the individual's personality, which decides their behaviour. For example, if a police car is behind you it would not cause you to stop although it might cause you to drive with more care, but if the blue light on the police car starts flashing, you would stop. The situation of the blue light brought about the behaviour, not any personality attribute of the individual – the same behaviour would probably have occurred whether you were dominant or submissive, sociable or unsociable. But in a different situation you might not stop. If, for example, you had just committed a crime other than a driving offence, you might try to escape. This is not to deny any influence to personality, but rather to say that reactions may depend on a number of factors. For example, the behaviour of a person in a school depends partly on their position – head teacher, teacher, secretary, caretaker, prefect, pupil or parent; partly on the situation – classroom, sports field, parents' evening, disciplinary, social; and partly on the personality of the individual. It might also be affected by the pressures of a peer grouping or by the values of the community (see Chapter Twelve).

The Cambridge study (in which a cohort of young boys was analysed and followed until adulthood) found (Farrington (1994)) that the really significant links were not with personality, but between offending behaviour and impulsivity (acting without stopping to think about consequences). This in turn may be connected with low physiological arousal as discussed in Chapter Seven, especially concerning EEG and the Autonomic Nervous System. Low arousal would lead to over-confidence, sensation seeking and risk taking all of which have been linked to offending behaviour (see Mawson (1987)). In the Cambridge study, low heart rate (one of the measures of low arousal) was linked with violent offending; when a boy appeared to come from a high risk background, one of the things which appeared most successfully to protect him from turning to offending was being shy, nervous or withdrawn, which Farrington (1994) suggests exhibits high arousal. This may then be one of the important causative links.

8.3.7 Some comments on treatment
The main use to which these so-called personality theories could be put is one of treatment. Some psychologists argue that drug therapy and electro-

convulsive treatment is of use in disabusing and re-training delinquents and criminals, but on the whole these methods are avoided or at least do not currently form the central part of any re-training techniques. The better opinion seems to be that greater understanding of personality gives rise to the possibility of controlling actions by behaviour therapy. In this, the psychologist uses the knowledge of the offender's personality, along with general information about other people with similar personality types, in order to choose the learning theory or conditioning which is thought to be most likely to give favourable results (see Chapter Ten for a discussion of cognitive behavioural technique).

For example, Trasler (1962) suggested that the learning of social behaviour was controlled by the desire to maximise pleasure and minimise painful or unpleasant incidents. If children are rewarded for good behaviour and punished for bad behaviour, they usually learn that the bad behaviour is not worth the pain or unpleasantness to which it gives rise: they therefore conform. Some individuals, such as extroverts (see 8.2.5), are less susceptible to this sort of conditioning and require more time or different methods. Others, such as extreme introverts and neurotics, may be over-susceptible to this type of learning, so that as soon as they are able to control their criminal tendencies they may start to re-learn them. The learning methods therefore differ for each type of personality.

Although it would be generally dangerous to use these theories to try to predict who will commit a crime (see 8.4), they may be useful in identifying how best to deal with criminals once they have transgressed. Many writers in this area have suggested that the criminality tends to be committed by those who possess certain personality traits such as not caring what others think, not caring about the consequences of acts when they affect others, weak or no personal ties, irresponsibility, and an out-going personality. If some of these factors do affect criminality, further criminality might be prevented by helping to alter or manage these personality traits. This may be done by, for example, making these individuals aware of the suffering they cause, making them face responsibilities, and teaching them to live in a social setting. In a few areas, some of these ideas have been tried at attendance centres which some offenders are obliged to go to as part of their probation and where some probation services provide group therapy (see Roberts (1995) and *Guardian*, 16 February 1990).

In Britain, probation orders can be accompanied by a range of conditions. The general ones which accompany almost all orders are that the probationer must be under the supervision of a probation officer for a specified period of time, report to the officer and receive home visits, and keep the officer informed of any change of address. Probation orders can also include additional requirements such as to undergo medical care, or to attend a particular place or see a particular person, or to take part or refrain from taking part in particular activities. These additional requirements have been used to implement schemes designed to deal with personality 'problems'. In the 1960s, probation orders frequently included a requirement to receive medical care. In the 1980s these additions to orders declined because doctors were unwilling to report failures to comply, which conflicted with the criminal justice view that these orders were to be seen as part of the sentence, any breach of which should be punished. More recently, psychiatric and psychological services have worked more in partnership with the probation service and there is a high rate of successful completion of probation orders and of any treatment conditions. Thus sentencers may now begin to use them more frequently (see Mendleson (1992)).

Probation orders are certainly seen as a positive alternative to incarceration. Roberts (1995) reports that the probation service has worked out strategies which are focused on particular types of offenders. For example, the Youth Offender Project run in Hereford and Worcester was aimed at persistent young property offenders who were given a mixture of social skills, information about legitimate services and how to access them, and exciting outdoor activities. The project was successful (30 per cent more successful than custody) for this group of offenders, though not for violent offenders, suggesting the need for a different strategy for each offender type. Raynor and Vanstone (1993) support the positive results which might be found in carefully targeted projects, particularly those built on cognitive behaviour, and Macdonald et al. (1992), after examining 95 projects, report positive results in at least three quarters of them. Programmes should enhance the offenders' ability to exercise responsible choices to avoid offending, and should treat them with respect so that they come to value themselves and their rights: it is important that offenders view such programmes as positive and helpful to them rather than just for control and punishment.

Similar strategies are also tried in some prison establishments, either as part of a group therapy session or in a wider context as the ethos of particular units such as Barlinnie in Scotland, opened in 1973, and the new wing in Hull. In these units the inmates are made to take some responsibility for their living conditions, they are trusted with dangerous implements like scissors and metal cutlery, staff and inmates talk through problems in the units together, and talk through the inmates' difficulties together. These units have taken on some of the most dangerous and uncontrollable inmates, and yet they have reported some quite surprising successes. Possibly their ideas should be used more widely in prison establishments. For a fuller account of such units see Wright (1982) or Boyle (1978) and (1984).

8.3.8 Criticisms of personality theories

Personality theories are more scientific than those put forward by the psychoanalyst, in the sense that they rely less on assessment and explanation of phenomena and draw more on mainly objective tests. They are more commonly based upon empirical research, which can be more easily assessed.

Most theories assume that each individual has a central or core personality which can explain reactions to most stimuli and will determine the likelihood of becoming criminally involved. However, different theories link different personality types to criminality, whilst the general use of empirical evidence makes it difficult to choose between them. On the other hand, there is much overlap: assertiveness and resentment of authority occur frequently as being linked to criminality.

More fundamental doubts arise from the central concept of the existence of a core personality. It assumes that a small number of characteristics can rule all an individual's actions and relationships. Many clearly believe that this core personality can be altered or controlled, otherwise their suggested treatment techniques would be rendered useless. Others assert that each individual is born with a particular core personality, or at least that it is developed at a 〈 early age (for example Eysenck and Trasler): for them very careful 〈 intensive treatment would be required to alter or control that inborn person ity. Some researchers have claimed that the core personality can be alter naturally by environmental change, by the passing of time, or the heighten maturity of the person (see Robins (1966)). Such a stance puts the wh〈 concept of a core personality in doubt, as the concept draws its strength fro the idea that it is permanent unless it is carefully treated by professiona However, if the core personality does alter naturally over time, it might help explain why many people who have a criminal record during their teens gro out of it in their early 20s as they mature and their personality alters. Th more basic immediate point is that so wide a range of interpretation of th basic concept must undermine confidence in theories based on personality.

Despite these doubts, common sense suggests that there must be some thing in the idea of a core personality – we all view Betty as different from Daisy or Freda and would say possibly that one is more reliable than the other, or that one is more friendly, and so on. Similarly, we all have an idea of how a particular person is likely to react to a certain situation, and that somebody else would react differently. If they do not act as expected, we would view it as 'out of character'. So we accept that although our basic idea of a person is that they portray a particular type of personality, we also accept that this can alter in small ways without losing its basic 'core'. We also accept that at certain times a person may not 'feel themselves': a normally cheery person may have an off day, but this does not alter our basic view of them. People are unique, partly because of their personalities.

To go beyond such pragmatic impressions of how criminality and personality might be related needs closer discussion of cause and effect than most of these theories provide. In almost all cases it is assumed that the relationship is direct (i.e., that criminality was a result of the personality attributes) whereas in fact the attributes may have arisen as a result of being arrested, convicted and punished, or both the criminality and the attributes may be the result of some third element. Even if the personality traits are affecting the criminality, it may not be in such a direct way as is implied. The personality traits may, for example, render the making of close relationships very difficult, which would isolate the person, who may then not feel as bound as other people are by societal norms. Alternatively, the traits may just render criminality more likely if certain other factors, for example environmental factors, are favourable to the commission of crime.

The extent to which personality attributes are accepted as a complete and reliable explanation of criminality is probably decreasing. The theories which contain a more sociological element have gained in popularity and acceptance. Despite this, personality must always play some part in the explanation of crime if only to help to understand why it is that not all people from certain social backgrounds and environments end up as criminals. Most sociologists accept this, but they would certainly question the idea of a fixed core personality and rather see personality as a continuing thread which is altered by experience and by relationships, and which of course can be affected by treatment methods.

8.3.9 An interesting use of personality tests

In recent years personality typing has been used, particularly in the United States of America, to help detect particular types of criminals. This method has been most useful in the solution of serial murders. In this section a brief introduction to some elements in this process will be touched upon.

Serial murder is not just the killing of a number of people: it is not just mass murder. Mass murder is usually the killing of a number of people in a fairly small geographical area in a relatively short space of time, such as the murders committed by Ryan in Hungerford in 1986. Mass murders can generally be said to arise from one outburst, and often culminate in suicide on the part of the perpetrator. The victims are usually chosen by chance and the outburst is often the result of a sudden and uncontrolled mood change. Serial murder, on the other hand, is a repetitive event. The murderer kills at a number of different times, frequently spanning a matter of months or years, and often the murders are committed at very different locations. It usually, though not always, involves one perpetrator and one victim (at a time). The victims are generally strangers or only slight acquaintances. The murders are often accompanied by sadistic acts, mutilation or both. To most rational people there appears to be no motive; most would say that these killings were the act of a mad man.

Holmes and De Burger (1989) claim that this description is not normally appropriate. They argue that such murderers are not suffering from any mental illness, and that in this type of murder there is characteristically a motive. Serial murders are not the result of purely uncontrollable outrages; they are not crimes of passion. But although there is a motive, most people would find it to be irrational. The motive is internal, not external; it does not arise from direct monetary gain or from a desire to do a job for money, as in the case of a mercenary or a hit man, nor does it arise because of a passionate belief in a cause as with a terrorist: it often arises for the pure pleasure and enjoyment of killing. Other motives may be the killing and elimination of a particular type of person – prostitutes, young women out at night, red-haired women, bearded men, tramps and so on. It may be the pure pleasure and thrill of killing; it may be the feeling of power over the victim, but there is always a motive which arises inside the murderer.

Many will question how such aggression and such clear antisocial behaviour can arise. The preceding sections introduced the idea that some forms of criminality were related to a tendency towards psychopathy. This is very different from the illness of psychopathy: it is generally caused by environmental factors and is often referred to as a sociopathic personality type. The earlier references were mainly to mild sociopathic problems, but this section is concerned with more extreme cases. Typically, they are asocial and therefore feel no guilt on breaking societal rules; they are driven by selfish, powerful and uncontrolled desires which they feel require immediate gratification no matter what others suffer. The perpetrator often has little ability to feel love or affection. The sociopath is also often aggressive and impulsive. This description of the personality type of a typical serial murderer is, of course, a characterisation, and in any particular case some of these factors may be missing and others may exist. The origins of this type of personality are probably numerous and certainly disputed. Some still believe that an individual is born with the possibility of acquiring such a personality, but all agree that upbringing, particularly relationships with parents and the amount of interpersonal violence to which the individual is subjected or witnesses as a child, has a very large part to play (see 8.2).

Serial murderers have been categorised into different types. Holmes and De Burger (1989) outline four main types:

1. Visionary Motive Type – This serial murderer commits crimes because commanded to do so by voices or visions. Peter Sutcliffe, the 'Yorkshire Ripper', claimed to have heard voices telling him to destroy prostitutes. This is the rarest type, and such serial murderers may be seen as suffering from a psychotic mental problem and therefore to be out of touch with reality. The victim tends to be a stranger and one who is believed to belong to a particular category of person. The act itself is usually spontaneous and disorganised and is committed only in response to the voices.

2. Mission-Oriented Motive Type – This type of killer has a goal, usually to rid the world of a particular type of person: in this case, however, the goal comes from within and not as a response to voices. These people are not psychotic but have a strong wish to solve a particular problem, to take control of it. Such a killer knows the action is wrong and that others condemn it. He is aware of what he is doing and of what others think of his crime. He is difficult to spot: he appears normal to all people who come into contact with him; he lives a normal life and is often very successful. He chooses groups which he regards as 'unworthy' – prostitutes, tramps, old people, women with long hair, black males. This may describe Sutcliffe, (some did not believe that he heard any voices) whose victims to begin with were prostitutes, and later were women out alone at night. The victims are usually strangers, chosen because they fit into a particular category. The act is usually well planned, well organised and efficiently committed.

3. Hedonistic Type – These killers basically kill for pleasure. According to Holmes and De Burger, there are two main sub-categories of hedonistic serial murderers, each of which derives its pleasure from different sources. The thrill orientated killer is possibly the most difficult to understand. This type enjoys the excitement of killing and so kills for pleasure. His victims are strangers chosen at random and with no specific characteristics. They become victims purely because they are in the wrong place at the wrong time. The killing is spontaneous and disorganised. There is often no pattern. There may be sadistic acts committed against the victims, but for this type of criminal

the important thing is the act of killing. The second sub-group is the lust killer. A central part of this crime is sexual. For many of them the sexual pleasure is heightened by the amount of pain and often sexual mutilation they can inflict. Lust killers gain sexual gratification by abusing others. They often have normal relationships and live normal lives, except that they have a problem with sexual gratification. For most lust killers the lead-up to the crime is part of the pleasure, so they fantasise about the crime and then take time in the selection of the victim, looking for specific traits, perhaps even following the victim for a period of time before the act. None the less, the victim is usually a stranger who happens to possess the desired characteristics. The act is usually planned and organised and the sexual and killing parts of the crime are often savoured, perhaps even including the disposal of the body.

4. Power/Control-Oriented Type – This type of killer is very difficult to distinguish from the lust or thrill-seeking types. Many of the same traits may appear: but this criminal acts out of a desire to show absolute power over another human by taking ultimate control of life or death. In order to prove control he may commit sexual acts, but the sex is only a form of power over the victim. The victim will be a stranger who has specific characteristics, the crime will be organised and planned. The killing is often very sadistic.

The above draws very crude and general pictures of these types of criminals. In order to help with a murder investigation the characterisation needs to be a lot more precise. The full profile is gained from a close examination of the scene of the crime; the scene of the discovery of the body, if different; the type of neighbourhoods in which these are situated; the last movements of the victim; the type of person the victim was; his or her physical appearance; the dissection of the body; and any information made available by the investigation. From these, the expert in behavioural science is able to piece together a description or profile of the type of person for whom the police are looking. Of course no profile can be exact, but as long as the police understand its shortcomings it is thought by many that the profile can be a useful tool in the investigation of these offences. Similar methods have been used in other serial offences such as rape and child abuse. In these cases the evidence of the victim is important, particularly if they can remember what the criminal said.

The profile is merely one of many ways of achieving a solution to horrific murders, and the inexact nature of the science on which it is based can reasonably be overlooked. The limitations of the methodology are noted by Omerod (1996); it is useful only in a few cases such as rape, killing or arson; the profile only describes a possible type of person and does not identify an individual; profiles could prove prejudicial, both in the minds of the police in looking for an offender and in the minds of a jury if a case comes to court. The profile can only supplement other investigative methods, both of finding offenders and constructing cases. Moreover, as the same methods are being used in the analysis of particular individuals and their reasons for committing certain offences, or to characterise the types of personalities which give rise to criminality, the subjectivity of the methodology limits its explanatory usefulness.

8.4 ASSESSMENT OF DANGEROUSNESS AND CRIMINALITY

8.4.1 Defining dangerousness

Most Western criminal justice systems include some form of assessing the danger posed by individuals who have been convicted of violent or other serious crimes. Such assessments help to decide how long those people should be removed from society, not as punishment but as protection for other members of the society. In some societies such removal is possible and occurs without any crime having been committed – in the form of civil committal to mental institutions, some of which occurs because such people are perceived as being dangerous either to society or to themselves, or both. This is only possible where the individual's mental stability has been questioned, and it is this rather than just the dangerousness which is the deciding factor. In all these instances, someone has to decide what is dangerous and whether a particular individual fits that description. It is therefore essential that there is a definition of 'dangerousness'. On the surface, this may appear to be a very simple task. Almost everyone has an idea of what they consider to be dangerous, and for most it involves at least an element of violence or threat to personal safety. For some, however, this idea is much wider – in America, for example, the Federal Court once ruled that the writing of a bad cheque was 'dangerous' to society because the economy would collapse if everyone did it (*Overholser v Russell* (1960) 282 F 2nd 195).

Some insight into the idea of dangerousness might be gained by consulting the law and discovering how it deals with the concept. In Britain there have been a number of provisions which have allowed perceived dangerousness of the criminal to play a major role in sentencing. In each case the basic concept is that of the protection of society rather than of dangerousness. The provisions are as follows:

Two new interrelated provisions were introduced by the Criminal Justice Act 1991 which allow sentencing to protect the public. Section 1(2)(b) allows the use of custody for a violent or sexual offence in order to protect the public and s. 2(2)(b) allows use of a longer sentence to protect the public (still within the legal maximum). Section 31(1) defines a sexual offence as any offence under various statutes including the Sexual Offences Act 1956 and the Sexual Offences Act 1967. The same subsection defines a violent offence as one which leads to or is likely to lead to the death or physical injury of a person, and includes an offence which is required to be charged as arson. Section 31(3) defines serious harm as death or injury whether physical or psychological. This means that these provisions should not be used where the person is likely to commit only minor offences. It is important to note that the Act does not say what level of risk is necessary before the provision can be used so that longer sentencing is possible even if the risk is only very slight. By s. 3(3)(b) the court is permitted to consider any information about the offender when it makes its prediction of future conduct, and presumably this could include expert testimony. The Act, however, leaves the sentencer to decide and does not even require that expert testimony is sought to decide on the issue of likelihood of future harm. Yet in the assessment of dangerousness judges are essentially lay personnel with no special training, and could act on a pure hunch or even on a dislike for the individual. In *R* v *Baverstock* [1993] 1 WLR 202, Lord Taylor of Gosforth CJ said that where the sentencer is considering a longer term than required by the seriousness of the offence the court should put counsel on notice – presumably to allow them to address this issue.

Secondly, life sentences, both mandatory and discretionary, can be used to protect the public from dangerous offenders. Life sentence is obligatory for those, over 18 years of age, found guilty of murder. When used in this way it is largely to mark murder out as different in kind from other offences. Risk and dangerousness therefore become an issue in relation to mandatory life sentences only when such prisoners are being considered for release on licence. Under s. 2 of the Crime (Sentences) Act 1997, there is now a second category of mandatory life sentence to be applied to persons over 18 convicted of a second serious offence. In England and Wales the Act defines a serious offence to include: an attempt, conspiracy or incitement to murder; soliciting a murder; manslaughter; wounding, or grievous bodily harm, with intent; rape or attempted rape; intercourse with a girl under 13; possession of a firearm with intent to injure; using a firearm to resist arrest; carrying a firearm with criminal intent; robbery while in possession of a firearm or an imitation firearm. In these circumstances, a judge on second conviction must impose a life sentence unless either there are exceptional circumstances relating either to the offence or to the offender which justify not passing such a sentence (these must be stated in open court), or, under s. 1, it would be inappropriate, having regard to the circumstances of the offence or the offender. The assumption here is that past behaviour is normally sufficient to prove dangerousness in the future.

In a number of other cases life is a discretionary maximum sentence. It is most commonly used in the following cases: aggravated burglary, arson, buggery, causing an explosion with intent to endanger life or property, causing bodily injury by explosions, criminal damage intended to endanger life, grievous bodily harm, incest or intercourse with a girl under 13 years of age, kidnapping, manslaughter, rape. In these cases the court is normally expected to pass a determinate sentence which indicates the severity of the offence. A court is supposed to use the life sentence only when the offence is serious enough to require a very long sentence, when the offender is unstable and likely to repeat such offences, and where if any further offences occurred they would involve serious consequences to others. These criteria appeared in *R* v *Hodgson* (1967) 52 Cr App R 113 and were confirmed in *Attorney-General's Reference (No. 34 of 1992)* (1994) 15 Cr App R (S) 167. In *R* v *Blackburn* (1979) 1 Cr App R (S) 205, the Court of Appeal said that the discretionary life sentence:

. . . should not be imposed unless there is clear evidence of mental instability as opposed to mental disorder which would indicate that the person was likely to be a danger to the public.

This indicates that the offender can be suffering from a mental problem which falls short of a mental disorder and could include merely personality disorders. Following *Pither* (1979) 1 Cr App R (S) 209, discretionary life sentences should be for those who cannot be appropriately dealt with under the Mental Health Act 1983, often because their mental instability or illness is not treatable. It is the untreatability of their instability which renders these offenders so dangerous.

The element of danger again becomes an issue at the time when a life prisoner is being considered for release or when a possible release date is being set. Such individuals are released on parole licence which will last the rest of their lives. In the case of mandatory life sentences the trial judge is permitted to declare the minimum period he or she feels should elapse before the offender is considered for release, but anyway is required to make a recommendation to the Home Secretary, through the Lord Chief Justice, informing the Home Secretary of the conviction and giving his or her views as to the period necessary to meet the requirement of retribution and deterrence, the 'tariff'. The Lord Chief Justice can comment on this information before it is passed to the Home Secretary, or more normally one of his or her junior Ministers, who then will decide whether the suggested 'tariff' is appropriate or needs to be increased or decreased. Since the decision in *R* v *Secretary of State for the Home Department, ex parte Doody* [1993] 3 WLR 154, the prisoner has a right to know the trial judge's recommendation, to make representations to the Home Secretary and to be given the reasons for any departure from the trial judge's recommendations. The case will then be reviewed by the local review committee (LRC) three years before the end of the tariff or after 17 years whichever is the sooner. If the LRC approve release then the Home Secretary may send this to the 'lifer panel' of the Parole Board. Under s. 29 of the Crime (Sentences) Act 1997, the Parole Board can only consider a case which has been referred to them by the Secretary of State, either as a class of cases or a particular case. If the Board recommend release then the Minister consults with both the trial judge and the Lord Chief Justice. Where the Board do not recommend release the prisoner must be held, but where they recommend release the Minister then has a discretion whether or not to release. Since April 1993 the Home Secretary has ordered that the parole dossiers, reasons for Parole Board decisions and the reasons for negative decisions by the Secretary of State will be made available to the prisoner. The central issue for both of these boards and the Minister is the safety of the public, part of this must therefore be a consideration of dangerousness.

In the case of discretionary lifers the 'tariff' is fixed in strict accordance with the recommendations of the trial judge. The problem then arises at the point of release. In *Weeks* v *United Kingdom* (1988) 10 EHRR 293 and *Thynne* v *United Kingdom* (1990) 13 EHRR 666 the old procedure practised in Britain was found to contravene art. 5(4) of the European Convention on Human Rights. These cases noted that in discretionary life sentences there would come a time when the punitive element of the sentence had been served and continued detention would be justified only on grounds of the potential dangerousness of the individual which must alter over time, and therefore the individual should have a right to have his or her case reassessed regularly to decide whether the dangerousness element had subsided. This requirement was recognised in s. 34 of the Criminal Justice Act 1991 under which the trial judge set a tariff and indicated the length of time which was required to be served before the prisoner can be considered for release and reflecting what was necessary for punishment. The process has been tightened by the Crime (Sentences) Act 1997, Chapter II of which effectively abolishes automatic remission, whilst under s. 28 the court may specify a time which must be served before consideration for release. But once this time has elapsed the case must be referred to the Parole Board. In other cases, once the specified time has elapsed the case may be considered by the Discretionary Lifer Panel of the Parole Board which was set up under the Parole Board Rules of 1992 and will consist of three members: the chair, who must be a person who holds or has held judicial office (in serious cases it will be a High Court judge), a psychiatrist and a third member. Under Part II, Chapter II of the Crime (Sentences) Act 1997, a person must be released on licence as soon as the Parole Board so directs. Where the Board decide against release, the lifer can require reconsideration after a further two years. The prisoner is normally permitted to see reports concerning him or her and can both appear before the tribunal and have representation. He or she is entitled to a decision with reasons within seven days of the hearing. This hearing is to assess the safety of releasing the individual and therefore the assessment of dangerousness is central to its decision. Neither for mandatory nor for discretionary lifers is there a definition of dangerousness or of factors to be considered.

Most recently, the Crime (Sentences) Act 1997 introduced minimum sentences for repeat offenders. When dealing with a person over 18 convicted of a class A drugs offence and who has at least two previous class A drugs convictions (at separate times), under s. 3, the court must pass a sentence of at least seven years. When dealing with a person over 18 convicted of a domestic burglary and who has at least two previous convictions (at separate times) for domestic burglary, under s. 4 the court must pass a sentence of at least three years. These minimum sentences apply unless there are specific circumstances relating either to the offence or to the offender which would render the minimum unjust (these must be stated in open court). The reason given for these minima is usually that they are necessary to protect the public from a person who has been proven to be a danger to the public in the past. There is no attempt to assess whether there might be any such danger in the future, nor any personal assessment.

Lastly, there are the provisions which allow restricted confinement of mentally disordered offenders. In the past the judiciary retained the power to decide when they would be released and did so at the time of sentencing, but in *X* v *United Kingdom* (1981) 4 EHRR 181 the European Court of Human Rights decided that such offenders should be guaranteed regular access to a tribunal to assess the lawfulness of their detention. This was later enacted and restriction orders are now available if there is a clear mental disorder recognised by the Mental Health Act 1983 and there is a special need to protect the public from serious harm (see s. 41 of that Act). It is generally used to prevent doctors discharging individuals who have committed an offence (which does not have to be serious) and where, having regard to the patient's previous record, there is a risk that further offences may occur which might lead to serious harm. Unless the restrictions are time limited the restriction lasts indefinitely and the patient can be discharged only by the Mental Health Review Tribunal or the Home Secretary. Such reviews must occur regularly. Discharge can either be conditional or unconditional; if conditional the person will be subject to recall. The fact that the authority to release is shared between the Mental Health Review Tribunal and the Home Secretary indicates the ambiguity of the decision: the former should consider mainly the need for, and likelihood of response to, treatment; whereas the latter should be interested in the safety of the public. These will not always coincide.

It is thus evident that the contribution of the law of England and Wales to a definition of dangerousness has not been very helpful: apart from the general requirement that there be an offence committed before the assessment of dangerousness could interfere with the liberty of an individual, each of the above categories seems to cover different ideas. Two broad themes arise. The first includes the possibility of a life sentence for serious offences, which include serious property offences as well as crimes against the person: the Criminal Justice Act 1991 covers the commission of violent or sexual offences and the Crime (Sentences) Act 1997 covers burglary, drug dealing, violent and sexual offences. The second strand is that the provisions consider the past conduct of the offender as indicative of possible future conduct. In the case of life sentences and restriction orders, general mental stability will be assessed while the past criminal record is merely part of that assessment. In the provisions of the Criminal Justice Act 1991, the extent to which past conduct is taken into account is a matter for the judge, as is the type of conduct to be considered and the weighting to be given to it. In the new provisions of the Crime (Sentences) Act 1997, the sole consideration for the passing of either the mandatory life sentence or the minimum seven- or three-year sentences is the offence: personal circumstances can be used only to argue against the imposition of these sentences. The presumption is that past behaviour alone predicts future behaviour.

Individuals have their own perceptions of danger and of unacceptable danger, often related to their sex, culture, social class etc., and some are deeply personal. To allow a judge unfettered powers to decide what is dangerous and remove someone's liberty on this ground would be unacceptable. Therefore certain frequently accepted boundaries are applied. For most people, any assessment of dangerousness such as to justify an individual having his or her liberty restricted would involve the individual in having already committed a serious crime, one they regard as involving danger or the potential for danger. Most would agree that crimes involving personal injury are the most serious and the most dangerous, and of these crimes those involving serious injury and/or injury to more than one victim would be the most dangerous. But it is not this simple. It is true that behaviour leading to injury is generally seen as the most dangerous type of conduct, but other factors need to be taken into account in the assessment of danger. There are, for example, many people killed on the roads due to breaches of one or other of the criminal laws – driving without due care and attention; speeding; dangerous driving; driving while under the influence of drink. Despite this fact, speeding, careless and even dangerous driving are often seen as crimes of low culpability and their perpetrators are not normally locked up. Even in the case of drunken drivers, it is rare that the individual is viewed as necessarily dangerous and in need of removal from society. Dangerous or careless use of firearms would generally be viewed as far more unacceptable even if no-one was actually injured, and deprivation of liberty would be far more likely to occur.

An interesting consideration is that some of the crimes which have the worst consequences in the light of the numbers of lives lost, or levels of serious injuries as well as loss of property, are committed by corporations or those acting for corporations: pollution of the atmosphere; harmful products; breaches of health and safety regulations. The social and economic consequences of this type of crime are probably worse for society than the consequences of traditional street crime. Yet most people fear street crime more than corporate crime, and most would probably view it as more dangerous. Corporate criminals are difficult to locate and convict, but even when this is done they would usually be subject only to a fine, often a fairly small fine. In the rare cases where they are imprisoned, it would only be for as long as was necessary to punish them; they would probably not be removed to protect the public from future dangerous behaviour (for a further discussion of this area see Chapter Three). From this it is clear that neither the law nor the general public seem to have any very clear view of what is dangerous.

Theorists have often tried to define dangerousness, and many have agreed with the idea expressed earlier that it must have something to do with personal security, and have correlated it with violence. This in turn necessitates defining violence. Mulvihill and Tumin (1969) define it as 'overtly threatening or overtly accomplished application of force which results in the injury or destruction of persons or property or reputation, or the illegal appropriation of property'. This would include accidental homicide, killing in self-defence (or under any other defence), and injury on the football field. The biggest problem with this definition is that it focuses on the act itself and therefore ignores the law – it includes many perfectly legal acts. In terms of illegality it might exclude some of the most atrocious behaviour – the acts of those in Nazi Germany. Mulvihill and Tumin's definition is not concerned with whether the violence was deliberate and it therefore includes accidental acts which happen to have the outcomes talked about in the definition. Under this definition anyone whom one would prefer not to encounter in the street, and a few one might not even place in that category, would be considered dangerous.

In the US 1973 Model Sentencing Act (see *Crime and Delinquency*, vol. 18, p. 335), s. 5 states that when a court is sentencing an individual for a felony it should be permitted to commit for a term of not more than 30 years when:

The defendant is being sentenced for a felony in which he:
(a)   inflicted or attempted to inflict serious bodily harm; or
(b)   seriously endangered the life or safety of another and he was previously convicted of one or more felonies not related to the instant crime as a single criminal episode,
and the court finds he is suffering from a severe mental or emotional disorder indicating a propensity towards continuing dangerous criminal activity.
Whenever the court feels that an individual falls within 1a or 1b it must send the individual for assessment at a diagnostic facility.

The legal limits of this power are fairly clearly defined. It is the predictor of dangerousness that is more difficult (see below 8.4.2.). In other words the legal definitions merely set limits within which the individual can be assessed and possibly incarcerated for a predicted dangerousness. The legal limits will not be accepted by everyone but are simpler to set and monitor than are any checks on the prediction of criminality. The section also illustrates that the mere fact of persistent acts of violence cannot be used to prove mental disturbance, otherwise the final part of the definition would have been unnecessary as being tautologous.

Some have taken a very narrow view of dangerousness including only overtly extremely violent and dangerous criminal acts such as murder, grievous bodily harm, or sexual crimes such as rape, child sexual abuse etc. (see Hollin 1989). Many would argue that this was too limiting as it would not permit the law to intervene when a dangerous or potentially dangerous act had been committed but before it had had disastrous consequences. These factors were taken into consideration by Megargee (1976). He defined violent behaviour as: 'acts characterised by the application or overt threat of force which is likely to result in injury to people'. He uses injury to mean personal injury and so excludes all purely property crimes where there is no physical force, either actual or threatened. By including the word 'threat' it covers the instance where there is a property or other offence carried out without actual violence but with a willingness to injure, for example armed robbery. The definition also covers situations where no one is actually hurt but where there is a strong possibility of injury, for example, shooting at someone or setting an explosion where it is 'likely' that injury will result but in fact none does. It does not cover the instance where a gun is fired and no one else is present as there is no likelihood of injury. By using the term 'force' it involves some element of intent or purposive use of power and therefore probably excludes injuries resulting from all unintentional or accidental violence. It would not cover the individual who opens a door and accidentally causes harm to someone on the other side or who crushes someone in a crowd. Most people would not view these activities as violent and it is necessary to include some element of intent even if not the intent to cause harm. Certainly such an element would be important to the usefulness of any definition in assessing dangerousness at least so far as the criminal justice system is concerned. Note this definition covers intentional acts of force which may be legal – such as killing in self-defence – as these are still violent. To exclude this behaviour one would need to define 'criminal violence' – the application or overt threat of force which is likely to result in injury to people and which is forbidden by law. Although this definition is not perfect it is one of the most useful to map out the area of behaviour in which we are interested. It is important to note that writers often have different conceptions of dangerousness and that this may well affect the value of the rest of their work.

Floud and Young (1981) came to a similar conclusion. They defined dangerous offenders as those who have inflicted or attempted to inflict serious bodily harm on other human beings and who are found to be suffering from a severe mental or emotional disorder indicating a propensity towards continuing dangerous criminal activity. Floud also suggested that the reason she so firmly supports longer sentences to protect the public is that it would then allow lower sentences for the run-of-the-mill offences – i.e., a lower tariff which would still mark the seriousness of the offence but exclude extra penalties for dangerousness.

Interestingly the provisions in the Criminal Justice Act 1991 incorporate the first part of Floud and Young's definition and, since it is the possible result of the crime which is perceived as dangerous not merely the crime itself, could be interpreted to include many of the more difficult areas, including both driving and corporate offences which either cause or are likely to cause injury. The Criminal Justice Act (probably) and more certainly the Crime (Sentences) Act 1997 which refers only to offences, ignore the second part of the Floud recommendations – that the court should be required to inquire into whether the individual is found to be suffering from a severe mental or emotional disorder indicating a propensity towards continuing dangerous criminal activity. This latter element is, however, a part of the calculation in the case of discretionary life sentences, both in their use and in recommending how much of the sentence should be served in order to protect the public.

8.4.2 Attempts to explain and predict violent crime

For many years theorists have been trying to predict who will offend and re-offend. Basically what many of these researchers do is to collect facts about convicted criminals: previous arrests and convictions; social and employment history; and, for juveniles, their school records, particularly truancy rates; drug use; family backgrounds etc. The factors which are most strongly related to recidivism are then singled out as those most likely to predict unacceptable behaviour. These factors are then tested normally in longitudinal studies to see whether the predictors stand up to the rigours of practical application. The studies do suggest a modicum of success – previous criminal records, drug habits and employment histories are the most often quoted predictors, but more recently others, such as family size and the age at which the child starts school, have been included. If these were found to occur in almost all recidivists then they might be used as predictors of dangerousness and so remove the question from the intuition of the judges, but the major problem with this method is that it tends to over-predict. It does very well in picking out groups of people who fit into a high-risk category, but with there will be a number of 'false positives'. Many of those with identifiers will not in fact be dangerous – they will not re-offe nately the predictors have been found to be particularly inefficient at disco- vering those most likely to commit serious crimes, particularly violent offences which is the category we most want to incapacitate. This is partly because of the lack of research material – there are insufficient serious violent offenders around to make a reasonably sized study group from which to glean the prediction characteristics.

More effective might be more personalised psychological predictors. Again there are problems with prediction but as they are more an assessment of the individual rather than a group of persons they may be more accurate. Psychoanalysts have, indeed, used a number of different approaches and theories to predict violent behaviour. Several will be briefly discussed here, but for a fuller coverage see Zillman (1979) or Siann (1985).

8.4.2.1 Instinct theories

Instinct theories assume there is an inner force which desires aggression and violence. Freud called it the death force or Thanatos. The life instinct, Eros, and Thanatos are in conflict and the aggression needs to be allowed to vent itself. Usually this is possible through acceptable means such as sport or competitive business, but if the force is not socially dissipated it will come out in the form of violence, either directed to others or at oneself - suicide. The work of Storr (1970) is an example of such an approach. But however interesting, these ideas are impossible either to prove or disprove, which limits their contribution to understanding in the particular area of criminol- ogy, and gives them little practical value.

8.4.2.2 Drive theory

Drive theories also assume that there is an inner force which desires aggression and violence, but in drive theory the inner force is acquired through experience, and is not innate. The general argument is that each type of behaviour is motivated by a drive, and as the drive increases above its normal levels, the individual takes action to reduce it. In the case of violence the basic assertion is that when individuals are prevented from getting what they want, they become frustrated. This frustration leads to aggressive or violent behaviour, which may be aimed at the obstruction to their desire or may be used on other targets (see Dollard et al. (1939) and Berkowitz (1974)). Although these theories are a little easier to verify – for example, by giving people a problem to solve and then moving them onto the next one just before they succeed, or by allowing them to watch all but the last twenty minutes of a film and watching the frustration and violence build up – they are not very useful as predictors of behaviour. It is unclear whether it is being claimed that all aggression is the result of frustration, or that whenever frustration occurs it always leads to aggression. Whichever it is, the interest of the theory is limited because it is not sufficiently precise to be useful as a predictor of dangerousness.

8.4.2.3 Personality and violence

There are a number of different ideas under this head. The first claims that people with psychopathic tendencies, sometimes known as sociopaths or antisocial personalities, are more likely than others to commit frequent acts of violence. Sociopaths are generally viewed as those who are unsocialised; they do not hold strong values and are less capable of forming loyal relationships with other individuals or with groups; they are selfish, irresponsible, impulsive, uncaring and do not tend to feel any guilt; they are easily frustrated and tend to blame others for their bad behaviour. As Checkley (1976) points out, the term psychopath or sociopath is fairly wide, and is often used to describe anyone who breaches the law, so that it becomes synonymous with criminal. He argues, however, that the true usage of the term can include businessmen, professionals, sportsmen, etc. (see 8.3.4). A brasher idea of sociopathy was expounded by Guze (1976), who said a person was a sociopath if he had been in trouble with the police (other than for traffic offences) and had at least two of the following: a history of excessive fighting; school delinquency; poor job record; a period of wanderlust; and being a runaway. For women, the fact that they had a history of prostitution could also be taken into account. He argued that sociopaths could not be treated, and therefore that they should all be locked up until middle age. This recommendation, if taken seriously, would apply to a large number of people who have never committed serious crimes and may never do so. It also confidently assumes that all sociopaths are readily identifiable without possibility of error. It seems to go much wider than the idea of dangerousness which was discussed above, and would involve the removal of many individuals from society with no sound proof that to do this would make society any safer. This is reinforced by Rafter's (1997) discussion of the evolution of the term 'psychopath' in criminology. She observes that the term is probably undefinable, being a 'misfit', 'on the borderline' between 'normality and abnormality'. For legal purposes a more precise definition would seem to be in order.

One of the most prominent explanations of violent behaviour was expounded by Megargee (1966). He argued that violence occurs when the push towards violence, which usually arises through anger, is stronger than the individual's ability to control it. The loss of control he saw as most dangerous, and most likely to give rise to criminal acts of violence in two particular personality types: the under-controlled and the over-controlled. When a potentially aggressive situation arises, the under-controlled make little or no attempt to control the feeling of violence. Such persons are likely to have many convictions for minor acts of violence.

On the other hand, people who are over-controlled will restrain their aggression in situations where most people might be provoked into violent reaction but will eventually reach a point where they may suddenly commit acts of extreme violence well beyond what might have been expected from the immediate provocation. The extreme level of violence which Megargee finds characteristic of this type of offender he explains by saying that most of us learn to match our level of violence to the level of provocation by practice.

We give vent to aggression in the form of anger or small outbursts on a frequent basis, and discover by experience what is acceptable. The over-controlled personality has no such practice, and may eventually respond with extreme levels of violence to quite minor provocation. Claims have been made for this analysis as a useful predictor of violence. Such claims must be dubious when it is not known what proportion of the population could be said to be over-controlled, but perfectly safe in the sense that they have never reached their breaking point, or at least have never done so in a criminally or dangerously violent situation.

Blackburn has taken the theory further. In 1971 he carried out MMPI tests on 56 murderers who had been detained in mental hospitals, and claimed that they could be analysed into four groups. Two of the groups were under-controlled and two were over-controlled. The under-controlled were:

1.   Psychopathic – poor self-control, high extroversion, hostility towards others and low anxiety;
2.   Paranoid aggressive – poor self-control, hostility towards others and psychotic symptoms.

The over-controlled were:

1.   Controlled-repressor – high level of self-control, low hostility and low anxiety;
2.   Depressed-inhibited – not impulsive, high levels of introversion and anxiety, hostility directed inwards and high level of depression.

He found similar results when he tested violent offenders who were not hospitalised. His findings have been upheld on a number of occasions, but McGurk and McGurk (1979) discovered that non-violent criminals could also be found to have fairly large numbers of the first three categories; only the depressed-inhibited were not found in the non-violent group. Their findings have also been replicated, and this suggests that personality inventories cannot be used in this way to predict dangerousness. This finding would be upheld by the previous discussion of the MMPI test – see 8.3.4.

It is unlikely that any method used to predict dangerousness is very accurate, and this must call into question the use of this concept in the criminal justice system.

8.4.2.4   Macho personality and dangerousness

The final personality difference which in recent years has been closely related to violence, and therefore possibly to dangerousness, is the macho personality as measured by the Hypermasculinity Inventory (see Zaitchick and Moscher (1993)). The macho personality views violence as manly, danger as intrinsically exciting, callous sexual activity aimed at women as acceptable, and interprets being tough as a form of self-control. Zaitchick and Moscher (1993) connected these personality elements with inter-male violence, callousness, violence and sexual attacks on women, gang violence and abuse of children. The utility of this test in predicting dangerousness could therefore be very strong but more scientific testing of the inventory is necessary before it can be reliably used to remove an individual's freedom.

8.4.2.5   Risk, mental disorder and dangerousness

In a recent study Steadman et al. (1993) worked in a team of 12 people including those trained in law, psychiatry, psychology and sociology who, after reviewing empirical and clinical research, concluded that there were five central factors to an assessment of risk of dangerousness. The factors are:

(a)   the level and type of social support available to the person;
(b)   how impulsive the individual is;
(c)   reactions, such as anger, to provocation;
(d)   the level of ability to empathise with others;
(e)   nature of any delusions and hallucinations.

They designed reasonably simple and apparently accurate tests which would assess each of these factors in mentally disordered groups, recognising that these might also be valid for testing other groups. In a pilot study they had some success in these clinically assessed factors, but there were discrepancies and the team felt that these might be the result of not having taken into account the situation or context in which any acts of violence took place. A wider analysis of their clinical risk predictors and if situational and contextual factors is being undertaken, and could help in making more accurate predictions of who is and who is not a danger to the public. Or at least it might help in deciding whether such predictions can realistically be carried out.

8.4.3   The dangers of prediction

As can be seen from the preceding section, the psychological prediction of dangerousness is very problematic and unreliable. In the United States, following a 1966 decision of the Supreme Court, 967 patients who had been diagnosed as dangerous were moved from hospitals for the criminally insane to ordinary mental hospitals, and in most cases this posed no problem. Only 26 individuals were returned to hospitals for the criminally insane; over 483 were later released into the community, and of these 83 per cent had no further arrests (Steadman (1972)). Clearly, most of them were perfectly safe. How could their detention be justified? Most countries do confine individuals to protect other members of society from harm. Can this be justified? A large part of the argument which follows is adapted from that made by Floud and Young (1981).

In most countries the penal system is largely based upon an idea of retribution, being intended as a punishment for a crime which has been committed. Where there is some recognition of the possibility of deterrence and rehabilitation, they have generally had to be accommodated with the time period laid down for retribution. Sentences are not generally lengthened simply to enable more time for rehabilitation, and are rarely lengthened for reasons of deterrence. The exception is that most States do considerably lengthen sentences, in certain circumstances, for reason of protecting the public. Clearly, protecting the public is a function of the criminal justice system, but the removal of the liberty of people based on a judgement, difficult to prove, that they may be a danger to others raises acute problems. Of course, in most States confinement to protect others does not take place unless the individual has first committed a crime. Is this a sufficient reason for such action? Does it make it acceptable? Should all rights be removed from an individual merely because of a single, or even a series, of transgressions? Once the individual has paid the debt to society, should they not be again presumed innocent until proven guilty?

It can be argued that such questions ignore the potential harm these individuals may inflict, and abrogates the responsibility to protect the innocent who might be harmed. This argument is most forceful where the lives or the health of others are at risk. An analogy is often made with quarantine – we confine carriers of infectious disease to protect others in society from becoming contaminated and thereby harmed, and so we should be willing to protect the public from dangerous criminals. In the case of disease, we do not protect society from all contagious diseases, only those most likely to have the worst consequences for those who catch them. Similarly, most people would never argue that the public should be protected from the petty criminal. That claim is made only in the case of those whose past conduct suggests they may inflict severe harm on others, usually physical harm to the person.

It has to be noted that the analogy is far from exact. It implies that the danger from a criminal is similar to the danger of catching a disease. Whilst there is a high probability that people exposed to the disease carrier will contract the disease, people suffering from a disease are not likely intentionally to try to contaminate others; they are confined because they cannot help but contaminate someone. There are therefore two differences. Firstly, there is a very high probability, and in most diseases a certainty, that if released the individual will contaminate someone and, secondly, that the contamination will be unintentional. If a supposed dangerous criminal is released, there is no such certainty and, as was seen above, often no strong probability that he or she will re-offend. The criminal has a choice, and that choice may depend upon many factors, including the situations faced on release. For any particular case there is the possibility that the released prisoner may not re-offend, and because there is no sound way of predicting future behaviour he or she has the right to be presumed innocent until the criminal law is actually transgressed.

This is a powerful argument until there is a further victim who may well be killed or suffer serious injury. At that point it will certainly be argued that the rights of the criminal should have been forfeited before anyone else was harmed. Such a reaction has a powerful emotional appeal, but that may not be a sound basis for legal action. If individuals are to have their liberty removed on some judgement of their future behaviour, it is clear that mistakes will be made. Some perfectly safe people will be incarcerated and some very dangerous people may be released. The problem is one of discerning the dangerous from the safe, and as yet the bases for prediction are unreliable. The arguments on both sides have merit; it largely becomes a moral argument of balancing the individual right to freedom against the collective call for safety. Most States allow some use of protective confinement and accept that some will have their liberty wrongly interfered with. Equally, most States allow such protective detention only in certain, usually well defined situations, and accept that they will thereby release some dangerous people. The secret is to find the right balance of reducing mistakes whilst understanding the justice of confinement to protect others.

Floud and Young (1981) argued that the way forward was by taking account of where the burden of risk should lie. Before individuals have committed a serious violent act, even if they fall into the dangerous group, they should retain their liberty and society should bear the risk that they may one day offend and cause some harm. But once people commit serious violent offences and also fall into the potentially dangerous group, then the burden of risk shifts to them and they should be locked up in case they do it again, i.e. you shift the risk of victimisation: before the crime if all of an 'at risk' group are locked up, many safe people will be incarcerated and the number of potential victims in society will be low; but once an individual commits a serious violent offence he or she should take the risk of being victimised and wrongly locked up rather than society taking the extra risk of releasing that person. Floud then argues that any detention above that necessary to mark the seriousness of the past crime should be limited to cases where the harm is severe, such as serious sexual or violent offences.

More recently there has been even more focus on risk as the central element in assessment of dangerousness. In the USA the 1991 Public Health Service report, *Healthy People 2000*, discussed the problems of violence and abusive behaviour from the health, rather than legal, perspective and focused on four main points:

(a)   A move away from a legal focus towards one based solely on risk, as assessed by health professionals.

(b)   Full realisation that all decisions in this area are on a linear continuum and cannot be split into simple yes/no decisions. Cases rarely clearly fall into one or other category so that decisions whether or not to release should be based on where on the continuum the risk should lie.

(c)   The level of risk should never be decided once and for all. A person's potential danger will alter over time and this should be recognised by allowing frequent reconsideration of treatment and release.

(d)   In all decisions there needs to be a balance between the seriousness of any possible criminal behaviour and the probability of it occurring. These assessments need to be based on specific risk factors.

Clearly much of the US suggestion accepts the need for protection of the public but allows it to interfere with the liberty of an individual only where this is proved to be necessary and only for as long as is necessary. This highlights a number of problems with our present system. Under ss. 1(2)(b) and 2(2)(b) of the Criminal Justice Act 1991 the judge in court will assess the amount of time necessary to punish for a particular offence and, where there is a need to protect the public (in violent or sexual cases), will also set the time necessary for such protection. This is a one-off decision which may not be assessed on any objective criteria or advice. With the exception of an immediate appeal it cannot be altered as the person changes and his or her danger to the public is either lessened or increased. In the case of life imprisonment the dangerousness of both mandatory and discretionary lifers will be assessed only once they have served the element necessary to punish for the crime committed. Most of this assessment should be concerned with their dangerousness, but how carefully the seriousness of the possible outcome is weighed against the probability of it occurring is impossible to tell. There are certainly no specific risk factors set out which need to be considered. In relation to mandatory and minimum sentences under the Crime (Sentences) Act 1997, there is no consideration of individual risk which is assumed if certain past conduct has occurred. This Act (and the 1991 Act) applies the first part of Floud and Young's test, but totally ignores the second part relating to individual assent. Finally in relation to restriction orders under s. 41 of the Mental Health Act 1983, these are largely medically assessed on grounds of the need for, and utility of, treatment as well as any consideration of dangerousness. In the method of their review they probably most closely approach the US suggestions, but still no specific risk factors are set out.

One suggestion is that the assessment should take account of both past conduct, particularly very harmful criminal activity, and a personal assessment, often of the offender's mental state or personality type. The second leg of this rather assumes a measurable tendency towards criminality which, as has been indicated above, is very often questionable and thus should never, alone, be used to predict dangerousness. It should be noted that there is no necessary link between mental illness and criminality (no more of those with mental problems commit crimes than do the general population) and that psychiatrists have found it impossible to predict criminal behaviour (see Pitch (1995)). However, it is argued that once the first part of the assessment has been completed then the second becomes necessary. For those who have a recognised mental illness, an evaluation of whether, and to what extent, their condition could be treated and whether such treatment could occur in the community is necessary. To safeguard the freedom of the individual, a careful analysis of the mental state might indicate that appropriate care and treatment measures rather than incarceration can reasonably ensure that the offender will not be, or is very unlikely to be, dangerous in the future. In other cases past behaviour may indicate no more danger than is normal, but without some assessment this would be impossible to ascertain. Without professional assessment it will be risky for the judge to release or to incarcerate only for a short period someone who has a past history of harmful offences. The tendency would be to refuse such release even where the immediate offence does not call for lengthy incarceration, which may breach basic rights to freedom. Professional assessment does not, of course, completely remove risk, but it makes possible a more balanced judgment between the need to protect the public and the desirability of maintaining individual rights.

Assessment of dangerousness and imprisonment associated with such assessment are both fraught with problems. Three areas in particular appear to need safeguards: first procedure; secondly the factors to be considered in the assessment; and finally the type of confinement.

The procedure of permitting a judge to assess this aspect at any stage appears to be questionable. This is unlike most other judicial decisions and there are good reasons for allowing the assessment to be made by a panel of persons, possibly including a legally qualified individual but definitely including a psychiatrist or psychologist. In cases where there is an element of dangerousness the judge could still pronounce on the seriousness of the offence committed and then pass the offender over to such a panel to make a preliminary assessment of its extent. There would then need to be a separate tribunal to hear appeals and to reassess the decision at appropriate intervals. This should represent a recognition that the decision being made is different in kind and effect from the judicial decision of punishment.

Secondly, there is a need for guidelines on how to assess dangerousness and how to balance the possible harm to the public against the probability of occurrence. Some guidelines are necessary as this is a very grave interference with liberty which should not be taken lightly. Open public debate about where the lines should be drawn would be helpful: at present we have almost no criteria and, in some cases, no need for professional advice. The public need to be protected from some very dangerous people but even these people also need their rights to liberty protected from unnecessary interference. The problems are legion but they need to be faced, particularly as the use of longer sentences for the protection of the public seems likely to become more common.

Lastly, there is the question of where to hold such individuals. Clearly some are mentally ill with treatable problems and are held in hospitals; others are in prison either because they are not suffering from a mental condition or because their condition is not treatable. Prisons are generally places we send individuals as punishment: should we be using them for dangerous offenders once they have served the part of their sentence necessary to punish? If they are detained to protect others rather than directly in relation to their behaviour, society should recognise this and place them in different institutions with more rights while retaining the level of security necessary to secure their removal from society. There seems to be little justice in imprisoning them in houses of punishment.

8.5 CONCLUSIONS

Most people would accept that every individual has a personality which is special to them. What is far more difficult to accept is that certain personalities will always or usually be criminal. It is therefore generally presumed that one cannot predict criminal behaviour by studying personality.

Acceptance of these statements does not render personality useless in the study of criminality; it merely limits the ways in which it is used. As was seen above in 8.3.7, 8.3.9 and 8.4, personality theories have had practical uses in the treatment of convicted criminals, the detection of certain types of criminals, and in deciding how to deal with certain offenders. These uses are limited, but none the less they are important and should not be ignored in any criminal justice system.

In the 1980s and 1990s there has been a strong tendency to reject any solutions based on reform or on helping offenders in the belief the 'nothing works', a case which was earlier expounded by Martinson (1974). This is based on the assertion that treatment is not effective and therefore should not be tried, even in a prison setting. Supporters of rehabilitative methods are necessarily cautious, but urge that such methods are certainly no worse than other ways of dealing with offenders, and may be better (Palmer (1990)). In any event, there are indications that there are advantages in recognising the particular problems of individual offenders, even if there is no alteration of criminal conduct, because their incarceration may be made less stressful both for inmates and prison officers (see Genders and Player (1993 and 1994)). What must be guarded against is any temptation to extend the length of imprisonment, or to put back release dates in order to continue treatment: treatment should not lead to sentencing. The aim should be for programmes to work alongside any punishment. What is being suggested is not strictly speaking treatment, but rather measures to encourage such offenders to confront their personality/psychological problems along with the social aspects. The object of such psychosocial interventions is to help individuals to cope without crime. Within this broad framework, as Lösel (1995) reports, different interventions have differing successes depending on the environment within which they are used and the punishment strategy which accompanies them. One of the major difficulties in improving the success rate arises from the tension between the two aspects of what the professional assessors are expected to do: the criminal justice system expects them to determine the responsibility of the individual so that the court can better decide how to punish; while the system, society and the offender all want the offender's behaviour to alter so as not to include criminality in the future. These functions may conflict and then there is little indication of how best to resolve that conflict (see Debuyst (1995)).

Besides using psychosocial interventions to assess the needs of punishment and/or assistance, it is important not to ignore the rights of offenders, victims and society (Hood (1995)). During the 1990s the uses made of such intervention, especially in assessing dangerousness, have moved towards ignoring the rights of individual offenders in the hope – probably the vain hope – of preventing further victimisation. It is an area in which politicians and judges can be tempted to take the popular line of removing the freedom of the offender to protect society, but there is also a need to ensure the protection of individual offenders. How this is resolved will depend on whether professionals (psychiatrists, other medical practitioners, social workers, lawyers and judges) as well as politicians are willing to reject solutions based purely on social control in favour of solutions which also take account of medical and social solutions. Even in findings of dangerousness, societal responsibilities should not be entirely abrogated.

REFERENCES

Aichhorn, August (1936), *Wayward Youth*, (first published 1925) New York: Viking Press.

Berkowitz, L. (1974), 'Some Determinants of Impulsive Aggression: Role of Mediated Associations with Reinforcement for Aggression', *Psychological Review*, vol. 81, p. 165.

Blackburn, R. (1971), 'Personality Types among Abnormal Homicides', *British Journal of Criminology*, vol. 11, p. 14.

Bowlby, John (1946), *Forty-Four Juvenile Thieves*, London: Ballière, Tindall and Cox.

Bowlby, John (1953), *Child Care and the Growth of Love*, (based by permission of the World Health Organisation on the Report: Maternal Care and Mental Health), Harmondsworth: Penguin.

Boyle, Jimmy (1978), *A Sense of Freedom*, London: Pan Books.

Boyle, Jimmy (1984), *The Pain of Confinement: Prison Diaries*, London: Pan Books.

Carlson, Neil R. (1986), *Psychology of Behaviour*, 3rd edn, Boston: Allyn and Bacon.

Cleckley, Hervey (1976), *The Mask of Sanity*, 5th edn, St. Louis, Missouri: C.V. Mosby.

Debuyst, Ch. (1995), 'Psychological Assessments Before and After Sentencing', in *Psychological Interventions in the Criminal Justice System*, Proceedings from the 20th Criminological Research Conference, 1993, European Committee on Crime Problems, Criminological Research, vol. XXXI, Strasbourg: Council of Europe.

Dollard, J., Doob, L.W., Miller, N.E., Mowrer, O.H., and Sears R.R. (1939), *Frustration and Aggression*, New Haven, Connecticut: Yale University Press.

Eysenck, H.J. (1959), *Manual of the Maudsley Personality Inventory*, London: University of London Press.

Eysenck, H.J. (1977), *Crime and Personality*, 3rd edn, London: Routledge & Kegan Paul.

Eysenck, H.J. (1987), 'Personality Theory and the Problem of Criminality' in B.J. McGurk, D.M. Thornton and M. Williams (eds), *Applying Psychology to Imprisonment*, London: HMSO.

Eysenck, H.J. and Gudjonsson, G.H. (1989), *The Causes and Cures of Criminality*, New York: Plenum Press.

Farrington, David P. (1994), 'Introduction', in David P. Farrington (ed.), *Psychological Explanations of Crime*, Aldershot: Dartmouth.

Floud, Jean and Young, Warren (1981), *Dangerousness and Criminal Justice*, Heinemann: London.

Freud, Sigmund (1935) *A General Introduction to Psycho-Analysis*, (first published in 1920), trans. by Joan Riviere, New York: Liveright.

Genders, Elaine and Player, Elaine (1993), 'Rehabilitation in Prisons: a Study of Grendon Underwood', *Current Legal Problems* 235.

Genders, Elaine and Player, Elaine (1994), *Grendon: A Study of a Therapeutic Prison*, Clarendon Studies in Criminology, Oxford: Oxford University Press.

Gilling, Daniel (1997), *Crime Prevention: Theory, Policy and Politics*, London: UCL Press.

Gleitman, Henry (1986), *Psychology*, 2nd edn, New York: W.W. Norton & Company.

Gross, Richard D. (1989) (first published 1987), *Psychology – The Science of Mind and Behaviour*, London: Hodder and Stoughton.

Guardian, 16 February 1990.

Guze, Samuel B. (1976), *Criminality and Psychiatric Disorders*, New York: Oxford University Press.

Healy, William and Bronner, Augusta F. (1936), *New Light on Delinquency and its Treatment*, New Haven: Yale University Press.

Hewitt, Lester E. and Jenkins, R.L. (1947), *Fundamental Patterns of Maladjustment*, Springfield Illinois: State of Illinois.

Hoghughi, M.S. and Forest, A.R. (1970), 'Eysenck's Theory of Criminality: An Examination of Approved School Boys', *British Journal of Criminology*, vol. 10, p. 240.

Hollin, Clive R. (1989), *Psychology and Crime: an Introduction to Criminological Psychology*, London: Routledge.

Holmes, Ronald M. and De Burger, James (1989), *Serial Murder*, Newbury Park, California: Sage.

Hood, R. (1995), 'Introductory Report, General Report of the Conference and Conclusions and Recommendations', in *Psychological Interventions in the Criminal Justice System*, Proceedings from the 20th Criminological Research Conference, 1993, European Committee on Crime Problems, Criminological Research, vol. XXXI, Strasbourg: Council of Europe.

Jung, Carl Gustav (1947), *Modern Man in Search of a Soul*, London: Routledge & Kegan Paul.

Kline, P. (1984), *Psychology and Freudian Theory*, London: Methuen.

Little, Alan (1963-64), 'Professor Eysenck's Theory of Crime: An Empirical Test on Adolescent Offenders', *British Journal of Criminology*, vol. 4, p. 152.

Lösel, F. (1995), 'Evaluating Psychosocial Interventions in Prisons and other Penal Contexts', in *Psychological Interventions in the Criminal Justice System* Proceedings from the 20th Criminological Research Conference, 1993, European Committee on Crime Problems, Criminological Research, vol. XXXI, Strasbourg: Council of Europe.

Lundman, Richard J. (1993), *Prevention and Control of Juvenile Delinquency* 2nd edn, Oxford: Oxford University Press.

Macdonald, G., Sheldon, B. and Gillespie, J. (1992), 'Contemporary Studies of the Effectiveness of Social Work' *British Journal of Social Work* 615.

McGurk, B.J. and McGurk, R.E. (1979), 'Personality Types Among Prisoners and Prison Officers – an Investigation of Megargee's Theory of Control', *British Journal of Criminology*, vol. 19, p. 31.

McGurk, B.J. and McDougall, C. (1981), 'A new Approach to Eysenck's Theory of Criminality', *Personality and Individual Differences*, vol. 2, p. 338.

Martinson, R. (1974), 'What Works? – Questions and Answers about Prison Reform', *The Public Interest*, vol. 23, p. 22.

Mawson, A. R. (1987), *Transient Criminality*, New York: Praeger Press.

Megargee, E.I. (1966), 'Undercontrolled and Over-Controlled Personality Types in Extreme Antisocial Aggression', *Psychological Monographs*, vol. 80, whole no. 611.

Megargee, E.I. (1976), 'The Prediction of Dangerous Behaviour', *Criminal Justice and Behaviour*, vol. 3, p. 3.

Mendelson, E. (1992), 'A Survey of Practice at a Regional Forensic Service: What Do Forensic Psychiatrists Do? *British Journal of Psychiatry*, vol. 160, p. 769.

Mulvihill, D. and Tumin, M. (eds), (1969), *Crimes of Violence: A Staff Report Submitted to the National Commission on the Causes and Prevention of Violence*, Washington DC: Supt. of Docs., U.S. Print Office.

Omerod, David (1996), 'The Evidential Implications of Psychological Profiling', *Criminal Law Review* 863.

Palmer, Ted (1974), 'The Youth Authority's Community Treatment Project', *Federal Probation*, vol. 38, p. 3.

Palmer, Ted (1990), 'The Effectivness of Intervention: Recent Trends and Issues', *Crime and Delinquency*, vol. 37, p. 330.

Pitch, Tamar (1995), *Limited Responsibilities: Social Movements and Criminal Justice*, trans. John Lea, London: Routledge.

Public Health Service (1991), *Healthy People 2000: National Health Promotion and Disease Prevention Objectives*, US Department of Health and Human Services.

Rafter, N.H. (1997), 'Psychopathy and the Evolution of Criminological Knowledge', *Theoretical Criminology*, vol. 1(2), p. 235.

Raynor, Peter and Vanstone, Martin (1994), *Straight Thinking on Probation, Third Interim Evaluation Report: Reconvictions within 12 months following STOP Orders, Custodial Sentences and Other Community Sentences*, Mid-Glamorgan Probation Service.

Roberts, J. (1995), 'Implementing Psychosocial Interventions Linked to Community Sanctions', in *Psychological Interventions in the Criminal Justice System*, Proceedings from the 20th Criminological Research Conference, 1993, European Committee on Crime Problems, Criminological Research, vol. XXXI, Strasbourg: Council of Europe.

Robins, L.N. (1966), *Deviant Children Grown Up: A Sociological and Psychiatric Study of Sociopathic Personality*, Baltimore, Maryland: Williams and Wilkins.

Schuessler, Karl F. and Cressey, Donald R. (1950), 'Personality Characteristics of Criminals', *American Journal of Sociology*, vol. 55, p. 476.

Siann, G. (1985), *Accounting For Aggression: Perspectives on Aggression and Violence*, London: Allen and Unwin.

Steadman, H.J. (1972), 'The Psychiatrist as a Conservative Agent of Social Control', *Social Problems*, vol. 20(2), p. 263.

Steadman, Henry J., Monahan, John, Robbins, Pamela Clark, Appelbaum, Paul, Grisso, Thomas, Klassen, Deidre, Mulvey, Edward P. and Roth, Loren (1993), 'From Dangerousness to Risk Assessment: Implications for Appropriate Research Strategies', in Sheilagh Hodgins (ed.), *Mental Disorder and Crime*, Newbury Park: Sage.

Storr, A. (1970), *Human Aggression*, Harmondsworth: Penguin.

Trasler, Gordon Blair (1962), *The Explanation of Criminality*, London: Routledge & Kegan Paul.

Waldo, Gordon P. and Dinitz, Simon (1967), 'Personality Attributes of the Criminal: An Analysis of Research Studies', *Journal of Research in Crime and Delinquency*, vol. 4, p. 185.

Warren, M.Q. (1970), 'The Case for Differential Treatment of Delinquents', in Harwin L. Voss (ed.), *Society, Delinquency and Delinquent Behaviour*, Boston: Little Brown.

White Paper (1990), *Crime, Justice and Protecting the Public*, Cm 965, London: HMSO.

Wolfenden Committee Report (1957), *Report of the Committee on Homosexual Offences and Prostitution*, Cmd 247, London: HMSO.

Wright, Martin (1982), *Making Good: Prisons, Punishment and Beyond*, London: Burnett Books.

Zaitchick, Matt C. and Moscher, Donald L. (1993), 'Criminal Justice Implications of the Macho Personality Constellation', *Criminal Justice and Behaviour*, vol. 20, p. 227.

Zillman, D. (1979), *Hostility and Aggression*, Hillsdale, New Jersey: Lawrence Erlbaum.

CHAPTER NINE
Mental Disorder and Criminality

9.1 INTRODUCTION

Mental disorder is sometimes referred to as mental abnormality, and many psychologists now refer to it as psychopathology. These three terms are used in the literature, but basically they refer to the same group of people. Where these terms are used, what is being discussed? Essentially, each term refers to states of mind which give rise to some form of problem, usually for the individual. The term mental disorder shows that the mind is in a state of confusion; it is not working properly; i.e., it is suffering from a disease. The term mental abnormality denotes that the state of mind is both uncommon and unpleasant; it shows a negative or bad element. People afflicted with such conditions are referred to as suffering from a psychopathology because it is an illness the symptoms of which are mainly psychological. 'Psycho' indicates the mental element and 'pathology' represents the illness, the overt symptoms produced by an underlying cause or disease. The main object of the psychologist is to treat the underlying pathology or illness. Different schools of psychology have differing ideas about the causes and cures for the various mental illnesses. Some stress physical manifestations – biological or neuro-scientific – where the use of chemical therapy and surgery is common. Others look more to cognitive or behavioural understanding and, possibly, alteration. These aspects will not be dealt with in this chapter. Here, we are interested in the connection between mental illness and criminality, and the way in which these diseases are viewed by the law.

Many studies have attempted to discover whether mental disorder or illness is associated with criminality. Most of these studies have been of people in prison, and ascertain how many prisoners are mentally ill. Thus Glueck (1918) and Bluglass (1977) respectively found that 12 per cent and 2 per cent of their samples were suffering from psychosis, 28 per cent and 14 per cent were suffering from mental subnormality, and 19 per cent and 13 per cent were suffering from psychopathy. Bluglass also assessed that 2 per cent were suffering from psycho-neurosis and 11 per cent were alcoholics or very heavy drinkers (figures drawn from Prinz (1980)). Teplin (1990) notes that recent studies conclude that rates of severe mental illness amongst the prison population range from 4–5 per cent to 12 per cent and that even the most conservative of these is two to three times higher than the comparable rates in the general population. This does not necessarily prove that the crimes committed by these people were induced by their mental problem. It does not even prove that the mental problem existed prior to the criminality. It could have been brought on through traumatic feelings of remorse or guilt, or through their treatment in prison. In order to prove a causative link, rather more is required. A better approach might be to study the criminal behaviour of psychiatric patients. Unfortunately, those studies which exist do not adequately explain their sampling or their diagnosis of various illnesses. A fairly good study was carried out by Rollin (1969). He found that 40 per cent of those admitted without recourse to the courts had a criminal record, and 36 per cent were persistent offenders. Of those admitted by the courts, 66 per cent had a criminal record and 44 per cent had previously had a custodial sentence. These figures do suggest some correlation between criminality and mental illness. If there is such a relationship, the way in which it develops depends on the types of mental illness. Before discussing that question, we need first to outline the way the criminal law and the courts have defined mental disorder and the significance of such recognition.

9.2 LEGAL IDEAS OF MENTAL DISORDER

There are a number of ways in which the legal rules take mental illness into account. It can be a general defence (see insanity 9.2.1) or a special defence to a particular crime like murder (see 9.2.4 and 9.2.5). Mental illness is also a factor which may be taken into account in sentencing offenders where the individual may obtain treatment instead of punishment (see 9.2.6), but in this case it is only available if there is a form of treatment which it is thought may help the offender. For a discussion of all the criminal law implications, see Smith and Hogan (1996); Cross, Jones and Card (1995); Ryan and Scanlan (1991); *Blackstone's Criminal Practice* (published annually); and Allen (1997).

9.2.1 Criminal law definition of insanity
Insanity is a defence long recognised in criminal law as being available theoretically in respect of any charge. In the past the accused who successfully pleaded 'not guilty by reason of insanity' was sent to a mental institution for an indefinite period. The detention had to continue until the Home Secretary was satisfied that this was no longer necessary for the protection of the public. Often the individual was never released. These severe consequences meant that in the past the defence was restricted to cases of murder, where the alternative was death. Following the abolition of the death penalty and the availability of the defence of diminished responsibility to an accused charged with murder, the defence of insanity became of less practical significance: between 1975 and 1988 there were only 49 findings of 'not guilty by reason

of insanity' (see Mackay (1990)). Its use may, however, be revived by the Criminal Procedure (Insanity and Unfitness to Plead) Act 1991. This gives the judge discretion about the appropriate sentence when an individual is found 'not guilty by reason of insanity'. The judge may now order detention in a hospital approved by the Secretary of State (with or without a restriction order); pass a guardianship order under the Mental Health Act 1983; pass a supervision or treatment order; or give an absolute discharge. This new range of orders suggests that accused persons should find the defense of insanity more attractive, but so far such pleas have not risen (Mackay and Kearns (1994)). The discretion does not apply where the charge is murder when the judge must order detention in hospital with a restriction on discharge without limit of time.

In recognising the defence of insanity, the criminal law is acknowledging that people can suffer defects of reason to a degree which makes it impossible for the law to hold them responsible for their actions.

The rules pertaining to this defence were first laid down in 1843 in *M'Naghten's case* 10 Cl & F 200. This was an advice sought by the House of Lords from the judges after the acquittal of M'Naghten of the murder of Sir Robert Peel's private secretary, following the finding that he was insane. Their advice, which subsequently has been known simply as the M'Naghten Rules, was to the effect that:

> every man is to be presumed to be sane and to possess a sufficient degree of reason to be responsible for his crimes, until the contrary be proved (to the satisfaction of the jury); and that to establish a defence on the ground of insanity, it must be clearly proved that, at the time of the committing of the act, the party accused was labouring under such a defect of reason, from disease of the mind, as not to know the nature and quality of the act he was doing; or, if he did know it, that he did not know he was doing what was wrong.

The case determined that it is a defence to any criminal charge for an accused to establish:

(a)   that he was suffering from a disease of the mind and as a consequence of this,

(b)   he was labouring under a defect of reason, and as a consequence of this,

(c)   he did not appreciate the nature or quality of his actions, or if he did appreciate the nature or quality of his actions he did not know that his conduct was wrong.

The judges also determined that if an accused, through a defect of reason arising from a disease of the mind, suffers from an insane delusion, criminal liability should be assessed on the basis that the facts as he or she believes them to be are true. For example, if an accused through an insane delusion had believed another was about to attack and kill him or her, then the killing of that other should be regarded as a possible act of self-defence. If, however, the insane delusion resulted in an accused believing another was stealing his or her wallet, then even if those facts were deemed to be true, the killing of the imagined thief would not be excused (unless the accused did not appreciate his conduct was wrong) since the law does not recognise killing simply to retain the wallet as being justifiable conduct.

The principal characteristic of a disease of the mind within the defence of insanity is that its cause lies internally within the physiology or psychology of the individual concerned, and is not brought about by external sources, e.g., drugs, concussion and so forth. It does, however, include diabetes, which if not treated with insulin may cause a defect of reason (*R v Hennessy* [1989] 1 WLR 187 and *R v Bingham* [1991] Cam LR 433).

The disease of the mind must produce a defect of reason in an accused. This is more than a temporary bout of forgetfulness or absent-mindedness: *R v Clarke* [1972] 1 All ER 219. An individual must be incapable of exercising any semblance of normal reasoning power and thus be unable to accept legal responsibility because:

(a)   He or she cannot appreciate the nature or quality of the act. Examples include:

(i)   An individual acting as an automaton, i.e., without conscious appreciation of his or her conduct. Such a person has not committed an *actus reus* because the act is not voluntary, this undermines the *mens rea*.

(ii)   An individual incapable of realising the consequences of his or her actions, e.g., strangling a small child simply to impose parental punishment without realisation that it will cause death. Here there is *actus reus* but no *mens rea*.

(iii)   An individual who is unable to appreciate the circumstances of an act may be unaware of its nature or quality. A rather prosaic example would be the case of an individual firing a shotgun at what is believed, because of a defect of reason, to be a scarecrow but was in fact a next-door neighbour. Here there is both *actus reus* and *mens rea* but no rational understanding and therefore no responsibility.

(b)   Although appreciating the nature or quality of the act there may be no realisation that the conduct was 'wrong', in the sense of contrary to law. Again there is both *actus reus* and *mens rea* but no rational understanding and therefore no responsibility.

The narrowness of the concept of defect of reason in the M'Naghten rules fails to take into account the greater understanding of the human mind which has been brought about through recent discoveries in psychology and psychiatry. It fails to take into account the possibility of an individual being aware of the nature or quality of an act and knowing that it is in breach of the law and yet feeling compelled to commit it, see *R v Kopsch* (1925) 19 Cr App R 50. In such cases there is both *actus reus* and *mens rea* but no rational understanding and therefore no responsibility. Perhaps this should be taken into account. For example, the individual may be acting under a delusion that the victim is planning to kill him or her or that the victim is possessed by the devil and will cause untold harm to others. In these circumstances it is certainly arguable that there is no real responsibility and therefore no criminal culpability. Such an 'irresistible impulse' may well constitute an 'impairment of mental responsibility' within the defence of diminished responsibility (see below)

As mentioned above the defence of insanity is not common and as it does not cover certain types of mental impairment its relevance and utility are now questionable. It is an all-or-nothing defence: if accepted it is a full defence to any crime; if not then, except in certain special instances (see 9.2.2 to 9.2.6 below), the accused is regarded as criminally culpable and will be convicted if the *actus reus* is proven. Thus although the defence is not very common it still shapes the limits of criminal responsibility and so is central to an understanding of the justice of applying sanctions and of the moral indignation to which crime should give rise. The definition is a legal construct and application of the rules leads to absurd distinctions. It can lead to separating mental problems which are clinically assessed as similar or as having similar effects on a person's mental capacity. The defence may cover individuals who suffer from transient problems such as sleepwalking or epilepsy (which are outside the Mental Health Act 1983) and yet does not cover those suffering, for example, from delusions which are clearly covered by that legislation. The failure of the definition to register real differences in responsibility has led to the insanity defence being severely attacked.

Packer (1968) has argued that without the insanity defence criminal culpability would have no meaning but so sweeping a view does not fit well with modern psychiatric and psychological knowledge. More plausibly the Butler Committee in 1975 suggested a complete redefinition of insanity to reflect the clinical understanding of responsibility: their suggestions formed the basis of the recommendations of the Law Commission in its draft Criminal Code Bill of 1989 (Law Commission No. 177). Similarly, in 1982 Norval Morris attacked the insanity defence stating that the issue was one of free choice and that what should be tested should be the degree of culpability measured on a linear continuum from the entirely rational (fully culpable) to the pathologically determined (no culpability). For Morris the level of culpability would be relevant for both deciding guilt and choosing the appropriate sentence. This approach, requiring an unlikely precision of 'scientific' assessment in each case, presupposes that criminal culpability and mental or psychiatric impairment are linked. Hochstedler Steury (1993) attempted to test this: the finding was that the intersection between the criminal and psychiatrically impaired populations was four times greater than it would have been if the two were entirely independent and she therefore concluded there was a link. On this basis, the justification for condemning criminal acts is reduced in a number of cases where the ability to choose the behaviour has been impaired. The definition of criminal culpability needs to take account of reduced or impaired free will in relation to both punishment and condemnation, but before this can occur the link between culpability, free will and mental impairment needs to be more clearly understood. Before the legal definition is altered there would need to be a very careful consideration of legal culpability in both criminal and civil law. There is a long and very prestigious history of linking justification for punishment, moral blame and criminal responsibility to free will and choice of actions (see, for example, Hart (1968)), but this literature generally fails to set out what should determine whether a person's free will has been interfered with. It could be that the present defence of diminished responsibility (see below 9.2.4) would indicate how best to formulate such a rule structure which could then be applied to all other crimes, not just restricted to allegations of murder (for a full discussion see Smith and Wilson (1993)). Any approach would still raise the difficulty of reconciling the need for a legal definition with what is required to make clinical sense.

9.2.2 Insanity and voluntary intoxication

An accused who, through drink or drugs, has produced a disease of the mind, e.g., delirium tremens, such as to produce a defect of reason, may be able to claim the defence of insanity. (For a discussion of the significance in law of intoxication, see 9.5 below.) A distinction must be made between the temporary impairment of the mental faculties produced by drink and drugs, and the repeated taking of such substances which, over a period of time, produces an impairment of the mental processes which may persist though the individual concerned is sober. Both situations are self-induced, but only the latter can possibly give rise to a defence of insanity (see the House of Lords decision in *Attorney-General for Northern Ireland* v *Gallagher* [1963] AC 349).

9.2.3 Non-insane automatism

To plead automatism one has to prove that movement of the limbs is not voluntary, but wholly unconscious or reflecting impaired consciousness. The mind must not be controlling the body at all (see *Bratty* v *Attorney-General for Northern Ireland* [1963] AC 386, *R* v *Isitt* (1977) 67 Cr App R 44 and *Attorney-General's Reference (No. 2 of 1992)* [1994] QB 91). A finding that the action is involuntary will lead to an acquittal. Where the automatism is the result of a disease of the mind the acquittal will be one of 'not guilty by reason of insanity', in other cases it will just lead to a verdict of not guilty. Any external cause of the automatism is seen as not a matter of insanity (see *R* v *Quick* [1973] QB 910): if the automatism is the result of a blow to the head or the administration of drugs for medication (such as insulin for hypoglycaemia) then a verdict of not guilty should be returned; if it is the result of internal factors such as epilepsy it should be treated as an insanity defence. There have been some interesting cases where automatism has been accepted. In *R* v *T* [1990] Crim LR 256, T, a young woman, was charged with robbery and causing actual bodily harm but acquitted as it was proved that three days earlier she had been raped: the psychologists suggested that at the time of the offence she was suffering from post-traumatic stress disorder which had caused a dissociative state and so she was not acting with a conscious mind. This is interesting as it could have been held that post-traumatic stress disorder was an internal state of mind, but it was held that it was caused by the rape which was external and therefore was simple automatism.

Self-induced automatism is a different issue. It is usually caused by voluntarily consuming drink or drugs, prescribed or otherwise. When the self-induced automatism is due to substances not normally considered to cause problematic behavioural changes, the defence of automatism will be available even if the substance was taken voluntarily as long as the jury do not find that the defendant acted recklessly (see *R* v *Bailey* [1983] 1 WLR 760). The issue is more fully considered under 9.5.2 but generally it is not recognised as a good defence.

9.2.4 Diminished responsibility

Since 1957, diminished responsibility has been available as a defence to those charged with murder. If this plea is successful, the individual will be convicted of manslaughter and the judge, in sentencing, can exercise discretion to reflect the degree of responsibility. The prosecution may also choose to charge a person with manslaughter on the basis of diminished responsibility. Under the Homicide Act 1957, s. 2, a plea of diminished responsibility will succeed if: the accused suffers from an abnormality or disease of the mind; that state of mind is caused by arrested or retarded development, some inherent cause, or by injury or disease; and that the abnormality substantially impaired the accused's mental responsibility for the acts and omissions in killing or being a party to the killing. 'Substantial' means that while the impairment need not be total it must be more than trivial in nature (see *R* v *Lloyd* [1967] 1 QB 175). The clearest formulation of the attributes of diminished responsibility are contained in the judgment of Lord Parker in *R* v *Byrne* [1960] 2 QB 396 at 403, where he said:

'Abnormality of mind', which has to be contrasted with the time-honoured expression in the M'Naghten Rules 'defect of reason', means a state of mind so different from that of ordinary human beings that the reasonable man would term it abnormal. It appears to be wide enough to cover the mind's activities in all its aspects, not only the perception of physical acts and matters, and the ability to form a rational judgment as to whether an act is right or wrong, but also the ability to exercise will power to control physical acts in accordance with that rational judgment. The expression 'mental responsibility for his acts' points to a consideration of the extent to which the accused's mind is answerable for his physical acts which must include a consideration of the extent of his ability to exercise will power to control his physical acts.

This definition leaves the description of the mental state of an offender and its effects on the responsibility for committing the crime to the professional (i.e, the expert medical or psychiatric witness) to a much greater extent than in the case of insanity. Furthermore, to justify a verdict of manslaughter on the grounds of diminished responsibility the abnormality need not be very marked: *R v Seers* (1984) 79 Cr App R 261, where the accused who suffered from a serious depressive illness was granted the benefit of the defence even though he could not be said to have been partially insane or on the borderline of insanity. Although the expert is charged with assessing the mental state of the accused, it is left to the jury to decide what weight to give that evidence, considered along with all the other evidence in the case; they are then entitled to reject or ignore expert evidence even if this was not contradicted. See the Privy Council decision in *Walter v The Queen* [1978] AC 788, which has been upheld in *R v Saunders* [1991] 93 Cr App R 245.

Diminished responsibility has been successfully used in a number of cases where one might not have expected s. 2 of the Homicide Act 1957 to have operated, for example, in cases where someone kills due to extreme anxiety, post-natal depression, pre-menstrual syndrome, reactive depression, grief, stress (particularly common in cases of 'mercy-killing'), impossibility or great difficulty in resisting impulses and alcoholism. This shows its flexibility as a defence and this is both its strength and its weakness. There are also cases where one would have expected the defence to be successful but where it failed, for example, the case of Peter Sutcliffe, the 'Yorkshire Ripper', where psychiatrists agreed that he was suffering from paranoid schizophrenia, an abnormality of the mind, which would amount to a lowering of responsibility and yet the jury refused to believe the defence. The discrepancy in decision-making suggests that the jury are making a moral rather than a medical decision. They take into account the offence committed and decide whether the individual deserves to be convicted rather than genuinely assessing the culpability of the offender. On the other hand, in many cases the expert psychiatrists are called on to pass an opinion as to whether the individual's ability to form the relevant mental responsibility was substantially impaired, making it a medical and moral, rather than a legal, issue.

All this contrasts with the position in relation to insanity (see above 9.2.1). There are problems with both positions. The issue for law, society and criminology is to determine for which crimes the various defences should be open. Is there any good reason why diminished responsibility should not be recognised in crimes other than murder? The legal reason is that it is only in cases of murder that there is a mandatory sentence: in all other circumstances diminished mental capacity can be marked in the sentence passed. Is this acceptable? Should we call someone guilty, with the full mental culpability to which that gives rise, when in effect his or her capabilities were affected by state of mind? Legally it would be very difficult to mark a finding in between guilt and innocence, but for a more realistic understanding of criminal culpability such a position may be necessary. The need is reinforced by the consideration that at the sentencing stage the rules of evidence are less clearly drawn which may give the defendant less protection, and by the inherent imprecision of any assessment to capacity or incapacity for intentional action (Pitch (1995)). Resolution of these issues has far-reaching consequences for the legitimacy of the law and for the concept of criminal culpability.

9.2.5 Infanticide

Under the Infanticide Act 1938, s. 1, the offence of infanticide can be charged only against a mother for killing her own child after its birth but before its first birthday. Alternatively, a woman charged with murder in such an instance may plead infanticide as a defence. In either case, if convicted or if the defence is accepted in relation to the charge of murder, she will be guilty of manslaughter. But note that the mother must adduce evidence that the balance of her mind was disturbed by, and not yet recovered from, childbirth or from lactation consequent on the birth of the child. This offence/defence reflects a belief in our society that the balance of a mother's mind may be disturbed by hormonal changes or imbalance resulting from giving birth to a child (but see also 7.1.1 above and 16.2.3 below). The introduction of this offence/defence into English law in 1922 and its re-enactment in 1938 was significant first from a practical point of view, because at that time the deliberate killing by a mother of her child would otherwise have amounted to murder (the penalty for which was death). Secondly, it was significant from a criminological point of view in that it was an implied recognition that the cause of the crime in question (i.e., the cause of the deliberate killing of her child by a mother) was biological or psychological. The implication was that these were matters that were beyond the mother's control, and that while she should not necessarily be absolved from liability, those 'causes' or 'influences' should possibly be taken into account by way of mitigation in so far as her punishment was concerned. It must be remembered that if a person either then or now was convicted of murder, the penalty or sentence was and is 'fixed by law'. The judge had, and still has, no leeway to consider mitigation. Previously the penalty was death; today it is life imprisonment. The fact that infanticide is rarely charged as an offence or relied on as a defence to murder today can be explained by a combination of factors: prosecutors are now more likely to exercise their discretion and charge a mother in this situation with manslaughter rather than murder, hence removing the need or opportunity to rely on infanticide as a defence; advances in medical treatment and after-care social services may have reduced the number of instances where mothers have become so adversely affected by childbirth or lactation as to kill their children; and there may be no prosecution, as the authorities may try to define the death as accidental in all cases where there is no clear proof to the contrary. Where infanticide is found, the Court of Appeal in *R v Sainsbury* [1989] 11 Cr App R (S) 533, observed that in all 59 such cases between 1979 and 1988 the offender had been dealt with by probation, supervision or hospital order. The implication was therefore that although the offence was serious, the mitigating factors were usually overwhelming.

The Butler Committee (1975) argued that infanticide was no different from other mental abnormalities, and suggested that in most cases where a mother killed her young child it had more to do with the stress of caring for a new-born baby than from hormonal imbalance consequent on giving birth. They suggested that infanticide be repealed and that such cases should fall in the defence of diminished responsibility. This ignores the fact that the two defences are different. For infanticide, one only needs to prove the existence of the condition, whereas for diminished responsibility one has to prove that it 'substantially impaired' the responsibility for the act (see Walker (1973)). Cheng (1986) supports this, pointing out that in only six out of thirteen recent cases of infanticide would the disorder have been sufficiently severe to allow a plea of diminished responsibility. It might still be argued that women should have to prove substantial impairment of responsibility, but at present, in law, diminished responsibility and infanticide are different. To resolve these problems the Law Commission in its Draft Criminal Code 1989 (Law Commission No. 177), clause 64(1), suggested that:

A woman who, but for this section, would be guilty of murder or manslaughter of her child is not guilty of murder or manslaughter, but is guilty of infanticide, if her act is done when the child is under the age of twelve months and when the balance of her mind is disturbed by reason of the effect of giving birth or of circumstances consequent upon the birth.

9.2.6 Mental Health Act definition of insanity

Mental problems may be taken into consideration in sentencing and can lead to the offender being sent to a hospital or psychiatric institution, or being required to seek outpatient help under ss. 36, 37, 41, 43 and 46 of the Mental Health Act 1983. The Act can only be used as an aid to sentencing if the psychologist can offer some hope of a treatment which may alleviate the mental problem. If no such treatment is available the judge must punish the offender in the normal way, even if there is some mental abnormality. Section 1(2) of the Act defines mental disorder as a:

mental illness, arrested or incomplete development of mind, psychopathic disorder and any other disorder or disability of the mind.

The term mental illness in that definition is not explained, and in practice, therefore, whether a person is to be placed in this category is a matter for clinical judgement. Furthermore, it still seems to have the meaning ascribed to it by Lawton LJ in *W* v *L* [1974] QB 711. In that case he said, at p. 719, that the words 'mental illness' had no particular medical or legal significance and so should be construed in the way any ordinary sensible person would do. If such a person would have said that to act in that fashion the accused must have been mentally ill, then so be it. This is likely to mean that a criminal act with no apparent motive will be construed as the act of a person who is mentally ill, and therefore as the act of someone who needs to be treated rather than just punished. Foucault would probably view this as the likely interpretation because it would perpetuate what he sees as the modern and dangerous practice of using psychiatric treatment as a form of control (see Kritzman (1988), especially Chapter Eight). The term mental illness was slightly more tightly defined by the then DHSS report (1976), which stated that:

Mental illness means an illness having one or more of the following characteristics:

(i)   More than temporary impairment of intellectual functions shown by a failure of memory, orientation, comprehension and learning capacity;

(ii)   More than temporary alteration of mood of such a degree as to give rise to the patient having a delusional appraisal of his situation, his past or his future, or that of others or the lack of any appraisal;

(iii)   Delusional beliefs, concerning self persecution, jealous or grandiose;

(iv)   Abnormal perceptions associated with delusional misinterpretation of events;

(v)   Thinking so disordered as to prevent the patient making a reasonable appraisal of his situation or having reasonable communication with others.

These legal and departmental descriptions are painted with broad brush strokes which lose accuracy when faced with the details of different mental conditions and with their possible effect on criminality. Mental illness can include at least all of the problems discussed in 9.3, but its exact meaning will depend upon the professional who is interpreting it. The Mental Health Act is restrictive in the mental disorders that it covers, since hospitalisation as a sentence is available to the court only if the disorder can be treated.

9.3   MEDICAL IDEAS OF MENTAL ILLNESS

It is important to consider some of the medical definitions of various illnesses and how they might affect a person's propensity to criminality.

9.3.1   Organic and functional psychoses

Psychoses are a set of related illnesses, but their outward manifestations are often very different. Organic psychoses are caused by some physical illness, either brain dysfunction at birth or by illness such as syphilitic infection. They may also be caused by accidents which have severe traumatic effects; by certain substances such as alcohol (see 9.5 below); by the severe changes in the brain which can be brought about with advancing years, (senile dementia); or by Alzheimer's disease. (One of the best known of the organic psychoses is that of epilepsy: see Chapters Six and Seven.)

Functional psychoses are those which seem to have no organic brain dysfunction as their root cause. It is still possible that they may be the result of severe biochemical disorders. It is these that are of most interest to criminologists. The best known of these disorders is schizophrenia; the less well known are referred to as affective disorders. Each of these is also made up of a variety of different illnesses.

9.3.2   Schizophrenia

This is the most frequent and important of the functional psychoses. The common use of the word to describe someone as having 'two minds' or having a split personality, where one of the sides to their personality is 'normal' and the other uncontrollable and bad, is inaccurate and incorrect.

More properly, the word schizophrenia means that the personality is disintegrated or splintered into very small parts which do not interact with each other in any well-defined manner. The most telling signs are the following:

(a) disorders in thinking, such as an inability to think straight, a tendency to jump from one thing to another with no train of thought;

(b) disorders in fitting feelings or emotions with thought or, generally, problems with emotions (anxiety, periods of unfeeling or flattened emotions, severe outbursts of rage and opposite reactions to various stimuli, e.g., laughing at something sad);

(c) a general withdrawal from social discourse. This often starts as apathy and slowly involves complete withdrawal, so that the individual lives in a private world (sometimes even refusing to hear or talk);

(d) a break with the real world in the form of delusions – giving real occurrences meanings that they do not hold, and usually related to paranoia or persecution (often a fear that everyone is stealing their thoughts, or that others are trying to drive them mad or ruin them).

Other factors which may appear are:

(a) periods of complete lack of movement which may give way to violence;

(b) hallucinations which are usually in the form of voices. Sometimes the voices command the commission of a crime;

(c) illusions such as believing that an everyday object is something fearful;

(d) defects in judgment, fantasy lives and peculiar mannerisms may also be present.

Not all of these would manifest themselves in one case: schizophrenia is best thought of as a series of disorders rather than a single illness. Basically, the personality is in tatters, and eventually there will be a complete break with reality. The causes of this illness are not fully understood. It is believed to have a lot do with the environment of the individual, although there may be links with genetic or biochemical factors.

Although the psychoses, and particularly the schizophrenias, are severe and can have very marked effects on behaviour, they are not generally closely related to criminality. In the studies mentioned above (9.1) only 12 per cent in Glueck's and 2 per cent in the Bluglass study were suffering from any form of psychoses, only some of which would have been schizophrenic. However, other studies have suggested a closer correlation between criminality and schizophrenia, particularly those studying life-imprisoned criminals (Taylor (1986)), or those who had committed specific serious offences and were referred for psychiatric treatment (Green (1981)). Lindqvist and Allebeck (1990a) reported on a longitudinal study of 644 schizophrenic patients discharged from Swedish hospitals in 1971 in which their officially recorded level of offending between 1972 and 1986 was noted. They found that 45 of the 330 men (a similar rate as for the general population) and nine of the 314 women (twice the rate for the general population) had committed offences. Although the rate for female schizophrenics looks significant the numbers are too small to draw conclusions. Most of the crimes committed by the schizophrenics were non-violent, mostly property offences, but the rate of violent crime was four times that of the general population. Although this is significant the violence was minor, mostly assault, and no killings were recorded. This trend is noted by Taylor (1993) who states that those with psychosis are more likely to commit property offences and petty assaults rather than serious violent acts. Furthermore Teplin et al. (1993) concluded that in their, admittedly limited, study severe mental disorder did not predict the probability of arrest for violent offences. Even the schizophrenics did not generally portray higher rates of violence although they found a small number in their total group who did. These studies are tentative evidence that there may be a link between crime and schizophrenia but the nature of the link is much harder to ascertain and is certainly not simply causative in nature.

Some crimes may be explained by schizophrenia. The most well known are crimes of violence which arise from a delusion or hallucination. One of the best known of these was Daniel M'Naghten, whose case gave rise to the famous M'Naghten Rules referred to above (9.2.1). M'Naghten suffered from delusions that he should kill the then Prime Minister, Robert Peel. He mistook Mr Drummond, the Prime Minister's secretary, for Robert Peel and killed him instead. He was found 'not guilty by reason of insanity'. This type of violent outburst may be suffered by the severely paranoid or by someone who has a morbid jealousy, and these people can appear completely sane and mentally able in all other respects. These people are particularly dangerous because they may well be classified as mentally normal, and they may also appear 'cured' while still harbouring the paranoia or jealousy. A more modern example is Peter Sutcliffe (the 'Yorkshire Ripper') whose paranoid schizo-phrenia may have played a role in his crimes (see Prins (1986)). Certain crimes, like matricide, have sometimes been linked with schizophrenia, although in 1993 Clark reported the results of a study which partially undermined this connection. Another type of violent crime committed by schizophrenics may involve severe cruelty, such as mutilation or killing slowly. Such crimes may also involve a sexual element, but it needs to be noted that they are rare. When they do occur, however, they are very newsworthy, and so people may perceive them as being more common. However infrequent, crimes of violence of this type are more prevalent amongst schizophrenics than amongst either other disordered groups or the general population.

Schizophrenics may well be brought before the courts for other, more minor offences, such as minor vandalism (criminal damage) or insulting people (breach of the peace). These and similar petty offences are probably all the result of their withdrawal from normal society. This suggestion is backed up by research carried out by Taylor in 1985. In a sample of psychotic offenders she discovered that only 20 per cent of the offending was directly related to the illness, but that when one took into account the indirect social and environmental effects, such as poverty, homelessness and social disability then over 80 per cent of the cases are explicable in terms of the illness. Schizophrenia also interferes with the ability of the individual to socialise which may have a causative effect on criminality. The links between schizophrenia, social problems and criminality are also suggested by Lindqvist and Allebeck's (1990b) finding that in the case of chaotic and socially disabled psychotics who offend there may be a link with substance abuse, alcohol or drugs. In the light of the increase in releases of the mentally disturbed into the community and the lack of sufficient and appropriate community care the effects of this combination of psychosis and social problems is likely to become more prevalent. It will then be dealt with as a criminal justice problem rather than as the social and medical problem which it really is.

9.3.3 Severe affective disorders: severe depression

There are two types of depression: major or psychotic depression and bipolar or manic depression. Major depression is characterised by a profoundly sad mood, strong guilt feelings, lethargy, appetite loss, loss of energy and loss of interest in both the individual and the outside world. These features may also be accompanied by irritability, tension, agitation, inability to sleep normally and sometimes a desire to commit suicide. Manic depression has all these characteristics, but they are alternated with moods of elation and excitement (manic periods). Each of these periods may last a few days or weeks, and they may be interspersed with periods of relative normality.

Like the schizophrenic illnesses, neither psychotic depression nor manic depression can explain all criminality, but they may explain a few particular cases. In the case of psychotic depression, the offence most commonly linked with it is murder followed by suicide. As was mentioned above, sufferers fairly frequently turn to suicide because of the misery they feel and the belief that nothing can be done to improve their position. In certain cases, they see the misery and helplessness also affecting their families, so rather than leave those they love to face 'such awful lives' alone they may kill them as well in order, they believe, to save them from further suffering. West (1965) studied 78 murders which were followed by suicide. Of these, he claimed, 28 were suffering from severe depression at the time of the offence. There have also been links between depression and lesser acts of violence against family members or others close to the individual. These are difficult to explain as in hospital these patients are not more violent than other mental patients or the general population (see Feldman (1993)). The violence is therefore presumed to be facilitated through social conditions, particularly close personal relationships. In the case of the manic-depressive psychoses, the type of crimes will be characterised by disruptive and often impulsive behaviour, which may be violent and may also be almost obsessive in its persistence: arson is sometimes linked with the manic state.

Of course, it is often difficult to ascertain whether the depression caused the crime. It may be that the individual merely happened to be depressed at the time of the offence without the depression being the cause, or that the depression resulted from the criminality. Whichever of these is correct the National Association of Probation Officers (NAPO) discovered that one in five prisoners, and a higher proportion of those on probation are mentally vulnerable and that 90 per cent of these suffer from depression. They noted that these difficulties were not being addressed, pointing out that only 2 per cent of probation orders included a requirement for psychiatric treatment, and in prison the vast majority of mental disorders are not treated. They also noted that many offenders suffered with mental health problems and of these many had chronic alcohol and drug problems. None of these difficulties was properly addressed by the criminal justice system (NAPO, 1994).

9.3.4 Neuroses

These are similar illnesses to psychoses, but do not involve a complete break with normality and so are not quite so disabling. The experts cannot agree on the precise difference between psychoses and neuroses. Some argue that the latter are merely less severe; others consider that psychotics live in a fantasy world, whereas neurotics simply cannot cope with the strains of the real world. Whichever is correct, the neurotic mostly lives a fairly normal life which is occasionally disrupted by the effects of the neuroses. They are in some respects difficult to diagnose because everyone suffers from similar traits from time to time. Everyone feels some form of 'let-down' or depression, and many feel anxious in certain situations. There is a thin line between these normal feelings and neuroses, which besides feelings of anxiety may also include phobias, obsession, hysteria and mild depression. The neurotic may be suffering from a number of these or may show signs that there is only one main problem.

Most neurotics will have no criminal tendencies (or at least none connected with their illness), but occasionally neuroses may be a cause of criminality. For example, obsessional and compulsive neuroses may be central in explaining a few crimes such as sexual perversions, like exhibitionism (only rarely obsessive) or fetishism (which may or may not be criminal), and pyromania (arson) or kleptomania (theft). In criminology it is the last of these, kleptomania, which is most frequently mentioned. Obsession is a compulsive and genuinely uncontrollable feeling, and often the sufferer realises the feelings are wholly irrational but is still unable to control them because the obsession pervades and overrules everything.

The term kleptomania has been largely devalued by its frequent use to describe otherwise uncharacteristic shop-lifting. The term should not be used simply to mean that the person had a strong desire, which he or she did not control, to take something. To be truly an obsessive thief there must be much more than this. Obsessional theft is often preceded by certain rituals, or the theft itself is ritualistic; clumsily performed with almost no attempt at concealment (possibly showing an underlying feeling of guilt which drives the thief on in order to obtain punishment); involves the taking of useless objects which may be hoarded, often does not satisfy any desire, and sometimes is even followed by a compensatory act.

9.3.5 The relationship between crime and psychosis

As the discussion so far indicates, the precise relationship between these mental illnesses and crime is uncertain. There is certainly no direct and simple link. There would appear to be some very severe cases where the mental element directly causes the criminality. As suggested in 9.3.2 there may in some cases be an indirect link: the illness may affect the individual in certain social ways which may, along with direct effects, make it more likely that a crime is committed. From the work of Link et al. (1992) it seems that there is an increased risk of violence in mental patients or those who have been treated in the past. However, the increase was only slight and not as important as some other factors, whilst the increased violence and illegality were usually manifested only in individuals with current psychotic problems and could be precipitated by inappropriate reactions of others to the psychotic symptoms. The uncertainties suggest that the provision of proper support in the community would be the most effective way of using the degree of current understanding.

What is possibly more important to the law is the effect of these illnesses on the mental element necessary for a conviction. It seems illogical that in cases where the offender is recognised to be suffering from a mental illness we convict as if there were full responsibility and then decide that punishment is not justified as the individual was not responsible and should be treated under the Mental Health Act 1983. A more logical stance would be to assess criminal responsibility and culpability at an earlier stage and in a more sophisticated way (for a discussion of this see 9.2.2). To burden the mentally ill with the label of criminality seems to be unfair and may inhibit their proper integration into society at a later date. It would be desirable for the law to deal with this anomaly but a major impediment arises because there are no hard and fast definitions of mental capacity and impairment nor can there be any precise assessment of whether, and how far, an individual was affected by a state of mind at the time of the offence. Lawyers do not readily embrace such uncertainty which makes a resolution of this issue unlikely in the foreseeable future.

Equally important is the need to recognise the way the criminal justice system is distorted by the policy of care in the community. All organs of the system are affected, from police through the courts to the punishment and treatment providers, and their actions in dealing with these people bear little relation to their intended criminal justice roles. The most affected are the police who often perform a heightened welfare role. These duties distort the functions of the criminal justice system and are performed by those who are ill-equipped to deal with people suffering from mental illness, where the associated problems are often social rather than criminal. The whole area has been the butt of much criticism – see, for example Wachholz and Mullaly (1993), who suggest that the police in performing these functions shore up the welfare State and the political order, helping to perpetuate the present system and avoiding the need to consider an alternative strategy. That is not to blame the police but rather an argument for a realisation of the problem and a call for a solution. Taylor (1993) suggests that the problem may be worsened because of hostility and despair in the psychiatric profession. These patients are very costly to deal with. The more socially incapable are not really dangerous but, when released, are difficult to integrate into society;

whereas the more dangerous, yet better adjusted, counterparts are more difficult to contain and it may be simpler to collude in their pretence of normality and release them. Each will cause problems for the criminal justice system, particularly if such releases are carried out without proper community backup. The problem will then appear to be one of crime whereas it may really be one of mental illness.

9.4 PSYCHOPATHY

9.4.1 Introduction
Psychopathy is a severe personality disorder, and could have been discussed along with other personality problems in Chapter Eight. It is included here because it is mentioned in the Mental Health Act and is often considered to be potentially extremely dangerous. Section 1(2) of the Mental Health Act 1983 defines psychopathic disorder as:

> a persistent disorder or disability of mind . . . which results in abnormally aggressive or seriously irresponsible conduct on the part of the person concerned.

It must be a disorder which has existed for some time otherwise it is not 'persistent'. However, Power (1988) refers to a case where a judge under the 1959 legislation sentenced a man to be detained in a mental hospital because two psychiatrists diagnosed him as psychopathic, even though the criminal problem had arisen only over a two-week period. As Dr Power points out, the judge must either have decided that the problem had been dormant for a long period, or that two weeks represented a 'persistent' disorder. The diagnosis rests on the types of behaviour which affect social functioning: it assesses whether the person has adjusted to society and, if not, whether they are a serious risk to themselves or to others. What is meant by 'abnormally aggressive' or 'seriously irresponsible' is not specified and will be left to the court to interpret, under the guidance of psychologists.

These offenders are dealt with under s. 37 of the Mental Health Act 1983, which allows them to be admitted to a mental hospital rather than sentenced to a punishment. Only three years after the passing of the Mental Health Act 1983, the Department of Health and Social Security (DHSS) and the Home Office produced a consultative document (1986) in which it was suggested that psychopathically disordered offenders would not be treated in the same way as other mental offenders or punished like ordinary offenders. This seems to be a reaction to the perceived increased dangerousness of these offenders and the fear that they might be released by the mental hospitals while still dangerous. Three proposals were suggested, each of which would have prevented the release of a psychopath by the hospital before a date set by the court. Although these proposals have since been dropped, they are an indication of the fear with which these people are often viewed because of their tendency towards impulsive behaviour. This type of attitude towards psychopaths is not new, but the Report of the Committee on Mentally

Abnormal Offenders (1975) stated that the long-term effect of punishing or threatening to punish psychopaths tends to be that they become more vindictive and gain more antisocial attitudes.

9.4.2 What is psychopathy?
It is important to note that psychopathy does not necessarily involve any impairment of the reasoning facilities, and psychopaths may be aware of their actions and have a normal interest in themselves and their surroundings. As Rafter (1997) notes, the term 'psychopathy' virtually defies definition when perceived as a personality defect, although it has more validity when seen as mental incapacity. A psychopath will normally suffer from distortions of, or a perversion of, feelings and affections as well as the possession of strange desires, habits, a strange moral disposition and odd behavioural patterns such as frequent and marked changes in mood and temper, impulsive behaviour and, in particular, violent outbursts. In short, a psychopath is unpredictable, unresponsive to help, and prone to extremely unacceptable behaviour. Hare (1980) names five elements which he says characterise the psychopath:

   (a)   an inability to develop warm, responsive, and affectionate relationships, a general lack of empathy;
   (b)   an unstable lifestyle;
   (c)   an inability to accept responsibility, particularly for their own unacceptable behaviour;
   (d)   they do not have psychiatric problems nor are they unintelligent;
   (e)   they have problems in controlling their behaviour.

The 1986 publication from the Department of Health and Social Security and Home Office may also be of assistance in understanding what psychopathy is:

   The core problem is impairment in the capacity to relate to others – to take account of their feelings and to act in ways consistent with their safety and convenience.

Psychopaths tend to be loners, and even if they live in or with a family they may have surprisingly separate and private lives. If they do live with their family, it is often the family who suffer most from their mood changes. This is particularly so if the family try to help them, as they are often hostile to those who offer help. Unlike their popular image, they are not constantly intent on harming people or causing pain, suffering and chaos. Instead, they are normally unable to stick to long-term plans, and the pain and suffering caused is often not intended and results rather from the fierce and severe mood changes and impulsive or violent behaviour. This is made worse by the fact that psychopaths seem unable to understand either pain or suffering in others, and this inability may render them unable to comprehend the reactions of others to their behaviour.

9.4.3   The origins of the disease

The outward manifestations of psychopathy may be related to some of the
central and autonomic nervous system functions discussed in 7.3 and 7.4. It
seems from work carried out by Hare (1970) that psychopaths often have
EEG patterns close to those of children, which suggest that they suffer from
cortical immaturity. Similar work has suggested that the illness is associated
with defective brain functions which are related to emotions. There is also
some suggestion that psychopaths suffer from low cortical arousal, related to
the ANS, which therefore needs and seeks excessive excitement which might
well involve criminal behaviour. Most people, whether psychopathic or not,
are right handed, and this means that the left cerebral hemisphere is
dominant and contains the speech centres of the brain. Hare and McPherson
(1984) point out that in psychopaths part of the speech function is carried
out by the right rather than the left cerebral hemisphere. This sharing of the
brain functions causes the two sides of the brain to be less well integrated,
affecting language and behaviour abilities as well as emotional processes and
responses. This might explain why psychopaths can lie without worry and
why they can hurt others with seemingly little feeling. Psychopaths have also
been found to suffer from a greater lack of autonomic activity than might be
found in the general population. This severe lack of autonomic activity also
shows markedly lower feelings of guilt, anxiety and emotional tension than
would be normal. Merely to list the possible origins of the disease is to
illustrate the uncertainty of present knowledge.

Farrington (1994) suggests that the problem is one of impulsive behaviour,
while Hollin (1992) also refers to the possibility that cognitive problems may
have a causal connection with the psychopathic personality. Interestingly, the
lack of learning occurs for physical or social disapproval but not for financial
penalties: it may therefore be more sensible, in terms of prevention, to punish
psychopaths financially rather than physically or by societal disapproval.
These learning problems may explain some of the difficulties which present
themselves in the psychopathic personality.

9.4.4   Psychopathy and criminality

What are the connections between psychopathy and criminality? A common
view is that the two are synonymous. Foucault suggests that some people are
said to have mental problems merely because we are unable to understand
their criminality and therefore unable to decide how to punish them. In such
cases he argues that psychology is being used to control people whose
criminality is perceived as irrational and therefore as more dangerous (see
Kritzman (1988), especially Chapters Eight and Eleven). When no other
explanation seems possible or likely, they term a criminal a psychopath,
particularly if that person's behaviour involves wanton violence. The label
'psychopath' is even more likely to be attached to those who will not respond
to punishment or treatment. It is possible that mild personality disorders
showing slightly increased psychopathic tendencies may explain a fair amount
of both criminality and recidivism (see 8.3), but there is a difference between
these and true psychopathic disorders. Many of the differences have been set

out by Cleckley (1976). First, the true psychopathic personality is unlikely to have planned the crime and is less likely to gain from it: in fact they may well lose. The crime may arise out of a wild and inexplicable mood change, and there is often no clear design. If psychopaths indulge in sexual offences or violence, there may be no pattern. The offences are committed at whim and other types of offences may be committed in the interim. The acts of a true psychopath are chaotic and repetitious, the offences often occurring in fairly rapid succession.

Even if it is not as marked as popularly believed, there is clearly a connection between psychopathy and criminality. One possible puzzle is that women are almost never classified as psychopathic. Guze (1976) suggests that women who portray similar traits are being classified as hysterics.

9.5 SELF-INDUCED MENTAL INCAPACITY

9.5.1 Introduction
This is usually brought about by the intake of drugs (in the broadest sense). Some of these drugs are legal and freely available (e.g., alcohol which is imbibed and glues or lighter fuels which are inhaled); some prescribed (e.g., barbiturates); some are only or normally available on the black market (e.g., amphetamines, LSD and opiates). Alcohol is more significant for criminality than other drugs, partly because its legal and common usage makes it easily available. Self induced incapacity may also be brought about by negligently or carelessly omitting to take the drugs necessary for some illnesses, possibly causing a form of automatism, e.g., not taking the correct medicine or food to prevent onset of a diabetic coma. Clearly, this is only voluntary if the individual is aware of what will result from the omission.

9.5.2 Criminal law, alcohol and drugs
In most instances, the voluntary taking of any drug will not affect the criminality of the individual and cannot be used as a defence. In crimes of negligence and of basic intent, the proof of recklessness is enough to establish the mental element necessary. The exception to this is offences of specific/ulterior intent, where a conviction is only possible on clear proof of the mental intent (e.g., murder). For a fuller discussion of this see *Blackstone's Criminal Practice* (published annually). In the 1997 edition, see A3.10.

Clearly, even in cases of specific/ulterior intent an accused who lacks the required mental element at the time of the commission of the *actus reus* through voluntary intoxication or self-induced automatism may still be held criminally responsible for such an offence. This may happen either if there was intent to execute the offence and drink was taken to give 'Dutch courage' to carry out the crime (see *Attorney-General for Northern Ireland* v *Gallagher* [1963] AC 349) or if, despite the intoxication, the court considers the individual was able to form the requisite intention to commit that offence.

An accused who is involuntarily rendered drunk and incapable of forming the *mens rea* of an offence (e.g., by 'spiked' drinks) or is an involuntary automaton (e.g., a person in a state of concussion) may generally have a defence even to an offence of basic intent: see *DPP* v *Majewski* [1977] AC 443. However, where a person, though involuntarily intoxicated, is capable of forming the required *mens rea* with regard to an offence, and the fact of his intoxication merely weakens his ability and will, then he is guilty of any offence he may commit. This remains true whether the offence is one which requires a specific/ulterior intent, a basic intent, or is negligence based (see *R* v *Bailey* [1983] 2 All ER 503 and *R* v *Kingston* [1994] 3 WLR 519). The fact of his intoxication is then relevant to sentence only.

Alcohol or drug abuse may result in mental impairment. If an accused, through the use of intoxicants or drugs, is rendered insane, the M'Naghten Rules apply (see 9.2.1). However, this is not the case if the use of such substances induces a temporary insanity in persons who are mentally unstable but not normally insane (see *Attorney-General for Northern Ireland* v *Gallagher* [1963] AC 349 and 9.2.1 concerning the law relating to insanity). There are also different categories of drugs: those which are known to have effects which may make the taker more aggressive or unpredictable; and those, like Valium, which are not normally associated with problematic changes in behaviour. In the latter case a defence of temporary mental impairment is possible (see above and *R* v *Bailey* [1983] 1 WLR and *R* v *Hardie* [1985] 1 WLR 64).

9.5.3   The effects of alcohol

The social and criminological effects of alcohol are significant. They occur because of the effect alcohol has on our bodies. First, alcohol is a depressant which renders the drinker less able to concentrate, less able to judge situations and less able to control emotions. When alcohol has been imbibed, the nervous message which represses the emotions is prevented from being transmitted, and so the individual is more susceptible to strong emotions of sadness, joy or anger. Because it lowers the ability to control emotions and lessens the ability to judge situations and to act rationally, there is obviously a marked behaviour change brought about by alcohol. Secondly, the change in behaviour may be brought about by the opposite effect: alcohol may stimulate the physical mechanisms involved in violent behaviour. This suggests that it increases the activity of the areas of the brain associated with aggressive behaviour. Lastly, alcohol may just provide a convenient excuse for aggressive behaviour, allowing the individual to attribute to heavy drinking the blame for aggressive behaviour in the expectation that the behaviour will be condoned or treated less seriously. All these effects can lead to what may be termed or considered otherwise uncharacteristic behaviour. For a full consideration of how these may operate see Pihl and Peterson (1993).

Despite these fairly drastic effects, alcohol is both freely available and socially acceptable. Most adults in this country use alcohol, but the quantity depends on their lifestyle and habits. Alcohol is used at most social occasions such as weddings, deaths, parties, presentations. Used in moderation, its effects can be beneficial in breaking down some inhibitions and so helping the socialising process. However, even the moderate use of alcohol may break down inhibitions sufficiently to release individuals to do uncharacteristic things. The danger is obviously most likely to arise when alcohol is consumed to excess, either on one occasion or habitually.

There are recognised to be a number of different types of drinker. One classification might be:

1. the light social drinker,
2. occasional intoxicant,
3. the heavy social drinker (i.e., one who engages in regular excessive use of alcohol),
4. alcoholic,
5. chronic alcoholic (i.e., one who is dependent totally on alcohol).

The demarcation between each is blurred: the point at which drinking moves from light and generally acceptable social drinking to heavy social drinking cannot be assessed in terms of amount, but rather by attitude. The heavy drinker is likely to attend social occasions for the alcohol, or while there, to be preoccupied in obtaining as much alcohol as possible. For such people, drinking tends to become more important and to occur at all times of the day, affecting efficiency in other aspects of life, such as work. One recent estimate by Taylor (1981) suggested that between 8-15 million working days are lost each year due to alcohol-related sickness. Other areas of life will also be increasingly affected. There will be lapses of memory and deterioration in relationships, particularly within a family. At this point other physical effects may occur, such as loss of appetite, hand tremors and reduction in sexual urges and vitality and sometimes suicide attempts or suicidal thoughts and feelings. Exactly how one defines an alcoholic or alcohol-dependent is difficult, but its essential element seems to be an inability to refrain from the use of alcohol.

9.5.4 Crime and alcohol

Alcohol has long been connected with antisocial activity, crime and criminality. As far back as the seventeenth century there was legislation against intoxication because it was perceived as the:

> . . . Root and Foundation of many other enormous Sins, as Bloodshed, Stabbing, Murder, Swearing, Fornication, Adultery, and such like, . . . to the Overthrow of many good Arts and manual Trades, the Disabling of divers Workmen, and the general Impoverishing of many good Subjects (An Act for Repressing the Odious and Loathsome Sin of Drunkenness, 1606; 4 James I, c. 5).

In more modern times, a similar root and branch belief in its evils led to its prohibition in the United States for thirteen years from 16 January 1920. Ironically, prohibition was one of the most crime-ridden periods in American history. But whatever the verdict on that large social experiment, there is a deep-seated belief that, whatever its benefits, drink causes criminality. Is this reputation deserved?

Alcohol is related to criminality in a number of different ways. First, there are some offences which have the drinking of alcohol as an essential component. These include simple drunkenness, being drunk and disorderly (in a public place) and driving whilst under the influence of drink in contravention of road safety regulations, which account for about 40 to 50 thousand prosecutions a year. Clearly, alcohol is part of these crimes; in fact it constitutes their commission. Of greater interest is how significant is alcohol in the commission of other offences. Assessments of this are more difficult, partly because the alcohol consumption of offenders is not recorded in the official statistics. Most information in this area is either an intelligent guess or calculated after studying a sample of arrested persons. Saunders (1984) calculated that alcohol was a significant factor in about 1,000 arrests per day or over 350,000 a year. In 1977 Aarens reported that in America 13-50 per cent of rape offenders had been drinking at the time of the offence; in 24–72 per cent of assaults the perpetrator had been drinking; and in 28-86 per cent of homicides the offender had been drinking when the killing took place. In cases of family violence in the United States, Flanzer (1981) estimated that 80 per cent of all cases involved drinking before, during or after the incident, and De Luca (1981) estimated that almost a third of the cases of violence against children in the home were alcohol related. Alcohol has also often been seen as a significant factor in relation to violent and sexual offences against women but, as Kelly (1988) warns, to accept that as an explanation would be to ignore the part played by accepted male values and behaviours which she argues are involved in the violence directed at both women and children. Other, more general studies have discovered a link between alcohol and general levels of criminal violence (see Collins (1988 and 1989); and Fagan (1990)). Murdoch et al. (1990) compared 26 studies from 11 countries and discovered that overall 62 per cent of violent offenders were drinking at the time of their offence (the range was 24 to 85 per cent in violent crime against 12 to 38 per cent in non-violent crimes). Also interesting was that 45 per cent of victims of violence had been drinking at the time they were victimised. The studies suggest that alcohol may be very closely related to violent criminality, but cannot establish that it was the cause of such criminality. Abram (1989) has suggested that both the alcohol use and the criminality may be the result of a third factor such as antisocial personality disorder.

The evidence does, however, suggest that some crimes, particularly of violence or criminal damage, are clearly related to alcohol and probably only take place because the normal inhibitory factors have been broken down by drink. Alcohol may not cause the criminality, but it does break down the normal inhibitions and therefore provides an excuse for the violence, i.e., normal rules don't apply because the individual is drunk. The violence may have arisen out of an argument; or drinking and violence may both arise out of other problems, such as family difficulties. In some cases the crime may well have been planned before the alcohol was consumed, and it was only drunk either to pass the time or to build up 'Dutch courage'. Clearly, alcohol use and criminality may both be caused by a third, common factor such as peer group pressure, broken homes and parental disharmony (see Glatt (1965)). Some writers have also suggested a connection between alcohol dependence, crime and physical attributes (for a discussion of this, see Chapter Seven). However, Teplin et al. (1993) found that alcohol use disorders such as alcoholism did not predict violence. This finding is backed up by Pihl and Peterson (1993) who found that in some circumstances alcoholics were less aggressive. However, in non-alcoholics they discovered a more complex relationship between alcohol and crime: in low doses alcohol seemed to increase sensitivity and probably reduced criminality; in high doses sensitivity was reduced and this sometimes led to violent criminality. They concluded that 'increased pain sensitivity, reduced response to cues of punishment and cues of frustrative non reward, and reduced response flexibility can all apparently occur as a result of drinking. The presence of such factors independently or collectively is likely to increase the probability of aggressive behaviour.' If this constituted one explanation of the relationship between alcohol and violence they also acknowledged that the effects of the drug may be affected by the state of mind with which the user approaches the alcohol and the surroundings in which this occurs. In a 1994 study, the National Association of Probation Officers (NAPO) asserted that almost half of all property crime was committed to sustain drug and alcohol addictions and that almost three-quarters of all those on probation committed their last offence to maintain such a habit. Mott (1990) suggests that the forceful link with criminality may not be the chemical effect of alcohol but rather the social context and wider culture involved in the consumption of alcohol.

It is obvious that crime and alcohol appear together in many different situations. It is difficult to assess whether the crime was the reason for the drink – to get Dutch courage or through guilt after the crime is committed; or drink was the reason for the crime – a breakdown of the inhibitory factors releasing the individual to transgress; or whether both crime and drinking are connected by other, often situational factors – both are encouraged by the peer group, or both can result out of depressing factors in home life.

9.5.5 Drugs

Drug taking does not have as long a connection with criminality as does alcohol. It was only at the beginning of this century that drugs were labelled as a major social problem and became regulated. Prior to that, many now prohibited drugs, especially the opiates, were used to treat even fairly minor ailments and could be purchased at the local pharmacy. In Britain the first attempt to regulate drugs appeared in the Pharmacy and Poisons Act 1868, but these controls were only very minor and piecemeal. Early in the twentieth century, there were strong international calls for the control of drugs which culminated in the passing of the Hague Convention of Private International Law 1912. Article 20 of this Convention called for:

> contracting powers to examine the possibility of enacting laws or regulations making it an offence to be in illegal possession of raw opium, prepared opium, morphine, cocaine and their respective salts . . .

Eight years later Britain passed its first full drug control legislation, the Dangerous Drugs Act 1920, which regulated the import, export and possession of the drugs referred to in the Convention. Some claim that outlawing the possession and sale/purchase of drugs led to an increase in addiction. Toch (1966) quotes an estimate that there was a 1,500 per cent increase in drug addiction in the opiates in the States between 1914 (the year they were outlawed by the Narcotic Act in that country) and 1918.

Despite its fairly short connection with the criminal law, many people now connect drug taking with criminality. Some of the difficulties with alcohol also pertain to drug taking. Clearly drugs can alter perceptions, break down inhibitions and generally alter behaviour, and so may be connected with crime in many of the same ways as alcohol. The same problems in calculating the significance of drugs as a cause of crime exist as in the case of alcohol.

Many drugs are illegal and so their possession, sale or consumption is an offence in itself. This leads to vast networks of organised crime which are built up on the proceeds from the sale of controlled substances. It also means that anyone wishing to use any of these substances is immediately criminalised, and this has brought many otherwise law-abiding citizens into contact with the criminal justice system. Some writers, like Morris and Hawkins (1970), claim that this has devalued the criminal law and possibly led to more people having a disrespect for the system and so being willing to commit other crimes. Four ways have been suggested (Nadelmann 1980) in which drugs are connected with crime, particularly violent crime.

First, users may commit crimes, including violent crimes, to get hold of the substances they want. Because of their illegality they are sold on the black market, often at high prices, encouraging addicts to commit property offences (theft, burglary, robbery etc.). Chaiken and Chaiken (1991) suggest that most drug-related crime falls into this category of non-violent property offences or, as Plant (1990) says, prostitution. Jarvis and Parker (1989) suggest that crime is causally linked to heroin use because of the need for recurrent supplies to feed the habit. Some users may be willing to use violence to secure the property or to obtain drugs from another who has them.

Secondly, drug use and criminal behaviour just happen to occur together because third factors may predispose individuals to both activities (such as an antisocial personality disorder), whilst there is strong evidence to suggest that crime leads to drug use rather than vice versa (see McBride and McCoy (1982); Auld et al. (1986)). In Scotland, Hammersley et al. (1989), carried out extensive research which suggested that criminal activity before drug use is much more important and reliable a predictor of later criminal activity than is the drug use itself. Furthermore they undermined the link between heroin and crime, finding a similar link with other drugs and, in particular, noting that moderate use of heroin seemed to have no greater connection with criminality than did cannabis or alcohol. Lastly, Pearson (1991) points out that there is certainly no clear proof that non-acquisitive crimes are increased by drug use. It seems not to be possible to resolve whether crime results from drug use or drug use begins as further proof of the deviant behaviour of an individual which may have a different cause.

Thirdly, dealers and others involved in the trade in drugs will tend to protect their 'business' interests by violent means, especially as they cannot call on legitimate forms of protection. The resultant level of violence and protection is difficult to estimate. Dorn et al. (1992) suggest that in Britain the market is not controlled by large, organised criminal syndicates so methods of protection will vary from area to area, although some argue (Pearson (1991)) that the British market is moving closer to that of the US.

Lastly, drugs are chemicals and their ingestion alters the chemical balance of the body and the brain, and this can affect behaviour. The way in which behaviour is altered varies from drug to drug and, as with alcohol, sometimes varies with the intensity of the drug taken and the frequency of use (for a fuller discussion see Pihl and Peterson (1993) and Fishbein and Pease (1990)). Interestingly the biological effects of opiates such as heroin, which are most commonly associated with criminality, tend to reduce aggressive and hostile tendencies. Despite this, opiates have been linked with psychopathic behavioural disorders and some have suggested that during use the individual commits markedly more crime, including violent crime (Fishbein and Pease (1990)). These differences can be explained only by taking account of the effects of the social and environmental conditions in which heroin is often used. On the other hand the immediate biological effects of cocaine and its derivative crack are more closely associated with violence. Their immediate effects may be positive, feeling elated, assertive and alert; but later this may turn to feelings of suspicion and paranoia, irritability, vigilance, nervousness, feelings associated with some psychotics and the effects may be violent criminal activity (Fishbein and Pease (1990)). As with alcohol, the genetic make-up of the individual and the social and environmental context may be as important as the chemical effects of the drugs. The level of criminal activity due to these chemical changes is probably relatively small as the level of use in Britain is still quite low.

To this catalogue might be added State involvement in the narcotics trade. Dorn and South (1990) have suggested that in the US there is some State-sponsored trading in drugs, notably by the CIA, and Frost (1986) looks at the situation in South America where such connections are less covert and easier to prove. The extent of these activities is impossible to assess but their use of normally legitimate services, such as banks, is especially threatening for the fabric of society.

9.5.6 Treatment

In discussing the connection of drugs and alcohol with crime, one needs to be aware of an important and unresolved conflict of approach. Some see both these activities as intrinsically wrong and *per se* in need of punishment; others see them as social and personal problems to be understood and treated as any other illness. The first solution has generally won out in the case of drugs, whereas the second has been most accepted in the case of alcohol.

Last century a number of attempts were made to 'help' or 'cure' habitual drinkers. In 1879 the Habitual Drunkards Act allowed justices to send these people to retreats, and in 1898, under the Inebriates Act of that year, they were given power to send them to certified Institutes for Reformation for up to three years. Very few retreats were ever established, and by 1921 they had all closed. More recently, similar provisions have re-appeared in s. 34 of the Criminal Justice Act 1972, as amended by sch. 6, para. 21 of the Police and Criminal Evidence Act 1984, which empowers the police to take drunkards to a medical treatment centre rather than arresting and charging them. This can only be done if they are arrested for an offence under s. 12 of the Licensing Act 1879 or s. 91(1) of the Criminal Justice Act 1967. Unfortunately, very few such centres have been made available. Similarly, although probation orders can have treatment requirements attached to them and treatment can be made available within prisons, such measures are insufficiently used (NAPO, 1984).

The problem of both drug and alcohol abuse has therefore largely been left to the criminal law to solve. In each case, due to pressure on police work, the problem is often ignored until a further crime is committed. Possibly these further offences could be prevented by an effective system of treatment provisions.

9.6 CONCLUSION

The central discussion in this chapter has been concerned with the mental state of the offender at the time of committing the offence. In some instances, the law recognises that the mental element affects the individual's culpability, and therefore allows it to be used in his or her defence. For example, insanity and automatism are full defences and diminished responsibility and infanticide are partial defences. In practice, insanity is used only in cases where the charge is murder, and in law diminished responsibility and infanticide can be used only when the charge is murder, and can be used only to reduce the conviction to manslaughter. Therefore, in most cases the full mental state of the defendant is not medically questioned or tested until after he or she is convicted. The defendant's mental capacity or understanding, which may reduce or interfere with the *mens rea* (mental intent) of the offender, are therefore often ignored until after there is a finding of guilt. At that point, the court may ask why the offender committed the offence and may well consider his or her mental capacity under the Mental Health Act 1983. If a psychologist then suggests that the offender is suffering from a mental illness which falls under that statute, the court may decide that the offender should be helped in a hospital and sentence him or her accordingly. If the mental element is seen to be sufficiently important to become an issue at the sentencing stage there may, in some cases, be an argument for its consideration at an earlier stage, before conviction. Some (such as Samuels (1988)) have even argued that mental disorder should be allowed as a full defence to criminality. Samuels suggests that if this was accepted the court could use the civil powers of the Mental Health Act 1983, and the local authority could then oversee the treatment received by such people. If this seems excessive there may be an argument for the introduction of a partial defence of mental incapacity to all crimes which would result in a finding of guilt, but with diminished culpability, similar to the diminished responsibility defence which is available in cases of murder (see Cranston Law (1983)). This would give the mental element further recognition, and also allow the medical evidence to be more carefully scrutinised than is the case when it is brought up at the sentencing stage. Of course, such a verdict would not be a full acquittal, but the disposals available to the court on such a finding would be limited to treatment or public safety measures rather than punishment.

Interestingly, the judges and legal system, helped by the medical and social professionals, seem to be moving the other way. As the medical profession turns away from being willing to define an offender as irresponsible, so the number of prisoners in ordinary prisons who suffer from psychological disorders or imbalances rises. Hodgins (1992) estimates that 22 per cent of the Canadian prison population manifest an 'antisocial personality disorder' and that at least 1 per cent are clearly psychopathic. This is causing immense problems for staff and inmates of these institutions. As suggested in the last chapter, it may be time for a rethink to address the responsibility and needs of offenders and to examine how the rights of offenders, victims and the public can be respected.

REFERENCES

Aarens, M. et al. (1977), *Alcohol, Casualties and Crime*, Berkley, California: Social Research Group, School of Public Health.

Abram, K. M. (1989) 'The Effect of Co-occurring Disorders on Criminal Careers: Interaction of Antisocial Personality, Alcoholism, and Drug Disorders', *International Journal of Law and Psychiatry*, vol. 12, p. 133.

Allen, Michael J. (1997), *Textbook on Criminal Law*, 4th edn., London: Blackstone Press.

Auld, J., Dorn, N. and South, N. (1986), 'Irregular Work, Irregular Pleasures: Heroin in the 1980s', in Roger Matthews and J. Young (eds), *Confronting Crime*, London: Sage.

Blackstone's Criminal Practice, published annually, Peter Murphy (ed.), London: Blackstone Press.

Bluglass, R. (1977), unpublished MD Thesis, quoted in J. Gunn, 'Criminal Behaviour and Mental Disorder', *British Journal of Psychiatry*, vol. 130, p. 317.

Butler Committee (1975), *Report of the Committee on Mentally Abnormal Offenders*, Cmnd 6244, London: HMSO.

Chaiken, J. and Chaiken, M. (1991), 'Drugs and Predatory Crime', in M. Tonry and J. Wilson (eds), *Crime and Justice: a Review of Research*, vol. 13, Chicago: University of Chicago Press.

Cheng, P.T.K. (1986), 'Maternal Filicide in Hong Kong, 1971-85', *Medicine, Science and the Law*, vol. 26(3), p. 185.

Clark, S. A. (1993), 'Matricide: the Schizophrenic Crime?', *Medicine Science and the Law*, vol. 33, p. 325.

Collins, J.J. (1988), 'Suggested Explanatory Frameworks to Clarify the Alcohol Use/Violence Relationship', *Contemporary Drug Problems*, Spring, p. 107.

Collins, J.J. (1989), 'Alcohol and Interpersonal Violence: Less than Meets the Eye', in A. Weiner and M.E. Wolfgang (eds), *Pathways to Criminal Violence*, Newbury Park, CA: Sage.

Cleckley, H (1976), *The Mask of Sanity*, 5th edn, St. Louis, Missouri: C. V. Mosby.

Cranston Law, N. (1983), 'Neither Guilty Nor Insane', *Medicine, Science and the Law*, vol. 23(4), p. 275.

Cross, Sir Rupert, Jones, Phillip Asterley and Card, Richard (1995), *Introduction to Criminal Law*, 13th edn, London: Butterworths.

DeLuca, John R. (ed.) (1981), *Fourth Special Report to the US Congress on Alcohol and Health*, Rockville, Maryland: National Institute on Alcohol Abuse and Alcoholism.

Department of Health and Social Security (1976), *A Review of the Mental Health Act, 1959*, DHSS Report, London: HMSO.

Department of Health and Social Security and Home Office (1986), *Offenders Suffering from Psychopathic Disorder*, London: DHSS and Home Office.

Dorn, N., Henderson, S. and South, N. (1992), *AIDS, Women, Drugs and Social Care*, London: Falmer.

Dorn, N. and South, N. (1990), 'Drug Markets and Law Enforcement', *British Journal of Criminology*, vol. 30, p. 171.

Fagan, J. (1990), 'Intoxication and Aggression', in M. Tonry and J.Q. Wilson (eds), *Crime and Justice: a Review of Research*, vol. 13, Chicago: University of Chicago Press.

Farrington, D.P. (1994), 'Introduction', in D.P. Farrington (ed.), *Psychological Explanations of Crime*, Aldershot: Dartmouth.

Feldman, Philip (1993), *The Psychology of Crime*, Cambridge: Cambridge University Press.

Fishbein, Diana H. and Pease, Susan E. (1990), 'Neurological Links between Substance Abuse and Crime', in Lee Ellis and Harry Hoffman (eds), *Crime in Biological, Social, and Moral Contexts*, New York: Praeger.

Flanzer, Jerry (1981), 'The Vicious Circle of Alcoholism and Family Violence', *Alcoholism*, vol. 1(3), p. 30.

Frost, C. (1986), 'Drug Trafficking, Organised Crime and Terrorism: the International Cash Connection', in V. Raanan, R. Pfaltzgraff, R. Shultz (eds), *Hydra of Carnage*, Lexington, Mass.: Lexington Books.

Glatt, M. (1965), 'Crime, Alcohol and Alcoholism', *Howard Journal of Penology and Crime Prevention*, vol. IX, p. 274.

Glueck, B. (1918), 'A study of 608 Admissions to Sing Sing Prison', *Mental Hygiene*, vol. 2, p. 85.

Green, C.M. (1981), 'Matricide by Sons', *Medicine, Science and the Law*, vol. 21, p. 207.

Guze, S.B. (1976), *Criminality and Psychiatric Disorders*, Oxford: Oxford University Press.

Hammersley, R., Forsyth, A., Morrison, V. and Davies, J. (1989), 'The Relationship between Crime and Opoid Use', *British Journal of Addiction*, vol. 84, p. 1029.

Hare, R.D. (1970), *Psychopathy: Theory and Research*, London: John Wiley.

Hare, R.D. (1980), 'A Research Scale for the Assessment of Psychopathy in Criminal Populations', *Personality and Individual Differences*, vol. 1, p. 111.

Hare, R.D. and McPherson L.M. (1984), *Journal of Abnormal Psychology*, vol. 93(II), p. 141.

Hart, H.L.A. (1968), *Punishment and Responsibility*, Oxford: Clarendon Press.

Hochstedler Steury, Ellen (1993), 'Criminal Defendants with Psychiatric Impairment: Prevalence, Probabilities and Rates', *Journal of Criminal Law and Criminology*, vol. 84, p. 352.

Hodgins, S. (1992), 'The Treatment of Mentally Disordered Offenders in Canada', in F. Lösel, D. Bender and T. Bliesener (eds), *Psychology and Law*, Berlin: De Gruyter.

Hollin, Clive, R. (1992), *Criminal Behaviour*, London: The Falmer Press.

Jarvis, G. and Parker, H. (1989), 'Young Heroin Users and Crime', *British Journal of Criminology*, vol. 29, p. 175.

Kelly, L. (1988), *Surviving Sexual Violence*, Cambridge: Polity Press.

Kritzman, Lawrence D. (ed.) (1988), *Michel Foucault: Politics, Philosophy, Culture: Interviews and other Writings 1977-1984*, New York and London: Routledge.

Lindqvist, P. and Allebeck, P. (1990a), 'Schizophrenia and Crime: a Longitudinal Follow-up of 644 Schizophrenics in Stockholm', *British Journal of Psychiatry*, vol. 157, p. 345

Lindqvist, P. and Allebeck, P. (1990b), 'Schizophrenia and Assaultative Behaviour: the Role of Alcohol and Drugs', *Acta Psychiatrica Scandinavica*, vol. 82, p. 191.

Link, Bruce G., Andrews, Howard and Cullen, Francis T. (1992), 'The Violent and Illegal Behaviour of Mental Patients Reconsidered', *American Sociological Review*, vol. 57, p. 275.

Mackay, R.D. (1990), 'Fact and Fiction about the Insanity Defence', *Criminal Law Review*, p. 247.

Mackay, R.D. and Kearns, G., (1994) 'The Continued Underuse of Unfitness to Plead and the Insanity Defence', *Criminal Law Review* 576.

McBride, D. and McCoy, C. (1982), 'Crime and Drugs: the Issues and Literature', *Journal of Drug Issues*, Spring, p. 137.

Morris, Norval and Hawkins, Gordon (1970), *The Honest Politician' s Guide to Crime Control*, Chicago: Chicago University Press.

Morris, Norval (1982), *Madness and the Criminal Law*, Chicago: University of Chicago Press.

Mott, J. (1990), 'Young People, Alcohol and Crime', *Home Office Research Bulletin*, vol. 28.

Murdock, D., Pihl, R.O., and Ross, D. (1990) 'Alcohol and Crimes of Violence: Present Issues', *The International Journal of Addictions*, vol. 25, p. 1065.

Nadelmann, Ethan A. (1989), 'Drug Prohibition in the United States: Costs Consequences and Alternatives', *Science*, vol. 245, p. 939.

National Association of Probation Officers, (1994), *Substance Abuse, Mental Vulnerability and the Criminal Justice System: A Briefing Paper From the National Association of Probation Officers*, London: NAPO.

Packer, Herbert (1968), *The Limits of the Criminal Sanction*, Stanford: Stanford University Press.

Pearson, G. (1991), 'Drug Control Policies in Britain', in M. Tonry and J. Wilson (eds), *Crime and Justice: a Review of Research*, vol. 13, Chicago: University of Chicago Press.

Pihl, Robert O. and Peterson, Jordan B. (1993), 'Alcohol/Drug Use and Aggressive Behaviour', in Sheilagh Hodgins (ed.), *Mental Disorder and Crime*, Newbury Park: Sage.

Pitch, T. (1995), *Limited Responsibilities: Social Movements and Criminal Justice*, trans. John Lea, London: Routledge.

Plant, M. (1990), *AIDS, Drugs and Prostitution*, London: Routledge.

Power, Dennis (1988), 'Psychopathic Disorder', *The Criminologist*, vol. 12, p. 202.

Prins, H. (1980), *Offenders, Deviants, or Patients? An Introduction to the Study of Socio-Forensic Problems*, London: Tavistock.

Prins, H. (1986), *Dangerous Behaviour, the Law and Mental Disorder*, London: Tavistock.

Rafter, N. (1997), 'Psychopathy and the Evolution of Criminological Knowledge', *Theoretical Criminology*, vol. 1(2), p. 235.

Rollin, H. (1969), *The Mentally Abnormal Offender and the Law: an Inquiry into the Working of the Relevant Parts of the Mental Health Act 1959*, Oxford: Pergamon.

Ryan, Christopher and Scanlan, Gary (1991), *Swot: Criminal Law*, 3rd edn, London: Blackstone Press.

Samuels, A. (1988), 'Mental Condition as a Defence in Criminal Law: A Lawyer Addresses Medical Men', *Medicine, Science and the Law*, vol. 28(1), p. 21.

Saunders, W. (1984), *Alcohol Use in Britain: How Much is too Much?* Edinburgh: Scottish Health Education Unit.

Smith, K.J.M. and Wilson, William (1993), 'Impaired Voluntariness and Criminal Responsibility: Reworking Hart's Theory of Excuses – the English Judicial Response', *Oxford Journal of Legal Studies*, vol. 13, p. 69.

Smith, John Cyril and Hogan, Brian (1996), *Criminal Law*, 8th edn, London: Butterworths.

Taylor, David (1981), *Alcohol: Reducing the Harm*, London: Office of Health Economics.

Taylor, P.J. (1986), 'Psychiatric Disorder in London's Life-Sentenced Offenders', *British Journal of Criminology*, vol. 26, p. 63.

Taylor, Pamela J. (1985), 'Motives for Offending among Violent and Psychotic Men', *British Journal of Psychiatry*, vol. 147, p. 491.

Taylor, Pamela J. (1993), 'Schizophrenia and Crime: Distinctive Patterns of Association', in Sheilagh Hodgins (ed.), *Mental Disorder and Crime*, Newbury Park: Sage.

Teplin, Linda A. (1990), 'The Prevalence of Severe Mental Disorder among Male Urban Jail Detainees: Comparison with the Epidemiologic Catchment Area Program', *American Journal of Public Health*, vol. 80, p. 663.

Teplin, Linda A., McClelland, Gary M. and Abram, Karen M. (1993), 'The Role of Mental Disorder and Substance Abuse in Predicting Violent Crime among Released Offenders', in Sheilagh Hodgins (ed.), *Mental Disorder and Crime*, Newbury Park: Sage.

Toch, Hans (ed.) (1966), *Legal and Criminal Psychology*, New York: Holt, Rinehart and Winston.

Wachholz, Sandra and Mullaly, Robert (1993), 'Policing the Deinstitutionalized Mentally Ill: Towards an Understanding of its Functions', *Crime, Law and Social Change*, vol. 19, p. 281.

Walker, Nigel (1973), *Crime and Punishment in Britain*, Edinburgh: Edinburgh University Press.

West, D.J. (1965), *Murder Followed by Suicide*, London: Heinemann.

CHAPTER TEN
Intelligence and Learning

10.1 INTELLIGENCE AND CRIME

10.1.1 Introduction

There are several links between IQ and the law. Some have little or no connection with the criminal law and will be dealt with only in passing; others have sometimes been very closely linked to criminality and form the basis of this section. There is very little discussion of high intelligence and criminality, and this will not be considered.

10.1.2 Legal definition of low intelligence

There are two distinct types of mental defect, amentia and dementia. Amentia literally means 'lack of mind', and describes a person who is born with a reduced intellect. These people are often known as subnormal. Dementia describes someone who once had a normal intelligence but later lost it through disease, decay or accident.

Under the Mental Health Act 1959, these conditions were referred to as subnormality and severe subnormality, and included people with low intelligence who were considered unable to live an independent life and unable to guard themselves against exploitation which might exist outside a State institution. Since the enacting of s. 1 of the Mental Health Act 1983, these problems have been referred to as mental impairment and severe mental impairment. They include a state of arrested or incomplete development of the mind which includes (severe) impairment of intelligence and social functioning, associated with abnormally aggressive or seriously irresponsible conduct on the part of the person concerned.

There are two important differences between these definitions. Firstly, there is a move away from the term subnormality towards mental impairment. This change has been severely criticised, both by individual experts and by bodies such as MIND, because it might be used to catch more individuals and therefore prejudice those of reduced intellect. Secondly, although both these definitions admit that assessment of mental inability cannot be tested on IQ ratings alone, they differ on the extra element required. The 1959 version included the ability of individuals to care for themselves; the 1983 version looks at their danger to themselves and, importantly, to others. It talks about abnormally aggressive or seriously irresponsible conduct. The 1983 version seems to move closer to a connection with criminality or criminal tendencies, something which has worried many professionals, as it may suggest that such tendencies accompany low intelligence. They find the wording to be particularly distressing because it is similar to that used to describe psychopathy in the 1959 Act.

These definitions are used to decide which individuals need treatment or help. They are used on both criminals, who may be forcibly treated if they fit into these categories, and non-criminals who may receive voluntary treatment. They indicate the way in which the law deals with severe problems in this area, and the recent alterations to the definitions may reflect the changes taking place in the view taken of the connection between intelligence and criminality.

The following table might give a better idea of the medical assessment of mental retardation:

Table 10.1: from Gleitman (1986), p. 587

CHARACTERISTICS OF THE MENTALLY RETARDED

Degree of retardation	IQ range	Level of functioning at school age (6-20 years)	Level of functioning in adulthood (21 years and over)
Mild	52-67	Can learn academic skills up to approximately sixth-grade level by late teens; can be guided toward social conformity.	Can usually achieve social and vocational skills adequate to maintain self support, but may need guidance and assistance when under unusual social or economic stress.
Moderate	36-51	Can profit from training in social and occupational skills; unlikely to progress beyond second-grade level in academic subjects; may learn to travel alone in familiar places.	May achieve self-maintenance in unskilled or semiskilled work under sheltered conditions; needs supervision and guidance when under mild social or economic stress.
Severe	20-35	Can talk or learn to communicate; can be trained in elemental health habits; profits from systematic habit training.	May contribute partially to self-maintenance under complete supervision; can develop self-protection skills at a minimum useful level in controlled environment.
Profound	below 20	Some motor development present; may respond to minimal or limited training in self-help.	Some motor and speech development; may achieve very limited self-care; needs nursing care.

It is not possible to assess exactly what percentage of the population is sufficiently mentally retarded to fall under this legal definition, but it has been calculated that only 3 per cent of the American population could be said to be retarded (Cytryn and Lourie (1975)). There is no reason to believe that the British population would not be similar. Moreover, for every 100 retarded persons it is suggested that 90 would be only 'mildly', 6 'moderately', 3 'severely' and 1 'profoundly' retarded (Robinson and Robinson (1970)). The legal definition clearly includes both the 'severe' and the 'profound' categories and might include some from the 'moderate' and 'mild' categories. In any event, only a very small section of the population is involved. If we consider the numbers of this already small group who have criminal tendencies, then our interest in this area would be minimal. The main area of the criminological study of mental capacity is therefore of those with reduced intellect, not severely impaired intellect.

10.1.3 How to measure intelligence

The link between reduced intellect and crime was made because it was assumed that intelligence was linked to the ability to learn and understand complex societal norms and rules. Furthermore, it was considered that those of low intellect were less able to control their emotions and their behaviour. It was not until the turn of the century that reasonably reliable tests to assess intelligence were produced. The first generally accepted test was constructed by Binet and Simon, and was called the 'Scale of Intelligence'. By 1908 they had assigned each test to a mental age. For example, an average seven-year-old could do certain tasks which would be too difficult for an average six-year-old. The level of the hardest tasks performed represented the mental age of the individual. These form the basis for the intelligence tests which are still used today. The validity of these tests has, for some time, been controversial and although we are not centrally concerned with this point, it should be borne in mind.

Binet devised the test so that he could pin-point children who had learning difficulties and give them special help. He set up special classes for these children in Paris, and discovered that with special teaching techniques they became both more intelligent (in this sense) and more able to learn. He claimed that this proved that intelligence was not inborn and unchangeable.

Intelligence tests were also used to discover whether there was a link between criminality and intelligence: some authorities who claimed to have discovered such a link argued for the limitation of the right of these people to have children (see 10.1.7).

10.1.4 Link between crime and intellect

The earliest reputable studies into the link between criminality and intelligence were perhaps those conducted by Goddard (1912), starting with an unscientific study of the Kalikak family; by using a subjective assessment of 'feeble-mindedness' it largely begged the question it claimed to prove. Goddard's later studies were more acceptable 'scientifically', as they used the objective IQ tests to measure for 'feeble-mindedness'. He studied the inmates of 16 reformatories, and found that the proportion of feeble-minded inmates ranged from 28 per cent to 89 per cent, the average being about 50 per cent. His results, which were published in 1914, led him to conclude that criminals were 'feeble-minded'. He went further and suggested that all 'feeble-minded' individuals were potential criminals. Since he argued that this condition was basically inherited, he recommended their institutionalisation or sterilisation to prevent them breeding.

Most research carried out at the time arrived at similar conclusions until, during World War I, the United States army began to test the IQ of their draftees, with the intention of declaring all the 'feeble-minded' as being unfit for military service. The unpalatable outcome was that about 50 per cent were 'feeble-minded'. The army could not accept this, and revised the level of 'feeble-mindedness' so as to catch fewer individuals. Following the war, theorists adopted the army's arbitrary revision. Goddard himself admitted that his previous findings were inaccurate, and even accepted that intellect was not purely hereditary but could be, at least partially, corrected by careful educational practices.

Investigations in the 50 years after 1920 largely failed to discover a connection between criminality and 'feeble-mindedness'. For example, the representative work of Mary Woodward (1955) concluded that 'low intelligence plays little or no part in delinquency'.

More recently, the possibility of a link has been revived and has had some support. The modern proponents of a link between intelligence and criminality have had a more scientific approach than their predecessors. Hirschi and Hindling (1977) found that low IQ was as good a predictor of delinquency as the more commonly accepted factors such as social class and upbringing. They argued that delinquency within a racial or social grouping is likely to be connected to IQ, so that low IQ Blacks are more likely to be delinquent than high IQ Blacks, and low IQ Whites are more likely to be delinquent than high IQ Whites. Similarly, lower-class delinquents will have lower IQs than lower-class non-delinquents. They discovered that delinquents on average had an IQ eight points lower than non-delinquents, and asserted that this difference was too significant to be ignored. They do not accept the idea that IQ is wholly related to hereditary factors, but argue that an individual's IQ potential may be affected by environmental factors. Finally, they do not claim that IQ has any direct effect on criminality. They speculate instead that the inability (or reduced ability) of low IQ juveniles to compete in certain fields leads them to look elsewhere for recognition (see, for example, the theories relating to school and criminality (13.6.2) and youth deviance (12.3)).

In Britain, one of the foremost pieces of research in this area is the Cambridge Study in Delinquent Development carried out by Cambridge University Institute of Criminology, directed by West. It was a longitudinal study (i.e., followed the subjects over a period of time) on boys from north-east London, who were under scrutiny from the age of 8 until the age of 25. The results of this study have been the material for a number of books dating from 1969. One written by West (1982) draws together all the findings. The survey included a number of factors which are commonly related to criminality, such as parental conflict, separation or instability, unsatisfactory child-rearing (such as neglect, cruelty, incorrect discipline or supervision), pupils who are 'troublesome' at primary school, low income families, large family size (which was found to be a particularly important predictor for those with a number of older siblings), and one or more criminal parents.

All those associated with the study were surprised to find that low IQ seemed as closely related to criminality as these other, more widely accepted, factors. The average IQ of future juvenile delinquents was 95 and that of future non-delinquents 101. This sounds a very small difference, but its significance is masked because it reflects averages. Close examination showed a distinct deficit of delinquent boys in the high IQ group, over 110, and a substantial excess of delinquent boys in the low IQ group, under 90. The far more frequent (almost twice as frequent) appearance of delinquent boys amongst the low scorers was sufficient to allow West to include this as one of the most important predictors of criminality. Even more interestingly, he discovered that low intelligence was particularly closely related to young convictions and recidivism. Furthermore, Gibson and West (1970) discovered that when they tested boys on both verbal and non-verbal intelligence tests, those convicted before the age of 14 exhibited a substantially lower IQ than the others.

Farrington (1992), again working with the Cambridge data, found that a third of those scoring below 90 on a non-verbal intelligence test at ages 8–10 later became convicted juvenile offenders. This is twice as many as those who scored over 90. This may suggest that those with low intelligence are less able to avoid conviction but it was also very closely related to high levels of self-reported delinquency. Low non-verbal ability was linked to low verbal ability and to low school attainment at the age of 11, both of which were linked to juvenile convictions. All of these were also connected to high truancy rates and early school leaving, though they were independent of other social links, such as large family size and low income (Lynam et al. (1993)).

If there seems to be a relationship between criminality and intelligence the nature of that relationship is both interesting and unclear. Apparently these individuals have difficulty in dealing with abstract concepts and reasoning, which reduces their ability to foresee the consequences of any actions either to themselves or to others. They may thus be less likely to be deterred by the possibility of detection, conviction and punishment, or by compassion or empathy for their victims. This lack of intellectual capacity may be linked to a number of factors. First it could be the result of different or reduced brain functioning. The frontal lobes of the brain control abilities such as abstract reasoning, comprehension of abstract concepts, forward planning and anticipation of problems, self-control – particularly of impulsive and socially unacceptable behaviour – and interest or concentration span. Moffitt and Henry (1989) have suggested that these functions are linked to low intelligence, offending and general antisocial activity, suggesting a causal link with brain dysfunctions (see 7.3.3). Secondly the abilities set out above are those found to be problematic in cognitive learning (see 10.2.6) and Farrington (1994) suggests that some families are less likely to develop abstract reasoning in their children. He argues that lower class, poorer parents tend to live more for the moment and talk mostly in concrete terms, making them less likely to help a child's abstract reasoning and possibly over-developing a child's impulsive behaviour. A third suggestion (Kohlberg (1976), Kohlberg and Candee (1984) and Smetana (1990)) links lack of intellectual capacity to failure to go beyond the first stage of moral development. In Kohlberg's scheme this is the preconventional stage which he says typifies many criminals (here people put their own desires first, only obeying law because of fear of punishment; it is associated with concrete, one-dimensional thinking). Beyond this are the conventional stage (people learn the law, accept it and obey it because it is law and ought to be followed) and the postconventional stage of a fully developed moral character (the individual can test the law against abstract concepts such as justice, fairness and respect for human beings and their rights).

Whether the link is with the brain dysfunction or the learning difficulties, it may well be possible to help such people with specially designed learning rehabilitative techniques (see 10.2.8). Certainly various studies (see, e.g., Gibson and West (1970)) which found that the low-IQ boys came from the poorer families strongly suggest that this lack of ability could be the result of inadequate schooling or little parental encouragement rather than an innate characteristic.

It is important to note that the link between genetics and intelligence, although not wholly rejected by these studies, is certainly relegated to a less important role than the effects of the environment and of learning on the development of the intellect. This conclusion is very different from that of researchers at the beginning of this century when faced with similar results.

10.1.5   Race, crime and intellect

In the United States, this type of research took on a disturbing form, in that it related low intellect to racial differences and then to criminality. This arose from the claim that, on average, Blacks scored about 15 points lower than Whites in IQ tests. An article by Jensen (1969) claimed to prove that at least 80 per cent of these differences were determined by hereditary rather than environmental factors. This research was drawn on by Robert Gordon (1976). In his study on delinquency prevalence rates (the proportion of a given age cohort that have committed delinquent acts by a specific age) he argued that the prevalence of low IQ for white youths was the same as, or very similar to, the delinquency prevalence rates for that group. He further asserted that the differences in the prevalence for low IQ between Blacks and Whites equalled the differences in the delinquency prevalence rates for Blacks and Whites. The rates of delinquency could, he argued, be substantially explained by assuming that all individuals with an IQ below a particular level were criminal. He went on to claim that some minority races such as the Chinese and Jews have similar low economic status to the Blacks but have a very low crime rate, often a lower crime rate than the more affluent Whites, and that therefore crime rate could not be related to poverty and environment. The conclusions he drew were: that IQ cannot be environmental; it must be hereditary; and low IQ must be related to criminality. His claim is that IQ causes delinquency, not only because it inhibits the ability to learn the socialising element of life but also because, as it is inherited, those with low IQs are going to be reared by parents with low IQ, who are therefore going to be less able to teach the socialising process.

This seems highly plausible, but it needs to be stressed that a large edifice has been built on weak foundations. The little evidence shown is practically untested, and very few control groups are studied. There is, for example, no proof that low IQ delinquents have low IQ parents nor any examination of the possibility that those with high IQ may be delinquent but evade detection or conviction.

A further problem with Gordon's research is the assumption that intelligence is inherited. Many researchers in this area have argued that it is the result of massively inferior environmental conditions of Blacks; wide and systematic discrimination, poorer living conditions, lower life expectancies, inadequate diets, bad housing and inferior schooling. To test the veracity of these conflicting claims, Loehlin, Lindzey and Spuhler (1975) tested the IQ of two matched groups – white children in deprived areas and black children in similarly deprived areas. They found that, although the IQ differences were not wholly eradicated, they were substantially reduced. They explained the remaining discrepancy as a result of the discrimination suffered by the black children, whereas Gordon and his followers claim it proves at least some hereditary basis for intellect. Another study looked at black children who, at an early age, had been adopted into white middle-class families (Scarr and Weinberg (1976)). They discovered the mean IQ of these children was 110, which is at least 20 points above the national average for black children. Such studies suggest a strong correlation between environment and IQ, which would suggest that if criminality is related to low IQ it is also related to the environment; and it may well be that the environmental factors caused both the low IQ and the criminality.

Caution is still needed. It is easy to leap to strong causal connections from the observation (Jones (1993)) that black people tend to live in areas of social stress with high crime rates, and also tend to be disadvantaged in terms of higher unemployment, lower living standards and greater poverty than Whites. But against this is the equally valid observation that Asians suffer on all these counts but have a markedly lower crime rate, lower than for Whites. The difference may be explained by a variety of factors: Asians experience greater socialisation within their own community (a powerful control mechanism – see Chapter Thirteen); they have not suffered discrimination as openly and frequently as Afro-Caribbeans; they have been more insular, relying on their own communities for jobs and housing; and they are not as stigmatised by the criminal justice agencies (especially the police) which deal with them in a less biased manner. Degrees of discrimination and bias are significant because they feed feelings of exclusion, anger and resentment (see Smith (1994)). Many of these factors will be considered at points later in this book; what is important here is to understand that the reasons for the higher crime rates of Afro-Caribbeans are very complex, as is their treatment in our society. To try to pin it on one factor such as lower IQ is both dangerous and misleading. Besides the points already made, such an approach fails to explain the low crime rates amongst this group earlier in their immigration and the current low crime rates of the older populations of Afro-Caribbeans. In any event, the assertions about lower IQs look less secure against the marked rise in the numbers of Afro-Caribbeans now attending higher education establishments; perhaps all that was needed was reduced discrimination and enhanced encouragement for youngsters in these communities. Such considerations reduce the plausibility of citing low IQ as a cause of criminality or as an explanation for differing crime rates in different communities. More likely are the social conditions and treatment of these groups since their arrival in Britain (for a further discussion see the later chapters in this volume, and see also Gelsthorpe and McWilliam (1993)). Interestingly, Jones (1993) suggests that the differential crime rates may soon alter – some improvement in the living conditions and prospects of Afro-Caribbeans (and more in higher education) may lead to a lowering in their crime rate, while increasing discrimination and social and economic disadvantage may unfortunately lead to higher crime rates in Asian communities.

10.1.6 Criticisms on intelligence and criminality
First, it is reasonable to expect that those with a lower IQ are less able to avoid detection. Also, once detected they will be less able to give a good account of their activities, so they are more likely to end up in court, where they may receive a harsher sentence because of their inability to explain themselves. It is also worth noting that criminal activity (such as embezzlement and white-collar crimes) which are likely to be mostly committed by individuals with high intelligence are generally less likely to be discovered, and are less likely to form the basis of a prosecution. All these factors may lead to the over-representation of those with low IQs in the statistics. If all that was studied was official criminality, then one could expect a high rate of low IQ individuals to be found. However, this cannot explain the similar findings in such self-report studies as found by the Cambridge Study in Delinquent Development.

Another criticism which has often been made of the IQ theory is that, far from testing innate intelligence or intellect, it assesses the individual's school level, i.e., measures levels of comprehension and vocabulary. This is certainly true of some of the older tests. The scores would therefore reflect educational attainment or cultural background rather than potential intelligence. If studies test educational attainment, then clearly those will suffer whose education is not as thorough. Some claim that non-verbal studies are therefore better indicators of ability than verbal tests, and some studies have found that delinquents perform better on these tests than on verbal ones. This was not borne out by the Cambridge Study in Delinquent Development, where they obtained the same results from both verbal and non-verbal tests. They also claimed to refute another criticism, namely that delinquents are less motivated in school generally and so would be less motivated to perform well in IQ tests; in their study the boys were generally equally motivated to succeed. This runs counter to other studies (West and Farrington (1973) replicated by Lynam et al. (1993)) that showed that non-verbal intelligence scores correlated well with juvenile offending and self-reported criminal behaviour, as well as early convictions, repeat offending, poor school performance and high truancy.

Others allege that IQ tests simply measure class bias. The types of skills which are measured are not objective, but rather represent a cultural skill which is most likely to be held by, and be useful to, a middle-class urban dweller. When Jane Mercier (1972) constructed simple behavioural and practical tasks, such as the ability to tie a shoe lace, to test intelligence, she claimed that the results were different. Those who under the usual IQ tests would be labelled 'low intelligence', often performed better than the normal high performers, and the low IQ lower-class individuals performed better on these tasks than did low IQ middle-class individuals.

There are therefore some inherent problems in making a link between criminality, delinquency and intelligence. The Cambridge study certainly suggests that there may be some link, but it is impossible to assess how direct it is. In any event, it is still possible that both low intellect and criminality are caused by some third factor.

10.1.7 The danger of linking criminality and IQ

The reason for mental deficiency or lower intellectual ability is still not fully understood. Years ago, the reason given was the Devil; a later explanation was heredity, and the modern reason is part heredity and part environmental or social. The move towards hereditary explanations derived from the acceptance of Darwin's theories of evolution. Proof of a link with hereditary factors was said to be obtained from studies such as that of Dugdale (1877) and Goddard (1912), where whole families were studied to discover their hereditary tendencies. All this led to apparent scientific justification for arguments that charitable works for these people were mistaken, since they encouraged them to reproduce and thereby cause a general deterioration of the human race. It was asserted that natural selection should at least be allowed to take its course, and so reduce the number of feeble-minded. Some wanted natural selection to be helped along by placing these inferior people in institutions, segregating them from normal people and not allowing them to breed.

A basis was thus provided for a strong opposition to any form of social welfare, as this would merely perpetuate the survival of lazy, immoral, devious and less intelligent people, slowing down the development of the nation. Only citizens who were hard working, careful and moral should be nurtured. Most countries bowed to this type of argument to a varying extent. The previous chapter referred to various measures which were used to punish and prevent crime. The method most specifically connected with low intelligence was sterilisation.

In America between 1911 and 1930 most States passed laws either permitting, or in certain instances requiring, sterilisation for behavioural traits thought to be hereditary. These laws were used particularly frequently against the feeble-minded and criminal, although they were also used to control alcoholism and certain sexual perversions (see Beckwith (1985)). Under these laws, at least 64,000 people were sterilised, and these sterilisations continued into the 1970s. In Virginia alone between 1927 and 1972 8,000 individuals were sterilised because they were feeble-minded (see Lilly, Cullen and Ball (1989)). Those sterilised in this way were without any means of support or anyone who would provide support. Therefore, it was generally only the feeble-minded poor who were so sterilised. The words of Justice Holmes in the Supreme Court of America when deciding the case of *Buck v Bell* (1926) 274 US 200, at 207, are indicative of this train of thought:

> We have seen more than once that the public welfare may call upon the best citizens for their lives. It would be strange if it could not call upon those who already sap the strength of the state for these lesser sacrifices, often not felt to be such by those concerned, in order to prevent our being swamped with incompetence. It is better for all the world, if instead of waiting to execute degenerate offspring for crime, or to let them starve for their imbecility, society can prevent those who are manifestly unfit from continuing their kind. The principle that sustains compulsory vaccination is broad enough to cover cutting the fallopian tubes.

In Britain, some sterilisation took place, usually of those in institutions. Some might even say there was a eugenics policy in operation in Britain between 1900 and 1930, but policies as far-reaching as those enunciated in *Buck v Bell* (above) were probably never explicitly adopted. It is, however, difficult to ascertain just how many people were sterilized in the early part of this century in Britain, as the official documents recording the numbers and the reasons for sterilisations are contained in a document which will not be available to the public until 2030 (see Robertson (1989), p. 164). It is probably true to say that sterilisation of criminals in this country tended to take place on what the officials like to refer to as a voluntary basis. In this vein, it has sometimes been offered to sex offenders and, in such cases, is not directly connected with IQ.

Although a full eugenics policy was never introduced into Britain, the ideas and arguments which eugenists encompass were well received in theories of penology. Segregation of the unfit, through imprisonment, had the same effect as sterilisation. At the turn of the century there were therefore many calls for long sentences, even of petty offenders. For example, Darwin (1914/15) wrote of persistent petty offenders:

> increased periods of detention of habitual criminals would produce both immediate social advantages and ultimate improvements in the racial qualities of future generations, and, if this be the case, the social reformer and the eugenist ought to be able to march together on this path of criminal reform. (p. 212)

This type of attitude led to longer sentences being more readily accepted, possibly more so in the case of the lower IQ criminal. Long sentences have lasted up until the present day in our penal system, although their survival may have a different basis.

In Germany there was a complete and very strong eugenics policy which involved either executing, or at least sterilising anyone who was feeble-minded, criminal or otherwise 'inferior'. Nazi Germany illuminates the very dangerous possibilities of a complete acceptance of theories of the sort outlined above.

Towards the middle of this century, the reason for lower mental ability moved on again. It became understood that although some severe forms can be inherited (e.g., mongolism or Down's syndrome), most were caused by disease, exposure to certain drugs, brain damage, lack of mental stimulation, malnutrition or other environmental factors. This moved the ideas of sterilisation out of vogue and encouraged concentration on the environmental causes. Acceptance of this might have beneficial consequences, such as both improved living conditions and educational opportunities for those worst off in our society.

However, in the work of Gordon discussed above (10.1.5), with its assumption that intelligence is inherited and that the lower intelligence of Blacks explains their higher rates of criminality, there is a tendency to return to the views held earlier this century. If such a shift is associated with a move away from a social welfare policy and towards more stress being placed on self-determination, self-betterment and success, it may indicate some reinstatement of a system of natural selection. The recent changes in the Mental Health Act are possibly indicative of such a change in the social and intellectual climate, and such developments need constant scrutiny.

Many liberal commentators detect ominous signs in some recent British cases in this area. In *Re F (Mental Patient: Sterilisation)* [1990] 2 AC 1, the sterilisation of an adult female was considered. The woman had a mental age of about four, and if she had become pregnant would have been unable to understand what was happening. It was felt that this would be bad for her health and well-being. The case was finally decided upon what were deemed to be the woman's best interests, but certain of the judges made comments which seemed to suggest that the sterilisation should be allowed if it were in the public interest. Some see the inclusion of public interest in such an area as a portent allowing for a return to earlier, insidious types of policies.

Gordon's work raises particular dangers, as it emphasises racial differences in IQs. He asserted that the Blacks were less intelligent and committed more crime than the Whites. But if one looks back at earlier American studies it was the Italians and other Southern and Eastern European peoples who were seen as the inferior, criminal races. It was then found that these people had an IQ 16 points below the general American population (see Pinter (1923)). These findings were instrumental to the passing of the Immigration Restriction Act of 1924, which controlled the immigration of Eastern Europeans into America partly because these people were thought of as biologically inferior. One of the rationalisations behind the immigration controls was this desire to keep the racial standards high, but there was already substantial evidence that the IQ differences were due to language problems and disappeared after about 20 years in America. This information seems to have been ignored, possibly because the majority wished to protect the economic *status quo* against a large influx of cheap labour.

Even earlier, the Irish had been seen as the criminal and inferior section of American and British society; now it is the Blacks. Prejudice may be fed by claims that these people are inherently less intelligent and therefore inferior, particularly if the lower intelligence is linked to criminality and therefore to social ills. For this reason, claims of this sort are very dangerous, particularly as the studies so far seem to suggest that it is largely due to environmental factors that Blacks have lower IQs and are more criminal. There seems to be a tendency to 'prove' that the poorest groups in a society, especially if they are easily identified by ethnicity or colour, are the most criminal and, according to some studies, the least intelligent. This might more plausibly suggest that criminality and intelligence have similar, environmental causes (see 10.1.5).

Such a claim is borne out by the work of Offord, Poushinsky and Sullivan (1978). Their study suggests that criminality and delinquency are both caused by external factors such as adverse family influences, and that the educational retardation itself is not causally related to criminality. The fact of an environmental cause of low intelligence is lent support by the work of Simons (1978) who discovered that when low IQ, lower-class children were placed in special educational classes they made gains of about 15 points, which would equal out even the worst predicted differences. Simons also claimed that if the IQ tests were carried out on very young children, before school had time to affect them, then the scores of lower-class and middle-class children would be similar. A few years later, once school had affected their relative rates of progression, the lower-class children would appear less intelligent. He therefore claimed that low intelligence was related to schooling and other environmental factors, rather than innate ability.

From this it can be seen that there are very real dangers in the full acceptance of some of the above theories. These have not deterred Murray and Herrnstein (1994) from suggesting significant links between crime, IQ and race, even arguing that the basis of differences in modern societies is, and should be, intelligence. Of course, it is not the theories themselves which are dangerous, but the use to which they are put. For this reason, particular care is necessary in carrying out and analysing such research, as well as in basing decisions upon it.

10.2 LEARNING

10.2.1 Introduction

Very few behaviours and actions are actually natural or instinctive; most must be learned. If an opportunity for advancement by criminality were to arise, an individual might well not recognise it, or not know how to take advantage of it, unless they had learned certain behaviours or ways of taking advantage of illegitimate opportunities. Basically, these theories see criminality as normal learned behaviour. Some behaviour is instinctive and is possessed by an individual at birth; the possession of this is determined by biological factors. Learned behaviour depends upon knowledge, skills, habits and responses that have been developed as a result of experience, or of the need to adjust to the environment.

Learning theories and their effects on individual behaviour are not new – one of the first proponents of a learning theory was Aristotle (384-322 BC). His ideas were based upon learning by association. For Aristotle, this meant the association between sensory experiences which were internal to the individual and upon which the outside world worked. The theory of association is still strong, but rather than the association being with internal sensations, it is now argued that it is a response to external stimuli or the association between stimuli.

It is important to note that learning theories are not closely connected with intelligence. Of course, the level of intelligence may affect the ability of a particular individual to learn complex types of behaviour, just as their physical make-up may affect their ability to perform certain activities. Learning theories are not concerned with either of these problems, but with the way in which learning takes place, and what affects the type of behaviour that might be learnt. The main learning theory to be connected with explanations of criminal behaviour is 'differential association', which was expounded by a social learning theorist called Sutherland (1939). This theory will be discussed later. First, it is important to understand some of the basic psychological theories on learning.

10.2.2 Learning structures

The old school of learning, sometimes referred to as the classical learning theory, can be characterised by the work of Pavlov (1927). Pavlov noticed that certain external stimuli always produced certain responses, and that these responses seemed to be natural. The example usually chosen is that a dog always salivates when it is given meat, but it does not salivate when presented with most other stimuli, e.g., a bell ringing. Pavlov tried to alter this. He persistently rang a bell when giving the dogs meat and after a time he stopped presenting them with meat and discovered that they still salivated when they heard the bell. By this experiment Pavlov showed that behaviours could be learned by association – the dogs had come to associate the bell with meat, and so the ringing of the bell triggered off a response to the expected stimuli of being fed. The conditioned response arose because the bell was now associated with food.

A certain amount of human behaviour may be explained in this way. For example, fear is a natural response in that it is a largely uncontrolled response to certain stimuli which can be quite varied. What an adult learns to fear may be the result of what was associated with that feeling in childhood. If a child fell and hurt himself he may come to fear heights; similarly, if he was punished he may come to fear whatever he was punished for. This might help to explain the use of punishment as a deterrent to certain activity. If a certain activity gives rise to punishment and/or unpleasantness, and so to fear, then the mere thought of the activity might later result in the fear, making it unlikely that the individual will take part in that activity. This type of learning is useful to our understanding of some behaviour, but it is of limited use because the individual is passive. The subject learns to correct its behaviours in response to the environment, and its learning can only take place because of the existence of certain innate reflexes which trigger off some responses, which could then later be triggered off by an associated different stimulus. Of much more interest is operant conditioning, which has also been referred to as instrumental conditioning.

In operant conditioning the individual interacts with the environment and thereby learns what behaviour will bring about the desired end. Skinner is probably the best known, though not the first, proponent of this type of theory, which is probably one of the most prominent learning theories in psychology today (Skinner (1938)). Its basis is that behaviour is learnt through the use of rewards and punishments. Behaviour which is rewarded will be reinforced and become more frequent in order to maximise the rewards, and behaviour which is punished or which meets with aversive consequences will be discouraged. Behaviour changes to secure more of what is liked, and less of what is disliked. Thus far, classical and operant learning are very similar, but in operant learning behaviour is not just affected by the environment, but operates on the environment to attain various ends. So, although people may learn that certain behaviour has unpleasant connotations, they may learn to avoid the unpleasant consequences whilst still enjoying the initial behaviour. A child might learn that stealing biscuits brings an unpleasant result, and so possibly stops the theft. The child may discover that by stealing in a different way, when everyone is out, it is not likely to be caught. The child thus learns that it might be able to gain the desired end and also avoid the unpleasantness by altering its behaviour to make the desired result most likely and the punishment least likely. If the risk seems worth it, the child may continue with the unacceptable activity. This theory is based on what the individual finds rewarding or unpleasant, and assumes that everybody seeks to maximise rewards and minimise punishment. Note that what is considered to be pleasant or unpleasant differs from person to person, but neither of these theories seems to assume that the individual has any clear understanding of what is learnt and why. There is little cognitive thought attributed to the subjects.

Cognitive learning is rather different from either of the above, each of which was based on responses. Cognitive learning considers the ability to understand. It might explain how people understand concepts and solve problems, and also how they arrange the information they obtain from response theories so as to give their behaviour meaning. It includes an understanding of the physical world as well as learning and shaping attitudes and beliefs about that world. In particular, it involves learning about other people, their behaviour and how we interact with them. It thus includes learning respect for the feelings of others, learning to take responsibility, learning to make rational choices about behaviour, learning to control impulsive desires and behaviours, learning to develop powers of moral reasoning, and learning how to solve interpersonal problems. Some theorists have suggested that criminals show lower abilities in one or more of these learnt behaviours (see Nelson et al. (1990); Akers (1990)).

These learning processes can take place through a number of different modes. In the above techniques, the learning was portrayed as taking place through direct experiences, but learning can also be observational or based on models. That is, learning can take place by watching the behaviour of others and seeing whether it is rewarded or punished. This type of learning may be used to build up new types of behaviour, or to reinforce or to weaken previously learned behaviour (see Bandura (1973)). Effective learning from observation or modelling probably requires the individual to practise or re-enact the behaviour, but such re-enactment can be mental rather than physical. A full learning will also include attitudes to behaviour. This type of learning is thought to be most powerful for children, who may model their behaviour on family, teachers or peer groups. In adolescence, the peer group is probably the strongest model, and the effects of this are discussed in Chapter Twelve.

Generally, for a particular type of behaviour to become part of a pattern it needs to fit in with the attitudes of the individual or the attitudes which fit the behaviour which needs to be learnt. Such attitudes are learnt from interactions with others. Most people act within what they consider to be acceptable: a strong negative attitude to crime is thus less likely to lead to violations than an ambivalent or positive attitude.

In any discussion of learnt behaviour, particularly observational or modelling, the effects of media images need to be considered, especially TV and films (here, this area will be referred to as TV). The assertion is that humans learn from the screen in the way they learn from face-to-face interactions. Where a link is said to exist between criminality and the media, it is usually perceived as influencing violent behaviour (see Bandura (1973)). The claim is that TV teaches methods and tactics of violence, and shows how aggressive behaviour can be rewarding. The main problems with the claims is that the influence of TV has never been proven to exist. Some recent studies do support the possibility of such a link. For example, Leyens et al. (1975) noted that there was an increase in physically aggressive behaviour in groups exposed to violent films, whilst in those exposed to neutral films there was actually a lowering of physical aggression. This does suggest that some behaviour may be affected by TV, but it does not mean that the learning process is the same as in face-to-face learning. It could be that TV teaches methods of violence to those who are already susceptible to it, and reinforces attitudes supportive of violence, but it may not go further than that. Many behavioural theorists discount or minimise the importance of the media. It is a fiercely disputed area (see 10.2.7, and Sparks (1983 and 1992), Harbord (1996)).

The effects of behavioural learning are often thought to be related to the environment in which individuals live, and to their social groupings, and it is at this point that Sutherland's theory becomes important.

10.2.3 Differential association

This term is inextricably linked with the name of Edwin H. Sutherland (1939). It is also clearly set out in Sutherland and Cressey (1978), which retains the basic theory but makes certain clarifying alterations. Sutherland was concerned with white-collar crime (for that part of his work, see Chapter Three). He attempted to explain why and how the upper classes turn to criminality, and to show that the same factors acted upon them as upon most other criminals. It was therefore an explanation which both he and others have used to explain criminality generally. In fact, some supporters of the theory believe it explains all criminal behaviour. This claim and others will be discussed in the consideration and evaluation of the theory.

Differential association is a theory of learning. Fundamentally, it asserts that crime is learnt by association with others. It has been said to have been conceived out of a refinement of the work of G. Tarde (1843–1904). Tarde's theory was one of imitation, stating firstly, that all men imitate each other. The amount of imitation which takes place is directly dependent upon how close are their contacts. Secondly, it stated that the lower classes tend to imitate the upper classes. Clearly, any statistical verification of these claims would be difficult, but it seems likely that they have at least some part to play in the explanation of criminality. People do tend to copy one another (see Wilson Vine (1960)).

Although Sutherland never gave much acknowledgement to Tarde, it seems he probably used this theory of imitation, expanded it, refined it and made it more popular. Instead of imitation, his theory was based upon a wider idea involving all the normal mechanisms involved in the learning process. He argued that all behaviour was learnt, and to decide whether someone would be criminal you needed to split criminal behaviour from non-criminal behaviour. The central hypothesis is that crime is not unique or invented by each criminal separately but, like all other forms of human behaviour, it is learnt from direct contact with other people. This leads into the second hypothesis: that behavioural learning takes place through personal contacts with other people. He does not rule out the possible influences of media, but claims that these are very much secondary to the direct personal interactions.

The learning takes place in small informal group settings, and develops from the collective experience and personal interaction as well as from particular situations. A third assertion is that the learning involves both the techniques for committing the offences and the motives, drives, rationalisations, values and attitudes for its committal, i.e., why it is committed. Finally, whether a person takes part in criminal activities depends on the amount of contact they have with criminal activities or with those who support or are sympathetic towards criminal activities. Non-criminal input or definitions generally come from law-abiding citizens and those who reinforce such behaviour, both by their actions and their words. Criminal input or definitions come from criminal offenders and those who may verbally approve of such behaviour, or those who may verbally disapprove of crime but who are nevertheless willing to participate in certain types of criminal activity. The attitudes and definitions are not as clear-cut as this, and there are often mixed emotions. For example, parents and others close to an individual may approve of, or at least not disapprove of, certain types of theft; to feed the hungry, to clothe children, or from certain types of victims like large stores or large employers. They might teach sympathy to these whilst still teaching that theft is generally wrong. All of these differing and sometimes conflicting definitions are experienced, and will lead to criminality if the individual is more exposed to views which are supportive of crime than to views which are against it. This is the central idea of the theory, and basically the idea can be summed up in the following words:

A person becomes criminal if there is an excess of definitions favourable to the violation of the law over definitions unfavourable to violation of the law.

The criminal activity may also be affected by the frequency, duration, priority and intensity of the definitions either for law-abiding or law-breaking behaviour. The longer and more frequently one is exposed to a particular type of behaviour or attitude, the more effect it is likely to have. The stress on priority is intended to denote that the earlier the attitude is experienced, the more forcefully it is likely to affect later behaviour. Finally, intensity has to do with the prestige of the person portraying a particular type of behaviour and the emotional reactions related both to the source and the content of the information. To an extent, this may explain why policemen and prison officers do not generally become criminal despite being in constant and close contact with criminals – they hold them in very low regard, and therefore only wish to learn from them how to remain as little like them as possible. Similarly, if a particular input brought with it great sorrow or great joy, this might affect the way in which it effects the learning process.

It is important to note that Sutherland does not consider that offenders are driven by different goals and desires from non-criminals, but rather that they choose different means of achieving those ends. Criminality may be entered into for financial gain or happiness, but most people manage to pursue financial gain and possibly even happiness in law-abiding jobs. To explain criminal behaviour by reference to its ends is therefore futile, as most non-criminal behaviour is driven by the same desires or ends. He therefore argued that it was the reason for choosing the particular method of reaching the end that was important.

Since its inception, the theory of differential association has been modified and changed in order to widen or to narrow its scope, depending on the intentions of the writer. For example, Glaser (1956) suggested that criminal learning was not only, or even primarily, based on associations between individuals, but that criminal learning involved identification with criminal roles and therefore a desire to emulate them. The identification could arise even though the individuals had never met. This could occur through factors such as the media and through role associations. Glaser formulated a differential-anticipation theory where he said that behaviour depends upon expectations, and that these arose from three sources:

(a) 'procriminal' and 'anticriminal' social bonds; that is the type of response people are likely to suffer on performance of various activities. Will they be punished or rewarded?

(b) Differential learning of desires, skills, problem solving and their understanding of whether to expect punishment or encouragement if they take part in a particular activity.

(c) Perceived opportunities, the balancing up of the possible gain, the possible punishment and the risk involved.

Each of these factors may be learned from social interaction or from other sources such as the media.

Other alterations to the theory have taken place but these will not be dealt with in this book. If the reader is interested, the main sources are: Defleur and Quinney (1966), Burgess and Akers (1966), and Adams (1973).

10.2.4 Evaluation

Criticisms concerning this theory abound, and only the most important will be dealt with here. The first few are intended to refute claims that it can be used to explain all criminality. Thus, it has been argued that it is impossible for this theory to explain the origins of criminality, because if the behaviour does not already exist, it cannot be learned by a second person (see Jeffery (1959)). Secondly, there are new and very inventive crimes which occasionally appear; certainly the mechanics for these could not have been learnt by differential association, although of course the desires and motives behind such crimes may have been learnt (see Parker (1976)). Thirdly, it does not explain the criminality of those who have never been subjected to criminals or to people who would hold criminal ideas. Such people could not have learnt criminality by inter-personal contact: if it was learnt at all, it would probably have been from the media, which Sutherland relegates to a relatively unimportant position in the learning process. One answer to the last point is that criminality may arise from having observed parents, or others close to the child. These, despite perhaps strongly teaching the child that, say, theft is wrong, none the less commit some dishonest acts, such as not telling a shop assistant that they have been given the wrong change; or while renouncing violence they take part either in domestic violence, or use overtly violent methods of punishment. In any event, as Wilson and Herrnstein (1985) note, the theory cannot explain why some individuals might learn criminal behaviour from a peer group while failing to learn non-criminal behaviour from a family (or *vice versa*).

A further criticism is that this approach cannot explain irrational, impulsive, opportunist or passionate criminals, who would then be acting due to one of those factors rather than as a result of anything they have learnt (see Nettler (1974)). The implication is that there are probably some crimes which could never be explained by differential association, which cannot therefore, constitute an all-consuming theory. Most of the criticisms have not been verified, and of course they do not necessarily bring the theory as a whole into question.

It is virtually impossible to measure the impact of differential association as an explanation of criminal behaviour, as the key concepts cannot be reduced to quantitative elements. It is, for example, impossible to make any objective measurement of whether there has been an 'excess' of definitions favourable to law-breaking of any particular type and for any particular person. It is hard enough, after the event, to try to reconstruct a person's thoughts and intentions immediately before they commit a crime, but impossible to go through their whole life and assess the effects on their actions of each input, both for and against crime committal. The difficulties are compounded when Sutherland attributes different weighting to certain material, and to factors such as intensity and priority. Most importantly, it is sometimes difficult to tell whether certain feelings and motives existed before a particular relationship was begun or only arose afterwards; e.g., did membership of a gang or group come about because of like thinking at the time, or has membership of the group given rise to that type of behaviour being learnt. Possibly even more telling is the fact that one can never be sure exactly what is a 'definition favourable to law-breaking', nor what is an 'excess' of such definitions. How much more of one than the other does it take for that activity to take over? Why, even if it could safely be asserted that an individual has an excess of definitions favourable to law-breaking, are most of that person's activities lawful?

Despite these great drawbacks, there have been various studies which go some way towards supporting a causal link between differential association and criminality (for example, Jensen (1972) and McCarthy (1996)). In most of these studies the main idea was supported in a fairly basic sense, but the research generally showed that differential association was only one of several causes of criminality. Factors such as the effects of a broken home, or of lax supervision within the family, or general emotional insecurity, were also present. Sutherland claims that what differential association helps to explain is why some people who suffer these other factors are not criminal whilst others are.

A further criticism is that differential association fails to account for the individual in the calculation. It seems to assume that these people are vessels into which is poured the definitions for and against law violation: their eventual behaviour is then decided by the balance. This allows very little room for the individual to assess these influences. Differential association does recognise some sifting, especially in the 'intensity', but it allows no room for free will, the personality of the individual, or for differences in types of response. Sutherland claimed that the response of each individual to a particular set of circumstances would depend upon the learning process already encountered. In some situations it is unclear whether it is a law-abiding or law-breaking situation, and it may depend upon the response of the individual. For example, finding a purse full of money might receive the response of an opportunity to better one's position, or could provoke the response of an opportunity to do someone a good deed. The way the person responds may affect the lesson learnt in that instance. Sutherland says that such responses depend upon earlier learning and would trace this all the way back to birth, to zero learning. Others would argue that there may be other factors concerned in this response.

Lastly, the theory is criticised because it does not explain why one person has one set of associations and another person has a different set, although the two may come from similar backgrounds. Sutherland considered this to be a red herring, and asserted that the important point was what was learnt from the associations, not why those associations occur. However, a secondary theory which he expounded, differential social organisations, may help to explain these differences. The theory of differential social organisations argues that every social setting, whether criminal or not, is organised. The likelihood of criminality is influenced by the social organisation of things like norms, values and acceptable behaviour. Such social organisation makes it more or less likely for inhabitants of a particular area to come into contact with definitions favourable to law-breaking. In this way it affects the individual's associations.

The numerous criticisms seem to suggest that the theory is of little value. The inability to test it, and the difficulty in applying it to particular circumstances, do reduce its utility. None the less, there are areas where it might be particularly pertinent. The most important is in the area in which Sutherland first expounded the theory – white-collar or corporate crime. As Steven Box (1983) has suggested, many businessmen may learn to, and be willing to, commit crimes to enhance the company where they would never consider other forms of criminality. It would seem absurd that a hitherto law-abiding individual arrives in a corporation and suddenly, for no reason, begins committing crimes. Far more likely is the idea that the individual slowly learns the 'realities of business', one of which may be that certain laws can be broken for the well-being of the firm. Furthermore, promotion procedures may reinforce such learning by rewarding those who internalise these 'realities'. For a fuller discussion of this, see Conklin (1989) and Box (1987).

Braithwaite (1988) and Fisse and Braithwaite (1993) proposed a system – reintegrative shaming – of crime control and punishment which seems to be at least partially built on Sutherland's ideas of differential association. In reintegrative shaming the key to altering future behaviour is to shame offenders, but to ensure that they are also provided with the means and the commitment to be accepted back into society as law-abiding persons. Basically the offender should be made aware of the effects of his or her actions, be held accountable and, possibly through restitution, be able to undo or make good the problem. This is usually mooted to occur in victim–offender mediation/conferencing schemes, which (see Chapter Two) have received considerable backing and have proved to be supportive of victims in some cases, especially as restitution payments have tended to be fairly reliably paid. They have arguably (Snare (1995)) been less useful for offenders since they seem not to have had an impact on rates of recidivism.

10.2.5 Differential reinforcement theory
This builds on differential association but includes all the elements of reinforcement and punishment which are central to operant learning, which

argues that most behaviour is learnt. Behaviour will be repeated when the positive reinforcers outweigh the negative reinforcers and the frequency will depend on the differential between these two. Clearly this includes taking account of all the positive aspects to which crime may give rise. These include the external gains such as the obvious financial and material gain as well as the less obvious reinforcement from peer groups either because they reward crime *per se* or because the gains to which the crime gives rise enhance the status of the individual. They also include internal gains such as the feelings of power, autonomy etc.: there is some evidence to suggest that in many people there is a physiological process which occurs in the brain when a risky and often difficult task is undertaken and which acts as a positive reinforcer of that behaviour (Gove and Wilmoth (1990)). The suggestion is that there is an '. . . internal biological system that rewards operant behaviours, and that this system does *not* simply reflect external reinforcement processes' (Gove and Wilmoth (1990), p. 263). The neurological 'high' produced by risky and difficult tasks is thought to be associated with the dopamine synapse (the same brain functioning associated with amphetamine, cocaine and heroin use) which when activated gives a good feeling. The strength of this effect varies between people, which would partly explain why an external positive reinforcer is enough for one person to commit an offence but not for another: the stronger this neurological effect the more likely one is to commit crimes to experience the rush. Negative reinforcers are also important. Examples of external negative reinforcers may be the possibility of arrest, loss of liberty, fear of injuring someone or oneself, fear of being ostracised by family and friends. Examples of internal negative reinforcers may be the production of adrenalin and other chemicals referred to in Chapter Seven. Clearly in any one individual the ways in which these elements may interact are very complex. For an example see Hollin (1992), p. 56.

This theory suffers from at least one very basic problem: it is tautological. The argument is that behaviour is repeated only if there is strong positive reinforcement for it; but the strong positive reinforcement is recognised only because of the repetition. It seems almost impossible to break out of this circle: that does not necessarily undermine the claim that it has an effect on the cause of crime, but it does question the proof of that connection. As will be seen later this may be dealt with if rehabilitative techniques are successful.

10.2.6 Social learning theory and cognitive social learning theories

Social learning theory is an extension of differential reinforcement theory in that it builds on the operant learning experience and adds cognitive experiences and learning to the equation. Its most well known proponent is Albert Bandura (see especially 1973, 1977 and 1986). There are many facets to this theory, which is one of the most complex criminological theories. The motivation associated with the theory includes the reinforcements connected with the operant learning theory as well as reinforcement gained from watching others (vicarious), and the sense of pride and achievement in what we do (self-reinforcement). The basis of the theory is that the learned behaviour is a combination of the physical acts and how to perform them (skills) and the attitudes and mental understanding necessary to the behaviour (including social skills, moral considerations and choice). Criminal behaviour can be learnt through practice, as in operant learning, or through watching the environment in which one lives, the activities of friends, family, neighbours, teachers etc., as well as in socially constructed environments such as books, magazines, television and films. Bandura would admit that all of these are included in the social learning of individuals and that therefore they all have an effect on criminality. Here a few of the elements of these theories will be considered

In order to perform a crime one must have the physical skill for the necessary tasks. These motor skills tend to be learnt from watching, or being taught by, others. Their presence or absence often dictates the type of crime to be entered into rather than whether a crime will occur. Bandura (1973 and 1977) bases much discussion on this idea of modelling and notes that whether it leads to criminal activity will depend on the message behind the behaviour as well as the behaviour itself. The physical attributes of the offender are also significant: constant aggressive models will not transform the behaviour of a physically weak person unless they are also given a way of carrying out the violence, such as a gun. Clearly as the offender becomes more competent, he or she will be better able to select weak targets and those where detection is less likely or will be able to avoid detection.

The level of social skills which individuals have learnt may be connected with the amount of crime they perform. Each person needs to learn how to understand both linguistic and symbolic communication, but some are never, or are insufficiently, taught by their parents or peers, or have been slow to acquire such skills. Whatever the reason, this situation has been linked to criminality, but whether that link is causal or not is still unclear (see Gaffney and McFall (1981)). Much of the research has been carried out on young offenders but is generally inconclusive: there seem to be stronger, though still not conclusive, links between lack of social skills and rape; but the strongest and almost irrefutable links are found between lack of social skills and child sexual abuse (see Hollin (1992)). Linked to this is the ability to assess and resolve social problems in socially acceptable ways. Slabby and Guerra (1988) suggest that criminals learn fewer solutions to interpersonal problems and often fall back on verbal or physical aggression to resolve difficulties.

Offenders usually need to be in a particular frame of mind for criminal behaviour to take place – this involves elements such as attitude, moral standards, feelings for and about other people, and ideas of responsibility, blame or control. Attitude is learnt from others; the esteem with which the messenger is regarded will affect whether the message is believed and learnt (see Feldman (1977)). Some have associated a low level of ability for moral reasoning with criminal activity, but this is not necessarily so (see Hollin (1992)). Thus, although most people would consider theft unacceptable, they may have fewer inhibitions about stealing small items from work; although killing is unacceptable, soldiers can be trained to kill in defined situations. Similarly, people label something differently in order to absolve them of the need to feel moral guilt: a terrorist is punishing the enemy, a burglar is carrying out a job. These euphemisms remove the problems to which full moral reasoning capabilities might otherwise give rise (Bandura (1986)).

There is also comparative moral reasoning: people may excuse their own lapses of conduct if they are aware of more heinous acts by others which have not been punished or not severely punished. They may see white-collar criminals go very lightly punished for stealing large amounts of money and therefore consider the small amounts they have taken as unimportant. Attached to this is a desire to believe that their acts are not very harmful by saying that the victim can well do without it, particularly easy if it is a large corporation or a rich individual, or someone covered by insurance. Offenders may also need not to empathise with their victims. This may involve putting the victims into a group with a derogatory label, often racial, or belittling them personally, e.g., 'He's an idiot' or 'She does not deserve x' (see Bandura (1977) and Kaplan and Arbuthnot (1985)). In other cases offenders see their actions as controlled by forces outside their control (Hollin (1992)). They often blame the victim: for example, in a personal attack, 'He should have given me what I wanted', or in rape cases, 'She was asking for it' and 'She led me on', and in property offences 'He should have been more careful where he left the car'.

Lastly, there is the question of rational choice, which some view as a separate theory (Cornish and Clarke (1987)) and others as part of the cognitive social learning theory (Akers (1990)). Rational choice assumes that there is a possibility of committing a crime, an opportunity, and then postulates that the offender weighs up the benefits (in terms both of increased wealth and personal benefits such as self-esteem or excitement) and the dangers (such as the possibility of detection and the possible punishments) and makes a rational decision whether to commit the crime. Those who see rational choice as a distinct theory argue that social learning theory is largely deterministic: that is, the individual learns and the resultant behaviour is largely determined by that learning. Others argue that the learning processes outlined above merely provide tools and that it is then up to the individual how and when to apply these tools.

Learning theories have problems; there is always an element of tautology as well as many unproven and possibly unprovable relationships. None the less, as will be seen in 10.2.8, the ideas set out here may be useful in designing certain strategies for preventing criminal behaviour.

10.2.7   Media and crime

In any discussion of learnt behaviour the effects of media images need to be considered, especially television and films (here this area will be referred to as TV). The effects seem particularly obvious in relation to learning concerned with observation or modelling but can also be apparent in moral and other aspects of cognitive learning. The assertion is that humans learn from the screen in the same way that they learn from face-to-face interactions. Where a link is said to exist between criminality and the media it is usually perceived as influencing violent behaviour, particularly in the young (see Bandura (1973)), or sexual offences where the claim is that pornographic literature and movies reinforce both the normality of the feelings and the acceptability of the activity. Here we will be concerned mainly with its effects on violence.

The claim is that TV teaches methods and tactics of violence, and shows how aggressive behaviour can be rewarding. Some recent studies do support the possibility of such a link. For example, Phillips (1983) suggested that in the USA there is a one-eighth increase in killings in the three-week period after a very heavily publicised boxing match. Bandura (1986) places great emphasis on the media, particularly television, as crucial sources of the observational learning of crimes against the person. Leyens et al. (1975) noted that there was an increase in physically aggressive behaviour in groups exposed to violent films, whilst in those exposed to neutral films there was actually a lowering of physical aggression. There was a similar conclusion in a study by Dr Susan Bailey who interviewed 40 of the most violent young offenders and 200 young sex offenders and found that 25 per cent had been exposed to violent videos, films and TV which she considered was a major factor in their violent behaviour. In evidence to the Broadcasting Group of the House of Lords, Sims and Gray (1993) listed more than 1,000 studies which had linked exposure to media violence with aggressive behaviour. In April 1994, 25 leading psychologists, psychiatrists and child care experts supported a paper written by Professor Elizabeth Newson which posited a connection between criminal violence and media violence and called for a restriction on the availability of 'video nasties', although no new data were provided (Newson (1994)). She makes a further interesting point: the amount spent on advertising shows that most corporations believe images to be effective in persuading people to behave differently but misses the fact that these images may impact differently on people's minds. A common weakness is that none of these studies explains how the learning is taken in.

In any event, others have denied such a link, or say that the correlation is much more complex than the above suggest. Messner (1986), much to his own surprise, discovered that exposure to TV was inversely related to rates of violent crime. Hagell and Newbury (1993) questioned the suggestion of a link between violent media images and criminality, after finding that persistent offenders do not watch more violence either in films or on the television than their non-criminal counterparts. However, the utility of this research for the immediate issue is diminished because they did not look specifically at very violent acts. Bailey (1990) studied the effects of media presentation of capital punishment in USA and discovered that it acted neither as a deterrent nor as a brutalising agent. The German Society for Media Research (VFM) (1994) exposed 500 individuals to violence in both newsreels and drama, and interim results suggest: that increased media violence led to reductions in aggressive behaviour but to increased fear of aggression and to an increased likelihood that people would sympathise with the victim; that social tolerance towards friends was marginally increased; that there was an adverse effect on stress management; and lastly that the effects differed with age, older people being more horrified by the violence, whereas younger viewers were more affected by the situation and whether there was a negative value placed on the violence they were watching (see Lewis and Von Gamm (1994)). This suggests that the context of the violence is essential to the effect (see also 10.2.6).

Whatever the evidence, there is clearly a willingness on the part of the public, the press and even professionals to accept a link between screen violence and criminality. In the Bulger trial, Morland J, without any evidence to support his assertion, stated that 'It is not for me to pass judgement on the boys' upbringings, but I suspect that exposure to violent video films may in part be an explanation'. This was seized on by the press, anxious for something to blame, as more or less positive proof. Press presentations implying clear links between screen violence and criminal behaviour, especially violent behaviour, are not uncommon: the press linked at least ten murders to Oliver Stone's film *Natural Born Killers*, with reports such as: 'Two young men have murdered four people – including three pensioners – in a real-life imitation of a brutal new Hollywood blockbuster' (*Sunday Mirror*, 11 September 1994). Again, these assertions, although making good stories, were unfounded. As was reported by the British Board of Film Censors in 1994, in all bar one of the cases the leader in the activities had already served a prison sentence for serious acts of violence, including, in three cases, murder (one had also been in a mental institution). In the other case the intention to kill had been stated to a friend many months earlier and the murderer had already sourced guns. No links to that film or any other have ever been proven.

From these brief and very selected reports it is clear that there is much disagreement about the effects of violence in the media. There are even stronger doubts (Wilson and Herrnstein (1985)) about any causal links. If the German research is to be believed media violence does not increase violence; indeed, it may actually have a therapeutic effect. This type of claim has also been made for obscene materials (Gillan (1978)). It has similarly been argued (Sparks (1983 and 1992)) that violent crime fiction actually reassures most audiences by portraying the victory of the good detective or the police over evil. It has tended to reinforce moral order and send the (mostly) misleading message that punishment will follow criminality. Harbord (1996) argues that the problem may not be the level of violence in the newer Hollywood output, but rather the lack of a clear moral message – everyone seems (relatively) bad and there is no-one to restore order and ensure justice is done. Altogether it could be that TV teaches methods of violence to those who are already susceptible to it and reinforces attitudes supportive of violence, but it may not go further than that. It is a fiercely disputed area amongst behavioural theorists.

These discussions almost always take place in the context of whether to censor such material. Because any benefits which may accrue from censorship have to be balanced against the loss of liberty which censorship involves, it is necessary to consider the size of the problem. Even if we assume some causative effect between violent crime and violence in the media, the level of increase is likely to be very low. Most studies, even if they found increased aggression, did not discover increased criminal violence: individuals may stop short of translating increased feelings of aggression into criminal violence. It seems that the number likely to commit criminal violence is likely to be very low and, if the German research is correct, restricted to those less capable of cognitive reasoning. The effects of the actions of this small number may still be appalling but they have to be weighed against the interference with liberty involved in preventing access to materials. Given the unlikelihood of decisive proof, the decision will come down to balancing benefits against harm or, more realistically, the political expediency of the situation. The views of those who may influence the direction of political expediency may themselves be fed by the news-media presentation of the arguments and issues, in particular very isolated cases like that of James Bulger (see, e.g., the *Sunday Express*) where a wholly unproven link was suggested and planted in the minds of the public as the explanation for this otherwise seemingly inexplicable behaviour. Under this pressure political expediency led the government to pass s. 89 of the Criminal Justice and Public Order Act 1994, requiring the British Board of Film Classification to take account (amongst other aspects) of the psychological impact of videos on viewers, especially children, and to consider the possibility that they might lead them to behave in a manner harmful to society. This gives Britain the most powerful film censorship in Europe. Whether this is judged as acceptable and to be welcomed largely depends on subjective value judgments which may have little connection with the evidence of 'scientific' studies. A more fundamental problem arises if, as many consider (Harbord (1996)), the new violence in films (and other art forms) largely reflects the reality of contemporary society: censoring the arts will not on its own alter social realities.

10.2.8 Practical implications for learning theories

The techniques and methods of learning theories can be used to re-train criminals in a more acceptable behavioural pattern. This may include teaching them some or all of the following: law-abiding attitudes and emotions; greater interactive or social skills; acceptable types of behaviour; acceptable reactions to certain stimuli which they may encounter; and life skills so they are more able to cope with everyday problems such as finding and keeping a job. The effectiveness of such learning depends on a number of factors, including the skill of the teacher and the willingness of the criminal to learn. McGuire and Priestly (1985) point out that one of the most important elements of success is whether the learning programme is shaped to particular individual needs, rather than based on the assumption that everyone would benefit from the same training.

A qualification of this method of countering criminality is that when the learning is only partially successful, it may lead to a heightened ability to avoid detection rather than a true change in behaviour. The individual may appear to learn by giving acceptable responses and the absence of further convictions might suggest success, but as the crimes would still occur, there is no real benefit to society. For real success, the individual has to internalise all aspects of the training, and be able to use a trained response when the stimulus is different from the training environment. This indicates understanding and a change of attitude. The implication is that for success, learning theories have to be applied by skilled staff to a willing individual over an extended period of time (Roberts (1995)).

Success also depends on whether the programme for treatment is focused on the problems which have been most to blame for the criminality of the particular person being treated. Programmes thus need to be designed for an individual, or a small group with very similar problems, rather than used very generally. Applied especially to high-risk offenders, such programmes could provide a positive and structured removal from society. Even so, such programmes would need to alter not only the outward behaviour but also the cognitive learning of factors such as attitude, values, self-control, social problem-solving, and moral reasoning. Hollin (1992) considers that such treatment is more likely to succeed if it is given in the community rather than in institutions. In this class he includes ideas such as probation, diversionary projects including intermediate treatment and reparation, more positive encouragement at school, and parent management training at the important level of the family. This has a difficult message in relation to offenders that some might class as dangerous: the public may want dangerous offenders removed from society in order to protect others, whilst the treatment most likely to succeed and render these individuals safe needs to be given in the community. One possible compromise is to require criminals to spend sufficient time in prison to mark the damage caused by their criminality, and then for them to be considered for therapy in the community. Where this is thought to be viable this option should be considered rather than further incarceration to protect the public. With care in the choice of persons it might prove to be a positive way forward, especially since most of these people are eventually released into the community: if there is a real possibility of changing their behaviour this would render them safer once this time arises.

10.3 CONCLUSION

Sutherland's theory is based on the idea that criminality is the normal result of normal learned behaviour. Just as some people learn non-criminal behaviour, so others learn criminal behaviour. In the learning process he says that the individual learns ideas, desires, motives, morality, goals, and whether types of behaviour are acceptable in particular social settings, as well as learning methods of carrying out those ideas or obtaining the goals. This is a wide-ranging theory of criminology, and although it cannot explain all crime, the learning process must play some part in almost all activity.

By making learning so central to the process such writers have claimed that those with low learning capacity are unable to grasp the moral and other elements which are so essential to law-abiding behaviour. This allows them to conclude that those of low intelligence are more likely to be criminal. Against this it can be said that social learning is not simply dependent on innate intellectual ability: behavioural learning is affected to a far greater extent by the social setting, social interactions, personal associations and the environment, than it is by innate intelligence.

The learning theories can thus have a powerful input to rehabilitation and make a positive contribution to the problem of criminality. To be effective, practitioners of this approach need to be able to interact with others concerned in the criminal justice process: the judiciary and the probation and prison services might consult with them more openly and more frequently. Any system which might result in a diminution in criminality needs to be cultivated. None the less it must be emphasised that the approach is not a panacea: its use needs to be confined to those situations and individuals where it seems most likely to give positive results, which might include some of those classed as dangerous in the discussion in Chapter Nine.

Although learning theories may have this positive aspect to offer the criminal justice system, they may also cause restrictive practices to be forced even on the law-abiding, e.g., censorship of the media, which as shown above, is difficult to justify on the basis of harm. This renders such censorship questionable. If one accepts the operant learning theories as paramount, such censorship may be acceptable to avoid a form of copycat behaviour. If the cognitive learning theories are embraced, the learning process is seen to be more complex and takes account not only of the skills but also of the moral standards, feelings of responsibility and respect for others which are portrayed in the media. Merely censoring violent media images is then less acceptable, being too simplistic. There is a need to take account of the whole media presentation, not just the fact of violence but the social and moral setting of that image. In this scenario fairly low levels of violence shown in certain contexts, depicting the behaviour as acceptable and enjoyable, may be more damaging than excessive violence shown in an unfavourable situation. On this basis, simple censorship becomes less valid or, at least, questionable. This is not to claim that the media do not play a part in the learning process, but rather to recognise the complexity of their role and to question the validity and justification of censorship.

The utility of learning theories may be greater than these uncertainties suggest. They could provide a fruitful method of altering the behaviour of offenders. They do not indicate that most offenders are in need of treatment, but rather that they have not been effectively taught to live within the rules which happen to exist within their society. The technique is therefore designed to reflect and encourage officially accepted forms of behaviour, values and responses to situations; the aim is not a 'cure' but to alter future behaviour. It is not implied that offenders were not responsible for their actions; the aim is to induce them to make more socially constructive choices in the future. These techniques could, moreover, be applied along with more traditional treatments, such as biological or drug therapies and/or working on the personality of the offender (Elchardus (1995)). It is, however, usually considered that cognitive learning techniques will be more likely to succeed if utilised in the community than in an institution (Hood (1995)). In the community offenders are in daily contact with the pressures which they are being taught to deal with, making it simpler to transpose the learnt behaviour into different situations, and perhaps ensuring that the new behaviour is better internalised.

Lastly, there is the notion that criminality is a normal and learned behaviour. How the learning process is seen to occur is of less importance. The fact that criminal behaviour is learned puts into question some of the theories of an innate criminal trait or criminal propensity. The fact that it is normal would suggest that there is nothing inherently bad about criminal behaviour. In so far as it is accepted, the theory implies that part of criminological study should be about why certain normal learned behaviours are criminalised and others are not. This is a theme which Sutherland studied in his discussion of white-collar crime, and is a subject which was discussed in Chapter Three and also in Chapters One and Fifteen.

REFERENCES

Adams, Reed (1973), 'Differential Association and Learning Principles Revisited', *Social Problems*, vol. 20, p. 458.

Akers, Ronald L. (1990), 'Rational Choice, Deterrence and Social Learning Theory in Criminology: the Path Not Taken', *Journal of Criminal Law and Criminology*, vol. 81, p. 653.

Bailey, S.M. (1993), 'Media and Violence', *Criminal Justice Matters*, vol. 6.

Bailey, William C. (1990), 'Murder, Capital Punishment, and Television: Execution Publicity and Homicide Rates', *American Sociological Review*, vol. 55, p. 628.

Bandura, A. (1973), *Aggression: A Social Learning Analysis*, New York: Prentice Hall.

Bandura, Albert (1977), *Social Learning Theory*, Englewood Cliffs, NJ: Prentice Hall.

Bandura, Albert (1986), *Social Foundations of Thought and Action*, Englewood Cliffs, NJ: Prentice Hall.

Beckwith, Jan (1985), 'Social and Political Uses of Genetics in the United States: Past and Present', in Frank H. Marsh and Janet Katz (eds), *Biology, Crime and Ethics: A Study of Biological Explanations for Criminal Behaviour*, Cincinnati, Ohio: Anderson.

Binet, Alfred and Simon, Theodore. See Gleitman, Henry (1986), *Psychology*, 2nd edn, New York: W.W. Norton and Company.

Box, Steven (1983), *Power, Crime and Mystification*, London: Tavistock.

Box, Steven (1987), *Recession, Crime and Punishment*, London: Macmillan Education.

Braithwaite, John (1988), *Crime Shame and Reintegration*, Cambridge: Cambridge University Press.

Burgess, R. and Akers, R. (1966), 'A Differential Association-Reinforcement Theory of Criminal Behaviour', *Social Problems*, vol. 14, p. 128.

Conklin, John Evan (1989), *Criminology*, 3rd edn, London: Collier Macmillan.

Cornish, D.B. and Clarke, R.V. (1987), 'Understanding Crime Displacement: the Application of Rational Choice Theory', *Criminology*, vol. 25, p. 933.

Cytryn, L. and Lourie, R.S. (1975), 'Mental Retardation', in A.M. Freedman, H.I. Kaplan and B.J. Sadock (eds), *Comprehensive Textbook of Psychiatry* II, vol. I, Baltimore: Williams and Wilkins.

Darwin, Leonard (1914/15), 'The Habitual Criminal', *Eugenics Review*, No. 6.

Defleur, Melvin and Quinney, Richard (1966), 'A Reformulation of Sutherland's Differential Association Theory and a Strategy for Empirical Verification', *Journal of Research in Crime and Delinquency*, vol. 2, p. 1.

Dugdale, Richard (1877), *The Jukes in Crime, Pauperism and Heredity*, New York: Putnam.

Elchardus, J.M. (1995), 'Problems of Therapeutic Interventions Regarding Certain Categories of Offenders, for Example in the Fields of Sexual Offences, Violence in the Family and Drug Addiction', in *Psychological Interventions in the Criminal Justice System*, Proceedings from the 20th Criminological Research Conference, 1993, European Committee on Crime Problems, Criminological Research, vol. XXXI, Strasbourg: Council of Europe.

Farrington, D.P. (1992), 'Juvenile Delinquency', in J.C. Coleman (ed.), *The School Years*, 2nd edn, London: Routledge.

Farrington, David P. (1994), *Psychological Explanations of Crime*, Aldershot: Dartmouth Press.

Feldman, M.P. (1977), *Criminal Behaviour*, London: Wiley.

Fisse, Brent and Braithwaite, John (1993), *Corporations, Crime and Accountability*, Cambridge: Cambridge University Press.

Gaffney, L.R. and McFall, R.M. (1981), 'A Comparison of Social Skills in Delinquent and Non-Delinquent Adolescent Girls Using a Behavioural Role-Playing Inventory', *Journal of Consulting and Clinical Psychology*, vol. 49, p. 959.

Gelsthorpe, L. and McWilliam, W. (eds) (1993), *Minority Ethnic Groups and the Criminal Justice System*, Cambridge: Cambridge University Press.

Gibson, H.B. and West, D.J. (1970), 'Social and Intellectual Handicaps as Precursors of Early Delinquency', *British Journal of Criminology*, vol. 10, p. 212.

Gillan, Patricia (1978), 'Therapeutic Uses of Obscenity', in Rajeev Dhavan and Christine Davies (eds), *Censorship and Obscenity*, London: Martin Robertson.

Glaser, D. (1956), 'Criminality Theories and Behavioural Images', *American Journal of Sociology*, vol. 61, p. 433.

Gleitman, Henry (1986), *Psychology*, 2nd edn, New York: W.W. Norton and Company.

Goddard, H.H. (1912), *The Kallikak Family, A Study in the Heredity of Feeble-Mindedness*, New York: Macmillan.

Goddard, H.H. (1914), *Feeble-Mindedness: Its Causes and Consequences*, New York: Macmillan.

Gordon, Robert (1976), 'Prevalence: The Rare Datum in Delinquency Measurement and Its Implications for the Theory of Delinquency', in Malcolm W. Klein, ed., *The Juvenile Justice System*, Beverly Hills, California: Sage Publications.

Gove, Walter R. and Wilmoth, Charles (1990), 'Risk, Crime, and Neuro-physiologic Highs: a Consideration of Brain Processes that May Reinforce Delinquent and Criminal Behaviour', in Lee Ellis and Harry Hoffman (eds), *Crime in Biological, Social, and Moral Contexts*, New York: Praeger.

Hagell, Ann and Newbury, Tim (1994), *Young Offenders and the Media*, London: Policy Studies Institute.

Harbord, Victoria (1996), '*Natural Born Killers:* Violence, Film and Anxiety', in Colin Sumner (ed.), *Violence, Culture and Censure*, London: Taylor & Francis.

Hirschi, T. and Hindling, M. (1977), 'Intelligence and Delinquency: A Revisionist Review', *American Sociological Review*, vol. 42, p. 571.

Hollin, Clive (1992), *Criminal Behaviour: A Psychological Approach to Explanation and Prevention*, London: Falmer Press.

Hood, R. (1995), 'Introductory Report, General Report of the Conference and Conclusions and Recommendations', in *Psychological Interventions in the Criminal Justice System*, Proceedings from the 20th Criminological Research Conference, 1993, European Committee on Crime Problems, Criminological Research, vol. XXXI, Strasbourg: Council of Europe.

Jeffery, Clarence Ray (1959), 'An Integrated Theory of Crime and Criminal Behaviour', *Journal of Criminal Law, Criminology and Police Science*, vol. 49, p. 537.

Jensen, A.R. (1969), 'How Much Can We Boost IQ and Scholastic Achievement?', *Harvard Educational Review*, vol. 39, p. 1.

Jensen, Gary F. (1972), 'Parents, Peers and Delinquent Action: A Test of the Differential Association Perspective', *American Journal of Sociology*, vol. 78, p. 562.

Jones, T. (1993), *Britain's Ethnic Minorities*, London: Policy Studies Institute.

Kaplan, P. J. and Arbuthnot, J. (1985), 'Affective Empathy and Cognitive Role-Taking in Delinquent and Non-Delinquent Youth', *Adolescence*, vol. 20, p. 323.

Kohlberg, L. (1976), 'Moral Stages and Moralisation: The Cognitive-Development Approach' in T. Lickona (ed.), *Moral Development and Behaviour*, New York: Holt Reihart and Winston.

Kohlberg, L. and Candee, D. (1984), 'The Relationship of Moral Judgement to Moral Action' in L. Kohlberg (ed.), *The Psychology of Moral Development*, San Francisco: Harper and Row.

Lewis, John and Van Gamm, Andrew (1994), 'Alton Turns Attention to Violence on 'Television', *Broadcast*, 15 April, p. 3.

Leyens, J.P., Camino, L., Parke, R.D. and Berkowitz, L. (1975), 'Effects of Movie Violence in Aggression in a Field Setting as a Function of Group Dominance and Cohesion', *Journal of Personality and Social Psychology*, vol. 32, p. 346.

Lilly, J. Robert, Cullen, Francis T. and Ball, Richard A. (1989), *Criminological Theory: Context and Consequences*, Newbury Park, California: Sage.

Loehlin, J.C., Lindzey, G. and Spuhler, J.N. (1975), *Race Difference in Intelligence*, San Francisco: Freedman.

Lynam, D., Moffitt, T. and Stonthame-Loeber, M. (1993), 'Explaining the Relation Between IQ and Delinquency: Class, Race, Test Motivation, School Failure or Self-control?', *Journal of Abnormal Psychology*, vol. 102, p. 187.

McCarthy, Bill (1996), 'The Attitudes and Actions of Others: Tutelage and Sutherland's Theory of Differential Association', *British Journal of Criminology*, vol. 36, p. 135.

McGuire, James and Priestly, Phillip (1985), *Offending Behaviour, Skills and Strategems for Going Straight*, London: Batsford Academic and Educational.

Matsueda, R. and Heiner, K. (1987), 'Race, Family Structure and Delinquency: a Test of Differential Association and Social Control Theories', *American Sociological Review*, vol. 52, p. 826.

Mercier, Jane (1972), 'IQ: The Lethal Label', *Psychology Today*, p. 44.

Messner, S.R. (1986), 'Television Violence and Violent Crime: an Aggregate Analysis', *Social Problems*, vol. 33, p. 218.

Moffitt, T.E. and Henry, B. (1989), 'Neuropsychological Assessment of Effective Functions in Self-Reported Delinquents', *Development and Psychopathology*, vol. 1, p. 105.

Mulvey, E. and Arthur, M. (1993), 'The Prevention and Treatment of Juvenile Delinquency: a Review of the Research', *Clinical Psychology Review*, vol. 13, p. 133.

Murray, C. and Herrnstein, R. (1994), *The Bell Curve: Intelligence and Class Structure of American Life*, New York: Free Press.

Nelson, J.R., Smith, D.J. and Dodd, J. (1990), 'The Moral Reasoning of Juvenile Delinquents: a Meta-Analysis', *Journal of Abnormal Child Psychology*, vol. 18, p. 231.

Nettler, Gwynn (1974), *Explaining Crime*, New York: MacGraw-Hill.

Newson, Elizabeth (1994), *Video Violence and the Protection of Children*, Child Development Research Unit, University of Nottingham.

Offord, D.R., Poushinsky, M.F. and Sullivan, K. (1978), 'School Performance, IQ and Delinquency', *British Journal of Criminology*, vol. 18, p. 110.

Parker, Donn B. (1976), *Crime by Computer*, New York: Scribner.

Pavlov, Ivan Petrovich (1927), *Conditioned Reflexes*, Oxford: Oxford University Press.

Phillips, D.P. (1983), 'The Impact of Mass Media Violence on US Homicides', *American Sociological Review*, vol. 48, p. 560.

Pinter, I. (1923), *Intelligence Testing: Methods and Results*, New York: Barnes and Noble.

Roberts, J. (1995), 'Implementing Psychosocial Interventions Linked to Community Sanctions', in *Psychological Interventions in the Criminal Justice System*, Proceedings from the 20th Criminological Research Conference, 1993, European Committee on Crime Problems, Criminological Research, vol. XXXI, Strasbourg: Council of Europe.

Robertson, Geoffrey (1989), *Freedom, The Individual and the Law*, Middlesex: Penguin Books.

Robinson, H.B. and Robinson, N.M. (1970), 'Mental Retardation', in P.H. Mussen (ed.), *Carmichael's Manual of Child Psychology*, vol. 2, New York: Wiley.

Scarr, S. and Weinberg, R.A. (1976), 'IQ Test Performance of Black Children Adopted by White Families', *American Psychologist*, vol. 31, p. 726.

Simons, Ronald L. (1978), 'The Meaning of the IQ-Delinquency Relationship', *American Sociological Review*, vol. 43, p. 268.

Sims, A.C.P. and Gray, P. (1993), 'The Media, Violence and Vulnerable Viewers', Evidence presented to the Broadcasting Group, House of Lords.

Skinner, B.F. (1938), *The Behaviour of Organisms*, New York: Appleton-Century-Crofts.

Slabby, R.G. and Guerra, N.G. (1988), 'Cognitive Mediators of Aggression in Adolescent Offenders: 1. Assessment', *Developmental Psychology*, vol. 24, p. 580.

Smetana, J.G. (1990), 'Morality and Conduct Disorders', in M. Lewis and S.M. Miller (eds), *Handbook of Developmental Psychology*, New York: Plenum.

Smith, David J. (1994), 'Race Crime and Criminal Justice', in Mike Maguire, Rod Morgan and Robert Reiner (eds), *The Oxford Handbook of Criminology*, Oxford: Oxford University Press.

Snare, A. (1995), 'Psychological Interventions Aimed at Resolving the Conflict Between the Perpetrator and the Victim, for Example Within the Framework of Mediation and Compensation Programmes', in *Psychological Interventions in the Criminal Justice System*, Proceedings from the 20th Criminological Research Conference, 1993, European Committee on Crime Problems, Criminological Research, vol. XXXI, Strasbourg: Council of Europe.

Snare, J. (1995), 'Implementing Psychosocial Interventions Linked to Community Sanctions', in *Psychological Interventions in the Criminal Justice System*, Proceedings from the 20th Criminological Research Conference, 1993, European Committee on Crime Problems, Criminological Research, vol. XXXI, Strasbourg: Council of Europe.

Sparks, Richard (1983), *Fictional Representations of Crime and Law Enforcement on British Television*, Cambridge: Institute of Criminology.

Sparks, Richard (1992), *Television and the Drama of Crime: Moral Tales and the Place of Crime in Public Life*, Buckingham: Open University Press.

Sutherland, Edwin H. (1939), *Principles of Criminology*, 3rd edn, Philadelphia: Lippincott.

Sutherland, Edwin H. and Cressey, Donald R. (1978), *Principles of Criminology*, 10th edn, Philadelphia: Lippincott.

West, D.J. (1982), *Delinquency: Its Roots, Careers and Prospects*, London: Heinemann.

Wilson, James Q. and Herrnstein, Richard J. (1985), *Crime and Human Nature: The Definitive Study of the Causes of Crime*, New York: Simon & Schuster.

Wilson Vine, Margaret S. (1960), 'Gabriel Tarde', in Hermann Mannheim (ed.), *Pioneers in Criminology*, London: Stevens.

Woodward, Mary (1955), 'Low Intelligence and Delinquency', *British Journal of Delinquency*, vol. 5, p. 281.

CHAPTER ELEVEN
The Sociology of Criminality

11.1 INTRODUCTION

Most of the explanations for crime so far discussed have focused on biological or psychological characteristics as causes of criminality. Claiming to be neutral and scientifically based, they mostly situate the causes of crime in the individual offender and so divert attention away from social or societal problems. In contrast, the theories which follow minimise these factors and instead concentrate on extraneous influences such as the environment, poverty and unemployment. The numerous theories linking criminality with these social factors focus on the problems related to vagrancy, unemployment, social controls, cultural values, and general poverty and despair. Their history stretches back over many centuries, but the accurate collection and keeping of data on criminality and other arguably related social factors only dates from the nineteenth century. In consequence, only this recent period is of interest to our study. Much of the early work in this area was published by social and political reformers, often as a small part of much wider treatises. In this country their views really began to be publicised after industrialisation had made drastic changes to population distribution, changing society irrevocably from an essentially rural culture. One aspect of this change was a shift from small, close-knit communities, whose aim was to grow sufficient produce to support themselves through consumption and sale. The changes produced a largely urbanised community having wide and diverse aims. Many, both at the time and since, have felt that the altered living style brought with it a marked change in criminal practices, leading to new problems of lawlessness. Crime in pre-industrial society was more dispersed and therefore tends now, though not necessarily then, to be perceived as being less acute. The concentration of population in urban areas was the start of our modern society and of the modern sociological explanations of crime.

Major problems were created by the fact that the system of control had not really changed, despite the transition from an agrarian society to an industrial one. The old controls were proving to be largely ineffectual in the new social situation. The difficulty in policing led many writers, including Chadwick (1839) to argue for a professional police force, particularly in the larger and fastest growing conurbations such as Manchester. Migration, population growth, rapid urbanisation and the emergence of extensive slum dwellings led many nineteenth century commentators to fear the formation of a dangerous sub-group, commonly referred to as the 'Residuum' (see Phillips (1977); Tobias (1972); and Jones (1982)).

The size of the problem is difficult to ascertain with any certainty. There were (and are) many problems with the statistics. Despite this, attempts were made both to assess the size of the crime problem and to explain the reasons for it. An early work which contained a significant discussion of criminality and society was published by Fredrick Engels in 1844. Engels, a German-born industrialist whose family partly owned a textile mill in Manchester, spent most of his adult working life in England and, with Karl Marx, is the founder of the communist ideology. Their concept of dialectical materialism became the underlying philosophy of Communism. Engels used some telling figures from the official statistics for England and Wales to show that the number of arrests for criminal offences rose steadily in the first part of the century from 4,605 in 1805 to 31,309 in 1842, a seven-fold increase in 37 years. Most of that increase occurred in the fast growing urban industrial areas of the North. Liverpool and Manchester alone accounted for 14 per cent of the whole. London, whose mid-century population was probably greater than all the other main towns put together, accounted for 13 per cent of the total number of arrests. The industrial areas of Scotland showed the same trend. In Lanarkshire, the population doubled once every 30 years whereas the crime rate doubled once every five and a half years (i.e., almost six times as fast).

Engels (1971) found this neither surprising nor difficult to explain. He documented the widening of class differences and the increased exploitation of the working class by the bourgeoisie, who were prospering under free competition. In his view, the workers became more brutalised, exploited and demoralised; as they lost any real control over their own lives, their resentment grew. He claimed that the growth of underlying class conflict was powerful and inevitable, and that criminality was an obvious result. He said:

> If the demoralisation of the worker passes beyond a certain point, then it is just as natural that he will turn into a criminal – as inevitably as water turns into steam at boiling point. (Engels (1844), from 1971 translation, p. 145)

He predicted that this class conflict would erupt into warfare (i.e., civil war) because the bourgeoisie had failed to understand its significance. This never happened in Britain. Although there were many bitter industrial conflicts, the last armed 'rising' against the State, the Chartist march on Newport in 1839, had already taken place before Engels was writing.

The idea of social conflict as an explanation of criminality was, however, taken up and refined by proponents of 'The New Criminology' into a full conflict theory (see Chapter Fifteen). Engels thought the answer to the problem of crime lay in idealistic political change, particularly in a breakdown of the system of exploitation. This would involve changing the whole of society, altering both its economic and social structures. Until recently, such a whole-hearted allocation of blame and such a drastic solution was generally uncommon amongst British criminological writers. Even those who saw societal reasons for criminality generally tended to suggest that it was caused by more specific elements, and proposed more limited 'cures' than those expounded by Engels.

One of the most common crimes in the nineteenth century was vagrancy. At times it became almost synonymous with the term 'dangerous class'. Vagrancy caused most alarm in the periods 1815-19, the late 1840s, the late 1860s and the mid-1890s. It was seen as a threat to the very fibre of society, as the vagrant's lifestyle did not espouse the Protestant work ethic, and was perceived to be a violation of respectability and religion. Vagrants were thought of as carriers of disease, and as criminals who often victimised respectable traders. Lastly, but significantly, in the acute economic distress of the late 1830s and early 1840s, they were thought to constitute a potential danger to stability in times of political tension. The Chadwick Reports (1839) are full of the iniquities of vagrants. It is important for us to remember, even though it was often lost sight of at the time, that not all vagrants were criminals; some were migrant workers following seasonal jobs; or they were navvies who moved with their jobs; or showmen and hawkers; or, as was the case with most female vagrants, they had lost their jobs and travelled to find work; or they were too poor to find homes or too old to work. Despite this more acceptable face of vagrancy, the vagrant was generally the first to be suspected of any crime which took place in a locality: they were believed to be the criminal class and were treated as such.

This view of the vagrant persisted despite the fact that they were rarely convicted of any really serious crimes – mostly drunk and disorderly, begging, sleeping out and stealing essentials such as clothes and food. Because vagrants were viewed as a social menace they were closely controlled, largely by means of the Vagrancy Acts of 1824 and 1838, which were given a wide interpretation in order to criminalise large areas of their lifestyle. The vagrant was thereby restrained before any real crime, apart from sleeping rough etc., had been committed. In this way, the British sought to control vagrancy which was seen as contributing to the crime problem, rather than seeking ways of solving that problem. This pragmatic approach epitomises many of the legal changes of this time: the heightened concern for the rights of property enacted or enforced laws against many activities of the poor, such as collecting fire wood, collecting coal, and using common pasture land. The intention was to control those who were seen as most likely to cause real problems, especially trouble related to crime, before they became too difficult.

In this way, British criminology was more practical than theoretical, and even slightly before Lombroso (see 6.3), but certainly after him, it adopted the positivists' view that certain factors, largely outside the control of the individual, determine behaviour (i.e., that there were large constraints upon the operation of free will). It is possibly partly because of this pragmatic approach that Lombroso's work did not have such a marked effect on British criminology as it had on the Continent. In Britain the pragmatic approach already existed, and people were already being punished both for their own and the collective good. The British criminological tradition has largely been to study and sometimes explain the *status quo* rather than to question it (for a criticism of the position, see Chapter Fifteen).

An example of this early pragmatic approach can be seen in Henry Mayhew's mid-century studies of London. Mayhew (1861–2) tended to see crime as an ecological phenomenon, but one which was tied in with the working classes and with social problems. He did not see criminals as a separate, dangerous class distinct from the working class. Rather, he recognised that many people were driven into poverty: some because they were unable but willing to get work, others because they became ill or otherwise incapacitated. Any of these positions might lead to criminality through need. In recognising social factors as the cause of criminality, he was not blaming the social structure in the same way as Engels. He did not argue for dramatic social upheaval. He saw that certain broad social changes, such as the move from rural to urban living, were necessarily latent causes of criminality. From this perspective, no blame could be placed either on the propertied classes or on the criminals themselves. They were seen as acting in a largely deterministic way which reduced the operation of free will. If the blame did not fall on urbanisation, then it might well fall on some other 'cause' such as immigration. In the mid-nineteenth century, it was the Irish immigrants arriving in the 20 or so years after the potato famine of 1846 that were seen as the cause of the problem (see Pike (1876)).

The significance of the essentially deterministic approach cannot be stressed enough. It is prevalent in the theories of most British and American criminologists up until about 1970, and can still be found in many theories today. It can be seen as a trend in most of the sociological explanations for crime. This is starkly illustrated by Hermann Mannheim's assertion that 'every society possesses the type of crime and criminals which fit into its cultural, moral, social, religious and economic conditions' (Mannheim (1965), p. 422). Similarly, the inertia which such a stance can produce can be demonstrated by the attitude behind the 1959 Home Office White Paper. In the opening paragraph, the White Paper noted that despite a rise in social standards in Britain since the Second World War, there had been no decrease in crime, which had continued to increase. It went on to say that it did not propose to deal with the 'deep-seated' causes of criminality, but rather set out the facts and the way government should deal with them or respond to them. In effect, it elected to accept the crime problem and merely to try to minimise its effects. This idea that a response might be made to crime without understanding it is one which has pervaded British criminology for a long time.

Despite this, some criminologists have attempted sociological explanations of criminality, albeit in a continuing deterministic fashion and with the clear aim of maintaining a pragmatic approach to the resolution of the problem.

11.2 THE ECOLOGY OF CRIME

11.2.1 Introduction

In this context, ecology is the study of peoples and institutions in relation to environment. The ecological school of criminology has a long history. Much of the work carried out in the last century studied the correlation between criminality, poverty and population density or type. It often used maps and charts to display the quantitative distribution of criminality: Henry Mayhew essentially studied the ecology of crime in London in the mid-nineteenth century (Mayhew (1862)). Perhaps because these early studies lacked any clear theoretical explanation for the distribution they discovered, they became overshadowed by more individualistic explanations. In the twentieth century, however, there has, from time to time, been a revival of interest in ecological theories, influenced by a general tendency to tie criminality with high population density and hence with cities. This popular belief is borne out by Ingram (1993) who concludes that urbanism is a significant predictor of criminality, whilst others (Campbell (1993)) have demonstrated that particular areas may be especially prone to criminal activity. In a broad sense studies in this area can be divided into two groups: the first draws on research in Chicago early in the century and is centred around the study of the areas in which delinquents reside (high offender rate areas); the second, more recent, studies the areas where crimes are committed (high offence rate areas). The two are not necessarily the same as criminals may offend at some distance from their homes. These two schools will be considered separately below.

Before doing so, however, it seems prudent to consider the popular conception that criminality is attached more to urban than rural areas. This is not straightforward: definitions of 'rural' and 'urban' are neither clear nor self-evident. Nor would the mere establishment of such a connection be sufficient: to be useful there must also be an explanation for the connection. If one goes back to the eighteenth century the popular conception of crime and many of the figures which are available for that time would suggest a greater concentration of criminal activities in rural rather than urban areas. By the middle of the nineteenth century, as mentioned above, Mayhew was implying that this had altered. Part of the reason could have been the changing construct of social organisation, including the way in which the criminal law was defined and enforced. Part of the apparent change in ecological factors associated with criminality may thus be due to such factors, and especially in the new methods of enforcement centred around a police force which concentrated both its manpower and its efforts in urban areas. When analysing the modern information it is important to keep in mind that some of the apparent differences may be explicable by reference to these social constructs and their operation rather than to actual differences in criminality or behaviour (for a fuller discussion see Chapter Fourteen).

Lastly it is necessary to register the fact that – despite the strong popular association of crime with towns, and the support given to this view by police data and victim studies – this is an area which has been very little researched. Most criminological study of the effects of the environment have concentrated on urban areas, ignoring rural areas. Indeed, any explanations of rural criminality have been constructed by contrast with theories tested in the urban environment, for example, that in urban areas there are less strong social bonds holding the society together (this is discussed under the control theories considered in Chapter Thirteen), and that there are fewer opportunities for criminality in rural areas (a factor considered below in 11.2.3). With these factors in mind it is now necessary to assess the way in which crime and environment may be linked and, hopefully, to consider why such links operate.

11.2.2 Environment and high offender rate areas
This area of study is closely associated with the Chicago School of Human Ecology (also referred to as The Chicago School). It had its roots in the department of sociology at the University of Chicago, and was most influential in the 1920s and 1930s. Chicago grew from a town of 10,000 inhabitants in 1860 to a large city with over two million inhabitants by 1910. Most of the increase was due to immigrants, many of whom came from Europe. The city was therefore a fruitful place for sociological work and the Chicago School studied every aspect of its life. All the information was recorded in meticulous detail, and used to test and formulate sociological theories. Much of this work was criminological, but before turning to those aspects, it is important to set the scene by introducing some of the basic sociological ideas upon which much of this explanation of crime is based.

The Chicago School was primarily the brain-child of Robert Park, who saw the city not just as a set of buildings in a particular geographic location, nor as formed by its institutions, but as a living ecological environment or as a kind of social organism. By this, he meant that the people and the institutions were so intimately bound together that they tended to interact as a whole. As with any ecological community, there were areas where the inhabitants were mainly of a particular type or types: racial or ethnic communities; immigrant communities; similar income and occupational groupings, etc. Within each community there were symbiotic relationships: the grocer needed customers and vice versa, whilst the inhabitants of different geographical areas needed each other to demand and supply work, etc. There were particular physical features of the city which were important to its inhabitants, the most obvious of which was Lake Michigan. The city was seen as an ever-evolving organism which was altering as people moved within it (Park (1952)).

Another member of the Chicago School, Burgess, elaborated on this model. He saw the city as an organism which grew largely from the centre in a series of concentric circles. The central area he named Zone I or the 'Loop'. It housed the business area with the major banks, large department stores, expensive shops, and the main administrative buildings of the city. It was an area in which few people lived. Zone II was what Burgess called the transitional zone. This was the oldest part of the city and was largely residential, but its housing was dilapidated and unlikely to be renovated as it was constantly in danger of being taken over or pulled down to make way for businesses, which in turn altered the character of the area. The worst housing in the city was in this sector, a lot of it split into rooms for rent. It comprised the ghetto area of the city and the poorest citizens lived there. Very often, the poorest ghetto dwellers were the newest immigrants. Zone III contained the workmen's houses, the homes of the skilled and semi-skilled workers. Many of these inhabitants had originated in Zone II but had since progressed to the slightly better housing of Zone III; it was the next place to which the successful immigrants would graduate. Zone IV had more desirable and expensive houses, and Zone V was the commuter zone or suburbia. In Chicago each zone was calculated at that time to be approximately two miles in width (Burgess (1928)).

Obviously, no city can be precisely categorised in this way. There are always pockets of less desirable housing near industrial areas and railways, but Burgess claimed that the general pattern was discernible. None of this was directly to do with criminology, but it laid the foundations for a particular criminological theory.

11.2.2.1   Shaw and McKay

In the early part of this century Chicago suffered an ever-increasing crime problem, and the search for an explanation to this became the major preoccupation of the Chicago School. Shaw began work in this area, but his most famous work was done in conjunction with McKay when they studied juvenile crime rates in Chicago (Shaw and McKay (1942) and (1969)). They recorded the number of juveniles (10- to 16-year-old boys) who appeared before the juvenile court, mapped out the areas from which they came, and then calculated the areas with the highest delinquency rates, defined as the number of juvenile crimes per hundred juveniles in the area.

They therefore measured official levels of juvenile crime and recorded the area where the delinquent lived, and not the area where the crime was committed. By this measurement, the neighbourhoods with the highest crime rates were those in the centre of the city, closest to concentrations of industry. These were sparsely populated and population was further decreasing as the land was being taken over by industry. Crime rates decreased as the neighbourhoods got further from the centre: on the zonal maps, Zone I or the 'Loop' had the highest crime rate, and the rate decreased as the zones moved outwards away from the centre.

Later they also measured the number of males from a particular area who had been sent to a correctional institution and the number of males who appeared in police records, and discovered that they followed the same pattern. Further, they claimed that the crime rate of a particular area over time remained constant, despite vast changes in the inhabitants of that area. The central zones retained their high crime rate even when the ethnic origins of the inhabitants completely altered. The implication seemed to be that individuals who once lived in the high crime rate zone became more law-abiding as they moved away from the centre. From all this they con-cluded that the delinquency rate was more a result of economic position and living environment than of racial or ethnic characteristics. More generally, Shaw and McKay claimed that official rates of delinquency and crime are highest in the centre of cities; decline with movement away from the centre; and do not depend upon the people who inhabit those regions. In making this claim, they were not saying that criminality was caused by location, but rather that it tended to occur in certain types of area or neighbourhood. They certainly did not claim that all members of a neighbourhood would be criminal, and realised that factors other than area affected individual decisions about participation in crime. Their theory is positivist, in that the individuals are seen as inert and their behaviour is largely determined by their environment or the level of social disorganisation.

They also noted that the crime problem of a particular area was related to such social problems as: high rates of suicide and truancy; a declining population concentrated into a small living space; infant mortality, tuberculosis and mental disorders. It was also related to such economic factors as: number of families living on State relief or who are dependent on charity; low rates of home ownership; and low rental values of properties. They did not connect criminality with poverty, on the grounds that rates of criminality did not significantly increase during the depression when poverty was at its peak. They point instead to social disorganisation, or what is sometimes termed differential social organisation (see also Sutherland's theory of differential association (10.2.3, and 10.2.4), and control theories in Chapter Thirteen). In the central areas of the city, or those around industry or business, there is a very rapid shift in population, which means that the residents see themselves as transients and do not take an interest in their surroundings. The social disorganisation means that the normal social controls of school, church and family may also be less forceful (see also Chapter Thirteen). Children may not spend much time in one school, and instability is disruptive to both their learning and their discipline. As criminal behaviour is more common in these areas, so criminal values are likely to be more common, and so each individual is more likely to come into contact with them and more likely to learn advancement by illegitimate rather than legitimate methods (Shaw and McKay (1969)).

Shaw published a number of books of life histories (e.g., *The Jackroller* (1930) and *Brothers in Crime* (1938)) which he claimed lent support to these views. For example, they suggested that there was no physical or personal difference between criminals and non-criminals; rather there was a difference in attitudes and opportunities in the neighbourhoods. The people in the criminal areas seemed more tolerant of criminal activity, and the social controls were less forceful. There were 'fences' and other factors which facilitated criminality, and which therefore rendered this type of lifestyle easier than in the more law-abiding areas.

Shaw and McKay claimed that all these factors led to an increased rate of criminality in certain areas of the city, those in the centre or near the industrial centres being the worst.

11.2.2.2 Evaluation and updating
The work of Shaw and McKay has been widely criticised especially for its methodology. In using officially recorded criminality, it is claimed that they

were basing their whole thesis on biased and inexact data. As was seen in Chapter Four, official crime statistics are inexact. A lot more crime occurs than is ever recorded. Certainly most self-report studies (see 4.3.1) suggest that crime is fairly evenly distributed across all classes (see Empey (1982)), making questionable a claim that it is centred on a small sector. Furthermore, the crimes of some sections of society are less likely to be discovered, or less likely to be defined as criminal or to require a legal sanction. It is generally the poor who are most likely to have their criminality detected and, once detected, most likely to face criminal charges and be convicted. These attacks become less forceful if one limits the research to the crimes which are most likely to result in prosecution, generally known as street crimes. When restricted to these, self-report studies do show more of this type of criminality in the lower classes, which might seem to remove some of the bias (see Hindelang, Hirschi and Weiss (1981)). But concentrating on street crime could be seen as defining crime as a lower-class activity.

The Chicago School theory, based on the idea of concentric circles, has also faced severe criticism, especially in Britain and the rest of Europe, where cities tend to be a lot older than in America. Even in America, this idea was often challenged. Lander (1954) in his study of Baltimore discovered that the industrial areas were to be found not in the centre of the city but on the outskirts, and questioned whether criminality was related to substandard housing, overcrowding or poverty. He suggested instead a correlation with a weakening of social controls (see anomie, Chapter Twelve and control theories, Chapter Thirteen). In Britain, although some studies have shown a correlation between areas and rates of crime (see, for example, the Notting-ham University study (1954)), they have not found a distribution based on concentric circles (see Burt's work in London (1925) and Mannheim's work in Cambridge (1948)).

Much of the more recent work in this country has centred on the effects of the slum clearances and the problem of the difficult housing estates which are often located on the outskirts of towns. Wilson (1963) found that the crime rate in Bristol was higher on some of the new purpose-built housing estates, usually council estates, on the outskirts of the city, rather than in the more dilapidated housing in the centre of the city. Despite this disagreement, both Shaw and McKay and Wilson point to social disorganisation as the cause of criminality. This claim for social disorganisation as a cause of criminality has been challenged by Sainsbury (1955), who said that in London, whilst suicide is related to areas of social disorganisation, criminality is related to areas of poverty. Obviously in some cities, like Chicago earlier this century, these two (poverty and social disorganisation) may have coincided, making it more difficult to discern which was the more important factor to crime committal.

Morris (1957), in one of the fullest accounts of ecological or area studies, attacks not only the concentric circle theory but the central idea that areas generate high levels of crime even if the make-up of its inhabitants changes. He found that certain areas of Croyden in Surrey, usually parts of council housing estates, did contain more delinquents, or as he refers to them, potential delinquents, than others. But he believed that this situation was artificially constructed by the authorities, who tended to house all 'problem families' in the same locality. The area was almost bound to house more criminals: those who had already shown a potential for crime or other undesirable behaviour were forced to live together. In his interpretation it was the socio-economic position of these families, the administrative procedures, and the class differences, and not simply the area, which led to the high criminality. Following this work, a number of British criminologists studied the effects of council house allocation and of restricted access to housing generally. Many confirmed the Chicago finding that the high crime rates were in city centres (see Baldwin and Bottoms for Sheffield (1976) and Davidson for Hull (1981)). Susan Smith (1986), in an extensive recent study of Birmingham, found a concentration of criminals residing in the inner city area. She argues that this stemmed from the unequal distribution of wealth and opportunity, forcing the least well-off to inhabit these areas, and at the same time contributing to high crime rates. The criminality is not, she claims, simply the reflection of a particular area. Such a simple correlation linking offender areas with social deprivation has been questioned by the work of Wikström (1991). Using housing tenure variables (owner-occupier, private rented etc.) as an indicator he found no simple causative link between social status/class and criminality. This suggests that the study of high offender areas is not merely the study of social class. A number of these factors will be discussed in this and later chapters.

Shaw and McKay's claim that all racial and ethnic groups had similar crime rates also excited criticism. They had themselves found (1942) that areas with large numbers of Oriental inhabitants had crime rates markedly lower than might be expected. Indeed, Jonassen (1949) used their data to prove marked ethnic differences in crime rates within areas. The particularly low crime rates amongst Oriental families has usually been explained by the strong family control and social organisation found in these groups (Chambliss (1974)). This would seem to uphold some of Shaw and McKay's arguments concerning social controls, or as they term it, social disorganisation.

Support as well as criticism also comes from a study by Bursik and Webb (1982). They attempted to test whether areas retained their delinquency rates despite almost complete changes in their inhabitants. Their conclusion was that all areas undergoing racial changes, whatever their previous history, experienced high crime rates. In these neighbourhoods the new race was generally black, and on their arrival all whites moved away, so that the change in the area was complete and very fast. Social disorganisation was therefore very great. But as these areas became more stable and more organised, the crime rates fell closer to their previous rates, suggesting that the important factor was not ethnicity, but the level of social organisation.

The connection with both social class and social disorganisation can be assessed by making smaller and closer studies of particular areas. One such is mentioned in Bottoms et al. (1989) and (1992) which compare three pairs of estates to discover why estates with seemingly similar housing facilities and very similar social variables (such as age, sex, social class, ethnic origin, size of household, rate of male unemployment, age of leaving full-time education and length of residence in present dwelling) might have very different offender rates (and notably differing offence rates). Thus comparing two low-rise housing estates they discovered a large, persistent difference in offender rates despite the fact that both estates had a very similar socio-economic status and both had a similar turnover of residents ruling out differences in social disorganisation as suggested by Shaw and McKay (above). (However, in the other two pairs of housing areas the high offender area did have higher rates of social disorganisation.) One clear difference was that the local authority in allocating housing placed those with the most acute housing need in the high crime rate area and also placed there families who had prior links with other residents in the area. Although both of these housing choices would seem to perpetuate the high offender rate, such a direct link between housing allocation and criminality was not accepted. It was instead argued that the allocation had its effect by influencing both the way in which the residents interacted, and the way in which outsiders perceived the area and its inhabitants. The first of these might affect the level of opportunity for criminal activity as well as driving some residents to apply for a move away from the area. The second might affect the attraction of the estate to housing applicants and also the way in which it was viewed by officials such as social workers, health workers and control agencies. Over time all these factors would influence the make-up of the area. The high offender rate area also had certain characteristics or area contextual effects (see Wikström (1991), above) which others have associated with high-crime areas, including: the effect on residents and potential residents of the labelling of the high rate area in a negative way; differences in the schools to which the children from each area would be sent; differences in peer groupings and the presence of a criminal subculture in the high-rate area; differing relationships with parents. It could be argued that these represent more individual explanations of the criminality, undermining the claims for environmental connections, but the whole socialisation process is closely linked not just to the immediate family but to the immediate environment and, in times of mass media, to the wider outside world. Individualised theories clearly help in particular explanations, but there is also a place for the environmental and wider social contextual elements in offender activity. For example, a follow-up study showed that the gap in offending rates had narrowed. The only large change (Bottoms et al. (1992)) was that the council now allocated homeless persons to both estates, which may have altered perceptions of the area and so altered other social factors such as crime. In effect, this whole study simply emphasises the complexity of the links between offending rates and environment.

11.2.3 Environment and high offence rate areas

In the 1970s there was a move towards studying offence areas rather than offender areas. One of the earliest British studies of this kind was carried out for the Home Office by Mayhew et al. (1976) and covered one of the theories concerned with this area – opportunity and crime. Bottoms (1994) refers to many studies which consider the differential offence rates between areas and concludes that there are marked geographical differences in offence rates, and that these can vary for different types of offences: one area may be high for burglary while another has a high rate of family violence etc. Moreover, even within high offence rate areas there will be some smaller locations which have still higher rates or greater concentrations of particular offences.

A related feature is multiple victimisation. For example, Farrell (1992) re-analysed the figures for the first British Crime Survey (1982) and discovered that, although only 32 per cent of individuals reported being victimised, 44 per cent of those reported more than one victimisation and multiple victimisation was more common for property offences than for offences against the person. Similarly Pease (1993) reports the preliminary findings of a re-analysis of the British Crime Survey data over time (from 1982 to 1988) stating that the differences between areas of their rates of offending has widened over time and that this change is largely explicable by the higher rates of multiple victimisations in some areas as opposed to others. Although this suggests that rates of offences are linked to geographic areas and the same areas are also linked with multiple victimisations, the connection is not definite because the findings are based on victim studies: a person could be a victim of several crimes but each of these could have taken place in a different area. Some work has already been done to clarify the connections by studying specific offences and their connection to multiple victimisations. Pease (1993) reported on the findings of a Northern Ireland study that 40 per cent of the non-domestic burglaries occurred in 1 per cent of the relevant premises (or in 16 per cent of the burgled premises) and that these premises were located in particular areas. Explanations are more difficult: possible hypotheses, such as those stressing opportunity theory (see below), need much more empirical testing before they can be pressed with confidence.

11.2.3.1 Opportunity and routine activity explanations of high offence rate areas
In the UK the first modern analysis of these variables was begun in the research and planning unit of the Home Office. In 1976 Mayhew et al. produced a short report in which opportunity became the central focus of research and suggested that levels of offending could be reduced by taking account of the situation in which the offence occurred. This was the start of a serious consideration of opportunity analysis which is related to a number of factors. One such is referred to as target attractiveness which considers the likely gains from criminal activity and the ease of performing the crime undetected (the level of surveillance). For example, Clarke (1983) reported that public telephones were much more likely to be attacked if they were located on the street rather than in pubs, launderettes and other buildings regularly frequented by the public. In earlier research Clarke (1978) noted that vandalism on double-decker buses was more likely to arise on the upper deck, and especially in the back rows. This area was the least likely to be supervised, particularly in driver-only buses. Introducing conductors produced interesting results: the levels of vandalism dropped but attacks against the conductors rose. Thus the criminality was related to other factors besides opportunity. This also shows that altering the environment will not necessarily prevent offending. The other most important element in opportunity

theories is the availability of the means to commit the offence so that a shooting will not occur unless there is a gun whilst on the other hand, the absence of a helmet makes motor bike theft less likely as the possibility of detection is high.

The routine activity theory is, in part, an extension of opportunity theory in that it includes, besides suitable targets and the level of surveillance, the need for a likely offender (see Felson (1994)). Thus it considers the day-to-day activities of victims and of those, such as neighbours, who might be able to offer surveillance. In an environment where most of the inhabitants are predictably absent for large parts of the day either because of work or other recreational activities there is greater opportunity for crime, especially if the targets have more portable and desirable goods. This links crime both with differences in lifestyle and with economic changes, both of which are recognised to alter over time and space. It is believed that rural communities have lower crime rates partly because of higher surveillance by neighbours etc. than in either urban areas or old rural areas which have now become commuter belts. Routine activity theory is therefore a wider-ranging theory than opportunity theory though they are both directed at similar aspects of offending.

It is also suggested (Sutherland and Cressy (1978)) that cultural and temporal changes cause different types of delinquency. For example, a study of Boston, USA (Euwies (1959)) had shown that in the poor and high delinquency areas there was a higher rate of property crimes than crimes against the person. In contrast in Cairo, Egypt, it was said that the position was reversed (high rate of crimes against the person and low rate of property crimes). The suggestion here is that both the level and the type of criminality are affected by the culture of the area.

Clearly the factors of opportunity and routine activity have a part to play in assessing whether a crime will occur but these are not the only important factors and the environmental aspects need to be seen in their wider social and other contexts.

11.2.3.2 Use of space and high offence rate areas

Studies have been made on where an offence occurs in relation to the offender's use of space on the hypothesis that offenders will commit offences in areas with which they are familiar, close to home, to work, to places of entertainment and so on. This theory has been most strongly postulated by Patricia and Paul Brantingham (1989, 1991 and 1993) who state that crime is most likely when the opportunity arises in an area which is well known by the offender. Building on this they have designed a programme of crime prevention for British Columbia which includes the following factors:

(a) Keep schools away from shopping areas.

(b) Provide school lunches or make sure that lunch is available with adult supervision.

(c) Plan routes taken to schools so that they do not go through areas where vandalism or other offending is likely.

(d)   Plan low-rise public housing with carefully marked private space, little public space, and few walls and other obstructions for offenders to hide behind.

(e)   Plan high-rise accommodation for the elderly with first-floor communal space and large windows for the supervision of entrances.

Bottoms (1994) refers to some research which tends to back up the claims made by the Brantinghams' work. If these factors are found to be important their contribution to reducing offending could be very great.

11.2.4   Practical applications of the ecological theory

Shaw and McKay's research essentially pointed to social disorganisation as the main reason for criminality. It led them to believe that treating or severely punishing individual delinquents would do little to alleviate the problem. For them, the solution is to be found in social organisation and stability. In an attempt to counteract the problems faced in these areas, Shaw established what he called the Chicago Area Project (1932). He set up 22 neighbourhood centres which were basically run and staffed by local residents, and encouraged and aided other organisations within the community. The intention was to reduce criminality by increasing social organisation and community feeling: youths were attracted into acceptable recreational activities; staff would help juveniles who got into trouble and watch out for difficulties which might be starting on the street; and residents were encouraged to take a pride in their community by improving their environment. Some of the projects ran for over 50 years and seemed to help the residents in many ways, but their effects on juvenile delinquency are difficult to assess. Schlossman et al. (1984) attempted with rather broken data and no real controls to calculate their effects: they confirmed that the projects had enabled communities to retain pride in and to care for their areas despite severe disadvantage; and further concluded that they were satisfied that the projects had had a positive effect on rates of offending, particularly juvenile offending. In contrast, when Miller (1962) studied the effect on criminality of a similar project in Boston, he found that it had had an almost negligible impact. The Chicago Area Project did not attempt to alter the political *status quo*, nor did it attack the distribution of power. It merely tried to help people live within, and cope with, the circumstances that already existed. For this reason some (for example Heidensohn (1989)) have argued that it could never succeed.

A more recent experiment to reduce crime by stabilising the area is reported by Taub et al. (1984). An area of Chicago was the target of investment for urban improvement from both the university and the city authorities. Multi-occupancy laws were enforced, cheap second mortgages provided for academic staff, a private security force patrolled the area, and emergency telephones were installed at frequent intervals. These changes allowed a high non-white community to become stable in its residents and increased house prices: it also altered the perception of the area and, after a while, reduced the crime rate (although this was still high). The changes, however, were dependent on active intervention by a large body and involved an alteration of the population of the area.

In Britain, other projects have taken a similar approach but with a slightly different slant on rectifying the problem. For example, Alice Coleman (1990) took a solely ecological approach in studying design problems in public sector housing. Coleman argues that the design of the area can induce bad behaviour which might well include criminality. Thus, to a far greater extent than Shaw and McKay, she argues that environment determines criminality, and her ideas are strongly positivist. She accepted three design factors which facilitated criminality – anonymity; lack of surveillance; and easy escape (which had been put forward by Newman (1982)). She argued that designs, particularly of public sector houses and housing estates, should be concerned to give the area character and allow easy surveillance. She and her research team from King's College London made certain more specific recommendations about public sector housing:

(a)   No more flats should be built. This was seen as necessary because the study had related many unpleasant factors, including bad behaviour and certain acts of criminality, with the number of dwellings per entrance, the number of dwellings per block, and the number of storeys.

(b)   Designs should have greater stabilising features. This was suggested because items such as overhead walk-ways and thoughtless use of space were found to be connected with bad behaviour and acts of criminality. Each dwelling or each block of flats should have its own enclosed garden rather than leaving the space completely open.

(c)   Any existing flats and housing estates should be altered so as to remove the worst of the design features and so cut down their adverse effects.

Coleman drew particular attention to the strong effects of these design factors when there are children living in the area. Her work has been widely accepted, and she has worked with a number of London boroughs and with the Metropolitan Police, designing new housing areas and redesigning blocks of flats so as to reduce their effects on criminality. She has had very marked success in a number of her projects. In the Lisson Green estate, the removal of walkways was followed by a 50 per cent fall in the crime rate, and the fall was maintained for at least a year (Coleman (1988)). Her most marked success has been in the Lea View estate, where the crime rate fell from a very high level to near zero when her design suggestions were implemented. The estate remained virtually crime-free for four years. In a similar Wigan House estate, where these improvements were not made, there has been no such drop in the crime rate (Coleman (1988 and 1990)). Coleman's urban designs are largely based on the idea that a 'defensible space' will limit criminal activity. The logic of this depends on people bothering to defend the space: the design presumes a reasonably strong community feeling and involvement. This presumption is implicit and hence never really discussed (see Merry (1981)). Furthermore, it is possible to have bad design with little defensible space and yet still have a low crime rate. The theory therefore needs an understanding and analysis of social context.

Much of what Coleman did might be termed target hardening. This became a useful tool of government in the 1980s – they could claim to be doing something about crime control and prevention. Target hardening in the UK largely grew out of work by Ron Clarke, former head of the Home Office Research and Planning Unit (Clarke (1980, 1992 and 1995)); see also Clarke and Cornish (1983) and Clarke and Felson (1993)). He believed that a criminal act required the combination of opportunity with the presence of a person disposed to criminality. For Clarke both factors needed to be present. The criminality side of the equation is centred on the person - why he or she chooses the criminal avenue. For the person the choice is rational and may be based on economic factors, excitement, impulse or limited information. The stress on the individual was typical of 1980s attitudes. It is, however, the first part of the equation which has been most seized on by policy makers – the need for the opportunity to arise. This notion also fitted well with thinking in the 1980s by aiming to make crime more difficult, reduce opportunities – target hardening. This gave government a fairly simple and often cheap initiative to make crime more difficult while seeming to be doing something very concrete: it did nothing about any underlying causes of crime.

Three studies serve as examples. First Painter (1988) studied people's experience of crime in a small area six weeks before and six weeks after street lighting was installed. Crimes fell from 21 before to three after. Secondly, Laycock (1985) tried property marking and discovered that in three villages in a Welsh valley burglaries were reduced, in one by 40 per cent, over a 12-month period. However, the area chosen was small and sufficiently cohesive that the prospective burglars were as aware of the property marking as were the prospective victims. The results from this close community might not occur in a large urban centre. Thirdly, Mayhew et al. (1992) show some of the limitations of this process. They compared the effect of the introduction of steering locks in both Britain and West Germany. In Britain these were introduced for all new cars and resulted in a reduction of the theft of such vehicles and an increase in theft of older cars without the locks. The effect was to displace crime from one target to another rather than to reduce the number of crimes. The West Germans required all cars, new and old, to have steering locks fitted by a particular date. This produced a clear reduction in the absolute number of car thefts of all kinds and the reduction remained significant for a number of years. The lessons, if any, of these three examples are far from uniform. Only the first involved actual State action; the second suggests that target hardening involves potential victims in protecting themselves; and the third indicates that other sectors of society, such as commercial corporations, may be expected to consider crime reduction in the design of their products.

Where target hardening or other environmental measures are taken by the State, they often help to enhance surveillance – the design of estates or the installing of street lights seen above. A more clearly surveillance-led initiative which has been gathering support in the 1990s is closed circuit television (CCTV). There is now an enormous literature building up on this subject (see, for example, Fyfe and Bannister (1996); Fyfe (1997); Taylor (1997); Norris and Armstrong (1997, forthcoming) and much work concerning the control of public space (Davis (1990) and Fyfe (1997a)). CCTV is perceived as a measure which can deliver control and deterrent effects because it relies on intensive surveillance. The hope here is that possible or prospective criminals (people who in the right situation might choose a criminal avenue) will worry about being watched; about the possibility of rapid intervention by the police; and about the clear evidence which the cameras will provide in any future court case. CCTV is a fairly expensive system to install and monitor; most schemes are initiated and paid for in partnership between local authorities and the private sector. They usually survey and therefore protect the fairly affluent shops in the centre of urban conurbations. They therefore tend to protect private commercial interests in the area, both by detecting and deterring crime and by making the public feel safer and therefore making them more likely to visit the locations. They have been claimed to be effective and are very heavily supported by the police (after all, they must aid their job of surveillance and making the public feel safe), but there are disadvantages. First, some claim that crime is displaced to surrounding areas and to other types of criminal behaviour: in Clarke's theory, one needed both a propensity to commit crime and an opportunity; these initiatives address only the second of these and do so only in a small area of the city/town. Secondly, CCTV may increase public indifference – people may be less inclined to report incidents if they believe the cameras should pick them up. Here the cameras are perceived not in a negative way – not as 'big brother' watching them – but rather as 'big father', solving all their problems for them. Lastly, such surveillance techniques raise problems concerning civil liberties issues: there are problems of privacy; they allow the State to regulate more intrusively the activities of a civil society; importantly, they may be used to control order rather than crime, being used to move on undesirable elements who are not necessarily committing any offences, and it is an approach which may erode the quality of life with its encouragement of a fortress existence (see Taylor (1997)).

A second, very different approach is to increase the likelihood of detection and so reduce the attraction of criminality. This is largely what is behind neighbourhood watch schemes which aim to increase the social awareness of residents and so help them to reduce crime in their locality. The schemes have wide popular appeal: by 1987, within four years of their first being set up, there were 42,000 schemes (see Evans (1992)). Such a proliferation is interesting, especially when their effectiveness is very unclear. Some of the schemes have probably been started because of the lower property insurance premiums payable on membership of a scheme. The acceptance by insurance companies is even more peculiar given the lack of proof in the schemes' validity. Husain (1988) studied two neighbourhood watch scheme areas just before the schemes were implemented and again a year after implementation; he also studied a possible displacement area and a control area. He concluded that neighbourhood watch schemes were not helpful in reducing criminality but he did not find any displacement. In contrast Pease (1992) introduced focused and more careful surveillance by neighbours into a council estate experiencing high burglary rates: the result was not only a reduction in burglary in these homes, but also a general reduction in the area, again suggesting an absence of displacement. The interim conclusion would seem to be that while the effectiveness of ordinary neighbourhood watch schemes is questionable, the more focused schemes could produce positive results.

Policing methods are also important in reducing criminality. Crime prevention has always been a police ideal and one which is said to be central to the policing role. Pease (1994) points out that the reality of what is done to effect crime prevention is often different. It has hitherto been largely neglected and never been given priority either in training or in financing the police. However, some positive policing initiatives have been set up under the Police and Criminal Evidence Act 1984 and its requirement for consultative committees, and may be of interest here. Both Mitchell (1992) and Fyfe (1992) discuss the operation of such schemes noting that there is no requirement to act on community initiatives written into the 1984 legislation. The success of the schemes is thus based on the consultative committees being genuinely representative and on police willingness to internalise some of their views. With these caveats they both considered that the system could operate and help in crime reduction within those areas, although there would still be the possibility that crime was being displaced rather than reduced overall.

Some of the impetus towards greater community policing and more visible police officers on the beat has come from this ecological approach to crime. Extra, or more obvious, surveillance is seen as a positive deterrent. Community policing could also have secondary side-effects helpful to the ecological approach: if the extra surveillance, possibly in unison with some of the other design changes, works then the reduced crime and enhanced safety can encourage more people to be out on the streets, adding still further to the level of surveillance.

Lastly, an important role which police could play was suggested by Goldstein (1990) and entitled 'problem-oriented policing'. It requires police to identify particular crime problems and then carry out research to discover how best to prevent them. In this way police attention would be focused and might lead to crime reduction. The identification of problems can now, with computerised information, be carried out for very small crime areas. In the 1980s these ideas were taken up in some areas and moulded into schemes which have had some success. Two such are reported by Heywood et al. (1992). In one a geographical crime database is used to store crime-related community data (including crime prevention measures being used by the public in specific areas, presence of street lights, demographic characteristics etc.) and use this information and spatial analysis to assess how best to incorporate crime prevention models. The second concerns a multi-agency approach, whereby a coordinating body gathers information collected by various agencies, discusses how best to tackle the problem, and then tries to put the ideas into operation.

It has been recognised that, as Kevin Heal (1992) has suggested, the purely physical changes suggested by the environmental approach are likely to be of only limited success. Their 1980s introduction was led by the very pragmatic desire on the part of the government and Home Office to tackle crime and to demonstrate a success. Towards the end of that decade, however, many theorists recognised that this could only ever be a very partial solution, and was likely to lead to displacement either from one area to another or from one crime to another. Any wider success would need to include psychological, and social measures as a recognition that environmental factors may not cause crime but rather offer the oportunity for it to occur.

11.2.5 Weighing the ecological approach

The ecological approach seems to have a popular appeal. The people living in each city usually associate particular areas with criminality. Those living in these high crime rate areas, especially the vulnerable or those who feel most vulnerable (often the elderly and women), perceive crime as a major factor affecting their lives and governing their activities. Almost all autobiographical accounts written by male criminals include a section about the area in which they were reared, and tend to associate that with their own criminality. Ecological ideas have also been given official recognition. Lord Scarman included environment, housing and inner city location as part of the reasons for the Brixton riots of 1981. These facts, together with some of the statistical evidence, strongly suggest that there is knowledge to be gained by studying the areas with high crime rates to see if factors can be identified which influence the level of criminality.

This is not necessarily to accept that the studies of the ecologists are correct in their approach or in their results. The limits of the usefulness of this research must always be recognised. It only really studies street crime or public crime, and never addresses the more secret and private crimes of child abuse or domestic violence. Nor does it address the crimes (apart from burglary) committed by or against the commercial businesses within these areas. It also almost exclusively studies male criminality and youthful criminality. Many of these studies show little awareness of these limitations: they might accept that they are mostly concerned with juvenile crime, but few recognise that they are studying male criminality. Thus gender issues or the power basis which may be involved are not addressed. Some of the differences may be seen when looking at autobiographies of female criminals which, instead of or as well as having accounts of the neighbourhood and its effects on their activities, generally include reference to the family.

Ecological studies, particularly the older ones, are further constrained by being based almost exclusively on official statistics. Again, the consequences of this are rarely given explicit recognition. In the absence of any attempt to assess the true rates of criminality, these studies are therefore open to the charge that they only measure official perceptions and reactions to activities in certain areas: they do not necessarily measure or relate to the criminal activities themselves (see labelling in Chapter Fourteen).

If we are trying to weigh the contribution to criminological understanding made by this approach, these limits must be recognised. And so must the possibility of change in the broad conditions on which much of the work has been based. For example, the close ties with youth in many of these studies may make them less and less important as the mean age of the population increases, but this can be said of many of the theories in this book. Also, as inner city regeneration occurs, such as in Cardiff, Liverpool and London dock-land areas, there may well be a change in the location of the high crime rate areas, although the reasons for their existence may remain the same. New technologies, changing the methods of industrial production, may reduce the concentration of population in cities. Such demographic changes have already begun, e.g., London's population has declined since the inter-war years, and the population of most rural areas in England and Wales has been increasing over the 1980s, often reversing a trend which has lasted for over a century. However, cities are likely to remain the areas of social conflicts of all sorts – riots, crimes and racial problems, as well as most labour disputes and demonstrations. Research into the crime rates of the city areas is thus likely to remain an important sphere of study in the future. None the less, it needs to be complemented by ecological studies into crime in rural areas.

The ideas expounded in the ecological studies have, as already indicated, led to many practical changes. Despite some success in the way such schemes or design changes have, in certain cases, cut down on levels of criminality, too much emphasis on this type of factor may have some unfavourable features. This is particularly so in cases where it leads to a form of victim blaming – saying crime is committed because victims are careless (see 5.6). With this reservation, some of the reforms have been fairly successful.

Possibly the most important implications of the work of Shaw and McKay lie not so much in the pure ecological area, but rather in the fact that they introduced or strengthened two ideas in accepted criminological knowledge: that which connects social control and criminality; and that of cultural support for behaviour. The first of these ideas was partially introduced by Durkheim, whose work will be considered in the next chapter, but was fully elaborated by the control theorists whose work will be considered in Chapter Thirteen. The second idea is a mixture of social learning theories, which were considered in Chapter Ten, and cultural and subcultural theories, which will be discussed in the next section and Chapter Twelve. All these approaches are mostly concerned with limiting or controlling observable behaviour and are less directed at motivation, intent and social pressure. The focus is on practical crime prevention and altering behaviour through reducing opportunity and increasing surveillance.

11.3 POVERTY AND UNEMPLOYMENT

11.3.1 Poverty and economic or income inequality
The theorists considered in the last section connected criminality with social disorganisation. In general, however, they found that the areas of greatest social disorganisation were also the poorest, but they failed to prove conclusively that it was disorganisation rather than poverty which caused the criminality. As was mentioned above, when Sainsbury (1955) did separate these elements he found crime was connected more closely to poverty than to social disorganisation, while others (e.g., Bottoms et al. (1992)) would also wish to include a link with ecological aspects.

In any event, the link between poverty and criminality is not as simple as Sainsbury's findings might suggest. Clearly, poverty *per se* does not cause criminality, as there are many tribes and peoples who are materially very poor but do not have a high crime rate. One possible hypothesis is that poverty is only a major factor in criminality if wealth is given great status in the society, and/or if it leads to some groups or individuals being deprived of the necessities of life. Bound up with this there are two related factors – economic or income inequality, and relative deprivation. Economic or income inequality exists where there is a substantial difference between the material or income level of those who have least in a society and that of other groups. It is the gap between rich and poor which is important: it is not necessary for there to be absolute poverty (if we could define such a term) in the society. The implication is that in a society with a relatively equal distribution, even if every member were poorer, the crime rate would be lower. Many writers (such as Stack (1984)) try to define the connection even more closely by suggesting that it is not just the inequality itself which affects the crime rate, but the feeling that such inequality is unfair (i.e., relative deprivation). This is especially likely to arise in societies where material success is put forward as an acceptable goal and citizens are officially told that individuals are equal. Confusion arises where the notion of poverty is discussed without consideration of such aspects as income inequality and relative deprivation.

Most of the theories which consider a simple link between crime and poverty are older and have been largely discredited. Today the viable theory is the possible link between crime and economic or income inequality. Box (1987) considers sixteen studies carried out between 1974 and 1985. Eleven of the studies found a close statistical link between income inequality and crime. The five which did not all related to homicide. Box concluded that for crimes other than homicide there seemed to be a very strong relationship, which may even be causal, with equality. In support, he quotes Carroll and Jackson:

> inequality has strong causal effects on crime rates . . . [although] . . . the effect of inequality on crimes against the person was not as pronounced as the effect on burglary. (Box (1987), p. 88, quoting Carroll and Jackson (1983), p. 186)

Even the exception of homicide has been questioned. Vold and Bernard (1986) refer to six studies which show a clear link between social inequality and homicide, but a much weaker link in the case of property offences.

The evidence of these studies suggests that most crime is linked to economic and income inequalities. Patterson's (1991) American research undermines these claims to a certain extent. She discovered no link between relative poverty or inequality and crime, not even property crime such as burglary, but did discover that significant absolute poverty was an indicator of higher crime rates, particularly violent crimes. She does not consider that the absolute poverty directly caused the criminality but rather that, the lack of money might have eroded the usual social controls. Her study may be of less validity in the British context as the level of welfare support has traditionally been stronger than in America but it should not be discounted,

particularly as the level of welfare provision for many individuals has been
eroded over the past 17 years and, as the Child Poverty Action Group point
out, there are now many people living below the poverty line. In any event,
this single work cannot dispose of the close statistical association between
crime and economic inequality indicated above. The issue will be revisited
through a discussion of relative deprivation in 12.2.

11.3.2 Unemployment

Unemployment is also associated with wealth or the lack of it. Unemployment is both an indicator of the general economic well-being in a State, and
of the equality of distribution of that wealth. Unemployment generally
increases in times of depression, and decreases in times of prosperity and
growth. If crime increases with unemployment, this might indicate a feeling
of unfair treatment ('why should I lose my job?'), but it might also show that
the resultant inequality in economic position, the pure fact of poverty, or
boredom and free time might be factors in the equation. Is there a relationship between crime and unemployment?

Not surprisingly, there is no simple answer to this question. Studies looking
at arrest or conviction data and their connection with unemployment often
find a fairly close relationship. Glaser and Rice (1959), for example, found
that at times of high unemployment recorded levels of adult crime (between
20 and 45 years old), especially for property offences, increased. They further
discovered that juvenile crime was reduced during these periods, a finding
which they attributed to parents being at home to control their children.
Other studies have disputed this last conclusion, and have indeed indicated
that it is in the juvenile groups that crime is most closely related to
unemployment. It is amongst the young adults that both unemployment and
crime are likely to be highest and prospects worst (see Block (1979)). The
young are unlikely to have job experience and therefore their prospects are
low; through no fault of their own they may feel useless and feel real anger
at the position in which they find themselves. When official crime statistics
are used, part of the explanation for a connection between juvenile crime and
unemployment may be that they are more likely to be arrested, prosecuted
and convicted. Some argue from this that the connection tells more about the
control agencies than about the criminals (see Box (1987)); it tells more
about why people are arrested than about why people commit crime.

Other studies are inconclusive. Some, such as Danziger and Wheeler
(1975), discovered that crime (they studied in particular aggravated assault,
burglary and robbery) was not related to unemployment. Others, such as the
British researcher Brenner (1978), reported a significant relationship between
crime and unemployment. However, in analysing these studies, Crow et al.
(1989), Box (1987), Vold and Bernard (1986) and Long and Witte (1981)
all conclude that on balance crime and unemployment are related; that this
relationship is not consistently strong; and that it is probably strongest and
most consistent in the case of young males. The last aspect is supported by
Allan and Steffensmeier (1989), who found that unemployment was most
clearly associated with the arrest rates of 14–17-year-old males (juveniles) for

property crimes. They went on to conclude that poor pay and hours (something they refer to as under-employment) were most closely associated with the arrest rates of 18–24-year-old males (young adults) for property crimes. Their use of arrest rates rather than criminality prompts caution, but none the less it is probably indicative of a connection between employment status and crime. A further link was proposed by Sullivan (1989), who found that those – the so-called core workers – who had access to or were employed in fairly secure jobs (by today's standards) were likely to get involved only in fairly petty and short-term criminal careers, while those who had access to or worked in a less secure employment structure, contract workers or temporary workers, were more likely to be involved in more serious criminality and over more protracted periods.

In Britain there has been a heated debate concerning links between unemployment and crime. In 1994, the Home Office proposed including rates of unemployment and of long-term unemployment as two of the predictors of high levels of crime in an area (others included rates of lone parent families and the number of council estates). The intention was to base police funding on these aspects. The then government were ideologically unconvinced of such links and quickly funded further research. Orme (1994) found no such links and so these predictors were withdrawn for funding purposes. Orme's report was heavily criticised: it took recorded notifiable offences as the indicator of criminality (as was seen in Chapter Four, this is a very imprecise base); it looked at large police force areas, which may have missed smaller problem communities; and it took the number claiming unemployment and related benefits as the indicator of unemployment, but this measure excludes most of those under 18, the largest criminal group. In contrast, Field (1990) noticed that potential offenders are most frequently found in poorer social groups whose access to and likelihood of having good secure employment are low (this links up with the work of Allan and Steffensmeier (1989)). In addition, while Wells (1995) discovered that property crime black-spots and unemployment black-spots tend to be the same areas, Dickinson (1994) found that cautions and convictions for burglary tend to fluctuate along with economic cycles and employment rates. These later studies had some defects similar to those in Orme's report, but neither of them was so clearly problematic. What is certain is that links with economic factors, particularly causal links, are not universally accepted. Indeed some, like Dennis and Erdos (1993), have argued directly against any causal relationship or link between unemployment and crime rates. They then assert an equally problematic causal link between criminality and fatherless households as the latter have been increasing over the last 30 years.

The balance of the evidence suggests that, despite government assertions to the contrary in the 1980s and early 1990s, there is some link between crime rates and rates of unemployment. What is less clear is the nature of the link. The issue acquired particular relevance in the 1980s and 1990s when the level of unemployment was consistently high, matching the mass unemployment experience of the inter-war years. We shall look briefly at two contrasting interpretations of the link between this experience and crime. Petras and

Davenport (1992) pointed out that the high levels of unemployment have had far-reaching destructive effects on individuals and communities. They link these destructive effects with the effects of the free-market economy, which they view as a form of social engineering which has further destructive effects on poor communities. Amongst the negative effects they identify: the exclusion of those most affected from the benefits of a consumer society, and their experience of poor health, high levels of suicide and early death. They also point to a substantial increase in criminal activity; very high levels of property offences, both acquisitive and destructive; and a rise in interpersonal violence. These have certainly occurred during this period, making the causative link at least highly plausible. In particular, the link between the unemployment of the 1980s and high rates of criminality amongst the young are forcefully suggested.

In a very different study of unemployment in parts of London, Hagan (1993) offers a quite different reading. He accepts an association between the overall rising trends in unemployment and crime, but argues that at a micro level it was early criminal behaviour and its continuation over time which tended to lead to adult unemployment. Criminal activity may remove individuals from the legitimate culture making it more likely that they would remain unemployed. Reinforced by peer-group pressures and parental criminal activity, criminality in youths would in turn lead to unemployment of youths: the stronger the criminal embedment, he claimed, the more likely that adult unemployment would follow. On this view, the individual's criminal behaviour is used to explain their unemployment whilst structural problems linked to unemployment are ignored.

These two approaches show very different aspects of the possible link between crime and unemployment. They may each be of some validity. The first suggests that, in areas of high and continuing unemployment, there will be strong pressure towards criminality amongst youths; the latter might explain why some remain in criminal and unemployed states rather than moving on from them. These are arguments about the *direction* of causation: from unemployment to criminality or vice versa. Others question whether there is a causative relationship at all. For example, Wilson and Herrnstein (1985) suggest that differences between individuals may precede, and be associated with, unemployment and criminality. This would make it possible for there to be correlation between the two without any necessary causation. Unemployment may not be a causative factor in criminality, but to suggest that unemployment, particularly at the levels suffered in Britain through the 1980s and early 1990s, stemmed only from elements internal to the individual seems unlikely. It is far more probable that the demise of the larger manufacturing industries and the major restructuring of the economy in line with a free-market enterprise-led economy would have had some influence. Through the 1980s and 1990s there was a widening gap between rich and poor. In 1979 there were 5 million living on less than half the average national household income (the basic measure of poverty in Britain), and by 1991 this figure had risen to 13.5 million (24 per cent of the population). Moreover, many unofficial estimates put the figure much higher. Official crime rates doubled over the same period. Much of the poverty is suffered by the unemployed, whose unemployment benefit has dropped by 20 per cent in real terms since 1979. The young have been hardest hit, being largely excluded from full benefit. The young are also the group most affected by State reduction in public housing (another result of a free-market economy) which Shelter estimates leads to about 150,000 young people becoming homeless every year. Since these trends particularly affect the young, and since all criminologists agree that delinquency is most prevalent among the young, particularly teenagers, it would be surprising if there were no link between unemployment, poverty, homelessness and crime. Such factors may not be causative – and, as we have seen, establishing causal connections in this area with so many variables is very tricky – but to suggest that they could be explained away on purely individualistic reasons is intuitively untenable, especially when all these factors have obvious connections with society. They are largely socially constructed problems, which in the case of unemployment, poverty and homelessness have been directly related to market society (Massey and Denton (1993)). One influential writer (Currie (1997)) has also argued for a causal connection between the free market and violent crime, both because of the greed and selfishness engendered by unregulated markets and because of the dehumanising effects of unemployment and poverty. Currie has further suggested that there may also be a tangential link – unemployment causes poverty and both of these lead some to feel disruption, hopelessness and depression encouraging drug use (and rates of opium use have been correlated with unemployment); in order to finance the drug use, they then turn to crime.

11.3.3 Evaluation of theories of poverty and unemployment

There is now widespread, though not total, acceptance that there is a strong relationship between criminality and economic or income inequality; that there is probably a relationship between crime and unemployment; and that this relationship is strongest in the case of young males. All of this may go some way towards explaining why the community project carried out by Shaw and McKay in Chicago did not succeed in reducing crime (see 11.2.4) – it did not attempt to alter the social and economic conditions, but instead tried to teach the people to come to terms with these problems. If the conclusions reported above are correct, the Chicago Area Project was doomed to fail because it did not address the need for a fairer and more even distribution of both wealth and opportunities (in particular jobs). Some would contend that the statistics clearly suggest that in a relatively egalitarian society crime would be reduced, and that this does not relate to the absolute levels of poverty or wealth of the people in such a society.

11.4 LOWER-CLASS CULTURE

11.4.1 Early class theories

The previous sociological theories in this chapter examined some views on the connection between crime and two broad social factors – ecology (particularly social disorganisation), and wealth distribution. This section examines some theories on the way crime is related to the people in society, not as individuals but as collective groups, and to the way of life of certain classes, particularly the lower or working classes. In such an approach, it is the lower-class culture *per se* which causes criminality. The argument is that, by conforming to lower-class values, the individual will break the law. The work of three criminologists, one American and two British, will be briefly discussed.

11.4.1.1   Miller
Walter Miller, an American writer, presents the idea that working class values include a delinquent subculture. He argues that there are distinctive working- or lower-class values, many of which are quite different from the middle-class values upon which our legal system is based. Adherence to the lower-class values in some instances more or less automatically leads to breaking the law. Those whose upbringing and behaviour falls within the lower-class norms are highly likely to be led to violate some aspects of the law (Miller (1958)).

Miller mentioned six key concepts, or as he calls them 'focal concerns', as epitomising lower-class values. These six demand a high degree of emotional involvement from the lower classes. They can be listed as follows:

1.   Trouble – a desire to avoid trouble but an admiration of those who dare risk getting into trouble.
2.   Masculinity or being tough – including physical confrontation or conflict which is often illegal.
3.   Being smart or able to stay a mental step ahead of the next person – gaining status without the need for physical confrontation.
4.   Excitement – might include taking risks in committing crimes.
5.   The power of fate – feeling they lack control over their lives.
6.   Autonomy – a desire to be independent from external controls such as the boss, parents, etc.

Miller offers no explanation for the origins of these social values. All he does is to mark their existence and explain that conforming to them will lead to criminality. He also refers to other factors. He notes, for example, that it is common in lower-class households for the father to be absent, often because he has breached the criminal laws. The home life is a female-dominated environment which, he says, leads lower-class boys to look for male role models outside the home. They often find them in street gangs which Miller calls 'one sex peer units'. These gangs take part in activities which uphold the lower-class 'focal concerns' and give the youths a sense of belonging and status.

11.4.1.2   Mays
From a similar standpoint, Mays (1954, 1968 and 1975), a British analyst in this field, argues that in certain areas, particularly older urban areas, the residents share a number of attitudes and ways of behaving which predispose

them to criminality. These attitudes have existed for years and are passed on to newcomers. Lower-class culture is not therefore intentionally criminal; it is just a different socialisation which, at times, happens to be contrary to the legal rules. He sees it not as a symptom of maladjustment but rather as a very well-adjusted subculture. The problem arises because the subculture is in conflict with aspects of the culture of the country as a whole, especially that which is enshrined in our legal system. Criminality, particularly juvenile criminality, is not therefore seen as a conscious rebellion against middle-class values. It arises from an alternative working-class subculture which has been adopted and altered over the years in a haphazard sort of way. The driving force may never have been to breach the criminal rules, but the result was sometimes to do so. He says:

> it seemed to me that excessive leisure time, the absence of adequate parental models and care, the presence of known adult offenders in the locality together with the boys' own natural desire to test themselves in acts of daring, bravado and danger, were a sufficient explanation for delinquent behaviour which invariably tapered off after leaving school and was almost certainly phasic in character. (Mays (1975), p. 63; see also Mays (1968) and (1975))

Like Miller, Mays does not discuss the origins of the social values, except in the negative sense of saying that it is not a hostile reaction against middle-class values. Or, more positively, that it is the set of values which best meets the social needs of that sector of society.

11.4.1.3 Morris
The third theorist is Terence Morris (1957), who is basically an ecologist. He argues that social delinquents abound in the lower classes, and that it is the class characteristics which have caused the criminality. Antisocial behaviour exists throughout society and in all classes, but the way in which it is expressed differs and depends upon membership of a particular class. Criminality he sees as largely a lower-class expression (Morris (1957)).

This is because the whole socialisation process in the lower class is more likely to produce criminality than the same process in the middle classes. The upbringing in the middle-class home is controlled by the family, is very ordered, and almost all activities are centred around the home and family. In the lower classes, the child's upbringing from a young age, about three or four, was split between family and home on the one hand, and peer group and street acquaintances on the other. The working class child is likely to have a less ordered and regulated upbringing and to be sent out to play in the street. The peer group is therefore a much stronger influence from a much earlier age. Like Miller and Mays he depicts the lower-class culture as driven by a desire for immediate gratification of both material and physical needs: self-control and deferred goals are much less common. Spontaneity and aggression are significant elements of this life. Furthermore, he argues that home life in working-class families is likely to be more strained and stressful, due to economic problems. If the parents adjusted well to these difficulties then the problems they caused for the child would be minimal, but often the parents did not adjust well. This gave rise to parental discord, which could be very damaging to the children and might further encourage them to escape onto the streets where the peer group has the greatest effect. Controls of these youths within their own community are negligible: they only come to be controlled when they commit a crime and the official systems of control step in. The essential message of Morris is that the whole ethos of the working class is more oriented towards criminality and antisocial behaviour.

11.4.1.4 Evaluation

Each of these three theories suffers from a common defect. They predict too much criminality, and cannot account for law-abiding behaviour within the lower classes. There is also an implicit prediction that individuals would continue in their criminal activity, or at least their support of such activity, throughout their lives. This conflicts with a widespread finding that most people's delinquency reduces considerably at about the age of twenty. This approach carries the implicit assumption that man is rigidly socialised and virtually unable to think outside the social constraints: if the social group accepts crime as normal and natural, the individual passively participates. Critics resist this argument and say that the individual usually needs a reason or a motive to act.

Mays attempted to answer criticism by asserting that people living in the lower classes who are non-criminal, or those who wish to protect their children from criminality, do not subject their children to the full lower-class values or, at least, not the more criminalogenic ones. It is a concession which leaves much of the original explanation in tatters. Mays goes on to assert that of those who embrace the full lower-class values, probably most do at some time commit a criminal act, but only a small number get caught. He seems to be saying that certain types of offences are thought of as normal, and although they might be easy to detect, they do not attract attention from the rest of the community and so are less likely to be either reported or solved.

If the defence offered by Mays does little to save the basic assertions linking crime to lower class culture, there is some support for the view that the working class is made up of two broad groups, one of which upholds middle class values whilst the other does not. A British study carried out by Nottingham University and published internally in 1954 under the title *The Social Background of Delinquency* studies a mining town in the Midlands which the researchers called Radby. They found that streets and homes with the same economic and social standing had very different delinquency rates. They documented two types of family existing in the working class of this town. The first accepted delinquency and often members of this group had criminal records; they accepted the lower-class values (these families were found to live in Dyke Street). The second did not accept delinquency and had virtually no criminal members; they did not accept the lower class values (these families lived in Gladstone Road). Although these elements may exist in separate streets as occurred in Radby, Mays argues that they may also exist side by side in the same street, and this he sees as particularly likely to occur in large cities. All these approaches suffer from at least two major confusions. First, there is the confusion between area and class, which are often used as more or less interchangeable terms. Secondly, and more fundamentally, there are the confusions arising out of an implicit treatment of the 'working class' as constituting a more or less homogeneous group. Even in the nineteenth century historians had recognised the existence of, for example, a 'labour aristocracy', where a strong desire was for 'respectability'. More recently, the whole notion of 'the working class' is often questioned. But for our purposes we only need to note that the dangers of sliding into an imputed homogenicity are quite general. To put it another way:

> . . . not everyone in a 'Catholic country' is devout, nor are even the devout always at mass or confession. (Heidensohn (1989), p. 21)

Certainly, in a criminal class (if there be such a thing) not everyone need be criminal, nor are criminals constantly involved in crime.

Furthermore, many of the definitions of class are based on concepts of the occupation of the traditional adult male breadwinner, which is not so relevant today. In many households both parents work, whilst there are also many single-parent households: neither of these groups necessarily falls neatly into the older definitions of class. The whole concept of class as used by the above researchers has become more problematic.

None the less several recent studies suggest that it would be premature to declare the total demise of a correlation between lower class and offending. After observing 1,000 Toronto school and street youths, Hagan and McCarthy (1992) concluded that class conditions still caused offending and delinquency (in its wider sociological concept). They considered that an important causative element in the correlation was something which they termed 'streetlife'. Their definition of 'streetlife' was based on a number of variables: parental class origins; family structure; parental control and conflict; school involvement, commitment and conflict; and the current class condition involved in life on the street. This definition is an amalgamation of old class ideas intermingled with certain aspects of control theory (see Chapter Thirteen) and strain theory (see 12.2). The clear correlation found between class and 'streetlife' and criminality was also identified by Foster (1990) and Farnworth et al. (1994). Foster discovered that in certain high crime rate areas, juvenile street crime was the norm and progressed on to crimes in the black economy as offenders got older. She found that although deviance was not supported by the community, particularly the older community, it was not really condemned either; there was a sort of ambivalence – it is wrong but not very harmful. This tolerance of minor criminality did not cross over into severe violence which was condemned. But mostly Foster was struck by the normality of the whole process. Farnworth et al. (1994) tried to explain the link, finding correlations when using measures of class; but strong correlations between serious street crime, delinquency and the concept of 'underclass'. The last is seen as long-term material deprivation with little possibility of being legally altered: it can be measured by such factors as persistent parental unemployment and long-term receipt of benefit. In any event, there is still some vigour in class theories as long as they consider other aspects of the equation, define class more clearly, and/or look for causative links rather than just assuming that a correlation automatically implies a causation.

11.4.2 Socio-economic status (SES)
Closely related to class are the numerous reports (e.g., West (1982) and Farrington (1992)) concerned with SES. They found that, even on their own, such factors as family income, housing, employment instability and family size related to criminality: large family size was seen as a particularly strong predictor. In these Cambridge studies a low SES was consistently associated with higher self-reported and official offending, although there was no such consistent link between parental occupational groups and crime. Again, the implication is that SES seems now to be associated with criminality, whereas old concepts and measures of class are less reliable predictors. But the reasons are uncertain: SES may be associated with deprivation or with unemployment, both of which were considered above. For example, Farrington (1986), reported that an erratic work record of the father is a good predictor of youth offending and an unstable or bad employment record for a young man is a firm predictor of criminality in early adulthood.

11.4.3 Modern associations of an underclass with criminality
In the introduction to this chapter there was mention of a connection between offending and an underclass in the nineteenth century. More recently very similar arguments have arisen. Much of the discussion in connection with criminality has emanated from an American writer, Murray (1990 and 1994), who has used both US and British examples to make his point. He is not alone in writing about what he consciously stigmatises as a new underclass and in considering welfare dependency as a social problem which causes many social ills. Much of the new right ideology which has had political prevalence in the past 20 years or so also centres around some of this debate, although not everyone has associated the problems of offending directly with welfare dependency. Murray suggests that the welfare provision has permitted some to survive outside the legitimate job market for too long. He directly echoes the early nineteenth-century arguments about pauperism in claiming that: those on welfare become dependent and take no responsibility for their own situation; that some young women have deliberately become pregnant to increase their welfare provision or to obtain housing. The final element Murray adds is criminality: men without families use crime to prove their masculinity. He makes the undemonstrated assertion that this can explain most of the officially recorded 60 per cent increase in violent offences which arose in Britain between 1980 and 1988. Murray should not be read without understanding his political subtext: the removal of benefits to force individuals to support themselves which, in his subjective judgement, would

restore their enterprise. Liberal welfare writers such as Frank Field (1990) attack Murray for having invented a Victorian-style undeserving poor, to be distinguished from the deserving poor who are trying to support themselves but may occasionally need a little help. In Field's view at that time, any dependent class has been politically and socially constructed by such new right policies as mass unemployment and regressive taxation. Whether as a Minister in the 'new' Labour government of 1997 he can effectively deconstruct this notion of dependence remains to be seen. In the face of increasing inequalities the unsocial activities of some in this group, while still condemned, can be seen as understandable. In particular, as mentioned above (11.3.2), the massive structural unemployment can have far-reaching destructive effects, including poverty, homelessness, illnesses, drug abuse and an undermining of social controls and constructs, all of which may then lead to increased criminality. On this analysis it is not the underclass, if any such group exists, that is the problem but the society which has excluded certain groups from the benefits of a free-market economy. Thus although a recent study (Farnworth et al. (1994)) claims to have found a relationship between chronic disadvantage and high rates of offending, this may only mean that the organisation of society has so reduced the options of these people that offending becomes a rational choice. An historical study of social deprivation (Kennedy (1997)) finds similar fears of social disorder and dangerous classes, requiring changes in society and in methods of social control. The underclass is not of itself more criminal, but criminality is generated when other social choices are closed.

11.5 CONCLUSION

The first two theories in this chapter (ecology and poverty and unemployment) relate criminality to 'objective' social and economic facts. They claim to prove that crime is statistically related to poverty or wealth distribution, or to social disorganisation. The incidence of a statistical link is, of course, highly important, but it does not necessarily mean that there is a direct causal connection. One objection arises from the frailty of the statistical base, especially the shortcomings (already rehearsed) of official statistics of crime. Another is that the statistical connection is inadequate to establish whether the real causal connection is with poverty, with relative inequality, or with some other factor. Part of the causal relationship may be tied up with feelings of unfairness which may put the individual into a stressful position. Strain will be discussed in the next chapter (12.2). More generally, the aspects examined in this chapter have been more concerned with practical crime prevention rather than causes. In the absence of any firm underpinning, however, this narrow approach is likely to fail as often as it succeeds, or to have substantial drawbacks. For example, the use of CCTV involves a great deal of surveillance of the law-abiding (the majority) in the hope of catching or deterring a few.

There were similar objections to any general acceptance of the Chicago School's claim that there was a close relation between social disorganisation and criminality. The final set of theories posited a connection between criminality and lower-class values. The claim made in some of the earlier studies was that different sectors of society live by slightly different rules, and some of the values of some sectors are criminal. Nowhere are these rules closely defined or proven to exist.

In more recent research there is consideration of the links between offending and class which gives some insight to how the situations may be linked. In later claims there is either an amalgamation of factors, some of which would have been considered separately under poverty or unemployment, or a very politicised claim about what causes the particular correlation between offending and class/SES/underclass which is claimed to exist.

Hagan (1990) puts in a plea that we should not lose sight of class as an element in offending. His concept of 'class' includes all elements discussed in this chapter and he sees great value in continued research into these areas. What he recognises is that class theories need to ascertain which elements of the social status may be most helpful in understanding not only why some people turn to criminality but also why many others in similar situations do not and why many of those who have taken part in early offending later move on to lead law-abiding lives as adults. In other words he looks for a theory sensitive to class disadvantage but which can take account of longitudinal life choices.

In all three of these areas, even where there is a strong statistical connection, it is not possible to prove a causal connection. In particular, none of the studies can explain why men seem to be so badly affected and women so little affected. These theories are largely building blocks from which more elaborate structures may be constructed.

REFERENCES

Allan, E. and Steffensmeier, D. (1989), 'Youth Underemployment and Property Crime: Differential Effects of Job Availability and Job Quality on Juvenile and Young Adult Arrest Rates', *American Sociological Review*, vol. 54, p. 209.

Baldwin, J. and Bottoms, A. (1976), *The Urban Criminal: A Study in Sheffield*, London: Tavistock.

Block, R. (1979), 'Community, Environment and Violent Crime', *Criminology*, vol. 17, p. 46.

Bottoms, Anthony E. (1994), 'Environmental Criminology', in Mike Maguire, Rod Morgan and Robert Reiner (eds), *The Oxford Handbook of Criminology*, Oxford: Oxford University Press.

Bottoms, A.E., Claytor, A. and Wiles P. (1992), 'Housing Markets and Residential Community Crime Careers: a Case Study from Sheffield', in David J. Evans, Nicholas R. Fyfe and David T. Herbert (eds), *Crime, Policing and Place: Essays in Environmental Criminology*, London: Routledge.

Bottoms, A.E., Mawby, R.E. and Zanthos, P. (1989), 'A Tale of Two Estates', in David Downes, *Crime and the City*, London: Macmillan.

Box, Steven (1987), *Recession, Crime and Punishment*, London: Macmillan Education.

Brantingham, P.J. and Brantingham, P.L. (eds) (1989), *Patterns in Crime*, New York: Macmillan.

Brantingham, P.J. and Brantingham, P.L. (1991), *Environmental Criminology*, 2nd edn, Prospect Heights, Illinois: Waveland Press.

Brantingham, P.J. and Brantingham, P.L. (1993), 'Environment, Routine and Situation: Towards a Pattern Theory of Crime', in R. Clark and M. Felson (eds), *Routine Activity and Rational Choice*, New Brunswick: Transaction.

Brenner, H. (1978), 'Review of Fox's "Forecasting Crime"', *Journal of Criminal Law and Criminology*, vol. 70, p. 273.

Burgess, Ernest W. (1928), 'The Growth of the City', in Robert E. Park, Ernest W. Burgess and Roderick D. McKenzie (eds), *The City*, Chicago: University of Chicago Press.

Bursik, Robert J. and Webb, Jim (1982), 'Community Change and Patterns of Delinquency', *American Journal of Sociology*, vol. 88(1), p. 24.

Burt, Cyril (1925), *The Young Delinquent*, London: University of London Press.

Campbell, B. (1993), *Goliath: Britain's Dangerous Places*, London: Methuen.

Carroll, L. and Jackson, P.I. (1983), 'Inequality, Opportunity and Crime Rates in Central Cities', *Criminology*, vol. 21, p. 178.

Chadwick Reports (1839), Royal Commissions on the Rural Constabulary Force, 'First Report of the Commissioners Appointed to Inquire as to the Best Means of Establishing an Efficient Constabulary Force in the Counties of England and Wales', 169 *Parliamentary Papers*, Reports, vol. 19, p. 1.

Chambliss, William J. (1974), *Functional and Conflict Theories of Crime*, MSS Modular Publications, Module 17.

Clarke, Ronald (1978), *Tackling Vandalism*. London: HMSO.

Clarke, Ronald (1980), 'Situational Crime Prevention: Theory and Practice', *British Journal of Criminology*, vol. 20, p. 136.

Clarke, Ronald (1983), 'Situational Crime Prevention: Its Theoretical Basis and Practical Scope', in M. Tonry and N. Morris (eds), *Crime and Justice: an Annual Review of Research*, vol. 4, Chicago: Chicago University Press.

Clarke, Ronald (1992), *Situational Crime Prevention: Successful Case Studies*, New York: Harrow and Heston.

Clarke, Ronald (1995), 'Situational Crime Prevention', in M. Tonry and D.P. Farrington (eds), *Building a Safer Society*, Chicago: Chicago University Press.

Clarke, Ronald and Cornish, D. (eds) (1983), *Crime Control in Britain a Review of Policy Research*, Albany: State University of New York Press.

Clarke, R. and Felson, M. (eds) (1993), *Routine Activity and Rational Choice*, New Brunswick: Transaction.

Coleman, Alice (1988), 'Design Disadvantage and Design Improvement', *The Criminologist*, vol. 12, p. 20.

Coleman, Alice (1990), *Utopia on Trial*, 2nd edn, London: Hilary Shipman.

Crow, Iain, Richardson, Paul, Riddington, Carol and Simon, Frances (1989), *Unemployment, Crime and Offenders*, a NACRO publication, London: Routledge.

Currie, Elliot (1997), 'Market, Crime and Community: Toward a Mid-range Theory of Post-industiral Violence' *Theoretical Criminology*, vol. 1, p. 147.

Danziger, S. and Wheeler, D. (1975), 'The Economics of Crime: Punishment or Income Redistribution?', *Review of Social Economy*, vol. 33, p. 113.

Davidson, R.N. (1981), *Crime and Environment*, London: Croom Helm.

Davis, Mike (1990), *City of Quartz*, London: Verso.

Dennis, N. and Erdos, G. (1993), *Families Without Fatherhood*, 2nd edn, London: IEA Health and Welfare Unit.

Dickinson, D. (1994), *Crime and Unemployment*, Department of Applied Economics: University of Cambridge.

Empey, Lamar T. (1982), *American Delinquency*, Homewood, Illinois: Dorsey.

Engels, Fredrick (1971), original 1844, *The Condition of the Working Class in England*, trans. W.O. Henderson and W.H. Chalenor (eds), Oxford: Basil Blackwell.

Euwies, Saied (1959), 'A Comparative Study of Two Delinquency Areas', *National Review of Criminal Science*, vol. 2, p. 1.

Evans, David J. (1992), 'Left Realism and the Spatial Study of Crime', in David J. Evans, Nicholas R. Fyfe and David T. Herbert (eds), *Crime, Policing and Place: Essays in Environmental Criminology*, London: Routledge.

Farnworth, Margaret, Thornberry, Terrence P., Krohn, Marvin D. and Lizotte, Alan J. (1994), 'Measurement in the Study of Class and Delinquency: Integrating Theory and Research', *Journal of Research in Crime and Delinquency*, vol. 31, p. 32.

Farrell, G. (1992), 'Multiple Victimisation: Its Extent and Significance', *International Review of Victimology*, vol. 2, p. 85.

Farrington, D.P. (1986), 'Stepping Stones to Adult Criminal Careers', in Dan Olwens, J. Block and M.R. Yarrow (eds), *Development of Antisocial and Prosocial Behaviour*, New York: Academic Press.

Farrington, D.P. (1992), 'Juvenile Delinquency', in J.C. Coleman (ed.), *The School Years*, 2nd edn, London: Routledge.

Felson, Marcus (1994), *Crime and Everyday Life*, Thousand Oaks: Pine Forge Press.

Field, Frank (1990), 'Response to Murray', in Charles Murray, *The Emerging British Underclass*, London: IEA Health and Welfare Unit.

Field, S. (1990), *Trends in Crime and their Interpretation*, London: HMSO.

Foster, J. (1990), *Villains: Crime and Community in the Inner City*, London: Routledge & Kegan Paul.

Fyfe, Nicholas R. (1992), 'Towards Locally Sensitive Policing? Politics, Participation and Power in Community/Police Consultation', in David J. Evans, Nicholas R. Fyfe and David T. Herbert (eds), *Crime, Policing and Place: Essays in Environmental Criminology*, London: Routledge.

Fyfe, Nicholas R. (1997), 'The "Eyes on the Street": Closed Circuit Television Surveillance and the City', in N.R. Fyfe (ed.), *Images of The Street: Representation, Experience and Control in Public Spaces*, London: Routledge & Kegan Paul.

Fyfe, Nicholas R. (ed.) (1997a), *Images of The Street: Representation, Experience and Control in Public Spaces*, London: Routledge & Kegan Paul.

Fyfe, Nicholas R. and Bannister, Jon (1996), 'City Watching: Closed Circuit Television Surveillance in Public Spaces' *Area*, vol. 28(1), p. 37.

Glaser, Daniel and Rice, Kent (1959), 'Crime, Age and Employment', *American Sociological Review*, vol. 24, p. 679.

Goldstein, Herman (1990), *Problem Oriented Policing*, New York: McGraw-Hill.

Hagan, John (1990), 'Poverty of a Classless Criminology – the American Society of Criminology 1991 Presidential Address', *Criminology*, vol. 30, p. 1.

Hagan, John (1993), 'The Social Embeddedness of Crime and Unemployment', *Criminology*, vol. 31, p. 465.

Hagan, John and McCarthy, Bill (1992), 'Streetlife and Delinquency', *British Journal of Sociology*, vol. 43, p. 533.

Heal, Kevin (1992), 'Changing Perspectives on Crime Prevention: the Role of Information and Structure', in David J. Evans, Nicholas R. Fyfe and David T. Herbert (eds), *Crime, Policing and Place: Essays in Environmental Criminology*, London: Routledge.

Heidensohn, Frances (1989), *Crime and Society*, London: Macmillan Education.

Heywood, Ian, Hall, Neil and Redhead, Peter (1992), 'Is There a Role for Spatial Information Systems in Formulating Multi-agency Crime Prevention Strategies?', in David J. Evans, Nicholas R. Fyfe and David T. Herbert (eds), *Crime, Policing and Place: Essays in Environmental Criminology*, London: Routledge.

Hindelang, Michael J., Hirschi, Travis and Weiss, Joseph (1981), *Measuring Delinquency*, Beverly Hills, California: Sage.

Home Office White Paper (1959), *Penal Practice in a Changing Society*, Cmnd 645, London: HMSO.

Husain, S. (1988), *Neighbourhood Watch in England and Wales: a Longitudinal Analysis*, Crime Prevention Unit Paper 12, London: HMSO.

Ingram, A. Leigh (1993), 'Type of Place, Urbanism, and Delinquency: Further Testing the Determinist Theory' *Journal of Research in Crime and Delinquency*, vol. 30, p. 192.

Jonassen, Christen T. (1949), 'A Re-Evaluation and Critique of the Logic and Some Methods of Shaw and McKay', *American Sociological Review*, vol. 14, p. 608.

Jones, David (1982), *Crime, Protest, Community and Police in Nineteenth-Century Britain*, London: Routledge & Kegan Paul.

Kennedy, D. (1997), 'Crime Waves, Culture Wars and Societal Transformations', *Crime, Law and Social Change*, vol. 26, p. 101.

Lander, Bernard (1954), *Towards an Understanding of Juvenile Delinquency*, New York: Columbia University Press.

Laycock, G. (1985), Property Marking: *A Deterrent to Domestic Burglary?*, Crime Prevention Unit Paper 3, London: HMSO.

Long, S.K. and Witte, A. (1981), 'Current Economic Trends: Implications for Crime and Criminal Justice', in K.N. Wright (ed.), *Crime and Criminal Justice in a Declining Economy*, Massachusetts: Oelgeschlager, Gunn and Hain.

Mannheim, Hermann (1948), *Juvenile Delinquency in an English Middletown*, London: Kegan Paul, Trench, Trubner and Co.

Mannheim, Hermann (1965), *Comparative Criminology*, London: Routledge & Kegan Paul.

Massey, Douglas and Denton, Nancy (1993), *American Apartheid*, Cambridge, Mass.: Harvard University Press.

Mayhew, Henry (1861-2), *London Labour and the London Poor*, vols. I–IV, London: Griffin, Bohn and Co.

Mayhew, Pat, Clarke, Ronald V., Sturman, A. and Hough, Mike (1976), *Crime as Opportunity*, Home Office Research Unit Study No. 34, London: HMSO.

Mayhew, Pat, Clarke, Ronald V. and Hough, Mike (1992), 'Steering Column Locks and Car Theft', in Ronald V. Clarke (ed.), *Situational Crime Prevention: Successful Cure Studies*, New York: Harrow & Heston.

Mays, John Barron (1954), *Growing Up in the City*, Liverpool: University of Liverpool Press.

Mays, John Barron (1968), 'Crime and the Urban Pattern', *Social Review*, vol. 16, p. 241.

Mays, John Barron (1975), *Crime and its Treatment*, 2nd edn, London: Longman.

Merry, S. (1981), 'Defensible Space Undefended: Social Factors in Crime Control Through Environmental Design', *Urban Affairs Quarterly*, vol. 16, p. 397.

Miller, Walter B. (1958), 'Lower Class Culture as a Generating Milieu of Gang Delinquency', *Journal of Social Issues*, vol. 14, p. 5.

Miller, Walter B. (1962), 'The Impact of a "Total-Community" Delinquency Control Project', *Social Problems*, vol. 10, p. 168.

Mitchell, David (1992), 'Initiatives in Policing London's Brixton since the 1981 Riots', in David J. Evans, Nicholas R. Fyfe and David T. Herbert (eds), *Crime, Policing and Place: Essays in Environmental Criminology*, London: Routledge.

Morris, Terence P. (1957), *The Criminal Area: A Study in Social Ecology*, London: Routledge and Kegan Paul.

Murray, Charles (1990), *The Emerging British Underclass*, London: IEA Health and Welfare Unit. The book includes a number of responses to Murray's thesis.

Norris, Clive and Armstrong, Gary (eds) (1997, forthcoming), *CCTV Surveillance and Social Control*

Nottingham University (1954), *The Social Background of Delinquency*, Internal publication.

Newman, O. (1982), *Defensible Space: People and Design in the Violent City*, London: Architectural Press.

Orme, J. (1994), *A Study of the Relationship Between Unemployment and Recorded Crime*, London: HMSO.

Painter, Kate (1988), *Lighting and Crime Prevention: the Edmonton Project*, London: Centre for Criminology and Police Studies, Middlesex Polytechnic.

Park, Robert E. (1952), *Human Communities*, Glencoe: The Free Press.

Patterson, E. Britt (1991), 'Poverty, Income Inequality, and Community Crime Rates', *Criminology*, vol. 29, p. 755.

Pease, Ken (1992), 'Preventing Burglary on a British Public Housing Estate', in Ronald Clarke (ed.), *Situational Crime Prevention: Successful Case Studies*, New York: Harrow & Heston.

Pease, Ken (1993), 'Individual and Community Influences on Victimisation and their Implications for Crime Prevention', in D.P. Farrington, R.J. Sampson and P-O.H. Wikström (eds), *Integrating Individual and Ecological Aspects of Crime*, Stockholm: National Council for Crime Prevention.

Pease, Ken (1994), 'Crime Prevention', in Mike Maguire, Rod Morgan and Robert Reiner (eds), *The Oxford Handbook of Criminology*, Oxford: Oxford University Press.

Petras, J. and Davenport, C. (1992), 'Crime and the Development of Capitalism', *Crime, Law and Social Change*, vol. 16, p. 155.

Philips, David (1977), *Crime and Authority in Victorian England*, London: Croom Helm.

Pike, Luke Owen (1876), *A History of Crime in England*, London: Smith Elder and Co.

Sainsbury, Peter (1955), 'Suicide, Delinquency and the Ecology of London'. From *Suicide in London*, Institute of Psychiatry, reprinted in W.G. Carson and Paul Wiles (eds), *The Sociology of Crime and Delinquency in Britain*, vol. 1, Oxford: Martin Robertson.

Scarman, Lord (1981), *The Brixton Disorders, 10-12 April 1981* (Scarman Report, 1981), Cmnd 8427, London: HMSO.

Schlossman, S., Zellman, G. and Shavelson, R., with Sedlak, M. and Cobb, J. (1984), *Delinquency Prevention in South Chicago: A Fifty Year Assessment of the Chicago Area Project*, Santa Monica Ca: Rand.

Shaw, Clifford R. (1930), *The Jackroller*, Chicago: University of Chicago Press.

Shaw, Clifford R. (1938), *Brothers in Crime*, Chicago: University of Chicago Press.

Shaw, Clifford R. and McKay, H.D. (1942), *Juvenile Delinquency and Urban Areas*, Chicago: Chicago University Press.

Shaw, Clifford R. and McKay, H.D. (1969), *Juvenile Delinquency and Urban Areas*, revised edn, Chicago: Chicago University Press.

Smith, Susan (1986), *Crime, Space and Society*, Cambridge: Cambridge University Press.

Stack, S. (1984). 'Income Inequality and Property Crime', *Criminology*, vol. 22, p. 229.

Sullivan, M. (1989), *Getting Paid: Youth Crime and Work in the Inner City*, New York: Ithaca Press.

Sutherland, Edwin H. and Cressey, Donald R. (1978), *Criminology*, 10th edn, Philadelphia: J.B. Lippincott Company.

Taub, R., Taylor, D.G. and Dunham J.D. (1984), *Paths of Neighbourhood Change*, Chicago: University of Chicago Press.

Taylor, Ian (1997), 'Crime Anxiety and Locality: Responding to the "Condition of England" at the End of the Century', *Theoretical Criminology*, vol. 1, p. 53.

Tobias, J.J. (1972), *Crime and Industrial Society in the Nineteenth Century*, Penguin: Harmondsworth.

Vold, George B. and Bernard, Thomas J. (1986), *Theoretical Criminology*, Oxford, Oxford University Press.

Wells, J. (1995), *Employment Policy Institute, Economic Report*, vol. 9, No. 1.

West, D.J. (1982), *Delinquency: Its Roots, Careers and Prospects*, London: Heinemann.

Wikström, P-O.H. (1991), *Urban Crime, Criminals and Victims: the Swedish Experience in an Anglo-American Comparative Perspective*, New York: Springer-Verlag.

Willmott, Peter (1963), *Adolescent Boys of East London*, London: Routledge & Kegan Paul.

Wilson, J.Q. and Herrnstein, R.J. (1985), *Crime and Human Nature*, New York: Simon and Schuster.

Wilson, Roger Cowan (1963), *Difficult Housing Estates*, London: Tavistock.

CHAPTER TWELVE

Anomie, Strain and Juvenile Subculture

12.1 ANOMIE AND CRIMINALITY

Chambers Twentieth Century Dictionary defines 'anomie' as: 'a condition of hopelessness caused by a breakdown of rules of conduct, and loss of belief and sense of purpose in society or in an individual'. In criminological terms it is normally used to depict a state of lawlessness or normlessness.

12.1.1 Durkheim
The term was first used last century as an explanation of human behaviour by the French sociologist and criminologist Emile Durkheim (see the 1933 and 1970 editions of his works). Much of his theory is derived from his work on suicide, rather than on general criminality, but his published ideas have had a lasting effect upon criminological writing. Durkheim describes how societies begin in simple forms of interaction and are held together by solidarity and likenesses. In such societies, the members have similar aims and roles. These generally homogeneous societies he called mechanical. The growth of societies, together with technical and economic advances, make the interrelationships more complicated and diverse. When this happens the functions and positions of individuals in societies will vary and each person's work becomes more specialised. Members of society also become more interdependent. Durkheim called these organic societies. He viewed these changes in society as being natural and unavoidable, leading to greater happiness for individuals because they would be released to enjoy goods produced by others. This transformation in most societies is a gradual occurrence leading to a healthy society. No one society is wholly mechanical or wholly organic. In even the most primitive societies there is some division of labour, and in the most complex there is some uniformity. Every society therefore exhibits elements from each of his categories.

In both types of society law plays an important role. In mechanical societies, its main function is to enforce the uniformity and the *status quo*. In organic societies, its main function is to integrate the diverse parts of the society and ensure that they co-exist without problems. Partly due to the different functions of law in the different societies, crime also plays a different part.

Durkheim recognised that there was criminality in all societies. He saw crime as a normal occurrence, and said that it is impossible to have a society totally devoid of crime. All societies generate some rules and provide sanctions in case these are broken. This would clearly not be necessary unless the activities so prohibited were 'natural' and likely to occur. Therefore, crime is a necessary feature of every society and, provided it does not exceed certain levels, the society is healthy. Durkheim argues that crime originates in society and is a fundamental condition of social organisation, therefore no social organisation can be without crime (this area of his discussion was picked up by the 'New Criminologists' and will be discussed in Chapters Fourteen and Fifteen). He claimed that the best examples of healthy levels of criminality were to be found in simple, mechanical societies.

An unhealthy level of criminality is more likely to arise in an organic society, and to be the result of the law being inadequate to regulate the interactions of the various parts of that society. The incomplete integration gives rise to anomie, one of the results of which is excessive or unhealthy levels of criminality. He used a number of examples, most of which arise from an unbalanced division of labour. These can largely be fitted into three categories. The first was a combination of financial crisis and industrial conflict. The second was rigid and unnatural class divisions, such that the oppressed may rebel. The third and final situation he mentions is where there is an abnormal division of labour, such that workers become alienated from their jobs and become disinterested in them.

In each of these three examples, before anomie can be said to exist the major factor which needs to be present is a financial or industrial crisis – this may be a depression as experienced in the 1930s, or it may arise from a time of unrealistic and precarious prosperity, or from an overly fast industrial growth. For later writers, anomie could exist without the prior need for such an upheaval. But for Durkheim upheavals were necessary. For him anomie was the result of a lack of societal norms or regulations over people's desires and aspirations. 'No living being can be happy or even exist unless his needs are sufficiently proportioned to his means' (*Suicide*, original 1897, reprinted 1970, at p. 246). The only way he saw of regulating or controlling the insatiable desires of humans was by public opinion or morality persuading individuals that what they have is all they morally deserve. A healthy society is therefore one in which the upper and lower limits of the acceptable and reasonable expectations of workers or members of each social class are carefully defined and enforced. He recognised that these societal rules and norms would change over time as economic standards changed. A slow and progressive shift would ease such adjustments, but abrupt or violent econ-omic disasters, or sudden growth of power and wealth, disturb the factors of control and produce anomie. When societal norms are overthrown, there may be resistance to new limitations, and so new norms take a long time to develop. It is at such times that suicide and homicide rates rise. (Later criminologists have attributed growth in crime generally to such changes; see Merton below.) To sum up: Durkheim viewed anomie as a state of lawlessness existing at times of abrupt social change, and affecting in particular the state of 'normlessness' which exists when the insatiable desires of humans are no longer controlled by society.

Durkheim's ideas have, to an extent, been attacked by some writers who claim that crime rates did not increase over the period of the French revolution or during the industrial revolution, periods depicted by Durkheim as being in a state of upheaval and anomie (see McDonald (1982)). The discrepancy in the figures arose because Durkheim based his theories on rates of suicide, which he found to be increasing, and assumed that crime rates were similarly affected. Sainsbury (1955) also found that suicide was related to social disorganisation, but crime was not. However, Durkheim's main thesis was that crime is associated with breakdown of social norms and rules giving rise to an absence of social control. There are two elements to this: the first is the breakdown of regulations, rules and informal limits, undermining confidence in the social structure; the second is that this structural problem leads to psychological feelings of isolation. The overall disorder and disorganisation, social and personal, shifts behaviour in the direction of crime. There may still be substance in this.

12.1.2 Merton

After Durkheim, the most famous criminological writer on anomie is the American Robert K. Merton. He drew on Durkheim's ideas to try to explain the crime problem in the United States of America. Instead of centring problems of anomie on the insatiable desires of human beings, he explains them as something which may exist when desires and needs, though limited, still go beyond what could be satisfied in socially acceptable ways. This is very close to Durkheim's idea of anomie in that it would suggest that to prevent an anomic situation arising, carefully structured norms must be enforced. The difference is that, for Durkheim, the moral norms to be upheld or enforced regulate the individual's desires, whereas for Merton, they would regulate and control the individual's willingness to use unacceptable ways to achieve those desires. Merton therefore argues that society will not be anomic if its members only use legitimate means of advancement, even if their desires are totally unrestricted; it is the relationship between desires and the means of achieving those desires which is fundamental (Merton (1949)). This link between desires and means has led to his theory being called a strain theory; one in which everyone is pressured to succeed, but those who are unable or least likely to succeed by legitimate means are under most strain to use illegitimate or illegal opportunities.

Durkheim said the individual's desires are derived from within the person; in Merton's view the desires of individuals are largely defined by society. Each culture and society has different elements which it considers worth striving for. In America and much of the Western world, this is wealth and, through wealth, material possessions. Wealth is encouraged far beyond its own usefulness, and great wealth is equated with personal value and worth. Those who lack money are looked down on, even if they may have other characteristics which might be given greater worth in other societies. Furthermore, Merton argues that Western cultures, and the American culture in particular, far from limiting desires actually encourages everyone to seek absolute wealth. Everyone is told that further enrichment is possible and that they should all strive towards it. If they do not, they are considered lazy and of less worth (Durkheim would have considered that this alone renders the culture anomic).

Merton maintains that the healthy society lays down accepted means of achieving the ends or goals. In Western cultures, the means of achieving those ends are supposed to be through hard and honest toil, not through theft and fraud. However, the latter means may well be more efficient. If society is to remain healthy, therefore, it is important that participating in the accepted means carries some reward. Merton argued that if society laid sufficient emphasis on conformity (e.g., via systems of reward for conformity or acknowledging any sacrifices made) then it would remain healthy. The philosophy behind this thesis might well be: 'It's not whether you win that matters, it's how you play the game'. However, if the emphasis is on reaching certain goals with no control of the way in which that is achieved, then society would be anomic. He accepted that this unhealthy attitude is prevalent in America, and embodied in commonplace attitudes such as: 'It's winning that matters, not how you play the game'. The 'American Dream' centres on wealth. How that goal is reached has become unimportant, so that the person who achieves wealth through unacceptable or dubious means is still rewarded with prestige, power and social status. Merton said that in such a society the regulatory norms are so undermined that many people either withdraw their support for the rules or withhold their support and live by expediency (i.e., using whatever means, whether legal or not, are most likely to achieve their goals).

Merton applied his ideas to provide an explanation of the pattern of crime as revealed by the official US statistics. Those figures, like those for England and Wales, show a marked discrepancy in criminality between the various strata of society. Each of them show a heavy criminal rate among the lower or working class of society, and a low rate among the upper, moneyed or powerful classes. Whether or not Merton simply accepted the correctness of the official statistics is debatable, but he did accept that there was more crime committed by the lower classes than any other sector of society. It was this discrepancy that he sought to explain.

His original study indicated a large amount of crime throughout American society, and his basic theory was then constructed to fit the statistics and the distribution of crime. Consequently, he argued that only part of American society was anomic, or at least that the anomic nature of that society only caused criminality to arise in one well-defined stratum, namely the lower class (for criticism of this, see Box (1981)). Criminality arose, not necessarily because of discrepancies between the goals and the approved means of achieving those goals, but because all the members of that society were led to believe that there was equality of opportunity. In practice, there were sharp constraints on such purported equality. The consequent feelings of unfairness could lead to criminality. Since the lower classes suffered most from educational and occupational discrimination, they were least likely to attain the 'American Dream' through the legitimate opportunity structures. It was these people who were most likely to escape from low paid and boring jobs by engaging in criminal activities. He argues that anomie becomes the differential application of opportunity rather than an application of social controls or norms; it is a strain theory. Frustration with the system, or possibly economic necessity, gives rise to strain and drives these people to resort to criminality.

Merton's theory is sometimes known as the 'means-end theory' of deviance. It involves an assessment both of desired goals and of structural means. He used their interaction to describe five types of social activity or reaction by individuals to the society in which they live. The first is conformity. In this reactive state, individuals accept both societal goals and society's means of achieving those goals, even when they cannot or clearly will not achieve them. In Merton's view it is because most people fall into this category that society remains basically stable and most people are not criminal. Merton's stress on this aspect probably arose out of his general acceptance of the official statistics. However, as was seen in Chapter Four, there is in fact more criminality committed by a much wider population base than officially recorded. The 'conformity' category is much smaller than envisaged by Merton and, even in stable communities, it may actually be a minority. None the less conformity to goals and means, even if it places individuals in a very unpleasant and undesirable position in society, is very common behaviour.

The other four types of behaviour are all categorised by Merton as deviant, although each covers a very different type of reaction. Of these, the first is called 'innovation', and comprises the individuals who accept social goals but reject the legitimate means of achieving them in favour of more effective but officially proscribed means. It is into this category that he fits most of the individuals who are included in the criminal statistics. Therefore, he sees innovation as most common among the lower class Americans because they are stigmatised because of their low skill, low pay and greater vulnerability to unemployment. The frustrations generated by this may give rise to crime as a means whereby higher status (i.e., wealth) can be reached more quickly. This reaction would be most likely to give rise to crimes against property, such as theft and burglary, or possibly to organised crime where the sole end is financial gain.

The second of Merton's deviant reactions, he calls 'ritualism'. In this category the goals are abandoned but the means are almost compulsively adhered to. This encompasses many lower-middle-class Americans who abandoned any dreams of bettering their lot in life but still stick rigidly to the rules of society. It is questionable whether this is actually a deviant state; it certainly does not involve any criminality. Merton suggested that, because the society sets the goals, lack of desire to fulfil those is itself deviant because it denies part of the culture.

The third deviant reaction he labels 'retreatism', whereby an individual rejects both goals and the means of achieving them. Merton felt that these people did not really belong to the society in which they lived. In this category he included the vagrant or tramp, alcoholics and drug addicts. It might also include racial or religious minorities, particularly if they are severely disadvantaged. All these people might well reject society's goals and the means of achieving them but feel no desire to fight for new ones. Their deviance is negative. The vagrant might well commit public nuisance offences. Alcoholics and drug addicts may commit offences while under the influences of such substances, and might also be driven to commit offences (usually property offences) in order to obtain those substances. The members of minority racial and religious backgrounds might also simply retreat and become introspective, committing no crime in so doing, but not really contributing to society. This behaviour might be viewed as unsociable but clearly cannot be considered deviant in a criminal sense.

Merton then includes 'rebellion' as the last of the reactions resulting in anomie. In this category again both goals and means of achieving them are rejected, but rebellion also includes a desire to substitute new goals in place of the conventional ones. What is involved is a conscious rejection of accepted goals, often combined with a cause or an ideal for which to fight. Their deviance has a positive end which is often pursued by negative means. In this category are the street gang members, the terrorist and/or freedom fighter. The rebellious reaction often involves destructive crimes, such as wilful damage to property and crimes of public disorder. It may even include murder, terrorist offences and any crime designed to attack the basis of the culture.

These five possible reactions of individuals to their society are not mutually exclusive. People may react differently at different times in their lives or in different spheres of their lives (such as at work, or within the family or peer group). For example, a person at work may be a true achiever and hard and dedicated worker who fits into the non-deviant and non-criminal role of conformity. In private, that same individual may use drugs, fitting into a retreatist and necessarily criminal response; and in the public sphere he or she may fight for a political ideal different from that presently existing, and involving a rebellious response which may or may not include criminality, depending on the behaviour chosen to express this political ideal.

Merton stated that his theory of anomie, or 'strain theory' as it is sometimes called, is only intended to explain certain types of criminality, particularly street criminality. This, to an extent, explains why he centres on crimes committed by the lower classes and crimes which may exhibit a lack of opportunity.

More fundamentally, Merton claims that American society, with its concentration on personal wealth and achievement at any cost, generates crime because citizens are encouraged to want and expect a lot but the societal structures necessary to deliver it do not exist. Recently a large part of this thesis has been given renewed attention in the work of Messner and Rosenfeld (1994), who argue that crime (in America) results from the culture of prioritising wealth, which is heavily supported by State institutions which give power to the economy. The cultural pull is the same as that marked out by Merton, but the structural analysis is rather different. For Messner and

Rosenfeld the State structure and social institutions (family, health and education) are designed to give strength to the economy. The American people are socialised to back these structures as supports for the economy – so education is not prized as an end in itself, for learning or personal development, but merely as a means to better paid employment. The culture and institutions centre on money and set values which support the free market. This encourages people to use the most efficient means available to them to attain the desired goals: the opportunities offered in the market economy are accepted by most as the approved and legal way of achieving this; but for some the most efficient means may be criminal. There is a wide range of criminal activities, from crude street crime such as robbery (often armed robbery) to more innovative forms such as insider dealing to defraud the stock market. Messner and Rosenfeld argue that other societies which are less focused on purely monetary values suffer less crime. However, Britain in the 1980s and 1990s has been moving towards a similar priority for market values: if their theory is correct, it does not bode well for British crime rates in the near future.

The policy implications of these approaches are largely outside the purview of the criminal justice system. They require wider political objectives – to provide greater educational and job training opportunities; to build up the possibilities for people to obtain jobs with good wages and reasonable hours; to encourage cultural ideals which focus on community and respect for humanity; and to ensure that more weight is given to the obligations of citizenship (so far as this involves respect for others) – being considered alongside individual freedom and rights.

12.1.3 Durkheim and Merton: a comparison

Durkheim and Merton did not see things in entirely the same light. The former places heavy emphasis upon a condition of 'normlessness' arising out of abrupt change; the latter sees anomie as an endemic condition. Merton says this can exist at any time in any society, as long as the factors mentioned above exist. A society can be basically stable while part, even a large part, of it is anomic.

Durkheim and Merton each document a slightly different idea of anomie. This can be problematic when other authors use the term unless the person using the word makes its meaning perfectly clear. There are two main differences. The first is the more fundamental. Durkheim states that the desires of individuals are natural and fixed, the level of criminal behaviour and of anomie is decided by the efficiency with which these desires are restrained, and that they are most likely to crumble and generate crime in periods of rapid change. Merton, on the other hand, says that society, not the individual, sets the desires and goals, and that same society also sets the acceptable means of achieving the ends. If rewards are only bestowed for obtaining the ends, the restraining means become weakened, encouraging the use of unacceptable and illegal means.

The second, and more practical difference, is that Durkheim talks about a whole society being anomic. Merton would consider that the condition only affects certain parts of the society (i.e., those parts which appear in the official crime statistics), and generally speaking those parts are drawn from the lower classes. Merton in effect focuses on the availability of legitimate opportunities to achieve wealth. These opportunities exist for the higher classes, but not for the lower classes. The absence of such opportunities gives rise to strain and . therefore criminality in the lower classes.

Some now refer to Merton's theory as a strain theory rather than anomie. This is because of his assertion that the motivation to commit crime arises when the legitimate means of achieving success are unavailable. The pressure to succeed exists, but the means are absent. The conflict or strain drives the individual towards a criminal way of achieving the success. This type of pressure is depicted again in subcultural theories (see 11.3). It can be seen as similar to, or closely related to, ideas of relative deprivation (see 12.2).

Most recently, anomie has been used as an explanation for the increase in crime during times of unemployment and recession (see Box (1987)). This last possibility fulfils Durkheim's need for a major upheaval before anomie can exist. Its effects are reinforced if the moral norms promoting acceptance of the rules of society appear to be missing. Some see this absence in the way the mass media, particularly TV, churn out the ideal of a materialistic existence as the norm to which all right-thinking members of society should aspire, even though few will ever achieve such a financial 'nirvana' through legitimate means. For Durkheim, these two factors would make the society anomic and so cause criminality to increase. Obviously, not all members of society will become deviant: some may resign themselves to a less comfortable existence; some may achieve the dream, or alternatively see their chances of doing so as very high, rendering criminality unnecessary. But for others the problem of anomie might be resolved by a resort to criminal conduct.

Merton concentrates more on the opportunity structures. He argues that even in a recession, people are told that there are opportunities and that they are fairly administered. These messages clash with the experience of many, especially the unemployed who have little realistic chance of achieving financial or occupational success. Many will accept their lot, or simply give up any dreams of attaining more than they already have; but there will be others who become sufficiently disillusioned and frustrated for criminality to provide both a release and an achievement. This is especially likely if they view their failure as a fault of the unfair operation of the system, rather than a reflection of their own ability. Although Merton saw this phenomenon as confined to the lower classes, there is no compelling reason why this should be the case. See, for example, the discussion of corporate crime in relation to this theory in Chapter Three. Each corporate body has a goal, usually financial, to achieve (i.e., high and ever-increasing profit). In times of recession, it is more difficult to achieve these goals, and the pressure to use unacceptable and criminal means is much stronger. The more the company, the firm or its executives are pressurised by the recession, the more compelling the temptation to offend by such things as tax evasion, VAT fraud, and cost-cutting in relation to health and safety (see Box (1987)).

Recently, themes such as those found in anomie have been appearing in the theories of Left Realists (see Chapter Sixteen) and in links between crime and modernisation. For a full discussion of these see Downes and Rock (1995), but the core is that there is a problem with the interplay between civilisation and modernity. The assumption is that as civilisation develops the external controls on people's actions become more sophisticated and diverse. Alongside this, people develop internal psychological controls or inhibitions to take into account the more complex standards of acceptable behaviour. Personal conduct as it affects others is thus presumed to have generally improved as civilisation progresses. This supposedly is seen in a general reduction in violence between about 1500 (the late medieval period) and the mid-twentieth century. It is then asserted that, unfortunately, that trend has regressed since the middle of this century, as exemplified both in wars and such brutality as experienced in Germany in the 1930s, or in the former Yugoslavia in the 1980s and 1990s. Ideas of modernity, on the other hand, centre on disruption caused by industry, social upheavals and economic upheavals to explain how controls, both internal and external, designed to prevent criminal activities may break down. The result is the increase in criminality, especially property crimes, in more modern cultures. Both the assumptions and the empirical basis for these sweeping assertions are questionable: they are presented here as one of the ways in which anomie might be used by present theorists to explain crime trends.

It can be seen that anomie, whether in the form defined by Durkheim or in that used by Merton, can have an effect upon the criminality of the State. Each approach explains why some people may be motivated to commit a crime. The theory of anomie therefore can be another useful tool of explanation and prediction for the criminologist.

12.2 STRAIN AND RELATIVE DEPRIVATION

In the previous chapter, the relationship between crime and both poverty and economic inequality was studied. It seemed that, whereas lack of wealth in itself was unlikely to be linked with criminality, there was a link with the unequal distribution of wealth. The possibility thus arises that it is the feeling of unfairness arising from that inequality that causes crime. The relative deprivation theory considers this point.

The idea is straightforward. Some individuals see their present position as comparing unfavourably with others; they desire more; they often feel they deserve more; but if there seems to be no legitimate chance of acquiring more, they may use illegitimate means.

The idea of relative deprivation was first formulated into a full political argument by Runciman (1966), although he did not use it as an explanation of criminality. He saw an individual as relatively deprived of X when:

(a)   he does not have X,
(b)   he sees some other person or persons as having X,
(c)   he wants X, and
(d)   he sees it as feasible that he should have X.

If relative deprivation is present, then feelings of envy and injustice will be present.

Some radical criminologists such as Stack (1984), have used this in explanations of criminality. In Stack's view, the problems caused by relative deprivation grow as more people fall into the category and as the gaps between these people and others grow. He argues that relative deprivation alone will not cause criminality. An individual might fulfil his desire by legitimate means, in this case generally through political struggle to rectify these imbalances. If there is a party which will fight for redistribution of income, or a union which will do the same, criminality is less likely to result. But those who believe that their plight is not addressed by these political means, or consider them irrelevant, may turn to other forms of redress, such as criminality. The criminality here is not a politicised act of trying to redress an unfair imbalance, but rather involves a person acting to try to better his position, often at the expense of others who may well be no better off, or only marginally so.

Relative deprivation as a theory of criminality carries with it the implication that the problem will not be fully redressed until there is a redistribution of income through policies such as full employment, high minimum wages and more equal wealth distribution. It is argued that the problem might be alleviated if fewer people felt politically marginalised and more believed that something might be done. From this standpoint, the criminality arises out of the unfair distribution of wealth which our system upholds.

A dramatic redistribution of wealth such as that envisaged in the previous paragraph would not necessarily stop the crime problem. Indeed, the same theory might well be used as an explanation of the new criminality. In relative deprivation, the feeling of deprivation may arise when an individual compares his situation with that of others or with that of himself at an earlier time. Those made worse off by the redistribution of wealth may feel unjustly treated, and be tempted to turn to criminality in order to regain their former position. The main difference is that the number in this group is likely to be smaller than the number who currently feel relatively deprived.

Box (1987) argues that the explanations provided by theories of relative deprivation are useful to explain higher crime rates in recessions. At such time, he argues, the strain to turn to criminality is stronger because the possibility of serious alterations in wealth distribution seem to be receding. In a society where wealth and possessions are important, and where the media stress this and strengthen people's desires, the feelings of envy and unfairness can only grow in a recession. The resultant strain is particularly strong in certain groups – the young; ethnic minorities; and women, all of whom feel politically marginalised because the solutions which might best address their situations are the least likely to be supported at these times. Criminologists who see this as an important element in criminality tend to advocate socialist solutions of greater equality of position and wealth as the only real solutions to the crime problem.

Currie (1985, 1995 and 1997) has noted that the result of the market economy has been deprivation, a widening of the gap between the rich and the poor and almost a trebling of the number officially included in the latter category between 1979 and 1991. These trends have been accompanied by a withdrawal of public support (financial and social) and an undermining of less formal support mechanisms and control structures such as family and community. He claims that the deprivations, exacerbated by the consumerism so central to a market economy, have fostered crime. To counter this and so address both the social and crime problems, he argues for a move towards full employment at good wages with reasonable hours by:

> . . . substantially expanding employment in public and non-profit making sectors of the economy, and developing policies for worksharing and reduction of work time. (Currie (1997), at p. 168)

This is expected both to provide more people with work and an income, and also to finance the staff for State agencies to support the less fortunate. In the current political climate the claim that such a programme would reduce strain, and with it crime, is unlikely to be tested.

Most of the above strain theorists centred on economic deprivation or relative deprivation, but other, more general strain theorists have different suggestions. So Agnew (1992) has taken a wider view and come up with what he terms a general strain theory which includes three distinct types of strain:

(a) Strain resulting from failure to achieve positively valued goals or goods, which could be seen as the most common form of strain theory used by criminologists in the past. This he once more split into three. The first subgroup arises when aspirations are not achieved and is the form which arises in the strain theories of Merton (see above 12.1.2), Cohen (see below 12.3.2) and Cloward and Ohlin (see below 12.3.3). The goals envisaged in this form have generally been middle-class aspirations. The second subgroup includes those who feel strain as a result of expectations not materialising into desired ends or goals. The expectation arises when people see others similarly placed achieving the desired goals: as their expectation is based on a realistic assessment, and not just on a vain hope or aspiration, the feeling of strain induced by failure is all the stronger. In this area, the desires are personal so the expectations may arise in all sorts of goals, not just those associated with middle-class values. In the final subgroup strain arises when the outcomes are not seen to be based on just decisions. This type of strain involves comparisons with other similar cases. Each of these assumes that the actors are pursuing some sort of goal. The first subgroup has been most studied by criminologists and yet Agnew notes that it is the other two which are most likely to give rise to anger and frustration: Agnew calls on researchers to include all three in testing strain theory.

(b) Strain resulting from the removal of positively valued stimuli. Stack (above) had considered this but was interested mainly in money and employment/unemployment whereas Agnew widens the scope to losing a person through death, divorce, moving away or through argument. All these could be equally traumatic experiences.

(c) Strain resulting from negative stimuli. Strain may arise when a person is faced with an unpleasant consequence or likely consequence such as psychological and other effects of child abuse or family break-up, threats, physical pain or attack, detection, criminal prosecution, punishment or even just embarrassment. This type of strain may give rise to criminality to escape (driving at speed, drug taking), to seek revenge, or to stop the unpleasant experience. Agnew, in earlier research projects, reports that he has found some correlation between crime and this type of strain.

The suggestion is that each of these types of strain is likely to give rise to negative emotions such as disappointment, depression, fear and, most importantly, anger. Agnew associates each of these with offending but the relationship with anger is the strongest. The effects will depend on the magnitude of the strain on the individual (a subjective test), how recent it was, how long it continued and whether incidents were clustered into a short period. Of course there is nothing fatalistic about the relationship and Agnew recognises that even very acute feelings of strain may not result in offending. Much will depend on cognitive abilities to reason the problem through and to place it in perspective, the availability of legal behavioural coping strategies which may work out anger, and emotional coping strategies such as throwing the anger into positive use by digging the garden or by calming the emotion with breathing exercises. The social environment can also help in coping with adversity. Zingraff et al. (1994), though not specifically concerned with strain theory, discovered that good performance, attendance and behaviour in school might help to prevent delinquency and offending even in neglected children or those who had been physically or sexually abused.

As can be seen from the above, Agnew in his general strain theory recognises that there are many non-criminal ways of dealing with strain. Perhaps this explains why many researchers had found only a very weak link between strain and crime. It thus becomes necessary to discover how criminal behaviour might be chosen. Agnew suggests the choice will be influenced by such features as: the importance of the goal to the individual and the presence or absence of other important goals; the differing abilities of the individual to cope through cognitive or problem-solving skills; social support; constraints to criminal activity such as social control (see Chapter Thirteen); fear of getting caught; and whether the wider social environment provides other opportunities or affects choices in other ways. Some of these clearly depend on the temperament of the individual, as well as learning abilities, peer groups and social control.

This is a far more rounded concept of strain and answers many of the problems associated with earlier theories. Agnew and White (1992) have carried out an initial testing of the theory with some positive results but no firm, conclusions can yet be drawn.

12.3 SUBCULTURAL THEORIES OF JUVENILE DEVIANCE

12.3.1 Introduction
The theory of anomie undoubtedly has had a profound effect upon criminology this century, but its explanations are more pertinent for some aspects of

crime than for others. The concept of anomie may be useful as an explanation of property offences, or those offences designed to enhance a person's social or economic standards. These are the crimes which aim to transport people closer to the glossy 'dream', the ideal of today's advertising agencies. The anomie theory is not nearly so useful as an explanation of the negative and damaging offences which are especially frequent in the officially recorded criminality of young persons, while the approaches of strain and relative deprivation only partially fill this gap. This section will thus concentrate on delinquency rather than criminality (see 12.3.2, 12.3.3 and 12.4).

There are two strong reason for concentrating on delinquency. As long ago as 1895 the Gladstone Committee in the UK gave official recognition and strong support to the view that the juvenile delinquent of today is the hardened and persistent adult criminal of tomorrow. By this hypothesis, if juvenile delinquency could be understood and possibly prevented, a large amount of adult criminality could be pre-empted and prevented. There is some apparent support for this notion in the criminal statistics, which show a large drop in the incidence of criminality for people over 21 years of age (in fact, the peak age of offenders is 15; after that age the numbers begin to drop). Furthermore, studies of both habitual adult and of juvenile offenders (e.g., West (1963) and Willmott (1966)) indicate that juveniles often reform and stop committing crimes in early adulthood.

The second reason for the preoccupation with juvenile crime is simply its scale. The fastest rising criminal statistics since the Second World War have been for this group, which now accounts for over one third of all officially recorded crimes. It has thus naturally been perceived as an increasing social problem, which has led to public concern and growing embarrassment for politicians and policy-makers. This perception is sharpened because the crimes with which youths are most often associated are those of wanton violence and destruction where a motive is often difficult to discover. The exact types of menacing behaviour have changed over time, but in Britain have been personified by such groups as Teddy Boys in the 1950s (see Pearson (1983)), muggers (see Hall et al. (1978)), and football hooligans in the 1970s and 1980s. It was also largely youths who were involved with the riots of the early 1980s (see the Scarman Report (1981)). Thus, amongst the criminality which engenders most fear in the community are some forms of youth crime, putting it at the forefront of many recent sociological discussions. With the demographic decline in the proportion of youths in our society, this factor may become less prevalent; the problems caused by this age group may diminish at least in proportion to other problems in society.

Most of the literature on this topic is American, and much of it has centred on gang delinquency and the notion that the gang is a delinquent subculture or part of a lower-class male subculture. The assumption was that most juvenile delinquency took place in gangs or groups, or that it was committed because of pressure from peer groupings. Likewise, it was assumed that the delinquent problem was largely confined to males from the lower or working classes. In part, these assumptions arose because the work was heavily dependent on the official statistics, which in itself leaves it open to criticism.

Official statistics may suffer from all manner of problems in recording, as well as biases arising from the application and policing of the law (see Chapters Four, Fourteen and Fifteen, and Vaz (1967)).

Some critics have argued that crime has the same causes at all levels of society (e.g., Bloch and Neiderhoffer (1958)). In their view delinquency occurs irrespective of social rank or status and is a result, or part, of the general difficulties associated with adolescence. These observers claim that, if there is in fact more delinquency in the lower classes, it arises because these boys face the added problem of trying to adjust to middle-class status: the delinquency is, however, of the same kind and has the same causes. Others, while acknowledging these arguments, point out that despite such opinions (and taking them fully into account) there is still more crime committed by lower-class males than by other groups in society. They see a need to explain the discrepancy.

The theories considered in this section are only interested in explaining certain types of criminality, largely street crimes – brawls, physical attacks which occur in a public place, theft and burglary, criminal damage or similar offences. They are thus limited in their explanation of criminality, although some could have been included in discussions of class theories (11.4) or strain theories (12.2), giving them a degree of validity outside peer culture.

12.3.2 Cohen

Cohen's major work, Delinquent Boys, was published in 1955. In it he claimed that crimes committed by the young could be explained by the subcultural values of the peer grouping. In other words, for the youths concerned, certain activities were correct by the standard of the subculture simply because they were wrong by the norms of the general culture (i.e., the culture of the middle class). Cohen alleged that youths committed malicious and negativistic crimes purely to attack middle-class values. He assumed that middle class values placed more weight on qualities such as drive and ambition; individual responsibility; personal achievement; rational planning and the ability to postpone the gratification of immediate desires for the expectation of future gain; the control of aggression and violence whether verbal or physical; constructive and healthy use of leisure time; and last, but certainly not least, the respect for property, particularly that belonging to other persons. Lower-class values often conflicted with those of the middle class, and included toughness, excitement and immediate gratification.

Cohen argued that, for the working-class boy, the socialisation at home often clashed with that at school leading to inner conflicts and confusion. He argued that the pervasiveness of middle-class values in important areas of the working-class boy's life meant that he had to internalise them. Cohen maintains that there are three possible solutions to the dilemma faced by the working-class boy. The first two he drew from W.F. Whyte's classic categories of college boy and corner boy (see Whyte (1955)). In the college boy solution, youths wholly internalise the values of the middle class and compete for success wholly on those terms – they must try to beat or match the middle class at their own game. Much more common was the corner boy solution, which involved youths accepting their limitations and living within them, making the most of what legitimately comes their way. Both the college boy and the corner boy reactions were essentially conformist and are similar to Merton's conformity referred to above (12.1.2).

The problem solution is the third response, which creates what Cohen described as the delinquent corner boy. Cohen's theory indicated that there are various stages through which a boy must pass in order to become delinquent:

1. He must be subjected to the competing input of working-class socialisation and middle-class values of success, and he must internalise the values.
2. Failure to succeed at school where middle-class values are applied. The innate ability of the youth may be equal to those who succeed; the failure may be due to not having been taught with the necessary skills, or with unfair application of the rules of success.
3. Guilt and shame, leading to a loss of self-esteem and a feeling of rejection.
4. Reaction formation, that is, withdrawal from school and a hostility towards middle-class standards and values.
5. Freedom to join with others in a similar predicament.
6. Negative and malicious behaviour under the new delinquent subculture.

The intentions of the new subculture are therefore non-utilitarian, malicious and negativistic, and those attitudes are epitomised by the boys' behaviour patterns.

Basically, this conduct epitomises the actions of someone who desires but is denied success in the middle-class sense. Even during reaction formation and the negative behaviour performed to show contempt for middle-class values, it is implied that the working-class boys secretly still desire the all-pervasive middle-class success values. Such secret desires may lead to psychological, and sometimes psychopathic, problems.

12.3.3 Cloward and Ohlin

Cloward and Ohlin (1960) also concentrated their efforts upon lower- or working-class youths. They accepted that delinquent acts do occur amongst adolescents from all classes of society, but that for middle-class youths it was far more of an individual struggle. Cloward and Ohlin attached more importance to the criminality of the lower-class juvenile because it illustrates the existence of gangs or subcultures which support and approve of the actions of the delinquent. Furthermore, the lower class delinquent is more likely to receive the support and approval, or at least will not suffer the disapproval, of the non-delinquent and adult members of their class; in fact the lower-class conventions may well support such activity. They therefore see lower-class crime as both more frequent than middle-class crime and as more dangerous, as it portrays a systematic attack on middle class values.

They point out some of the problems with Cohen's arguments by showing that he relies too heavily on the idea that the working-class boy desires middle-class success. They say that this may be true of the college boy if he fails, but it does not apply to most lower or working class boys. They argued that, although these boys might have dreams and aspirations far beyond their expectations, they did not necessarily covet status in terms of middle-class values. Therefore, like Merton, they saw most lower- or working-class boys as goal oriented, and saw their problem as a discrepancy between the available means and the desired ends. They called their theory 'Differential Opportunity Structure'.

In formulating their theory they draw extensively on the ideas of Merton (see above 12.1.2), who argued that crime results from exclusion from legitimate means of achieving success, and of Sutherland's Differential Association (see above 10.2.4), which argues that criminal behaviour is learned from group relationships. Drawing on these theories, Cloward and Ohlin argued that crime occurs because of blocked legitimate opportunities: the type of criminal behaviour which will arise depends on the area and peer grouping or gang with which the individual is connected.

First, Cloward and Ohlin set out the circumstances in which adherence to the conventional and legal behaviour patterns becomes unnecessary. They argue that individuals will only withdraw from legitimate behaviour if the legitimate means are seen to be unfairly applied, i.e., if they feel that the system has caused them to fail. The society professes equal opportunities for all, but the reality is very different. Basically, there are too many people with the natural and necessary ability for the best positions and the highest paid jobs, so selection may be based on subjective criteria such as accent, class, ethnic origin, religion and 'who you know'. The lower-class boys see their legitimate opportunities of success being unfairly blocked by the conventional institutions in society, such as the school and employers. The resultant strain and feeling of unjust deprivation can lead to a withdrawal of support for official norms. This leaves the lower-class youth free to join with others in a similar predicament to form gangs, and possibly to take part in criminal acts without feeling guilty about the morality of his actions. Unlike Cohen's explanation, no psychological problems need arise.

The opportunities for committing crimes are unevenly distributed in society. It is the characteristics of the neighbourhood which most influence the opportunities for committing illegal acts. The most important character-istics are: first, the extent to which conventional, or legitimate behaviour and illegitimate behaviour and values are integrated and accepted; and, secondly, the extent to which there has been integration of offenders of all ages in the neighbourhood. Cloward and Ohlin list three types of illegal opportunity which may be available to the lower-class juvenile: criminal; conflict; and retreatist (the latter is sometimes also known as 'drug-oriented'). It is for this classification that Cloward and Ohlin are probably best known, as it draws together Merton's anomie and Sutherland's differential association theories.

The 'criminal gang' is a juvenile gang whose most important activity is the illegal taking of property. It will only develop in an area where there are opportunities for such offences as stealing and for the receiving and handling of stolen goods. Cloward and Ohlin argue that this environment is most likely to exist if there is adult criminal activity within the neighbourhood. Such misbehaviour by adults provides both the structures and the model roles for criminal activity. It will be further enhanced if there is a stable relationship or understanding between the criminal and (largely) non-criminal adults in the area, especially if there is an interdependence between the two; for example, a shopkeeper who may occasionally be willing to buy and sell stolen items.

All of this means that the neighbourhood gives certain limited criminal activities an air of respectability and apparent legitimacy. The area is relatively stable, but is applying norms different from those present in the rest of society. In such areas the juvenile gangs are most likely to be driven to relatively orderly criminal activity for financial goals. Unpredictable individuals will not be accepted as members; they will therefore be driven to one of the other two types of behaviour.

One of these is the 'conflict gang'. The areas most likely to spawn conflict gangs are usually transient or unstable, often because of shifts in population or because of lack of pride in the community. In such environments, neither criminal nor legitimate role models readily exist for young boys. As a result, they may lack purpose in life, become negative and violent, and form a conflict gang. Lacking social control, whether criminal or legitimate, the result is often a feeling of anger and a desire to prove their worth and status. It is this that turns them to violence.

Cloward and Ohlin's third type of gang – the retreatist or drug-oriented gang – may exist in any neighbourhood where drugs can be obtained. The members of these gangs are 'neither fish nor fowl'; they have failed both in the legitimate and the criminal spheres. Some of these 'failures' may become the stable corner boys referred to by Cohen, but some become members of these retreatist gangs. Which way an individual turns will depend upon their own personalities as well as on their associations and the availability of drugs. Cloward and Ohlin recognise that many gangs probably partake in some drug use, but in most this will only be a peripheral activity. In fact, to talk of 'retreatist gangs' may be a little misleading, as it is rare for a gang culture to centre around drug-taking: more usually the rejection from another gang or absence of other gangs leads the individual to respond by retreating into a more individual pattern of drug abuse.

Cloward and Ohlin predict a growth of conflict-type violent and aggressive behaviour. They see this as a response to the collapse of community spirit in lower-class areas, possibly due to the political changes in slum organisation or clearance. They also documented a recent increase in the modernisation and organisation of American adult crime which they said reduced the opportunities for youths to commit property crimes, driving them towards conflict and retreatist cultures, i.e., towards aggression or use of drugs. The latter argument is not convincing, as there will usually be opportunities for youths to commit less sophisticated crimes.

12.3.4 Evaluation
Some critics have argued (see Box (1981)) that these theories suffer from a basic implausibility. They require lower-class youths to experience strong

disappointment with the dominant culture when it does not deliver them to success, whereas, it is argued that most working- or lower-class boys never expect or aspire to any great success under those values. Such an approach might suggest that it is the lower-stream grammar school boys and mid-to upper-range comprehensive boys (or as Cohen calls them, the 'college boys') who are most likely to suffer disappointment because of their relative lack of success. It is an hypothesis which raises its own set of possibilities and problems. As will be seen from the sections concerning school and control theories (see Chapter Thirteen), there is much evidence that school itself does not cause rebellion against middle-class norms, but boredom may lead to outbursts of energy which may be of unacceptable and possibly even criminal behaviour. For example, Corrigan (1979) in his study of two schools in Sunderland argues that delinquency, particularly fighting and wanton destruction, is a role played by the youths to make their lives more exciting.

In addition, the explanations described in this section provide no convincing basis to account for the fact that many of the youths tend to reform or stop committing criminal acts at the end of their teens and the onset of adulthood. They mostly remain members of the same social class, and there is no obvious reason to believe that they all find their lot improving and enjoy sudden success at the age of about twenty. If the initial juvenile criminality is due to a reaction against the middle-class norms, or at least influenced by them, why does this behaviour change although there is little or no change in those values? Cohen might make a plausible response to this paradox by saying that it is the standards applied at school which first cause the delinquency; leaving school alleviates the problem, and criminal behaviour therefore stops, or at least reduces. The rate of criminality does begin to decline at sixteen, and drops rapidly at around age twenty, so there could be some weight in this explanation. It might also be that the young feel more outrage at what they may see as unfair workings of society, and as they mature they slowly come to accept the *status quo* or limit their opposition to passive resistance. It may also be that as they grow older they become more domesticated, and acquire responsibilities which leave them less free to participate in criminality. Perhaps adult frustration comes out in different ways, such as in domestic violence (crime), or in anti-social rather than criminal ways. Farrington (1991), in arguing this, also suggests that the problem originates much earlier than these subcultural theories suggest: childhood behavioural problems become juvenile criminal behaviour and then adult anti-social activities.

Both Cohen and Cloward and Ohlin draw to a large extent on the strain or anomic theories of Merton. They usefully show how that theory might be adapted to explain crimes which do not appear to be motivated by greed. They draw on Merton to explain how the strain might result in crimes of protest as much as in crimes of purpose.

12.3.5 The British situation
It was initially indicated that most of these theories originate in the US: their relevance to British criminality must be considered. One consistent theme was that of the delinquent subculture, peer group or gang. Do such gangs

exist in Britain? In most British studies, strong and structured juvenile gangs, particularly gangs whose central intention is to commit delinquent acts, are largely absent (see for example Mays (1975), and Downes (1966)). It also seems that most British juvenile delinquency is committed in twos and threes, and while each of the participants is likely to be part of a particular circle of friends (or peer group), not all members of this circle of friends will necessarily commit criminal acts (see Downes (1966), and Jensen and Rojek (1980)). Therefore, the idea of a strong and leading delinquent gang inadequately describes the position in Britain, although there are examples of looser peer groupings which commit some acts of criminality (see Corrigan (1979)). A further problem, particularly associated with Cohen's theory, is that recent British studies of gangs do not uphold the idea that gang members derive heightened self-esteem from association with other members (see Jensen and Rojek (1980)).

Similarly, it is not obvious that any easy translation can be made into a British context of Cloward and Ohlin's notion of splitting delinquency into three types: criminal; conflict; and retreatist. The pattern of behaviour they called criminal existed in the districts where there was a well-defined criminal opportunity structure, partly drawn up from Mafia-type organisations which can be seen to exist in many urban areas in the United States. In Britain such groups are seemingly infrequent (see Downes (1966)). Much adult British crime tends to be committed in small groups, and membership tends to be transient and brought together for particular crimes or 'jobs'. There is, of course, organised crime, particularly in drug-trafficking, prostitution, gambling and 'protection', but this is (or has been) less pervasive in Britain. The inference is that, in the absence of a structured adult criminality, fewer adolescents will aspire to a criminal career. A more common influence may possibly come from the workman who steals from work and sells the goods fairly openly within the community, giving youngsters the impression that stealing is normal (see Willmott (1966)). This apparent normality may contribute to the high levels of delinquent theft. Any full explanation would also need other elements, such as the desire for excitement included in biological and psychological theories of delinquency (see Chapters Six and Seven).

The US concept of conflict delinquency is closely related to Cohen's notions of gang fights and protection of 'turf' in America. Such activity is said to be virtually non-existent in Britain, although the activities of drug dealers may be altering this pattern. There are of course fights, but rarely between two structured gangs and rarely over their 'turf' or 'patch'. This interpretation may not be giving sufficient weight to the obvious exception of football violence and fights between the old Mods and Rockers, but that apart, most British fights are said to be spontaneous and between looser peer groupings (see Willmott (1966) and Corrigan (1979)). Acts of destruction, which are also mentioned by Cloward and Ohlin, are clearly visible in British juvenile crime. They are especially prevalent in high-rise buildings where there is little sense of community and a lot of social disorganisation.

The third category, retreatism, has perhaps become more important in recent years as more British youths turn to alcohol and drug abuse. However, even in America this is, as Cloward and Ohlin say, a less structured group activity.

The perhaps surprising conclusion – given the pervasive nature of the British class systems – is that the strong class-based and subcultural theories of both Cohen and of Cloward and Ohlin are of only limited relevance in Britain. Nonetheless, when allowance is made for cultural differences, similar strains do appear with similar, if less rigidly group-oriented, results (see, for example, Willmott (1966)). In this respect, the American theories may be of substantial relevance to juvenile crime in Britain.

In any event, ruling out these very structured concepts of peer influence does not remove the possibility that youths are encouraged to offend partly due to influences of their peers, using the word in a much looser idea of friends. West and Farrington (1973) found a relationship between the offending of young boys and those of their friends, despite also finding that delinquents and offenders are generally unpopular. The unpopularity may be explained away: a general unpopularity is not inconsistent with being popular with other delinquents. In 1977 the same researchers claimed that withdrawal from a delinquent or criminal peer group (of friends) was an important indicator of an end to the offending of an individual. A correlation between offending and peers was found to be strongest when the individual felt most attached to his or her peers (emotional closeness and a tendency to see the peers as role models), felt most peer-group pressure to conform and was in frequent contact with them (see Agnew (1991)). Interestingly Agnew found that the effects were strongest when an individual formed a close attachment to a peer group which committed serious offences. Each of these suggest a link between offending and the offending of peers and close friends. It has also been suggested (Hirschi (1969)) that although offenders tended to have delinquent friends, both were caused by a third factor, such as the breakdown of one or more of the social controls. Others (Wilson and Herrnstein (1985)) claim that the peer group has an effect which precipitates criminal behaviour because the peers supply attitudes which tend to favour criminal behaviour.

Interpretation of the information is difficult, especially, and crucially, in terms of causation. Does it mean that offenders forge close friendships because they are isolated and rejected by non-offenders or because they seek out those who indulge in similar activities or is the criminal activity committed only because of encouragement from friends? Since many young males commit offences in pairs or other groupings does this mean that the dynamics of these friendships influence the criminality, or simply that the offenders are out together when they decide to offend when they might have decided to do something else, such as catch a bus? Is peer-group influence only a factor because the shared experience makes it more pleasurable and, if so, why is it more pleasurable? Is there a causal relationship, a link, a chance incidence or some combination of these?

12.4 MATZA AND SYKES

In 1957, David Matza and Gresham Sykes produced a theory of delinquency which, because he later extended it, has come to be generally attributed to

Matza alone (Sykes and Matza (1957); Matza (1964) and (1969)). Although it was designed to explain juvenile crimes, and most of this section will be devoted to that area, the central thesis may be extended to cover some adult crime, and some of the examples in this section are designed to show how this might be possible. Matza's main theme concerned what he called drift. In contrast to the theories so far covered Matza's theory of drift involves an element of free will, individual choice and judgment on behaviour. This admission of free will into his doctrine is, to a certain extent, a return to the classical school of criminology which existed before positivism became popular.

The analyses of the positivists seem to imply that there should be much more criminality: they cannot explain why those we think of as criminals are law-abiding in most respects; nor can they explain why most criminals reform in their early 20s; and they cannot account for the fact that in areas where the social forces militate towards criminality most people are in fact law-abiding. Sykes and Matza argued that individuals are not committed to criminality. The concept of drift basically situates the individual as drifting at will between law-abiding and delinquent or criminal behaviour, being never committed to either type of behaviour. The state of drift is reached because of what Matza terms neutralisation. Neutralisation arises from the fact that every criminal law has its limits, usually denoted by official defences to the activity, and therefore every law is qualified. Matza suggests that the juvenile uses these limits, extending their interpretation in ways which allow the action without guilt or remorse: it can be justified both to self and others by pleading, say, self defence, duress or even insanity. Part of this process also involves a distortion of other areas of the dominant value system. A minor element of the dominant value system encourages individuals to seek excitement and adventure. These objects are normally made subordinate to more dominant ideals such as hard work. Matza argues that delinquents take these subordinate values, extend them, and use them in inappropriate ways and times. Thus violence may be acceptable in boxing or possibly other sports, but the delinquent, without generally approving of violence, may extend the times and places where it is acceptable, for example by using it in gang fights or pub brawls. Similarly, no action is absolutely condemned; even killing is permitted as self defence or by accident, and it may be positively required at times of war or for the purposes of judicial execution. In those who take part in criminal activities, such reasons are given a wider interpretation than those accepted by the conforming members of society. The justifications for the criminality are therefore in a perverse way derived from the norms of the dominant culture. In Matza's theory, the individual does not fully accept or internalise any set of rules or norms, but has rather learnt a set of 'definitions favourable to violation', while still tacitly subscribing to many of the middle-class rules.

Matza and Sykes (1957) list five justifications (before the act) or excuses (after the act) which delinquents (and others) may use to explain or neutralise criminal acts:

(1)   Deny responsibility, usually by claiming that the act was a result of uncontrollable factors: an accident, parental neglect, poverty, broken home,

being led astray by friends. This type of excuse is not restricted to juveniles and is often seen in offences committed by white-collar and, especially, corporate criminals. Such offenders frequently claim that they were forced to act by their superiors; or acted only out of a sense of responsibility to some larger entity (see the claims of Colonel Oliver North); or that it was the fault of subordinates who had been negligent (see the attempt to pass responsibility in the case of the sinking of the Channel ferry called the *Herald of Free Enterprise*).

(2)   The criminal may claim that no-one was actually harmed, either physically or financially. If items are stolen from wealthy individuals, or from employers or large shops, it may be said that they can afford the loss or that the insurance company will pay. The same person might well perceive theft from an identifiable fellow individual as immoral. Again, this may be used to explain a lot of white-collar and corporate crime. A quite different set of activities, gang fights, pub brawls or domestic violence, are often seen by their perpetrators as private and therefore not criminal. Domestic violence may even be perceived as being for the victim's good. In all these cases the perpetrators may be basically law-abiding but have an extended view of acceptable behaviour.

(3)   The claim that the victim deserved the harm caused and so is not a true victim (e.g., the victim is also criminal and so should not complain; or the victim started the trouble and so 'only got what was coming'). Similarly, in the case of sex crime: 'she was asking for it because of the way she was dressed'; and in domestic violence, that the victim deserved the violence as he or she had misbehaved.

(4)   An offender might claim that since everyone has at some time committed a criminal act, no-one is in a position to condemn him.

(5)   The approval of the group or gang (or the corporation) may be said to be more important than those of the family or of society. Thus, where the group calls for delinquency it is justified.

In part, these justifications underline Matza's main point that the individual has in a particular instance chosen delinquent behaviour. The way in which free will is exercised is influenced by a variety of factors, but the youth is not bound by the constraints of a group. A person can react and respond to opportunities to commit crimes, or can decide whether a particular time, place and environment is well suited to breaking the rules. The group, subculture or gang may make such activity more likely by promoting it, but it does not make the behaviour mandatory. For Matza, there is a major flaw in the works of both Cohen and of Cloward and Ohlin: in each case the individual who turns to the peer group gives up or escapes the constraints of conforming to official behaviour for the equally demanding and constraining requirement of conforming to the subcultural values. Matza rejects this idea, and gives the individual greater freedom to choose whether to commit a criminal act and to do so for a personal reason, rather than merely as a requirement of a group.

12.4.1 Evaluation

Matza's ideas became widely accepted. This can be partially explained by the time in which they were posited. The end of the fifties and the early sixties were seen as a period in which society began to change. In both America and Europe there had been a very conventional acceptance of family life and legality. This began to be questioned by such movements as the Southern Christian Leadership Conference (SCLC) led by Martin Luther King, and the civil rights movement. This was also reflected in the arts, which were exploding with radical and rebellious ideas, evidenced in literature by the 'angry young men' and in music by 'rock and roll'. The cultural change extended the acceptable areas of behaviour. Convention, for example, had made alcohol the only acceptable social drug, whereas acceptability began to be extended, in certain sectors of society, to marijuana and in some cases the more psychedelic drugs. Despite its wide acceptance, it is necessary to assess its usefulness.

Matza asserts that neither the individual nor the peer group is totally opposed to the norms of the dominant social order. He suggests that it would be impossible for a juvenile subculture to evolve in which the members' views were diametrically opposed to adult (or middle-class) values, as the latter are too closely connected with the juveniles to allow such a wholesale breach with dominant culture. His central starting point is rather the significance of individual 'drift', to which is added the importance of peer group setting, particularly during adolescence. Although the members of the peer group may not be individually opposed to adult values, the desire to feel 'strong', 'virile' or 'masculine', or to prove loyalty to the group, may lead them outwardly to express opinions or partake in activities contrary to the adult values.

Matza's is not a pure subcultural theory because, despite its close connection with a delinquent group, the delinquency arises out of the state of drift which is an individual feeling. Juveniles are subject to both conventional values, as promoted by adults, and delinquent influences, as arise in the peer group or subculture. They respond to both these pressures; some of their activities mostly derive from one and some mostly from the other. Unlike Cohen, or Cloward and Ohlin, where the delinquency was a direct result of the peer group, in Matza's theory it can exist apart from it. For him, the subculture permits delinquency but it does not demand it.

Matza's views are, to an extent at least, upheld by the findings of Short and Strodtbeck (1965). They claimed that their research showed that gang boys, lower-class boys (who did not belong to gangs) and middle-class boys all, in a general sense, held middle-class goals and behaviour in high esteem. The biggest difference was that the gang boys had a low evaluation of middle-class values which proscribed certain behaviour. They were, for example, more tolerant of petty thieving and violence. The gang members were thus licensed to take part in certain delinquent activities without abandoning middle-class values in general. Matza attributed this ability to stretch social values to his concept of neutralisation; Short and Strodtbeck attributed it to a lack of commitment to such social institutions as the family, school and work. They argue that this stretching of social values is not necessarily determined by social class; anyone who loses close contact with social institutions might turn to criminality regardless of their social class (see also Chapter Thirteen in which the effect of these social institutions is discussed).

The negative element of some juvenile delinquency can also be explained by Matza's theory. An individual in a state of drift and wishing to prove his ability to control his life might perform an action merely because it is criminal. No prediction is attached to this: there is simply the possibility that an individual might decide to perform a criminal act and might also be able to exercise some choice over the type of criminality.

Indeed, Matza's theory differs in a number of ways, most of which seem to carry a great deal of empirical as well as intuitive conviction, from the other theories in this section. It is not so wedded to the idea of a gang or subculture with the sole aim of committing criminal acts. It is the individual who is delinquent, although environmental and social factors may well render such activity more likely. In this way, delinquency can be strongly reinforced by a subculture or gang, which thus continues to act as a factor in Matza's construction. However, the distinctive feature to emphasize is that Matza sees most delinquents as being neither committed to criminality, nor to law-abiding behaviour: they have some area of choice as to whether they will perform criminal acts when both the opportunity and the temptation arise.

12.5 CONCLUSION

This chapter has sought to introduce a variety of sociological and pseudo-sociological explanations of crime. Recent developments which stand somewhat apart from the others are Agnew's general strain theory (see 12.2), which allows a subjective assessment both of what is important and of differing personal ways and abilities of coping with strain, and Currie's explanation of how relative deprivation can create tensions leading to criminality. The increased emphasis on personal, as against social and cultural, factors represents an exciting new facet to strain theory and one which needs rigorous empirical testing. The other writers surveyed in this chapter all stress various aspects of the relationship between individuals and society, emphasising the greater likelihood of criminal activity arising whenever this relationship is seriously lacking in harmony. Several manifestations of possible antagonism or conflict between individuals (or specific groups) and the dominant values and behaviours of society have been explored. The explanations have been broadly categorised under three main concepts: anomie; strain; and subculture. To a large extent, these explanations have in common a strong tendency to situate these disjunctures primarily – but not exclusively – in the lower orders of society, and to find them to be especially potent amongst young males in those groups. They fail to address the reasons why women, who suffer from the same social conditions, are not similarly affected and do not also turn to crime in large numbers. This failure reduces the explanatory power of these theories (see also Chapter Eleven). Consequently, the contribution these explanations make to understanding criminal behaviour is greatest when working-class, youth crime and delinquency is being considered.

The policy implications are various. In the criminal justice sphere they mainly seem to be aimed at preventing the problem manifesting itself as criminal activity. The implication seems to be that offenders, following one or a few violations, should be removed from society for a period of time. This is both an expensive option and one which is invasive of personal freedom, but many see it as a necessary preventative measure. Other possible policies might be to require proof of acceptable lifestyles and conduct before any access to welfare, and/or a type of fortress existence whereby the 'worthy' are protected from the activities of the 'underclass' who are left to prey on each other. The latter proposal assumes that the population can be clearly and fairly divided up into moral groups: this seems unlikely on any proper study of society and criminality, including white-collar, corporate and domestic crimes. Other policy implications largely lie outside the criminal justice system: provision of greater educational and job training opportunities; increased job opportunities involving good wages and reasonable hours; an expansion of the public sector to provide services to the less well off; promoting feelings of inclusion of all citizens; and encouraging cultural ideals which focus on community and respect for others.

REFERENCES

Agnew, R. (1991), 'The Interactive Effects of Peer Variables on Delinquency', *Criminology*, vol. 29, p. 47.

Agnew, Robert (1992), 'Foundation for a General Strain Theory of Crime and Delinquency', *Criminology*, vol. 30, p. 47.

Agnew, Robert and White, Helen Raskin (1992), 'An Empirical Test of General Strain Theory', *Criminology*, vol. 30, p. 47.

Bloch, H. and Neiderhoffer, A. (1958), *The Gang, A Study In Adolescent Behaviour*, New York: Philosophical Library.

Box, Steven (1981), *'Deviance Reality and Society'*, 2nd edn, London: Holt Rinehart and Winston.

Box, Steven (1987), *'Recession, Crime and Punishment'*, London: Macmillan Education.

Cloward, Richard and Ohlin, Lloyd (1960), *Delinquency and Opportunity*, London: Collier-Macmillan.

Cohen, Albert (1955), *Delinquent Boys: The Culture of the Gang*, New York: The Free Press.

Corrigan, Paul (1979), *Schooling the Smash Street Kids*, London: Macmillan.

Currie, Elliot (1985), *Confronting Crime: An American Challenge*, New York: Pantheon Books.

Currie, Elliot (1995), 'The End of Work: Public and Private Livelihood in Post-employment Capitalism', in Stephen Edgell, Sandra Walklate and Gareth Williams (eds), *Debating the Future of the Public Sphere*, Aldershot: Avebury.

Currie, Elliot (1997), 'Market, Crime and Community: Toward a Mid-range Theory of Post-industrial Violence', *Theoretical Criminology*, vol. 1, p. 147.

Downes, David M. (1966), *The Delinquent Solution*, London: Routledge & Kegan Paul.

Downes, David and Rock, Paul (1995), *Understanding Deviance: A Guide to the Sociology of Crime and Rule Breaking*, 2nd edn, Oxford: Clarendon Press.

Durkheim, Emile (1933) (original 1893), *The Division of Labour in Society*, Glencoe, Illinois: Free Press.

Durkheim, Emile (1970) (original 1897), *Suicide*, London: Routledge & Kegan Paul.

Farrington, David P. (1991), 'Antisocial Personality from Childhood to Adulthood', *The Psychologist*, vol. 4, p. 389.

Hall, S., Cutcher, C., Jefferson, T. and Roberts, B. (1978), *Policing the Crisis*, London: Macmillan.

Hirschi, T. (1969), *Causes of Delinquency*, Berkeley, Ca: California University Press.

Jensen, Gary F. and Rojek, Dean G. (1980), *Delinquency*, Lexington, Mass.: D.C. Heath.

McDonald, Lynn (1982), 'Theory and Evidence of Rising Crime in the Nineteenth Century', *British Journal of Sociology*, vol. 33, p. 404.

Matza, David (1964), *Delinquency and Drift*, London: Wiley.

Matza, David (1969), *Becoming Deviant*, New Jersey: Prentice Hall.

Mays, John Barron (1975), *Crime and its Treatment*, 2nd edn, London: Longman.

Merton, Robert K. (1949), *Social Theory and Social Structure*, New York: Free Press.

Messner, S.F. and Rosenfeld, R.R. (1994), *Crime and the American Dream*, Belmont, Ca: Wadsworth.

Pearson, G. (1983), *Hooligan: A History of Respectable Fears*, London: Macmillan.

Runciman, W.G. (1966), *Relative Deprivation and Social Justice*, London: Routledge & Kegan Paul.

Sainsbury, Peter (1955), 'Suicide, Delinquency and the Ecology of London', from *Suicide in London*, Institute of Psychiatry, reprinted in W.G. Carson and Paul Wiles (eds), *The Sociology of Crime and Delinquency in Britain*, vol. 1, Oxford: Martin Robertson.

Scarman, Lord (1981), *The Brixton Disorders, 10-12 April 1981* (Scarman Report, 1981), Cmnd 8427, London: HMSO.

Short, J.F. and Strodtbeck, F.L. (1965), *Group Process and Delinquency*, Chicago: University of Chicago Press.

Stack, S. (1984), 'Income Inequality and Property Crime', *Criminology*, vol. 22, p. 229.

Sykes, Gresham M. and Matza, David (1957), 'Techniques of Neutralization: A Theory of Delinquency', *American Sociological Review*, vol. 22, p. 664.

Vaz, Edmund (ed.) (1967), *Middle-class Juvenile Delinquency*, New York: Harper and Row.

West, D.J. (1963), *The Habitual Prisoner*, London: Macmillan.

West, D.J. and Farrington, D.P. (1973), *Who Becomes Delinquent?*, London: Heinemann.

West, D.J. and Farrington, D.P. (1977), *The Delinquent Way of Life*, London: Heinemann.

Whyte, William Foote (1955), *Street Corner Society: The Social Structure of an Italian Slum*, 2nd edn, Chicago: Chicago University Press.

Willmott, Peter (1966), *Adolescent Boys of East London*, London: Routledge & Kegan Paul.

Wilson, J.Q. and Herrnstein, R.J. (1985), *Crime and Human Nature*, New York: Simon and Schuster.

Zingraff, Matthew T., Leiter, Jeffrey, Johnsen, Matthew C. and Myers, Kristen A. (1994), 'The Mediating Effect of Good School Performance on the Maltreatment–Delinquency Relationship', *Journal of Research in Crime and Delinquency*, vol. 31, p. 62.

CHAPTER THIRTEEN
Control Theories

13.1 INTRODUCTION

The term control, and particularly social control, can be taken to have all sorts of meanings. To most politicians or political theorists it would mean the control of political opposition, or possibly its suppression. To most sociologists it includes all the social processes which militate for conformity, from infant socialisation, through school and job to the public and State control systems such as the police, the courts and the punishment systems.

Most of the theorists discussed in earlier chapters have assumed that conformity is normal or natural, and criminality is abnormal. It is then often argued that there is no justification for individuals to break the law unless something abnormal is present. Some base that abnormality in the individual, such as biological abnormalities or personality defects. Others see criminality as a social problem, arising out of social disorganisation, unemployment, culture conflicts or strain. At least one such factor is seen as being necessary before the natural order of conformity can be broken. The control theorists largely attack that central assumption. Their basis is that every individual is born free to break the law. It is criminality which is natural, and conformity needs explanation. The main question here is therefore: why don't we all break the law? Conformity is seen as the result of special circumstances, and criminality is to be expected if these special circumstances break down. For example, there is nothing natural about driving on one side of the road, and yet motorists do keep to the required side. It is not natural to buy rather than take food when one sees it, and yet in our society most people buy rather than take. There is clearly nothing natural about conformity, as most of our formative years are spent learning what is permitted behaviour and what is not, and often why the difference exists. Parents at home, teachers at school and other individuals in the community, particularly the social control agencies such as formal religious bodies, the police and the courts, spend a lot of time and effort in controlling each of us.

Each society makes rules and tries to restrict its members to partake only in activities which are acceptable to the social order. Control theories explain how societies persuade people to live within these rules. It is important to note that conformity is always seen as fragile, as something which might be broken at any time if the reason for conformity is weakened, lost or momentarily broken. Criminality is therefore the breakdown of the socialisation process.

All this is open to a variety of interpretations, but this chapter will concentrate on the more influential. To illustrate some of the diversity the work of Reiss and Reckless will be mentioned, but the main thrust of this chapter will be on Hirschi and others who have drawn on his work. Most of these worked with juveniles, but unlike the subcultural theories in Chapter Twelve, many of these can also be used as explanations of adult crime.

13.2 EARLY CONTROL THEORIES

Control theories draw on both psychological and social factors to explain criminality. The psychological aspects can be seen most clearly in the earlier work of writers like Reiss and Reckless.

Reiss (1951) discussed the effects of 'personal control' and 'social control' on delinquency. Here, 'personal control' denotes how well the juvenile manages to resist using socially unacceptable methods to reach his goals. This assessment of the individual control is based in the psychological diagnosis of the development of the super-ego, and therefore indicates a Freudian basis. In this case conformity meant that the individual accepted the rules and norms as his or her own, or submitted to them as a rational control of behaviour in a social setting – a healthy super-ego. Delinquency denoted the opposite of this.

'Social control' is the ability of social groups or institutions to make norms or rules effective. Conformity resulting from social controls tends to involve submission to the rules and norms of society. Reiss's work was concerned with predicting juvenile crime. He tried to base predictions on the willingness of the individual to submit to social controls, particularly in school, but found this to be an invalid predictor. A much better predictor he found in the psychiatrists' analyses of the individual's super-ego or internal controls (see 8.2).

Reckless (1967) and (1973), posited a containment theory in which the main thread is that there are pushes (drives) and pulls which tend to tempt a person towards delinquency. Prevention requires the exercise of control by factors which insulate the individual against such temptations. Drives, pulls and insulation could all arise either within the individual or outside him.

Psychological desires or propensities, such as restlessness and aggression, might be the internal elements which push the individual towards criminality. External factors which may push towards criminality could be social pressures such as poverty, family conflicts and lack of opportunities. Pull factors are generally external and might include the availability of illegitimate opportunities, criminal peer groups and, he claims, some mass media images (but see 10.2.2).

Similarly, insulators or containments against criminality might be both internal or external. Internal insulators could include the psychological position of the individual such as the development of the super-ego; a sense of direction; the ability to find alternative legitimate fulfilment; and a commitment to values or laws and feelings of responsibility. External insulators may be illustrated by having a meaningful role to play in society, reasonable expectations, a sense of belonging and identity, supportive relationships, especially in the family, and adequate discipline.

The most distinctive element in the writings of Reckless is that of the self-concept. This is internal, and his claim was that those individuals with a strong and favourable self-concept were best insulated against the drives and pulls towards criminality. A favourable self-concept might be illustrated by saying that the individuals view themselves in a positive way: as having values to live up to; as being law-abiding; and as having an idea of being of use and value to society and those in it. Parents affected an individual's self-concept most strongly, but other influences came from teachers and others in authority.

Reckless argued that this theory had a number of advantages – he claimed it could be applied to individuals; the various constraints could be measured; it could be applied to explain both conformity and criminality; and it could be used for the treatment and prevention of criminality. He carried out a number of studies which seemed to suggest that the theory was vindicated by being a good tool for predicting delinquency (Reckless (1967) and (1973)). However, one carried out in conjunction with Simon Dinitz (Reckless and Dinitz (1972)) found that of the boys the containment theory predicted would become delinquents, only 40 per cent had had contact with the police in the following four years. Other studies also throw these claims into doubt (Schwartz and Tangri (1965)).

Despite these doubts and assertions that the key terms are ill-defined and too general, strengthening people's self-esteem has been used to train them away from criminality. McGuire and Priestly (1985) claim that strengthening an individual's morals and feelings of altruism raises their feelings of worth and self-esteem, which decreases the likelihood of future criminality. This would involve using the learning techniques discussed in 10.2, and has been seen to achieve some success.

13.3   INDIVIDUAL CONTROL

Most of this chapter will be devoted to the social control theories. These are strongly based on external controls, often state or societal, as providing the impetus to legality, the bond to society which will tend to reinforce legal behaviours. In this the control is largely external and structural. Gottfredson and Hirschi (1990) have moved away from this towards a control theory based almost exclusively on individual aspects. It is interesting that Hirschi should be one of the leaders in this new move as he is also one of the central figures in the structural or social control theory.

The approach suggested by Gottfredson and Hirschi in their book, *A General Theory of Crime* (1990) and their re-discussion of it in 1993, unlike the ideas on individual control discussed earlier (Chapters Seven to Ten), does not propose a biological or genetic reason for criminality. Their focus is on self-control formed by early childhood socialisation, particularly in the family, and provides a wide theory of criminality, not dependent on legal definitions. It purports to explain all acts of 'force or fraud taken in pursuit of self-interest' (p. 15), which probably includes all property offences and acts of violence. There are two dependent aspects: the lack of self-control of the individual; and the opportunity for committing crimes. If the opportunity to commit a crime arises then the person with low self-control will commit it, whereas the person with high self-control will not. As they present their theory, low self-control is the central aspect, but will operate to give rise to criminal acts only if the opportunity arises.

By self-control they mean a subjective state whereby one individual is more vulnerable to the temptations of the moment than is another. It is an assessment of how restrained each individual feels about his or her actions. A person who lacks self-control will like quick, easy tasks where the outcome is clear and positive, will lack diligence and tenacity and will be impulsive; unable to postpone gratification; insensitive; self-centred and indifferent to the needs and sufferings of other people; risk-taking; short-sighted; non-verbal and short-tempered; easily frustrated; and physical, preferring physical activity to mental or cognitive experience. The assumption is that most of these traits come together in the sort of person who will find it difficult to resist the temptation to criminality. Furthermore, the traits arise at a young age, well before the usual age of criminal responsibility, and endure until death.

Although Gottfredson and Hirschi recognise that most crime is committed by the young and that the rate of offending declines as the age rises, they deny that there has been a change in criminality, arguing that the individual will still have low self-control but the problem may manifest itself in non-criminal activities. They also recognise that women commit less crime than men, but do not accept that women necessarily have greater self-control: they see the explanation in closer socialisation by their families when they are young. They also account for the sex difference by asserting that women may not get as many opportunities to commit offences as their male counterparts, and so their criminality may come out in non-criminal activities. The claim is thus that low self-control means criminality, but this may or may not manifest itself in criminal activity: the opportunities open will be the strongest factor operating on how criminality will manifest itself. If it does not lead to offending, it will come out in other imprudent activities such as heavy drinking or smoking, unemployment, a bad work record, failure in marriage, unwanted pregnancies, and even a greater likelihood of being involved in road and other accidents. Low self-control, when it coincides with opportunity, is supposed to predict all of these. If valid, this theory would explain differences in offending over time (for the same offender and for different offenders), in different locations, and between individuals.

In their theory the low self-control is not learned: no class or racial group intentionally teaches it. On the contrary, almost all socialisation is designed to teach self-control. The implication would appear to be that lack of self-control must be inherent. This would send us back to the earlier discussions but Gottfredson and Hirschi are very careful to exclude this possibility. Instead they state that any person can be effectively socialised but that individual differences can influence the prospects of effective or adequate socialisation. But this simply shifts the ambiguity which they attempt to resolve by asserting: that the object of offending is always to maximise immediate pleasure; that without socialising most individuals would try to maximise pleasure; and thus teaching self-control is an essential precondition for law-abiding behaviour. The adequacy or otherwise of the socialisation – monitoring the behaviour of the child, recognising deviant or unacceptable behaviour and punishing such behaviour – determines how well self-control is developed. This aspect of the theory is therefore external, the self-control is externally shaped by socialisation or the lack thereof, but once the level of self-control is formed it is internal. In their view most of this socialisation occurs in the family, relegating other frequently cited socialising influences, such as peer groups and school, to peripheral roles in the formation of self-control. Peer pressure comes after self-control is formed and is merely confirming: school can only reinforce (not replace) the family socialisation because those with already low self-control are ill-equipped to learn new skills. The heavy stress on the family has been attacked by some feminists because it tends to blame the mother, often in reality the foremost socialiser, as the person at fault for improper socialisation (see Miller and Burack (1993)).

The second requirement for an offence to be committed is that the opportunity be present. Gottfredson and Hirschi (1990) say very little about opportunity, other than asserting that: it must clearly maximise immediate pleasure; involve simple mental and physical tasks; and involve a low level of risk or detection. The first two of these fall in with the definition of low self-control and so are unsurprising; the last is rather odd and appears to contain a contradiction. In defining self-control, being impulsive, short-sighted and enjoying risk are mentioned, and yet opportunity is maximised when risk is minimised. By saying little more about risk, which must be partially externally determined, they might be said to have moved the focus of their theory even more towards the personal and away from social structure (for a fuller discussion of this criticism, see Barlow (1991)). In the 1993 piece written by Hirschi and Gottfredson, there is a little more explanation of opportunity. Using the example of driving under the influence of drink, they argue that people of low self-control will do so when there is easy access to alcohol and a car is available, but when alcohol sales are restricted there may be no risk of such activity even for those of low self-control – the opportunity has been removed by a situational construct. In some cases this situational construct may depend on the offender: embezzlement from a bank requires one to be an employee and/or to have the necessary computer skills. Presumably, though this is not made clear, whether that opportunity is taken will depend on the degree of self-control. These examples demonstrate a partial recognition that there are social and structural aspects to opportunity but even these are represented as depending on the individual's situation and level of self-control. Thus while accepting that Barlow is right in stating that they largely devalue structural aspects of opportunity, they see this as a strength in the theory rather than a weakness.

Another attack came from Grasmick et al. (1993) who tested the theory and found partial support for it, particularly the opportunity element. They then argued that the explanation of low self-control needed supplementation by variables which might increase the desire to commit a criminal act. For example, strain theory would allow recognition that the motivation for crime is not equal for all. Gottfredson and Hirschi both in 1990 and 1993 reject this call and state that it is fundamental to their theory that people are not more or less prone to criminality, not more or less desirous of its ends. They wholly reject any deterministic explanation claiming that they merely set out what factors increase a probability to offend not a propensity to do so. Criminality is equally attractive to all. They also attribute the failure of Grasmick et al. (1993) to discover a stronger correlation with low self-control to a faulty methodology using a self-report approach instead of direct observation of behaviour to assess self-control as had been done by Keane et al. (1993). However, their preference – direct observation – would appear to take the very behaviours the theory is trying to explain in order to test it. Gottfredson and Hirschi do not see this as problematic but others do: certainly Ackers (1991), who attacked the theory for being tautologous, would see this as a problem. Gottfredson and Hirschi respond that as long as criminal behaviour is not used as one of the indicators of low self-control when searching for a link with criminality there is no difficulty. It is legitimate to look for:

whining, pushing, and shoving (as a child); smoking and drinking and excessive television watching and accident frequency (as a teenager); difficulties in interpersonal relations, employment instability, automobile accidents, drinking, and smoking (as an adult). None of these is a crime. They are logically independent of crime. Therefore the relation between them and crime is not a matter of definition, and the theory survives the charges that it is mere tautology and that it is nonfalsifiable.

This is plausible, but not fully convincing and adds to the other questions about an approach which otherwise has strong possibilities for explaining behaviour.

The similarities between Gottfredson and Hirschi's theory and cognitive learning theories is very marked (see 10.2.6). Both base the criminality heavily on certain learned behaviour and attitudes; both accept that there is a rational choice made to offend, both would recognise a heavy input from the family. There are also powerful differences. The cognitive learning theorists recognise differences in motivation; and are ready to accept that these could be learned, not only through cognitive learning, but also through other methods of acquiring motivation such as the strain theories or deprivation. The cognitive learning theorists also consider that an individual continues to learn and develop all through life. Gottfredson and Hirschi reject the notion of differences in motivation and claim that low self-control is fully shaped very young and that it is not really altered by later experience.

Apart from other inferences, these differences would point towards different ways of treating convicted criminals. One example would be over the efficacy of punishment. For example, Keane et al. (1993) briefly discuss how punishment could be used to deter criminal action through its likelihood, its severity and the rapidity of its application. The certainty of punishment has usually been claimed to be the strongest deterrent, but in empirical tests has not been found to be very effective. Keane et al. argue that one reason is that deterrence theory depends on offenders making rational choices, weighing up the possible gains against the possible losses, including detection and punishment. Some people do not act in such a rational manner: indeed, the very definition of low self-control (immediate gratification etc.) would exclude such calculating behaviour. If this is correct then punishment is almost never likely to deter, no matter how certain, severe or quick (unless it is so inevitable as to negate the opportunity, like the presence of a police officer at a house to be burgled). From data collected by the Home Office this was recognised by the government in its 1990 White Paper leading to the Criminal Justice Act 1991 which moved towards abandoning deterrence, and favouring just deserts, as an element in punishment. Unfortunately before the 1991 Act and its reliance on just deserts could be fully tested, part of it was repealed by the Criminal Justice Act 1993 which reinstated deterrence by allowing consideration of previous offences and increased sentencing if previous sentences had not deterred the criminal behaviour. If Gottfredson and Hirschi are correct the 1993 Act would seem to be wholly illogical.

The theory may therefore have a useful place in assessing punishment. It may also be relevant in assessing treatment or alteration of behaviour. Gottfredson and Hirschi's suggestion of low self-control being formed early and more or less permanently implies that after a certain stage it can never be altered. The only ways of preventing criminality would then seem to be either to remove opportunity (for some discussion of this see Chapter Eleven), or to remove the individual (see dangerousness in Chapter Eight). The possibility of intervening before criminality is fully formed seems impractical if this takes place at a very young age, whilst a programme of educating everyone in good parenting skills to ensure appropriate family socialisation seems even more forlorn. The only bright possibility would seem to be widespread provision of nurseries with a caring socialising programme.

13.4 SOCIOLOGICAL CONTROL THEORIES

One of the earliest sociological control theories was Durkheim's theory of anomie (see 12.1.1), but the more modern study of this area is often connected to Hirschi (1969). He argues that human beings are born with the freedom to break the law and will only be stopped from doing so either by preventing any opportunities arising, which would not be possible, or by controlling their behaviour in some way. Law-breaking is natural, and we need to explain law-abiding behaviour. This looks very like the starting point of the classical writers like Beccaria and Hobbes, but Hirschi is not arguing that criminality is an expression of free will, only that it occurs and is normal behaviour. Control theory does not mean that people who perform criminal activities lack morality; they just exhibit a different morality. Nor is it argued that people are born wicked; that people are born criminals. Instead, it is asserted that at birth they know nothing about acceptable and unacceptable behaviour, and will just follow their natural desires. Of course each individual might learn, by a process of trial and error, their own standards for behaviour, but where humans live together in a community they generally feel the need for a little more order than this would produce. Each new member, whether it be a new-born child or a person who previously lived in another community, is socialised into the activities which the community finds acceptable by use of carrots and sticks, rewards and punishments. Classical theorists only recognised fear as the agent of conformity; people could only be deterred if they feared a nasty punishment: control theorists recognise both punishments and rewards. The implication is that the amount of crime is partly constrained because people are reluctant to cause pain to those who love them, and are unwilling to risk losing their possessions and, often more importantly, their reputations. People are not permanently law-abiding or permanently law-breaking. Depending on the controls in their lives they may, at some time, become willing to take part in criminal activities or may turn away from criminality to a law-abiding lifestyle.

Law-abiding citizens are seen to have four elements: their attachments with other people; the commitments and responsibilities they develop; their involvement in conventional activity; and their beliefs. The first of these elements, and some have said the most important, is attachment, the strong social and psychological attachments with other people and institutions in their community. Strong attachments make criminality less likely, and such attachments therefore often need to be socially reinforced. The first and strongest attachments are seen to be with the family, although others will be formed with those in authority, for example, teachers and employers as well as the looser friendships and other personal relationships.

The second element is that of commitment – the more social investments an individual makes to spouse, children, education, job, financial commitments, property investment etc., the less likely that individual is to risk losing all or some of this by committing a delinquent act. It is a cost/benefit sort of argument. If commitments lose importance for the individual, or if they never make what they consider to be important commitments, then they are relatively free to commit delinquent acts. It is not only those who objectively have no commitments who may be able to commit crimes, but also those who do not value what others might assess as important. Furthermore, as shown in 13.7.3, commitments of this sort can sometimes lead to criminality.

The third element is involvement, and refers to the amount a person's life has been given over to a particular legitimate activity. Do they take part or involve themselves in the extra-curricular activities of a school? Do they have many friends, and does most of their social life revolve around a group of friends from work? Criminal acts are less likely if participation in conventional or legitimate activity is important to the individual.

The final element is the individual's beliefs. This is used as a sociological rather than a psychological term. Hirschi does not see beliefs as a set of deeply held convictions, but rather as something the individual chooses to accept. Unlike deeply-held convictions, acceptance of a particular stance can be changed quite easily by being subjected to different arguments; therefore these beliefs need constant social reinforcement. Rejection of rules or values does not necessarily involve criminality, as this may be prevented under one of the other controls. For example, a person may not believe that it is morally wrong, or at least not criminal, to blaspheme, but may refrain from doing so to avoid upsetting others. As Hirschi puts it, 'delinquency is not caused by beliefs that require delinquency, but is rather made possible by the absence of (effective) beliefs that forbid delinquency' (1969, p. 26). Learning and understanding moral issues can help to promote a situation where criminality is less likely (see 13.2 and 10.2).

All four control elements interrelate and are, theoretically, given equal weight: each helps to prevent criminality in most people. However, to present Hirschi's four elements as if they were generally accepted would be to give too great a feeling of consensus. Other writers posit slightly different elements. As an example, the seven sources of control listed by Roshier (1989) will be quoted. He claims that these seven factors can be used as rewards to persuade us to conform or, by their denial, as punishments to threaten us. The seven sources are as follows:

1.   Affection – The human need for affection is very strong and almost universal. Therefore, many people will refrain from criminality in fear of losing it. It depends on the affection being used to show disapproval of unacceptable acts.

2.   Status – The way people outside the family view us, e.g., colleagues and peers. Individuals need to elicit feelings such as respect and admiration from others. In most cases, fear of a bad reputation will act as a barrier to criminality. Equally, if the other person or group admires law breaking, it can militate towards criminality. Box (1983) has suggested that status might be a very powerful weapon against corporate crime, where the perpetrators often rate their reputations very highly.

3.   Stimulation – Many obtain this directly through a job or from leisure activities; or vicariously through friends; or through fiction and the media. Punishment, whether by fines, community service or prison, removes or reduces these possibilities.

4.   Autonomy – Most people need to feel their independence and power over their own destiny; they need the power to choose how to live some part of their lives (see 12.4). If law-abiding ways of self-expression are not present, then it may be that people will resort to criminality.

5.   Security – a desire for comfort and physical safety. Punishments often threaten this security by threatening the discomfort of prison, or by removing from us the money which can provide these comforts.

6.   Money – This is necessary for what it can obtain. Wealth may bring with it status, autonomy and security, and can be used to increase the number

and types of stimulation available. It is therefore very important to conformity and control, which has meant that the fine is the most frequently used punishment in developed societies. The desire to obtain money is, of course, also a major stimulus towards criminality, one way of controlling this is to remove the profits of crime, e.g., by confiscating monies on conviction of certain offences.

7. Belief – this is very similar to Hirschi's last element of conformity (see 13.4).

All these elements can act towards conformity, but several can also encourage criminality. The outcome in any individual case will be discussed below.

13.5 CONTROL BALANCE

Control balance was first mooted by Tittle (1995, and modified in 1997) and provides the control area with a general theory to explain deviance. Tittle defines deviance as any activity which the majority find unacceptable or would disapprove of; it is thus a much wider concept than those of crime and offending, and it occurs when a person has either a surplus or a deficit of control in relations to others. Those whose position in society allows them to exert more control over others and their environment than is exerted over them, enjoy a control surplus. A control deficit arises in people whose position in society means that they are more controlled by others than they are able to control. Tittle suggests that any control imbalance (surplus or deficit) will be likely to lead to deviance which may be criminal in nature. A deficit of control may lead to resentment, envy, loss of any stake in society removing the need to conform, and humiliation. Each of these has been frequently linked to criminality, the link here being the attempt, through crime, to redress the deficit by increasing control and autonomy. At the other end of the spectrum a surplus of control is said to be corrupting, and may lead to a desire to extend that surplus which will enhance autonomy and feed a desire to dominate. The link with criminal activity rests in the belief that the subservience of others largely removes the risk of being caught: a more specific claim is that any breakdown of subservience provokes angry outbursts which can explain some domestic violence (see Hopkins and McGregor (1991)). This dual aspect seems to provide explanations both of street crime (most likely to be associated with a control deficit) and corporate or white-collar crime (most likely to be associated with a control surplus). The approach may be of use in analysing sex differences in offending.

Tittle does not assume that an imbalance alone will lead to criminality, recognising the importance of rational choice in any human behaviour, including criminal activities. Motivation arises for those with a control surplus because they want to extend that surplus (greed) and prove their power, and for those with a control deficit because they want to minimise the deficit (need) and hit out against it. For deviance or criminality to occur the motivation has to be triggered by provocation and facilitated by both opportunity and the absence of constraint. A person with a control surplus who is greedy and has an opportunity to offend and not be caught (so offending would be a rational choice) may still not be moved to do so unless there is a reason, a provocation, an insult from a subordinate person or a large personal gain. Similarly, a person in deficit who is faced with an opportunity to commit an offence may still not offend unless motivated by something which tips the balance. Moreover, internal moral controls (see Chapters Eight and Ten) may mitigate against criminal behaviour even when all these factors favour it.

Linking crime with power and its acquisition is not new. Many see violent crime as involving an element of control or power over the victim, and sex crimes have often been analysed in this way (see Lansky (1987) and Scheff and Retzinger (1991)). It is also possible to analyse property offences in this manner – burglars have a sort of power over their victims, the power to decide what to take and leave, how much mess and upset to cause etc., and for some this may be part of the attraction (see Katz (1988)). What Tittle adds is an ambitious attempt to predict the type of deviance/offending behaviour by reference to the amount of control deficit or surplus (Table 13.1). The exact boundaries between the types of deviance are difficult – perhaps impossible – to establish in the absence of any clear measures of degrees of control. This greatly reduces the practical utility of the categorisation: perhaps all that can be claimed is that the more serious the control imbalance, the more serious the outcomes for the individual and the community.

Table 13.1: Offending behaviour by reference to the amount of control surplus or deficit

Amount of control surplus	*Behaviour*
Small	*Exploitation* – price fixing; bribery; protection rackets; blackmail.
Medium	*Plunder* – destruction of the environment for personal gain; destruction caused to the community by organised gangs controlled by others.
Large	*Decadence* – large-scale flaunting of wealth.
Amount of control deficit	*Behaviour*
Small	*Predation* – theft; burglary; violence (basic street crimes).
Medium	*Defiance or escapism* – protest against control (could include the above); or withdrawn (escapist) deviance such as drug abuse, suicide, mental illness, or alternative cultures or political movements.
Large	*Submissive deviance* – compliance with everything because one is too frightened to exhibit any challenge.

None the less, the control balance theory does help with some of the more complex problems which vex criminologists: for example, it could be used to explain sex differences in deviance. There is still a tendency for women to be controlled to a greater degree than men, and in more spheres of their lives. Because of this women suffer control deficits more frequently than do men, and those deficits tend to be large so they would fall into the range of submissive deviance (see Table 13.1: subordinating themselves entirely and without thinking of complaint) or defiant/escapist areas and far less frequently into the predatory area. Fewer women are presumed to have a control surplus so they would be under-represented in the areas of exploitation, plunder and decadence. Tittle suggests that males, on the other hand, tend more to inhabit the centre of the spectrum, many being in balance and then successively reducing in numbers as they move out to the edges of the spectrum. They would thus be more heavily represented in the predation and exploitation areas of the continuum and less so in the submissive and defiant/escapist areas. This would explain the low level of predatory criminal activity which every measure of female crime has always discovered. Such an interesting analysis of offending and general deviance is illuminating and at the least deserving of attention.

If it could be operationally established, Tittle's theory offers immense possibilities for a greater understanding of crime in general: it offers the possibility of being able to view all types of offending (deviance) and all types of offender (rich and poor; male and female; powerful and weak; racially discriminated against and racially dominant) as similar, and as equally destructive of community and equally damaging to victims. Such a universal approach has obvious attractions.

Braithwaite (1997) takes the theory further by proposing a policy approach which, he claims, would minimise the destructive effect of control imbalances. To do this he simplifies the theory: he considers that the most problematic aspects of control imbalance are the aspects of the theory which attack freedom. These he identifies as the predatory, exploitation and plunder aspects, all of which he sees as essentially predatory. It is questionable whether this limitation is justifiable: the areas of defiance and submission could also indicate a loss of liberty, especially if they induce actions by limiting freedom of choice. At the other end, decadence certainly carries implications for the freedom of other people. It is therefore questionable whether the simplification which Braithwaite suggests is either necessary or useful to his policy suggestions.

His solution is seen to be in an approach which bases policies on the need to redistribute control. A more egalitarian society, he claims, will reduce control surplus and control deficit, and so help to reduce deviance generally and offending in particular. It is recognised that some control will be necessary to an ordered society, but this should be exercised in a way which respects those subjected to the control. The optimistic conclusion is that such even-handedness, both in the exercise and in the distribution of control, will ensure its willing acceptance. The prospects of such harmony would certainly recede still further if the generalised approach was converted into specific suggestions.

13.6   FACILITATING AND CHOOSING CRIMINALITY

If these control elements break down, it explains why a person may be free, on an individual level, to participate in criminal activity, but it does not explain why such a choice might be made (for a full discussion see Box (1981)).

13.6.1   Facilitating criminality

Some forms of criminal behaviour involve particular and necessary skills. Other crimes may require essential specialist tools. But for most crimes neither of these constraints is absolute. A more general restriction might result from the fact that some crimes may be possible only if the opportunity arises. For example, to defraud the Inland Revenue it is normally necessary to earn money, and it may be feasible only if you are self-employed or if your employer at least acquiesces in the crime by not telling the truth.

Some people might refrain from committing crimes until they are given some sort of social support to offend. They may deviate only when they are in a group which encourages it, or when they have friends who would support the activity. This is not the same as the peer group pressures of the last chapter, as the group does not cause the criminality, does not necessarily push otherwise law-abiding people to commit crimes. The group simply provides the supportive atmosphere in which those who already lack social controls might find that they can commit crimes. Some individuals who are sufficiently free of the social controls to allow them to take part in criminal activity may none the less wish first to be able to justify this to the wider community; social support can provide this justification. The justifications often take the form of one of the techniques of neutralisation discussed in 12.4.

Possibly the oldest and often most important element to be considered by potential law-breakers is the likelihood of getting caught. A secondary consideration is the possible punishment which might be faced, and especially the probability of that punishment being administered. Thus many motorists break traffic regulations knowing what the penalty is, but will drive within legal limits when they are aware there is a police car in the vicinity. The activity is only deterred if the individual believes that the criminality is likely to be detected. This belief may be wholly erroneous, but it leads the potential criminal to ask: is the benefit worth the risk of being caught and the punishment to be faced if I am caught? In control theory this analysis will only lead to criminality if the individual perceives detection to be low and is otherwise willing to perform a crime – unlike the classical theorists, it is not postulated that everyone is bad and will only be deterred by fear of detection and punishment. If a law is unjust (e.g., an edict that no red-haired person should drive), or is seen to operate unjustly, it may encourage people to ignore or evade its application. Differential application of the laws, even to people who are guilty, can give rise to disrespect for the law (see 13.8.2).

13.6.2   Choosing criminality

Despite the factors which affect the ability of the individual to commit a crime, the individual still needs to choose to turn to criminal activity. In classical criminology this was not a problem, as all people were naturally evil and therefore crime was inevitable unless it was controlled by deterrence. In modern control theories man is not naturally either evil or moral, but needs a reason for choosing criminality. The theory predicts that this choice will be made when law-breaking behaviour is more attractive than law-abiding behaviour. Law breaking may offer the possibility of more money or more goods. It may act as a way of satisfying physical desires, which most people manage to satisfy through willing participation in legally recognised activities, or to control or suppress. It may permit people better to meet what they see to be their roles: a man to show his masculinity by being tough; or a provider to feed or clothe his or her dependants. In some groups, criminal acts may bring with them recognition and position, and this is often a motivation. Again, the person may be encouraged into criminality by a peer group which is supportive of such behaviour. Criminal activity may be seen to be, and may prove to be, exciting or meet a desire to take risks (see Lofland (1969)). This is especially attractive to those who cannot afford to, or are not given the chance to take part in legitimate and possibly dangerous or exciting, but often expensive leisure activities. Lastly, as Matza ((1964), see 12.4) suggested, an individual may find criminality useful in order to take control over something and make it happen. All these may provide the final reason for the choice. Most of these are legitimate goals and values set by conventional society, but in some instances a person may perceive that they may be better reached by criminal rather than law-abiding means.

13.7 COMMUNITY BASED ORIGINS OF CONFORMITY

In this section some of the many possible origins of conformity will be considered. Much of the work in this area has been done with juvenile offenders, but consideration will also be given to adults. A number of the earliest control theorists tended to concentrate on psychological controls, giving particular importance to interpersonal relationships, especially those of family, close friends or peer groups. Control theorists who have a more sociological view would also add things such as race and sex divisions (sex will be discussed in Chapter Fifteen), as well as giving more attention to the institutional control agents.

13.7.1 Family
The most commonly quoted control factor is the family, which includes consideration of the effects of family breakdown (particularly early maternal separation), and the quality of the family relationship.

The effects of a family breakdown, whether it occurs naturally through the death of one of the parents or arises from traumas such as desertion or divorce, has long been considered a factor affecting the criminality of the children of the family. Views, such as those of Bowlby ((1946) and (1953), see 8.2.2) which concentrated upon the absence of the mother, are often strongly psychological. Haskell and Yablonsky (1982) assessed eight studies which researched the relationship between crime and broken homes, finding that between 23.9 and 61.5 per cent of delinquents came from broken homes while only 12.9 to 36.1 per cent of non-delinquents came from broken homes.

If this suggests some relationship between delinquency and broken homes, other studies found no such connection. Christie (1960) studied male delinquents and found no correlation between criminality and broken homes. This might have led to a feeling that broken homes were unimportant to criminality, except that Monahan (1957) had already suggested that broken homes were found far more frequently among male black delinquents than among Whites and among female delinquents than among male. Evidence of other studies suggests that broken homes may well be more important to these two groups. In 1986, for example, Pitts claimed that there was a link between criminality and homelessness. West Indian youths tended to become homeless more often than their white counterparts. In the case of female criminality, many writers, such as Box (1981), have related the low crime rates of females with the higher levels of control exercised over them. The implication is that they are likely to be more adversely affected by anything which interferes with such controls, such as family breakdown (but see also 16.6). Chilton and Markle (1972) have questioned this differential effect of family breakdown; they found that the rate of family breakdown is anyway much higher in the case of black than white families, and this may explain why more black delinquent adolescents than Whites come from broken homes.

Two recent studies in Britain reported that broken homes and early separation predicted convictions up to age 33 (Kolvin et al. (1990)) where the separation occurred before age five, and that it predicted convictions and self-reported delinquency (Farrington (1992a)). Morash and Rucker (1989) found that although it was single-parent families who had the children with highest deviancy rates (used in the wider context), these were also the lowest income families: the nature of the problem – broken home, parental supervision, low income – was unclear and could have been structural (see Chapter Eleven). Altogether, the evidence from this wide range of studies is confused and conflicting. Wells and Rankin (1991) tried to reach some sort of conclusion by using a careful method called meta-analysis to compare 50 studies concerning broken homes and delinquency between 1926 and 1988. The result seemed to be that officially recorded delinquency had a stronger relationship with broken homes than did self-reported delinquency and that broken homes had a significantly higher prevalence of delinquency than did two-parent homes (10–15 per cent higher). The relationship was constant over sex and racial connections, but this fairly strong relationship was only true for minor offences and did not hold as strongly for serious offences. Some have recently suggested that the factor of broken homes is less important than the quality of the relationship between the child and parent or parents. In 1982 McCord claimed that the real link between broken homes and offending turned around whether the mother was loving: for males brought up in broken homes with unloving mothers the prevalence of offending was 62 per cent against 22 per cent in similar homes with loving mothers. Similar differences were found in non-broken homes which suggests that it is the relationship with the mother which is crucial rather than the status of the home. There are a number of problems underlying much of this research: for example, some of it may test conviction rates and these may be unconsciously skewed by decisions on prosecution or conviction (see Wells and Rankin (1991), above). The only firm conclusion is the need to be wary of the interpretation to be placed on any correlation between criminality and broken homes (see labelling, 14.2).

In part, the proposed connection with maternal affection relates back to the suggestion, reported earlier, that mothers may be primarily responsible for the relationship between families and criminality. Given without qualification the implication is that much of the blame for offending rests with the failure of women to adopt the appropriate relationships with their children. This rather simplistic connection needs to be questioned. Why is the relationship with the mother of such great importance? Should the implication be that power relationships in homes should be altered so that the burden of primary carer should be shared? As Morash and Rucker (see above) would suggest, the statement also ignores possible structural reasons – low income etc. – which may affect the ability of a mother (or other primary carer) to show affection and to have time for parental supervision (see Chapter Eleven).

There is also a problem because much of this research was conducted a long time ago or is reporting on longitudinal studies where the family break-up occurred well into the past and might since have changed. The concept of family is itself not unproblematic, particularly today. In the past in Britain it was basically defined by white Western society to mean two heterosexual adults, of different genders, married to one another, together with any children which were biologically theirs. However appropriate it may have been in the past, this definition is now much too restrictive when we have large numbers of single-parent families, extended families, unmarried parents, single-sex parents, adopted children etc. As society comes to accept these different families as 'normal', the effects of family breakdown or difference may be far less traumatic on the children and thus perhaps be less connected to criminals and deviant behaviour. In other words it may not be the families themselves but the way in which they are affected by external assessment of them that is crucial to offending.

The second way in which family has been related to criminality is in the quality of the relationship between parents and children. In this area, delinquency is connected to low levels of supervision by adults in the family, less affectionate relationships within the family, low levels of interaction between the parents and the children, less family harmony, and to the way in which discipline is carried out. There is general agreement that delinquents are less attached to their parents than are non-delinquents, they do not identify with their parents as closely, they care less about them and what they think, do not interact as much with them and are less likely to ask their advice. Many theorists link these factors with criminality, for example Nye (1958), Hirschi ((1969), see 13.4) and West (1982). All three denied that broken homes were important factors in criminality; instead they pointed to the harmony of the relationships within the family and how well the parents and children interacted. Hirschi points out that where children believe that their parents are not going to find out where they are or what they are doing, they are more likely to commit a crime than if they are worried that their parents may find out. The closer the relationship with the parent, the more likely they were to believe that the parents would discover it and disapprove. The parental relationship can thus act as a control even when the parent is not present. Hirschi suggested that generally, delinquency was inversely related to the quality of the relationship between parents and children, and therefore the bond of attachment the child has with the family. This relationship was important in all racial and social settings.

A close relationship with parents only tends to produce a low rate of criminality if the relationship is used to supervise the child's behaviour to ensure conformity with conventional standards. Even parents who participate in criminal activity might teach their children conventional values and behaviour (Box (1981)). They may hide their criminality from the child and still use the attachment formed to encourage law-abiding behaviour. Similarly, not all conventional parents use the ties of affection to teach conformity; some may have lax or ineffectual training techniques, and others will just not bother. Most importantly, it does not necessarily mean that middle- and upper-class parents are likely to perform these tasks better than lower-class, unemployed or black parents. Neither the way in which this task is performed nor its success simply depends upon the social position of the family (see Box (1981)). It may, however, be related to certain social facts within the family. In some homes, both parents may work long hours either from choice or from necessity, in which case they may form less firm family bonds. Wilson (1980), discovered that parents who were lax in their supervision were more likely to have criminal children, but that often the poor supervision arose more from social conditions. West (1982) found similar results, but also closely related family size to criminality. He suggested that the difference might stem from the fact that the large family size gave rise to problems in providing individual supervision, and that the level of parental supervision was often more closely related to social pressures than to the choice of the parent in upbringing.

More recently Farrington (1992b) has claimed that both juvenile and adult convictions are related to poor parental supervision, and also that offenders – then or later – had poor relationships with their partners. What was important was the whole relationship, including discipline, encouragement and supervision. It must also be noted that although the parents may perform all these functions well and although there may be strong ties of affection between parent and child and the parent may try to use these to teach law-abiding behaviour, if the child does not view that parent with prestige, then they will be less likely to learn from them (see differential association, 10.2.3).

Lastly, West and Farrington (1977) in the Cambridge Study discovered that less than 5 per cent of the families were responsible for approximately half of all offending. This was unlikely to be due to genetics or biological factors, so they and others such as Robins (1979) have suggested that criminal, antisocial and alcoholic parents will tend to have children with behavioural problems including a higher offending rate. The implication is that the children learn the behaviour and attitude patterns of their parents.

In the more modern, post-positivist control theories, the relationships within a family are seen as dynamic, and therefore their effects on criminality may alter. This factor may help to explain the differential criminal involvement at different ages and stages of development. Generally, one would expect the ties to be stronger at very young ages when the child is most dependent upon its parents and when it is least likely to question them. Also, at this time the parental relationship controls most other contacts, for example with friends and others. As the child reaches adolescence, the parental bond and power may recede, and the child is likely to form closer bonds with peers which might then influence their behaviour more strongly. Furthermore, in adolescence the frustration from feelings of lack of autonomy may be greatest and the desire to take charge of some part of their lives might become powerful. After adolescence, family ties – perhaps with a spouse and children as well as parents – may once more become more important.

Family structures have also been used to examine sex differences in criminality. Thus some explain the lower crime rates for women by the fact that they are far more closely controlled and watched, as well as more severely punished for minor transgressions of societal mores (Nye (1958)). Another sex-based consideration of family socialisation arises from the observation that the power balance within the family is important – hence power–control theory (Hagan (1989) and Hagan et al. (1990)). The argument is that in patriarchal families girls will be socialised as home-makers and diverted away from risks, whereas boys will be socialised towards the outside world, be prepared to take risks and to enjoy the challenge of so doing. Where sons and daughters are given equal treatment in upbringing, it is the daughter's outlook which shifts towards a greater propensity for risk-taking, thus increasing the likelihood of turning to crime. These studies are useful in recognising the sex-based nature of much socialisation within the family, but are flawed in being too simplistic. For example, Hagan assumes that egalitarian families take the traditional male upbringing as the norm rather than borrowing from both traditional forms of rearing. The latter might still have the effect of creating more equal crime rates for males and females, but it would be less likely to increase the overall crime rate and might actually decrease it if the greater control over daughters was also used for boys and the greater self-control inculcated in girls was also taught to boys.

Box (1987), has suggested that in times of recession there is likely to be a weakening of family bonds. Unemployment and shortages of money put tension onto those who are made to suffer them, leading to higher divorce rates, increased family violence, and other behaviour which adversely affects family attachments. Therefore, he claims, in times of recession family attachments will be weaker, and so people will be freer to commit criminality if that is what they decide they wish to do.

Most of this is based on the assumption that families will normally try to socialise their children towards law-abiding behaviour and that it is rare for any family intentionally to socialise its children towards criminality. Offending by the child is seen to be the result of a mistake or incapacity by parents to perform this function properly. There are, however, activities of the family which have been very closely related to criminality and have sometimes been said to have a socialising effect towards such behaviour. Such accusations are usually made against families in which there is abuse or neglect. Zingraff et al. (1994) refer to a number of studies where such a link is discovered although the link is not explained. They also note that other studies suggest that these effects can be altered by other positive socialising input. On this basis the family, although seen as highly important in both the positive and negative effects it may have, is not the one unique factor which shapes the control theory.

13.7.2 School

The effects of school have long been associated with criminality. In earlier chapters the position of intelligence and criminality was discussed (10.1), as was the connection between school and criminality as part of the strain theories (Chapter Twelve). Here, the effect of attachment to school on the behaviour of the pupil will be considered.

Hirschi (1969) compared the attachments to parents, particularly the father, with attachments to school. He discovered that pupils who did not have strong attachments with their parents were less likely to form attachments with the school. However, in cases where there was a weak parental, but a strong school, attachment, the crime rate tended to be low. He suggested that this indicated that school attachments were more important than parental attachments, but this may just suggest that whatever the attachment to law-abiding behaviour, if it is strong it is likely to be effective.

The suggestion that school affects criminality was upheld in two famous pieces of research: one carried out by Hargreaves and reported in 1967. He claimed that streaming by ability, with low expectations and rewards for the lower streams, led to pupils in these streams becoming disillusioned with school and therefore failing to form bonds with teachers. Such pupils tended to form close peer group bonds with those who had similar feelings of hostility, which freed them to participate in delinquent activity. The reason for the low streaming was unimportant; the essential element was the response of the pupil to being written off in this way by the education system. Hargreaves (1980) has more recently indicated ways in which these problems might be reduced. He suggested that petty rules concerning things such as dress and smoking should be relaxed, lower-stream classes should not be allocated the less able teachers, rewards should not only be given to the very able, and teachers should not wash their hands of the most troublesome pupils. Such changes, he argued, would lessen the chances of school being the cause of delinquency, as it might not alienate so many pupils.

The second study was carried out by Rutter et al. (1979) who compared 12 large comprehensive schools in London and discovered that problems associated with schools tended to arise together: schools with high delinquency rates also had high truancy rates and low academic success rates. Such schools also tended to have large numbers of pupils drawn from families of low social class, but even after allowing for the class differences there was still a difference in delinquency and truancy. These factors were more responsive to differences in the relative amounts of punishment and praise used by teachers than by the physical surroundings: much of the effect thus turned around the way in which children were controlled and encouraged. Although neither of these studies is conclusive, they each find a connection between school and offending, and each connects it with discipline and reward. They may thus be important for control theory since if schools reward only a small number of very bright children (usually for academic achievement) and they discipline others harshly (even for fairly small transgressions) they may, by alienating some pupils, negate the otherwise controlling and socialising environment of the school.

Often, the willingness to submit to, or become attached to, the authority of school may be strongly affected by the perceived utility of the school. If the pupil views the school as being instrumental to their career or success, they are more likely to invest time in school activities. Adolescents who do not consider that the skills they may learn in school are going to be of use to them may become antagonistic towards it, especially in the year or so leading up to their leaving school. During this period, they feel the futility of school more sharply than before and may also find the low streaming increasingly difficult to accept because of the low esteem in which they are viewed by others, and which they feel for themselves. This may all lead towards criminality (see Box (1981)). In 1987 Box went further than this in suggesting that in times of recession this alienation is even more likely. Low job prospects reduce the normal restraint of not wishing to jeopardise the chances of employment after leaving school.

It seems probable that school does have a large role to play in teaching children conforming behaviour, and in providing bonds or reasons for remaining law-abiding. If schools are sufficiently welcoming and encouraging they may be able to help to counter some of the negative aspects of socialisation elsewhere such as in the family. For example, Zingraff et al. (1994) found that children who suffered abuse and/or neglect in the home were not necessarily more likely to be delinquents because of the influence of other socialising processes, such as school. This suggests that schools, when they operate well, can help to reduce the possibility of offending by providing a strong control link with conformity. If schools are to do this effectively, some prior socialisation is essential: and since, as already seen, it cannot always be assumed that this has already been provided by the family, there is a strong case for universal nursery education. This would greatly enhance the ability of schools to perform their socialising task: equally their ability in this respect will obviously be greatly reduced if pupils feel rejected by the school. The relevance to all this of the political priority given to education in the late 1990s is as yet unclear. The strong tendency to attribute the shortcomings of some schools to the inefficiency of teachers may not be constructive, especially since the inefficiency is largely defined in terms of academic results.

13.7.3 Peer groups, colleagues and neighbourhood
Peer groups have already had a large amount of attention given to them in Chapter Twelve, and neighbourhoods were discussed in Chapter Eleven. Their relevance to control will be considered here.

In the last chapter, peer groups, usually gangs, were used to explain why young people turn to criminality. In control theory, they are not necessarily gangs, and can be loose groupings of friends or just single companions. Furthermore, in control theories peer groups can, like all other attachments, act for or against law-abiding behaviour. If a strong attachment is formed with a peer group for whom conventional behaviour is very important, this can be a strong pull towards conventional, law-abiding behaviour. There are, however, certain peer groups whose members clearly support delinquency, or who at least do not censor such behaviour. In these groups, it may be that some types of criminality are actively encouraged and given prestige, or merely that they are tolerated and not actively discouraged. In either situation, if individuals become attached to such a group they may feel freer to commit criminality if there are other motivations for wishing to do so. This type of connection with criminality was upheld by Conger (1976). It is important to note that contact with a criminal peer group may only arise because the individual is willing to commit crimes. In this case the group only facilitates the activity by, for example, teaching the skills required.

Box (1983) and (1987) takes these ideas and applies them to adults in one of the few books in which this is done. He refers to corporate crime as being committed partly because colleagues encourage each other. They discover that certain activities, though unacceptable in all other areas of their lives, might be perfectly acceptable and even expected as part of their working lives. Company loyalty and the corporate requirement to make a profit both set up an environment in which it might not make good business sense to remain entirely within the law. Also, certain accepted business practices, for which people might gain acquiescence, or even prestige from their colleagues, may be illegal or near the edge of the law. As long as they succeed in the business objective and are not caught, they will be accepted and might even gain promotions. In most cases, the chances of being caught committing a corporate crime are very slim (see, for example, Carson (1970), Leigh (1980) and Box (1983)). Furthermore, if caught they rarely face any great stigma or penalty: they are often fined only a small amount and their peers do not ostracise them, nor do their careers necessarily suffer. A number of commentators have suggested that because these people have a very great stake in conformity, they could be easily controlled if detection were more certain, and punishment – monetary, social, professional – greater (see especially Box (1983) and Hagan (1987)). Heckathorn (1990) adds that group disapproval (such as the disapproval of colleagues) could provide a further effective measure of control. It is clearly an area where a great deal could be gained by greater controls on these people's activities and by encouraging ethical working practices.

The adult effects of peer groups also enter other areas of the work environment. In some jobs certain violations against the employer may be seen as a 'perk of the job'. In offices, colleagues generally accept that local telephone calls are acceptable on the employer's phone bill unless they are officially banned. In some labouring jobs certain items may be fair game, and the employer actually include their loss in any estimates submitted. In adult peer groups as well as youth peer groups, especially in work, certain activities might be acceptable and, in some cases, actually encouraged.

The effect of the neighbourhood on criminality was largely discussed in Chapter Eleven. In some areas this was seen as a force towards criminality. Very often the reasons given for this were similar to control theories – a lack of community to watch over children, mobility and therefore anonymity. Neighbourhood watch schemes have been seen as one counter, both by increasing control and by cultivating mutual concern. Similarly, Coleman (1988) suggested changes in building design to make criminality less likely. The big difference is that in control theory, the area is seen as being more criminologenic not because these factors cause criminality, but because they fail to persuade the inhabitants towards conformity. This may appear to be merely semantic, but it has some important effects. One of the main problems with the Chicago School and other neighbourhood theories was that they predicted too much criminality. This problem is avoided in control theory, because if the control constructs in an area are weak it means only that a person would be free to commit crime; it does not mean that they will, or will want so to do.

Informal stable social controls may have an effect in countering otherwise expected criminal and antisocial behaviour. Sampson and Laub (1990) set out to discover whether adults who might be predicted to have high rates of criminality might be controlled by secure and stable adult bonds. They used stable marriage and job security as indicators of adult bonds and chose to study a cohort of adults who had exhibited childhood behavioural problems and often also indicated juvenile criminality. As was seen in Chapters Eight and Ten, there is a strong continuity from childhood delinquency to juvenile crime and adult crime antisocial behaviour (as measured by items such as alcohol abuse, divorce etc.). Sampson and Laub claimed that this expected continuity could be broken by the informal social controls of stable marriage and job security. Shover (1996) agrees, noting that the forging of new stable relationships was a powerful factor in the ending of a criminal career. If these stabilising aspects could counter the behavioural problems of childhood, they might be able to counter other negative indicators such as living in a disorganised community or an upbringing which accepted criminal behaviour. Policies which encourage high levels of secure employment and stable and enduring marriages may therefore have a place in countering criminality.

Last in this section we will consider the effect of religion on criminality. Many theorists have noted that an attachment to religion may well help to reduce criminality and deviance (see, for example, Cochran and Ackers (1989) and Grasmick et al. (1991)). The claim is that religion positively increases the desire for law-abiding and conforming behaviour and, negatively, fosters the fear of damnation. Others, such as Cochran et al. (1994), whilst admitting a strong correlation between religious practice and conformity, have none the less questioned the place of religion in controlling behaviour. They attempted to test the causal connection shown by the negative correlation between religion and offending and discovered that it did not hold for assault, theft, vandalism or illicit drug use. Two explanations were offered.

Either those who commit crimes have low boredom thresholds which makes religion unattractive to them: thus it is not that religion promotes conformity but that those who are likely to be religious are likely to be conforming. Or that religion provides the backdrop in which the individual will form relationships with other individuals and it is these relationships, not the religion itself, which form the social bond for conformity (social control theory).

13.7.4 Race

Race has already been addressed at a number of points in the book. The connection between race and intelligence was addressed in 10.1, and the possibility of race being connected with criminality was considered again in Chapter Eleven. Here its connection with control theories and crime will be briefly considered. The official statistics for England and Wales suggest that certain racial groups commit more crimes per head of their population than others. The West Indians are generally seen as the group with the highest crime rate, while the Whites, Asians and Chinese have much lower rates. These statistics are not entirely representative of the real crime rates, but even taking account of all bias and of self-report studies, it does appear that some groups are more crime-prone. Control theory may offer an explanation of this. The higher West Indian crime rate relates only to those born and brought up in this county and not to the original immigrants who have a low crime rate while these differences in recorded crime rates are only fairly recent, despite there having been a sizeable black population in Britain for over a hundred years. These considerations should make anyone cautious about any assertions of an inherent link between any particular race and criminality: we need to look more closely at social circumstances. The Asian community tend to have a higher number in the business or professional classes and, as will be seen in the next section and Chapter Fourteen, these classes appear less in the crime figures, perhaps because they are less closely policed. The West Indians often live and work in the worst areas of Britain and, as was mentioned above, will therefore be in neighbourhoods where control over children is most difficult to perform and where the institutional control structures are least strong. They may also be sent to schools where scholastic achievement is low, and be in the lower streams. This low streaming may have more to do with social influences than with innate intelligence. West (1982) suggests that poor families with a large number of children living in overcrowded and deprived accommodation, and attending poor schools, are more likely to have low IQ children and these children are more likely to become delinquent. West also implies that these are the children whom teachers find most difficult to control. They have high rates of truancy, and are disorderly or inattentive when they are in school.

A further element which is likely to play a part in the race differentials in crime committal is racial prejudice. Prejudice in the general population makes it harder for these groups to secure good employment, especially in times of recession. This may lead to feelings of rejection, anomie, loss of self-esteem, low status, poverty, lack of autonomy, and insecurity both of person and property. The last is exacerbated by the conviction of many blacks, whether warranted or not, that the police are less than zealous in dealing with racially motivated attacks by whites on blacks. All these lessen the strength of many of the control mechanisms of society.

Control theory writers thus imply that racial differences in crime rates may, like other crime, be explained by the level of control mechanisms.

13.8   OFFICIAL OR INSTITUTIONAL CONTROL AGENTS

The criminal justice system is a composite of a number of the main institutions or means of social control. The ones which will receive consideration here are the police and punishment, but others such as prisons, customs and excise or factories inspectorate could have been added. It is worth noting that, on top of the official State control agencies, there are unofficial control agencies such as private security firms, debt collection agencies, store detectives and other private detectives. These will not be considered here, although they may have an effect on the level of crime. It would be interesting to question where these agencies get their legitimation as control agents.

In an ideal society coercive State control systems would be unnecessary. Each individual would feel constrained to live within the rules because that is best for the society as a whole, and therefore for each individual within that society. The reality falls somewhat short of this, and therefore central or State control systems are seen as necessary to deal with the cases where the less formal controls have failed. They are based on a coercive type of control. Rather than persuading individuals to conform and thereby earn acceptance in society, they threaten them with what might occur if they do not. If they do not comply with State rules, individuals are threatened with punishments, which are meant to be sufficiently unpleasant to deter people from certain forms of behaviour (for an historical analysis, see Cohen and Scull (1983)). They are administered against those who have committed unacceptable criminal acts because they have committed those acts, and are chosen and administered by people who are empowered under the law of that State to perform such functions. They are intended to show society's displeasure at the acts which have been performed by the individual who is being punished.

Seemingly, most of the agents of criminal justice are centred on bringing transgressors to justice and punishing them. Before any of the agents of social control are considered, it is worth noting that it is possible to have a State control agency which is not centred on the use of coercive power – the factory inspectorate generally see their role as one of education, persuasion and promoting law-abiding behaviour rather than one of prosecuting and punishing for non-compliance. This, however, is not the role of most of the State agents of control.

13.8.1   Police
The police are one of the last and most drastic elements of social control. They will only be required to intervene to control social behaviour if other, less severe and less formal, agents of social control have failed. They are intended as an objective and rational legal authority whose function is to

control those who are a threat to society and to other people. They are seen as necessary because any control system has to have sanctions in order for it to function. In the case of the criminal justice system, the sanction is punishment. Punishment will only act as a deterrent if it is likely to be used. Box (1983) suggests that the low possibility of being detected, prosecuted and punished is one of the factors which leads to high rates of corporate crime. If all crimes were detected and cleared up, one could therefore expect a large drop in the levels of criminality. Unfortunately, this is not the case. As was seen in Chapter Four, many crimes are never reported to the police, and for many of the others the police never catch the perpetrator because: no-one is found; the perpetrator is found but not convicted; or the wrong person is convicted. These all lead to higher rates of criminality. Feldman (1977) contends that if there is to be effective deterrence of a particular type of behaviour, detection needs to occur at least more often than non-detection. For the individual, undiscovered criminal behaviour acts as positive reinforcement of that behaviour, making it more likely to be repeated. Detection and punishment act as negative reinforcements, making the behaviour less likely. Detection is essential to control.

As a result, control theorists have recently given some attention to detection. In general, they see actual detection rates as being less important than perceived detection rates; if people believe they are likely to be caught, they will be less likely to commit the act than if they believe that their deed will go undetected. Modern control theorists have therefore concentrated on increasing the risk of being caught. In an effort to increase detection rates, the police and local communities have sometimes chosen to use technical surveillance devices such as Closed Circuit Television (CCTV) to deliver control and deterrent effects – people will think twice because of the possibility of a rapid response by the police. This is a policy move away from dealing with crime through treatment and rehabilitation of offenders towards a 'new behaviourism' where the State is less interested in the causes of crime than in its prevention, and is less concerned with trying to change social conditions than with the more modest aim of 'changing behaviour sequences' by reducing the opportunity to commit crime with impunity (Cohen (1985)). CCTV therefore works at the level of deterrence, not crime causation. As already indicated (11.2.4), these surveillance techniques raise problems concerning civil liberties. For an informed discussion of the theories of surveillance see Mathiesen (1997). As well as increased use of technical surveillance devices the police have also tried to increase detection and prosecution by more efficient policing. Such endeavours are not easy to implement, however, and in some instances have been found to be counter-productive. Thus, in the early 1980s, police used saturation policing in certain high crime rate areas in Britain: the purported object was to prevent crime by achieving high detection rates. Unfortunately, the detection rates, relative to the man-power expended, were not high and, more seriously, the locals viewed the policy as very unjust: the policy, indeed, was seen as one of the main factors in sparking off the 1981 riots in Brixton (London), Liverpool and Bristol (see Scarman (1981)). Similarly, police practice was an instigating factor in the riots in Brixton and Broadwater Farm (London) in 1985 (see Gifford (1986)). Each of these was also tied up with the appalling relations between the police and the black community. In these areas the police are very much seen as interfering outsiders and as applying subjective laws in a subjective manner against the interests of the black community. Where policing practice is, whether rightly or wrongly, seen to be unacceptable to the locals, the ensuing conflict is a constant threat to law and order and reduces their effectiveness in crime detection (see Reiner (1985); Institute of Race Relations (1987); and Gifford et al. (1989)). Also, some other recent police methods, such as those used for the policing of marches and strikes, and certain uses of the computer and other technology, have been seen as being intrusive into the civil liberties and freedoms of law-abiding citizens to a degree unacceptable in a democratic society.

Such reactions tend to lead to the alienation of the police from the community they are supposed to protect, reducing the ability of the police to fight crime (see Cohen (1985); *Striking Back* (1985) and Scraton (1985)). These difficulties are aggravated when, despite increases in the numbers of police and in their funding, recorded crime in the last decade has been rising, whereas clear-up rates have declined (Kinsey et al. (1986)). All these policing problems have meant that police detection of crime has been made less effective, which perhaps acts as a catalyst to criminality. This suggests that the effectiveness of the police as agents of social control has been blunted. If this means that potential criminals perceive that they are likely to go undetected, they may be more willing to commit crimes. In this context it is not surprising that there has been a continuing debate over how police should perform their functions. A common police method has been to target certain areas or certain groups for closer policing because they are believed to be more criminal. For the reasons outlined above, the results can be ambiguous or even conflicting, and some believe that the costs in terms of alienation outweigh any benefits in the form of (often temporary) higher detection rates.

Other types of policing may be more productive and get the backing of local residents, as has been the case with community policing. That is proactive policing, a system whereby the police consult with and work with the local community, often to help rebuild informal social controls. Using such methods, the police are acting more in an enabling role than in a coercive control role (see Moore and Brown (1981)). Unfortunately, the manpower necessary to keep community policing going is thought to be prohibitive for some forces, where it is therefore viewed as inefficient. Other ideas which have been mooted are the increasing of police powers to improve the possibility of detecting crime, or raising efficiency by greater professionalism to enhance their powers of detection (see Scarman (1981)). Each of these might increase the detection rates of the police, but their effectiveness might vary in different parts of the country. It may be best to allow local communities more say in the way they are policed by increasing the accountability of the police to them. Methods of attainment are matters of dispute and debate, but there is no doubt that the ability of the police to detect crime is an important factor in the control of individuals in a society.

Police can also help in strategies designed to decrease criminal opportunity. Some of the initiatives in this area were discussed as part of the consideration of the neighbourhood in 13.7.3 above. Recently, the police have enhanced the work they do in preventing crime and in teaching individuals how to avoid being victimised, for example, visiting schools and talking to children, giving advice on locks and safety features, and by the support of neighbourhood watch schemes. Each of these can help in preventing crime and has a part to play in control, but the central police role in our society remains that of coercive control.

This does not necessarily need to remain the case and some recent initiatives would, if implemented, reduce the present emphasis on coercion. Most present policing reacts either to calls from the public or to situations they discover on the street. A drawback of reactive policing, especially when the police no longer live in the areas which they police, is that they often do not really get to know and understand their areas – they get to know the criminogenic parts but not necessarily the neighbourhood or district as a whole. Their whole lives are separate from those they control most. In reacting to incidents or to problems they may implement apparently logical policies which backfire because of inadequate understanding. This was seen in the riots in the early 1980s (see Scarman (1981)) and still happens in some areas, often those with high minority populations (see Gifford et al. (1989)). To remedy the problem it has been recognised that this does not need to be the shape of policing in the future. Police could be involved in society in a more proactive way.

Such a development would, however, require drastic changes. This is clear from the proposals of its leading advocate (Goldstein (1990)) in the US where it is termed problem-oriented policing. A great deal is involved in a move from simply reacting to immediate problems and becoming involved in the community in a rounded way. It means much more than seeking out those who violate the law and bringing them before the courts for justice. It requires large-scale data collection which needs then to be broken down to be applied to more manageable problems. The deconstruction of the wider problems is only possible if the police understand the structural, personal, and interactionalist difficulties of their communities as well as those elements of the equation which impact on the crime problem. For example, police could: work closely with those who have been victimised to see whether they can help themselves to avoid repetition and in areas with high offence rates try to alert all inhabitants (for problems associated with this see Chapter Five and 11.2.4); target particular environments or work with architects to prevent building designs which are favourable to offending (see 11.2.4); help to reinforce the less formal institutions of social control such as the family, school and neighbourhood (see above); work with local government and other agencies such as the welfare and medical agencies to try to resolve disputes and conflicts before they escalate into serious criminal problems requiring the intervention of the criminal justice system. The implication is that the police would not be fully tied to the criminal justice system and would use their powers in this domain only when that was of utility to the community as a whole, preferring the proactive use of less formal control aspects to reduce crime. Such a programme would certainly require a very different training programme for officers, and possibly a different sort of officer. It takes ideas like community policing, foot patrols, consultation with local people etc. to its logical and fully developed conclusion, which is probably several steps too far for its full application.

None the less, partial implementation is possible: some British examples already in operation were discussed in 11.2.4. In addition, particular policing problems have also been approached from this wider perspective. One such is domestic violence where some police forces work hand-in-hand with social services and with treatment programmes, offering counselling and trial separation to try to prevent repetition. In this way they sometimes approach domestic violence from a less criminal justice oriented mode than many other crimes. This is often attacked by feminists as an indication that domestic violence is not being treated seriously. This suggests that where a problem-oriented solution is introduced only for certain crimes it may lose credibility. Other forces have prosecuted the offenders, but then used the punishment system to treat them, sometimes in an enclosed prison environment and sometimes in the community. In the absence of a general problem-oriented solution this last approach is likely to find more support. There have also been attempts to divert some offenders, particularly the young, away from the full rigours of the criminal justice system. These efforts have recently been attacked as failures, but it may simply be that these policies have not addressed the full problems faced by the youths and the communities from which they come. Perhaps to work they need a fuller adoption of the ideas of problem-oriented policing such as in the projects described by Heywood et al. (1992) and discussed in 11.2.4. It is not a question which will be easily resolved.

Such a solution, if solution it be, has to confront the fact that it invests the police with a much greater control role. Communities need to decide whether they wish to embrace it in the hope of discovering answers to the crime problem. For it to operate the police would need the complete trust of the communities and this would involve changing a number of aspects of modern policing and the control of the police. First it necessitates much more open policing than at present, providing information both about their policies and individual actions. It would also require strong local and legal accountability which should extend to both individual and operational decisions. Lastly, it requires a more open recognition of some of the problems to be discussed in Chapters Fourteen and Fifteen so that sections of the community do not become isolated. One of the central themes of Goldstein's project is that minorities and the weak in society should not become marginalised and alienated. With all these caveats, policy-oriented policing is one of the brightest possibilities to have been suggested.

A major problem with any interventionist State model comes from the possibility of targeting whole groups and categories (see Mathieson (1983)) by the use of TV cameras, development of advanced computerised systems holding sensitive information for control purposes, and new covert intelligence and surveillance techniques which pry deeply into certain people's lives. Goldstein finds this unacceptable but some in society may consider that some such measures are vindicated as being necessary to prevent greater evil. The outcome needs to be a balance between societal interests, smaller-group interests, and the individual interest in privacy etc. That the problem-oriented policing model could foster such interventionist measures should not be ignored.

13.8.2 Punishment

In classical criminology it was thought that a system of punishments set to fit the crime would, through fear, prevent crime (Beccaria). It is generally assumed that this model entails universally harsh punishments. This is not strictly necessary to the theory: all it logically requires is proportionality of sentence for the crime committed. In practice, however, punishments based on this viewpoint tend to be fairly harsh, both to dissuade the potential offender, and to ensure that the law-abiding individual has not lost out to the criminal.

It is generally recognised that there needs to be an idea of justice involved – criminals should not be allowed to gain, materially or psychologically, from their criminality (see Finnis (1968)), nor should they be punished more than necessary. This leads to a cost-effective type of punishment system. The State needs to decide how much punishment is necessary in each particular case to gain the desired end – reform of that criminal. Furthermore, each criminal has to decide whether the costs of criminality – punishments – are worth the benefits of crime. On this basis, it is considered important to remove from the individual the profits of the crime. As Feldman (1977) puts it:

> Clearly, a £20,000 haul which is retained will help to mitigate a prison sentence; the latter would be experienced as more negative if no money was retained from the offence.

Unfortunately, our system is often less effective as a control mechanism because it leaves the criminal to enjoy the ill-gotten gains.

Such an approach suggests that the level of punishment should be related to the crime, but in almost all societies the punishment is also individualised. Most courts ask not only what punishment is applicable to this offence, but also what should *this* offender suffer or, often, what does *this* offender need. Our system takes account of the offender's physical, mental and, especially, social situation. If this individualised system is seen as working unjustly in favour of particular groups, particularly in favour of otherwise advantaged groups, the ability of punishment to deter, and thus to control, is diminished. Similarly, if in any individual case punishment is perceived to be unfair, then its control element may be lost. Suppose A, B and C all commit the same crime: A gets away with it; B is convicted and faces a very severe sentence; and C is convicted but is only very lightly sentenced. It would be unsurprising if B were to feel aggrieved and lose respect for the law, unless B could be shown that there was good reason for the treatment of the other two – A had left the country, perhaps, and C was a minor. But if the difference is seen by B to be arbitrary – A was not suspected because she was a woman, and C was dealt with leniently because he was more articulate – then the way in which the law dealt with B may have an effect opposite to that intended. Probation is particularly prone to distinguish between offenders. Indeed, its whole intention is to meet the needs of the individual offender: to help them towards law-abiding behaviour rather than to punish them for their behaviour. For this reason, the courts in sentencing, and the probation service in making out social inquiry reports, need to ensure that they are seen to be acting in an even-handed manner. Failure to do so gives substance to the common claim that individualised dispositions of the court, such as probation and discretionary life imprisonment, as well as strong mitigation, sometimes go too far and lose sight of the need for punishment to deter and ensure that people 'pay' for their crimes.

One of the elements of this individualised sentencing which is often applied by judges is that the previous character of the offender, in so far as there is no previous criminal record, should be taken into consideration in mitigating the sentence. Feldman (1977) points out that this may be counter-productive. To give greatest effect as a control mechanism, punishment should be inflicted early on in the behaviour. Someone who has committed numerous acts before being detected has already acquired a criminal habit, making the punishment less effective than if it had been administered after the first criminal act. Similarly, a first offender who does not receive very harsh punishment may conclude that the criminality is worth it: by the time severe punishment is forthcoming, the behaviour may be too entrenched for the punishment to have an effect. Arguably, our system of using mild punishments first may reduce their effectiveness as controls.

All the above assumes that there is a deterrent element to most punishment, but, as will be seen in Chapter Fourteen, in labelling individuals as offenders one may actually precipitate their further involvement in crime: for example, by reducing their chances of providing for themselves through legitimate means. In 1988 Braithwaite put forward a theory of the notion of reintegrative shaming (see 10.2.4) which suggests one way of avoiding this. Offenders are, through shaming, made aware of the suffering they have caused, but are then eased back into social acceptance.

It can be seen that in choosing any system of punishment the intended effects need to be considered very carefully. Unfortunately, there is almost never one desired effect of punishment towards which any system is leading, making a clear policy difficult to obtain and making it difficult to assess success (see Rothman (1983)). Any system tends to be an amalgamation of a number of ideas and objectives, which often prevents any one of them being successful (for a fuller discussion of sentencing see, for example, Honderich (1989); Harding and Ireland (1989); and Walker (1985)).

The part played by official control agents is therefore quite complex. For their intervention to act as a deterrent, it is necessary to use the controls fairly and reasonably firmly.

13.8.3 Diversion and its net-widening control effects

One of the quickest-spreading control factors in Britain has arisen in the last 20 years or so and has blossomed largely out of the processes of diversion.

Diversion is now an enormous industry and it occurs at all levels of the criminal justice system. Before a court appearance it takes two forms: first, the police or other primary law enforcement agency (such as factory inspectors, Inland Revenue inspectors or Customs and Excise) can unofficially or officially divert individuals away from the full rigours of the criminal justice system by cautioning them. In these instances the offender has to admit the offence, and some may do so even when they are innocent to avoid a court appearance or to get it over and done with. Similarly, the prosecution may decide not to prosecute, or agree to prosecute for a lesser crime to which the individual is willing to plead guilty. In Britain these forms of diversion are usually complete in themselves, but there is now a form of diversion called 'diversion plus' where the individual may be asked to do something extra (normally, in the case of Customs and Excise or the Inland Revenue to make an extra payment over that actually owed). More recently some police have been using a scheme whereby offenders are offered reparation on top of the diversion. In the case of juveniles such schemes were not found to be very promising: victims felt pressured as reparations seemed to be pushed just to ensure acceptance of diversion by offenders. For these reasons the scheme was not adopted by the government (see Home Office (1990)). However an adult scheme set up in Kettering has had more success and managed to avoid the conflicts between offender and victim interests (see Dignan (1991)).

There is also diversion at the court stage where again there may be a willingness to plead guilty to some of the lesser offences hoping for a lesser sentence (again this is not the formalised US system of plea bargaining: judges here are not allowed to make promises). Finally there is diversion at the sentencing stage, away from a punishment model towards a treatment or community model. This may be in the form of a mediation and reparation scheme. One, the Leeds Reparation Scheme, has involved serious offences but most are concerned only with minor offences. More normally it involves probation with or without some counselling or other intervention such as community service, supervision order, curfew order or attendance centre order. Each of these appears to be more helpful to offenders than to victims. Each has been vigorously attacked by some authors and politicians as encouraging increased criminality by an excess of liberal permissiveness.

Other attacks suggest that such systems, far from keeping individuals outside the criminal justice system in fact suck more and more within their control. The most notable proponent of this 'net-widening' effect is Cohen (1985), who argues that community programmes and social diversion suck children in at a younger age, often before they have offended but are merely 'at risk'. In the 1970s cautioning was systematically used to deal with individuals who would otherwise have been dealt with informally. As a result the wider welfare model has been used to deal with children whose behaviour falls short of criminality. Something similar also arises at the sentencing stage. On pure punishment grounds a sentence of say six months might be appropriate, but by deciding on diversion a probationary sentence may be passed which might remain in force for one or two years. This, too, increases the numbers controlled at any one time. Moreover, those who offend whilst on probation may, in some circumstances, be sentenced not only for the most recent offence but also for the initial offence, which again leads to more people being contained in the criminal justice system.

There is also a difficulty of what Cohen terms 'thinning the mesh' whereby not only are the numbers controlled increased but the level of intervention in their lives is increased. In older probationary systems the level of intervention was fairly low: to ensure that the offender tried to live an industrious life, he or she would be recommended to pursue certain types of activities. Newer schemes offer additions which the court can choose to attach to the sentence (see the Criminal Justice Act 1991, s. 8, which substituted new powers under the Powers of Criminal Courts Act 1973, s. 2). Requirements include: residential requirements; community service; an order to take part in certain activities, especially those of a probation centre; and treatment for mental conditions. There are also specific requirements which may be used in cases of sex offenders and those suffering from drug or alcohol dependency. The control system is interfering to a much deeper level in the lives of individuals. Finally, in this respect, is the problem that most of the non-custodial interventions are used not as alternatives to incarceration , but have tradition-ally replaced the fine, the punishment which intervenes least in the lives of offenders. The Criminal Justice Act 1991 tried to remedy some of this last problem but its effectiveness in doing so has been largely undermined by the provisions of the Criminal Justice Act 1993 which removed the unit fine system which permitted the poor to be more appropriately fined, and allowed previous offending to be taken into account.

The result, Cohen claims, is that there is a dangerous blurring of the formal and informal control system so that officially organised State intervention is becoming very wide and very controlling, especially of the poorer sections of society, as well as penetrating deeply into society. These wider control systems have not reduced the prison population but simply led to general increases in the numbers controlled and the extent of control. Cohen sees this as dangerous, unnecessary and unacceptable.

One newer method which tries to increase diversion from court without running into Cohen's problem is the systems management approach, usually operated in connection with juveniles (see Thorpe et al. (1980)). This is intended to do for the criminal justice system what problem-oriented policing should do for the operation of the police. Basically systems management systematically analyses all the elements of the criminal justice system – how the agencies interact, how and why particular suspects pass through the process – starting with detection and working through to final disposal. A knowledge of both how and why decisions are made could constructively affect final outcomes to secure diversion from court. Systems management schemes constitute an elaborate series of processes: the first diversion is taken by the police, the next level is a non-statutory multi-agency panel, sometimes called the cautioning panel, sometimes the juvenile liaison bureau. The panel has representatives from the police, probation, social and educational services and any other important local bodies dealing in child care. These panels try to divert as many juveniles as is safe either by use of a simple caution or the caution-plus model, social work intervention or reparation to the victim. The panel is thus another gate through which the case has to go before a prosecution is arrived at, but any case not diverted then goes to the Crown Prosecution Service for its decision on whether to prosecute. If the case goes ahead, and if a pre-sentence report is requested, the reports try to target offenders most likely to be incarcerated and find realistic alternatives. Often they will recommend intermediate treatment (IT) for such juveniles. In the 1980s many intensive IT schemes were set up in order to divert juveniles from custody. Many of these try to confront offenders with the negative aspects of their actions and teach them how to avoid such outcomes (see cognitive learning theory in 10.2.6). They were helped in this endeavour by the fact that the Criminal Justice Act 1982 required courts to use imprisonment only as a last resort: any offer of a realistic alternative makes it more difficult to incarcerate juveniles (a similar measure was introduced for adults in the Criminal Justice Act 1991, s. 1, thereby allowing similar strategies to be used for adults). Lastly the system requires the outcomes and each stage of a case to be carefully monitored to ensure the attainment of the minimum acceptable intervention. By this method they try to avoid net widening whilst not abandoning some of the useful social interventions which may be available.

If all this shows some possible ways of improving the criminal justice system, it also illustrates the complications of pursuing them. In particular, the proposed remedies will themselves have side-effects which are difficult to foresee and some of which will be unwelcome. An awareness of the dangers should not, however, inhibit the search for improvements.

13.9 EVALUATION OF CONTROL THEORIES

The concepts which make up the control theory are based on logical connectors which have been linked with crime for a long period. They have therefore received much research. Most of this research has, to a large extent, upheld the basic theory (see, for example, Travis Hirschi's own study in 1969, Empey and Lubeck (1971) and the 1979 British study by Johnson), but other empirical studies have been more sceptical (see, for example, Rankin (1977)). Grasmick and Bursik (1990), in an interesting study, tried to test the various elements of control theory to ascertain which had most validity and was most likely to produce conforming behaviour. Shame (or the internal deterrence of conscience) had the strongest deterrent effect: that is, if an individual believed something was wrong and would be ashamed of doing it, this factor was most likely to pull him or her back into conformity. This finding is supportive of socialisation processes such as those discussed in 13.7 and in Chapters Eight and Ten, and also lends support to policies based on shaming (13.8.2) as well as cognitive learning programmes (see 10.2.6). Legal punishments, if believed to be fairly certain, were another strong inhibitor of criminal activities. Surprisingly, disapproval of 'significant others' was least important, perhaps because the respondents thought it unlikely that 'significant others' would find out. At all events, there is now a substantial body of research based on control theory which lends some support to its use as a means of understanding and influencing conforming behaviour. Policies based on these findings could play a constructive role.

Of course, control theories cannot explain all types of criminality or delinquency, but no theory could ever do that, since crime is too disparate a feature of human behaviour. For example, Box (1981) suggests that they probably do little to explain collective behaviour such as football hooliganism. If this is committed in a 'youth culture', at least part of the explanation for it probably lies outside the control theories. Box further suggests that their explanatory power is limited to primary deviance, which he defines as occurring when an individual:

(a) deviates episodically and infrequently,
(b) does so without much organisation or sophistication,
(c) has no self-image of deviancy, and
(d) is not viewed as essentially deviant by the authorities.

Others have not accepted these limitations, but he poses them because he claims that once an individual has frequently transgressed the law, there are probably no further effective ties to conformity. This is true to a certain extent, but even habitual criminals generally only transgress certain laws, and the control constructs may be strong enough to prevent them from branching into different crimes. This emerges from research into the behaviour of criminals in prison, many of whom disapprove very strongly of certain types of offenders such as mass murderers or sex offenders. Such offenders normally have to be held separately on Rule 43 for their own protection.

Box also claims that control theory cannot explain what he sees as the most serious crimes – those of the powerful, such as Watergate, or oil sanction busting in Rhodesia. He assumes that these are not explained by control theories. This is not necessarily the case, as these criminals may be willing to transgress because they are unlikely to be caught and therefore the attachments, commitments and involvement in conventional society are not in jeopardy. That would be wholly rational behaviour under the control theory. Control theory may therefore be useful in a wider context than Box is willing to concede. Of course, there will always be crimes which people are willing to commit no matter how great their stake in conformity, because the potential gain is very high. There will also be a small number of criminals who commit criminal acts because they are suffering from some sort of mental or physical problem.

Further criticism has come from writers such as Agnew (1993) who claim that the social control model ignores aspects of motivation which they see as crucial to offending. The model would, they urge, be improved by taking account of theories of strain and differential association or social learning. Thus critics claim that, even in the absence of strong controls, there may be no offending if the motivation is insufficiently strong; and even in cases where the social control is strong, there may be offending if the motivation is sufficiently strong. They therefore would contest, not the theory itself, but its claim to be so all-embracing and to stand alone.

In response it could be said that (conceptually) control balance theory encapsulates both motivation and rational choice. A more practical difficulty is that the qualities of the social controls which promote or nurture law-abiding behaviour and those which promote and nurture law-breaking behaviour have not yet been properly identified. As a result, the practical utility of the theory is somewhat lessened. Until the theory can pin-point more accurately the specific types of attachments, commitment, and involvement that will encourage law-abiding behaviour, and suggest how they can be promoted, the theory is only of limited help to our understanding of criminality. The insistence of its advocates that each of these variables is subjective further reduces its usefulness. It is not possible to generalise from a substantially subjective theory. It was in an attempt to meet some of these objections that 13.7 above discussed the way in which a few of the more important social constructs, such as family and school, affect criminality.

Despite these shortcomings, control is possibly one of the most promising intellectual developments yet to emerge in the struggle to understand and explain criminal behaviour.

Many policy suggestions arise from this field. In particular, the ideas support policies which will assist families, schools and other socialising organisations to carry out their functions. These might involve State-financed family and marriage counselling; more financial support for families; greater funding for schools, including funding to support extra-curricular activities; and efforts to develop closer ties between schools and families. There are also implications for the way the State sector deals with offenders. Control theories suggest that cognitive learning processes should be carefully considered in sentencing decisions (particularly involving probation) and in prisons and other institutions where offenders are held. This would involve a new belief in treatment/psychosocial processes and the willingness to invest in them. The approach also suggests broader policy goals: if, for example, real and stable employment was more readily available, more adults would be tied into more conventional lifestyles and diverted from criminality.

In the area of State control, policy is more difficult to delineate. This chapter suggests that the police and other agencies of control should be more closely integrated with each other, with agencies of social support and with the community they are there to serve. This would involve more consultation and accountability than is presently the case. The approach also indicates that, in relation to punishment, very tough measures could lead to feelings of resentment and rejection which in the long run could exacerbate offending (see also Chapter 14). At the very least, the studies examined suggest that the law and order rhetoric of the past 20 years or so needs careful analysis and assessment (see Currie (1996) and Raup (1996)). Policy based on reintegrative shaming or on cognitive learning might be more appropriate and effective.

Overall, the kind of policies prompted by control balance theory lean towards 'liberal' or 'progressive' solutions. They point to moving towards the equal distribution of control and of being controlled; to control being exercised with respect for others; and to State encouragement of and support for strong social bonds, strong communities and social support within the community. These ideological leanings will be sufficient for some to reject them out of hand. This, however, is to refuse to consider the evidence of the studies and – more fundamentally – to lose sight of the fact that all these policy suggestions assume that the *status quo*, the present middle-class values etc., are worth upholding and should be heavily inculcated into the whole population. The 'progressive' texture is seen by some as disguising an element of persuasive mind control which depends heavily on the ethics of the values being supported. These values are heavily attacked in the next two chapters.

REFERENCES

Ackers, Ronald L. (1991), 'Self-control as a General Theory of Crime', *Journal of Quantitative Criminology*, vol. 7, p. 201.

Agnew, Robert (1993), 'Why do they do it? An Examination of the Intervening Mechanisms between "Social Control" Variables and Delinquency', *Journal of Research in Crime and Delinquency*, vol. 30, p. 245.

Barlow, Hugh D. (1991), 'Explaining Crimes and Analogous Acts, or the Unrestrained Will Grab at Pleasure Whenever They Can', *Journal of Criminal Law and Criminology*, vol. 82, p. 229.

Beccaria, Cesare (1964), *Of Crimes and Punishments* (first published 1776 as *Dei delitti e delle pene*, 6th edn, trans. Fr. Kenelm Foster and Jane Grigson with an introduction by A.P. D'Entreves, London: Oxford University Press.

Bowlby, John (1946), *Forty-Four Juvenile Thieves*, London: Ballière, Tindall and Cox.

Bowlby, John (1953), *Child Care and the Growth of Love* (based by permission of the World Health Organisation on the Report: Maternal Care and Mental Health), Harmondsworth: Penguin.

Bowlby, John (1973), *Separation: Anxiety and Anger*, London: Hogarth Press.

Box, Steven (1981), *'Deviance, Reality and Society'*, 2nd edn, London: Holt Rinehart and Winston.

Box, Steven (1983), *Power, Crime and Mystification*, London: Tavistock.

Box, Steven (1987), *Recession, Crime and Punishment*, London: Macmillan.

Braithwaite, John (1988), *Crime Shame and Reintegration*, Cambridge: Cambridge University Press.

Braithwaite, John (1997), 'Charles Tittle's Control Balance and Criminal Theory', *Theoretical Criminology*, vol. 1, p. 77.

Carson, W. (1970), 'White Collar Crime and the Enforcement of Factory Legislation', *British Journal of Criminology*, vol. 10, p. 383.

Chilton, Roland J. and Markle, Gerald E. (1972), 'Family Disruption, Delinquent Conduct, and the Effect of Subclassification', *American Sociological Review*, vol. 37, p. 93.

Christie, Nils (1960), *Unge Norske Lovovertredere* (Young Norwegian Lawbreakers), Oslo: Universitetsforlaget.

Cochran, John K. and Ackers, Ronald L. (1989), 'Beyond Hellfire: an Exploration of the Variable Effects of Religiosity on Adolescent Marijuana and Alcohol Use', *Journal of Research in Crime and Delinquency*, vol. 26, p. 198.

Cochran, John K., Wood, Peter B. and Arneklev, Bruce J. (1994), 'Is the Religiosity–Delinquency Relationship Spurious? A Test of Arousal and Social Control Theories', *Journal of Research in Crime and Delinquency*, vol. 31, p. 92.

Cohen, Stanley (1985), *Visions of Social Control: Crime, Punishment and Classification*, Cambridge: Polity Press.

Cohen, Stanley and Scull, Andrew (eds), (1983), *Social Control and the State: Comparative and Historical Essays*, Oxford: Basil Blackwell.

Coleman, Alice (1988), 'Design Disadvantage and Design Improvement', *The Criminologist*, vol. 12, p. 20.

Conger, R. (1976), 'Social Control and Learning Models of Delinquent Behaviour', *Criminology*, vol. 14, p. 171.

Currie, Elliot (1996), *Is America Really Winning the War on Crime and Should Britain Follow its Example?* NACRO, 30th Anniversary Lecture, London: NACRO.

Dignan, James (1991), *Repairing the Damage: an Evaluation of an Experimental Adult Reparation Scheme in Kettering, Northamptonshire*, Sheffield: University of Sheffield, Centre for Criminological and Legal Research.

Empey, Lamar T. and Lubeck, Steven G. (1971), *Explaining Delinquency*, Lexington, Mass.: D.C. Heath.

Farrington, D.P. (1992a), 'Juvenile Delinquency', in J.C. Coleman (ed.), *The School Years*, 2nd edn, London: Routledge.

Farrington, D.P. (1992b), 'Explaining the Beginning, Progress and Ending of Antisocial Behaviour from Birth to Adulthood', in J. McCord (ed.), *Advances in Criminological Theory*, vol. 3, New Brunswick, NJ: Transaction.

Feldman, M. Phillip (1977), *Criminal Behaviour: A Psychological Analysis*, Chichester: John Wiley and Sons.

Finnis, J (1968), 'Old and New in Hart's Philosophy of Punishment', *Oxford Review*, vol. 8, p. 73.

Gifford, Lord (1986), *The Broadwater Farm Inquiry*, London: Karia Press.

Gifford, Lord, Brown, Wally and Bundy, Ruth (1989), *Loosen the Shackles: First Report of the Liverpool 8 Inquiry into Race Relations in Liverpool*, London: Karia Press.

Goldstein, Herman (1990), *Problem-Oriented Policing*, New York: McGraw-Hill.

Gottfredson, Michael R. and Hirschi, Travis (1990), *A General Theory of Crime*, Stanford, Calif: Stanford University Press.

Grasmick, Harold G. and Bursik, Robert J. (1990), 'Conscience, Significant Others, and Rational Choice: Extending the Deterrence Model', *Law and Society Review*, vol. 24(3), p. 837.

Grasmick, Harold G., Bursik, Robert J. and Cochran, John K. (1991), 'Render unto Caesar What Is Caesar's: Religiosity and Taxpayers' Inclinations to Cheat', *Sociological Quarterly*, vol. 32, p. 251.

Grasmick, Harold G., Tittle, Charles R., Bursik Jr, Robert J. and Arneklev, Bruce J. (1993), 'Testing the Core Empirical Implications of Gottfredson and Hirschi's General Theory of Crime', *Journal of Research in Crime and Delinquency*, vol. 30, p. 5.

Hagan, J. (1987), *Modern Criminology: Crime, Criminal Behaviour and its Control*, New York: McGraw-Hill.

Hagan, John (1989), *Structural Criminology*, New Brunswick, NJ: Rutgers University Press.

Hagan, J., Gillis, A.R. and Simpson, J. (1990), 'Clarifying and Extending Power–Control Theory', *American Journal of Sociology*, vol. 95, p. 1024.

Harding, Christopher and Ireland, Richard W. (1989), *Punishment: Rhetoric, Rule, and Practice*, London: Routledge.

Hargreaves, David H. (1967), *Social Relations in a Secondary School*, London: Routledge & Kegan Paul.

Hargreaves, David H. (1980), 'Classrooms, Schools and Juvenile Delinquency', *Educational Analysis*, vol. 2, p. 75.

Haskell, Martin R. and Yablonsky, Lewis (1982), *Juvenile Delinquency*, 3rd edn, Boston: Houghton Mifflin.

Heckathorn, Douglas D. (1990), 'Collective Sanctions and Compliance Norms: A Formal Theory of Group-Mediated Social Control', *American Sociological Review*, vol. 55, p. 336.

Heywood, Ian, Hall, Neil and Redhead, Peter (1992), 'Is There a Role for Spatial Information Systems in Formulating Multi-agency Crime Prevention Strategies?', in David J. Evans, Nicholas R. Fyfe and David T. Herbert (eds), *Crime, Policing and Place: Essays in Environmental Criminology*, London: Routledge.

Hirschi, Travis (1969), *Causes of Delinquency*, Berkeley: University of California Press.

Hirschi, Travis, and Gottfredson, Michael R. (1993), 'Commentary: Testing the General Theory of Crime', *Journal of Research in Crime and Delinquency*, vol. 30, p. 47.

Home Office (1990), *Crime, Justice and Protecting the Public: the Government's Proposals for Legislation* (Cmd 965), London: HMSO.

Honderich, Ted (1989), *Punishment: the Supposed Justifications*, Cambridge: Polity Press.

Hopkins, Andrew and McGregor, Heather (1991), *Working for Change: The Movement Against Domestic Violence*, Sydney: Allen & Unwin.

Institute of Race Relations (1987), *Policing Against Black People*, London: Institute of Race Relations.

Johnson, R.E. (1979), *Juvenile Delinquency and its Origin*, Cambridge: Cambridge University Press.

Katz, Jack (1988), *The Seductions of Crime: Moral and Sensual Attractions in Doing Evil*, New York: Basic Books.

Keane, Carl, Maxim, Paul S. and Teevan, James J. (1993), 'Drinking and Driving, Self-control, and Gender: Testing a General Theory of Crime', *Journal of Research in Crime and Delinquency*, vol. 30, p. 30.

Kinsey, R., Lea, J. and Young, J. (1986), *Losing the Fight Against Crime*, Oxford: Basil Blackwell.

Kolvin, I., Miller, F.J.W., Scott, D.M., Gatzanis, S.R.M., and Fleeting, M. (1990), *Continuities of Deprivation?*, Aldershot: Avebury.

Lansky, M. (1987), 'Shame and Domestic Violence', in D. Nathanson (ed.), *The Many Faces of Shame*, New York: Guilford.

Leigh, L. (ed.), (1980), *Economic Crime in Europe*, London: Macmillan.

Lofland, J. (1969), *Deviance and Reality*, New Jersey: Prentice-Hall.

McCord, J. (1982), 'A Longitudinal View of the Relationship between Parental Absence and Crime', in J. Gunn and D.P. Farrington (eds), *Abnormal Offenders, Delinquency, and the Criminal Justice System*, Chichester: Wiley.

McGuire, James and Priestley, Phillip (1985), *Offending Behaviour: Skills and Strategies for Going Straight*, London: Batsford.

Mathieson, T. (1983), 'The Future of Control Systems: the Case of Norway', in David Garland and Paul Young (eds), *The Power to Punish: Contemporary Penalty and Social Analysis*, London: Heinemann.

Mathiesen, Thomas (1997), 'The Viewer Society: Michel Foucault's "Panopticon" Revisited', *Theoretical Criminology*, vol. 1, p. 215.

Matza, David (1964), *Delinquency and Drift*, London: Wiley.

Miller, Susan L. and Burack, Cynthia (1993), 'A Critique of Gottfredson and Hirschi's General Theory of Crime: Selective Inattention to Gender and Power Positions', *Women and Criminal Justice*, vol. 4, p. 115.

Monahan, Thomas P. (1957), 'Family Status and the Delinquent Child: A Reappraisal and Some New Findings', *New Forces*, vol. 35, p. 250.

Moore, C. and Brown, J. (1981), *Community Versus Crime*, London: Bedford Square Press.

Morash, M. and Rucker L. (1989), 'An Exploratory Study of the Connection of Mother's Age at Childbearing to her Children's Delinquency in Four Data Sets', *Crime and Delinquency*, vol. 35, p. 45.

Nye, F. Ivan (1958), *Family Relationships and Delinquent Behaviour*, New York: John Wiley.

Pitts, J. (1986), 'Black Young People and Juvenile Crime: Some Unanswered Questions', in R. Matthews and J. Young (eds), *Confronting Crime*, London: Sage.

Rankin, J.H. (1977), 'Investigating the Interrelations among Social Control Variables and Conformity', *Journal of Criminal Law and Criminology*, vol. 67, p. 470.

Raup, Ethan (1996), 'The American Prison Problem, Hegemonic Crisis, and the Censure of Inner-City Blacks', in Colin Sumner (ed.), *Violence, Culture and Censure*, London: Taylor & Francis.

Reckless, Walter C. (1967), *The Crime Problem*, 4th edn, New York: Appleton-Century-Croft.

Reckless, Walter C. (1973), *The Crime Problem*, 5th edn, New York: Appleton-Century-Croft.

Reckless, Walter C. and Dinitz, Simon (1972), *The Prevention of Juvenile Delinquency*, Columbus: Ohio State University Press.

Reiner, R. (1985), *The Politics of the Police*, Brighton: Wheatsheaf.

Reiss, Albert J. (1951), 'Delinquency as the Failure of Personal and Social Controls', *American Sociological Review*, vol. 16, p. 196.

Robins, L.N. (1979), 'Sturdy Childhood Predictors of Adult Outcomes: Replications from Longitudinal Studies', in J.E. Barrett, R.M. Rose and G. L. Klerman (eds), *Stress and Mental Disorder*, New York: Raven.

Roshier, Bob (1989), *Controlling Crime: The Classical Perspective in Criminology*, Milton Keynes: Open University Press.

Rothman, David (1983), 'Social Control: The Uses and Abuses of the Concept in the History of Incarceration', in Stanley Cohen and Andrew Scull (eds), *Social Control and the State: Comparative and Historical Essays*, Oxford: Basil Blackwell.

Rutter, M., Maughn, B., Mortimore, P., Ouston, J. and Smith, A. (1979), *Fifteen Thousand Hours: Secondary Schools and their Effects on Children*, London: Open Books.

Sampson, Robert J. and Laub, John H. (1990), 'Crime and Deviance Over the Life Course: The Salience of Adult Bonds', *American Sociological Review*, vol. 55, p. 609.

Scarman, Lord (1981), *The Brixton Disorders, 10-12 April 1981* (Scarman Report), Cmnd 8427, London: HMSO.

Scheff, Thomas and Retzinger, Suzanne (1991), *Emotions and Violence: Shame and Rage in Destructive Conflicts*, Lexington, Va: Lexington Books.

Schwartz, Michael and Tangri, Sandra (1965), 'A Note on Self-Concept as an Insulator Against Delinquency', *American Sociological Review*, vol. 30, p. 922.

Scraton, P. (1985), *The State of the Police*, London: Pluto.

Shover, Neal (1996), *Great Pretenders: Pursuits and Careers of Persistent Thieves*, Boulder, Co: Westview Press.

Striking Back (1985), Cardiff: Welsh Campaign for Civil Liberties.

Taylor, Ian (1997), 'Crime Anxiety and Locality: Responding to the "Condition of England" at the End of the Century', *Theoretical Criminology*, vol. 1, p. 53.

Thorpe, D.H., Smith, D., Green, C.J., and Paley, J.G. (1980), *Out of Care: the Community Support of Juvenile Offenders*, London: George Allen and Unwin.

Tittle, Charles R. (1995), *Control Balance: Towards a General Theory of Deviance*, Boulder, Co: Westview Press.

Tittle, Charles R. (1997), 'Thoughts Stimulated by Braithwaite's Analysis of Control Balance', *Theoretical Criminology*, vol. 1, p. 99.

Walker, Nigel (1985), *Sentencing: Theory and Practice*, London: Butterworths.

Wells, L.E. and Rankin, J.H. (1991), 'Families and Delinquency: a Meta-Analysis of the Impact of Broken Homes', *Social Problems*, vol. 38, p. 71.

West, D.J. (1982), *Delinquency: Its Roots, Careers and Prospects*, London: Heinemann.

West, D.J. and Farrington, D.P. (1977), *The Delinquent Way of Life*, London: Heinemann.

Wilson, H. (1980), 'Parental Supervision: A Neglected Aspect of Delinquency', *British Journal of Criminology*, vol. 20, p. 20.

Zingraff, Matthew T., Leiter, Jeffrey, Johnsen, Matthew C. and Myers, Kristen A. (1994), 'The Mediating Effect of Good School Performance on the Maltreatment – Delinquency Relationship', *Journal of Research in Crime and Delinquency*, vol. 31, p. 62.

CHAPTER FOURTEEN

Labelling, Phenomenology and Ethnomethodology

14.1 INTRODUCTION

'The New Criminologies' is rather a misnomer. The ideas upon which much of this school is based are by no means new: they are drawn from the works of Plato and Aristotle, Machiavelli, Hobbes, Alfred Schultz, Karl Marx, and the Chicago School. Moreover, since the theory began to appear about thirty years ago it is perhaps no longer 'new'. In many texts the approach is referred to as radical criminology, conflict criminology, Marxist criminology or symbolic interactionism. Whatever the label, the contents are much the same. They first began to be propagated at the end of the fifties and, although they are still frequently drawn on, writers of this school were most active and influential in the limited period between 1960 and 1975.

It is unsurprising that they arose during this period, which was generally a time of questioning authority and the *status quo*. The sixties are known for their campus conflicts in both Europe and America, as well as the wholesale rejection of many of the values of the immediate post-war years. The human rights movement began to become more popular and stronger; the young began to question the conventional way of life and conventional values; in America there was protest over the Vietnam war, and both here and elsewhere there was a growing pacifist movement; in Britain the Northern Ireland problem grew from a civil rights campaign into a violent conflict; and the women's rights movement and feminist arguments began to arise. Just as most of these movements or trends were reactions against the accepted values, explanations and ways of life, so the new criminologies were, to a large extent, a reaction against the positivism which had arisen in and taken over criminology. To understand the new criminologies, it is important to understand some of the theoretical, empirical and institutional elements against which these people were working.

As has already been seen, positivists believe that criminality is caused by something outside the control of the offender: it is the result of a biological, psychological or social fault. They therefore reject, or at least severely limit, the idea of a rational man able to exercise free will and to choose and direct his actions. In doing this, they cease to describe the world and the activities of a society by means of those who participate in it. Instead, they seek out what they consider to be the profound and compelling causes which subconsciously direct the participants' behaviour. The cause of the behaviour makes the individual choose to act in a particular way, and so the cause becomes the choice. As has been evident in many of the preceding chapters, if a particular factor arises markedly more frequently in criminals than in non-criminals, then the positivists tend to see that factor as a cause of that criminality (see Chapters Six to Twelve). In criticism, the new criminologists point out that it merely indicates seeming contacts between criminality and the various factors. They claim that it is not sufficiently supported by theoretical explanation to establish whether the connection is causal and how the causation works in practice.

If the positivist tradition is so obviously flawed, why was it accepted for so long and by so many people? Much of its appeal rests on its claim to be 'scientific'. The links between crime and the various factors seemed to be scientifically tested, and thus as 'objective': the presumed freedom from political or other bias made them more acceptable. These general considerations are reinforced by particular institutional traditions. For example, in Britain the judiciary is used to being asked to interpret and apply the law objectively without questioning its validity or fairness. A scientific and objective basis for explaning criminality is thus especially acceptable to it, the more so if it is postulated by other professionals. The positivist approach also appeals to substantial sectors of the general public: it makes them feel safe from becoming criminal themselves, whilst not simply condemning the individual who is criminal. 'Unlike myself, a criminal is not normal, or has experienced an upbringing/environment different from mine: they need help and I need to be protected against them.'

New criminologies reject this stance. Some of the reasons for this rejection will gradually emerge from our discussion, but others can immediately be made explicit. One argument against the positivist school is that it is too simplistic. It seems to treat the criminals as if they exist almost in a vacuum. Most criminal activities involve, either directly or tacitly, the cooperation or at least knowledge of many people or even groups, such as purchasers of stolen goods. When a member of a corporation does some illegal act within that institution, it is generally done with the knowledge and often the blessing or even direction of supervisors. A criminal act is not an isolated act, so the new criminologist would argue that to explain most criminality in positivist terms is neither realistic nor illuminating.

A second argument against positivism can be found in the rejection of the idea that criminal behaviour can be reduced to a purely scientific or technical question. The criminal act was seen as an abnormal act, and it was necessary to bring the criminal back to normality, either by correcting some psychological defect, or by teaching how to cope with some biological or social problem and become law-abiding. The implicit assumption was that crime is not really a rational choice, and therefore anyone making that choice must be different and need help (for a very strong questioning of this stance see Foucault's views, reproduced in Kritzman (ed.) (1988), pp. 125-51). Furthermore, positivists seemed to assume that if something was called a crime, it was necessarily wrong because the State said it was wrong. New criminologists probe behind this claim, and argue that many acts are defined as crimes largely to protect and reflect the interests of the powerful and to retain a political and ideological *status quo*. In the 1960s much of this was brought into question: many faced criminal charges for what they saw as oppression, and notions of 'helping' them back to normality seemed irrelevant. At a time when the *status quo* was being questioned in all other fields of life, it would have been surprising if it had not been challenged in the sphere of criminality. For the new criminologies, crime is related to the law-abiding, especially the powerful, as well as to those who violate the law.

The new criminologies largely agree on the basis for rejecting positivism, but they differ over what should replace it. The new criminologies, as the plural suggests, embrace different ideas and schools of thought. Here the study will be split into four areas or 'schools', namely: labelling or interactionism; phenomenology and ethnomethodology; conflict; and radical criminologies. It is not claimed that this is the only, or the correct, way to present the materials, but it is hoped that it will make them easier to follow. It is, however, important to emphasise that these areas are interlinked and do not constitute separate theories. Two of these perspectives (labelling or interactionism, and phenomenology and ethnomethodology) will be dealt with in this chapter, and two (conflict, and radical criminologies) in the next.

14.2 LABELLING OR INTERACTIONISM

Labelling theories and interactionism were the spring-board for many of the proponents and ideas of the new criminology. Two preliminary points need to be noted. Firstly, labelling or interactionism represents, not a single theory, but rather a number of different ideas drawn together under one method. This method is sometimes also called social reaction theory and, as this term suggests, it looks towards society's reaction to the deviant more than to the person of the deviant. Secondly, and possibly more important, its proponents never claimed that it caused criminality in a direct way. They saw it rather as widening the area to be considered in criminological theories, in particular to include the actions and positions of those around the criminal, and the effect these may have upon the criminal.

Although the ideas of labelling theory only took root in British criminology in the 1960s, they have a fairly long history. In 1936 Frederick Thrasher, in his work on juvenile gangs, recognised that the official label of 'deviant' had potentially negative effects upon the youths. Two years later, Frank Tannenbaum (1938) argued that calling someone criminal might result in him living up to the description. These references passed without causing any intense interest, and the real work on labelling theory did not begin to emerge until the work of Edwin Lemert (1951) and Howard Becker (1963 and 1973).

Labelling, or interactionism, is a derivative of the widely used sociological idea of interactionist social theory. Interactionist theory analyses the way social actors, usually individuals, have conceptions of themselves and of the others around them with whom they interact. This gives meaning to the behaviour of individuals, as it places their action in their understanding of the world. Of course, many conceptions which each person holds will be drawn from their culture or position in society, but the interactionists attach importance to the meanings which the individual places on various occurrences. Labelling theory is drawn from this, but centres its study on how symbols, namely labelling someone, can be used, or can be seen, to influence someone's action.

Rubington and Weinberg (1973) say that in the traditional criminology the researcher is concerned with why a person commits crimes and how one can prevent criminality, or further criminality. In interactionist criminology the researcher, they claim, must take at least two perspectives. First, to look at the problem from the perspective of society and ask under what circumstances does a person get set aside and called criminal. How does the labelling come about? How does the label affect the actions of others towards the individual? What value do they put on the fact of deviance? Secondly, to look at the problem from the perspective of the person labelled and ask how they react to the fact of being labelled. Do they adopt the criminal role set for them by others? Does it affect the circles they live in, and alter their self concept to take account of the deviant role assigned to them?

This sets out two facets of the interactionist or labelling perspective, but it clearly has more. We shall briefly comment on these two facets, and add a third. Thus we shall ask: what behaviour should attract the label of 'crime', and why? This is the third question to add to the two already indicated: how do official agencies and society use and apply these labels, and what effect does labelling have on the individual?

14.2.1 Labelling behaviour: societal reaction

Howard Becker (1963 and 1973) pointed out that no behaviour is deviant or criminal until it is so defined and thereby labelled by a section (the section in power) or by the whole of the society. To call something a crime is therefore only a reaction to a particular type of behaviour, a reaction that marks the behaviour out as unacceptable to other members of society. Each society creates deviants and criminals by making rules whose breach will constitute deviance or criminality. The rules of any particular society at any particular time are not inalienable. For example, abortion was generally illegal in Britain up until 1967; now in certain defined circumstances it is legal and acceptable. Rules differ from society to society. Thus the proponents of labelling or interactionism consider that the conventional morality of rules (even criminal laws) should be studied and questioned, not merely accepted as self-evident truths. This covers a wide range of approaches to the criminal justice system, from reform to left realism to anarchic abolitionism (see Pitch (1995), pp. 44–45). A more usual view is that nothing is criminal until someone reacts to it in such a way as to define it as such and treat its transgressors as criminal:

there is no such thing as an act which by its very nature is criminal and reprehensible. Even the most commonly recognised crime, murder, is not universally defined in the sense that anyone who kills another is, everywhere and always, guilty of murder. Some killings are excused on the grounds of extreme provocation or of self-defence. Some are actively condoned and glorified – killing in war. Therefore the same act – killing – cannot be understood without reference to other people's reactions. In this theoretical analysis, the creators and enforcers of rules need to be subjected to a critical scrutiny which should not be confined to those who violate the rules.

This perspective on the setting of criminal laws goes against the more traditional normative idea under which an activity is a crime if it breaches the norms of behaviour accepted by those in the society. The problem with the normative idea is the idea of a consensus of all people in a society, since normative theory assumes that the views of all persons carry equal weight. In interactionism, this assumption is challenged by scrutinising the reactions of individuals and groups to see whose reactions are given most weight.

Downes and Rock (1971) discuss the effects that power and position can have upon the way in which a person's act may be defined by others in society. They argue that if actions are performed by powerful people, there is a reluctance to define the action as criminal, although it may be criticised. Even if the activity is made illegal, it may be defined as an administrative infraction rather than a crime. This can most clearly be seen in the area of corporate or white-collar crime, where very often morally reprehensible and damaging activity is not defined as criminal. They argue that this tendency arises not only because of the power of the person carrying out the acts, but also because of the proximity of the actor and the person who is setting out the reactions of the society. The closer these two are, the more likely the action is to be excused and explained away as fairly normal. The further apart they are, the more likely the action is to be classified as criminal and a harsh penalty set for those who transgress.

It is not only the powerful who fight for certain legal positions. All sorts of pressure groups argue for all manner of legal changes. For example, although in 1967 abortion was legalised in certain situations, there have always been pressure groups who argue for changing this. On the one hand, many groups may fight for the woman's right to choose, and therefore for abortion on demand and up until 28 weeks. Other groups will be arguing for the rights of the foetus or, as they would call it, the child, and either push for no abortion at all, or for much tighter regulation of the laws. Each is arguing to protect rights: one the rights of the mother and the other the rights of the foetus (or child). Any changing of the law results in some redistribution of benefits. One or more type of person loses by being prevented from doing as they want or being criminalised for their behaviour, and others gain by having their rights protected. The group that wins is the one which is successful in obtaining the support of those in a position to decide.

Some behaviours become criminalised due to fairly small pressure groups or interest groups, but later become so accepted as criminal that almost all in a particular society would accept them as inherently bad. One of the best examples of this is the regulation of drugs. Until early this century, almost all drugs were legally available on demand. Many were used in the treatment of fairly minor ailments, and were commonly given to children. A small but strong international group led, in 1912, to the Hague Conference calling for the possession, sale, etc., of such drugs as opium, morphine and cocaine to be made illegal. In 1920, under the Dangerous Drugs Act, they became illegal in Britain. Many in the country at the time would have opposed such a law, but now the possession of these substances for other than medical purposes is generally regarded as bad or wrong in itself. Musto (1973) claims that the change in attitude towards drugs was, in America at least, brought about by the manipulation of scare stories. At all events, it is clear that the view of the wider society may well change from time to time.

The approach of interactionism has its own problems. The researchers are often effectively placing their own values on others. For example, they often assert that the powerless would draw the line defining criminality in a different position, which is not necessarily the case. In some respects this is as problematical as assuming a normative structure, but in the case of interactionism the theorists are at least more aware of the problematic position of labelling certain behaviour as criminal and other behaviour as non-criminal. This awareness is significant: it should make them less willing to condemn people for their behaviour and less willing to assume that something is wrong or bad *per se*. Because they do not view crimes as different in kind from other behaviours, the proponents of this school tend to study deviance rather than crime. They have looked at activities, some criminal, some not, which have led groups in society to view the perpetrators in a bad light.

14.2.2 Labelling the individual

The leading proponents of this area are Lemert (1951) and Becker (1963 and 1973). Lemert saw the main problems arising when a label attaches and the individual identifies with that label. Becker (1963) took the view that in making rules or crimes, society created deviance and by applying the rules to particular people and labelling them as criminals and outsiders, society creates the criminals. In this section we are concerned with how society decides who to label; in the next we will consider the effects of such a label on the individual.

The question is: 'who do we label as criminal'? The trite answer is 'those who transgress the criminal law'. Such a response requires enormous qualifications. As should have been clear from Chapter One almost everyone has transgressed a criminal law but many have never been punished for so doing. Therefore the answer might be that we label and punish only those who are caught. This is partially true, and can explain some of the concentration on street as opposed to boardroom or domestic criminality. As pointed out by Downes and Rock (1971), one of the factors affecting societal reaction to a particular activity is the visibility of the offence. If an offence is obvious and committed on the street, both the public and police are going to be more aware of it than if it happens in the home or in boardrooms. For this reason, its negative effects will be more obvious, and it is more likely to be officially controlled. Where this street activity becomes particularly prevalent and established as a 'problem' these factors are even stronger, as can be seen from the reaction to football hooligans. The types of crimes which are targeted in this way, and the public fear of them, can be artificially controlled. As was seen in Chapters Three and Five the media may build up a particular crime as being more important and more prevalent than the facts would suggest. This may alter its perception by society and therefore influence the reaction of society to it. Similarly the police, by deciding to target particular crimes, may make it appear that there is a problem in a particular area. For example, when Anderton took over as chief constable in Manchester he began a crusade against homosexuality and used his police to seek out and prosecute this group. Manchester, which had hitherto believed it had an insignificant homosexual problem, suddenly discovered a large problem. The activity had always existed, but only now was it was being policed and reacted against. Similarly there may be a decision on the part of the police to patrol certain areas more closely. They are then likely to discover more crime there, which may justify their initial judgment that this is a high crime rate area; or it may simply mean that the apparently lower crime rate of other areas reflects a less intense level of policing.

Even this is too simple an answer, because many people who are caught committing a crime are either not reported to the police or have no action taken against them. Therefore, the label 'criminal' is only put upon someone in fairly rare circumstances, and their criminal activity is only a small part of the process. The way in which actions which have been defined as criminal are policed and controlled is at least as important.

In some cases the police are not the enforcement agency. This has already been seen for corporate crime. Here the control agencies, such as the factory inspectors, mostly use persuasion and rarely press criminal charges (see Carson (1970)). In most offences, however, the enforcement agencies are the police, the courts, judges, probation officers and prisons. There are claims by labelling theorists that the police show sexual, racial, religious and/or class bias in performing their duties (see for example Smith and Gray (1986) and the Institute of Race Relations (1987)). On figures produced by the Home Office there is a clear difference in racial and sexual inclusion in the criminal justice system which is at least suggestive of bias (Skogan (1990); Home Office (1992a); Home Office (1992b)). On figures produced by the Commission for Racial Equality, or on their behalf, the bias is even more evident and exists at a number of levels in the system (see Hood (1992); Commission for Racial Equality (1992a); Commission for Racial Equality (1992b)). Like other agents of the criminal justice system, the police are, not surprisingly, likely to be influenced by a variety of external circumstances. Thus Piliavin and Briar (1964) discovered that the police response on catching a juvenile committing a crime varied: if a juvenile was demure and respectful he was more likely to be released with no further consequences; whereas if he was nonchalant, rude, argumentative and generally unhelpful he was more likely to be arrested and prosecuted. This was particularly the case if the demeanour of the juvenile was backed up by their appearance, social grouping, race and peer grouping. Such bias was also found by Sean Damer (1974) when he discovered that the inhabitants of certain neighbourhoods were characterised or labelled as criminal, and that in slum clearances, if the population of such an area were moved, their reputation moved with them and they would, in both the old and new neighbourhoods, be subjected to close policing. The labelling process also involved the locals who lived near the new estate and perceived the newcomers as trouble even before their arrival.

Finally, the wrong person may be arrested, accused and eventually even convicted. This may happen if those in power decide to punish a scapegoat, that is, knowingly punish the wrong person, or if there is a mistake. At all stages of this 'mistake' there may be effects for the wronged individual, who may be treated differently by others on the basis that there is 'no smoke without fire'. All these areas of bias can again become important in the court appearances and the encounters with probation officers and other officials. The use of the word 'criminal' perhaps has as much to do with the reaction of society to the behaviour and to the individual as it does to the fact of an offence having been committed.

14.2.3   Social reaction: the individual and self-concept

The third part of the social reaction theories is that if someone is subjected to a label, this may be internalised by the person labelled, and this might affect behaviour. Becker (1963 and 1973) and many other labelling theorists who expound this idea are not saying that this caused deviance. Labelling theorists have never argued the simplistic misrepresentation that they are sometimes accused of – they have never said: if you catch me stealing, call me a thief and convict and sentence me for theft, I will internalise the label and will call myself a thief and act accordingly. They were seeking to comprehend a situation by taking account of all the participants, and of their interactions. How others treat and view people affects the way they view themselves (see Matsueda (1992)). A person may have a particular self-image, but unless this becomes accepted by others in the society it is difficult to sustain and may have to be relinquished. This is seen as crucial because each individual conducts his or her life according to their self-image.

This part of the labelling theory is possibly the best documented and most widely discussed. Most writers use the concepts of primary and secondary deviance. The former is seen as rule breaking, and generally has nothing to do with labels because the deviant act is neutralised, normalised or denied (see Lemert (1967 and 1972)). Neutralisation involves justifying the action in some way, possibly by saying that the employer owes him the money; or he is only borrowing the money; or that the violence was committed in self defence. (For a fuller discussion of neutralisation, see 12.4.) It could be normalised if others around them also commit similar acts, making them seem slightly disreputable rather than criminal. For example, a worker may see that everyone pilfers a little from work, or a youth may see that most of his peers shop-lift. They come to see such acts as normal rather than criminal, and believe that they have a reasonable defence or justification (the employer or the shop can afford the loss, etc.). Even people who have committed many crimes may fit into this category of primary deviance, especially if they have not been convicted and have therefore been able to maintain their self-image.

Primary deviance is not featured in many labelling explanations because those concerned have not yet changed their self-image in response to societal reaction to their behaviour. When the label criminal is officially applied to someone who is still a primary deviant, many labelling theorists say that the individual is falsely so defined (see, for example, Garfinkel (1965)). By this they do not mean that the individual is innocent, but rather that the individual has not accepted the view of society that it is not only the activity which is wrong, but also that the individual offender is a criminal. That is, society now views the person as less worthy and as the type of person who will get into trouble; but the term primary deviance implies that the person concerned does not share this view. They see criminality as neither part of their character nor of their lifestyle. However, calling them criminals may change this.

Secondary deviance is behaviour which results, at least in part, from the problems of self-identity and societal reactions. Secondary deviance may have a number of causes, but these writers suggest that it can be better understood through the effects of labelling which may have made it more likely. Those covered by the concept of secondary deviance are generally those who persistently break the law, both as a way of making a living and as a way of life. In fact, most of the criminological studies so far carried out, by positivists as well as by the proponents of labelling, have concentrated on this group because the examples of criminals are mostly drawn from prisons and similar institutions. One strength of the labelling school is that they are more aware that their findings mostly apply only to secondary deviants.

It is the members of society, and particularly the police, courts and other agents of social control, who are responsible for giving an individual a label. It is also society, largely through the same agents, who can determine the effects that label will have on the individual. The individuals so labelled are treated differently from others, and the effect of this depends partly upon their ability to deal with the consequences and how they then view themselves. The individual accepting the label becomes a secondary deviant. For some, this acceptance may arise after only one transgression and label; for others it may take a number of transgressions and penalties. Secondary deviance may also, but rarely, arise when the perpetrator, although undiscovered, believes that if caught he will be labelled and accepts that self-inflicted label. Becker calls this secret deviance (Becker (1963 and 1973)). No one of these types covers the whole of deviance, and therefore each is important to our understanding of the social interaction involved.

The effects of being labelled a criminal, and especially whether this is accepted as a self-image, depend upon two factors: firstly, the way the person is treated as a result of the deviance; and secondly, the way the person manages to handle these effects. It is important to note that labelling theorists see the act of labelling only as a first step in the process; the fact of being officially labelled is often not sufficient to affect the individual. For any stigmatisation to give rise to a deviant identity it must be disseminated through society, or a part of society which is significant to the person concerned.

If people know about the criminal label it is likely to affect the way in which they treat the individual. For many, the criminal label is likely to be the overriding identifying label. A person previously known mainly as a parent or a schoolchild, or whatever, is now primarily known as a thief. The individual may then start to wonder whether the conception of him as bad or as a thief is actually more real than the perception he had of himself previously.

Many people have a stereotype of offenders as less worthy than others, and often reject them because of their criminality. For example, offenders may be refused work because they have been convicted. This may be rational (e.g., being rejected as a child-minder because of convictions for child abuse) or irrational (e.g., if a conviction for child abuse results in rejection for a job as a cashier, despite excellent qualifications). Such people are considered less worthy or in some other way different from others in society because they are criminal. The same reasoning may also cause them to be treated differently in other spheres of their lives, cutting them off from friends and even relatives, and from the law-abiding sectors of society. This may force them into association with other law-breakers, which may further consolidate the criminal label as well as providing an opportunity to learn new crimes and criminal values. So an occasional drug user may, after the intervention of official agencies of control, become separated from the legal and acceptable sections of society and, by associating with others in the same predicament, learn the attitudes, aspirations and activities of this new subculture, becoming more inclined to use drugs and perhaps becoming involved in other illegal activities. Furthermore the police may help to consolidate the criminality by visiting them when crimes similar to those they committed arise in their area – 'if they did it once, they may well do it again'. All of these effects are amplified if the State incarcerated them for their crimes. But, as the repeated use of the word 'may' indicates, there is nothing unavoidable or deterministic about such reactions. Indeed, some become determined to 'learn from the error of their ways' and to win back their reputation. The argument of the interactionists is, however, that many do internalise the label, and thus criminality arises out of the reaction of society to them.

The incarceration of offenders is generally seen as the most vehement societal condemnation and constitutes the strongest case for labelling theorists. Prisons are often referred to as the breeding-grounds for criminals, and the labelling perspective on this is a part of that claim. Prisons give people the opportunity of learning how to commit other crimes, but more important from our viewpoint is that they provoke criminality by reinforcing the alienation of these people from society. Prison removes many of the elements of life necessary for a normal existence, and tends to mark people as ex-convicts. Many prisoners accept the label, see no possibility of change, and on release commit further crimes: prompting the question of whether these further crimes arise as (in part) a consequence of the label and the punishment. Others do not accept that their actions were genuinely criminal and so will never accept the label: still others will try to return to as normal an existence as possible and probably will not re-offend.

Such reformist intentions are made the more difficult to implement because, on release from prison, the stigma follows the individual into the community. All the problems with acceptance into a community, finding a job and police surveillance are amplified in the case of an ex-prisoner. They stem from the label, and they all keep the individual slightly apart from law-abiding society, which it becomes difficult to rejoin. The paradox is that the processes and means of social control which in the last chapter were said to lead to law-abiding behaviour are the very same processes that the labelling theorists argue lead to further criminality – the control and labelling leads to a redefinition of the self, resulting in an acceptance of a criminal self-image (see for example Lemert (1967 and 1972); Sagarin (1975); and Gove (1980)).

A similar conclusion can be drawn from the school of thought which applies social reaction theories to groups. By a process known as deviancy amplification, one group labels another as deviant, leading to the societal alienation of the deviant group (Wilkins (1964)). As the excluders reinforce their action against the deviant group, excluding them from normal social interactions, it leads to more crime by the deviant group. This heightened criminal activity merely re-affirms the original label, apparently confirming the initial alienation and justifying even less tolerance of the deviants. Basically, the postulate here is that crime increases, not because controls have failed, but because they are working, creating something like a vicious circle. Such a process could help to explain the extreme problems which have arisen at particular times in certain communities. For example, police action in stopping and searching youths suspected of street robberies in Brixton in 1981 was widely blamed as a central factor in causing the very much more serious crime which arose during the weekend of riots. If the allegation is true, this might be said to be an instance of amplification causing criminality, but it might also be explained by means of a wider conflict theory (see Chapter Fifteen).

One test of the labelling hypothesis describes a situation in which a population of a certain area are moved to live in a new council estate, and how they are labelled as trouble by both the others living in the area and by the authorities (Damer (1974)). The deviancy amplification hypothesis suggests that such treatment should have led to the newcomers being excluded from normal interactions, pushing them towards more deviant behaviour, confirming the label, reinforcing the rejection, and so on. Damer claims that this did not happen: the inhabitants fought back against the label, which did not serve to amplify the deviance. On the other hand, a study of Mods and Rockers felt that society's reaction to them was important (Cohen (1972)). The argument was not that the way society viewed them caused all their unacceptable behaviour, but rather that the intense focus of media and official attention caused a panic in the rest of the population. The result was that even if their actions were not unduly harmful, they met harsh reactions from the control agencies (police and courts) which may then have helped them as individuals along the road to acquiring a negative self-image.

14.2.4 Evaluation

It cannot be disputed that interactionism has had profound effects on later criminologists who have used some of its methods. Despite this, the central claims of the theory have faced significant criticism.

First, they are accused of perpetuating the same sin of determinism as does positivism. The charge here is that interactionism seems to assume that, given certain factors there will be a certain outcome. They are thus said to fall into the trap they are trying to escape. The usual answer is that labelling is not a theory of causation, but rather a method of interpreting what happens. It is not claimed that labels create certain types of behaviour, but rather that they and the effects that they have may be one of the factors considered in any offender's decision to choose criminality. Some may view this as a somewhat unsatisfactory answer but, in view of the fact that it was never claimed as a causative theory, or even a theory at all, it is perhaps acceptable.

A second difficulty with these theories is that they tend to class the offender almost as the victim, and one loses sight of the fact that there are victims of their crimes. When they remove the normative element of the offence, they make the act appear morally neutral. It is made to seem that the disapproval of the act is confined to those in authority. However, many in society would argue that certain things are bad in themselves (e.g., violence). If the moral elements of actions are removed, the person who suffers the crime is deprived of the status of victim. They are not really victims, but only constructed victims.

Thirdly, as was mentioned above (14.2.3), the processes which interactionism marks out as possibly adversely affecting those labelled criminal can have a positive effect on the law-abiding. In terms of numbers, the positive effects it may have in preventing law violation in others may outweigh any negative effects on the offender (see Vold and Bernard (1986)). In any event, the effects of labelling are not easily predicted. A study of the labelling effect of the impact of arrest in cases of domestic violence (Sherman (1992)) found that those with steady jobs were deterred but the reaction of the unemployed was, if anything, to increase the violence against their partners following an arrest. Perhaps, however, these findings are more relevant to the power relations embodied in control balance theory (see 13.5) than they are to labelling.

A fourth criticism often levelled at the labelling theory is that it does not withstand empirical testing. Far from stating a fact which existed, it could be said that labelling was conveying a social and sometimes a political message. The assertion that social reaction to a label may encourage a person's criminal career is very difficult to test. Indeed, the proponents of labelling themselves argue the criminality is often a deep-rooted problem before people are officially labelled. None the less, attempts at testing have been made. The results are ambiguous: some uphold or go some way to upholding the theory (see, for example, Cuthbertson (1975) and Jenson (1980)); others lend it little support or actively claim to disprove it (see Hepburn (1977) and Foster, Dinitz and Reckless (1972)). Other areas of the theory may seem to be more easily empirically tested, e.g., whether the police show bias in picking up or charging certain types of people. In the Piliavin and Briar (1964) study such bias was found to exist, and a more recent study by Sampson (1986) appears to back this up, but others such as Gove and Hirschi (both reproduced in Gove (1980)) found that the seriousness of the offence was the main factor taken into consideration, and that factors which were non-legal were only marginally considered.

The last point is lent some support by research (Mawby (1979)) which attempted to test whether labelling had an effect on crime rates. The hypothesis was that the police, by labelling particular areas as more criminal and policing them more closely, would discover more crime and thus complete a self-fulfilling prophesy about high crime areas. This assumption was not upheld: area differences in crime rates were not markedly altered by differences in police actions. However, things may be different when the label is attached to a personal attribute of the offender. This occurs in areas such as race, sex or even possibly age. In these cases there may be more substance to the labelling perspective. In relation to race, there is recent evidence that racial differences may have affected decisions at various levels in the criminal justice system (Hood (1993); Home Office (1992b); Commission for Racial Equality (1992b); Skogan (1990)).

Lastly, the radical criminologists have attacked interactionism for not going far enough. They say that it ignores the fact that the criminality and the use of labels are rooted in the unfair system of capitalism. Taylor, Walton and Young (1973) are exponents of this view and say that, although the labellers argue that those in power will tend to construct and apply the rules, they ignore the full impact and political importance of this use of power. This is a standpoint which will be expanded in considering radical criminology in Chapter Fifteen.

Whatever validity there is in the idea that labelling affects behaviour, it has had a number of positive effects. It has shown that the perspective of the various actors is essential to understanding criminality, and that the criminal law is not a given and unchallengeable set of rules. These insights need to be included in discussions of causes of deviance. The stress on the mutability of the criminal law has given more force to arguments for change. Thus, since the beginning of the sixties there has been discussion about what some writers see as unnecessary criminal laws, often called (some would say mis-called) victimless crimes. In a few cases these offences have been decriminalised, for example, abortion within certain bounds, and homosexuality between consenting men over the statutory legal age and in private. Others have been seriously considered for decriminalisation, such as the use of certain so-called 'soft' drugs (for further consideration of this area see Chapter Two).

Similarly, the individual aspect of labelling theory has been one of the elements which has led to a greater use of measures to divert people from criminal actions. This has had a profound effect throughout the criminal justice system where diversion appears at many levels. We have already

(Chapters Eleven and Thirteen) discussed some general preventative measures, but labelling directs attention to more individualised methods of diversion, such as cautioning and diversion from custody. Each of these is attractive to the authorities because it reduces labelling, but also because it is cheaper to deal with people in less formal ways and to punish them in the community rather than incarcerate them. Cautioning is a logical extension of the labelling theory: the individual no longer becomes heavily involved in the criminal justice system and is no longer labelled by others as an offender. Official cautioning demonstrates that offending will not escape official control whilst allowing the individual a second chance of averting a public and stigmatising label.

Despite its positive intention of diverting offenders, particularly young and new offenders, away from the system, diversion of this sort has major problems for any criminal justice system. First it is secret and so it is very difficult to be sure that non-discriminatory reasons are being used for decisions. In a study produced by the Commission for Racial Equality (1992b) there is very strong evidence to suggest that racial prejudice is allowed to affect cautioning decisions. Secrecy also raises uncertainty that the individual, who must admit the offence before a caution can be used, has done so freely. Pressure may be brought, even if only that with the admission the individual will be released and very little else will be done. Moreover, it is not always clear why one offence is cautioned and another is not, which, together with wide differences in cautioning rates from one force to another, makes for unacceptable inconsistency. The final problem is that cautioning, far from preventing individuals from being officially treated, has actually widened the net of the criminal justice system: many who would previously have been dealt with on the street are now brought into the station for official recognition (for a full consideration of the net-widening effects see 13.8.3 and Cohen (1985)). On this analysis a process which was intended to reduce the numbers of those officially recognised and labelled has led to more people being involved and labelled.

Similarly, the intention of diversion from custody was to avoid the heavy stigmatising effect of incarceration (and also perhaps to save money because punishment in the community is a cheaper alternative). Various alternative punishments have been made available: community service for those who are 16 and over; probation for those who are 16 and over (now a sentence of the court: Powers of Criminal Courts Act 1973, s. 2(1) as amended by the Criminal Justice Act 1991, s. 8); a combination of these two (introduced by s. 11 of the Criminal Justice Act 1991); attendance centre order for those between 10 and 20; supervision orders for those between 10 and 17; and curfew orders with or without electronic monitoring (tagging), both of which are provided for in s. 12 of the Criminal Justice Act 1991 but neither of which is presently in force. Each of these allows the offender to be diverted away from incarceration which in theory would reduce the stigma and labelling. Unfortunately many commentators suggest that they have had the opposite effect. The reason is again net-widening (see 13.8.3 and Cohen (1985)). Although these measures may divert the individual from the most controlling

how the phenomenon is constituted or built up. Phenomenology therefore studies the way in which things are grasped by an individual's consciousness. It does not question whether the knowledge is correct, but merely studies how it came into being. Phenomenology sees all action as intended, that is to say, that people choose their behaviour in terms of goals, projects, reasons, motives, purposes, etc., which they have in their minds. This means that a person's mind or consciousness is intended; in other words, it is conscious of or about something. In its simplest form, then, we can always say what it is we are conscious of; we can put a name to it. Even if we only say it is uncertain or muddled, we have named it, and in this sense can always name the object of our consciousness or of our intention. The intention of the mind or consciousness is necessarily very closely related to the actions, which it substantially controls. People's actions are controlled by what their minds intentionally see, wish, believe or hope to be true: the mind controls actions.

The way in which the intended objects of someone's mind are made up depends upon the society in which that person is based. Therefore, the intentions of the mind are not wholly of the individual's making; the intentions hold meaning for him, but they are created from the social factors which he experiences. Each person lives in a society and their intentions are modified, endorsed or defeated by others in that society with whom they have contact.

Phenomenology takes these intentional objects and, firstly, tries to define the intentions or meanings experienced by individuals and to relate them to the objects which gave rise to them. For example, if the intention or meaning is fear, then the intentional object is that which is feared. Secondly, phenomenology uses this description to construct or constitute the process by which the specific meanings arise in the person's mind or consciousness. If an individual performs any action, theft for example, then the phenomenologist relates that action or theft back to the views and meanings held by that person at each stage of the process which leads up to the theft.

From this it can be seen that the phenomenologist is trying to do something very different from that done by most sociologists. He is trying to question the whole process of sociological theorising. He tries to comprehend how people come to have the experiences they do have. The phenomenologist intends to put into language the typical experiences of the everyday world experienced by typical people for typical reasons.

14.3.3 Ethnomethodology

Ethnomethodology draws upon these phenomenological concepts and methods in order to describe social occurrences. Rather than a theory it is a general method of sociological study, used in criminology and all other areas of sociological study. It does not purport to give explanations of criminality, although application of its methods may lead to greater understanding of the area. It seeks to give an accurate account of what has occurred or is occurring in any social interaction, and to provide a sense of structure for the interaction itself. Essentially, it is concerned with the sociological study of everyday activities by concentrating on the methods used by individuals to report their common-sense practical actions to others. Its interest is centred on how the individual experiences and makes sense of social interaction.

In many traditional sociological approaches there is a basic idea that the society is underpinned by a shared set of rules. Some researchers seem to contend that these rules are invisible, in the sense that they are so basic as to be generally understood and accepted without realisation; or they are assumed to be so obvious and evident that they do not require discussion. Often it seems that the only way of examining the rules is to discover when they are breached and to explain these breaches. The structure of society would be threatened unless such breaches are relatively infrequent. This idea presumes that there is a common culture within every society which is so basic as to be acted upon without question, and that the society would tend to disintegrate if its rules were broken so frequently that they lost their common acceptance. Garfinkel, one of the main writers in ethnomethodology (his work is very complex; see Heritage (1984)), carried out certain experiments designed to undermine these common rules to see whether the result would be a breakdown in ordinary social life. These are called his disruption experiments. Each took a social setting, and introduced behaviour which was totally alien to that setting and breached these unspoken rules. He found that the social setting did not disintegrate. He deduced from this that the idea of sociological explanations based purely upon the presumption of a common culture was insufficient. In searching for the other elements necessary for the understanding of society, he called upon the use of phenomenology, which moved the centre of the discussion to the individual. For ethnomethodology, the experience of the person actually involved in the activity is essential: my world as I see it is the one which will allow an understanding of what I do.

Unlike phenomenology, where everything has to be questioned rather than accepted, ethnomethodology starts from how things are viewed by the ordinary person, whose perceptions are thus accepted as they appear, and not questioned. There is an assumption that if another person could swap places with me, and have exactly the knowledge I have, then they would see the world as I see it, share my interests and understandings and, more importantly, act as I do and *vice versa*. This is not to argue that there is no structure to life, but rather that the structure can only be understood in its context and by taking account of the thoughts, actions and knowledge of the participants.

The ethnomethodologists, unlike other earlier criminologists, view the social structure as part of the understanding of the activity. They generally accept that there is a basic structure to everyday life, and that most people's activities in any day are largely predictable or taken for granted. Nonetheless, they argue that since the social structure is understood slightly differently by each individual, no real understanding can come of what has occurred until the social structure which exists for that person, how they view the world, is also understood. These meanings they see as being essential to an understanding of human behaviour. For example, murder is always the same action, but rarely do two murders have the same meaning. If John kills Mary, he may do it in order to escape from the scene of a crime; he may do it to prevent her escape from a crime (a police officer); he may do it as an act of passion; he may do it as a drunken driver; he may do it as a freedom fighter or a terrorist; he may do it as a soldier. In all these instances he may perceive his act in one way; the control authorities may perceive it in another; and different sectors of society may perceive the act in still different ways.

To ignore these perceptions, particularly that of the actor, is to rob the act of its meaning and possibly to misunderstand or fail to understand the crime. Take a seemingly wanton killing where the parties are unknown to one another. It may be that if we ask the perpetrator he or she will explain that the crime was committed for political reasons and was justly done to undermine an unjust system. The dead person is then a casualty in the war, a necessary loss to obtain a greater good. The control agencies in the State in which the crime was committed, or against which the crime was committed, may term it an act of terrorism, an assassination, or treason. They will probably also claim that there is no reason for the violence and that its perpetrator is a common criminal, not a political prisoner or a prisoner of war (this is the situation in Northern Ireland). By such denials, the meaning of the act for the perpetrator is also denied, and the criminal is portrayed as a vicious and dangerous person who kills for no rational reason. Others, either individuals or States, may wholly support one of these meanings or accept partial explanations from each. For example, they may understand and accept the meaning given by the criminal, i.e., the political nature of the act, but deny the use of violence to support it. All this gives a crude idea of the intentions of the ethnomethodologists especially: in the example, the different positions are easily defined; normally they would not be so obvious. To criminology, the most important element of the ethnomethodologists' work is practical and involves clear interpretations of the positions, actions and thoughts of the actors in the crime.

The above description only covers the part of the method of the ethnomethodologist known as indexicality – any human activity is interpreted differently depending upon the context in which it is seen or the position of the viewer. A specific illustration of the use and implication of the approach is seen in its profound questioning of criminal statistics. It had long been accepted that the statistics did not represent the full criminal population or even the full catalogue of criminal incidents; that there was a large and worrying dark figure of crime statistics. Nonetheless, these statistics had been portrayed as reasonably objective and able to act as a reliable basis for indicating trends in crime and suggesting associations. Phenomenology and ethnomethodology questioned this interpretation of the statistics, which they saw as the result of interpretation by those in authority and of social organisation. If, in the past, the statistics had been treated as clear and unquestionable indications of such matters as the crime rate, they were now to be viewed as just one interpretation of the world. The seemingly objective numbers embody decisions made by people influenced by preoccupations, prejudices, or simply by past practices: they thus represent a large number of very subjective decisions. It is therefore important to follow the numbers back to see how they are constructed. For example, criminal statistics partly record and reflect the routine occurrences in the courtroom or in the police station.

Thus, in the courts the staff will categorise and standardise their work so that the cases are more predictable and more easily dealt with. They will try to force all cases into categories. To understand the statistics is to understand the people who made them as much as their subject matter. To accept them without this questioning is to miss a very important element of their make-up. Indexicality requires that a similar process be entered into in most other studies of human behaviour, including the criminological.

Ethnomethodologists press beyond this, recognising, for example, that some interpretations given by actors may not give meaning to the act if they are constructed after the event, after the individual has reflected upon the action. They may be constructed for the audience or to help the individual to accept the action himself. As Matza (1964) pointed out, criminals often construct self-deceiving reasons for their actions in order to neutralise the action and perhaps to hide the real reason even from themselves.

Ethnomethodologists also question the interpretation of certain actions as typical of certain patterns of behaviour or structures. Garfinkel (1967) called this documentary interpretation. Many theorists, researchers and control agents have tended to make a leap from superficial appearances to identifying someone as a trouble-maker, a delinquent, etc. By thus earmarking him they diminish the importance of the difficult and possibly conflicting social, political and economic factors which may be involved. In this way, criminal identities are imputed to individuals by various control agencies. The ethnomethodologist is interested to discover and describe how such imputations are arrived at.

The other area of interest in this context is that of rules or social norms. The argument here is that there is no such thing as a rule outside its social setting or its social interaction; it needs that interaction to give it meaning. As people in various social contexts come together, their interactions form into patterns which are then recognised as having a life of their own. By this understanding of the world, social order is people in a social context giving meaning to otherwise meaningless situations and thus making order out of chaos. One consequence is that phenomenology and ethnomethodology recognise that there is not one social order but many – schools, hospitals, courts, prisons, peer groups, families, communes, etc., as well as many smaller social interactions such as that between prostitutes and clients, or between police and accused. The setting in which a thing occurs may be vital to the way in which it is viewed: in one it may be deviant while in another it is normal. From this viewpoint, behaviour outside the general pattern is difficult to interpret: its perpetrators may be ignored or avoided as harmless; or they may be seen as threatening, and so be labelled as dangerous and deviant. If A knocks B to the ground with a punch in a boxing ring, A is the winner and, in some people's eyes, a hero; if it occurs on the streets as part of a pub brawl, it is a crime, and A is a criminal to be punished. If it occurs in the home between husband and wife, then again it is a crime, but A is far less likely to be convicted and punished, and he, and many others, will consider it is a private incident between himself and his wife; and the police may be reluctant to get involved both for this reason and because they suspect that the wife will refuse to give evidence or will change her statement in court. The setting is important. It is argued that in this way the building up of rules can be studied, and the categories of deviant and criminal might be better understood.

In the criminal law some of these methods can be used to question the justice of what goes on at each stage of the proceedings. For example, suppose a person pleads guilty at trial to assault involving actual bodily harm. He may accept that he did hit the victim and is therefore technically guilty. At this point the court is only interested in the facts for the purposes of sentencing, and will call on the police to state the circumstances of the offence. The police may give a set of 'facts' about the incident quite different to the incident as seen by the offender, and may not give evidence which may reduce the blameworthiness of his action. At this point the offender generally has no opportunity of setting the record straight, as it is assumed that the guilty plea is to the facts as seen by the police. The defence lawyer is given the opportunity to speak, but often does not say what the offender wants laid before the court. He usually only addresses mitigating factors and not the facts, and although the judge can invite the offender to speak, this is rare. The law, or the legal players in the court, have denied the offender the opportunity of setting his or her perception of events before the court. This may distort the court's actions in sentencing the offender. The criminal justice system is neater without this complication; after all, the offender is guilty.

14.3.4 Evaluation
In this area of study the way in which individuals make sense of their own world and actions is of paramount importance. But in everyday life there is not normally time, nor is there the need, for people fully to examine or recognise their thought-processes, nor would they necessarily recognise any description of these. The fierce difficulties of validating or testing the description is a major obstacle to the widespread use of this approach.

The methods of the phenomenologists and ethnomethodologists could still be used by other sociologists to test their own work for personal and subjective weighting. They could be particularly useful in delineating the way in which certain words and phrases are used. Sociologists tend to use words such as rules, norms, delinquent, or criminal without always defining exactly what they mean by those words. The reader is left to use commonsense (or perhaps prejudice) to perceive the concept, and this perception may not match the author's intentions. Even if readers successfully hit on the intended usage, their construction of it may be different from that of the author. Properly applied, the approach can give more precision to empirical socio-logical study. For example, is the phrase 'labelling process' a term that those studied would use, or is it a sociological construct? If it is a construct, then do all sociologists use it in the same way, and what phenomena were referred to by the people in the study that the sociologist subsumed under this phrase?

Traditional criminology has largely ignored ethnomethodology and phe-nomenology because the practical ends are not obvious, and because the reflexive need to question their own research is both awkward and time-consuming. The most that is usually done is to warn of the dangers of taking, for example, official statistics at their face value; and often the writers then go on to do just that. For these reasons, phenomenology is usually thought of as interesting but irrelevant. Many traditional criminologists would argue that there is a reality which can be discovered from a study of society and that constantly to question this is both unnecessary and unproductive. Each time it was done it would need to be re-tested in, logically, an endless process. Some deduce from this that if we are interested in such questions as who becomes criminal and why, then, for practical reasons, it is necessary to start from the world as it is. To this, the ethnomethodologists would reply that there is no such thing as one real world or one social reality; it depends upon the person, context, time and place.

The two views seem to be totally incompatible, and yet each has some element of truth. Accepting the absolutist view strips each occurrence of its particular facts and each actor of his particular reasons. The object is to search for general explanations, but this can distort the actual activity and force too much explanation under one head. Accepting the ethnomethodologist makes impossible any general understanding of particular actions; each must be described in its particular context and from the particular view of one person. It therefore makes it difficult to look at issues in their generality, to typify them and to study their distribution. It may teach us a lot about the particular, but little about the subject matter in general. Neither is a perfect method, but each has something to offer, so it is perhaps unfortunate that the phenomenological method has been almost totally ignored in favour of the simpler and more obviously practical absolutist methods.

As indicated earlier, the time when it is most dangerous to deny the individual position, and therefore to deny ethnomethodology, is when it should be used to challenge the way in which those in authority use their power to force individuals and actions into categories without giving full weight to the meaning and explanations of the people who actually carry out the activity. When people plead guilty, they may be saying they committed this act in these circumstances. They may well not be pleading guilty to the circumstances as seen by the police. This can have serious effects for offenders, and their legal position should not be jeopardised. If the offender is heard, the judge can rule on the legal importance of the information and the jury upon the factual basis. If some evidence does not appear in court, then it is difficult to say that there has been a fair trial.

14.4 LEFT IDEALISM

Left idealism has grown out of labelling perspectives, and to a lesser extent the phenomenological movement, which had began and largely flourished in the USA whereas left idealism is a largely European movement (see Lea and Young (1984)). Rather than claiming that there is a labelling perspective shaping the criminal law and its implementation these theorists see the influence of those in power in a far more all-encompassing way. The State and those who shape it touch not only the criminal justice system but all aspects of life and do not just set out the rules but influence the way of thinking of all those in a society. By shaping the way of thinking they also structure the behaviour of the people. The criminal justice system is there to deal with those who fail to conform, to coerce them into conformity. The reason that there are more poor than rich in the system is the result, firstly, of defining lower-class behaviour as criminal and, secondly, because of biases in arrest and other aspects of the criminal justice system.

On this reading all the agencies of the State and the powerful – government, schools, the media – are utilised to convince the masses that capitalist, patriarchal and racial protectionist perspectives are necessary to their well-being and to the survival of society and of themselves. Images are constructed of how 'normal' members of society should behave: compliant, contented and accepting their position in society. These images are deemed to be excessively simple, ignoring the pluralistic reality of cultural diversity, sexual difference, diverse family models, racial and class difference. Attempts to undermine this conformity are rejected by labelling any variation as deviant and investing the State agencies of social control with the job of ensuring that all conform either by persuasion (the media and the school) or by coercion (the criminal justice system).

Left idealists see no real causes of crime, but certain types of behaviour are constructed as criminal by the powerful in society. The behaviours so labelled will tend to be those most commonly associated with the less powerful in a society. The criminal law is here constructed not in order to prevent crime but to discover it amongst the lower classes who will be divided against themselves and fear crime from amongst their own number. The powerless will be persuaded to attack crime as the most important evil, leaving the powerful to their own activities, however unjust, unhindered by constraints (Reiman (1979)). The function of the criminal justice system is then not to solve crime but to unite the people against certain individuals, defined as deviant, and so to retain the legitimacy of the underlying social order. Prisons are not there to reform criminals but rather to stigmatise them and cause them to be viewed as the enemy (see Foucault (1980); Reiman (1979)). Police are not there to prevent and apprehend criminals but rather to retain the social order, being used to control strikes, demonstrations or any other activities which threaten to undermine the community as defined and constructed. They are also used to widen the net of social control so that it captures more of those who are seen as possible deviants (see Cohen (1985)). Finally, in order to do this, the authorities, particularly the police, will need to be invested with the necessary powers and relatively free of control: accountability to local and national governments is otiose when it is their interests which are being served (Scraton (1985)).

This view of social order, of law and of the criminal justice system seems all too simplistic and focused. It denies the reality which most people experience. The individual nature of criminality is not just a construction by the State and most criminal behaviour is not directed against the constructed social order. Similarly the criminal law is not just directed at keeping the less powerful in their place. Most of this group need the criminal law for protection. They are commonly the victims as well as the perpetrators of criminal activity. They use the criminal law and enforcement agencies to protect them. The left idealists ignore the fact that most in a society would support the prohibition of most of the behaviour which is defined to be criminal. All this is not to deny that there are definitions of illegality which show social control by the powerful and a reluctance to control their own activities. It is the fundamentalism of left idealism which is in question.

Left idealism picks up on labelling theory and tries to invest it with a single-minded construction of society as a whole. In this it fails but it does usefully draw attention to the possibility that labelling might be part of a wider interest, intended rather than accidental. It is thus likely to be more illuminating in discussions about particular aspects of the criminal justice system rather than as a guide to the nature and origin of the system as a whole.

REFERENCES

Becker, Howard S. (1963 and 1973), *Outsiders: Studies in the Sociology of Deviance*, 1st and 2nd edns, London: Macmillan.

Carson, W.G. (1970), 'White Collar Crime and the Enforcement of Factory Legislation', *British Journal of Criminology*, vol. 10, p. 383.

Cohen, Stan (1972), *Folk Devils and Moral Panics*, London: MacGibbon and Kew.

Cohen, Stanley (1985), *Visions of Social Control*, Cambridge: Polity Press.

Commission for Racial Equality (1992a), *A Question of Judgement: Race and Sentencing*, London: Commission for Racial Equality.

Commission for Racial Equality (1992b), *Cautions v. Prosecutions: Ethnic Monitoring of Juveniles by Seven Police Forces*, London: Commission for Racial Equality.

Culbertson, R.G. (1975), 'The Effect of Institutionalisation on the Delinquent Inmate's Self Concept', *Journal of Criminal Law and Criminology*, vol. 66, p. 88.

Damer, Sean (1974), 'Wine Alley: The Sociology of a Dreadful Enclosure', *Sociological Review*, vol. 22, p. 221.

Dignan, Jim (1991), *Repairing the Damage: An Evaluation of an Experimental Adult Reparation Scheme in Kettering, Northamptonshire 1987–89*, Sheffield: Centre for Criminological and Legal Research, Faculty of Law, University of Sheffield.

Dignan, Jim (1992), 'Repairing the Damage: Can Reparation be Made to Work in the Service of Diversion?', *British Journal of Criminology*, vol. 32, p. 453.

Dignan, Jim (1992a), 'Just Deserts or Just Outcomes? Reparation Comes of Age', *The Magistrate*, vol. 48(3), p. 49.

Dignan, Jim (1994), 'Reintegration Through Reparation: a Way Forward for Restorative Justice?', in A. Duff, S. Marshall, R.E. Dobash and R.P. Dobash (eds), *Penal Theory and Practice: Tradition and Innovation in Criminal Justice*, Manchester: Manchester University Press.

Downes, David and Rock, Paul (1971), 'Social Reaction to Deviance and its Effects on Crime and Criminal Careers', *British Journal of Sociology*, vol. 22, p. 358.

Forsythe, Lubica (1994), 'Evaluation of Family Group Conference Cautioning Program in Wagga, NSW', Conference Paper Presented to the Australian and New Zealand Society of Criminology 10th Annual Conference.

Foster, J.D., Dinitz, S. and Reckless, W.C. (1972), 'Perceptions of Stigma Following Public Intervention for Delinquent Behaviour', *Social Problems*, vol. 20, p. 202.

Foucault, Michel (1980), 'On Popular Justice', in *Power/Knowledge*, trans. and ed. C. Gordon, Brighton: Harvester.

Garfinkel, Harold (1965), 'Conditions of Successful Degradation Ceremonies', *American Journal of Sociology*, vol. 61, p. 420.

Garfinkel, Harold (1967), *Studies in Ethnomethodology*, New Jersey: Prentice Hall.

Gove, Walter R. (1980), *The Labelling of Deviance: Evaluating a Perspective*, 2nd edn, Beverly Hills, California: Sage.

Hepburn, John R. (1977), 'The Impact of Police Intervention Upon Juvenile Delinquents', *Criminology*, vol 15, p. 235.

Heritage, John (1984), *Garfinkel and Ethnomethodology*, Oxford: Polity Press.

Home Office White Paper (1990), *Crime, Justice and Protecting the Public*, London: HMSO.

Home Office (1992a), *Gender and the Criminal Justice System: A Home Office publication under section 95 of the Criminal Justice Act 1991*, London: HMSO.

Home Office (1992b), *Race and the Criminal Justice System: A Home Office publication under section 95 of the Criminal Justice Act 1991*, London: HMSO.

Hood, Roger (1992), *Race and Sentencing: A Study in the Crown Court*, Oxford: Clarendon Press.

Husserl, E. (1964), *The Paris Lectures*, The Hague: Martinus Nijhoff.

Institute of Race Relations (1987), *Policing Against Black People*, London: Institute of Race Relations.

Jenson, G.F. (1980), 'Labelling and Identity: Towards a Reconciliation of Divergent Findings', *Criminology*, vol. 18, p. 121.

Kolakowski, Lesek (1974), *Husserl and the Search for Certitude*, New Haven, Conn.: Yale University Press.

Kritzman, Lawrence D. (ed.), trans. Alan Sheridan and others, (1988), *Michel Foucault: Politics, Philosophy, Culture, Interviews and other Writings 1977–1984*, London: Routledge.

Lea, John and Young, Jock (1984), *What Is To Be Done about Law and Order?*, Harmondsworth: Penguin.

Lemert, Edwin M. (1951), *Social Pathology*, New York: McGraw-Hill.

Lemert, Edwin M. (1967) and (1972), *Human Deviance, Social Problems, and Social Control*, 1st and 2nd edns, Englewood Cliffs, New Jersey: Prentice-Hall.

Mackay, R.E. and Moody, S.R. (1994), *Neighbourhood Disputes in the Criminal Justice System*, Edinburgh: Scottish Office, Central Research Unit, HMSO.

Mackay, R.E. and Moody, S.R. (1996), 'Diversion of Neighbourhood Disputes to Community Mediation', *The Howard Journal*, vol. 35(4), p. 299.

Marshall, T. and Merry, S. (1990), *Crime and Accountability*, London: HMSO.

Matsueda, R.L. (1992), 'Reflected Appraisals, Parental Labelling and Delinquency', *American Journal of Sociology*, vol. 97, pp. 1577–1611.

Matza, David (1964), *Delinquency and Drift*, London: Wiley.

Mawby, R.I. (1979), *Policing the City*, Farnborough: Saxon House.

Morris, Allison, Maxwell, Gabrielle M. and Robertson, Jeremy P. (1993), 'Giving Victims a Voice: A New Zealand Experiment', *Howard Journal of Criminal Justice*, vol. 32, p. 304.

Musto, D. (1973), *The American Disease: Origins of Narcotics Control*, New Haven, Conn.: Yale University Press.

Pelikan, Christa (1991), 'Conflict Resolution between Victims and Offenders in Austria and in the Federal Republic of Germany', in Frances Heindensohn and Martin Farrell (eds), *Crime in Europe*, London: Routledge.

Piliavin, Irving and Briar, Scott (1964), 'Police Encounters With Juveniles', *American Journal of Sociology*, vol. 69, p. 206.

Pitch, T. (1995), *Limited Responsibilities*, trans. John Lea, London: Routledge.

Reiman, J. (1979), *The Rich Get Richer and the Poor Get Prison*, New York: Wiley.

Rubington, E. and Weinberg, M. (1973), *Deviance: the Interactionist Perspective*, 2nd edn, New York: Macmillan.

Sagarin, Edward (1975), *Deviants and Deviance*, New York: Praeger.

Sampson, Robert J. (1986), 'Effects of Sociological Context on Official Reaction to Juvenile Delinquency', *American Sociological Review*, vol. 51, p. 876.

Scraton, Phil (1985), *The State of the Police: Is Law and Order Out of Control?*, London: Pluto.

Sharrock, Wes and Anderson, Bob (1986), *The Ethnomethodologists*, London: Tavistock.

Sherman, P. (1992), 'The Variable Effect of Arrest on Criminal Careers: The Milwaukee Domestic Violence Experiment', *Journal of Criminal Law and Criminal Justice*, vol. 83, p. 1.

Skogan, W. (1990), *The Police and Public in England and Wales*, Home Office Research Study No. 117, London: HMSO.

Smith, David J. and Gray, Jeremy (1986), *Police and People in London*, London: Policy Studies Institute.

Strang, Heather (1993), 'Conferencing: A New Paradigm in Community Policing', Paper delivered to the Annual Conference of the Association of Chief Police Officers.

Tannenbaum, Frank (1938), *Crime and the Community*, New York: Colombia University Press.

Taylor, Ian, Walton, Paul and Young, Jock (1973), *The New Criminology*, London: Routledge & Kegan Paul.

Thrasher, Frederick (1936), *The Gang*, 2nd edn, Chicago: University of Chicago Press.

Vold, George B. and Bernard, Thomas J. (1986), *Theoretical Criminology*, 3rd edn, New York: Oxford University Press.

Walker, Nigel (1973), 'Caution: Some Thoughts on the Penal Involvement Rate', in Louis Blom-Cooper (ed.) (1974), *Progress in Penal Reform*, Oxford: Clarendon Press.

Wilkins, Leslie (1964), *Social Deviance*, London: Tavistock.

CHAPTER FIFTEEN
Conflict Theories and Radical Criminologies

15.1 INTRODUCTION

Mainstream or traditional criminology which, as has been seen, had dominated criminological study up until the sixties, is largely rejected by the conflict and radical criminologists who will be discussed in this section. Traditional criminology was pragmatic, had little theoretical discussion, a strong correctional bias, a pathological interest in criminals and a weak reformist interest. Its proponents tended to be drawn from psychologists, psychiatrists and forensic scientists with a few conventional sociologists drawn in, and the work centred around clinical positivist studies. All this was to be questioned and often rejected by the conflict theorists, and wholly rejected by the early radical criminologists. But although they broke with the old or traditional criminology, their perspectives were not entirely new and drew upon earlier theorists, such as Marx, who will be considered here. Others, some of whom we have looked at in earlier chapters, had anticipated or suggested much of what was to come. For example, Mays (1954) and Morris (1957) both studied the confrontation between working-class values and the structure of middle-class authority (see 11.4), and could be seen as forerunners of the new criminologists.

Many of the writers to be discussed in this chapter were heavily influenced by the interactionist and phenomenological perspectives (see Chapter Fourteen) which had also challenged mainstream criminology. Radical and conflict criminologists drew on their rejection of the consensus model, on their focusing of discussion on the meaning of crime, and on their move away from a study of the individual pathology of convicted criminals. However, they rejected the interactionist tendency to accept the class *status quo*, as well as what they saw as the interactionist failure to deal with the use of power to control people. The new criminologists went on to suggest a possible alternative, which they argued would be more humane.

15.2 CONFLICT THEORIES

15.2.1 Introduction

Most theories so far considered are based on the order, or consensus, idea – social order is the consensus of the people in that society. The conflict view gives more recognition to the fact that within any sizable society there are groups with conflicting needs and values. From this emerges a general discussion of the struggle which may arise over power, status and the desirable, but often scarce, resources of society. The conflict may be between individuals and/or groups. For reasons of exposition we have stressed the difference between views which emphasise conflict and those which emphasise consensus, but at the outset we need also to remind ourselves that there are dangers in attempting to draw too firm a distinction between these two models. As Coser (1968) has pointed out:

> One is . . . ill-advised to distinguish sharply a sociology of order from a sociology of conflict, or a harmony model of society from a conflict model. Such attempts can only result in artificial distinctions. The analysis of social conflicts brings to awareness aspects of social reality that may be obscured if analytical attention focuses too exclusively on . . . social order; but an exclusive attention to conflict . . . may obscure the central importance of social order and needs to be corrected by a correlative concern with the ordered aspects of social life. (pp. 235–6)

It is therefore important not to forget that each has an important place to play in the understanding of society and social interactions.

Conflict theories have a long history. Their most famous exponent was possibly Karl Marx, but the ideas of conflict go back much further than the last century. In the fourth century BC, Plato and Aristotle wrote of social disorder and conflicts within Greek politics: parts of the theories of Hobbes and Machiavelli also centred on this concept. It is obviously misleading to refer to this as a new idea or perspective, but the theorists of the sixties gave the ideas new lease of life. The present purpose is to consider certain theories which seek to describe how conflicts within society may lead to criminality, or more exactly how they explain the type of criminality which will occur. This will not involve studying the older texts, though reference will be made to some of them where they illuminate later writings.

15.2.2 Marx, Engels and Bonger

In the first half of the nineteenth century Marx and Engels were already predicting a collapse of the existing idea of an accepted social order (see Marx and Engels (1848), Marx (1904), and Engels (1971)). They further saw this decline as an inevitable aspect of a capitalist society. The unfair division of labour and capital would eventually lead, through conflict, to the overthrow of capitalist ideals. The State was based upon capitalism and it would have to be replaced by communism. Conflict was inherent in capitalism, which promoted an unfair distribution of desired and scarce resources (housing, wealth and particularly property); that this unequal distribution would worsen over time; and that one consequence would be social conflict. For Marx and Engels such discord had a political basis: the oppressed would seek a revolutionary solution and overthrow the political oppressors. Crime was one of the means of opposing the oppressors but, for Marx in particular, it was a most imperfect form of opposition to the system.

There is an implication that if capitalism is overthrown there would be no conflict. This sweeping idea arises again in the work of Taylor, Walton and Young (1973). In their final chapter, they argue that the implementation of the pure Marxist idea of the reaction against capitalism would transform society and social relations, eradicating crime completely. This ignores the oppression which in the twentieth century has been committed in the name of communism; as these regimes began to be dismantled from the late 1980s, such oppressions are seen to have been a clear part of their government. Their interpretation has other weaknesses. For example, it implies that the criminal activities of oppressed people reflect a positive, purposive, conscious and political reaction against the powerful in capitalist society. Apart from other considerations, this ignores the fact that, as was seen in Chapter Five, many victims come from the same class as the criminals. It also requires too great a political awareness and motivation from the common criminal (for a full critique of these ideas see Downes (1979)). If there are serious drawbacks to the Marxist perspective, this should not obscure his innovative use of the concept of conflict, nor the fact that some later writers have constructively used it to suggest a cohesive basis for criminological explanation.

For example, Bonger (1969, originally published in 1916) believed strongly in the social instincts of humans. Left to themselves, people would naturally form into communities and live in social harmony, but once a system of exchange arises, people have to compete with their neighbours. In the ultimate system of exchange, capitalism, the process leads to the means of production being controlled by a few people, leaving most deprived and their economic position controlled by others. The poor are taught to seek material pleasures and are encouraged to compete against each other for this purpose. Such acute self-interest which can be expressed lawfully or through criminal action, only arises because of the capitalist State and would disappear if society were run upon other grounds. The poor might then commit crimes to address their poverty, either out of need or because of the injustice of the system. Bonger also recognised that the rich would commit crimes which might be related to a 'necessity' to protect their business or personal interests; or be related to their power, either because the power presented them with the opportunity or because it enabled them to commit crimes with relative impunity.

Bonger thus attributed many different and often quite surprising crimes to economic determinism. Clearly crimes such as theft, other property offences, political crimes (designed to obtain political power) could plausibly be related to this economic struggle. Prostitution or soliciting were similarly attributable because of the low economic status of women. Low status and their powerlessness in capitalist societies was also used to explain crimes committed against women, such as rape. Other crimes which could be included on similar arguments were infanticide, violence and domestic violence. Interestingly, the economic subjugation of women did not mean that the female crime rate was very high, and in fact Bonger argued that the economic and social liberation of women would give rise to an increase in their crime rate relative to men. As will be seen in the next chapter, recent official figures lend support to this claim, although it cannot be accepted unquestioningly.

Basically, Bonger attributed criminality to an economic determinism. He did not rule out the possibility that other factors might have some effect on it, but asserted that they could not have a causal basis in the absence of this economic determinism.

15.2.3 Sellin

As was seen in 10.2.3, Sutherland's theory of differential association was built on the concept of differential social organisation. It is possible to relate this to a conflict theory in that it does not assume that society is built on a consensus. Sellin's conflict theory has a similar basis. In 1938 he wrote about culture conflict which was based on the conflict of conduct norms, where each separate culture set out its own norms (rules of behaviour) and instilled them into its members. The norms learnt by any individual were therefore dictated by the culture in which that person was situated. He argued that, in a healthy homogeneous society, these were enacted into laws and upheld by the members of that society because they accepted them as right; they represented the consensus view. Where this did not occur, culture conflict would arise, and could take, Sellin saw, two forms: primary and secondary.

Primary conflicts were those which arose between two different cultures. He proposed that these might arise in three situations:

1. where two societies were in close proximity there might well be border conflicts;
2. where one group moved into the territory of another, or at least where they use their power to extend their legal norms to cover the territory of another culture;
3. where members of one culture migrate or move into the territory of another, where they will be made to accept the norms of the host culture.

Primary culture conflicts have been most used in looking at the problems which arise from immigration.

Secondary conflicts are those which arise within one culture, particularly when it develops subcultures, each with its own conduct norms. The laws would usually represent the rules or norms of the dominant culture. The norms of other groups may even be criminal under the law, so that by living within their subculture's rules of behaviour, they may be breaking the criminal rules of the dominant culture. Note that, unlike the subcultural theories of Cohen (1955) or Cloward and Ohlin (1960) (see 12.3), the norms of the subculture do not arise in order to question the middle- or upper-class values, or to represent a different means of achieving the cultural goals of the middle and upper classes, but rather they represent intrinsically different values and norms (see 11.4, especially Miller (1962), 11.4.1).

15.2.4 Vold

Like Sellin's secondary conflicts, Vold's ideas are based on the conflicts within a culture, but instead of subcultures Vold looks at conflicts between interest groups which exist within the same cultures (Vold (1958)).

He argued that people are naturally group oriented, and those who have the same interests come together to form a group in order to push for these interests in the political arena. Unlike subcultures, these are likely to be transient, only coming into existence and only continuing in existence for as long as is required to reach their desired ends. Members are brought together out of belief in a desired end, but become more attached to the group as they work with other members towards that end. Members become psychologically attached to groups, especially as they invest more of their time and effort in them. If the end is achieved, members will probably lose their allegiance to the group, and it may dissolve. Vold's theory thus comes from a social-psychological perspective.

Central is the idea that different groups have different and often incompatible interests which give rise to conflicts. Where groups are of a similar strength, then often these conflicts are resolved by compromise, lending stability to a society. Where they are of differing strength, one may win by using the full power of the State to enforce their interest. Where this involves the passing of a criminal law, the dominant group is backed by the police, lawyers and courts to protect its interests, whilst these same forces are used against the interests of the politically weaker groups and in some cases actually criminalise such interests. Members of losing groups are very likely to fall the wrong side of the law, as defined by these powerful groups. Crime is not the result of an abnormality, but rather is the natural response to an attack on their way of life, or on a way of life in which they believe.

Vold gives a number of illustrations of this type of conflict, and includes particularly crimes of political movements aimed at political reform. The ultimate example of this is a revolution in which whoever loses is the criminal – if the revolution succeeds, then the previous government is criminalised: if it fails, then the revolutionaries are criminals. From this it can be seen that such criminality has little to do with who, if anyone, is right, and more to do with winning. In the struggles to obtain the suffrage for women, many were punished as criminals. They are now more commonly seen as martyrs for the cause, in that their 'crimes' were justified because of the ends. A second category which Vold includes concern labour conflicts, either between management and labour unions which might involve certain illegal behaviours on the part of one or other – the legality of each side's actions will depend upon how successful they have been in getting their interests legally protected – or between labour unions. The final area which he mentions as giving rise to such criminal tensions is racial conflict, where there may be violence involved in the challenge to racial segregation and institutional prejudice.

Vold claims that a significant amount of criminality results from group conflicts; the crime is justifiable to reach a greater good. This approach only claims to explain this type of criminality, and does not explain individual criminality, which Vold sees as far less rational. This restriction limits the usefulness of the theory, as most criminality does not arise out of any clearly defined group interest. Most falls into the category of individual activity or the activities of unorganised collections of people who just happen to be in structurally or socially similar situations.

15.2.5 Dahrendorf and Turk

Both of these writers look at the relationship between authorities and their subjects. For Dahrendorf, power is the crucial factor; whereas for Turk it is based on social status.

Dahrendorf (1959) attacked the Marxist idea for taking account of only one form of power, namely property ownership. Marx located conflict in an unjust economic system and saw it as something which could be eradicated. Dahrendorf, in contrast, saw it as located in the power differences, and especially in the distribution of authority, in a State, and as being necessary to a healthy society. All healthy societies need a difference in the levels of power or authority of the individuals, so that the cultural norms or rules can be enforced. If one is to have rules, one needs sanctions to enforce them, and to ensure that the sanctions are effective someone has to have the power to use them. This is bound to lead to conflict.

Turk (1969) also recognised that social conflict was a real and inescapable part of social life, and that someone had to be in authority. For Turk, if there was no conflict in a social order it was unhealthy. It might indicate either that there was too great a consensus in the community, or that individuals were being excessively controlled or coerced by those in power. Too much conflict would also be undesirable, as no society can be healthy without a fairly high level of consensus. Turk therefore saw social order as being based on a coercion-consensus model, and the authorities must ensure that the balance between the two is not lost.

Turk was interested in the conditions under which the cultural and social differences between authorities and subjects result in conflict. In doing this, he first distinguished between cultural norms and social norms. Cultural norms set out verbally what behaviour is or is not expected; the social norms represent what is actually being done, what the actual behaviour is. For the authorities, the cultural norms are usually laws, and the societal norms are the enforcement of those laws. For subjects, the cultural norms may be subcultural and the social norms the actual behaviour patterns of the individual. Clearly, the cultural and social norms of the authorities may differ from those of the subjects, but Turk also envisaged the possibility that within each group cultural and social norms might not correspond. He therefore saw four possible situations:

1. Authorities actually enforce the laws (so the cultural norms and social norms correspond) and the beliefs and the behaviour of the subjects are very

close (again, cultural norms and social norms correspond). In this case, the cultural norms of each group are the same and there is no conflict; if they are different, there is a high degree of conflict. For example, if the State believes in banning alcohol and actually tries very actively to enforce that ban, but the subjects believe that it should be freely available and actively use it, then there is a very high likelihood of conflict. This is substantially what happened during prohibition in the United States of America.

2.   The authorities are very lax in their law enforcement (so that although the cultural norms exist, they are not acted upon, i.e., the social norms do not correspond) and subjects do not act on their beliefs (again, although the cultural norms exist, the social norms do not correspond). In such a situation, the conflict potential would be very low. Until recently, this was the situation with the blasphemy laws. Although blasphemy is an offence, the authorities do not actively enforce it, and although many people do not believe in the Christian religion, they do not actively try to breach the law. If a situation does not give rise to tensions between the groups, the conflict level is low.

3.   Authorities actually enforce the laws (so the cultural norms and social norms correspond) but subjects, although holding different cultural norms or beliefs, do not act upon them (although the cultural norms exist, the social norms do not correspond). Suppose the authorities imposed and enforced laws against 'soft' drugs but the subjects, although not opposed to soft drugs, made little use of them: conflict would be limited to that minority of cases where subjects did use the drugs.

4.   The authorities are very lax in their law enforcement (so that although the cultural norms exist, they are not acted upon, i.e., the social norms do not correspond) but the beliefs and the behaviour of the subjects are very close (the subjects' cultural norms and social norms correspond). The State may, for example, have legislated against 'soft' drugs but does not enforce the law; and the subjects oppose the law and actively participate in the use of 'soft' drugs. The result is still lower potential for conflict than 3 above, because subjects found using the drugs are unlikely to be prosecuted.

The disjuncture between cultural and social norms is not the only factor which may induce conflict; the organisation and sophistication of both authorities and subjects also affects the degree of conflict. Authorities, other than mobs, must by their nature be organised to obtain and retain power. On the other hand, subjects often lack organisation; but those which are organised – by, for example, being members of a close-knit gang – will be better able to resist the power of the State. Turk argued that if those who were acting illegally were organised, there would be a greater conflict between them and the State. Interestingly, in sentencing an individual, the court always treats organised crime more severely, which suggests that the State sees it as more of a challenge to its authority, and therefore more threatening and worrying.

Sophistication exists when one side understands the behaviour of the other and uses that knowledge to manipulate them. If authorities are sophisticated, they will be able to persuade subjects that acting within the law is in their best interests, and hence reduce the need to rely on coercion in order to achieve obedience to the law. Sophisticated criminals will be able to hide their criminality, pretending to be law-abiding whilst acting in a criminal way; the less sophisticated will be in frequent conflict with the State. The conclusion would seem to be that the more sophisticated are both State and criminals, the less conflict would arise.

In the case of criminals Turk suggested four groupings representing four levels of conflict:

1. Organised and unsophisticated; for example, youth gangs. These would give rise to most conflict.

2. Unorganised and unsophisticated; for example, vagrants or careless individual thieves, whose crime was obvious but not threatening, and therefore less of a conflict.

3. Organised and sophisticated; for example, corporate criminals and some organised crime, where the crimes are less visible and the criminals less obvious. In such cases, conflict arises less often and is less likely, but the crimes are threatening and carry the potential for conflict.

4. Unorganised and sophisticated; for example, a lone embezzler or a con artist, where the crime has low visibility and where the threat from a single criminal is low. The conflict is the lowest in these situations.

These seem fairly logical but may not be borne out by actual study, that is, criminalisation may be upon different lines. Turk suggests that three other factors also affect whether a person is criminalised, and these might also affect the above analyses.

First, different enforcement agencies may have different views. Turk divides them into first-line enforcers, such as the police and factory inspectorate; and higher-level enforcers such as prosecutors, juries and judges. If none of these believe that the behaviour should be criminalised, enforcement is very unlikely. If they are all committed to the prevention of the behaviour, then enforcement will be high, with the likelihood of high arrest and conviction rates, and severe sentences. If the first-line enforcers are committed but the higher-level enforcers are not, then there will be high arrest rates but low conviction rates and lenient sentences. If the first-line enforcers are not committed but the higher-level enforcers are, then arrest rates will be low but when a person is arrested, they are likely to be convicted and receive a heavy sentence. Turk saw the police and other first-line enforcers as the most important element determining criminalisation.

Secondly, the relative power of enforcers and resisters is important. If the authorities and enforcers are powerful but the resisters, those who have behaved in a criminal way, are powerless, then the authorities are more likely to arrest, convict and harshly sentence them. Such subjects are likely to have their behaviour officially defined as criminal unless their crimes were unimportant and not worth the bother. If, however, the enforcers and resisters are of approximately equal power, then the enforcers may be more reluctant officially to label the individuals as criminals, making their criminalisation less likely. If the power of the resisters becomes sufficiently strong, they may be able to persuade the authorities to decriminalise the activity.

Finally, Turk said that the 'realism of the conflict moves' affected the likelihood of criminalisation. If those who broke the law were realistic, making their crime less visible; avoiding antagonising the enforcers by accusing them of being corrupt, unjust or violent; and not upsetting or alarming the public, the offensiveness of the activity would be reduced. If they behaved less 'realistically', they would provoke calls for the strengthening of the enforcement agencies. On the other hand, the enforcers should be realistic by refraining from doing anything which might reduce public support; they should make their procedures fair, and follow due process; they should not punish so severely as to evoke public sympathy for the criminals; and they should ensure a high level of consensus for both their cultural and their social norms.

Turk's conflict theory can be applied to a wide range of 'criminal behaviour' occurring in different social structures. It recognises that many laws are political and not purely legal constructs; nor do they represent any absolute morality, but are invented by those in authority or in power. He also deals with the political nature of enforcement, and how, at each stage, all the factors which have been discussed affect the level of conflict in a society and the criminalisation of individuals. In this way it is a broader and possibly more useful conflict theory.

15.2.6 Quinney

15.2.6.1 Quinney's social reality of crime
Quinney's writings change quite dramatically over time. He began in 1970 by postulating a social reality of crime which was based largely on phenomenological ideas (see 14.3), moved on, in 1974, to a Marxist theory based on materialism, and then, in 1980, postulated ideas which clearly show a theological base. Each will be dealt with here, but from a conflict perspective, the most important is his social reality of crime.

Quinney (1970), expressed this in six propositions:

1.   Crime is a definition of human conduct that is created by authorised agents in a politically organised society (1970, p. 15). This proposition arises from the labelling perspective (see 14.2) that behaviour only becomes labelled as criminal due to others' reaction to it.

2.   Criminal definitions describe behaviours that conflict with the interests of segments of society that have the power to shape public policy (1970, p. 16). This derives from the ideas of both Vold and Turk, in that it recognises that the interest groups which have power will be able to get behaviours they find unacceptable criminalised, and that they are more likely to do this when there is sufficient conflict of interest between the different segments in the society.

3.   Criminal definitions are applied by the segments of society that have the power to shape the enforcement and administration of the criminal law (1970, p. 18). Those who have the power to legislate probably also have the power to enforce, and to shape the enforcement in ways that make it unlikely that they will be criminalised.

4. Behaviour patterns are structured in segmentally organised society in relation to criminal definitions, and within this context persons engage in actions that have relative probabilities of being defined as criminal (1970, p. 20). Quinney believed that, within a segment of society, individuals shared the same values, norms and ideals, but that these differ from segment to segment. Some segments may be organised and strong, such as employers or unions; others may be more loosely organised, such as racial and religious groups or the women's movement; and others have virtually no organisation or power, such as the young, neighbourhoods and prisoners. Each segment of society has its own behavioural norms; those with least power in any society are least likely to have their interests represented in law making, and are most likely to find their activities criminalised.

5. Conceptions of crime are constructed and diffused in the segments of society by various means of communication (1970, p. 22). Once an offence has been created, it needs to be accepted before it can become a generally established 'social reality'. It needs to be communicated to society, and one of the most important and effective means for this is the media. Different segments of society may try to push forward different crimes as being the most damaging and dangerous. For example, those who have property will wish for property protection to be seen as a high priority on the list of crimes; environmentalists, consumer groups and unions may see some of the activities of large companies and businessmen as the most dangerous crimes, and promote the control of such behaviour. The successful dissemination of these various views requires the segment of society promoting them to be able to ensure strong media coverage and acceptance of their views.

6. The social reality of crime is constructed by the formation and application of criminal definitions; the development of behaviour patterns related to criminal definitions; and the construction of criminal conceptions (1970, p. 23). The previous ideas can be summarised in this final element. The powerful segments of society successfully create and communicate their construction of reality, so it becomes condoned or sanctioned by others. They then use that to argue that they are selflessly protecting others for the common good, whilst they are really serving their own ends and their own interests.

The theory can be best summed up in Quinney's own concluding remarks:

> The reality of crime that is constructed for all of us by those in a position of power is the reality we tend to accept as our own. By doing so, we grant those in power the authority to carry out the actions that best promote their interests. This is the politics of reality. The social reality of crime in a politically organised society is constructed as a political act.

15.2.6.2 Quinney and Marxism
In this way, Quinney sees the capitalist State as causing a criminalogenic society but, writing from a Marxist standpoint, he is not satisfied with explaining the criminality. He adds that it is important to work towards

changing the establishment and replacing it with a socialist society in which individuals would have a more fulfilling and authentic existence, which would lead to crime reduction (Quinney (1974)). To this end, Quinney set out six propositions:

1. American society is based on an advanced capitalist economy.
2. The state is organized to serve the interests of the dominant economic class, the capitalist ruling class.
3. Criminal law is an instrument of the State and ruling class to maintain and perpetuate the existing social and economic order.
4. Crime control in capitalist society is accomplished through a variety of institutions and agencies established and administered by a governmental elite, representing ruling-class interests, for the purpose of establishing domestic order.
5. The contradictions of advanced capitalism – the disjunction between existence and essence – require that the subordinate classes remain oppressed by whatever means necessary, especially through the coercion and violence of the legal system.
6. Only with the collapse of capitalist society and the creation of a new society, based on socialist principles, will there be a solution to the crime problem. (Quinney (1974), p. 16)

The influence of the writings of Marx, Engels and Bonger is very clear in these propositions. One of the main differences appears to be that, whereas the older Marxist view depicted crime as an unsatisfactory response to a political problem, Quinney politicised crime by seeing it as the only available response of the powerless to the small and elite section which used its control of power for its own ends. Later, in 1977, he moved closer to the idea that crime, though natural, was an imperfect and irrational response to oppression unless it amounted to rebellion. For example, he pointed out that a capitalist economy naturally generated a surplus work force, the unemployed, which it had to support through the Welfare State while still making a profit. Those thrown into this position may find that welfare does not adequately provide for their needs, so they turn to crimes in order to survive. He argued that nearly all crimes of the working class were carried out in order to survive. As such, he saw them as a natural choice, but argued that it was imperfect and irrational; what they should be doing was overturning the capitalist system and replacing it with democratic socialism.

In 1977 Quinney set out a typology of crimes. There were crimes of domination which would be committed by those in power, and crimes of accommodation and resistance which were most likely to be committed by the oppressed. Crimes of domination included physical domination, such as police or other official brutality; crimes of economic domination, such as corporate crime and organised crime; and crimes of governmental misuse of power, such as sanction-breaking or Watergate. Crimes of accommodation include predatory crimes, such as theft and embezzlement, and personal crimes, such as murder and rape. Crimes of resistance generally involve a political struggle against the State, for example, terrorism.

15.2.6.3 Quinney's theological conflict ideas

Although he retained a socialist perspective, Quinney began, in 1980, to place importance upon the spiritual as well as the social and political predicament of people under capitalism. He argued that a capitalist society taught people to be cold and calculating, and to have and show less feeling and less compassion. A genuinely just society would need to consider the divine and sacred meanings of existence; otherwise the essence of humanity would be ignored. Even a turn to socialism would not be sufficient if it ignored this divine element of justice.

15.2.7 Chambliss and Seidman

Chambliss and Seidman (1971) began with the argument that as society becomes more complex, the interests of individuals within the society begin to differ, and they are more likely to be in conflict with one another and need help to resolve these disputes. According to them these differences arise because people's values are affected by the conditions of their lives, which become more varied as societies become more complex. Initially, the resultant disputes may be resolved by reconciliation or compromise, but as the society becomes more complex, the more reliance is placed on rules enforced with sanctions against those who violate them. This form of normative society requires formal institutions with the power to make and enforce sanctions. Both the institutions and the rules will probably be provided by the most powerful. The establishment of a sanctioning authority would lead to further social stratification, giving some people or groups more wealth and power than others. The powerful groups would then have an interest in perpetuating their supremacy by using coercion if necessary. Although this is not a clear Marxist analysis, it is not counter to many who put forward such ideas.

In even more complex societies, there would be an increasing need for bureaucratic organisations to apply these sanctions. These bureaucracies would have their own interests, which might differ from those of the sanction-makers. They therefore saw the law in action reflecting the interests of both these groups.

These authors set out to discover whether the consensus model or the conflict model best represented what really went on in law-making and law enforcement. They were interested in whether the power of the State was used in a fair and even-handed way merely to resolve disputes in an attempt to reduce conflict (as was suggested in most of the more traditional legal explanations based on a consensus model), or whether the power of the State, being used to protect certain interests, actually causes the conflicts (as suggested in conflict models such as the one they postulated). Their conclusion is that in State law-making it is the views of interest groups or pressure groups which are heard, not the public interest. The groups with greatest power and wealth will be most reflected in the law.

Turning to judges' decisions, they examined the space where the law was uncertain and it was left to judges to decide upon its meaning. Judges claim that they are drawing upon unquestionable ideas of justice as embodied in other laws or legal decisions: and therefore that they are not making laws.

However, as Chambliss and Seidman point out, many judicial decisions are not unanimous, and the dissenting judgements are equally based on pre-existing legal rules and are equally valid. They assert from this that what the judges do, mostly unconsciously, is to decide a case on their own personal values and then fit their decision into a legal rule. Their assertion that they are deciding in the public interest only means that they decide in what they see as the public interest, which again is an application of their own value system. As people's values are affected by their life conditions, those of judges will reflect their position in society. Judges tend to come from affluent backgrounds; they are often drawn from the most successful lawyers, which often means they represented most affluent clients. Having thus moved in the more affluent, influential and powerful circles, they often have a similar set of values to these affluent clients and important people. Indeed, Chambliss and Seidman claim that lawyers with views which are less in keeping with the powerful are less likely to be promoted, and therefore again the power base is protected. A similar view of the judiciary may also explain why corporate and white-collar criminals generally obtain relatively low sentences, despite having committed what some might consider very serious crimes, and despite the fact that severe sanctions may have more of a rehabilitative effect upon these people than upon other criminals.

Chambliss and Seidman also studied the workings of the police as the first enforcement agency, and one of the most important elements of the bureaucratic machinery. They were charged with the job of law enforcement and had an interest in obtaining reputations for fighting crime, but with as little difficulty for themselves as possible. Furthermore, law enforcement agencies depend for their resources upon those with most power. The authors deduced what they considered to be logical implications from the facts. For example, the more powerful an individual, the more problems they could cause for any enforcement agency; it is thus prudent for the agencies mostly to process those who are politically weak and powerless, and refrain from processing those who are politically powerful. Even within the individual criminal and professional criminal groups, there was a police interest influencing actions. Criminals such as thieves, drug-users and even organised criminals are useful to the police as informants and may gain immunity in return for information. The suggestion was that an amount of crime is tolerated because the police need it in order to trace other criminals.

The general conclusion from Chambliss and Seidman is that both the structure and the enforcement of the law favour the powerful in society, and that the public interest is only of importance if it agrees with the well-being of these groups. The law and its enforcement are therefore against the powerless, and actually form a source of conflict. They conclude that the conflict perspective is the one which is upheld by empirical study.

15.2.8　Conflict and explanations of criminality

In the 1960s, many theorists had ceased to search for an explanation of the cause of criminality and had focussed on other elements. Control theories explained conformity; labelling said it was a question of how and why names became attached; ethnomethodology tried to restore the view of each individual in the event; and even conflict theory is primarily a theory of the behaviour of the criminal law.

However, conflict theorists do also address the issue of crime causation. Bonger argued that it arose out of the dehumanising effect of capitalism: the more people were affected by capitalism the more likely they were to be criminal. Turk considered it to be explained by the existence of different cultural and social norms within a society, which makes the actions of some necessarily criminal. Quinney spoke of the way in which crime was politicised so that crime was the way in which the powerless could express their dissatisfaction with the political *status quo* and try to bring about change. In his later writings, Quinney saw it as the natural, if irrational and pointless, reaction to being oppressed. Finally, Chambliss and Seidman saw it as a natural reaction to exploitation; people's actions were directed by their positions and conditions.

Conflict theory in itself has a causative side. In saying that States tend only to regulate the damaging behaviours which are most likely to be carried out by the powerless, they are basically saying that powerlessness can be viewed as a cause of criminal behaviour. The powerless group is often poor, but it is important to note that they are not saying that the poor are criminal because they are poor, but rather because they suffer a relatively strong deprivation of both wealth and power. This idea of crime causation was considered in 12.2 under relative deprivation, where Runciman (1966) and Stack (1984) both argued that individuals who felt that they were badly off relative to others were likely to join with others to seek a political solution, or to better their own position in a non-political and selfish way which might actually victimise others who cannot afford it. Box (1987) upholds this type of analysis and says that the problem grows as people are more marginalised through things such as unemployment and depression. Conflict balance theory might also be interpreted as supporting the main elements of this argument (see Tittle (1995 and 1997) and 11.5).

In Marxist conflict theory the existence of an unemployed group, the 'reserve army of workers', was seen as a necessary part of a capitalist society. Creating such a deprived group is bound to cause tensions and conflicts to arise and, as the group is the least powerful in society, they are least likely to have their views listened to, and are under most strain to become criminal (Box (1987)). These groups will suffer the worst relative deprivation but Willis (1978) suggests that the creation of both a manual labouring class and such an unemployed class have knock-on effects. Youths, whilst still at school, will relate the hopelessness of the situation to themselves and come to see school as irrelevant to their position, and refuse to conform. They may get involved in a delinquent subculture or a criminal subculture and become alienated from school life. This prepares them for accepting the manual jobs or dole queues which await them on leaving. The hopelessness of their situation again leads them into conflict with authority.

15.2.9 Evaluation

Most of the conflict perspective is one of the behaviour of the criminal law – that is, official crime rates depend on the enactment and enforcement of criminal laws. They particularly turn on the idea that the behaviours of the powerless in any society are more likely to be criminalised, and this same group is more likely to be arrested, convicted and harshly sentenced.

The first part of this assumes that it is only the interests of the powerful which are protected. This invites the riposte that most of the criminal law actually protects individuals and society in general from potentially very harmful behaviour, such as murder and personal violence. The conflict theorists would point out, however, that many acts which are as injurious as those criminalised are in fact perfectly legal, and that these tend to be behaviours which would be carried out by the powerful in society.

There is also an assumption that, if the power structures were altered, then the new powerful group could pass laws to protect its interests or values. For example, if drug users and distributors became more powerful they might be able to legalise the use of drugs, and so alter the criminal laws to protect their enjoyment and interests. If non-smokers become much more powerful, they may succeed in preventing smoking in public places and so increase their freedoms at the expense of smokers. If paedophiles became powerful, they might be able to legalise sexual encounters with children. In each case there would be a shift in the criminal laws, and either certain behaviours presently criminalised would be decriminalised, or certain behaviour presently legal would be criminalised. In each case the changes would benefit those who had become powerful enough to push them through, whilst being to the detriment of some other less powerful sector of society.

The second basic idea of the conflict theorist dealt with the enforcement of the criminal laws. As was seen in 14.2.3, there is conflicting evidence about the level of differential enforcement of the criminal laws, but it is likely that it has some part to play in law enforcement.

Conflict theories see two ways of changing the emphasis of the distribution of criminality. First, new interest groups could be formed which would promote their own welfare or, secondly, there could be a complete revolt which overthrows the present legal order and replaces it with something different. Generally, the Marxists are arguing for the second, which will be addressed in the next section. On the first, the rise of new interest groups, there is no inherent reason for expecting that the changes in the law which they introduce will necessarily lead to a reduction in the final number of criminals. They might simply replace present crimes with different ones, redistributing criminality by making criminals of those whose behaviour is presently legal, and vice versa. Whether any particular individual views it as fairer will, by definition, depend on their values, which in turn depend upon their social and structural positions in society. Possibly their most important contribution to criminology is this realisation. It leads to the questioning of the previously accepted methods which relied on acceptance of the criminal laws as objectively defined. Conflict ideas have now led to many studies of the law enforcement agencies as well as of the individuals whose behaviour is presently defined and repressed as criminal. In this way, the theories have had a significant effect upon the whole area of crime and crime causation.

15.3 RADICAL CRIMINOLOGY

15.3.1 Introduction

The most recent of the 'New Criminologies' is radical criminology, which has been described variously as Marxist, socialist, left-wing and critical. Whatever the label used, it generally encompasses similar ideas. It is important to note that it is not Marx's criminology, although it has clearly been influenced by Marx and sometimes reflects his views (see especially Bonger in the last section). More often, they expound a more contemporary radical view which is only fairly broadly grounded in Marxism. It is also important to note that nearly all are very critical of the systems in what are, or were until recently, socialist States in Eastern Europe and the USSR. Such States, although drawing upon a Marxist base, have their focus on correctionalism and personal pathologies, and in many ways are closer to traditional criminology.

Radical criminology has evidently also been influenced by conflict theories, some of which have gone on to develop a radical criminologenic perspective (see Quinney (1980) and Chambliss (1975)). Conflict theorists, however, do not generally go as far as radical theorists. They recognise a range of interests and power bases, whereas radicals recognise only capitalism. Furthermore, conflict analysts stop short of rejecting the need for a legal order and for legal definitions of crime; they generally fight for policy reforms rather than revolution. Having said this, radical and conflict theories and theorists do overlap, making it difficult to draw clear lines between the two.

15.3.2 Early radical criminology

Section 15.2.2 above introduced the basic ideas of Marx and Bonger. Briefly, they proposed that human nature itself is not criminal. Capitalism causes people to become criminal. Capitalism teaches individuals to be greedy, self-centred and exploitative. The law and legal systems are the tools of the owners of the means of production, and are used to serve their interests in keeping their activities legal even if they are harmful, brutal or morally unacceptable. They are also used to control the activities of the people, so that they do not challenge the position of the owners of the means of production. The people are made to compete for an inadequate number of jobs, pushing them towards self-interest in order to survive. Some turn to crime in order to survive, but this was seen as an irrational and unsatisfactory form of rebellion against the system; the only true and worthwhile action is revolution. This over-simplified statement of the position is clearly rather unsatisfactory, but will serve our purposes. Modern radical criminologists have reached varying conclusions based on these ideas.

It is useful to begin with a consideration of the early radical ideas as expounded in America by Quinney (1974) and in Britain by Taylor, Walton and Young (1973). Quinney's ideas on radical criminology developed from the conflict model, and were considered briefly in 15.2.6.2. He saw the unequal economic situation which exists in a capitalist State related to an equally unequal power and political basis, both of which grow out of the economic base. The economically powerful are also the politically powerful, and criminality grows out of this power base in order to protect it. From this analysis, he argued that the powerless should be led and aided in a political struggle to overturn this power base. A complete overhaul of the present system was needed, and its replacement with a new set of social realities based on equal power distribution. He particularly argued that the law and the legal system were illegitimate, as they served the interests of a few in the name of everyone. The law, far from being an inevitable part of our society, was unnecessary and oppressive, and should be abandoned in favour of a popular ideal of justice and right. On this analysis the very concept of law, not just the present legal rules, is illegitimate.

One of the many problems with this was that both the law and the legal system claim general support from most members of society. Accepting this, Quinney argued that the government and the powerful manipulate the people through propaganda disseminated via education, the media, State departments, the courts, and through academic disciplines such as traditional criminology which lends legitimacy to the State and owes its existence to the same State which pays for the research. Street crime, being visible and frightening, merely lends legitimation to this manipulation and draws attention away from the crimes of the powerful. As Quinney saw the law as illegitimate, he also saw the need to obey the law as being questionable, and certainly viewed crime as a natural choice in many instances. Moreover, he considered that traditional criminals could quite easily be viewed as rational, as having made a legitimate, free and often political choice. In 1977 he hoped he was seeing the beginning of change in the questioning of support for the State and the legitimacy of law through movements for rights. Against this, and at the same time, he admitted that much conventional criminality reproduced capitalist oppression and was unacceptable, as it preyed on the oppressed.

Taylor, Walton and Young (1973 and 1975) arrived at similar conclusions to Quinney, but they did so via the different path of interactionist criminology. They started with the idea that all human behaviour should be considered normal and natural and not seen as a pathology. In this, deviance and criminality are simply diverse human behaviours. Criminality was therefore a social construct invented by the powerful to protect themselves; in reality it was unnecessary. If crime is only needed due to the types of social and political structures we live in, then, they believed, the abolition of crime was a real possibility under certain, socialist, arrangements. If inequalities of wealth, power, property and life-chances were abolished, their abolition would also remove correctionalism, which was an evil, as it assumed that deviation or different ways of living were caused pathologically. They wished to move towards a time when human diversity would be tolerated and not subjected to the control of the criminal law.

These theories have been widely criticised. To rid a society of all laws makes the weak into prey for the strong, possibly in a different way from a capitalist regime, but in ways which are for most as marked and unpleasant as those attributed to capitalist regimes. The disintegration of the so-called socialist States of Eastern Europe was a rapid demonstration of this. Radical theorists seemed to view crime as a rational choice for the oppressed, and often ignored the fact that the criminal was frequently preying upon those equally disadvantaged. Most people, whether in a socialist or capitalist State, would wish to be protected from certain harmful behaviour, especially that which is physically harmful. Possibly the worst indictment of these theorists is that they often argue for the wholesale destruction of existing systems, but offer little but rhetoric for their replacement. Despite these very heavy drawbacks, they do force criminologists to consider the legitimacy of the very heart of their science, not just its make-up but its very existence.

15.3.3 Recent radical criminology

Radical criminology has lately become a more disparate area of study which can only be briefly sampled here to give a flavour of the present radical perspective.

In 1975, Chambliss began to give his earlier conflict ideas (see 15.2.7) a more radical perspective. He argued that acts are only defined as criminal to protect the ruling economic class which can harm others with impunity, whilst these others are punished by the law. As the disparity between them widens, so the coercion is strengthened. He also argued that crime reduces surplus labour by providing jobs in such areas as law enforcement and welfare. Crime diverted the oppressed from their exploitation by turning their indignation towards criminal members of their own class. In 1978, Chambliss added to this theoretical model an in-depth study of criminality in Seattle. In his results he claimed that the high levels of crime and racketeering in American society were related to the distinctive features of its capitalism. He concluded that crime and corruption were rife throughout American society, and entitled his work: *From Petty Crooks to Presidents*. Much of this criminal activity he traces to the Marxist oppression he had earlier documented.

In British criminology, Hall, Cutcher, Jefferson and Roberts (1978) studied the concept of mugging and how it was constructed. Mugging does not exist, in the sense that there is no offence defined as such. It is an idea invented by the media to encompass a collection of violent and property offences which occur on the street. The researchers noted that these offences had come to be associated with black youths, and these people came to be portrayed as unacceptable and dangerous. They then attempted to trace the origin of the concept of mugging, and maintained that it was artificially constructed in an overtly political way in order to divert attention from other problems. They depicted the real problems as lying in conflicts over power, wealth, the economy, class struggles, racial tensions and Northern Ireland. It is the politicised explanation of the construction of the concept of mugging which gives this study its radical perspective. In so far as it is valid, this is interesting, as it indicates the way in which the powerful supposedly control the masses by propaganda designed to win their support in a law and order ideal. Unfortunately, the authors offer little proof of such a conspiracy; rather than a political ploy it could merely be a media hype designed to sell papers.

Another British study which draws on the radical perspective in a number of respects is that of Box (1987). He linked crime with recession and the effects of income strains. Marx had predicted that capitalism would lead to a reduction of the propertied producers and an increase in the number of workers, and to large scale unemployment. Box's study is interesting because it attempts to document the effects that the strains of an economic squeeze might have, not only on the worst off in society, but also those whose position is worsening, including large corporations. He identifies a process which narrows the productive base and widens unemployment, and relates this process to crime as a rational choice. He also considers income inequalities and links them to criminality; in a recession they are visible.

The radical elements in this are easy to see, but two factors are worth mentioning. First, he sees the strains caused by recession as affecting many sections of society. The effects will not be limited to property crimes committed by those most in need, but also lead to apparently less rational outbursts of violence, frustration and anger in reaction to the brutalising effects of the severity of capitalism during a recession. The harder times will also influence the extent to which workers 'fiddle' from both their employers and clients. Such crimes are committed by all sections of the work-force, ranging from fiddling small amounts through to high level embezzlement and frauds on shareholders. Box also thought that recession increased crimes of domination committed by the powerful as the pursuit of profit became more difficult. Lastly, Box argues that recessions lead to repressive crimes committed by agencies of the State, particularly the police and prison officers in confrontation with criminals, protesters and strikers. He postulates that at times of economic crises there is a greater need to control the oppressed classes, and therefore a growth in the police as the first-line enforcement agencies who are responsible for this work, felt to be necessary due to the heightened fear caused by greater criminality on the streets. Box noted a similar rise in corporate criminal activity at these times, but in this case, the first-line enforcement agencies – the factories inspectorate – actually decreased. This does suggest some sort of control decisions made on grounds other than actual needs. His ideas therefore cover a number of areas, and although he falls well short of suggesting a wholesale rejection of law, his critique does have radical elements.

Not all Marxist and radical criminologists wholly reject law as a tool of social order. What they do is to suggest that in its present form it is merely used to repress certain factions, the poor whose criminality can be seen as an expression of frustration at their position and the class inequalities of the system, whilst leaving the rich and powerful largely unregulated. These theorists attack two main aspects of crime: first the areas defined and controlled; and secondly the whole structure of capitalist societies which they argue need to be dismantled. It is only through remedying the structural unfairness that crime might be remedied: full employment, workplace equality, wage equality, welfare, health, education and social services for all on an equal footing. For radical criminologists, without addressing the crimes of the rich, the use of power through the criminal law to control the poor and the structural inequalities within society, crime will always be a problem. Concepts of crime need to address these issues if they are to be seen as anything other than a scapegoat used by governments when faced with problems such high unemployment, social decay and economic difficulties.

15.4 CONCLUSION

It is important to give space to these writers, as one of their effects has been to widen the study of criminology. Although many of the objects of their concern and comment fall outside the scope of this work, the wide-ranging questioning conducted by these radical theories provided, amongst other things, a basis for challenging the whole criminal justice system. Two examples out of many will be chosen here. The work of Cohen (1985) studies the way in which control agencies are essential to the modern State as we know it, but emphasises that theories of control must encompass the problems set out by critical and radical criminologies and, to retain conviction, must be able to answer some of the accusations presented by radical writers. Cohen is largely critical of the new criminologies, but he accepts their importance in any modern study of criminology. In a book edited by Carlen and Cook (1989), various essays point to the inequalities engendered in our present punishment system, especially in the use of the fine as a punishment. Without wholly denigrating the punishment system, they use new criminological ideas to question the present practice. Again, the criminal justice system is placed in the dock and questioned from the viewpoint of the less privileged.

An interesting practical example is also worth noting. It arose in Liverpool in a number of cases between 1987 and 1988, although similar cases have been heard elsewhere. The cases involved the policing of Liverpool 8 (Toxteth) and some incidents which arose out of it. Over a two-year period, a number of black youths were arrested for violent disorder arising in a few different incidents. Here, only one example will be followed. On this occasion, as on many others, a stolen car came into Granby Street in the Liverpool 8 district. This gave rise to trouble, partly because the locals felt that this occurred too frequently and could not be a coincidence. They felt that chases were engineered to culminate in this district, and could have been stopped before their arrival. Trouble ensued between some of the local youths and the police, during which a brick was put through the window of the police car. There were no arrests at the time. Two days later three youths were arrested. Before the arrests took place, one of the youths arrested had made a complaint about the behaviour of the police at the incident; he was cited by the police as leading the trouble which they alleged ensued. This particular youth had been previously convicted of other offences, including violent disorder. On these occasions he had always been unhappy with the way in which his defence had been conducted, as the lawyers had always refused to attack the police, and had ignored the racial elements which were involved in the cases. On this occasion again, the lawyers he spoke to in Liverpool advised him against bringing up these factors, as they explained that, in attacking the police, his own record would come to light and then, they felt, he would be convicted. As a result of this advice he felt that his case would not be represented in the way in which he wished, and therefore he brought up black lawyers from London to conduct his defence (all the other youths similarly believed that the only way their cases would be conducted in the way they wished was by using these same black lawyers from London). These lawyers brought evidence both about his complaint against the police which they felt was relevant to the case, and about the type of policing which occurred in the district (Margaret Simey, who chaired the Merseyside Police Authority from 1981-1986, gave evidence about this). There were nine or ten prosecution witnesses (mostly police officers) who all refuted the allegations about the policing on that night. During the trial, the defendants took a very active part in their own defences, interrupting proceedings to get their lawyers to ask the relevant questions or to explain something to them. They were acquitted.

Some of the factors which the defendants brought forward many traditional lawyers would have claimed were irrelevant to the legal issues before the court, but the defendants, and clearly the jury who acquitted them, felt that they were of the utmost importance to what happened and why. Had they been denied the representation that they viewed as essential to their case and to presenting what they viewed as all the relevant facts, they would probably have been convicted. A strict interpretation of the legal rules and traditional legal practice involved would have denied them their full hearing and a chance to have the facts as they saw them placed before the court. This and other cases are referred to in the Gifford Report (1989). They show how the law and practice have been used to deny some sections of the community, the less powerful sections, a proper hearing. They show what can happen when this practice is broken. They show that a radical approach to the problem can have positive results.

All these examples show that the various cultures which exist within a society are in conflict, and that neglecting this conflict leads to unfair outcomes and a perpetuation of the difficulties. Radical criminology is designed to highlight these problems and bring them to the fore.

Conflict and radical criminology have both had important effects on the way in which criminologists later theorised about crime, offender, victim and State. They raised questions which ought to be considered in any serious criminological debate, but they have had little effect on social or penal policy, at least in Britain. Mainstream criminology could not avoid addressing the challenge from the radical and critical criminologists. The mainstream tended to accept the law as given and then look for some sort of pathological explanation for offending behaviour (biological, psychological, ecological or social). Implicit in this approach was the notion that the *status quo* was essentially satisfactory, while it also started from the presumption that offenders were 'different' or that offending behaviour was 'different'. Against this, radical criminologists claimed that many of the problems lay in the artificial construction of the law and the biased way in which it was administered. When mainstream criminology, particularly the positivist school, replied that it was taking a scientific stance and dealing with factual data, the riposte was that the data were tainted with a specific moral and structural bias: by ignoring this the positivists were not the objective scientific observers they claimed, but were – probably unconsciously – actively upholding a particular set of subjective values. By questioning the fundamental assumptions of mainstream thinking, radical theorists encouraged criminologists to look more closely at the definitions of the criminal laws, to think more carefully about why punishment was administered, and to examine the power basis of punishment and the politics of punishment. Some of the work on social exclusion and social problems has led to policy suggestions and impacted on other aspects of political and social inquiry. There is now a greater readiness to question the operation of law and to recognise that the law in books often differs from the law operated on the streets. One policy result was the Police and Criminal Evidence Act 1984, which increased the accountability of the police by requiring consultation, and increased the protection given to suspects by clearly setting out police powers and requiring strict procedures to be met in the exercise of those powers. The effects were, however, largely offset because, in the law and order environment of the 1980s, those powers were steadily extended, while the procedural safeguards were used to argue for, and obtain, even greater powers for the police (see especially the Criminal Justice and Public Order Act 1994). In the end the suspect has probably been the net loser.

At the same time, many of the abuses raised by the radical school remain unaltered: in July 1997 a case was brought before the court following an identity parade which had been set up using white people, blacked up to have dark faces, to sit in with a dark skinned suspect; and none of the officers who were involved in the wrongful conviction of the Guildford Four or Birmingham Six have ever faced trial for their alleged brutality and perjury. The list could be extended. It could reasonably be argued that the legal system has failed to deal with the real issues brought up by radical and critical criminology, and there is some substance to Steinert's (1997) point that State and mainstream criminologists have more or less deliberately silenced the radical school of thought. If so, it is to be deplored. It is true that the issues raised stem from a radical political philosophy and question the very basis of Western society, but they obviously have enough substance to command serious attention and cool assessment. Trying to explain the behaviour of individual offenders is not enough: it is also necessary to consider the interactions between individuals and between them and institutions. It is comfortable to accept and largely work within the dominant theoretical, political and social boundaries of the time, but this can lead to complacency and the avoidance of dealing with the underlying assumptions. The best defence for existing values is to uphold them by reasoned debate. To deal with Steinert's assertion that '"Progress" in criminology has meant breaking through the limits of the discipline' does not require the acceptance of the theoretical or political positions of the critical and radical school: it does require reasoned engagement with such views.

REFERENCES

Bonger, Willem (1969) (originally published in 1916), *Criminality and Economic Conditions*, Bloomington: Indiana University Press.

Box, Steven (1987), *Recession Crime and Punishment*, London: Macmillan.

Carlen, Pat and Cook, Dee (eds) (1989), *Paying for Crime*, Milton Keynes: Open University Press.

Chambliss, William J. and Seidman, Robert B. (1971), *Law, Order, and Power*, Reading, Mass.: Addison-Wesley.

Chambliss, William J. (1975), 'Toward a Political Economy of Crime', *Theory and Society*, vol. 2, p. 152.

Chambliss, William J. (1978), *On the Take: From Petty Crooks to Presidents*, Indiana: Indiana University Press.

Cloward, Richard and Ohlin, Lloyd (1960), *Delinquency and Opportunity*, London: Collier-Macmillan.

Cohen, Albert (1955), *Delinquent Boys: The Culture of the Gangs*, New York: The Free Press.

Cohen, Stan (1985), *Visions of Social Control*, Cambridge: Polity Press.

Coser, L. (1968), 'Conflict: Sociological Aspects', in D.L. Sills (ed.), *International Encyclopedia of the Social Sciences*, vol. 3, New York: Macmillan.

Dahrendorf, Ralf (1959), *Class and Class Conflict in Industrial Society*, London: Routledge & Kegan Paul.

Downes, D. (1979), 'Praxis Makes Perfect: A Critique of Critical Criminology' in D. Downes, and P. Rock (eds), *Deviant Interpretations*, Oxford: Martin Robertson.

Engels, Fredrick (1971) (original 1844), *The Condition of the Working Class in England*, trans. and ed. W.O. Henderson and W.H. Chalenor, Oxford: Basil Blackwell.

Gifford, Lord, Brown, Wally and Bundy, Ruth (1989), *Loosen the Shackles: First Report of the Liverpool 8 Inquiry into Race Relations in Liverpool*, London: Karia Press.

Hall, S., Cutcher, C., Jefferson, T. and Roberts, B. (1978), *Policing the Crisis*, London: Macmillan.

Marx, Karl and Engels, Frederick (1848), 'Manifesto of the Communist Party', in *Marx–Engels Selected Works*, vol. 1, London: Lawrence and Wishart.

Marx, Karl (1904) (originally published 1859), *Critique of Political Economy*, New York: International Library.

Mays, John Barron (1954), *Growing Up in the City*, Liverpool: University of Liverpool Press.

Miller, Walter B. (1962), 'The Impact of a "Total-Community" Delinquency Control Project', *Social Problems*, vol. 10, p. 168.

Morris, Terence P. (1957), *The Criminal Area: A Study in Social Ecology*, London: Routledge & Kegan Paul.

Quinney, Richard (1970), *The Social Reality of Crime*, Boston: Little Brown.

Quinney, Richard (1974), *Critique of Legal Order: Crime Control in Capitalist Society*, Boston: Little, Brown.

Quinney, Richard (1977), *Class State and Crime: On the Theory and Practice of Criminal Justice*, New York: McKay.

Quinney, Richard (1980), *Class State and Crime: On the Theory and Practice of Criminal Justice*, 2nd edn, New York: McKay.

Runciman, W.G. (1966), *Relative Deprivation and Social Justice*, London: Routledge & Kegan Paul.

Sellin, Thorsten (1938), *Culture, Conflict and Crime*, New York: Social Research Council.

Stack, S. (1984), 'Income Inequality and Property Crime', *Criminology*, vol. 22, p. 229.

Steinert, Heinz (1997), '*Fin de Siècle* Criminology', *Theoretical Criminology*, vol. 1, p. 111.

Taylor, Ian, Walton, Paul and Young, Jock (1973), *The New Criminology*, London: Routledge & Kegan Paul.

Taylor, Ian, Walton, Paul and Young, Jock (1975), *Critical Criminology*, London: Routledge & Kegan Paul.

Tittle, Charles R. (1995), *Control Balance: Towards a General Theory of Deviance*, Boulder, Co: Westview Press.

Tittle, Charles R. (1997), 'Thoughts Stimulated by Braithwaite's Analysis of Control Balance', *Theoretical Criminology*, vol. 1, p. 99.

Turk, Austin T. (1969), *Criminality and Legal Order*, Chicago: Rand McNally.

Vold, George B. (1958), *Theoretical Criminology*, New York: Oxford University Press.

Willis, P. (1978), *Profane Culture*, London: Saxon House.

CHAPTER SIXTEEN
Criminology and Realism

16.1 THE BIRTH OF REALISM

The ideas, analyses and explanations already surveyed might seem sufficiently comprehensive and all-embracing to exclude any significant additions. Yet recent years have seen the emergence in Britain and the USA of an approach which is considered to be sufficiently distinctive and covering a sufficient scope as to be given its own title: realism. The genesis of realism lies essentially in the perception that crime *rates* have tended to rise remorselessly in advanced societies, and that established policies for dealing with crime have failed to stem this increase. Realism accepts these perceptions and aims to analyse the position in ways which will lead to more effective solutions.

Given so ambitious a project, it is not surprising to find that those starting from realism's basic presumptions have not all arrived at the same analysis and solutions. Broadly there are two main schools of realism: one which draws its philosophic stance from the politics of the right, and one drawing on leftist political values. In the account which follows more attention will be paid to the left realists because their influence so far seems to have been stronger in Britain, and the central writers (Jock Young, Roger Matthews, Pat Carlen and John Lea) are British. The right realists have their greatest effect in the United States where the strongest proponent of these views, James Q. Wilson, is based.

As indicated, the realist approaches have originated in a restatement of the object of criminology as the need to explain not just crime, but its apparent long-term increase. From this altered perspective, there are substantial difficulties with all the ideas discussed in preceding chapters. Most of these have turned around two basic concepts: the criminal either is seen as choosing criminality, or is seen mainly as an instrument. Theories which emphasise the choice by an individual attribute the criminal decision to a wide variety of possibilities such as a lack of moral fibre; a failure to make a proper internalisation of basic standards; or antagonism towards the oppression of the State. Those who see the criminal as merely the tool, stress that the criminal actions are preordained either by internal biology or by external forces of society or circumstance. They all have in common a desire to explain criminality, the aetiology of crime. Most commentators are now agreed that any plausible explanation would have to contain a mixture of causes, sometimes a biological/social mix, sometimes a psychological/social mix and sometimes a mixture of different social theories. As has been seen in preceding chapters this has sometimes led to mixed responses. So in Britain in the last 15 years or so there has been what can be seen as a strange *mélange* of policies. The Conservative government first tried to impose a 'get tough' policy to crime and enforcement. Punitive approaches were central and involved, amongst other things, a 60 per cent increase in the budget for the police (whose performance – crime clear-up rate – none the less dropped) and a massive prison building programme at a time when the rise in prison population was slowing down. The government also tried to implement a 'privatisation' of certain aspects of the system, sometimes with apparently perverse effects (Group Four). And yet at the same time, all this has been accompanied by a massive increase in the use of cautioning, especially for the young, and of a less intrusive and less punitive system for youths generally. The continuation of tough measures was signalled early by the new Labour government in 1997. The Home Secretary, Jack Straw, then suggested steps such as the possible confiscation of passports and driving licences for those on probation; giving the courts powers to name and shame juveniles; and greater responsibility placed on parents of juvenile offenders.

What does seem to be irrefutable is that, whatever the policies, crime rates have continued to rise. The level of criminality has altered radically upwards since the war. Not only have the get tough and control policies not managed to stem the rise, but the existing theories also seem unable to provide an explanation. For example, unless there has been a vast biological change, theories in biology, even if it is accepted that they can explain some crime, cannot explain the increase. Nor, without some grave and widespread difference in the psychological health of individuals in a community, is it possible to explain it on this factor. The existing biological and psychological theories in criminology do not refer to such general physical and mental changes. There is more plausibility in some of the other ideas which have been examined. Thus social theories are often concerned with deprivation and other social ills which, at least in real terms, have become more apparent in the past 40 years. But although social background and upbringing may have altered, it is questionable whether they could explain the increase in criminality. It could be said that the ideas examined in earlier chapters can reasonably claim to give an insight into the aetiology of crime but none can begin to understand the recent changes. Nor do they, either separately or together, suggest an appropriate policy initiative or series of initiatives which might be useful for tackling the problem. Policies are either too expensive, too narrow or absent. Moreover almost all of these theories are relevant only, or largely, to men. They never explain why women living in similar conditions or with similar biological make-up do not offend as frequently as men.

There have been various responses to these shortcomings. As the crime problem could not be fully explained some theorists and politicians called for greater State intervention in the form of greater numbers of police and a firmer criminal justice approach. These measures were predicted to be of minimal utility (Heal et al. (1985)) and when introduced they have had almost no impact: the crime rate continues to rise.

A more fundamental response has been to deny the existence of the rise. It is argued that the increase is only an aspect of the official rate rather than a reflection of actual crime. Official statistics are officially constructed and do not necessarily give a true view of the problem. It is claimed that there is bound to be an increase as the result of a number of official responses: the authorities making new laws (if there are more laws to obey there are more to break); the authorities altering the way crimes are recorded; the authorities increasing enforcement and so including individuals who were not originally included but who had always committed crimes; the authorities increasing the awareness of and fear of crime leading to an increase in reporting and hence the appearance of greater criminality; more enforcement officers leading to greater numbers of crimes being detected; increased opportunity due to more affluent lifestyles and more goods to steal. There is obviously some substance in these claims, as seen in the preceding two chapters, but they are not sufficient to explain away the rise. They explain only a part of the rise.

This analysis of the shortcomings of existing theories and policies signalled a need for new approaches and new realistic goals. These have been provided by the two new theories: right and left realism. Realism of both types is intended to denote an acceptance that there is a real crime problem; a recognition that it has destructive effects on communities; that there is a need to discover realistic policies to counter the crime problem; and recognition that no miraculous solutions will ever be found. Both approaches also recognise the need to monitor the success of interventions so as to guarantee their cost-effectiveness and are critical of the present approach of the police. The similarities stop there.

16.2   RIGHT REALISM

16.2.1   The basic concepts of the theory

James Q. Wilson is the foremost proponent of right realism (see Wilson (1985)) and writes about criminology from the standpoint of new right philosophy and politics. Two broad consequences follow; right realism does not challenge the criminal law as currently defined by the State (i.e., the relatively powerful in society), and it centres its efforts on attacking 'street crime' to the exclusion of all other offences.

Wilson accepts that there is a real rise in the crime rate. Although he suggests that some of this can be explained by the greater number of young males, the most criminalogenic group, he recognises that this alone cannot explain the rise. He thus turns to other aspects, and has been instrumental in pressing for a substantial shift in the terrain of discussion.

The right realist debate does not abandon aetiology altogether, rather it centres on certain aspects, especially the behavioural and conditioning theories. Wilson worked with Herrnstein (Wilson and Herrnstein (1985)) to devise a bio-social approach to crime. They recognise that circumstances do not cause everyone to participate in crime and so use individualistic biological and psychological explanations to explain why some are more prone to criminality. The biological section of their reasoning returns to body-type theories and to genetics. The psychological aspects seem to centre on learning, particularly conditioning within the family. It is unclear exactly how they see these as interacting but it seems that both the conditioning and the biological predisposition play a part in the ability of individuals to assess rewards and punishments. By punishments they do not mean the very uncertain actions of the State as it is likely that the activity will go undetected and, even if detected, punishment is not guaranteed. Instead they refer to the internalised conscience of the individual which is learned from the family and other social interactions. From this basis, the approach attacks certain types of family, particularly the single-parent family, for ineffective socialisation. At the same time, the ability to learn is affected by the constitution of the individual and the effectiveness of the input from family, peers, school, work etc. The conclusion is that biology sets the population who are at risk of becoming criminal, whilst socialisation, or its failure, helps to decide whether this will be realised. The possible punishments will then be assessed and balanced against the potential gains. As affluence increases the available opportunities for lucrative offending, so the choice to offend also becomes more likely.

Wilson thus uses biological and conditioning factors in his initial analysis but then largely abandons them. This is justified, not because they are not important, but because they do not offer reasonable policy suggestions for moving forward with the debate. It is not, or not yet, possible to alter the biology of an individual in the way which would be necessary were his assumptions in this area correct. Nor is it possible rapidly to improve the socialisation offered by families, or quickly rid society of single-parent families (although both in Britain and the USA the New Rights have seen this as a policy objective and one which should be tackled as part of a welfare problem). Nor can other socialisation influences which may militate towards criminality – the freedom, materialistic and individualistic nature of society – be easily altered. Therefore, despite having acknowledged broad causes of criminality, right realism does not propose to tackle these. Instead the aim is to reduce the problem via pragmatic intervention, accepting that this can be of only limited benefit, but stressing that it is feasible and ought to work. Wilson also sees no gain in merely increasing policing or other strictly law enforcement measures – this is merely costly and has never produced strong positive results.

His solution does, however, partially rest on the policing function. He and Kelling (Wilson and Kelling (1982 and 1989)) argue that the main and most effective use of police is not as law enforcers but rather as a body to keep order within society. They claim that reduction in order within a neighbourhood gives rise to the conditions in which crime can proliferate. Disorder heightens fear, which alters the area so that the law-abiding become less visible and less likely to perform a surveillance role. Also disorder, where it goes unchecked, shows a breakdown of controls which encourages crime. On the other hand, the maintenance of order by the police allows community control mechanisms to flourish, encouraging the maintenance of both order and law-abiding behaviour. The constructive function of the police is then seen to be not reducing crime, but providing the environment in which criminality is not able to flourish. To do this they have to be less centrally concerned with breaches of the criminal law and more interested in regulating street life in a wider perspective. They should centre on behaviour which may not seem to be the most criminalogenic but which reduces respect in the area and reduces the desire of the locals to enforce controls – behaviour such as soliciting, gang fights, drunkenness, disorderly conduct and pornography. In themselves these may not be harmful, but they harm the community and therefore need to be controlled. Right realists, far from legalising these behaviours, call for them to be more stringently controlled. Similarly, in fighting drugs they suggest no increase in activities against the dealers and the addicts who are beyond help: the effort should be concentrated on enforcement against small users, the least culpable and harmful in themselves but the ones identified as attacking the fibre of the community. Lastly, in calling for a restoration of order Wilson and Kelling see no problem in allowing police to interfere even where the behaviour is not strictly criminal. Here they advocate action against empty properties, rowdy children, groups of teenagers on the streets, litter, noise, harassment and intimidation which falls short of criminality and other indicators of social decline. Such action is justified because these conditions lead to high crime rates. Right realists do not therefore argue for structural alterations but rather for the individual behaviours to be controlled whether or not these are strictly criminal. They do so by arguing that these non-criminal behaviours are often those which interfere most with the enjoyment of life for many people, particularly many poor people. Essentially the argument is that it is individuals, not society, who are at fault and the solution is to clamp down upon the individual behaviour of those at risk.

These measures to restore order, as those to control crime, should be most directed against the areas which are just beginning to turn into high crime rate areas. Areas which have gone so far that they are beyond saving should not have money and resources devoted to them: the focus should be on those which can be altered. Where the community controls are just beginning to lose their force there is still a possibility of restoring order.

In the less hopeful areas, and for those already criminals, the strategy involves a more direct attack on crime itself. In areas where there is already an irrevocably high crime rate there should be a more crime-orientated approach. The police should detect and prosecute offenders. Similarly, at an individual level, recidivists should be harshly treated. They should be punished not on the seriousness of the crime they have just committed, but on the weight of their criminal record. This is very similar to the old extended sentences (abolished by the Criminal Justice Act 1991) for those repeating serious offences and has given rise to the 'three strikes and you're out' policy in the US, whereby on a third offence – however trivial – an individual is removed from society for an extended period.

As already indicated, a major part of the right realist's thesis is that crime is the result of an individual choice and can be prevented or contained by pragmatic means which make the choice of criminal behaviour less likely: reducing the opportunity; increasing the chances of detection; raising feelings of being detected partly through close policing, especially of disorder; and, most importantly, definite punishment – the threat of severe, certain and swiftly imposed punishment. Imprisonment is seen as especially effective in neutralising or incapacitating offenders and terrorising others into law-abiding lifestyles. The stress on prisons simply as punishment goes alongside a belief in the need to move away from treatment and training in these institutions, which, it is asserted, does not work. This approach was encapsulated in the statement from the Director-General of the Prison Service in 1983 that prisons were to serve four functions: keeping untried and unsentenced prisoners in custody until they were to be brought to court; keeping sentenced prisoners in custody; providing as full a life as possible within the confines of custody (largely meaning regular baths, toilet facilities etc.); and helping prisoners keep in touch with their families. To this basic security and control Woolf (1991) added justice, to ensure that the dignity of those working in and incarcerated in prisons was upheld. Woolf did not restore any purpose, such as rehabilitation and reform, for prisons apart from secure containment. This rejection of the previous prison ideals has meant that it is easier to apply the simple economic drive of efficiency and cost-cutting and hence has made prisons more amenable to the application of market forces in the guise of private prisons. All of this fits well with the right realist ideal of simple punishment to disable present offenders and deter others. It also renders possible the distancing of government ministers from responsibility for the prisons, especially the operational aspects of containment, and makes it more difficult to employ any other initiatives in the institutions. It returns to the right realist belief that crime, responsibility and family are all interrelated (Young (1996)).

16.2.2   Criticisms of the theory

First, the theory is very limited in the area of behaviour in which it is interested: street crime. This excludes any consideration of corporate or white-collar offences and is likely to exclude more powerful offenders from the arena. Furthermore, right realists accept official definitions of crimes as given, and fully concur in the validity of official priorities and assessments of seriousness. This presupposes that these assessments are not politically constructed and that most people's experience of crime is limited to harm caused by street crime; both of these assumptions are obviously open to challenge. Such criticism does not deny the importance and impact of street offences. All realist approaches recognise that these are the areas of offending which most visibly and directly affect individuals.

Secondly, in searching for explanations of criminality it ignores all social economic, structural and materialistic ideas and concentrates solely on the individual and the behavioural conditioning which is most strongly connected with the family. These criteria are not arrived at after careful empirical analysis and they ignore many pieces of research which undermine the claims; the individualistic nature is not strongly proved. For example, Matthews (1992) found little support for the hypothesis that there is a connection between crime and incivilities or order. Incivilities seemed to be marginal to the process of urban decline. Far more important were other social indicators and the general level of services available to an area. As many writers have noted the decline of such areas is far more dependent on structural, socio-economic and other similar factors. To put the blame on incivility and increases in single-parent families, ignores the wider social issues. If this is so, solving these minor disorder problems would not solve criminality and in fact the limited targeting of areas suggests that what is far more likely to occur is not a lowering of criminality but a displacement of this activity to areas which Wilson and Kelling write off as being beyond help. This outcome is even more likely if one were to accept the individual nature of criminality which Wilson and Herrnstein claim.

This displacement of crime is more interesting, and more worrying. Wilson and Kelling admit that there are certain areas which are beyond helping, and their proposals seem likely to move the offending into these areas and away from those which still have some control mechanisms and, in their terms, are better equipped to deal with the difficulty. Thus the worst areas are written off, and the underclass and extremely poor who live in these areas are further marginalised and disadvantaged. They are to be heavily penalised when they step out of line (as in Clinton's 'three strikes and you're out' policy in the USA) and left to rot in high crime rate areas even if they do not. Their plight is seen as of their own making because they have not been sufficiently condemning of minor transgressions, they have not inculcated discipline into their offspring and used controlling, often physically controlling (corporal punishment), mechanisms to condition behaviour. Wilson and his colleagues ignore the social aspects, preferring to blame people. It is an approach which conveniently allows them to escape from financial investment in improvements for these areas. There is, in any event, a basic contradiction in their approach. Their central tenet is that criminality is a choice – a rational choice and a wrong choice which must be punished. The choice must be punished because it is an individual choice not affected by the social, political or cultural environment. It is thus inconsistent for them to argue that such choices are likely to arise, or more likely to arise, only in certain environments: if crime is an individual internal choice, how can more policing of 'order' within particular areas help to control behaviour?

This policing of order not of crime allows intervention on grounds which would not be entirely legal, or necessarily just. Such an approach has been heavily attacked by Kinsey et al. (1986) who say that the only true indicators of police performance are the clear-up rates. Moving towards an order model reduces the possibility of making reasonable assessments of police efficiency. More worryingly, if the police are allowed on such a loose mandate to control all manner of activities, it is very difficult to make them accountable and ensure they act with integrity. It also opens the possibility of discriminatory decisions by police officers, or at least of claims of such by members of the public. Kinsey et al. also note that some of the areas which Wilson and Kelling portray as being merely instances of the maintenance of order are in fact cases of law enforcement – fights between youths, domestic disputes, soliciting, drunk and disorderly. It may be that what they are advocating is to treat them as problems of order and so to try to stamp them out without recourse to the courts and official mechanisms. This, too, could endanger the system of criminal justice. On the other hand, if crime is caused by the lack of order in these neighbourhoods, the negative impacts noted by Kinsey et al. may be worth suffering in order to achieve a lower crime rate.

Although these policies have an immediate commonsense attraction, they could be very damaging to society as a whole. They might reduce crime and fear of crime in some areas, but one consequence would be totally to marginalise other areas. In the abandoned areas constraints towards being law-abiding are reduced still further and the inhabitants, even if law-abiding, will be subjected to ever-increasing levels of crime and victimisation. This is surely unacceptable.

16.3   LEFT REALISM

16.3.1   Introduction
The last two chapters (Fourteen and Fifteen) concerned the response, mostly from the left, to existing deterministic theories. An important part of this response was to emphasise the role played by the powerful in society. These persons, it was asserted, also committed crimes; but in addition it was largely they who shaped the criminal laws, criminalising types of behaviour which were more common amongst the less powerful. In much of this, often called left idealism, the theorists presented the criminal almost as the 'victim' of society rather than as the positive and cognitive offender. More positively, they widened the scope to point out that the study of crime, like that of all social activities, should encompass all the actors: the criminals and law-breakers, the enforcers, the police and the other organs of State control. Many of the theories considered crime at societal level, shaped by wide social aspects (a macro level) and not just the immediate micro level, shaped by smaller local social aspects. Left realism aims to look at the micro and macro levels. It considers crime as it would be perceived by many, either through their own experiences or through those of family and friends and through media images. It then tests these feelings about criminality and tries to include them in its explanations. Left realism also widens the plane of the debate to the plight and situation of victims and to the informal, community systems of social control.

Part of the impetus for this whole school came from feminist writing concerning victimisation, particularly of women but also more generally the victimisation of the disadvantaged, often by the disadvantaged. Each of these victim studies exposed the conflicts within the working class. Hitherto radical and critical criminologists had seen the working class as a unified whole, victimised by the powerful. Recognition of intra-class and sex-based victimisation was a major force in moving critical and radical criminologists towards a consideration of the realist debate. This rooting of the school also leads us to one of its central tenets – crime is a real problem, often a problem for the poor and the marginalised.

The most important writers in this field are British, e.g., Jock Young, Roger Matthews, Pat Carlen and John Lea. Two books are invaluable to the discussion of this subject; each is a collection of essays published in 1992: *Rethinking Criminology: The Realist Debate*, edited by Jock Young and Roger Matthews; and *Issues in Realist Criminology*, edited by Roger Matthews and Jock Young.

16.3.2 The essence of left realism

In the author's judgment the essential element in left realism is its holistic approach to the question of criminology. The ideal is to identify the links between all facets and all the actors. The recognition of all aspects and actors in the subject is then used both for a macro and micro study of the subject. It is this approach which marks the school out from all others. This is not to devalue other aspects of the school but to recognise that many of these almost flow from the holistic approach: this is the strong theoretical aspect at the centre.

Left realism thus starts from the proposition that crime, like other social events, involves various subjects (offenders, victims etc.) who are engaged in a variety of social actions and reactions. Most earlier theories concentrated on just one or two aspects: the criminal, or the criminal and the victim, or the criminal and the State, particularly the control agencies. Left realism takes over some of the ideas which emanate from these theories, but rejects any notion that crime can be studied from a narrow range of its aspects. Left realism is unwilling to compartmentalise the debate in this way and insists that there is a multiple relationship which should not be severed. More specifically, it recognises four main aspects: offenders; victims; formal control (the police and other agencies of social control); and informal control (the public). These four facets are posited as the points of a square. The essence is to study the interrelationships between them: the approach is sometimes characterised as 'the square of the crime'.

Positivist criminology has tended to centre wholly on the criminal and the reasons why he or she committed offences, whether these be social or biological. Labelling theory and radical criminology centred on the State as constructing both the area of behaviour to be delineated as criminal and the way in which actors would become embroiled in the system, as well as the reaction of the State to certain behaviours. Whilst recognising the worth of each of these approaches, left realists accept neither because they are too restricted. Full understanding requires consideration of: why people commit crimes; why the State delineates certain activities as unacceptable; why it controls behaviour in certain ways; the interaction between all the actors, offender, victim, enforcement officer etc.; how moral and social approval and disapproval interplay both with offending and with the definitions of offending; social interaction of groups in society and their impact on offending; structural aspects of offending; reasons for administrative decisions. All these questions interlink to give a full and meaningful comprehension of crime. Such totality of knowledge is beyond our reach but approximations can, at least, be sought. In pursuit of this the importance of the square of crime will be considered in relation to various aspects of the issue.

16.3.3 The reality of crime rates and fear of crime

Like those on the right, left realists recognise the rise in crime. They also accept that there has been a rise in the fear of crime. However, neither of these is seen as unproblematic or to have only a single, or narrow, dimension. Thus the notion that the crime rate has risen may be simple, but its significance for an understanding of the reality of crime is highly complex. In part, this is because the crime rate is affected by the way in which the four corners of the square develop and react, the way in which the various aspects come together to provide a fuller understanding of the intricate social relationships between the poles of the square.

Officially recorded crime rates are affected by changes in the points of the square. So an increase in the normal offending group, young males, is likely to lead to an increase in offending. Similarly a change in the number of people who own desirable goods, or who are on the streets at high crime rate times will increase the number of potential victims and again is likely to increase the number of offences. A change in activity by members of the public can also alter the situation. For example, if there are fewer non-offenders on the streets there is a lower level of surveillance and hence a lower level of control: these conditions heighten the opportunity for offending which is thus likely to rise. The figures will be similarly altered by changes in the official agencies of enforcement: an increase in policing, for example, is likely to give rise to an increase in officially recorded crimes. It should be noted that the last of these examples differs from the rest because it refers only to officially recorded offending whereas the others referred to actual levels of crime.

It is more significant to note, however, that to consider the effects in this disjointed way loses the force of left realism. It is important to register the impact of each point of the square, but it is essential to attempt to see how they fit together to form a social whole, a social relationship. The explanation for the crime rate must try to include all these considerations and the way in which they interact.

The texture of what is meant can be illustrated from a very brief consideration of burglary. There is in the officially recorded offending statistics, a rise in the levels of burglary over time. This may be partly a product of changes in the social behaviour; or there may simply be more burglaries because there are more youths, or because there are more desirable goods owned by more potential victims. Or more burglaries can arise because of a more general acceptance of a consumerist society where people's worth is measured by the level of their ownership constituting a sort of pressure towards property-based offending. Or it may be partly a product of the way in which the behaviour is defined, policed and reacted to by official agencies. It may also be partially a product of an increased sensitivity to crime on the part of the public, which could be described as unofficial reactions to behaviour.

The last of these can be briefly expanded to suggest some of the more subtle possible interactions and also to show how it interacts with the others. Thus society may, over time, become less tolerant of certain activities. The shifts in attitudes towards drug use can illustrate the point. To look first at opiate use; although it was popularly accepted and widely practised in the nineteenth century, it became officially defined as criminal (unless prescribed by a physician) early in the twentieth century and fairly quickly became popularly rejected and defined as unacceptable behaviour. Today such activity is very widely rejected but still practised by many individuals. The level of use may or may not have altered; certainly the reasons for the use today and in the nineteenth century are likely to be very different, and so are the main users. But it is largely the changed reactions of society, both officially and unofficially, which makes it appear as if there is an increase in such use. Certainly, until recently, there has been a marked increase since the Second World War although, as the British Crime Survey has shown, it is not as widespread as popular opinion suggests (Ramsey and Percy (1994)) and there is some suggestion that this is now levelling out (South (1994)). There is as yet no comparable levelling out of the fear and intolerance.

The area of soft drugs is somewhat different. Again use was accepted and practised in the nineteenth century and became labelled criminal early in the twentieth century, leading to some rejection of it. However, today tolerance of use and possession in small quantities has risen; the official definition has not altered, but control both by enforcement agencies and the public is less interfering and more accepting. Use since the Second World War has risen very markedly (South (1994)) but is now more tolerated so that it is not perceived as a problem. Interestingly, the official figures do not necessarily show this difference in tolerance; enforcement is statistically more common against soft drugs like cannabis than against hard drugs, but the stronger penalties are reserved for the opiates and other hard drugs.

Changes in crime rates are thus normally the result partially of an increase in the behaviour itself, and partially as a change in the reaction to that behaviour. Also important are the social control constructs of both State and people: what people define as crime both as a community and officially. It is the way in which these fit together to form the pattern of offending which shapes the crime rate.

It seems that today we have a situation in which most of these factors are pulling together, that is, there is an increase in criminal behaviour as well as an increased intolerance of such behaviour. Thus the officially recorded rise in crime rates to some extent mark an actual rise in the activity, but they also mark a difference in what individuals will tolerate. There is both a rise in the recognition of the activity (whether official or not) and an increase in the official definitions of crimes (both in new crimes and in interpretations of, and willingness to record, crimes which are already in existence). These tendencies were seen in the discussion of drugs above, but there will also be slight differences in their application to various areas: it is necessary not only to study the general interactions but also how these come together in an explanation of the change in statistics for particular activities over time and in particular environments.

As well as the need to study tolerance and the activity, account needs to be taken of control. Again, as shown in the discussion concerning drugs, there may be a difference between the tolerance either officially (in defining crime) or unofficially (in reporting, complaining about, or being fearful of it) and in the control of the activity (the level of control which occurs for any particular offence, either official or unofficial). An activity may be less tolerated than it was in the past but that does not mean that its control will be more certain: control may remain constant or even decrease. As a consequence the agents of control – police (and other official agents), the family, school, media, peer group etc. – are less able to exert pressure or influence to persuade against offending behaviour. The criminal justice system may be less capable, through detection and punishment, of persuading individuals against offending than it was in the past. Similarly, the unofficial control system can decline or increase in its efficiency which will affect the actual rate of criminal activity.

16.3.4 The fear of crime

At the start of this section it was noted that left realists also acknowledge that rising crime rates have a destructive effect. Part of that effect occurs because of the fear to which the increase gives rise. As was noted in Chapter Five, there is a strong claim that some of the fear of crime is irrational in that the groups least likely to suffer victimisation are most fearful of it. Again as was noted earlier, the fear felt by these groups may not be as illogical as it first appears; it may be partly because of their fear that they conduct their lifestyles in ways which tend to reduce their victimisation (see 5.4 and Pearson (1993)). Furthermore, although they are not victimised by street crimes as readily as are their male and young counterparts, they are more frequently victimised in more hidden ways: domestic violence, rape, harassment and sexual violence or street crimes which are for various reasons less likely to be reported (Jones et al. (1986)).

More important for left realists is the different impact which crimes have on various people. An attack on one person or group may have very different effects from that on other groups. A woman who is attacked may suffer greater physical and psychological effects merely because of feeling unable to defend herself and so being made aware of her physical vulnerability. Women and the old lack power generally in society and their victimisation furthers this experience, reinforcing their believed impact of the criminal victimisation. In addition, if women are less tolerant of interference they will view minor infractions as more intrusive: the impact of the crime is thus more marked than is indicated by the bald rate of the crime figures.

In left realism, the notion of impact goes wider than this, because certain groups, particularly the poor and often racial minorities, are seen to be most at risk of high levels of victimisation. Victimisation tends to be focused geographically into the poorest areas and also on certain groups, for example, minority races. These groups are often least able to cope with the impact of such victimisation, because they have no financial or other resources: due to their poverty they are less likely to be insured and so unable to replace goods stolen. They are also the groups which suffer most from other social ills such as poverty, physical and mental illness, bad housing, unemployment, racism. Adding criminal victimisation to these other problems extends their generally negative experience and enhances its impact.

Victimisation, fear and the impact of crime are therefore as complex as the relations which are at play in the discussion of the crime rate. The impact and the destructive effect of criminality, together with the fear of crime, are largely affected by internalised feelings. They are also influenced by the support structures both in the community and from the State, which can help in handling the victimisation. All these factors converge to give rise to the destructive nature of victimisation.

16.3.5 Causes of crime

Views on the causes of crime constitute a central element for left realism. Writers from this school often give priority to the need to remove or reduce the causes of crime, over the need for investment in dealing with offending after it has occurred. The causes they emphasise rest on viewing the wider social context of the offending behaviour. The immediate causes thus need to be studied in relation to their wider social placing, the reactions of State and informal control systems to social problems, and the behaviour of the offender and the impact on the victim.

Left realism accepts that many factors help to cause crime, and that no one explanation of any individual's choice to offend is likely. They certainly reject all single, simple causative relationships, and deterministic explanations. This said, the main cause which is recognised by left realists is social and relative deprivation. As was seen in Chapters Eleven and Twelve, this is very different from single causative factors like unemployment or absolute poverty. By relative deprivation what is meant is not the simple situation of having nothing but rather the injustice to which it gives rise – especially the injustice compared to others, and especially if it is felt that the problem could have been avoided. Relative deprivation is also different from absolute poverty in other ways – it can occur at any level in the economic chain and will be discernible whether the State is relatively poor or relatively affluent. Clearly the poor, particularly those who are unemployed or otherwise marginalised from the material benefits of society (racial minorities, single-parent families and others), are most strongly affected by deprivation and therefore may be most prone to criminality as a result of this factor. The more a State is economically divided the stronger will be their relative deprivation, and the more likely it is that offending will result. They are not, however, alone in this: the very wealthy may aspire to even greater riches and through greed be moved to criminality. A further complication which attaches to relative deprivation is that it is not possible for an outsider to state categorically whether someone is experiencing deprivation in a way which will lead to criminal behaviour: it is the individual's own subjective assessment of his or her position which is the essential aspect. Social injustice may be clear to the outsider but still go unrecognised by the individual; only when people feel relatively deprived will they become more likely to choose offending as a sensible way out of their problem.

The way in which relative deprivation affects crime thus rests, to an extent, on anomie. Either the available opportunities are insufficient to meet the desires (which may be a factor in the crimes of the poor) or the community has failed to persuade people to internalise limits to their desires (the pure greed which ensues can explain the crimes of both rich and poor). The more a society stresses the desirability of having certain goods, the more people are encouraged to acquire, not just basics but the luxuries, the more pressure is placed on everyone to acquire these indicators of success and merit. It is not relevant that such success is illusory (as it often is): relative deprivation is felt at all levels of the economic and social structure if the socially approved targets are not attained. One result of this is to increase criminality. To take one example, the pressure on the young to conform to certain fashions is very strong. They are told to obtain not just certain clothing but brand-named clothing. They will turn to crime to obtain it (see Burnley (1990)). In the United States there are recorded instances of youths committing murder to secure a pair of Nike trainers. Young (1994) asserts that the crime rate was at its highest during the *laissez-faire* capitalism of the nineteenth century and attributes this to both the push to succeed and the political belief that this could be done by one's own hand. Similar politics of self-help, self-interest and pure economic and capitalistic endeavours are prevalent in Britain now, at a time with very high crime rates. And some left realists would argue that these tendencies are organically connected.

Most of the above would suggest that relative deprivation may be a good explanation for property offences but that it has nothing to offer in accounting for other types of offending. This is mistaken. Strain theory, discussed in Chapter Twelve, can help to explain the connection. This suggests that relative deprivation leads to frustration, creating a state where criminal activity is more likely to occur. The injustice suffered, or believed to be suffered, as a result of relative deprivation raises feelings of unfairness. These are exacerbated if there seems to be no possibility for a person lawfully to act to correct the injustice; if there is no legal way of addressing the problem there is a temptation to act in a criminal fashion. The feeling of injustice and strain is particularly strong where there is a belief that the deprivation was avoidable. For example, it may be believed that with investment jobs could be available, or that the State could act to reduce income inequalities: again this feeling could operate where the object is to relieve relative, rather than absolute, poverty. This injustice may thus be felt even by the rich where measures taken by government adversely affect their position, and in a way which they perceive as unfair. The strain may also be heightened if there is no end in sight to the unfairness, no end to the relative deprivation. This may be particularly relevant in the 1990s when many of those who are most economically and politically marginalised see no pending amelioration to their position and therefore possibly view criminality as their only sensible option. The usual controls which might otherwise mitigate against such action are weakened if they can offer no positive alternative. This points to a final element in strain. The immediate problem of losing a job or failing to obtain goods which are desired may be insufficient to move someone to criminality. Immediate deprivation may be insufficient unless the feeling of anger at the injustice is particularly strong. In many cases the relative deprivation, anomie and strain will take some time to work towards a choice to offend.

One other element which may be necessary is an environment in which criminal activity is made more possible, a place to sell stolen goods, to sell drugs, and peers with whom to share the experience. For left realists social structures and subcultures are crucial not only in determining whether criminality is chosen, but also the type of criminality. In other words, the relative deprivation, anomie and strain set the scene and the subculture helps to shape which solution is chosen. In this interpretation, subcultures do not cause crime *per se*, they facilitate it once the individual is facing problems. They are not necessary to criminality, but if they are supportive of certain behaviours then in many instances they make such a solution more likely (Hagan (1994) posits such a connection for crime in the USA). Understanding the phenomenon requires an understanding of both the reasons for the predicament and the structural facilities available. Any idea which ignores one part of this is unlikely to be of utility, and any solution which is so based is unlikely to succeed. One implication is that both causes and solutions need to be focused on particular problems and particular areas; ideas cannot simply be mechanically imported across international boundaries, possibly not even across city or neighbourhood boundaries. There is no one solution for all crime, not even for all crime of a particular type.

As indicated, left realists do stress the social and structural factors. But if biological factors are thus marginalised, they are not ignored. The final choice may rest, to a very limited extent, on biology: is the individual sufficiently strong to carry out the offence, sufficiently confident to break the law? Biology is essentially a limiting factor here. The relative deprivation, anomie and strain cause the climate in which an individual may choose criminality but negative biological factors may prevent offending.

16.3.6 The fact of crime
Realists have noted that offenders are not simply predators, nor are victims and the public simply innocents. There is what they describe as a shape to crimes – each offence or group of offences is seen to have a particular structure. For example, drug dealing is usually seen as a pyramid. One central and important dealer sends materials out on a large scale to a chosen few, each of whom passes them on to a few more. The chain expands until the drugs arrive with the large number of users at the base of the pyramid. Each person within the pyramid is an offender. Each relies on others for some desired purpose. There is a strong consensus in each of the relationships and in the structure as a whole. Adding an international dimension complicates the shape: the main dealer will pay certain parties to arrange for the production of the drugs and there may well be double pyramid shape (a

bow-tie). Drug offences are largely consensual. Other groups of offences are partially consensual and partially predatory or coercive. Property offences rely on the public being willing to buy or handle stolen goods – this section of the relationship is consensual – but there is also a predatory or coercive element when the goods are actually taken from the victim. The hidden economy which exists in the distribution of stolen goods is usually local to the offenders, but the more general inference is that property offences occur because there is a fairly large number of people willing to participate. Without this such offences would become less attractive. There are then offences which are wholly predatory or coercive; most offences of violence fall into this category. In order to tackle crime in the most effective and efficient way much more needs to be understood about these relationships, which section of the chain might be easiest to tackle, and whether this might prevent the offending.

Over time the fact that a crime or crimes have occurred can have an effect on the interrelationships between the four aspects of the square. Victimisation can have profound effects on people's lives causing very real shifts in behaviour. Repeated victimisation is particularly debilitating in this way. Repeated burglaries can undermine the quality of life for a whole family. Repeated violent or sexual attacks can cause one of a number of psychological syndromes: rape trauma syndrome, battered woman syndrome, child sexual abuse accommodation syndrome, child abuse syndrome, parent abuse syndrome, post-traumatic stress syndrome. Each of these affects the victim in extreme ways. Whether such effects materialise will, to an extent, depend on the official and unofficial response to the victimisation once it is reported.

Similarly, once an individual has offended, whether the offending is repeated may depend on the response to the initial action. Official, administrative and community responses will all be factors and interact to change the experience, and possibly the behaviour, of the offender. In particular it may depend on whether the offender is detected and, if so, how his or her rationalisations concerning the action are treated. Such detection may be by peers in which case their response, rationalisations and acceptance are likely to be very different from those which would arise were the police to detect the offending. The end result might be very different.

As seen above, realism views all offenders as having chosen to offend. Offending is not determined by circumstance, situation, biology or psychology – left realists reject positivism. They also reject an organised and wholly rational decision to act against the system – the left idealist stance. This moral choice may alter over time. The second crime may be more or less directed. The causes of crime, too, alter over time and are affected by their relationship with the other aspects of the square of crime.

As well as a temporal, left realists also recognise a spatial, dimension to criminality. Some aspects of crime may be very wide-ranging – drug trafficking is an international offence, top-level dealing may be distributed throughout the country – while other aspects, such as street selling, will be largely located within certain defined areas, often small areas of a city. Burglary and handling usually share a spatial area. Violent attacks are often centred on particular areas. Some of these areas converge to give high crime rate districts where offending, particularly predatory offending, is common. Many people then avoid these districts, making offending still easier as it reduces surveillance.

All that has been said might suggest that left realists accept the present boundaries of the criminal law. This is not the case. They see nothing intrinsic in most behaviour which renders it necessarily criminal; even killing is not always against the law. The way crime is and should be defined should reflect the important aspects of the relations between the points of the square of crime. Left realists neither unquestioningly accept present definitions of crimes, nor do they take the relatively simplistic stance of left idealism or critical criminology. They do not assume that there is always a power analysis: official and unofficial interests have to be considered as does the fear of crime. They would also wish to split criminal activity down into its many constituents and assess its nature and its impact upon each facet of the square of crime before arguing either to criminalise or decriminalise any behaviour. Here the complexity of human activity is given full weight and all discussions are assessed in a wide social context. Thus some drugs might be passed over to regulatory agencies whilst others need tight control by the criminal law. Again, discussions about legalising soliciting and brothels must confront a possible need to protect the women who appear to enter these markets consensually, but their participation may have been coerced by their socio-economic deprivation. White-collar and corporate crimes have only relatively recently been addressed by left realists. In the assessment of the second Islington Crime survey, Pearce (1990) found a high incidence of feelings of victimisation by these criminal activities in that community: as a result both definitions of these activities and their enforcement are more securely placed on the agenda of left realists.

16.3.7 Control of crime
Like other aspects, the control of crime will be unsuccessful unless it addresses the problem from all sides. It must involve action being taken to resolve problems at each point of the square – changes in policing, better community involvement, empowering and supporting victims, and dealing with the causes of offending.

The policing role must prioritise justice, which is the opposite of the suggestions made by the right realists who place the retention of order above justice in policing. Left realists view justice as essential as otherwise communities or sections of them will become further alienated from society, increasing their marginalisation and acting to increase the causes of crime discussed above. It would enhance feelings of relative deprivation, and increase the strain on individuals both of which left realists associate with criminality. Factors such as this were documented as causes of the Brixton riots in the early 1980s where Scarman (1981) stated that interventionist and saturation policing had been the factor which had tilted the balance towards riotous behaviour. His report led to the Police and Criminal Evidence Act 1984 which was supposed to be a fairer system, one including checks and balances and so (it was hoped) reinstating justice. Measures designed to arrive at order or crime control at the expense of justice are more likely to exacerbate than solve the problem.

It is also recognised that any intervention by the State is bound to carry with it costs to victims, offenders and the community. The aim is to reduce the harmful effects, both those of the criminal activity and of control. This does not mean that policing should necessarily be removed or reduced, merely that it should be made more accountable, particularly accountable to the needs of the local area and to the law. It also means that enforcement should be more fairly distributed. Some areas are perceived as being targeted for too much control. Street crime in certain inner-city areas is often policed in this way and it is particularly unacceptable when the targeting is of particular groups or of minor transgressions, minor drugs offences or youth status crimes. It will be recalled that this is exactly what the right realists would focus on: here it is believed to be the source of the problem rather than the solution. Other areas are perceived as being too little policed: crimes such as white-collar or corporate offences fall into this category. Seeing these offenders more controlled would also add to the feelings of justice in the system and further enhance the effectiveness of the system. Other activities which might benefit from closer State control include racial violence and harassment, child abuse and domestic violence. Again policing of these areas would enhance the quality of life of some of the population and imbibe an element of justice into the control system.

It follows that policing and other official control should be mindful of a number of factors: exactly what it is trying to achieve; the financial costs of intervention; the costs of its action to both the local community and to the criminals and victims; the costs of the criminal activity to the quality of life of the community and victims; and whether the likely outcome would justify the costs. In all of this the interests and desires of the community should be paramount. In this way control can be better, more justly targeted and should give rise to a better quality of life for the whole community. Once justice is carefully provided for, any State intervention needs to be carefully tailored to the problems faced in various areas. It needs to take account of the structural and cultural aspects of the problem, and be designed to help, rather than undermine, community control. This is also necessary to the fight against crime because, without public support and willingness to provide information, the job of policing would become impossible.

Community control is the second limb of the fight against crime. This has two aspects, one is the informal control mechanisms such as those discussed in Chapter Thirteen, the other is the willingness of the public to cooperate with the official control agencies in order to solve crimes and catch offenders. Again each of these is most likely to flourish where there is justice in the system of official control. Left realists argue that the problem with this system is that it is least effective where it is most needed. In areas of high crime rate the informal systems of control are least evident and least able to exert any impact on the situation of offending. Left realists also attack some of what is done to bolster up the self-help systems. Many of these involve monetary input to make the targets less easy to attack, but such investment is least available where it is most needed. Indeed, it is noted that investment in more affluent areas serves to reduce crime in those locations but all too frequently causes an increase in other districts, particularly in the poorest areas. Right realists do not consider this to be a problem as they suggest heavier policing and sentencing tactics in such areas: a solution not possible for left realism which relies on justice. The private techniques which are employed in some areas are thus questioned on the basis that they further marginalise the least powerful, economically and politically. Left realists argue for different schemes which can unite society in a common cause, not further marginalise some whilst protecting the better off. This often means that they would support much greater community involvement in crime prevention and policy development.

The victims of crime are held to deserve special treatment. Their plight needs to be recognised both by the criminal justice system giving them the respect they deserve, and by society providing the social support which they may need. Their concept of the victim is wide, including social as well as criminal victimisation. Here it seems they believe that if the social rights which victims can expect are reinforced together with their position in society, they would cooperate and perform the social duty of giving evidence etc. There is therefore a payoff for the extra value given to victims. It may also mean that we can expect certain standards of care from the population to avoid being victimised.

Last, but in the eyes of left realists most important, is the need to address the causes of crime which they perceive as being most important. Relative deprivation is the central element. Crime occurs when there are no legal means of addressing this problem or when those legal means are less pleasant and less likely to meet with success. On this reading, society needs to provide the more deprived with jobs, housing, and such community facilities as hostels, youth clubs, drop-in centres, clinics, nurseries etc. However, beneficial provision will not immediately give rise to an alleviation of the problem. Just as in discussing causes of crime, negative structural changes were seen to take some time to work their way through subcultural levels, so too amelioration of problems will not give rise to quick positive results. Changing deep-seated attitudes like relative deprivation takes time measured in decades rather than days. Even then it depends on the nature of the positive input and on the make-up of the area in age, sex, race and in long-term unemployed, structural unemployment, and youths who have never worked. Many factors will bear upon recovery, just as many have a bearing on criminality and the choice to offend.

16.3.8 Assessment of left realism
Left realists claim that their theory is strongly based on the social reality of crime and on providing realistic, affordable and acceptable solutions to the problem. It is therefore in this vein that they should primarily be assessed. It is thus pertinent to note that their reality, despite embracing the four aspects in the square of crime, is largely constructed from victimisation studies (for

a full discussion of these see Chapter Five). Moreover, left realists stress local rather than national studies on the grounds that these record not only the description of crimes but also explanations of the reality of crime. They ask more questions concerning issues such as: racial harassment and domestic violence; age, sex, ethnicity; the full impact of crime on particular victims; other disadvantages which people feel they suffer (a class situation); criminal activities of the interviewee. Local surveys also focus on a small geographical area encouraging the claim that they are better placed to understand the specific nature of a community's problems. The most commonly quoted studies, Islington and Merseyside, are both inner-city surveys which tend to give a class dimension to the problem of victimisation.

On this basis left realists have attempted to dispel claims that fears of crime are either irrational or that they are constructed outside the realities recognised and experienced by people. Their essential criticism of earlier views which dismissed the irrationality of a widespread fear of crime is undoubtedly well-founded, but their own tendency to replace this by establishing the rationality of fear is open to a similar comment. The assumption seems to be that fear can be assessed as lying on a linear continuum between rationality and irrationality: this represents too simplistic a view of fear (Sparks (1992)). On the one hand, it could be said that most people harbour fears which appear to be irrational – fears of spiders, flying, open spaces etc. But this is not to deny or remove the reality of the fear. On the other hand, attempting to establish rationality by measuring the risk of victimisation ignores the fact that most people have neither the information nor the capacity accurately to calculate the risks: their fear is not the product of some sort of actuarial assessment. The demand to know more than is practicable is part of modernity's desire for certainty and for control of the extended world (see, e.g., Holloway and Jefferson (1995)). In this sense left realism, by putting too much stress on measures of crime, understates the importance of other influences which are not necessarily irrational. These would include: awareness of the political or economic marginalisation of an area; attack on, or control over, a group or groups; media, especially local media, comment (Smith (1986)); and the extent to which crime is discussed in a particular area or amongst particular groups. Left realist writers would not deny much of this, but in striving to place too much weight on the rational (in the sense of reasonably calculated) basis of fear they expose themselves to doubts and criticism. This could undermine the acceptance of their basic point: that, contrary to earlier views, the fear of crime is not irrational, and is a reality for many groups in society.

However, in trying to tie the rationality of fear to risk and behaviour the thesis becomes again problematic. We do not entirely live our lives in relation to how much we may suffer from particular dangers, and we are quite willing to accept some dangers while rejecting others which may be far less serious. Some parts of socialisation actually encourage 'living on the edge' and the taking of risk. This last may be a very sex-based aspect of our society, male socialisation accepting and encouraging risk-taking where the socialisation of women does not, or does to a lesser extent (Walklate (1995)). Although perhaps declining, this is still an important aspect of our society and one not considered by the left realists (see also Chapter Thirteen, especially the section concerning control within the family).

In any event, victimisation studies are necessarily limited. Some of these limitations are recognised by the left realists when they argue that they take account not only of the reality as understood by victims but also of factors of which they are unaware. The effect is to take the impressions of the victims seriously (as being real) but then to superimpose a degree of structural analysis (the material conditions within which that reality is experienced) which the victims would probably not recognise. Young (1996) attacks them on this basis, claiming that left realism fails to grasp the subtleties of crime and victimisation. Even apart from this the approach empowers and disempowers victims within the one theory. The dilemmas to which this gives rise can be seen in the empowering of the local community to participate in deterrence and policing policies.

Left realism empowers because it presumes that by democratic process the community can participate in policies concerning their local policing and deterrence. This presumes sufficient interest for communities to become involved, and also presumes a level of understanding and knowledge of the crime problems of the area which may not always exist. Left realists reasonably justify the empowering of the public since more than 90 per cent of serious crimes of which the police become aware are reported by the public and most of the information necessary to a solution of such crime is also gained from the public (Lea et al. (1987)). They then argue that such public support might not be forthcoming if people do not believe that the policing is for them, rather than of them, and if they are not able to see justice in the system: without public support the police could not operate. The conclusion is that the best policy for the police is to cultivate relationships with the public. For left realists this can be best achieved by fairly strict legal control of powers, limiting areas of individual discretion; minimal police-initiated activity and maximum public-initiated activity; a recognition of the inherently political nature of policing; and some accountability at a local political level.

There are problems with all items of this programme. To begin with, a legally controlled system will not in itself remove unfairness: the level of the injustice will then depend on the formulation of the rules. On the positive side will be the transparency of a legally controlled system, making it easier to alter: on the negative side, the inevitable continuance of some injustice will lead to some groups feeling marginalised. It is, in any event, not possible – as the left realist writings seem to imply – to remove all exercise of discretion. The real problems with misuse of discretion probably occur at the lowest ranks, are undocumented and are notoriously difficult to control (see Fyfe (1992)). This problem is carefully illustrated by social interactionist considerations (see Chapter Fourteen). The initial contact between the police and criminals, victims and the public, takes place out on the street and much of this behaviour remains hidden from legal controls. Furthermore the impact of any policies, however accountable, may be thwarted because they are decided by the prejudices and personal approach of the individual officers on the street. This is not to argue that political accountability should not be used to control the police, nor even that it will be ineffective, but to recognise its limitations. By avoiding this the left realists are open to attack as having too simplistic an approach and not recognising the limitations of the utility of their suggestions.

Similarly, the equation that fairer policing will give rise to wider acceptance of police and control is questionable. It belies the complexity of these relationships and thus exaggerates the left realist case. Increasing the justice felt by a community might increase the general willingness of the community to impart information but this does not necessarily mean that there will be an increase in the type of information necessary to effective policing or that it will flow from those who hold most information about this social phenomenon. Much information now arises from informants whose information is affected by very different interests, often financial. Increased legal controls and political accountability may lead to controls over the police which actively reduce their ability to solve serious crimes. There is undoubtedly truth in left realist claims concerning justice and the cooperation of communities, but this should not be overstated. Furthermore, left realists largely argue for a minimalist approach to policing and presume that this will be the type of policing chosen by communities. In reality this may not be the case. Many in the community might wish to have more proactive and interventionist policing. Presumably left realists, with their preferred democratic ideals, are not really arguing that they will impose the minimalist approach on society and that only within this would communities have discretion or have a democratic voice.

A policy largely directed by local democratic needs would tend to be heavily based on victims' real understanding of their position. The likely outcome is that, like most other theories, left realism would be largely concerned with street crime as this visible face of offending is the element most likely to be prioritised by any community. This is not quite so intense a problem as it used to be: the second Islington crime survey (Pearce (1990)) revealed some awareness of corporate victimisation. But such corporate crimes, especially as the offenders are likely to be outside the locality, or even the country, will never be as sharply seen as immediate street crimes. In any event, corporate violations also show some of the problems which may be associated with minimal intervention. In regulatory offences such as environmental pollution and breaches of factory legislation, much of the offending takes place over a period of time and, is perhaps most effectively detected and controlled by interventionist policing. These considerations have led some left realists to suggest that in the area of corporate crime the best approach is through a proactive control policy coupled with encouraging the public to report such offences or suspected offences (Pearce and Tombs (1992)). If the agencies which police these crimes actively responded to such public participation this might alter the power base between public and capital, enhance the feelings of justice with in the whole system, and increase the efficiency of the wider criminal justice system. However, such a solution probably rests on abandoning the strict calls for minimalist interventions in all crime control, an issue which is not embraced by all left realists.

Nor do left realist writings sufficiently confront some of the ambiguity of democracy. It could, for example, be said that their form of democracy and devolved power simply means more local responsibility for crime control and law and order, while real power is held and policy set at central government level (Reiner and Cross (1991)). Moreover, left realist reliance on a democratic basis might permit the largest groups to dominate the minority groups in any area, or a more powerful group to dominate a less powerful group. For example, if there is minimalist policing based on policies formed by the local community, this might lead to issues such as domestic violence and child abuse remaining marginalised: they are both less visible and may also conflict with the perception of crime held by most of the community. Thus although left realists espouse an understanding of the marginalisation of women, it would seem that their policies are unlikely to protect them. Similar difficulties may exist in racial and other issues. Perhaps these are areas and issues where policy is best set from outside the community and which are not most effectively addressed by the minimalist interventions espoused in most left realism.

None the less, the call for greater community say in the management and control of crime is one element which has taken root in recent years. It has spawned all manner of suggestions – Neighbourhood Watch, mediation and conferencing (see Chapter Five, Wright (1995)) and the Safer Cities Programme (see Tilley (1992) and Sutton (1996)) amongst others. These bring with them immense difficulties and few certainties. Many of the suggestions of the left realists imply or openly suggest the need to move towards a criminal control system based partially in the community (a form of Communitarianism) where the community is the provider and upholder of social justice. The idea most left realists seem to have is that in this way democracy and justice are better served for all, but it is important to note that this does not always herald a fairer or more egalitarian society. The democratic aspects were discussed above, but it needs to be recognised that much communitarian thinking and motivation stems from the conservative right. Thus Murray (1990) suggests the removal of centralised welfare provision, leaving such functions to communities. He argues that local communities will provide the necessary welfare, housing, and education and crime control, but this effectively denies the differential needs of various communities dependent on whether they are affluent or poor. Such an approach would seem certainly to serve to increase the divide between rich and poor.

A left realist approach would need to confront these dangers as well as the democratic attractions of locating crime problems and solutions at the level of the community. One such danger, as Lacey and Zedner (1995) point out, is romanticising the past: for example, Murray from the right has an idealised version of simple, crime-free communities of days gone by. There are thus two questions to be confronted: what is a community; and might empowering them for criminal purposes carry broader social risks? On the first issue there is a problem of whether a community is a geographical or a social construct. The spatial element has often been seen as central to criminal studies, but, as an examination of some of this research indicates, the notion of community which was used was fluid. There were:

two estate-based projects; two neighbourhood anti-burglary projects; an area-based street offences project; a town-wide anti-cycle theft initiative; a borough-wide racial harassment project and a drug-related crime prevention project. (Crawford (1995) note 3)

Currie (1988), Crawford (1995), Gardiner (1995) and Gilling (1997), amongst others, see spacial community as problematic and have all considered not just geographic ideas of space but also more abstract concepts of community. These have included unified sets of attitudes or values; the presence or absence of a structural or institutional basis; and a social or economic homogeneity. Of course, if all that is involved is an exhortation to encourage the informal social control of neighbourhoods then we are back to pure control theory and a definition is less important. But more is generally expected here (see Graham and Bennett (1995)). If significant power is to be placed in communities it is necessary to define them.

It then becomes much more questionable whether definition of the social order should be done by reference to crime. Certainly, this carries with it particular difficulties from the point of view of left realism. If crime is the central defining concept then issues such as health may be reduced in importance, or communities may be constructed from their views on crime rather than from other social aspects, such as unemployment, housing, racism or the need for social amenities. The focus on crime as the problem may thus allow social problems such as economic constructs to be ignored. Even within the area of crime control such moves could be socially divisive. Affluent areas may opt for private policing, making them reluctant to contribute to official law enforcement agencies; those who refused – or who were unable – to contribute to the private forces would be left without protection; and crime might simply be driven from these areas into other, less select areas. Such approaches would also do little to promote – might indeed inhibit – action on domestic violence, corporate crime and white-collar offences. The emphasis of private community schemes is overwhelmingly on control (within their area and social group): if traditionally important issues, such as prevention, are also to be addressed, communities would have to be given the power and finance to alleviate social problems which often accompany crime. This questioning of the drawing in of community, so important to many left realists, is not intended to reject its whole basis but to ensure that it is utilised with these issues clearly to the fore.

One of the strengths of left realism is that it does recognise the importance of State agencies other than the police – agencies such as the social services; schools; medical agencies; factory inspectors; Inland Revenue; Customs and Excise; local authorities. These may be called upon in official capacities to deal with particular offences, offenders or victims. For example, in drug abuse the medical profession may be called on, or the Customs and Excise may be involved; in child abuse both the medical profession and social services will play a large role; sexual and physical assault will include medical as well as police agencies; corporate offences may involve factory inspectors or environmental agencies etc.; and local authorities might be involved in policies to help reduce crime in particular areas. Left realists argue that where more than one agency is logically involved the local authority should play a coordinating role to ensure an accountable and logical approach to crime. In addition to these State bodies, a role is seen for less formal organisations such as the family, media, religious organisations and youth clubs which help to facilitate moral standards. All this sounds very acceptable but the precise role for these agencies, and the balance between them, is not clearly stated or addressed. As with policing, it presumably depends on local accountability which, as already seen, is not without its associated problems.

In any event, most of these agencies are primarily concerned with the areas of detection, prevention and decisions to prosecute. Left realism rather neglects many of these aspects of the criminal justice system. This is a serious drawback, especially when one of left realism's strongest attacks on other criminological theories is that they fail to take account of the whole picture. Left realism thus falls foul of one of its own testing criteria for an acceptable approach to crime: there seems little point in addressing injustice at one stage in the system while leaving it to fester in others. It may be that one of the reasons for this gap in attention arises because centring on later stages of the criminal justice system would necessitate a less local approach and could not be resolved by use of local political controls: being forced to confront the later stages of the criminal justice system might usefully force these writers to reconsider the all-embracing utility and acceptability of local political accountability over and above other forms of control.

Lastly, the central aspect of the approach is a call for the need to reduce relative deprivation through a package set to decrease feelings of marginalisation. However, the realists have not fully explained how the discontent which may arise out of relative deprivation may lead individuals to choose criminality. They have centred on subcultural aspects, but the only way in which relative deprivation, discontent and subculture appear linked to crime is through some sort of predisposition, something they attack in the theories of others. Furthermore, all the suggestions to attack relative deprivation etc. are based on structural and economic factors of absolute deprivation, although it is not fully explained how attacking these has an impact on feelings of relative deprivation. Presumably part of the hope is that attacking the physical problems might lead to structures which will encourage stronger ties in the community, moving the subculture slowly towards being more supportive of legal as opposed to illegal activities. But this, like other aspects of left realism, could be said to place too much belief in the idea of community without really defining what is meant by this concept. How small an area? Who is included? Will it simply further alienate those not included?

Some, such as Steinert (1997), bemoan the willingness of earlier critical and radical criminologists to move to left realism, which they see as insufficiently focusing on crime because of its concern with broad social issues. Others welcome the school as including alternative analytical accounts of State-defined aspects of crime and criminal justice (see Garland (1997)), and it is probably true that the left realists do posit one of the most convincing and potentially most useful approaches to date. The approach does, however, have its problems and an uncritical acceptance of their solutions would be counter-productive. But it is reasonable to point out that, as the theory matures, more of these difficulties are being addressed.

REFERENCES

Brown, David and Hogg, Russell (1992), 'Law and Order Politics – Left Realism and Radical Criminology: a view from Down Under', in Roger Matthews and Jock Young, *Issues in Realist Criminology*, London: Sage.

Burnley, Elizabeth (1990), *Putting Street Crime in its Place*, London: Centre for Inner City Studies, Goldsmiths' College, University of London.

Crawford, Adam (1995), 'Appeals to Community and Crime Prevention', *Crime Law and Social Change*, vol. 22, p. 97.

Currie, Elliott (1988), 'Two Visions of Community Crime Prevention', in T. Hope and M. Shaw (eds), *Communities and Crime Reduction*, London: HMSO.

Fyfe, Nicholas R. (1992), 'Towards Locally Sensitive Policy? Politics, Participation and Power in Community/Police Consultation', in David J. Evans, Nicholas R. Fyfe, and David T. Herbert (eds), *Crime, Policing and Place: Essays in Environmental Criminology*, London: Routledge.

Gardiner, Simon (1995), 'Criminal Justice Act 1991 – Management of the Underclass and the Potentiality of Community', in Lesley Noaks, Michael Levi and Mike Maguire (eds), *Contemporary Issues in Criminology*, Cardiff: University of Wales Press.

Garland, David (1997), '"Governmentality" and the Problem of Crime: Foucault, Criminology and Sociology', *Theoretical Criminology*, vol. 1, p. 173.

Gilling, Daniel (1997), *Crime Prevention: Theory, Policy and Politics*, London: UCL Press.

Graham, J. and Bennett, T. (1995), *Crime Prevention Strategies in Europe and North America*, Helsinki: European Institute for Crime Prevention and Control.

Hagan, John (1994), *Crime and Disrepute*, London: Sage.

Heal, K., Tarling, R. and Burrows, J. (eds) (1985), *Policing Today*, London: HMSO.

Holloway, W. and Jefferson, T. (1995), 'The Risk Society in the Age of Anxiety', Paper presented to the British Criminology Conference, 1995.

Jones, T., Maclean, B. and Young, J. (1986), *The Islington Crime Survey: Crime Victimisation and Policing in Inner City London*, Aldershot: Gower.

Kinsey, Richard, Lea, John and Young, Jock (1986), *Losing the Fight against Crime*, Oxford: Basil Blackwell.

Lacey, N. and Zedner, L. (1995), 'Discourses of Community in Criminal Justice', *Journal of Law and Society*, vol. 22, p. 301.

Lea, John, Matthews, Roger and Young, Jock (1987), *Law and Order. Five Years On*, London: Middlesex Polytechnic, Centre for Criminology.

Matthews, Roger (1992), 'Replacing "Broken Windows": Crime, Incivilities and Urban Change', in Roger Matthews and Jock Young (eds), *Issues in Realist Criminology*, London: Sage.

Matthews, Roger and Young, Jock (eds) (1992), *Issues in Realist Criminology*, London: Sage.

Murray, C. (1990), 'Underclass', in Murray, C. (ed), *The Emerging British Underclass*, London: Institute of Economic Affairs.

Pearce, Frank (1990), *Commercial and Conventional Crime in Islington*, London: Middlesex Polytechnic, Centre for Criminology.

Pearce, Frank and Tombs, Steve (1992), 'Realism and Corporate Crime', in Roger Matthews and Jock Young, *Issues in Realist Criminology*, London: Sage.

Pearson, G. (1993), *Hooligan: A History of Respectable Fears*, London: Macmillan.

Ramsey, Malcolm and Percy, Andrew (1994), *Drug Misuse Declared: Results of the 1994 British Crime Survey*, Home Office Research Study No. 151, London: HMSO.

Reiner, R. and Cross, M. (1991), 'Crime and Criminology in the 1990s', in R. Reiner and M. Cross (eds), *Beyond Law and Order*, London: Unwin Hyman.

Scarman, Lord (1981), *The Brixton Disorders, 10–12 April 1981*, Cmnd 8427, London: HMSO.

Smith, Susan (1986), *Crime, Space and Society*, Cambridge: Cambridge University Press.

South, Nigel (1994), 'Drugs: Control, Crime and Criminological Studies', in Mike Maguire, Rod Morgan and Robert Reiner (eds), *The Oxford Handbook of Criminology*, Oxford: Clarendon Press.

Sparks, Richard (1992), 'Reason and Unreason in "Left Realism": Some Problems in the Constitution of the Fear of Crime', in Roger Matthews and Jock Young, *Issues in Realist Criminology*, London: Sage.

Steinert, Heinz (1997), *'Fin de Siècle* Criminology', *Theoretical Criminology*, vol. 1, p. 111.

Sutton, Mike (1996), *Implementing Crime Prevention Schemes in a Multi-Agency Setting: Aspects of Process in the Safer Cities Programme*, Home Office Research Study No. 160, London: HMSO.

Tilley, Nick (1992), *Safer City and Community Safety Strategies*, Home Office Police Research Group, Crime Prevention Paper 38.

Walklate, S. (1995), *Gender and Crime*, Hemel Hempstead: Prentice Hall.

Wilson, James Q. (1985), *Thinking about Crime*, 2nd edn, New York: Vintage Books.

Wilson, James Q. and Herrnstein, Richard J. (1985), *Crime and Human Nature*, New York: Simon Schuster.

Wilson, James Q. and Kelling, G. (1982), 'Broken Windows: the Police and Neighborhood Safety', *Atlantic Monthly*, March, p. 29.

Wilson, James Q. and Kelling, G. (1989), 'Making Neighborhoods Safe', *Atlantic Monthly*, February, p. 46.

Woolf, Lord Justice (1991), *Prison Disturbances April 1990: Report of an Enquiry by the Rt. Hon Lord Justice Woolf (Parts I and II) and His Honour Judge Stephen Tumin (Part II)*, Cm 1456, London: HMSO.

Wright, Martin (1995), 'Victims, Mediation and Criminal Justice' *Criminal Law Review*, p. 187.

Young, Alison (1996), *Imagining Crime: Textual Outlaws and Criminal Conversations*, London: Sage.

Young, Jock (1994), 'Incessant Chatter: Recent Paradigms in Criminology', in Mike Maguire, Rod Morgan and Robert Reiner (eds), *The Oxford Handbook of Criminology*, Oxford: Clarendon Press.

Young, Jock and Matthews, Roger (1992), *Rethinking Criminology: the Realist Debate*, London: Sage.

Young, Jock and Matthews, Roger (1992a), 'Questioning Left Realism', in Roger Matthews and Jock Young, *Issues in Realist Criminology*, London: Sage.

CHAPTER SEVENTEEN

Positivist Explanations of Female Criminality

17.1 INTRODUCTION

In the past, women were virtually invisible in the literature on crime. Until recently, the problems posed by female criminality were generally ignored in most text-books or were added as a foot-note to the discussion of male criminality. In these accounts the experience of women has generally been marginalised, and their criminality has been distorted to fall in with whatever male theory was being expounded. In such accounts criminality was assumed to be a male characteristic, and therefore explaining male criminality explained all criminality. This chapter will deal with these areas and discuss their inadequacy as explanations for female criminality. The second chapter on women and crime (Chapter Eighteen) will discuss the newer explanations, some of which are said to be linked with female liberation, others with feminism generally or with a clear gendered analysis of crime. Accordingly, this book discusses two main explanations of female crime. The present chapter will consider the more traditional positivist theories; the next chapter will concentrate on the thesis which has developed out of 'feminism', and its alleged link to female criminality.

In both these areas, until the last twenty years, the lack of literature on female criminality is often astounding. One reason given for this lack of interest is that females have traditionally been seen as being intrinsically law-abiding. It is certainly true that, from the statistics available, crime appears to be a largely male, and young male, activity. Although sex crime ratios (the proportion of men and women offending) differ depending on what crimes one is considering, men are generally represented more · frequently than women. Even in shop-lifting, a crime which is traditionally linked with women, there are more males than females convicted. In Britain, of those convicted of serious crimes 80 per cent are male, and women make up only about 3 per cent of the prison population, suggesting that their offences tend to be less serious. The figures of sex ratios in the United States are similar to those for Britain. Indeed, Sutherland and Cressey (1978) claim that these sorts of figures are fairly global, indicating the law-abiding behaviour of most females, making gender possibly the easiest predictor of criminality. If one were put into a room with twenty people chosen at random, half male and half female, and were told that ten of them were convicted criminals, the best single predictor would be sex.

It could be that female crime remains undetected vastly more frequently than male crime. This seems unlikely, as the two largest areas of hidden crime are white-collar and corporate crimes, which women have less opportunity to commit, and domestic crimes such as spouse battering and child physical and sexual abuse, both of which are more commonly carried out by men than by women. It is true, however, that when women do commit crimes of violence these are often committed in the home.

The different involvement in crime of men and women is one of the most striking and consistent criminological truths, and it is therefore surprising that it has not been more widely studied in order to ascertain what causes this difference, and therefore possibly what causes conformity and criminality. As we shall see in this chapter, the female is generally overlooked in the explanation of criminality, and even in the explanation of conformity – where one would expect women to be the central consideration – they are often marginalised in favour of discussion from a purely male perspective.

17.2 BIOLOGICAL, HORMONAL AND PSYCHOLOGICAL THEORIES

17.2.1 Introduction

Physiological and psychological theories subsume a number of explanations which basically attribute female criminality to individual characteristics (physiological, hormonal or psychological) which are either unchanged or only marginally affected by economic, social or political forces. These theories often conclude that criminality is due to the inherent nature of particular 'abnormal' women who are bad and begin their life with a propensity for criminality; that is, in everyday language, they are considered to be 'born criminals'.

All criminology writers seem to make moral, social or value judgments. The judgments tend to be more evident where their arguments are based upon assessments of individuals. Not surprisingly, they are for this reason often subjected to strong criticism nowadays, but it should be remembered that many of these theories are very old. Their arguments and assumptions may appear alien to the modern obsession with being 'scientific', but were more acceptable at the time they were written.

Because these theories are centred upon the individual, they all suggest a 'cure' based upon adjustments to the individual. These 'cures' range from sterilization in order to prevent crime in future generations through to psychoanalysis. Little, if any, consideration is given to the role, status or socio-economic position of women in society. The neglect of social factors has an immediate attraction for anyone wishing to retain the *status quo* in society, helping to explain the popularity of these theories amongst the better-off sections of the community. Such an approach also lent support to the idea that the penal system should 'reform' prisoners whilst in custody. Criminals were thought of as persons who suffered from something which could be 'cured'. It takes time to 'cure' or to 'help' people, and so it is necessary to incarcerate them for long enough to have the desired effect. In this way, these theories also influenced the lengths of prison sentences.

None the less, it is important to bear in mind that at the time they were written they represented novel and innovative thinking. For our purposes, the study of female criminality will begin with the work of Lombroso (see Chapter Six for his thesis on male criminality), whose writing on this topic started in 1895. At that time, little had been done to study the criminal individual, whether male or female, and merely to begin such work was innovative. His theories were topical, as they could be seen to have their basis in the then relatively new and still controversial arguments of Darwinism. It is therefore not surprising that they became popular and widely accepted. With hindsight it is now all too easy to point out flaws in his rather simplistic arguments, but it is not possible wholly to discount his ideas on physiological reasons for female criminality, which must therefore be discussed. After Lombroso, a selection of the work of other writers illustrates the way in which physical and psychological explanations of female crime have progressed to the present day.

17.2.2 Lombroso

Although Lombroso's work on female criminality is now largely discredited in its pure form, its relevance continues because several influential later writers base their ideas upon his work. Lombroso is also a good starting-point because he states explicitly what is only implied by later theorists.

His basic idea is that all crime is the result of atavistic throwbacks, that is, a reversion to a more primitive form of human life or a survival of 'primitive' traits in individuals. Although Lombroso wrongly includes in 'atavism' such non-hereditary factors as tattooing, his use of the term is generally correct. He argues that the most advanced forms of human are white males, and the most primitive are non-white females. He studied the physiology of both criminal and non-criminal females (this is one of the few occasions on which he studied a control group). Any traits found more commonly in the criminal group he described as atavistic: large hand size; low voice pitch; having moles; being short; having dark hair; being fat, and so on. All his tests were carried out in Italy, and some of the so-called characteristics can be seen to be particularly prevalent in certain areas, most markedly in Sicily. He gave little consideration to the fact that within Italy Sicilians were generally poorer than other groups and that their social conditions rather than their physical appearance may have led to their criminality. In later writings he did compromise by admitting that the 'born criminal' accounted for only 35 per cent of criminals, and that some crime was committed by pseudo-criminals who might be pushed into crime by adverse environment, passion or criminal associations. But his main arguments explaining persistent criminals were based on atavistic traits.

On this basis, women portraying certain 'atavistic' characteristics would become more criminal than others. However, if crime was to be explained merely by primitive traits, female crime would be greater than male crime because, according to Lombroso, all females are less advanced than males. Lombroso's theory therefore seems to point towards a higher female than male crime rate, whereas the female rate was, and is, according to the statistics, lower. He explains this apparent anomaly partly by maintaining that prostitution was the female substitute for crime and partly by attributing the lower female crime rate to women's proximity to lower life forms. He claimed that women had a smaller cerebral cortex which rendered them both less intelligent and less capable of abstract reasoning. This, he argued, led to a greater likelihood of psychological disturbance (see Freud, 17.2.6 below) and was also more likely to lead to sexual anomalies than crime. He further maintained that because females are more simplistic than males, women, like lower animal life, are more adaptable and more capable of surviving in unpleasant surroundings. This might explain why he largely ignores the poverty of the environment in which criminal women often lived. In his view, with this ability to adapt, they can survive male manipulation and male control and, in this respect, are seen as a stronger though less well-developed sex. This ability to survive evidences an inability to feel pain and a contempt of death, making them insensitive to the pain and suffering of other people. However, in most women the coldness is controlled or neutralised by pity, weakness, maternity, and, he argues, most importantly by underdeveloped intelligence and lack of passion. On the other hand, criminal women, and all men, possess passion and intelligence. So criminal women have a cranium closer in size to that of men, and have more body hair and other masculine physical traits which are not signs of development in women. Rather they represent anomalies, being unnaturally masculine and showing signs of atavism. He argues that passion and any over-activity in women must be a deviation from normal, as their nature is normally passive. The more passive a woman, the more highly developed she is, and the further from being a 'born criminal'.

Lombroso was not himself consciously race- and class-biased, but the whole idea of a passive female gives rise to criticism of his theory being prejudicial. A racist criticism arises because Lombroso's atavistic traits are necessarily more prevalent in certain races, particularly the non-Whites (traits such as large cranium, square jaw and dark hair). Such traits necessarily appear more commonly in certain races and although five characteristics had to be portrayed before a person was labelled a born criminal, the possession of one of these traits by a whole race puts every member of that race closer to the category of 'born criminal'. This has led to his theories being criticised as racist, although they were probably not written with this intention nor seen in that light at the time they were written. His approach can also be said to be rooted in class because in order to have a wholly passive female, devoted only to family and home, it is necessary to have a society in which someone works in order to support these women. Of course, when Lombroso wrote, this was the way society was structured, and was seen as normal, acceptable and just. Both the racist and class bias can be illustrated by looking at the application of his traits to Italy. There was a distinct prevalence of 'atavism' amongst the Sicilians, who were both darker skinned and poor labourers.

Lombroso's ideas re-appear as threads in theories right up to the present day. Partly this is because he and his followers provided the basis of the positive school of criminology (see Chapter Six), but Lombroso also influenced at least two main areas of criminological thought, namely, the notions that crime can be explained by reference to biological and inherited characteristics; and that crime is caused by a pathological or chemical abnormality which needs to be treated. Later writings based on Lombroso tend not to express these ideas quite so directly, but they often make similar assumptions.

17.2.3 Recent biological factors

Cowie, Cowie and Slater (1968) carried out an extensive study of the inmates of a female approved school. They looked at both social and genetic variables and concluded that genetic factors are the main causes of criminality. Furthermore, they proposed that genetic factors also dictate the types of criminality which the sexes might become tied up with. The suggestion seems again to be that girls would tend towards sexual delinquency more frequently than boys, whilst the latter would tend towards criminality. The proof which they propose is very flimsy and would not stand up to close scrutiny.

Other studies have tried to establish a link between chromosomal abnormalities and criminality, but again the proof for these claims is lacking (see 6.6.1). Healy and Bronner (1936) had suggested that an 'abnormality' in sex roles would be related to gender abnormalities. In other words, a masculine woman would be the result of possessing a male 'Y' chromosome, and they assessed that criminal women are large for their age and that prostitutes often show high rates of lesbian tendencies. It has, however, never been shown that a Y chromosome is linked with height or lesbianism, nor is it necessarily linked with enhanced masculinity in the way in which writers such as these seem to use this phrase.

Other analysts (see Money and Erhardt (1972); Rose, Holoday and Bernstein (1971); and Marsh (1978)) have blamed increased male hormones. Most writers in the physiological or psychological arena have remarked on the passivity and basic lack of aggression on the part of females, asserting that this explains their lack of criminality. It has been suggested (Money and Erhardt (1972), and Rose et al. (1971)) that the genetic passivity of females is related to the different brains of men and women and the difference in hormones between men and women. Clearly, it is difficult to experiment on hormonal change in humans, so all tests have been done on animals, mainly rats. Soon after birth a rat's brain becomes either male or female. If there is a predominance of female hormones (oestrogens), the brain becomes female; if a predominance of male hormones (androgens), the brain becomes male.

If, early in life, a female is injected with androgens, she becomes aggressive and indistinguishable from a male, and an early castrated male will be more passive later in life. It has been claimed that these tests, and some rather more complex ones involving monkeys, show that the same may well be true for humans.

The extrapolation of any finding from rats or monkeys to humans is necessarily very risky. It remains unclear what, if any, the effects are of hormones, particularly in early life. Behaviourists such as Marsh (1978) try to claim that differences between the sexes are purely a result of socialisation. It could be argued that upbringing over many generations has actually over-emphasised what was originally a negligible difference between the sexes. It is very difficult to ascertain which, if either, of the social or the genetic has had the greater effect.

17.2.4 'Generative phases' of women

This biological theory is based on changes connected with the menstrual cycle. The argument is that at times of menstruation women are reminded that they can never become men, and the distress to which this gives rise makes them increasingly prone to delinquent acts. The best known proponent of this idea is Pollak (1950), who also suggests that the hormonal disturbance resulting from pregnancy and the menopause may be a cause of female crime, but his claims have never been proven. If he is correct, most women could spend about 75 per cent of their adult lives in a hormonal state which predisposes them to criminality. In 1961, Dalton believed she had proven the thesis when she discovered that 59.8 per cent of imprisoned women studied committed their crimes in the 16-day period covering pre- and post-menstrual hormone imbalance. This, of course, means that 40.2 per cent (almost half) of women committed their crimes at other times (during the other 12 days). It is questionable whether these figures prove anything, but if they do, it could merely mean that women are more likely to be caught committing crimes at these times. Results are therefore inconclusive.

Although it is unclear whether women generally suffer a higher incidence of criminality during their generative phases, it is clear that the law takes account of these elements in deciding some cases. Menstruation has been used as a partial defence plea, and both menstruation and menopause have been accepted as factors which should reduce sentences (see also 7.1.1). Here the case of menstruation will be considered, but similar factors apply to menopause. Although both these 'generative phases' have been commonly used in such relatively minor cases as shop-lifting, more serious cases will be considered here. Susan Edwards (1988) notes that in the nineteenth century pre-menstrual tension (PMT) was frequently discussed as being an important element of a defence in cases of violence, killing, arson and theft. Both she and Luckhaus (1985) refer to cases in the early eighties where PMT was successfully pleaded. In one of these, the woman faced a murder charge which was reduced to manslaughter due to diminished responsibility attributed to PMT, and had received a probationary sentence with a proviso that she undergo hormone treatment (*R* v *Craddock* [1981] 1 Cl 49). Only a few months after the first offence, the same woman was charged with threatening to kill a police officer and of possessing an offensive weapon. Although convicted, PMT acted as a factor to reduce sentence and she was again placed on probation and required to undergo an increased hormone dose (*R* v *Smith* Court of Appeal (Criminal Division) Lexis Enggen, 27 April, 1982; Craddock and Smith are the same person). In another case a woman, charged with murder, was convicted only of manslaughter due to diminished responsibility; there was no custodial sentence, not even the requirement of hormonal treatment (*Christine English, The Times,* 12 November 1981). Clearly, in the cases of these women the law accepted that PMT, although not amounting to a full defence and therefore not the only reason for the occurrence of the crime, was the most important reason for the behaviour. PMT was accepted as a partial excuse and as a reason for lenient sentencing; the total effect was the acceptance of the controversial idea that PMT amounted to a causative explanation. This is an interesting acceptance in the light of the fact that medical evidence is divided about the existence of such a syndrome and its effects. If there are effects, they appear to be mainly psychological, such as tension, irritability, depression, tiredness, mood swings and feelings of loneliness, although Dalton (1984) has included some relevant physical effects such as epilepsy, fainting and even hypoglycaemia (see 7.2.2 and 7.3.2).

In the case of post-natal depression there is, of course, the special case of infanticide (see generally 7.1.1 and 9.2.4 for a definition of this defence). Again, in this instance the law accepts as a partial excuse the fact that a women's mind and behaviour are affected by the hormonal changes in her body. If a mother kills her child within its first year as a result of post-natal depression or lactation, she would have a partial defence to murder which would render it infanticide. This is clearly only a defence open to women, and is the only sex-specific defence recognised in the criminal law. Some of these killings may possibly be the result of exhaustion through caring for the child, guilt through not feeling affection for it, or the effect of other social pressures, all of which could equally well be suffered by a man if he was the person primarily in charge of the care of the child (for a full discussion of this see Wilczynski and Morris (1993)). The Law Commission's Draft Criminal Code suggested (clause 64(1)) that these social reasons for infanticide be recognised but only in the case of women (see Mackay (1993)). But a man cannot rely upon the same defence and would have to argue that his mind was unbalanced in some other way in order to plead diminished responsibility.

Certainly when one looks at the figures there appears to be an unfairness, Marks and Kumar (1993) show that the rates of killing of children under one have remained constant since 1957 at about 45 per million per year. This is higher than for any other age group and represents about 30 killings a year. They further discovered that women who kill such children are dealt with much more leniently (most are subject to probation) than are men (who are frequently imprisoned), even when the level of violence used by the women is greater. The leniency could arise because the charge of infanticide is available for women. Dell (1984), has shown that in cases of manslaughter the sentencing has been steadily becoming more and more severe, but Maier-Katkin and Ogle (1993), suggest that even when women are convicted of manslaughter they are treated leniently (often with probation) which suggests that it is not so much to do with a special defence being available but is connected with greater compassion for these women. Whatever the reason the men suffer much more serious sentencing for relatively similar cases. It is questionable whether such imbalance is just. The solution should not be to remove the defence of infanticide which recognises the severe pressures of new motherhood and reduces the stigma and the punishment. Perhaps there is scope for extending this defence: in the case of women to include 'circumstances consequent on the birth' as suggested by the Law Commission in the draft Criminal Code Bill; and in the case of men for severe stress caused by the birth and care of a child. In some of the most severe cases there may even be worth in pleading insanity and obtaining a finding of not guilty by reason of insanity, see Maier-Katkin (1991).

As was seen in Chapter Seven the hormonal imbalances suffered by men do not normally affect either their conviction or their sentence. Women, however, can successfully plead such imbalances even in the most serious cases where they take the life of another person (see also (9.2.4)). For the individual women involved, this is probably an advantage as they will either elude an unpleasant label or an unpleasant sentence, or both. For women in general, its effects are not so positive. It allows the continuation of the idea that women are incapable of controlling themselves and that their actions can be explained through medical reasoning – they are mentally or physically sick, or both (see Wilczynski and Morris (1993)). Widely used, the implication of this reasoning would be that women should be treated for this 'sickness' rather than punished. It removes from women the idea that they may choose the criminality, that it might be a rational decision arising out of a social, economic or political situation. As PMT is such a medically controversial area, and as it is not possible to give it an exact diagnosis or definition, its use is even more problematic. If it were relegated to a plea in mitigation, to be taken into account in sentencing, it would be much less threatening. In most cases, this is how it would be seen. In the case of a murder charge there is no discretion in sentencing, and therefore to allow the judge any discretion PMT must be used to reduce the charge to manslaughter.

17.2.5 Thomas
The work of Thomas acts as a stepping-stone between physical and psychological explanations. In his early work (1907) he reiterates much of Lombroso's theory concerning the passivity of females and the abounding energy and creativity of males. He argues that this divergent development can be seen best in civilised white races where human selectivity is more refined. Again, like Lombroso, this assumes the white 'upper class' definition of femininity; it is arguable whether such an assumption, in 1907, sprang from a conscious class or race bias. For Thomas, it was a biological fact that certain types of women are more criminal than others and, if nothing else, these must

be severely punished in order to protect society. In the later work (1967, first published 1923) he argues for a form of rehabilitation by controlling the mind rather than just deterring by punishment, sterilization or other physical preventive measures.

Thomas moves away from Lombroso's idea of female criminality being due to masculine tendencies towards saying that, for civilised cultures, female criminality is an illegal or unacceptable use of female traits. Female criminals are considered to be amoral, that is, without morality, not immoral, which implies loss of morality. They are described as being cold, calculating people who have not learned to treat others with pity and evidence of maternal concern. They use the less developed and colder sides of their natures in order to gain something for themselves through sexual promiscuity, soliciting, prostitution, or other 'unacceptable' and sometimes illegal means.

For Thomas, there are four basic wishes which drive every individual: the desire for new experience (for example, hunting or dangerous sports); for security (the fear of death); for response (maternal and sexual love); and for recognition (dominance within the group). Thomas argues that for females generally, it is the response wish which is most marked. In 'normal' law-abiding women, this wish for response is fed by retaining her chastity as a good way of obtaining a devoted husband who can give her security and a family to love. For 'amoral' women the need for love drives her to commit any act in order to gain affection; her own sexual and other feelings take a minor role. Female criminality is thus largely seen as being based on sexuality, leading Thomas to emphasize prostitution and soliciting to explain all unacceptable and criminal behaviour. If the 'amoral' and generally lower-class female was controlled and taught the same standard as her 'normal' middle- and upper-class counterpart, she would be law-abiding. Social conditions are ignored: if women adhered to their model role in society, there would be no female crime. Re-educating those who failed to come up to the conventional role was the change advocated by him. These ideas were common at the time and were extensively used in the control of women by the authorities. Women were channelled, both culturally and by the State correction system, into female roles (see Smart and Smart (1978) and Rafter (1983)).

17.2.6 Freud
The next milestone on this road is the writings of Sigmund Freud (1973, originally written in 1925 and 1931). Lombroso's and Freud's understanding of the concept of the born criminal is quite different. Lombroso distinguished between born criminals and other people, but Freud saw everyone as a potential criminal in the sense that all human beings are born with immoral and anti-social instincts. The other main difference is that for Lombroso the criminal was a product simply of hereditary factors, whereas for Freud it was a mixture of inherited factors and the effect of external experiences. So, Freud recognises that although all humans are born with criminal designs, most will learn to control them; it is those who do not learn such control who end up as criminals. For Freud, the inability to learn social habits is partly hereditary

and partly related to up-bringing. His successors often argue the human personality is shaped by its social environment alone and that heredity plays no part (see Chapter Eight for a discussion of this), but Freud places a large part of his argument on heredity. Here, it is intended to focus upon Freud's theory of female criminality.

As with a large portion of Freud's work, the central tenet of his theory tends to be sexual; that is, that the explanation or motivation for the female criminal is largely sexual neurosis. Due to the lack of a penis the female feels, and often is, inferior, better suited to the less demanding destiny of being wife and mother rather than breadwinner. He says that a woman, whilst she is still a child, recognises that she has inferior sexual organs and believes this to be a punishment. She then grows up envious and revengeful. The feminine behaviour of most women can be traced to their lack of a penis. They become exhibitionist and narcissistic, and so try to be well-dressed and physically beautiful in order to win love and approval from men. Freud argues that the genetic differences between men and women lead to a difference in sexual functions which make women passive and masochistic, as their sexual role is receptive:

> It is perhaps the case that in a woman on the basis of her share in the sexual function, a preference for passive behaviour, and passive aims is carried over into her life to a greater or lesser extent . . . (p. 149)

He further argues that women generally do not develop a strong conscience. Men develop one as a result of controlling their Oedipal complex. An Oedipal complex is a man's or boy's incestuous love for his mother which is repressed due to a fear of a jealous reaction from his father. The fear is that the father may ultimately castrate the son – this is the most feared punishment. As a result, boys generally by the age of about five develop a very strong super-ego or conscience. As girls and women cannot be castrated, they do not possess the fear necessary to overcome the Electra complex (their desire for their father and hatred of their mother).

> In the absence of fear of castration the chief motive is lacking which leads boys to surmount the Oedipal complex. Girls remain in it for an indeterminate length of time; they demolish it late and, even so, incompletely. In these circumstances the formation of the super ego must suffer; it cannot attain the strength and independence which give it its cultural significance . . . (p. 163)

Normally this would lead to a higher crime rate for women, but due to the passivity (mentioned above) and their very strong desire for love and affection, particularly from their fathers or other men, they are controlled. They do not break men's laws, for to do so would lead to disapproval and a withdrawal of male love and affection. Their problem is two-fold. Due to their preoccupation with envy, they are self-centred and concerned only with trivial personal and family matters: and because of a weak super-ego they cannot understand justice. They thus should play no part in production and property ownership.

In Freud's world, deviant women are those who attempt to become more like men, those who compete or try to achieve acclaim within the masculine spheres of activity, or those who refuse to accept their 'natural' passivity. These women are driven by the desire to claim a penis, which leads to aggressive competition. This ultimate desire is, of course, hopeless, and they will end up by becoming 'neurotic'. Such women need help to enable them to adjust to their intended sex role. The birth of a child would be seen as particularly therapeutic as the baby is seen as a substitute for a penis, according to Freud.

Like Lombroso, Freud mostly ignores social, economic and political factors: unlike Lombroso, who centred his theory on physical characteristics, Freud's theory uses psychology and mental disease to explain female criminality. Nevertheless, the concept of a well-adjusted woman is based very much on traditional ideas of sexuality and society. It thus suffers from the same sex and class problems as the earlier theories, but was probably more demanding because of its 'scientific' basis.

17.2.7 Pollak

Pollak's theory (1950), was sex-based. He was doubtful that women commit as little crime as the official statistics showed. He thus advanced a theory of 'hidden' female crime. Pollak follows Freud in explaining female crime by reference to sexual neurosis. Women are traditionally shy, passive and passionless, but can simulate a sexual orgasm to hide their true feelings. They can take part in sex without any physical passion, and they can learn to hide their monthly menstruation. All this means that within the sexual sphere they learn to manipulate, deceive and conceal – this, he claims, decides the inherent nature of women, making them likely to be the instigators of crime which is then actually perpetrated by men. Where they do themselves commit crimes, these are related to their feminine nature and explained either on psychological (mental) grounds (for example, shop-lifting is the result of kleptomania, an uncontrolled urge to steal), or on sexual grounds (for example, soliciting for prostitution or sexual blackmail). Other crimes committed by women can be hidden and underhand, for example, poisoning or infanticide. In so far as this description of female crime is valid, he seems not to have considered the possibility that lack of social, political and economic power may have forced women into taking an underhand or manipulative way to enforce change, and so better their position and standing in society.

Lastly, Pollak claimed that women appeared less before, and were more leniently treated by, the criminal justice system because they were differentially treated by all officers of the law. This preferential or, as he saw it, chivalrous treatment arose from the fact that men generally had a protective attitude towards women. Men thus disliked making accusations against women because they did not want women to be punished. This chivalrous treatment, he claimed, stretched from police through the jury to the judge, and thus resulted in a great under-conviction of female criminals. This is a thread picked up by much later writers, although in rather more refined form.

17.2.8 Modern applications

Each of the above theories seems to assume that women are more or less totally different from men in every respect: biology; psychology; needs; desires; motivations. They often link criminality in women to old, unquestioned popular assumptions about problem women – usually associated with their breach of the societal norm of wife, mother and homemaker. Implicit in such views are concepts of women as sources of evil, causing the downfall of mankind: their criminality is then represented as more destructive of social order than anything man could do. This almost pathological fear of female non-conformity and criminality is reminiscent of the 'witch-hunts' of history, which, as Heidensohn (1996) suggests, is a powerful and recurring popular image of 'deviant women as especially evil, depraved and monstrous . . . used by "scientific" criminologists . . . as the basis of their theories, theories which . . . not only had a stigmatising effect, but have also had unfortunate consequences for the treatment of women offenders'. However, Heidensohn may provide us with one of the reasons why female criminality is so feared: women are relied upon to maintain order and to continue present societal structures, so deviance from this role is seen as especially threatening. The socialising role of women in the family and in society is also limiting on them, because it means that they are expected to, and often do, have a far greater stake in conformity. In addition, since the pressures of these roles limit their opportunities to offend, such action by women becomes viewed as more peculiar, and hence less acceptable, than it would be for men.

In studying male criminality, it was clear that mental illness or strong psychological problems were useful explanations only in rare cases where the mental problem was clear. In female criminality, it has been assumed that a wide range of crimes can be explained by such mental factors and that the sexual basis of the mental problem is strong, whereas it was absent in explanations of male criminality. In male criminality, even sex crimes are generally explained on some basis other than the sexual. Even rape is very rarely associated with an incomplete resolution of the Oedipal complex; more often it is said to be a crime of power or violence which just happens to assume a sexual element. In court it is often ascribed to sexual frustration (usually caused by the female dressing or behaving in a 'provocative' manner) or to drink, and is thereby more understandable. Female criminality is, however, often explained in a clinical or sexual way. Campbell (1981) discusses how shop-lifting, traditionally a female crime (although in fact more males than females commit it), has frequently been connected with both mental problems and sexuality. The sexual nature is interesting, as it is a crime which does not obviously possess any sexual elements. Female shop-lifting has often been attributed to kleptomania despite the fact that such a mental disease is very rare (see 9.3.4). Campbell also refers to the perceived sexual nature of shoplifting: women are supposed to obtain sexual excitement from the act; or perform the crime to still repressed sexual desires; or in order to be punished for such feelings. The prevalence of these ideas, until at least the 1960s, partly continued because of the number of single, divorced or widowed women who performed such acts; the possibility was ignored that this particular group faced unusually harsh economic and social stresses.

Gibbens and Prince (1962) also studied shop-lifting and explained male lower-class youthful shop-lifting by reference to the gang or peer group and/or the desire to appear fearless and masculine. In the case of the small number of middle-class boys, they suggested that they suffered homosexual tendencies which meant that the reasons given for women would apply to this group too. Women were seen to commit these acts due to depression, resentment, to keep up appearances, and meanness. The first two of these reasons have clear mental and clinical applications and are postulated with little proof of their validity. The last two do appear to have a more socially based reasoning, although 'keeping up appearances' is something which may turn on a sex-based theory, the desire to attract a male partner.

Several psychologically based pleas have now emerged for the legal defence of women. The most interesting addition to this catalogue is the use of post-traumatic stress syndromes; the one most applicable as a defence is the battered woman syndrome; whilst the rape trauma syndrome has been used as a tool to back up both the defence and the prosecution cases. Similar syndromes have been clinically discovered in both men and women but are more frequently used in the courts in cases involving women. In the case of the battered woman syndrome the defence is to a charge of murder and the claim is that what may look like a premeditated crime – or at least one in which self-defence and provocation as presently defined would be difficult to use – can be psychologically explained. Some have attacked the use of, and the need to use, such defences and suggest that the traditional defences such as self-defence should be forced to take account of women's culture and experience (see O'Donovan (1991)); or that in assessing the reasonableness of the accused's actions and beliefs they should be explicitly subjective (how would a person in her circumstances and with her emotional condition assess the situation?). If these approaches were taken there would be less need to use psychological defences, particularly the syndromes which rather stretch and alter the legal concepts which they are used to prove (see Freckleton (1994)).

The resurgence of women's sex roles and their treatment by the criminal justice system is evident in the treatment which women obtain from the application of the criminal law. The actions of criminal women are, as mentioned above, often viewed as having breached the idea of the female role in society, justifying, some claim (see Carlen (1983)), subjecting them to increasing sanctions as they move through the system. Although most studies do not find a gender bias in sentencing (see Heidensohn (1996) and Daly (1994)), Kennedy (1992) amply documents a criminal justice system which is generally biased against women, possibly because they are alien to it. Furthermore, for young female offenders, the system seems to want to try to show them the error of their ways, ostensibly to help them, by applying welfare approaches to resocialise them. These welfare models are more invasive of their private lives than those applied to young males, and treat such women more as sexual miscreants than as criminals.

From the above, it should be clear that clinical and sexual reasons for female criminality have been accepted even where those crimes have no clear

sexual basis. In the case of male criminality, such explanations were reject
even where the crime appeared to have a very real sexual link. There would
appear to be different standards being applied to explaining male and female
criminality.

17.3 LEARNING THEORIES

In Chapter Ten the idea that criminality was the result of differential learning
theories was mooted. Sutherland (1939) argued that criminality was the
result of normal, learnt behaviour (see also Sutherland and Cressey (1966)
and 10.2.4) and claimed that criminality is not innate, but is learnt from
interaction with other persons; the learning process includes both the motives
for its commission and the methods of carrying it out. Criminality will result
if the definitions favourable to law-breaking outweigh those unfavourable to
it. In modern industrial societies, people are encouraged to pursue self-
advancement and are not inculcated with a sense of social responsibility. As
a result, although some still learn that the pursuit of aims by legitimate means
is the morally acceptable way to behave, many at all social levels will learn
that the achievement of the goal is the only important factor: they thus learn
both legitimate and illegitimate modes to this end. In general, Sutherland
and Cressey maintain that their theory is of general application and
applies to rich as well as to poor, and to women as much as to men. The
class equality continues throughout the book, but gender equality wavers
under the need to explain why the male crime rate is so much higher
(see Sutherland and Cressey (1966), pp. 138-143). Sutherland does this
by excluding females from this absorbed pursuit of self-interest. He argues
that females of all classes and ages are socialised into the same sex role:
they are taught to be nice rather than egotistical; they are all brought up
to behave in a non-criminal fashion which is only true of some men; and they
are more closely supervised and controlled. Women, on this interpretation,
seem to be excluded from the pursuit of wealth which pervades the rest
of society.

Although not referring to any innate trait in women, Sutherland implies
that women are more law-abiding because they are excluded from the
dominant and, he seems to say, male culture. He avoids the potential clash
between this and his claim to disprove innate criminality by arguing that
differences of gender explain different socialisation of males and females.
Because of their sexual difference, girls and boys had different capabilities and
interests which are channelled and developed through different training and
education, which leads to differential behaviour. Sutherland might have been
better sticking to a strict application of his original theory. The criminality of
females is more likely to rest upon their access to deviant or criminal inputs
than on their gender. Sutherland removes from women the education
necessary to criminality or to competitive law-abiding behaviour. He only
allows them learning which fits their perceived roles as mothers and carers;
any criminality has to arise out of this.

17.4 SEX ROLE THEORIES

tion

World War, this general line of thought is further developed
___ are often referred to as the masculinity (or masculinity/
femininity) theories. These centre not on sex itself, but on a recognised and
accepted role for each sex. Under this approach, proper socialisation is
explained purely as a function of the individual's physical sexual nature:
maleness gives rise to masculinity and femaleness to femininity. It is only
when this 'natural' process breaks down that women become criminal. These
writers generally portray women as passive, gentle, dependent, conventional
and motherly, a picture of woman that is not different from that painted by
many of the biological determinant theorists. In these later writings, similar
behaviours are being considered, but the role is learned. The argument is that
people ascribe to themselves the roles of the group to which they belong.
They are socialised into these groups from birth; it is easier and less
problematic to accept and act within them. Gender roles are among the
strongest learnt social roles in our society and, although not entirely static,
they remain fairly constant although they may vary widely between different
ethnic groups.

17.4.2 Masculinity/femininity theories

The American sociologist Talcott Parsons (1947 and 1954) explained the
different levels of delinquency between males and females as being due to the
basic structure of American society and families. The father is the breadwinner, and he works outside the home in order to provide for the family. The
mother is involved with the care and upbringing of the children and looking
after the home. Boys see the different functions performed by each sex and
realise that they are expected to emulate the father, who is largely absent
during their upbringing. They feel that they need to prove independence from
the mother and act as unlike her as possible. Parsons argues that her role is
clearly less prestigious than that of the breadwinner and therefore the boy,
wishing to become important, assumes that passivity, conformity and being
good are behavioural traits to be avoided. This leads to an aggressive attitude
which can lead to anti-social, rebellious and criminal activities. Girls, on the
other hand, have a close adult model, the mother, to emulate which allows
them to mature emotionally and to learn slowly and surely to become
feminine. It is not just the ready presence of an adult model of the same sex
which leads to conformity, but also the fact that that model will portray a
passive and monolithic nature, making conformity and a law-abiding life
more likely.

Grosser (1951, to be found in Gibbons (1981), pp. 239–241) uses this
analysis and applies it to explain juvenile delinquency. Boys see they must
become future breadwinners and so become interested in power and money,
which might lead them to steal to provide, and to fight to obtain power and
prestige. Girls see they must become the home-makers, and so close relationships are more important to them. Girls are more likely to participate in

sexual promiscuity than criminality; any criminality will be committed to win the affection of men, such as theft of clothes and make-up which may make them more attractive to the opposite sex.

This thesis was taken up by Cohen (1955), first to formulate his theory on male delinquency with which we have already dealt in 12.3.2, and secondly to argue that, although it is true that girls are essentially law-abiding, there are some who will break the law. He further argued that such law-breaking, when it did occur, was related to their feminine role in that it was either sexually promiscuous or directed at the task of finding an emotionally stable relationship with a man. He argued that women would avoid masculine aggressive behaviour.

Reiss (1960) similarly claims that the sexual activity of females may lead to criminality. Young girls may be willing to participate in sexual activity, both because by having a close relationship with a male they obtain prestige among their peers, and because they consider it necessary to maintain a close relationship with the boy. However, if complications, such as pregnancy or sexually transmitted diseases develop, the young girl will lose all prestige both from her male and female peers. Loss of prestige in this way may lead to criminal activity. Here, criminality is the result of sexual behaviour which arises due to the need to fulfil a particular sex role – that of having a relationship with a male, which may also involve other types of criminality such as stealing clothes and make-up.

Dale Hoffman Bustamante (1973) notes that females are rewarded for conforming behaviour, whereas males, although being taught to conform, are often rewarded when they breach the rules. She argues that this teaches men, but not women, that though conformity is generally desirable, it can be rational to breach the rules in some cases. Women are shown that the only way forward is by conformity. She notes that media images can also be influential: male heroes can be portrayed as rule-breakers or benders (cowboys in Western movies, police in adventure films); heroines, at least until recently, have generally been pictured as girlfriends, mothers and housewives. She says that sex role skills are important as they dictate what type of crime an individual will be capable of committing. Women are less likely to use weapons because they rarely learn how to use them, but they may use household implements to threaten their victims. This is also consistent with the fact that female crimes of violence are often committed against family members or close friends. Property crimes, she argues, often take the form of forgery, counterfeiting or shop-lifting which may arise from the stereotyped role of women as paying the bills and doing the shopping. She notes that amongst children and teenagers in America, girls are more likely than boys to be arrested for the juvenile crimes of 'breach of curfew' (which is an offence in some States in America) and 'running away'. This she explains by saying that girls are more likely to be noticed if they are out alone than are boys, and parents are more likely to worry about their daughters than they are about their sons.

The sex-role stereotyping is so strong that in some cases even where a theory is being postulated which runs counter to this idea, a feeling of the sex role may be present. Smart (1976) proposes a feminist critique of explanations but at points she lapses into a sex role orientation. For example, she explains receiving stolen goods, when committed by women, in terms of a passive act carried out for a loved one, and the goods are likely to be hidden somewhere in the house. The offence is thereby ascribed to relationships and to passivity, both of which fit in with sex-role stereotypes.

Masculinity/femininity theories are based upon behavioural theories (see earlier 17.2), social learning theories (see earlier 17.3), control theories (see below 17.6), and they are sometimes related to biological theories (see earlier 17.2).

17.4.3 Empirical testing of masculinity/femininity theories

However the masculinity/femininity based theories arise, they all argue that criminality is inexorably connected to sex. Such theories have more recently undergone a certain amount of empirical testing. Some of the tests consider the link between female crime and masculinity/femininity. In 1979 Cullen, Golden and Cullen reported that they had tested 99 men and 93 women. The test was a self-report study of both delinquency and self-perceived 'masculinity' (it did not test for 'femininity'). The masculine traits used were independence, objectivity, dominance, competitiveness and self-confidence. Subjects were asked to choose their positioning on a four point scale for each trait (from 'to a large extent' to 'not at all'). Possession of high masculinity was linked to greater criminality both of males and females, but males committed more crimes than females even when matched for masculinity. The conclusion to be drawn is that abnormal levels of 'masculinity' alone cannot explain female crime.

Again in 1979, Widom conducted a study which used tests of both masculinity and femininity traits. She studied 73 women awaiting trial and 20 controls, matched for status, race and education. Widom split her samples into four categories; androgenous – high masculinity/high femininity; masculine – high masculinity/low femininity; feminine – low masculinity/high femininity; and undifferentiated – low masculinity/low femininity. Masculinity was found to be a very poor predictor of criminality, but femininity was found to be inversely related to law-breaking. Thus, high femininity led to conformity but low femininity led to criminality.

A further piece of research reported in 1979 by Shover et al. looked at over 1,000 people and tested them for masculinity and femininity traits. Unfortunately, the questionnaire was arguably rather unsophisticated. It consisted of ten questions, five to test for masculinity:

1. I expect to pay for activities when on a date.
2. I expect to fix things like my car.
3. If I marry, I would expect to provide most of the income for my family.
4. I expect to ask someone for a date rather than being asked.
5. If I marry, I would expect to take responsibility for major family decisions such as buying a home or a car.

and five to test for femininity:

1. If I marry I would expect to be mainly responsible for housework, whether working outside the home or not.
2. Before going out at night, I expect to tell my parents where I am going.
3. I expect to take care of younger children in the family or neighbourhood.
4. I expect to get married and raise a family rather than get a job in the business world.
5. If I marry I would expect to move to another city if my spouse changed jobs.

It can be seen that these questions are inexact and reflect a subjective analysis of what is understood by 'masculinity' and 'femininity', concepts which are inherently difficult to define exactly or at all. The main virtue of the test was that it was applied to over 1,000 people. Any judgments on the value of the results needs to balance the defects of the tests against their substantial scale.

The researchers found that masculinity traits were largely unrelated to either property or aggressive crimes. They did find, however, that women were more likely to be aggressive if they were less feminine, that is, there was an inverse relationship between femininity and aggression. (These and other tests are more fully dealt with by Naffine (1985).)

17.4.4 Evaluation of masculinity/femininity
The three studies surveyed provide very inconclusive results. They neither prove nor disprove the hypothesis that increased 'masculinity' leads to crime. While there is some suggestion that the female crime rate is inversely related to femininity, this is by no means proven, nor is it necessarily a causative relationship. All the results must be treated carefully. The first two studies dealt with very small numbers, while the third involved a large number of subjects but embodied dubious methods of assessing 'masculinity' and 'femininity'. However, all definitions of these necessarily rather elusive and subjective concepts are likely to be primitive and/or subjective. Masculinity and femininity are ideas understood in a commonsense way by almost all people in all societies, but as scientific criteria they are more evasive. Because the male rate is so much greater than the female crime rate, any tests which seem to suggest that masculinity leads to crime and femininity leads to law-abiding behaviour are understandably attractive at first glance. But the tests all confront the difficulty that, both theoretically and empirically, there seems to be no unexceptional criterion by which to measure 'masculinity' and 'femininity'. Even so, it may be cautiously suggestive that these tests question the correlation between masculinity and crime, but do find an inverse relationship between crime and femininity. The implication is that masculinity is an unreliable indicator but that a very 'feminine' woman may be less likely to commit crime than is her less feminine counterpart.

Many doubt whether even such tentative implications have much validity. The constructs of masculinity/femininity are themselves seen as patriarchal and thus are rejected by many feminists. In particular, their use as an explanation of crime is challenged because one of the defining elements of femininity is usually given as conformity. In addition, it has been claimed that on most other behavioural measures (other than crime) men and women are more alike than different (Nicholson (1984)). Partly as a result of feminist writings, a newer field studying masculinity and its connection to criminality is beginning to emerge (see Jefferson and Carlen (1996)).

17.5   STRAIN THEORIES

The strain theory as applied to men was discussed in Chapter Twelve, which described the anomic theories of Durkheim and the way they were adapted and almost completely altered by Merton to explain the American way of life. In Merton's analyses, individuals are taught to desire certain things such as material success, but the legitimate means of achieving this – education and thence employment – are either not available or have only a limited relevance for the bulk of the American people. Those with limited opportunities were then frustrated into committing criminality to obtain the goals. This formulation was adopted by Cohen to explain male lower-class and youthful criminality but, as seen above (17.4.2), females were excluded from this form of strain: the only thing which they ought legitimately to desire was a mate or male companion, and therefore their criminality would revolve around that aim. In Cohen's scheme the whole of American culture is basically gendered; ambition, wealth, rationality and control of the emotions are the outward signs of a successful person, but only a male person. For women, success is to form a close relationship with a successful man. A lack of ambition, inactivity, irrationality and emotional instability are signs of a failed and defective male; they are the very identity of women. The other main proponents of the strain theory, Cloward and Ohlin, also relegate women to a position which excludes them from the main masculine culture. Because women are not subjected to financial pressures, they do not suffer strain in the same way and so have no need of criminal gangs or cultures to redress the balance.

As Box (1987) has pointed out, females have increasingly become economically marginalised. More women are now the only, the major, or the joint breadwinner, and therefore the pressures or strains of economic requirements are increasingly placed upon them. As women often inhabit low paid and insecure areas of employment, or are unemployed, they have tremendous pressures upon them to provide. Within this context it is instructive to note that women are more likely than men to be poor: Child Poverty Action Group in 1989 calculated that 5.1 million women as opposed to 3.4 million men were living on or below social assistance level; from the official social security statistics over a number of years it is clear that two thirds of adults supported by the social assistance income support scheme are women; Steven Webb shows that the Family Expenditure Survey reveals that women are over-represented in the lowest deciles, both on the basis of their individual incomes and when taking account of the incomes of other household members. In the latter case, two thirds of adults in the poorest households are women. This is not a peculiarly British situation: in the whole of Europe (except The Netherlands) Eurostat figures show that female-headed households suffer much higher rates of poverty – this is particularly so in the UK, Ireland, Portugal and France (all figures are reproduced in Feminist Legal Research Unit, Liverpool (1994)). These increased strains may help to explain some of the increased female criminality, especially in the traditionally male criminal areas (see Box and Hale (1983)). Applying strain theory to females could, however, predict too much criminality, as they are the most economically marginalised, and therefore if they were also to enter the competition for success one might expect their criminality to exceed that of men. Some of the reasons for the lack of such an immense increase in female criminality may be found in Tittle's control balance theory (see 13.5).

There is no doubt that to view the criminality of women as related only to their desire for a partner is too narrow. Clearly, women play a real role in society in general, and often fall under similar strains to those suffered by men. If there is a vast difference in their criminality, it must be ascribed to some other reason.

17.6 CONTROL THEORIES

Theorists in this school claim that it is not necessary to explain criminality, as this activity is natural. What is to be explained is conformity: why don't more people break the law? This question was addressed in Chapter Thirteen; here its specific relation to female criminality needs to be considered.

In 1958 Ivan Nye argued that delinquent behaviour is natural, whereas conformist behaviour has to be learned, first through childhood socialisation, and later through prohibitions and punishment inflicted by social institutions. The difference between male and female criminality is, according to Nye, generally explicable by the fact that girls, and later women, are subjected to much closer socialisation than their male counterparts. They are often more severely punished for minor transgressions of social rules. It is because of this close learning process that girls accept and live by conforming behaviour more completely than do boys. Delinquency results when there is a lessening of social control.

Hirschi (1969) set out the main thesis of control theories, whereby society controls people by means of four methods: attachment to conventional and law-abiding people; commitment to conventional institutions such as work, school or leisure activities; involvement in these same activities; and belief in the conventional rules of behaviour. These should lead to conformity. This idea is set out as a gender-neutral idea, but Naffine (1987) suggests that for a number of reasons it remains a male-gendered theory. First, she notes that if Hirschi was really interested in conformity he would have studied females, as the largest and strongest conforming group, to see why they were law-abiding, and yet he studied men. Secondly, Hirschi sets out as factors of conformity the traditional male role idea of breadwinner, such as responsibility, hard work, commitment to employment and making a rational decision to remain law-abiding rather than risk all of that. Conformity in males is thus depicted as positive, but females are said to conform because of their passive natures – conformity has become negative. Naffine claims that Hirschi alters the nature of the conformity because he conceives it as male rather than female. When the theory has been used to explain female conformity, the element of conformity is altered and has been devalued. She cites Hagan, Simpson and Gillis (1979) as an example of this. They surveyed both boys and girls and discovered that girls were more conforming than boys, then proceeded to discuss girls as passive and negative because they are conforming, whereas males were exciting, rational and positive in their law-breaking. Although using the control ideas, the negative depiction of conformity in this study runs counter to Hirschi's portrayal of conformity as positive when applied to males.

Control theory does not necessarily involve this strong gendering and negative view of the female. It is clear that some other tests have not included such factors. For example, Hindelang (1973) ran a replica of Hirschi's study but included females. The finding was that the control theory could predict criminality in both girls and boys, although the prediction for males was slightly stronger than for females. This suggests that the positive view of conformity could be attached to female as well as male behaviour. However, the greater conformity of women seemed to come from their being denied full access to the outside world of work, which was seen as being kept largely by men for men. Women were controlled more closely in the home and almost forced to conform, as their opportunities were very narrow.

Certainly Box (1981) viewed the control theory as gender neutral and as a useful tool to explain the greater conformity of females than of males. He argued that greater social bonding, a stronger perception of the risk involved in delinquency, and greater support for conformity among peers all make for more conforming behaviour and make the choice to conform rational and intelligent, a positive choice. Historically, Nye (1958) explained low female criminality by reference to women's close control in the family and society. Hagan (1989, see also Hagan et al. (1990)) also sees family socialisation as important, but notes that in some respects upbringing has altered and that this may explain changes in crime rates for women: in patriarchal families, girls, in contrast to boys, will be socialised as home-makers and away from risks; whereas egalitarian families increase the propensity of girls for risk-taking and so of their likelihood of turning to crime (see 13.7.1).

Heidensohn (1985 and 1996) proposes control theory as offering the best account of female criminality or, more particularly, female conformity. She argues that women are controlled in the home by their caring role of mothers and wives. She sees this role as being reinforced by social workers and health visitors stressing the rights and welfare of the child, through the idea of community care for the elderly and disabled, and through the way society assumes dependency of women in certain areas. She notes that although it is obviously a simple fact that women are dependent, the legitimation of the position by the State helps both to perpetuate this position and to control their behaviour. Even if they are at work, their free time is often constrained by having to perform the household tasks as well as their jobs, while because they are often in the least secure employments they are deterred from behaviour which might jeopardise their position. Lastly, male violence also acts as a very real control; domestic violence may keep them in their place in the home, and street violence also tends to keep women in the home, especially when their presence on the streets at night may actually be taken as being a temptation to prospective attackers (as in certain rape cases). Heidensohn (1992 and 1996), while confirming this thesis, also considers the changes that have and may come about as women attain positions of control in criminal justice.

The already mentioned work of Tittle concerning control balance might also be used to analyse gender differences in offending (for a full discussion see 13.5). He notes that in most areas of their lives women are controlled, often very heavily. As he sees control deficit as one aspect of deviant behaviour, this would appear to predict that women would be heavy offenders, but he notes that large control deficits result in submissive behaviour rather than predatory offending. Also, as women's lives less frequently motivate them towards deviance they tend to be law-abiding. This theory and its possible use in explaining gender differences in offending needs to be more closely considered.

The way in which controls act in our society generally means that females have less opportunity to take part in criminal behaviour and are possibly more at risk if they so do. This makes criminality a less rational and available choice in the case of females than it is in the case of males. The argument here is that it is not women's natures which make them more conforming; it arises rather in the way others control them, together with fewer opportunities. This will be discussed again in connection with female emancipation and its effects on criminality.

17.7 CONCLUSION

Unfortunately, no conclusive scientific tests have been found to ascertain what link, if any, psychological and physiological factors have with crime. Thus, although theories based upon these ideas can be very strongly attacked, they cannot be wholly discounted. Behavioural scientists and those involved in social sciences have tried to offer other explanations for criminal behaviour and so have largely displaced biological differences; the claim is that either upbringing or environment have emphasised what was originally a very small or non-existent biological difference. As was shown above, a theory (in this case the masculinity/femininity theory) can be said to arise either from upbringing or from biological factors, but both arguments may be questionable if their central tenet is not sound. The only definite conclusion is that biological arguments have been largely discounted as major reasons for crime. The more socially based theories seem to offer more plausible explanations.

However, social explanations of criminality have not provided very plausible answers to the question of why women commit crimes, nor do they satisfactorily explain why females are more conforming than their male counterparts. It may be that the tendency to see male crime as normal necessarily overshadows the study of the much less common female offending (Heidensohn (1996)). Female criminality is, in any event, most directly damaging to people they know and live with rather than to the wider society, so that theories based on societal conflict seem less immediately relevant. Studies which are implicitly based on masculinity and on presumptions that the offenders will be male, mean that the behaviour of women, if included at all, is – unconsciously – seen through a masculine prism. Even in more recent research where there has been an attempt to include feminism, this remains predominantly the case (see Bourgois (1996)). The most promising ideas so far come from control theories, and from strain theories as long as these are applied in a gender-neutral manner. Each of these theories suffers from the idea that they are basically determinate, that is, that if certain factors arise, criminality will occur, or if others arise, law-abiding behaviour will result. This will be questioned in the next chapter.

More immediately, we can note the effects that some of the most primitive views of women have had upon the criminal justice system. First, as Klein and Kress (1976) point out, women who transgress their feminine role in a sexual or permissive way will be likely to be harshly treated, whereas those who take part in property crimes are not taken seriously (such a claim has been questioned by Hedderman and Hough (1994)). This is said to be because, being economically unimportant, they represent no threat to society and can thus be treated more leniently than their male counterparts. Where women are criminalised and treated harshly by their imprisonment, they are often placed into regimes which are based upon old and often discredited physical or psychological theories. For example, Dobash, Dobash and Gutteridge (1986) explain that the Holloway Project Group, which was set up at the beginning of the 1970s officially to plan the redevelopment of women's prisons, accepted the psychological and physiological explanations for female criminality and set up the prison regime to link in with this idea. The use of medical help was essential to this basis. Smart (1976) points to the fact that prison staff also try to inculcate female offenders into the role of mother and housewife by pressing the domestic rather than vocational skills and by encouraging them to take an interest in their appearance. All this is seen to accept either the biological/ psychological ideas of female criminality or the sex role stereotyping which will dictate that the more feminine and domesticated a women is, the less likely she will be to commit criminal activities. Despite the questionable status of these theories, they have been, and are, accepted and acted upon by the authorities.

REFERENCES

Bourgois, Philippe (1996), *In Search of Respect: Selling Crack in El Barrio*, Cambridge: Cambridge University Press.

Box, Steven (1981), *Deviance Reality and Society*, 2nd edn, London: Holt Rinehart and Winston.

Box, Steven and Hale, Chris (1983), 'Liberation and Female Criminality in England and Wales', *British Journal of Criminology*, vol. 23, p. 35.

Box, Steven (1987), *Recession, Crime and Punishment*, London: Macmillan Education.

Campbell, Anne (1981), *Girl Delinquents*, Oxford: Basil Blackwell.

Carlen, Pat (1983), *Women's Imprisonment*, London: Routledge & Kegan Paul.

Cohen, A.K. (1955), *Delinquent Boys: The Culture of the Gang*, Glencoe: The Free Press.

Cowie, J., Cowie, B. and Slater, E. (1968), *Delinquency in Girls*, London: Heinemann.

Cullen, F.T., Golden, K.M. and Cullen, J.B. (1979), 'Sex and Delinquency', *Criminology*, vol. 17, p. 301.

Dalton, Katharina Dorothea (1961), 'Menstruation and Crime', *British Medical Journal*, vol. 2, pp. 1752-3.

Dalton, Katharina Dorothea (1984), 2nd edn, *The Premenstrual Syndrome and Progesterone Therapy*, Droitwich: Heinemann Medical.

Daly, K. (1994), *Gender, Crime and Punishment*, New Haven, Conn.: Yale University Press.

Dell, Susanne (1984), *Murder into Manslaughter*, Maudsley Monograph Series No. 27, London: Institute of Psychiatry.

Dobash, R.P., Dobash, R.E. and Gutteridge, S. (1986), *The Imprisonment of Women*, Oxford: Basil Blackwell.

Edwards, Susan (1988), 'Mad, Bad or Pre-Menstrual?', *New Law Journal*, p. 456.

Feminist Legal Research Unit, Liverpool (1994), *For Richer, For Poorer?: Feminist Perspectives on Women and the Distribution of Wealth*, Liverpool: Feminist Legal Research Unit, Liverpool University.

Freckleton, Ian (1994), 'Contemporary Comment: When Plight Makes Right – the Forensic Abuse Syndrome', *Criminal Law Journal*, vol. 18, p. 29.

Freud, Sigmund (1973), 'Femininity', from papers originally written (1925) and (1931), reproduced in J. Strachey and A. Richards (eds), *New Introductory Lectures on Psychoanalysis*, Harmondsworth: Penguin.

Gibbens, T.C.N. and Prince, J. (1962), *Shoplifting*, London: Institute for the Study and Treatment of Delinquency.

Grosser, George H. (1951), quoted in Don C. Gibbons (1981), *Delinquent Behaviour*, 3rd edn, Englewood Cliffs, New Jersey: Prentice-Hall.

Hagan, John (1989), *Structural Criminology*, New Brunswick, NJ: Rutgers University Press.

Hagan, J., Gillis, A.R. and Simpson, J. (1990), 'Clarifying and Extending Power-Control Theory', *American Journal of Sociology*, vol. 95, p. 1024.

Hagan, J., Simpson, J.H. and Gillis, A.R. (1979), 'The Sexual Stratification of Social Control: A Gender-Based Perspective on Crime and Delinquency', *British Journal of Sociology*, vol. 30, p. 25.

Healy, William and Bronner, Augusta F. (1936), *New Light on Delinquency and its Treatment*, New Haven: Yale University Press.

Hedderman, Carol and Hough, Mike (1994), *Does the Criminal Justice System Treat Men and Women Differently?*, Home Office Research and Statistics Department, Research Findings No. 10, London: Research and Planning Unit.

Heidensohn, Frances (1985), *Women and Crime*, London: Macmillan.
Heidensohn, Frances (1992), *Women in Control?*, Oxford: Oxford University Press.
Heidensohn, Frances (1996), *Women and Crime*, London: Macmillan.
Hindelang, M.J. (1973), 'Causes of Delinquency: A Partial Replication and Extension', *Social Problems*, vol. 20, p. 471.
Hirschi, Travis (1969), *Causes of Delinquency*, Berkeley: University of California Press.
Hoffman Bustamante, Dale (1973), 'The Nature of Female Criminality', *Issues in Criminology*, vol. 8, p. 117.
Jefferson, Tony and Carlen, Pat (eds) (1996), 'Masculinity, Social Relations and Crime', *British Journal of Criminology*, vol. 36(3), Special Issue.
Kennedy, Helene (1992), *Eve Was Framed*, London: Chatto & Windus.
Klein, D. and Kress, J. (1976), 'Any Women's Blues: A Critical Overview of Women, Crime and the Criminal Justice System', *Crime and Social Justice*, vol. 5, p. 34.
Law Commission (1989), *Report and Draft Criminal Code Bill*, Law Com. No. 177, London: HMSO.
Lombroso, Cesare (with Ferrero, G.) (1895), *The Female Offender*, London: Unwin.
Luckhaus, Linda (1985), 'A Plea For PMT in the Criminal Law', in Susan Edwards (ed.), *Gender, Sex and the Law*, London: Croom Helm.
Mackay, R.D. (1993), 'The Consequences of Killing Very Young Children', *Criminal Law Review*, p. 21.
Maier-Katkin, Daniel (1991), 'Postpartum Psychosis, Infanticide and the Law', *Crime, Law and Social Change*, vol. 15, p. 109.
Maier-Katkin, Daniel and Ogle, Robbin (1993), 'A Rationale for Infanticide Laws', *Criminal Law Review*, p. 903.
Marks, M.N. and Kumar, R. (1993), 'Infanticide in England and Wales', *Medicine Science and the Law*, vol. 33, p. 329.
Marsh, Peter (1978), *Aggro: The Illusion of Violence*, (with a forward by Desmond Morris), London: Dent.
Money, John and Ernhardt, Anke A. (1972), *Man and Woman: Boy and Girl*, Baltimore: Johns Hopkins University Press.
Naffine, Ngaire (1985), 'The Masculinity-Femininity Hypothesis: A Construction of Gender-Based Personality Theories of Female Crime', *British Journal of Criminology*, vol. 25, p. 365.
Naffine, Ngaire (1987), *Female Crime: The Construction of Women in Criminology*, Sydney: Allen and Unwin.
Nicholson, J. (1984), *Men and Women*, Oxford: Oxford University Press.
Nye, Ivan (1958), *Family Relationships and Delinquent Behaviour*, New York: Wiley.
O'Donovan, Katherine (1991), 'Defences for Battered Women Who Kill', *Journal of Law and Society*, vol. 18, p. 219.
Parsons, Talcott (1947), 'Certain Primary Sources and Patterns of Aggression in the Social Structure of the Western World', *Psychiatry*, vol. X, p. 167.

Parsons, Talcott (1954), *Essays in Sociological Theory*, Glencoe, Illinois: Free Press.

Pollak, O. (1950), *The Criminality of Women*, Philadelphia: University of Pennsylvania Press.

Rafter, Nicole Hahn (1983), 'Chastizing the Unchaste: Social Control Functions of a Women's Reformatory, 1894-1931', in Stanley Cohen and Andrew Scull (eds), *Social Control and the State*, Oxford: Martin Robertson.

Reiss, Albert J. (1960), 'Sex Offences: The Marginal Status of the Adolescent', *Law and Contemporary Problems*, vol. 25, p. 309.

Rose, R.M., Holoday, J.W., and Bernstein, S. (1971), 'Plasma testosterone, dominance, rank and aggressive behaviour in male rhesus monkeys', *Nature*, vol. 231, p. 366-8.

Ryan, Christopher and Scanlan, Gary (1991), *Swot: Criminal Law*, 3rd edn, London: Blackstone Press.

Shover, Neal, Norland, Stephen, James, Jennifer and Thornton, William (1979), 'Gender Roles in Delinquency', *Social Forces*, vol. 58, p. 162.

Smart, Carol (1976), *Women, Crime and Criminology: a Feminist Critique*, London: Routledge & Kegan Paul.

Smart, Carol and Smart, Barry (eds) (1987), *Women, Sexuality and Social Control*, London: Routledge & Kegan Paul.

Sutherland, Edwin H. (1939), *Principles of Criminology*, 3rd edn, Philadelphia: Lippincott.

Sutherland, Edwin H. and Cressey, Donald R. (1966), *Principles of Criminology*, 3rd edn, Philadelphia: Lippincott.

Sutherland, Edwin H. and Cressey, Donald R. (1978), *Criminology*, 10th edn, Philadelphia: Lippincott.

Thomas, William I. (1907), *Sex and Society*, Chicago: University of Chicago Press.

Thomas, William I. (1967) (first published 1923), *The Unadjusted Girl*, New York: Harper and Row.

Tittle, Charles R. (1995), *Control Balance: Towards a General Theory of Deviance*, Boulder, Co: Westview Press.

Tittle, Charles R. (1997), 'Thoughts Stimulated by Braithwaite's Analysis of Control Balance', *Theoretical Criminology*, vol. 1, p. 99.

Widom, Cathy Spatz (1979), 'Female Offenders: Three assumptions about self-esteem, sex role identity and feminism', *Criminal Justice Behaviour*, vol. 6, p. 365.

Wilczynski, A. and Morris, A. (1993), 'Parents Who Kill Their Children', *Criminal Law Review*, p. 31.

CHAPTER EIGHTEEN

Women's Liberation and Feminist Theories

18.1 INTRODUCTION

In the previous chapter, it became obvious that one of the most striking features about female criminality and conformity is the lack of research and information available. The female and gender issues were ignored, and attention focused on male criminality and the male. The exclusion of half the population from study is very likely to lead to distortions even, perhaps especially, if that half is likely to be much less represented in the behaviour studied.

When the female was considered, she was generally seen as being inferior to the male. Although conformity was generally to be appreciated, when women conformed, it showed their inferiority. This inferiority was of the same type, whether it was seen as arising out of biological, psychological or social reasons. The male was seen as independent, autonomous, intelligent, active, assertive, rational, unemotional, competitive, achieving and objective. The woman was seen as dependent, passive, uncompetitive, immature, unachieving, unintelligent, emotional, subjective and irrational. The male qualities were portrayed in a positive manner even when they led to negative outcomes such as criminality, and the female attributes were portrayed as negative even when they led to positive outcomes such as conformity to the legal rules.

This view of women was challenged by feminists in various ways. Some tried to prove that liberation has made women more like men and more able to compete on an even footing. Others attempted to force established theorists to rethink their ideas by taking into consideration a feminist perspective and allowing a more gendered approach to the whole question of criminology. Much of the research in these areas is in its infancy.

18.2 FEMALE LIBERATION

18.2.1 The proposition

In the last chapter, some of the theories suggested that people are not born criminal, but learn criminality or conforming behaviour from associates and from the environment in which they are brought up. Some writers, although recognising that in-born characteristics play a part, attach most importance to the efforts of the society in which a person is brought up. If one accepts that it is through close conditioning that a woman learns to conform, and that it is this close supervision which prevents criminality, then any lessening of the control would lead to increased criminality. On this basis, some, such as Adler and Simon, have claimed that the increase in female criminality in the last 30 years is the result of reduced control, which they argue is the direct result of the women's liberation movement.

Adler (1975) contends that there is very little actual difference between the potential criminality of men and women: previous differences in criminal activity were due to sex-role differences. The women's movement has, she says, led to a change in women's social position in all legitimate spheres. This has also brought with it an increase in women's criminal activity, particularly in areas which have traditionally been associated with men, e.g., crimes of violence and robbery. In fact, for Adler female criminality is an indicator of the degree of liberation achieved by women; more female crime means more female liberation. Women's liberation has brought out their competitive instincts, making them more assertive, more aggressive and generally more 'masculine'. The movement is also seen as having opened up structural opportunities for women in both legitimate and illegitimate fields. She argues that wherever men had previously been active in a particular area women saw it as prestigious and appealing: to emulate men, they were drawn into all previously male activities, including criminality. This is Adler's explanation of the increase she perceived in female crime: essentially, that women are acting more like men. It is an interpretation which largely accepts the traditional idea that criminality is a masculine and male preserve: to take part, women have to act more like men. She accepts that prior to liberation women were passive, but this was simply because of sex-role differences. The conclusion would seem to be that women are becoming more masculine and therefore more criminal. Such a view would need to confront the fact, seen in 17.2.5, that there is no proven correlation between masculinity and criminality; indeed, some of the more masculine females were seen to be less likely to become criminal.

Simon (1975) argued, rather differently, that the women's movement has given rise to an increase in the opportunities for women to commit crimes and thus to an increase in their crime rates, but that the increase is mostly in financial or property crimes. Because they go out to work, they are more likely to participate in the type of crime for which their occupations provide them with opportunities for crime. She also contends that the extra interest that education and employment have given women reduces their feelings of frustration due to victimisation and exploitation, which also reduces their motivation for violent crime, particularly murder. Simon is at variance with Adler on two major points. Firstly, she argues that liberation will make women less violent as the frustrations, both within and outside the home, will be removed. Secondly, Simon does not argue that women are self-consciously competing with men to become criminals; rather, their criminality arises out of an increased opportunity to which liberation gives rise.

Many other writers (for example Henson (1980)) have put forward similar arguments, but in all these cases their basic thesis assumes that there has been a sharp increase in female crime since the women's movement. Before one can assess their arguments, it is essential to discover whether this basic presumption is sound. Most writers agree that there was a rejuvenation and strengthening of the women's movement in the early 1960s: has there been a large increase in female criminality from this time?

18.2.2 Female crime statistics

Any attempt to answer this question runs into all the problems about the statistics: not only about their reliability, but also about their manipulation and interpretation. Adler in her book examines the Federal Bureau of Investigation's Uniform Crime Figures (for America) and notes large increases in female criminality between 1960 and 1972. For example, arrests for robbery were up 277 per cent (for men, the increase was only 69 per cent); burglary increased by 168 per cent (63 per cent for men), and so on. From this she assumes that in America, female crime increased much faster than male crime at a time when the liberation movement was very strong. She looked at similar figures for juveniles. For example, arrests of adolescent females for negligent manslaughter had increased 450 per cent, whilst those for young males had dropped by 36 per cent, and she drew the conclusion that there would be a large increase in female crime in the near future. She also used the figures and arguments to predict large rises in female criminality in Europe, India and New Zealand, without having taken sufficient account of the differences in culture and legal practices in these countries. These propositions are not really proven. It can be misleading to make assumptions by comparing two sets of figures without assessing other factors which may have been relevant. Furthermore, it is generally accepted that great care must be taken if juvenile crime is used as an indication of future adult crime. The two phenomena are different, both in their causes and very often in their participants. It is important that a rather more careful study of the figures is made. Thus Crites (1976) points out that Adler's 450 per cent increase in arrests of adolescent females for negligent manslaughter represented a rise from two to eleven cases for the whole of the United States, hardly meriting the significance Adler gives it.

Carol Smart (1979) puts forward a more refined assessment. She turned to the official statistics for England and Wales and, whilst noting their obvious shortcomings, attempted to make use of them to test whether female criminality is caused by emancipation. She noted that indictable offences by women had nearly doubled from 1965–75, and that the bulk of such increases had taken place in crimes of violence. Male crime had also increased, but the percentage increases for the same period were a lot smaller than for women (see Table 18.1). But large percentage increases can arise from small changes in the absolute numbers. For example, there was a 500 per cent increase in murder by women between 1965 and 1975, but it went from *one* case to *five* cases in that period. Generally, she argues, it is false to compare percentage increases in male and female crimes. Female crime figures tend to start from a small absolute base: but in male crime the absolute figures are high at the outset, so that even a relatively large increase will only show a small percentage (for example, from 10,000 to 11,000 would only be a 10 per cent rise but would include 1,000 more cases, whereas from one to five is a 500 per cent increase but only four more cases). A result such as depicted in Table 1 could, for this reason, be deceptive.

Table 18.1: Proportionate increases in indictable offences by males and females between 1965 and 1975 in Britain

Offence	Male %	Female %
Class I (sex offences and violent offences)	100	225
Class II (burglary and robbery)	55	149
Class III (theft and handling stolen goods)	46	66
Total of *all* indictable offences	83	95
(Smart 1979; Table 2)		

Smart also claims that, to see the general trend, it is necessary to consider increases over a number of decades. Table 18.2 shows a fluctuation in crime figures over the period 1935–75. It also portrays a general increase in female compared with male crime over this period. More significantly for the present purpose, it shows that the period immediately preceding women's liberation generally shows a higher increase in female crimes than the period when emancipation would be expected to have an effect.

Table 18.2: Number of males and females found guilty of indictable offences per 100,000 of the male and female population respectively

	1935	1940	1945	1950	1955	1960	1965	1970	1975
Male	370	428	512	553	502	747	971	1,423	1,694
Female	47	68	86	76	69	93	149	201	278

Source: HMSO, Criminal Statistics, England and Wales

(Smart 1979; Table 4)

This questions the earlier assumption that the increase in female crime is a phenomenon of the last 30 years. Moreover, it also argues that the sex distribution of criminals (i.e., the number of males as a percentage of all criminals and the number of females as a percentage of all criminals) has remained almost constant throughout this period (see Table 18.3). All these figures, she argues, refute the claim that there have been more increases in female crime since the women's liberation movement began to have world-wide prominence in the 1960s.

Table 18.3: The relative female-to-male contribution to persons found guilty of committing indictable offences, per 100,000 population aged 15–64, 1951–79, England and Wales

Year	All indictable crimes	Crimes of violence against the person	Crimes against property
1951	0.13	0.08	0.13
1956	0.13	0.05	0.14
1961	0.14	0.04	0.16
1966	0.15	0.06	0.17
1971	0.15	0.06	0.18
1976	0.19	0.09	0.22
1979	0.18	0.09	0.22

(Box and Hale 1983; Table 2)

Smart's claims are questioned by Austin (1981). He argues that although Table 18.2 above shows that indictable crime generally, and Class III offences in particular, show greater increases in 1955–65 than in 1965–75, Class I and II offences show a greater increase in 1965–75. In other words, it is in more serious crimes – crimes of violence, burglary and robbery, which have traditionally been considered male crime areas – that the largest increases have occurred since the women's liberation movement. Thus, he argues that the movement has had an effect on female crime, even if that effect is not as strong as is often claimed by proponents of the link between female crime and the liberation movement.

Table 18.4: Females found guilty of indictable crimes, England and Wales 1951–79, rate per 100,000 population aged 15–64

Year	All indictable offences	Violence against person*	Property offences†	Standardised 1951 = 100		
				All	Violence	Property
1951	1.04	0.0002	0.96	100	100	100
1956	0.92	0.0002	0.84	88	100	88
1961	1.54	0.0003	1.44	148	150	150
1966	2.01	0.0006	1.90	193	300	198
1971	2.94	0.0010	2.72	283	500	283
1976	4.21	0.0020	3.70	405	1000	385
1979	4.00	0.0025	3.51	385	1250	366

*Includes murder, manslaughter, conspiracy to murder, causing death through dangerous driving, grievous woundings, malicious assaults, etc., i.e., official categories 1–15 in Criminal Statistics England and Wales.

†Includes robbery, burglary, theft, handling, fraud and forgery, i.e., official categories 28–31, 34, 39–49, 51–53, 54, 60–61, in Criminal Statistics England and Wales.

(Box and Hale 1983; Table 1)

The area is clearly full of statistical traps for the unwary. One of the fullest British discussions on the numerical increase in female crime and the question of whether or not it is linked with women's emancipation came in 1983 from Steven Box and Chris Hale. They attack the whole idea of a link between female criminality and liberation, and reject most previous arguments on the grounds that earlier writers commit one or more of the following errors:

1. A failure to take into account changes in the number of females available to commit crimes in each particular year. Most researchers look at the numbers of crimes committed in various years without looking at whether the number of women has changed, and particularly without discovering whether the number of women between 15 and 65, that is, those likely to commit crimes, has changed. There is more reason to be concerned if more crimes are being committed by the same, or a fewer, number of women than if the increase in crime is matched, or exceeded, by an increase in the number of women (see Table 18.4).
2. Failure to take into account the change in male crime. If this is also increasing, then although female crime may be increasing *absolutely* (i.e., when compared with female crime in previous years) it may not be increasing *relative* to male crime. If both increase at the same rate then, although there may be a need to be concerned about crime in general, it is uncertain whether

there should be concern about female crime in particular. This problem can be dealt with either by comparing percentage increases in female crime and male crime (as was done by Smart in Table 18.1) or by looking at the share of crime that each has had over a certain period (see Table 18.3).

3.   Failure to break down the broad categories of crime recorded in the criminal statistics into different types of crime, particularly into those which are more theoretically relevant. All too often authors rely on gross data, such as the American Crime Index or the British category of indictable offences, whereas the theoretical assertions refer to more specific crimes within these broad categories. For example, some analysts look at Class I offences as an indication of violent crime, but the Class I statistics also include sex crime and other categories: for this purpose, they should confine their attention to the more specific crimes of murder, grievous bodily harm, assault, theft and so on.

4.   Failure to specify theoretically and measure rigorously the other dependent or independent variables which may have had an effect on the statistics. This would include, for example, changes in the law, or in the recording of statistics or in court practices.

5.   Failure to apply relevant statistical tests to the data so that significant changes and relationships between the independent and dependent variables can be identified. That is, they do not try to test how much of an effect each of the factors may have had.

They argue that all the previous studies have done is to show an historical overlap between women's liberation and an increase in female crime (if they have managed to show anything). Something more than just concurrence is necessary before one can convincingly show a causative element.

These surveys of statistical data cast serious doubt on the notion that there is a causative correlation between female crime and female emancipation. If, however, the arguments based on criminal statistics are left to one side for a moment, there are still those who propose that women's liberation must have affected female crime. They say it has led to an increase in legitimate opportunities for women, allowing them even after marriage to leave the home and go out to work, which necessarily leads to increased criminal or other socially unacceptable opportunities for women.

18.2.3   The women's liberation movement

The women's movement is not wholly or even largely concerned with women's positions and standing in the working environment. Nonetheless it seems that popular opinion sees this as their main area of concern, and it is in any event plausible to consider whether their clearly important efforts in this area are likely to have affected female crime. Smart (1979) argues that if criminal opportunities are directly related to the release of women from the home environment and into work, the results would show up in increases in specific crimes. In particular, the increases would fall into the area of white-collar crime rather than that of violence, robbery or burglary. Yet it is not white-collar crime which appears to have increased. It is difficult to know what to make of this since, as was seen in earlier chapters, white-collar crimes remain largely hidden. Its relation to female crime is further obscured, because it appears to be only the middle-class professional or clerical worker whose employment opportunities have been noticeably improved by the so-called liberation movement. Lower down the social scale the main change has been in the number of married women doing mostly part-time, low paid work. Otherwise, working-class women have always had to go out to work, and in fact the working position and opportunities of these women in the last twenty-five years has in some respects been worsening. For example, the liberation movement has done little to help those affected by increased unemployment amongst working-class women. Yet, Smart argues, it is the working-class women who are increasingly appearing in the criminal statistics.

If Smart is correct in her analysis, then it is difficult to detect any direct causative connection between women's liberation and the level of female crime. The indirect effects of the liberation movement are even more difficult to assess and, as yet, have been rarely studied. For example, there is no really careful study of whether and how convicted girls and women were affected by the movement. Smart does argue that the movement may have had an indirect effect by shaping the way in which law enforcement agencies perceive and treat women. It may have made them more likely to suspect, charge, prosecute, convict and sentence women than was previously the case. Her conclusion, that in order to study the real effect of women's liberation we must look wider than pure statistical analysis or its direct effects, seems difficult to refute.

There have been some attempts in this direction in both America and Britain. We shall look briefly at one study from each country, starting with Josefina Fiqueira-McDonogh's 1984 American study. She tested three hypotheses about the importance of feminist aspirations on behaviour:

1. *The 'equal opportunity' hypothesis:* a high level of feminist aspirations (for example, equality between the sexes) will press women towards a greater involvement in the male's sphere of activities, both legitimate and illegitimate (Adler (1975); Simon (1975); see above).

2. *The frustration hypothesis:* a high level of feminist aspirations under conditions of *lagging* opportunities will lead to a greater involvement of women in illegitimate behaviour (Austin (1983); see above).

3. *The competitive hypothesis:* a high level of feminist aspirations will lead females to high levels of legitimate activity to compete with males for available legitimate opportunities.

She obtained her data from male and female high school students who completed self-administered questionnaires. The groups chosen had been drawn from a variety of social and economic backgrounds. The subjects were born in 1964 and so were brought up in an environment which was likely to be aware of the liberation movement and of women's rights generally. As well as collecting figures on criminal activity, the study was based on information on various other aspects. First, on feminist orientation or the effects of women's liberation (looking at public attitudes – work, political leadership; private attitudes – division of labour in the family; and self-personal perceptions of aggression and success). Second, on class, race, and social aspirations (looking at conventional aspirations – both raising a family and going to college; career – obtaining a job, particularly a high status job; material factors – owning cars, clothes, money, being able to travel). Third, on school involvement, grades at school, social activities (particularly interaction with opposite sex, groups of people and close friends, steady boyfriend); and finally sexual activity. After using a model which aimed to test the causation interactions between all these items she states in her conclusion:

> The findings support best a subcultural deprivation explanation of delinquency. Lower-class position depresses aspirations leading to lower school performance and high social activity which strongly predict delinquency. *The contribution of feminist orientation to the predominant explanatory path is minimal.* (our emphasis)

Support of sexual equality in public opportunities and private life showed no effect and a negative effect respectively. Only where there was a personal identification with feminist attitudes was there any slight positive effect on delinquency. All three original hypotheses received some confirmation. Feminist orientated girls had higher career aspirations, performed better in school and were less involved in sex. They fell within the competitive hypothesis which predicted no extra crime as a result of liberation. This hypothesis was most strongly supported by the results. The equal opportunity and frustration hypotheses drew some support from aggressive and success-orientated girls. The overall results showed that the feminist movement had given rise to a number of positive effects and very few negative effects. It also suggested that the best way of curbing the small negative results is by encouraging high school performance and reinforcing career and/or conventional aspirations rather than by trying to curb the aggressive, success-orientated aspect.

This empirical study gives rise to quite strong results which seem to disprove a correlation between women's liberation and the female crime rate. It must be remarked, however, that it was a self-report study and also that it was conducted on juveniles, and as Smart (1979) points out, any extrapolation from juvenile delinquency to adult crime must be handled with great care: the types of crimes committed by adults and juveniles are very different, as are their general lifestyles and environments.

The British study by Steven Box and Chris Hale (18.2.2) looked at crime in general and used a very careful breakdown of the official statistics. Box and Hale find that, taking the female population which is available to commit crimes and looking purely at crimes of personal violence between 1951 and 1979, there was a dramatic increase (see Table 18.4). However, the ratio of male to female convictions for crimes of violence has remained fairly constant, whereas for property crimes the female share has been increasing in relation to the men (see Table 18.3). Because the results were so different,

Box and Hale attempted to look at the absolute change in female crime *and* to compare this with changes in male criminality over the same period. They recognised that such comparisons encounter substantial difficulties. In particular, changes in social attitudes could affect the data. For example, changing sex roles, the perception of sex as a factor and the greater attention given to female crime by the media may have resulted in a more uniform application of criminal procedure to both sexes. Changes in the statistical data may also have made a difference. Until quite recently the police did not record female accomplices, but now they do. This means that the higher figures partly reflect a bureaucratic or policy change rather than a genuine trend.

As a measure of the significance of women's liberation in the general population they considered four factors:

1. fertility;
2. female undergraduates plus graduates;
3. female labour force participation; and
4. unattached women (single/divorced/widowed).

(1) and (4) were used as indicators of female release from family ties; (2) and (3) show their entry into other spheres of activity. They also attempted to test for the lower economic groups by looking at the rates of female unemployment, but this may be rather misleading as many eligible women do not register, and their willingness and ability to do so has almost certainly changed over the last 29 years.

Box and Hale found no statistical relationship with crime in any of the four indicators of female liberation in the 29-year period. They did, however, find that crime was affected both by the number of registered unemployed and by the level of employment of women police officers. The latter is part of a general increase in the number of women employed in all parts of the criminal justice system, although there are still relatively few in senior positions (Home Office (1992)). Thus over the three decades studied there was a four-fold increase of women in the police force, which indicated the extent to which the force has increasingly recognised demands for sex equality, and this recognition probably extended to the routine processing of female suspects. Thus, one aspect of the spread of equality may have been to visit the same consequences on female criminals as would apply to men. They concluded that they were unable to find any correlation between increases in crime and female emancipation, but they do recognise that other indicators of liberation, or testing more specific areas of crime (for example shop-lifting), could give rise to different results. The outcome of their study was therefore inconclusive, in that it could not definitely prove or disprove a correlation between women's liberation and female crime, but it did suggest that any correlation was unlikely and, if it existed at all, was only an indirect effect of the movement.

These two studies thus point towards the absence of any strong direct causative link between female liberation and women's criminality, either amongst juveniles or amongst adults. Admittedly, the study in juvenile crime was conducted in America and may not apply in Britain but, until an analysis of that type is conducted here, it and other United States studies which reach similar conclusions are the best indicators of what the relationship is likely to be.

Recent developments in control balance theory (see 13.5) also support these views. They suggest that, even if the women's liberation movement has caused there to be a difference in the power or control of women, particularly in the opportunities for paid employment, this would not necessarily lead to a large difference in female crime rates because other traditional socialising aspects may remain, or because women may be less likely to choose such behaviour. The overall implication is that to assume that women's liberation would necessarily lead to greater female criminality is both too deterministic and too simplistic (for a fuller discussion see 18.3.1 below).

18.3 FEMINIST THEORIES

18.3.1 Old ideas re-assessed

In the last chapter, many of the theories which have been posited for explaining male criminality were studied to discover how they fitted female criminals into the picture. Most of them viewed male criminality in a far more positive light than they did female criminality, and applied very negative explanations to both female criminality and female conformity. Here, it is proposed to re-assess some of these ideas and discover whether there is anything more positive which they may have to offer to explain female criminality.

Sex-role socialisation theories of criminality have been found to be very unreliable predictors of criminality (see 17.4 and 18.2). The assumption that masculinity leads to criminality because of its aggressive, positive, rational and objective qualities is not found to be the case where women are concerned; in fact some of the women with high masculinity factors seemed to have a lower tendency towards offending. Similarly, femininity, when portrayed by women in the form of a passive and pliant female, does not reliably predict conformity. The simple negative view of femininity as compliant and passive is a stereotype which can no longer be credibly employed. Possibly the view proposed by Gilligan (1982) would be a step in the right direction. Although she accepts a very traditional view of the sexes, she at least credits women with a positive set of values. She sees the male approach as an ethic of rights, one in which individuality and differentiation are to be valued. The female approach she sees as an ethic of responsibility, that is, consideration of others before oneself, consideration of relationships and feelings, kindness, compassion and an idea of mutual dependence and attachment. Here Gilligan accepts a traditional role for women, but does so in a gendered and feminist way. She accepts a difference between masculinity and femininity; but rather than investing the former with all the positive traits she attributes both masculinity and femininity with positive, though different, values. Although to test whether these revised masculinity and femininity factors made better predictors of criminality and conformity would be interesting, there is a major prior question. Are these personality variables inherently connected with male and female, or are they merely constructed that way by society? Is femininity just a product of the exploitation of women within the society?

In Chapter Twelve sub-cultural gang theories, largely of the 1950s and 1960s, were considered. But, for three main reasons, these were then applied only to young males: these theories saw male crime as normal and so female conformity would be odd; social conflict was thought to be less central to female offending; and male researchers empathised with male offenders (Heidensohn (1996)). The male researchers presumed that women did not participate in such activities. More recently, feminist literature has forced virtually all criminological areas at least to acknowledge its existence so that more recent work in these areas has tried to include females and feminism or gender. Thus when Bourgois (1996) looks at gangs of crack dealers in Spanish-Harlem and at their environment, he takes gender and feminism as one of his analytical tools but is still drawn to explanations based on economy more than feminist interpretations (thus when one gang member beats his pregnant wife this is explained as frustration at not being able to provide for his family, ignoring the possible power and gender aspects which might be present). Despite stated intentions, the voice of women and feminism is still muted in such studies. Other research centres on female gangs or sub-cultures. Both Shacklady-Smith (1978) and Welsh (1981) found that girls did join gangs, often mixed-sex gangs, while Messerschmidt (1995) discovered female gangs of girls from ethnic minorities connected with other (usually) female gangs in a way similar to that which had been documented for some male gangs. These women defined and pursued their own ideas of femininity, claiming that their criminality was consistent with these ideas as it allowed them to experiment and take part in exciting activities which they chose for themselves and within boundaries which they set themselves. This may not be mainline feminism but it recognises constructs of gender similarities and differences being created by boys and girls on the street. Here then there may be a place for masculinity/femininity and gang cultures, but on very different grounds to those discussed in the largely male-orientated literature (see Messerschmidt (1993 and 1995) and Jefferson and Carlen (1996)). This is an interesting example of the way in which feminist perspectives permit a broader and more inclusive academic debate than has hitherto been possible within the strict confines of mainstream criminology. In this way feminist theories have helped to emphasise how both masculinity and femininity could well form a central area of research for criminologists.

In contrast, as we have seen (17.5), strain theorists such as Cohen (1955) dismissed women from serious consideration by claiming that a woman's only role was as a seeker of a partner and a family. This was questioned by the more feminist approach of Box and Hale (1983) when they pointed to the economic marginalisation of women which clearly placed them under great strain (see 17.5). Steven Box (1987), after reviewing 50 American and British studies linking crime and unemployment, concluded that the most plausible explanation for the increase in conventional crimes committed by females is that more women become economically marginalised during a recession. This economic element of their plight has also been addressed by Pat Carlen (1988). In an intricate study of 39 women she discovered that poverty (a desire or need for money) was a frequent reason for their criminal behaviour. Of the 39 women interviewed, 32 were poor and had been so for all but brief interludes in their lives, and five others had been poor at some time. Most had only achieved short periods of prosperity from their criminality. But the women themselves did not attribute their crimes to poverty. Although over 80 per cent admitted being poor and 95 per cent had been poor at some time, only 30 per cent saw it as the main reason for the criminality, and only 50 per cent mentioned it as one of the factors leading to criminality. No doubt economic marginalisation does cause a certain amount of criminality amongst women, and a proper application of the strain theory may well be useful in describing these cases, but it is only of limited use. Bettina Cass (1985) also points to the link between poverty and criminality, but the more important issue might be quite different. Thus she indicates that in six States studied (including Britain, America and Australia) women were more likely than men to be poor, and being female and unattached carried with it a profound risk of becoming poor. Since women are generally economically worse off than men, how can we explain female conformity? The problem that the strain theory needs to address is why females, despite being more economically marginalised, are less criminal than males. If an answer is found to this problem, it will not only benefit explanations of female criminality but also explanations of male criminality.

Various refinements to strain theory have been suggested which may be of assistance. One is that, as with male criminality, the strain might be caused by feelings of relative, rather than absolute, deprivation. Or that relative deprivation may be less strongly experienced by women than by men. This is possible since feelings of relative deprivation are necessarily subjective, and reflect social and cultural values. And many would say that social structures affect men and women in different ways and to different degrees. It may be that some combination of relative deprivation, subcultural theories and strain may help not only to explain the rate of female offending but also to explain some of the differences between male and female rates of offending. In any event, it needs first to be further clarified exactly what needs to be explained. All writers on criminality are agreed that male and female crime rates are very different. But how different? Over the 1980s official statistics show that women have been responsible for only 20 per cent or less of indictable (more serious) offences but are more frequently involved in offences of handling or of theft (Hedderman and Hough (1994)). On the other hand, self-report studies suggest that the discrepancy is much less, perhaps that one third of offences are committed by women (see Rutter and Giller (1983)). There are also areas where the involvement of women looks more serious. The NSPCC suggest that in the early 1980s, where children were physically injured, natural mothers accounted for more cases of suspected abuse than did natural fathers (33 as opposed to 29 per cent) although fathers were more implicated when account was taken of the parent with whom the child lived (Creighton and Noyes (1989)). The figures all show that there is a discrepancy, but it may be neither as simple nor as great as the official statistics suggest, and that there may be some offences where women are more evident. Explanations must take account of all these factors.

In Chapter Seventeen the effects of differential association on women were also discussed (17.3) and were seen in the light of their different socialisation. Sutherland (1939) claimed that girls did not take part in gang activities, and that they remained relatively free from peer group pressure leading to illegal behaviour, but other authors have disagreed. In addition to the works cited at the beginning of this section, Carlen (1988) discovered that over half of her sample had been members of mixed gangs involved in antisocial and criminal activities. Clearly, the criminality of their peers had strong effects upon the criminality of these women. Furthermore, Campbell (1981 and 1984) has produced two lengthy works which indicate that women do join gangs and participate in violent behaviour. The findings suggest the possibility that a straight application of the differential learning theories might be as useful to explaining female criminality as it is to male criminality (see 10.2). Interestingly, Campbell found that the girls in the gang were very conventional in their outlook and their aims – to find a stable relationship with a man, have a family, and live happily.

Ngaire Naffine (1987) suggests that a different application of differential association theory might also be useful to explaining female behaviour, especially their conformity. She notes that Sutherland mentions altruistic cultures in which cooperation and care are paramount. These cultures he considered to be peaceful and law-abiding. She suggests that Sutherland might have made greater use of this altruistic, and therefore conforming, female culture to explain female conformity. If this is done, it does lead to a very traditional view of women which many would find difficult to accept, particularly if there were any suggestion of it being an innate trait rather than learned by differential associations.

Following on from this is the question of the control theories in which conformity is both learned and based upon the investment made in conformity. As was seen in section 17.6, this can be seen as a male gendered theory. However, as pointed out by Hindelang (1973), Box (1981), Heindensohn (1985 and 1996) and Tittle (1995 and 1997), this is not necessarily so and control theory may be as, or more, useful in explaining female criminality and conformity. Women in modern society are as committed and responsible in their public lives as are men and, because of their differential socialisation, they are also more concerned than their male counterpart about the effects of their behaviours on those close to them, particularly dependent children.

Most working-class women, Carlen (1988) claims, are controlled by two mechanisms. First at work, where the rewards of employment outweigh the rewards of crime. Secondly in the home, where their parents or husbands keep fairly close control over them. They have a psychological commitment to a family, and so remaining in the family would be more important than the rewards which might be gained if they were to turn to crime. Women who have been brought up in care (particularly if this occurs from their early childhood) lose this commitment, or never fully gain it. They see themselves as having little or nothing to lose by engaging in criminality, and so the temptation of criminality is not so well controlled as for other women. The effect of residential care on women was strong in Carlen's study (second only to poverty) and might be said to have come about from a change in the control of these women.

Carlen also claims that once they are brought before the courts for their first offence then, if they are already in care, the authorities often see the only possible punishment as custodial, particularly if they have been difficult to control whilst in care. Moreover, once released from care the women are badly equipped with the skills necessary to cope with an independent existence. This inadequacy, she claims, may cause these women to engage in acts of criminality either because other deviants are the only easy form of companionship available, or because they feel that they only need to consider themselves and are willing to enter into almost any activity to enhance their own position. Ironically, many of the women had been taken into care in order to provide greater control of their up-bringing and to teach them conformity, particularly sexual conformity. Yet just this type of attempt to inculcate conformity and traditional values actually led to criminality.

If female conformity is seen as arising out of the way in which women are controlled, then this may be used by some as a cogent reason for opposing more freedom for women. It may result in some people arguing that women should be made to face their responsibilities in the home, particularly in child-rearing. This type of attitude can be seen in the reasoning of the Conservative government in the late 1980s for not providing greater nursery and child care facilities – women should face their responsibilities in these areas, and so keep themselves in conformity and teach their children conformity. Right realists, as we have seen, would go still further, placing the blame for the general rise in crime on parents, particularly mothers and especially single mothers (see Wilson (1985)).

Possibly if there is a lesson to be learnt from the association of the greater conformity of women with their being more closely controlled, it is that it might better be used to control men. From study of the victims and criminals on the street, many victims are female and are victimised by men (male victims are, of course, also victimised by men). It would seem logical to socialise men and boys in a more controlled way, teaching them conformity. Such a crude application of these ideas would carry with it clear dangers. One of the most obvious might be that it would merely increase domestic violence against wives, sisters and children. Less crude controls, such as inculcating in boys stronger ideas of caring and responsibility and weaker ideas of self, might, however, lead to some reduction of male violence and male criminality.

As already indicated (13.5), control balance theory may be relevant in this respect. In particular, Tittle's notion that deviance will occur when a person either has a surplus or a deficit of control in relations with others would be useful if it could be made operational. Women have traditionally been seen as falling into the latter category, as suffering a severe control deficit. This can be seen in their general treatment in society, especially in terms of harassment, being regarded as objects, the lack of support by authorities, and typically having little control in all kinds of situations (see Brooks Gardner (1996) (harassment on the street); Dobash and Dobash (1992) (domestic violence); Hanmer et al. (1989) (rape and other violence); Smith (1989) (rape); Smart (1977) (female victims of violence are often on trial as much as the male perpetrators); Binney (1981) (domestic violence and lack of support by authorities); Hagan (1989) and Hagan et al. (1990) (gendered social control)).

In domestic violence in particular, the rationale for non-intervention has probably been that the family is a private place where the male has power and can choose which methods are necessary to assert his control; a clear illustration of the traditional view of women as being in substantial control deficit and often unprotected by the State. But, as Tittle points out, to assume from this that women will turn to criminality is to accept a deterministic aspect to behaviour: he sees a place for motivation and other concepts of choice. The imbalance in control is not seen as being itself sufficient to predict deviance: the individual must also be motivated, provoked and criminality must be facilitated by both opportunity and the absence of constraint. Of particular importance here may be a commitment to moral ways of behaving which may constrain deviant or criminal activity. At present, because of the very heavy control deficit women suffer, it is argued that they would tend to choose defiant or submissive behaviour which may be destructive, particularly of themselves, but which need not be criminal. Defiant activity may be positive, as can be seen from women collecting together to redress the balance (see the suffragette movement, Strachey (1978)) or to help each other against male control (see women's refuges, Binney (1981)) and to change control bases (see how women have helped to change the criminal justice approach to the way rape and domestic violence are dealt with, Jones et al. (1994)), or to defy male violence in more open ways (see the Greenham Common protests, Cook and Kirk (1983)). More destructive deviance may also arise – drug or alcohol abuse, suicide, mental illness or forms of activity which challenge the dominant culture (see above the discussion of female gangs: Messerschmidt (1995)). As their control imbalance is corrected because of changes – brought about in part by feminist pressures but also by other changes in society – they may move into an area where, if they choose deviance, they are perhaps more likely to commit predatory types of behaviour which will often be criminal. This is still not to be taken for granted: the other influences of motivation, opportunity and moral constraint may still be decisive. The important point is that deterministic outcomes should not be assumed: control balance and alterations in the power bases are the backdrop against which individuals may feel a need to deviate or offend, but they will do so only if they choose such behaviour.

From this it can be seen that careful use of male-orientated theories of criminality may be appropriate in explaining women's criminality, and may also help to focus on the strengths and weaknesses of these areas. Adding a feminist or gendered perspective may then further illuminate both female and male behaviour, conforming and offending. Feminist research in these areas needs to be expanded, perhaps particularly the sort performed by Carlen which is sympathetic to women's own views of their behaviour.

18.3.2　Radical feminists

Many radical feminists take a similar stance to the radical criminologists discussed above, except that they consider the position on a gender rather than a class basis. They are concerned with what they see as the failure of the law and legal system to protect women, particularly from violent crimes. They connect this to the patriarchal nature of societies and to power relations, especially within the family. From this point of view crime must be studied in relation to the general position of women in society, and the involvement of women, whether as victims or criminals, cannot be understood outside its social context. Some have proposed that crime should be deconstructed into its essential components which could then be related to the particular social aspects which seem best suited to explain the behaviour (Smart (1990)) so that, for example criminology would study rape and child sexual abuse in the social context of sexuality. Such deconstruction can be misleading (thus rape and sexual abuse may really be acts of power) and is also unnecessary since the general position only requires an understanding that crime is related to the sexual, economic and political powerlessness of women in society.

Klein (1995) suggests an even more radical recreation of crime and how to study it – 'commitment to women's lived experiences and concerns' rather than the mere building and testing of academic criminological theories. Women, and all people to be studied, should be treated with dignity and respect; they should be included as participants not just objects. This type of study requires more than just quantitative studies, it needs qualitative accounts (Daly and Stephens (1995)). It involves a critical questioning of the presumption that justice is an objective ideal or value, and raises the possibility that the system of criminal justice is heavily inclined towards particular types of order. The implication is that equal access to the presently defined concept of justice does not necessarily guarantee justice so far as certain groups are concerned, requiring reconsideration of the nature of justice in the light of feminist and other, particularly racial, constructs. This could be made explicit partly through feminists' research into the legal divide between public law and private law, especially as the changes in private/public space are becoming very complex in today's society. In another approach Daly (1994) used a court study to consider whether justice was distributed differently between different groups and individuals, while others have questioned the heavy use of the criminal justice system to police self-damaging behaviours or to control mothers who use drugs (see, for example, Maher (1990)).

Some radical feminists view the very nature of law as necessarily gendered and patriarchal, and question both its validity and the enforcement mechanisms which are used (Smart (1989 and 1990)). The suggestion is that the essential nature of criminology represents an attempt at social engineering and continued patriarchy, leading to a belief that, whatever the intentions, there is something inherently dangerous about both law and the study of its social control in the form of criminology. This is obviously similar to the Marxist attacks on the nature of law being an attack on certain classes, and it suffers from similar problems. First it ignores the fears and control over women that come out of their victimisation which would exist even without laws to control it and might even exist in a non-patriarchal society. Secondly it assumes that the State is patriarchal in all its endeavours and must always stay so.

Other writers, although accepting the essentially patriarchal nature of the State, would still choose to use the law for their own ends, to protect women. Many of these have fought passionately for the alteration of the law in various guises. To take but one example, MacKinnon and Dworkin have argued hard for the protection of women by the further criminalisation of pornography, a form of expression which they view as degrading to women, whom it portrays as submissive, as subjects, and as second-class citizens. Its criminalisation they see as necessary to restore to women their dignity, equality and power (MacKinnon (1993 and 1994); Moore (1993)). Similar arguments can be found in other claims to alter the law (see Chapter Two). Through altering the criminal law and the focus of control one might be able to empower women and so increase their position in society.

Another strand of radical feminist criminology looks generally at crime from the perspective of women. This includes how they experience victimisation (much of this has informed left realist criminology), how they experience their own criminal conduct, how they experience law enforcement and sentencing. It is an approach which challenges the whole of the criminal justice system to acknowledge women's experiences, and for criminology fully to take notice of these. In doing so they hope to empower women within the criminal justice system as well as through society. It is a politicised approach which questions one of the main bases of our present society, patriarchy.

18.3.3 Gender issues

A side-effect of focusing on female criminality has been that the whole area of crime, both male and female, has become a gender issue. To some degree all aspects of the criminal justice system are being re-assessed from a gender perspective. Much of the work has centred on the police (see above) and on the use of sentencing powers. NACRO (1987a; 1987b), for example, suggest that the sentencing of women is more harsh than for men, though this is questioned by Daly (1994) and seems not to be borne out by the prison statistics where the ratio of men to women is 30:1. Nor is it accepted by some academics. Hood (1992) found no evidence of harsher sentencing of women; Hedderman and Hough (1994) agreed with the qualification that apparent leniency for women may just be reflecting the seriousness of the actual offences, and noting that some women may have been very harshly treated. They also observe that, despite the fact that most convicted women are dealt with in the community, there was a more limited range of community sentences available for women in some areas. It has also been suggested that in the past apparent leniency was due to differences in the records of the offenders (Farrington and Morris (1983)). The reasonable conclusion is that, although it may seem that women are dealt with leniently there are instances of very hard treatment of women (see Kennedy (1992)). What is clear is that the position of women is often very problematic, and that the criminal justice system seems less clear about how to deal with them (Carlen (1990)). Lastly, when women are punished by being imprisoned the impact of this on many women is greater than on men: there are fewer facilities for education and training; fewer female prisons means that many are kept at long distances from their families; prison is more likely to lead to the break-up of the family in the case of women than men (Shaw (1991) and Green (1991)); women exhibit their disquiet with their predicament in ways which are less serious for the authorities. They do not riot but there are higher levels of self-mutilation, and more tranquillisers are used in women's prisons than in men's. Women's experience of the system is clearly different from that of men and its study may help to illuminate the understanding of the process and to reach solutions to some of our crime problems.

Another area where women's experience of the system is different from that of men is in their victimisation. In victimisation their experiences at the hands of men has come out into the open more frequently than was previously the case. This has led to some changes in women's position and highlighted some major problems. The two areas most frequently studied are rape and domestic violence.

In the case of rape, the feminist view of the victim has led to some improvement in her position: first, she is theoretically allowed anonymity and protection from having her character tested, although in practice few women actually are protected (see Adler (1982)); secondly, by setting up more sympathetic units in police stations for her to attend (rape suites) and generally altering the police response to a rape victim. These changes have encouraged some improvement in reporting, although the incidence of rape is still far higher than is officially recorded, as any rape crisis centre will confirm (see Jones et al. (1994)). Feminist calls in this area have now gone further, for example, towards calling for a change in the law, often in the definition of rape.

In the case of domestic violence, again there have been some improvements. First, there are now special provisions set out to protect women and children against this type of behaviour: the Domestic Violence and Matrimonial Proceedings Act 1976, ss. 1 and 2 and the Domestic Proceedings and Magistrates' Courts Act 1978, ss. 16–18. Some critics contend that these Acts have worsened matters: they allow these offences to be less seriously dealt with than would be the case in street violence. Secondly, although the focus on such activity as an offence, and as caused by the male, has led to some increased reporting of such offences, it still remains one of the least reported offences (see Hanmer and Saunders (1984) and Dobash and Dobash (1992)).

Feminist studies of rape have pointed to a power-based reason for the commission of these offences rather than their being grounded in sex. These findings suggest consequential changes in the control and socialisation of men in order to cut down on the likelihood of such offences (see Wilson (1980) for the position as regards rape and Dobash and Dobash (1980 and 1992) for the position as regards domestic violence). And Walby (1986) has linked all male violence towards women and children with power inequalities due to both economic and political weaknesses experienced by both women and children.

Clearly the separate study of women and their experience in crime has had a three-fold effect. First, it has led to different explanations of female criminality and conformity, and secondly it has led to a general gendering of crime and therefore gendered explanations of certain male criminality. It is important that gender issues are seen as relevant to both male and female criminality and are not relegated to a narrow relevance in female issues. In some significant respects men have also been sex-stereotyped in criminological theories, creating a need to study gender for both males and females. Thirdly, it has led to a recognition of a different 'experience' of crime, victimisation, and the criminal justice system. Recent realisation of this led left realists to base much of their research and many of their proposals on victim studies which are tailored to discovering women's experience of crime. This has been achieved because of the work of feminist criminologists. But if left realists recognise gender differences, their use of and application of such information is not always acceptable to feminists (see Schwatz and DeKeseredy (1991); Carlen (1992)). More generally, feminist research has still not been widely accepted nor has its potential in addressing both male and female criminality.

18.4 CONCLUSION

A number of studies have shown that female emancipation is likely to have some indirect effect upon officially recorded cases of female criminality. Smart and Box and Hale suggest a correlation between changing perceptions of women by bodies who enforce the criminal law and the increase in recorded female crime. They suggest that 30 years ago women were less likely to be suspected of crime; when suspected they were less likely to be charged and prosecuted; and finally, when prosecuted they were less likely to be convicted, than they are today. Today they are more generally seen as being equally capable of committing both legitimate and illegitimate activities. In other words, belief in the constitutional idea that women are somehow, physically or psychologically, incapable or unlikely to be criminal is weakening. This effect may be evidenced by the fact that NACRO (1987a and 1987b) discovered that the proportionate use of imprisonment for women has more than doubled in the last ten years, and that women are increasingly being sent to prison for less serious offences than men (although this finding has been questioned – see 18.3.2).

Box and Hale found that the major factor accounting for most of the increase in property offences seemed to be economic. As women become economically worse off, particularly through unemployment, they become less unwilling to commit crime.

Clearly, neither psychological/physical factors nor 'women's emancipation' is going to explain female crime satisfactorily. Other reasons will have to be postulated. For these it may be necessary to draw upon the studies so far applied to male criminality. Most types of crime committed by women are also committed by men and, to a large extent, both sexes live in the same environment and are subject to the same types of peer group pressures and effects on upbringing. From this standpoint, crimes by each should be explicable along similar lines. It is also true, however, that the causative effect of each factor may differ for men and women as it does for men from different backgrounds or with different peer groups. It may therefore be necessary to analyse and compare more closely the roles of men and women in society so as to ascertain which factors can be said to cause criminality.

To understand female criminality fully it is first essential to study all explanations of crimes. Women are as likely as men to be primarily affected by their environment, their peers, their upbringing, labelling, general social interactions, anomie, and all the other factors that were mooted in earlier chapters. Beyond this, there are explanations of women's crime (and especially of some particular crimes) which are based on factors peculiar to, or predominant amongst, women (such as reasons argued for infanticide and theories based on the menstrual cycle and other typically female body functions). But, in contrast to the view of earlier generations of legal theorists, present analysis suggests that specifically feminine characteristics (whether biological, psychological or behavioural) do not constitute the main explanation of women's crime.

Unfortunately, this does not seem to have filtered into the consciousness of magistrates and the judiciary, as was evidenced by Edwards' (1984) study of various courts, where she discovered that women were being sentenced for both their criminality and their denial of their gender roles. In her words their behaviour was 'medicalised'; there had to be something wrong with women before they could be capable of such activity. This approach follows women into prisons where the study by Dobash, Dobash and Gutteridge (1986) found that women's prisons are heavily concerned with controlling women and inculcating them with domestic routines so that they can learn traditional domestic roles rather than educational and work skills.

These last two criminal justice responses to female criminality show a need for more research into the extent of, and reasons for, women's criminality. They also pin-point a need to test the responses of the criminal justice system to gender issues. In the case of juveniles the criminal justice system now recognises the need for different treatment: there is a similar need for such recognition of gender differences.

From the above it is clear that feminist studies have had some impact. They have influenced left realism, altered some experiences of women in the criminal justice system, and ensured more consideration for women, feminism and gender in general criminological theories. These effects have been limited, however. Mainstream criminology remains largely sexist, in that it is focused on crime and criminal justice, areas which are for the most part still defined and inhabited by men (Young (1996)). As Hahn Rafter and Heidensohn's (1995) work clearly shows, in all corners of the world feminist, gendered, masculinity approaches and racially informed theories have much to offer social science generally and criminological discourse in particular. These approaches and new ways of looking at society and criminology imply the need to deal with many aspects, such as societal control; law and criminal justice; urban security; concepts of justice; victimisation; and criminal behaviour.

REFERENCES

Adler, Freda (1975), *Sisters in Crime: The Rise of the New Female Criminal*, New York: McGraw-Hill.

Adler, Zsuzsanna (1982), 'Rape - The Intention of Parliament and the Practice of the Courts', *Modern Law Review*, vol. 45, p. 664.

Austin, Roy L. (1981), 'Liberation and Female Criminality in England and Wales', *British Journal of Criminology*, vol. 21, p. 371.

Binney, Val, Harkell, Gina and Nixon, Judy (1981), *Leaving Violent Men: A Study of Refuges and Housing for Battered Women*, London: Women's Aid Federation.

Bourgois, Phillippe (1996), *In Search of Respect: Selling Crack in El Barrio*, Cambridge: Cambridge University Press.

Box, Steven (1981), *Deviance Reality and Society*, 2nd edn, London: Holt Rinehart and Winston.

Box, Steven (1987), *Recession, Crime and Punishment*, London: Macmillan.

Box, Steven and Hale, Chris (1983), 'Liberation and Female Criminality in England and Wales', *British Journal of Criminology*, vol. 23, p. 35.

Brooks Gardner, Carol (1996), *Passing By: Gender and Public Harassment*, Berkeley, Ca: University of California Press.

Campbell, Anne (1981), *Girl Delinquents*, Oxford: Basil Blackwell.

Campbell, Anne (1984), *The Girls in the Gang*, Oxford: Basil Blackwell.

Carlen, Pat (1988), *Women, Crime and Poverty*, Milton Keynes: Open University Press.

Carlen, Pat (1990), *Alternatives to Women's Imprisonment*, Milton Keynes: Open University Press.

Carlen, Pat (1992), 'Criminal Women and Criminal Justice: The Limits to, and Potential of, Feminist and Left Realist Perspectives', in Roger Matthews and Jock Young (eds), *Issues in Realist Criminology*, London: Sage.

Cass, Bettina (1985), 'The Changing Face of Poverty in Australia: 1972–1982', *Australian Feminist Studies*, vol. 1, p. 67.

Cohen, A.K. (1955), *Delinquent Boys: The Culture of the Gang*, Glencoe: The Free Press.

Cook, A. and Kirk, G. (1983), *Greenham Women Everywhere*, London: Pluto Press.

Creighton, S.J. and Noyes, P. (1989), *Child Abuse Trends in England and Wales 1983–1987*, London: NSPCC.

Crites, Laura (1976), 'Women Offenders: Myth v Reality' in L. Crites (ed.), *The Female Offender*, Lexington Mass.: Lexington Books.

Daly, Kathleen (1994), *Gender, Crime and Punishment*, New Haven, Conn.: Yale University Press.

Daly, Kathleen and Stephens, Deborah J. (1995), 'The Dark-Figure of Criminology: Towards a Black and Multi-Ethnic Feminist Agenda for Theory and Research', in Nicole Hahn Rafter and Frances Heidensohn (eds), *International Feminist Perspectives in Criminology: Engendering a Discipline*, Buckingham: Open University Press.

Dobash, R.E. and Dobash, R.P. (1980), *Violence Against Wives*, London: Open Books.

Dobash, R.E. and Dobash, R.P. (1992), *Women Violence and Social Change*, London: Routledge & Kegan Paul.

Dobash, R.P., Dobash, R.E. and Gutteridge, S. (1986), *The Imprisonment of Women*, Oxford: Basil Blackwell.

Edwards, S. (1984), *Women on Trial*, Manchester: Manchester University Press.

Farrington, David P. and Morris, Alison M. (1983), 'Sex Sentencing and Reconviction', *British Journal of Criminology*, vol. 23, p. 3.

Fiqueira-McDonogh, Josefina (1984), 'Feminism and Delinquency', *British Journal of Criminology*, vol. 24, p. 325.

Gilligan, Carol (1982), *In a Different Voice*, Cambridge: Harvard University Press.

Green, P. (1991), *Drug Couriers*, London: Howard League for Penal Reform.

Griffin, S. (1971), 'Rape: The all American Crime', *Ramparts*, vol. 10, p. 3.

Hagan, John (1989), *Structural Criminology*, New Brunswick, NJ: Rutgers University Press.

Hagan, J., Gillis, A.R. and Simpson, J. (1990), 'Clarifying and Extending Power-Control Theory', *American Journal of Sociology*, vol. 95, p. 1024.

Hahn, P., Rafter, Nicole and Heidensohn, Frances (eds) (1995), *International Feminist Perspectives in Criminology: Engendering a Discipline*, Buckingham: Open University Press.

Hanmer, J. and Saunders, S. (1984), *Well-Founded Fear*, London: Hutchinson.

Hedderman, Carol and Hough, Mike (1994), *Does the Criminal Justice System Treat Men and Women Differently?*, Home Office Research and Statistics Department, Research Findings No. 10, London: Research and Planning Unit.

Heidensohn, Frances (1985), *Women and Crime*, London: Macmillan.

Henson, S.D. (1980) 'Female as totem, females as taboo: an inquiry into the freedom to make connections', in E. Sagarin (ed.), *Taboos in Criminology*, Beverly Hills, California: Sage.

Hindelang, M.J. (1973), 'Causes of Delinquency: A Partial Replication and Extension', *Social Problems*, vol. 20, p. 471.

Home Office (1992), *Gender and the Criminal Justice System*, London: HMSO.

Hood, Roger (1992), *Race and Sentencing: a Study in the Crown Court*, Oxford: Clarendon Press.

Jefferson, Tony and Carlen, Pat (eds) (1996), 'Masculinity, Social Relations and Crime', *British Journal of Criminology*, vol. 36(3), Special Issue.

Jones, T., Newburn, T. and Smith, D. (1994), *Democracy and Policing*, London: Policy Studies Institute.

Kennedy, Helena (1992), *Eve Was Framed*, London: Chatto and Windus.

Klein, Dorie (1995), 'Crime Through Gender's Prism: Feminist Criminology in the United States', in Nicole Hahn Rafter and Frances Heidensohn (eds), *International Feminist Perspectives in Criminology: Engendering a Discipline*, Buckingham: Open University Press.

MacKinnon, Catherine (1993), 'On Collaboration', in Stevi Jackson (ed.), *Women's Studies: a Reader*, London: Harvester Wheatsheaf.

MacKinnon, Catherine (1994), *Only Words*, London: Harper Collins.

Messerschmidt, James W. (1993), *Masculinities and Crime — Critique and Reconceptualisation of Theory*, Maryland: Rowman and Littlefield.

Messerschmidt, James W. (1995), 'From Patriarchy to Gender: Feminist Theory, Criminology and the Challenge of Diversity', in Nicole Hahn Raften and Frances Heidensohn (eds) *International Perspectives in Criminology: Engendering a Discipline*, Buckingham: Open University Press.

Moore, Wendy (1993), 'There Should Be a Law Against It . . . Shouldn't There?', in Stevi Jackson (ed.), *Women's Studies: a Reader*, London: Harvester Wheatsheaf.

NACRO (1987a), *Women in Prison*, London: NACRO.

NACRO (1987b), *Women, Cautions and Sentencing*, London: NACRO.

Naffine, Ngaire (1987), *Female Crime: The Construction of Women in Criminology*, Sydney: Allen and Unwin.

Rutter, M. and Giller, H. (1983), *Juvenile Delinquency: Trends and Perspectives*, Harmondsworth: Penguin.

Schwatz, Martin D. and DeKeseredy, Walter S. (1991), 'Left Realist Criminology: Strengths, Weaknesses and the Feminist Critique', *Crime, Law and Social Change*, vol. 15, p. 51.

Shacklady-Smith, L. (1978), 'Sexist Assumptions and Female Delinquency', in C. Smart and B. Smart (eds), *Women, Sexuality and Social Control*, London: Routledge & Kegan Paul.

Shaw, R. (1991), *Prisoners' Children: What Are The Issues?*, London: Routledge.

Simon, Rita J. (1975), *Woman and Crime*, Lexington Mass.: Lexington Books.

Smart, Carol (1977), *Women, Crime and Criminality*, London: Routledge & Kegan Paul.

Smart, Carol (1979), 'The New Female Criminal: Reality or Myth?', *British Journal of Criminology*, vol. 19, p. 50.

Smart, Carol (1989), *Feminism and the Power of Law*, London: Routledge.

Smart, Carol (1990), 'Feminist Approaches to Criminology, or Postmodern Woman Meets Atavistic Man', in Lorraine Gelsthorpe and Alison Morris, *Feminist Perspectives in Criminology*, London: Routledge.

Smith, L.J.F. (1989), *Concerns about Rape*, Home Office Research Study No. 106, London: HMSO.

Strachey, R. (1978), *The Cause*, London: Virago.

Sutherland, Edwin H. (1939), *Principles of Criminology*, 3rd edn, Philadelphia: Lippincott.

Tittle, Charles R. (1995), *Control Balance: Towards a General Theory of Deviance*, Boulder, Co: Westview Press.

Tittle, Charles R. (1997), 'Thoughts Stimulated by Braithwaite's Analysis of Control Balance', *Theoretical Criminology*, vol. 1, p. 99.

Walby, S. (1986), *Patriarchy at Work*, Cambridge: Polity.

Welsh, S. (1981), 'The Manufacture of Excitement in Police–Juvenile encounters', *British Journal of Criminology*, vol. 21(3), p. 257.

Wilson, H. (1980), 'Parental Supervision: A Neglected Aspect of Delinquency', *British Journal of Criminology*, vol. 20, p. 203.

Wilson, James Q. (1985), *Thinking about Crime*, 2nd edn, New York: Vintage Books.

Young, Alison (1996), *Imagining Crime: Textual Outlaws and Criminal Conversations*, London: Sage.

CHAPTER NINETEEN
Envoi

One trend which has been widely shared by most modern industrial countries in recent years has been a rising concern over crime. There is a widespread public perception that lives and property (and, some believe, organised society itself) are increasingly threatened by a seemingly irresistible tidal wave of lawlessness. 'Law and order' has become a significant political issue, made none the less important because it is so little specified and analysed in public debate. It is against this general atmosphere of concern that the survey of crime and criminology offered in this book has been undertaken. One objective has been to offer some perspective and understanding of the complex issues involved.

In part this can be done by indicating the extent of our ignorance on some of the most basic aspects. Thus, even the brief critique of the official crime statistics which was offered in Chapter Four makes it clear that in a quite literal sense we do not know how much crime is now committed in Britain. Problems of definition and the many problems over unrecorded, or mis-recorded, crime make comparisons over time even more problematic. It can only be said that crime as revealed in the official statistics has increased (or decreased or altered) historically: but for most practical purposes this may be sufficient if, and it is a major qualification, *if* there is an awareness of the limitations and defects of the statistics. Unfortunately, neither the media nor many politicians, exercise such restraint.

The judgement on the statistics may be said to constitute a negative conclusion: but the more general characteristic of the survey is that no conclusions have emerged. This should not be surprising. One impression which should have emerged with some clarity is that explanations in crimi-nology have been, and still are, drawn from a wide variety of sources and disciplines. Biology, anthropology, philosophy, law, theology, psychology, sociology and social administration have all made their contributions. In attempting to assess these contributions it has been shown that each of the subjects could offer some justification for its involvement. Synthesising their approaches is, however, extremely difficult, if only because they often use different definitions and language, as well as having different methods and objects. No doubt what is needed is some generally accepted, over-arching theory, but it would be foolish to pretend that any such serious candidate is in sight. And would any single theory suffice to answer such different questions as, for example: what is the explanation of crime?; who are, or will become, the criminals?; and, what causes changes in the types of crime? One way forward is by decomposing the problem into its constituent parts. It is thus encouraging to see that many studies now focus on specific activities or groups.

If the study of the subject is confused by the Babel of discourses which it has attracted, a still more fundamental obstacle exists in the intractable nature of the basic subject-matter. This is not crime as such, but human beings and human nature. The wide variety of human experience, and the motives, attitudes and behaviour which it produces (or is produced by) necessarily makes generalisation elusive and unreliable. And there is a similar complicating variety in the forms of social organisation and cultures. It should again have emerged with some clarity from the rapid forays made in this book that it is wholly insufficient to relate crime simply to some presumed homogeneous national, institutional and cultural milieu. Many studies have indicated the importance of differences within societies and have identified a multiplicity of subcultures and social arrangements. There is a continuing need to recognise the forces which lie behind the control mechanisms, forces such as patriarchy, racism and class.

These reflections are not meant to indicate the impossibility of progress in this field. On the contrary, they are meant to give a realistic assessment of the task which still needs to be done as a prelude to considering where we have reached, and to suggest some possible ways forward. There certainly have been substantial advances made in what is still, in any systematic sense, a young area of study. One of the reasons for presenting this survey in a partially chronological way is to highlight the changes. If it is hardly in the nature of the subject and its material that it will ever become a science, there is no doubt that the approaches to it have become more 'scientific'. In most areas of interest, laboratory-type experiments are, and are likely to remain, out of reach; but there is a much greater awareness of the need to collect and use evidence more carefully through, for example, using control groups as a check on findings arising from studies of criminals or other social groups. There has also been a greater awareness of the value of using victim and local studies as ways of ascertaining the problems which crime causes for people.

One factor which has possibly retarded progress in the general field of criminology has been the relatively unsophisticated use of statistical methods. A number of the studies which have been looked at in this book derive their significance from attempting to measure one or other aspect of crime or criminals or victims. Yet, perhaps because of the academic background of the researchers, the statistical manipulations are relatively rudimentary, and the use of even common statistical techniques for testing the results virtually non-existent. In this respect we are now entered on a period of substantial change and progress from at least two directions. First, many of the people working in this area are now better equipped for making fuller use of their material in this way – one characteristic of the so-called New Sociology, for example, is its greater use of statistical, and even mathematical, methods. And secondly, technological advances – and especially the development of the computer – have revolutionised both the amount of material which can be collected and, even more, the ways in which it can be analysed and manipulated.

Such advantages can at present only be hopes for the future. They are not without their problems. One set arises from the use of quantitative approaches to meet the need to provide policy changes to tackle the 'crime' problem. One consequence is that the more theoretical or conceptual work is being ignored. For example, feminist and much socially based research has given us an awareness of the limitations of purely quantitative studies: there will always be a need for qualitative research to give an understanding of people's lives, and as a reminder that it is people, and not just objects or concepts, which criminologists have to study. The increasing use of quantitative data is doubtless reflected in the present work, but it is hoped that students will seriously consider any theoretical suggestions which may give an insight into behaviour and society's need to control it.

In addition, many aspects of this book have tended to indicate that the area for study, crime and criminal justice, is not even stable or universally accepted. In Chapter Two it was pointed out that the criminal justice system was intended to make society safer for its citizens. However, it should now be clear that this is done on a narrow definition of what citizens need protection from, and what security means. Radical, critical and feminist research indicates the schisms in these areas – it sets a rigorous task for criminology: a recognition of the problematic areas of its discourse; the possibility that what we have at present is crime as defined by a few, mostly powerful, rich, white men; a criminal justice system which serves the interests of particular groups in society rather than the whole range of disparate groups; a narrow and traditional understanding of control etc. Criminology as manipulated by State agencies has tended to claim that it has addressed these issues by merely taking on board small aspects of this agenda – for example, by slightly altering the way police and courts deal with rape and/or domestic violence – rather than being willing to reconsider the whole area to be studied. Another indication of the narrow approach of the criminal justice system is the limited view it has of justice: in Chapter Two a number of seemingly very different models of justice were set out (see especially crime control and due process in 2.6), but each accepted justice as an objective or value-free concept. Criminology must now meet the challenge that such simplistic acceptance of the basic tools and concepts of its field of study is not always either useful or necessary.

All this is probably particularly true of British criminology, which takes a very pragmatic view of the area to be studied and the policies which this suggests. As a result, many policy alterations in Britain turn around controlling the opportunity for crime as being the simplest target – for example, by target hardening or removing from society those considered to be threatening. The wider consideration of the underlying social and psychological aspects tends to be down-played. It is an approach which beyond a certain point becomes too expensive, both in terms of freedom and finance. The unrestrained rhetoric of the 1980s and 1990s calls for law and order have moved us closer to this point and suggest the need to search for additional strategies, some of which will involve a more far-reaching questioning of overall social structures. Such a search could usefully draw on some of the theories considered here but there is (mid-1997) little sign of a strategic shift in policy. The new Labour government's central concern is still that it should not be seen as 'soft' on crime. The Home Secretary (*Guardian*, 31 July 1997) has announced proposals to give courts the power to confiscate the passports of those given non-custodial sentences and to introduce driving bans for certain non-motoring offences; to extend house arrest curfews by electronic tagging to juveniles; to give courts power to 'name and shame' juveniles; and to implement the minimum sentence for repeat offenders of some serious crimes but not those for burglary (see 2.12). It has not been a main objective of this book to examine specific policies, or to make explicit policy proposals, but towards the end of most chapters there is a brief section on policy implications.

The immediate objective of this book is, and must be, more modest. It is to introduce students to the broad area covered by criminology and to convey some understanding of the development and present state of the subject. More ambitiously, it aims to convey some of the writer's enthusiasm and concern for problems which are both intrinsically fascinating, and of major significance for our times.

Index

Authors whose work is discussed in the text appear in the index, cited only authors do not.